FRANKLIN PIERCE: MARTYR FOR THE UNION

Franklin Pierce

MARTYR FOR THE UNION

Peter A. Wallner

PLAIDSWEDE PUBLISHING
Concord, New Hampshire

ACKNOWLEDGMENTS

Researching and writing a biography is a daunting challenge for any historian. Not only does one need to learn all there is to know about his subject, but the process requires considerable background work in the times in which he lived, the issues he confronted, and the people he knew. A successful conclusion to such a quest is impossible without the support and assistance of family, friends, colleagues, professional historians and librarians. I was fortunate to receive an abundance of such help.

The research process began at the Tuck Library of the New Hampshire Historical Society where William Copeley and David Smolen cheerfully accommodated my almost constant presence for the past five years. As a Society employee I was also encouraged by colleagues Del Delampan, Wes Balla, Mark Foynes, Sharon King, Donna-Belle Garvin, Joan Desmarais and Bill Veillette. The Tuck Library is conveniently located in Concord next door to the New Hampshire State Library. The State Library staff was also most efficient and helpful.

As this second volume focuses on the Pierce presidency, I made a number of lengthy trips to Washington, D.C. The Library of Congress was my home base while in the Capital and I benefited greatly from the pleasant and efficient staff. I also ventured to the National Archives, but found most of their material on the Pierce administration available on microfilm at the National Archives-Northeast Region in Waltham, Massachusetts to which I made many productive visits. Other successful research ventures took me to the Dimond Library of the University of New Hampshire, the Massachusetts Historical Society in Boston, and the American Antiquarian Society in Worcester, Massachusetts. Wherever I went I found professional and gracious assistance.

An entirely unexpected benefit of publishing this biography in two volumes was the number of people who came forward after reading volume one to offer me research leads or actual material. It is doubtful that I would have uncovered this information on my own. Therefore, I am especially grateful to Larry Brown of Albany, Georgia, Paul F. Hughes of Greenland, New Hampshire, Barry A. Billings of Nashua, New Hampshire, and Rev. David Jones of St. Paul's Episcopal Church in Concord, New Hampshire for steering me to some valuable material. Others who offered assistance in a variety of ways include Craig Schermer, Dr. Kent Bicknell, Chip Morgan, Rev. Richard J. Kelley, Harold Ivan Smith, John F. Prout, Dr. Mitchell R. Young, James J. Kiepper, Dean Dexter, William W. Upton, and Dr. Jane Venzke. For the cover portrait and the images in the book I am indebted to Hillary Crehan of the White House Historical Association, Barbara Moore of the Library of Congress Photoduplication Service, and Lorayne Billings of the New Hampshire Historical Society.

The final volume benefited greatly from the critical readings of Donald B. Cole and Michael J. Connolly who also assisted with the first volume. Donna-Belle Garvin also read parts of the manuscript. Their suggestions were direct and insightful, but the author alone is responsible for any failure of fact or interpretation.

As with volume one, I am indebted to the team at Plaidswede Publishing. The efficient and cheerful persistence of copy editor Martha Carlson-Bradley, and the expertise of book designer and typesetter Sid Hall made the final book what it is. My special thanks to publisher George Geers who has been behind this project from the beginning.

To the many volunteers of the Pierce Brigade who support the Pierce Manse in Concord, and to the Hillsborough Historical Society which operates the Pierce Homestead in Hillsborough, New Hampshire I offer my appreciation and thanks.

To Karen and Rich

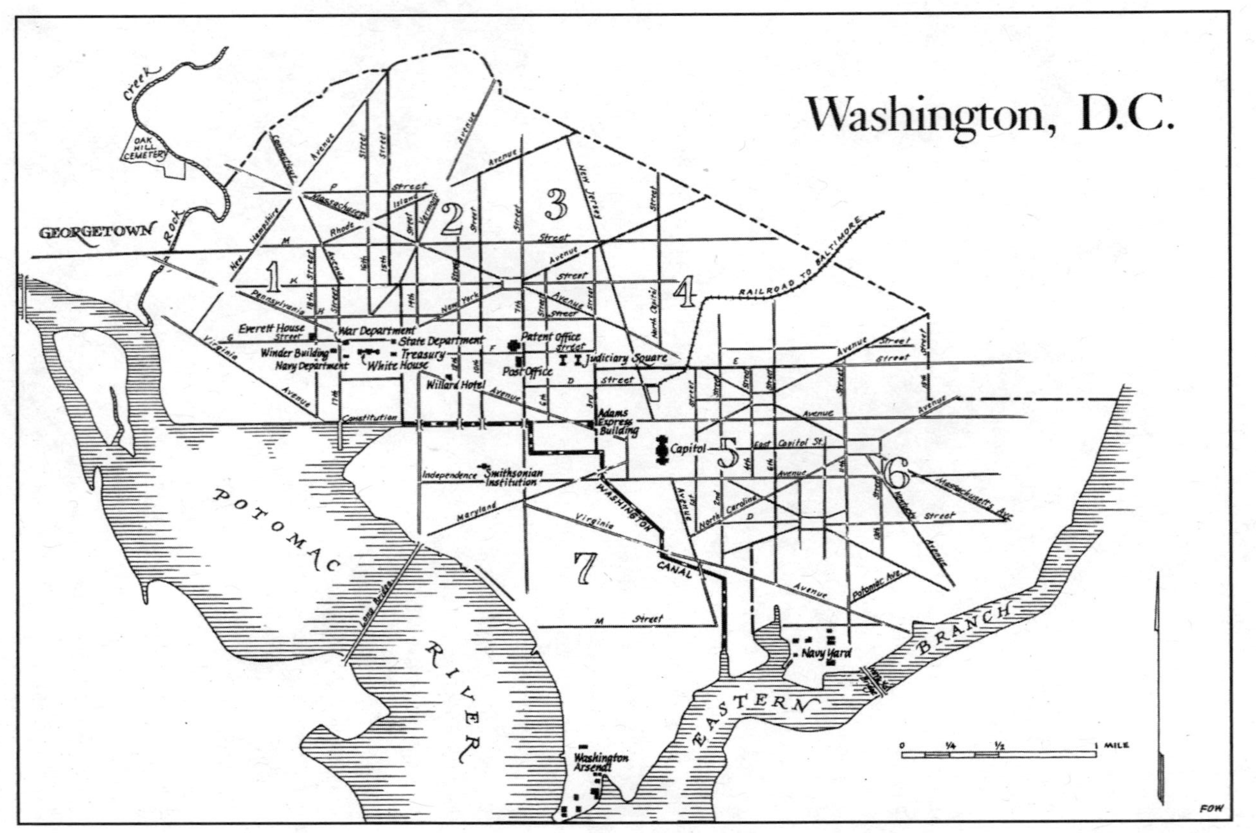

Washington, D.C.
GEORGETOWN
OAK HILL CEMETERY
Rock Creek
RAILROAD TO BALTIMORE
Everett House
War Department
State Department
Winder Building
Treasury
Navy Department
White House
Willard Hotel
Patent Office
Post Office
Judiciary Square
Adams Express Building
Capitol
Smithsonian Institution
WASHINGTON CANAL
Navy Yard
Washington Arsenal
Long Bridge
POTOMAC RIVER
EASTERN BRANCH
0 1/4 1/2 1 MILE
FOW

INTRODUCTION

On the evening of April 15, 1865, following receipt of the news of the death of President Lincoln by an assassin's bullet, the citizens of Concord, New Hampshire, took to the streets, motivated by a mixture of sorrow and anger and seeking the solace of friends with whom to share their inexpressible grief. After gathering before the State House, the crowd of nearly four hundred began to march south on Main Street, drawn toward one residence in particular. Along the way they called at the homes of neighbors who had yet to display the flag as a gesture of patriotic reverence for their fallen leader. Around 9:00 p.m. the mob reached its destination, the house rented by the former president, Franklin Pierce. Throughout the war Pierce had been an outspoken critic of Lincoln and his war policy, and on this night no flag graced his front porch. The mob called for Pierce, who came outside to confront them. As one man in the crowd shouted, "Where is your flag?" Pierce began to speak. For fifteen minutes he addressed his neighbors in the clear, commanding voice they knew so well. Speaking extemporaneously, Pierce quieted the crowd and peacefully dispersed them to their homes, many undoubtedly departing shamefacedly.

Did Pierce reflect that night on the course his life had taken? Barely twelve years earlier, New Hampshire's then-favorite son had stood before a crowd of nearly thirty thousand at the Capitol in Washington, D.C., and in the same strong, clear voice delivered a thirty-minute inaugural address entirely from memory. Now a pariah to many of his own neighbors, Pierce may have thought back to his boyhood in nearby Hillsborough and to his father, Benjamin, a Revolutionary War veteran, who became a sincere Jeffersonian and a political force among the yeoman farmers of the granite hills of western New Hampshire. Benjamin moved effortlessly into the Jacksonian Democratic party of Isaac Hill and Levi Woodbury, and young Frank began his own meteoric rise to political prominence following his graduation from Bowdoin College. Adopting his father's reverence for the Union and the Constitution, Frank was elected to the state legislature at twenty-four, was chosen speaker at twenty-six, elected to the U.S. House of Representatives at twenty-eight, and chosen by the legislature for the U.S. Senate at thirty-two. His personal charm, sincere interest in the lives of his constituents, and his brilliant oratory won him many friends throughout the state.

On this night in April 1865 Pierce may have thought back to his resignation from the Senate in 1842 at age thirty-seven to practice law and raise his family in New Hampshire. How would his life and that of his wife, Jane who disliked politics, have been different if he had stuck to that decision? But politics was in his blood, and the state party needed him to lead it through a minefield of divisive issues. As state party chairman, he brokered a long-standing dispute between the radical and conservative wings, allowing the Democratic Party to continue to claim the support of independent farmers while at the same time fostering the growth of corporations, particularly railroads and banks. Radical abolitionism burst forth as a political force while Pierce was in Congress. As state party leader, he confronted the slavery issue, which threatened to split his party as it had local communities and church congregations. Though he viewed abolitionists as dangerous fanatics, Pierce, nevertheless, abhorred slavery and his party was able to mollify the majority of state voters by endorsing the Wilmot Proviso, while at the same time maintaining strict adherence to the Jacksonian principles of states' rights and limited power to the federal government, which tended to protect the South's peculiar institution. As a result, the New Hampshire Democratic Party of Franklin Pierce remained the most consistently victorious state party in New England.

That fact was not lost on national party leaders, who convened the 1852 national convention in Baltimore. Though seeking a compromise candidate who could reunite the party following the national election debacle of 1848, party leaders did not consider Pierce among the more than a dozen candidates before the convention. But two groups—Pierce's political supporters from New Hampshire, known locally as the Concord clique, and former Mexican War generals—

masterfully manipulated the convention delegates into making him everyone's second choice. Pierce was nominated as the second dark horse candidate in U.S. history. His relative obscurity, balanced by his patriotism for serving as a general in the Mexican War, and his consistency in defending party principles attracted all factions to rally behind him. Pierce was swept into office, winning twenty-seven of the thirty-one states over his better-known but more controversial Whig opponent, Winfield Scott.

Pierce assumed the presidency with the goodwill of most of America but under a cloud of personal grief over the recent tragic death of his last surviving child, Benny, in a train accident. How would his skills as a political organizer, his past success as a conciliator, and his strict adherence to Jacksonian doctrine translate to his role as president? Most significantly for the future of the Union, could President Pierce fulfill the pledge made in his inaugural address to do nothing to upset the repose that had existed on the issue of slavery since the adoption of the Compromise of 1850? Some two hundred Americans died the night following Lincoln's death, as rioting citizens took out their wrath on those who had spoken ill of the dead president. The mob in Concord may not have intended the same fate for Pierce, but they certainly demonstrated their disapproval of the course his public life had taken and signaled the ignominious end of his forty-year political career.

FRANKLIN PIERCE: MARTYR FOR THE UNION

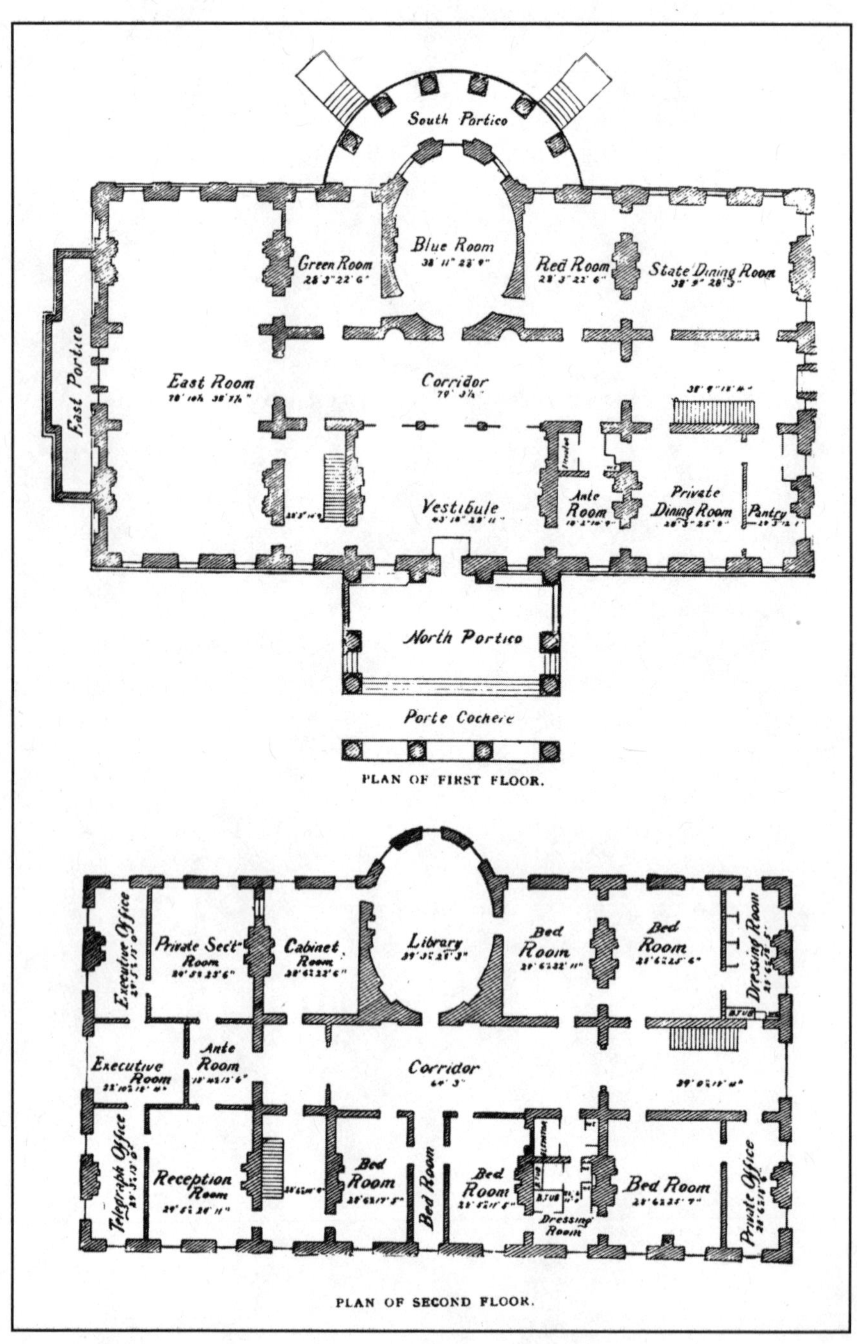

Franklin Pierce's White House

1

LAUNCHING AN ADMINISTRATION

THE NEW PRESIDENT AWOKE on March 5 in an "Executive Mansion"—it was not yet officially called the "White House"—that was about to undergo its first major refurbishment since the building itself had been rebuilt after the British burned it in 1814. In early 1853, Congress appropriated $25,000 for repairs to the White House interior and another $12,000 for improvements to the South Grounds. Some work had been completed at the end of Fillmore's administration, including new gravel walks that crisscrossed the grounds, gas lighting at every entrance, and exterior painting. All of the interior work would take place during Pierce's first year in office.[1] The most expensive and significant change was the new central heating system, installed in June 1853. Three new furnaces, fueled by coal fires, heated water-filled copper coils, which "heated the air around them which rose to the rooms."[2] The improvements corresponded with changes in the way the Executive Mansion was managed. Congress now paid for the expense of lighting the house and grounds, as well as the salary of the doorkeeper, his assistant, and the gardener. But it wasn't until 1855 that Congress agreed to pay for fuel and maintenance on the new heating system, which would prove to be a major drain on the president's $25,000 salary, as the inefficient system was costly to operate. The president was also responsible for paying the wages of his personal secretary, bodyguard, and White House servants and all expenses related to entertaining, including the salary of the steward and butler. The marshal of the district, the position coveted by Pierce's close friend Benjamin Brown French, was responsible for assisting the president in organizing and hosting state occasions, such as the president's annual New Year's levee.[3]

The city itself had undergone some changes since Pierce left the Senate in 1842 but remained "a shambling, dilapidated, ill-planned town set off by a few fine buildings and squares."[4] The new Patent Office Building and the new hall of the Library of Congress opened in 1853. The Washington Monument was being built and would rise to a height of 120 feet during the Pierce administration, but other than the Smithsonian Institute and the Botanical Gardens, the mall was an immense empty space. The streets remained mostly mud and dust, and there was no sewage system. Excrement was deposited in above-ground boxes, which were then emptied by city workers into "poudrette factories" in two locations in the city, from which "putrid gasses" offended the olfactory senses of the residents. For water, the city still relied on wells. The White House had its own unfenced spring in Franklin Square, and the purity of its water was the envy of everyone. Congress had recently authorized the building of a sixteen-mile-long aqueduct to bring fresh water from the falls of the Potomac into the city, but this project was not completed until after Pierce left office.[5]

Office space for federal employees was also inadequate. The White House was surrounded by four buildings that housed the State, Treasury, War, and Navy departments, but all were too small for the growing federal bureaucracy. Employees of the War and State departments spilled out into rented space around town. The newest department, the Interior, had no building of its own and was required to share space in the new Patent Office building.[6]

Inside the White House the president had only to walk down the hallway from the family living quarters to the executive offices, which were on the second floor. The White House and grounds were open to all, and visitors came and went at will. The front entrance under the columned portico opened into a wide reception hall decorated with busts of Columbus, Vespucius, Lamartine, and other notables. The entire first floor was open to the public and included the large East Room and the Green, Red, and Blue rooms, which served as parlors. On the southwest corner of the first floor was the State Dining Room. These rooms were completely renovated in 1853, with new woodwork, plastering, paint, carpets, drapes, and gas lighting. In the basement were the kitchen, servants' quarters, and storerooms.[7]

A visitor desiring to see the president entered the grounds through the North Gate, which opened every morning at 8:00 a.m. and closed at sunset. At the North Portico the visitor was greeted by the doorman and asked to sign the register before proceeding into the large reception area, where Pierce's bodyguard, Thomas O'Neill, was seated. The guest then turned left to the long stairway leading to the executive offices. At the top of the stairs the visitor entered the anteroom; this along with the president's large, private office and the office of his secretary made up the entire executive office suite. Doors connected the three rooms, and each had its own door into the hallway. When the anteroom was filled, guests spilled into the hallway and down the stairs. The president worked at Andrew Jackson's old, high desk. There was a mahogany table around which the cabinet members sat during meetings. A portrait of Old Hickory above the fireplace overlooked the office. The rest of the second floor was closed off from the public for the family quarters. This seven-room suite included a library (a newly designed space created by Mrs. Fillmore), a family dining room, Jane Pierce's two-room suite, and the president's bedroom on the southwest corner. During that first year, a new bathroom was installed adjacent to the president's bedroom, with hot and cold running water and a tub. Previously, residents of the White House had to use portable bathtubs with water heated in kettles. The only other private space was the White House garden on the east side of the building, from which the public was excluded. Each spring and summer the garden was ablaze with color from blooming lilacs, camellias, fruit trees, dogwoods, quince, redbuds, and roses. This would be home to the Pierces for the next four years. They owned no other residence and did not visit Concord again until the fall of 1856.[8]

Pierce and his twenty-five-year-old secretary and former law clerk, Sidney Webster, got right to work that first day, Saturday, March 5. The president had an enormous and thankless task ahead of him. Some eighteen thousand federal offices were to be filled with loyal Democrats, and estimates were that thirty thousand hungry office seekers were in Washington, lobbying for positions.[9] As a courtesy to the new president, the Senate would remain in session for the first month to receive his nominations for the hundreds of positions that required Senate confirmation.

As promised, Jefferson Davis arrived in Washington that day and met immediately with Pierce and Caleb Cushing to discuss joining the cabinet as secretary of war. Though continuing to express some reluctance to join a coalition cabinet, Davis ultimately agreed.[10]

The next day Pierce spent a quiet Sabbath and attended the 4½ Street Presbyterian Church. It would be a firm rule of the president, likely influenced by Jane, to conduct no business on the Sabbath. Monday, March 7, saw a return of the horde of office seekers, but on this day there were still formalities associated with the inauguration of a new administration. In the morning Pierce met with twenty-two of his former brigade officers from the Mexican War, whom he had invited to the White House to share in his success. At noon Senators Walker and Phelps arrived and informed Pierce that the Senate had convened and was awaiting his communication. Sidney Webster then followed the senators down Pennsylvania Avenue to deliver eight messages from the president. Seven were for the confirmations of his cabinet, and the eighth recalled all previous nominations of the Fillmore administration that had not yet been acted upon by the Senate. All were confirmed unanimously, and Davis and Dobbin, escorted by the officers of the army and navy respectively, proceeded to the Senate to be sworn in. The other members of the cabinet were sworn in at their offices later in the day.[11] The formalities over, the cabinet met the next day and almost daily over the next six weeks to confer on dispensing patronage. A visitor from New Hampshire was impressed with the cabinet members when introduced to them by Pierce in his office:

> Mr. [James] Dobbin [Navy] first came in—then Mr.[James] Guthrie [Treasury] the very antipodes of each other in personal appearance. Mr. D. spare, small, prompt, precise: Mr. G. large, tall, heavily moulded, heavily moving, imprecise, strong everyway: then [James] Campbell [Postmaster General]—lips tobacco stained, full built—smooth features, very priest like, but an open honest air—Gov. [Robert] McClelland [Interior], spectacled,

> quite professor like in general appearance—Gov. [William L.] Marcy [State], large, heavy, commanding, seared & iron-y features; he certainly reminded me of Webster—Gov. Davis [War], tall, slender, moving a little stiffly, but not haughtily, quite the opposite from the impetuosity of bearing so characteristic of him on the battle-field. Introduced to Gen. [Caleb] Cushing [Attorney General] last, well built, ruddy-cheeked, moving, active, more of the man of the world than either of the others;—all gentlemen & very pleasing to me in their address—easy, courteous, affable.[12]

The cabinet members were as different in their political views as they were in appearance and personality; they represented not only different geographic regions but different factions of the Democratic Party and even different parties, if Cushing's Whig roots are considered. Their selection would seem to be a formula for dissension and likely to bring failure to the administration, but they would prove to be one of the most able and unified cabinets of the nineteenth century. For the first and only time in U.S. history, a cabinet remained unchanged for an entire presidential administration. There were disagreements, even feuds. Davis and Marcy were incompatible, neither was fond of Guthrie, and Marcy did not trust Cushing. Sidney Webster, who observed the working of the cabinet for four years as Pierce's secretary, later recalled, "The elements of that Cabinet were such that, if left without a controlling chief, it would have broken asunder in a week."[13] What held them together was their mutual respect, even fondness, for Pierce. Often characterized as "pliable and yielding," Pierce was, in fact, rigidly consistent and inflexible in applying the principles that had marked his entire political life: a strict interpretation of the Constitution, limited power to the federal government, and the right of the states to control their own domestic institutions. His personal integrity and honesty , which was almost "obtuse," coupled with a uniquely charming and generous personality won the loyalty and affection of each member of a disparate cabinet, which held together through four tumultuous years.[14]

Pierce had strong views as to the role of the president. He believed the Constitution gave the president broad responsibility to conduct foreign affairs but very limited control of domestic matters, which more properly belonged to the Congress. The president was responsible, however, for carrying out the laws of Congress, and, to Pierce, this meant honest and efficient stewardship of the people's money. In his inaugural he pledged "a devoted integrity in the public service, and an observance of rigid economy in all departments. . . ." These were not idle words, for Pierce fully intended his to be a reform administration, one that eliminated waste, inefficiency and corruption in the executive branch. He would insist on the "qualities" of "diligence, integrity and capacity" in all government workers "for the preventing or punishment of fraud, negligence, and peculation. . . ."[15] As he had in his nine years in Congress, Pierce would consistently apply the highest standards of necessity and frugality to any appropriation or proposed act of Congress. To his credit, Pierce had chosen cabinet members who, though different in political orientation, all shared his belief in honest, efficient government and who did not view their own positions as an opportunity for personal gain. In this respect, the Pierce administration would stand out as a glowing exception to the prevailing ethical standards of the time, when public office was considered an invitation to public plunder.[16]

But the first application of these high standards would prove to be the most difficult and, as it turned out, the most controversial. As the cabinet met to dole out jobs, the president established the general guidelines. Anyone who supported the party during the most recent presidential election was eligible. An individual's previous political indiscretions, such as opposing the Compromise of 1850 or bolting the party to support Van Buren in 1848, were forgiven. A pledge to support the Baltimore platform, with its strong plank endorsing the compromise and the Fugitive Slave Act, was sufficient to qualify one for preferment by the administration. Pierce added his own insistence on appointing only those who met high standards of competence and honesty. In one case, Pierce rejected a candidate recommended by Attorney General Cushing because "I do not think his professional reputation warrants his being pressed for the position." He concluded this memo by saying, "In a word the question should be what is best on the whole for the public service & the administration."[17] Beyond this, positions would be dispensed with consideration to geographic balance, and when possible a Democratic congressman, senator, or local leader would be consulted on appointments to federal offices in their district or state.[18]

The president was the chief personnel officer of a government of some fifty thousand officers and employees in three separate branches of administration: the foreign service, the civil service, and the armed service. There were three separate classes of appointments. Those requiring Senate confirmation—chief accounting officers, territorial governors, ministers and consuls to foreign countries, judges of the federal courts, postmasters, collectors of the customs at the nation's 152 ports of entry, district attorneys, and land agents, a total of 929 positions in all—got the personal attention and endorsement of the president. A second class of appointees—chief clerks, clerks and messengers, field agents—were selected by their department head (cabinet officer), but with the knowledge and consent of the president. Subordinate field employees—minor customs officers, postal workers—were appointed by the local agent in charge, the postmaster or customs collector, for example.[19]

On March 9, Pierce and Secretary of War Davis sent to the Senate a list of nominees for promotion in the army. This was almost entirely based on seniority. Beginning on March 15 and almost daily thereafter for the next three weeks, nominations for other offices were sent to the Senate. Among the first was Charles H. Peaslee for the post of collector of the port of Boston. Peaslee was part of the Concord 'clique,' a three-term congressman, and head of the National Campaign Committee in Washington in 1852. Choosing a New Hampshire political ally to serve in Boston raised some eyebrows in Massachusetts, but Peaslee fit Pierce's criteria of honesty, competence, and loyalty and would serve as collector throughout the Pierce administration. Massachusetts Democrats were not ignored, as longtime Pierce allies Charles G. Greene was named naval officer in Boston, and Benjamin F. Hallett, former national chairman of the Democratic Party, was chosen U.S. attorney for the district of Massachusetts, a position which put Hallett on the front line in future fugitive slave cases. Another of Pierce's close friends, Judge Nathaniel G. Upham of Concord, was sent to London as commissioner to negotiate the settlement of claims made by British or American citizens against the governments of the two nations.[20]

An open seat on the Supreme Court was quickly filled with the nomination of John A. Campbell, a states' rights, pro-Union lawyer "of unswerving integrity" from Alabama. The seat had been vacant since another Alabamian, John McKinley, had died the previous summer. President Fillmore had sent three separate nominees to the Senate in the intervening months, but the lame-duck president was unable to get the Democratic majority in the Senate to agree to any of them. Finally, in frustration and with an understanding of the enormous number of positions the new president had to fill, the members of the Supreme Court, in an unprecedented move, recommended Campbell to Pierce. He concurred and the Senate unanimously confirmed Campbell on March 25, 1853. This would be the only Supreme Court vacancy filled by the Pierce administration.[21]

One of the greatest challenges proved to be the selection of the ministers and consuls to foreign capitals. As with many presidents, Pierce would prove to be his own secretary of state at times, particularly in the appointment of foreign ministers. Secretary of State Marcy admitted his lack of experience in foreign affairs in letters to the former secretary of state, James Buchanan and, at first, seemed overwhelmed with the broad responsibilities of his office.[22] Pierce clearly stated in his inaugural, "My Administration will not be controlled by any timid forebodings of evil from expansionism" and he claimed that "the acquisition of certain possessions . . . [is] eminently important for our protection."[23] Having endorsed the goals of the expansionist wing of his party, which called itself "Young America," Pierce was determined to select foreign ministers and consuls who represented the administration's prodemocracy, proexpansionist goals in foreign lands. Ten positions abroad were of the highest grade, ranked as "envoy extraordinary and minister plenipotentiary"; the term "ambassador" with its monarchical connotation was not used until late in the nineteenth century. Of these ten positions, five were in Europe (Great Britain, France, Prussia, Russia, and Spain), and five were in the Western Hemisphere (Mexico, the Central American states, Brazil, Chile, and Peru).[24]

First up, Marcy chose A. Dudley Mann to be assistant secretary of state. The youthful Mann was already an experienced diplomat and committed to the cause of expansion and Young America. Next, Pierce reappointed John Randolph Clay as minister to Peru. Clay had been in Peru since 1847 and had previously served in diplomatic posts in Russia and Austria. His choice was viewed as a favor to the retiring President Fillmore. That same day, Pierce also sent the nomination of John Slidell, a former Louisiana congressman and minister to Mexico, to the Senate as minister to the Central American states. This was a potential hot spot, as the United States had a strong interest in a trans-Isthmian canal, and Great Britain was extending its influence in the area. All three nominees were approved unanimously, but Slidell turned down the appointment. Pierce turned instead to Arkansas Senator Solon Borland, whom he knew from the Mexican War, and Borland was promptly confirmed.[25] The final major post among the first wave of nominees went to Senator Pierre Soulé, of Louisiana, as Minister to Spain. Soulé was born in France and had been jailed in his native country for revolutionary activity. After fleeing to the United States, he began a legal and political career in New Orleans as a states' rights Democrat. He was also strikingly handsome with a dynamic personality, and he had impressed Pierce when he visited Concord in late June 1852, as part of the delegation sent by the national convention to inform Pierce of his nomination. Soulé's appointment was praised in the press at the time, but Marcy had opposed it, and Soulé would prove far too radical and impetuous to be a successful diplomat.[26]

Among diplomatic appointments of the second rank, the most noteworthy was Nathaniel Hawthorne as consul to Liverpool. Pierce rewarded his old friend by giving him one of the most lucrative posts at the president's disposal. Not only would Hawthorne collect a decent salary, but he was also entitled to fees for every ship coming to Liverpool from the United States or leaving from Liverpool to the United States. The appointment allowed Hawthorne and his family to visit Europe for the first time, where his literary reputation, particularly in England, was even higher than in the United States.[27]

Hawthorne left immediately for Washington, to lobby for his own confirmation and to visit Pierce. Though he was confirmed unanimously, Hawthorne expressed disappointment at not being able to spend more time with Pierce, who was overwhelmed with guests and the pressures of patronage: "Frank was as free and kind, in our personal interviews, as ever he was in our college days, but his public attentions to me were few and by no means distinguished—only inviting me once to tea, and once to go to a methodist meeting with him; while [other people] were invited to dinner and made much of."[28] Before heading back to Massachusetts, Hawthorne escorted Jane Pierce on a boat trip on the Potomac River to Mount Vernon, a rare excursion from the White House for the First Lady, who was still in deep mourning following the death of Benny and who had only recently settled into her new home. Jane had remained in Baltimore until March 22, when she finally moved to Washington, accompanied by Abby Means, her girlhood friend and widow of Jane's uncle. Means, more outgoing and accomplished socially than Jane, would serve as White House hostess for the first half of the Pierce administration. Despite the special attention shown to Jane, Hawthorne continued to view her harshly: "To confess the truth, I did not in the least regret being almost shut out of the White House; for of all dismally dull and heavy domestic circles, poor Frank's is certainly the most intolerable."[29] The two old friends would not see each other again for more than five years.

Another glimpse of the president's social activities is provided by B. B. French, a friend of Pierce's for over twenty years and treasurer of the national campaign committee in 1852. French wrote in his journal on March 27, 1853, "Thursday evening we all went to the President's levee. It was a throng and the President did the duties of receiving the immense crowd in the most urbane and gentlemanly manner possible—the ladies all fell in love with him! Mrs. Pierce (poor afflicted woman) was not present, and Mrs. Means (formerly Abby Kent) did all the feminine honors with that grace & dignity which always marked her, even in her girlhood. We were boy & girl together in Chester, N.H., where we were both born, & now we are here amid the hurly-burly of Washington."[30]

French was also a candidate for a job in Pierce's administration and had his sights set on the post of marshal of the District of Columbia.

His journal and letters reflect the anguish Pierce must have felt in trying to satisfy the wishes of his friends. French records, "On Monday p.m. the President . . . with his private Secy. Mr. Webster came to my door and invited me to walk with them. We walked about ½ mile down East Capitol Street, & our talk was of office. Gen. Pierce commenced by saying[,] 'Major, I want to say something to you about this office of Marshal. You cannot expect me to appoint you merely because we have been so many years personal friends.'"[31] Pierce explained the difficulty in offering French the job he sought when so many other prominent local Democrats were promoting other candidates. French responded by asking if Pierce had any other position in mind for him, to which Pierce replied, "I desire to provide for you, and it is now necessary that I should have another private Secy. to sign land patents, as Mr. Webster is so constantly engaged that he cannot possibly do it. It will be but temporary, and if you will accept it you shall be appointed."[32] French declined at first and set about procuring as many signatures as possible to convince Pierce to nominate him marshal. The effort failed, however, and a week later French again met Pierce at the White House, where he was told that he would not be appointed marshal. French found that Pierce "was so earnest" in his desire to have French accept the temporary position of assistant secretary that he finally agreed, with the understanding that "it should not be in my way for a more lucrative and better office. He promised me it should not &, so we separated."[33]

The perceptive French may have sympathized with the president's plight, recording, "He appeared worn down by fatigue, & I told him I would not undergo what he is undergoing to be President of the U.S. He said it was hard & he wished all the offices were elected."[34] French wrote to his brother, Henry, in New Hampshire, "If anyone had told me three months ago that I should be seated here, in the 'White House' as Assistant Private Secretary to the President . . . ."[35] Henry was appalled: "I cannot conceive how you could accept, or he offer you this sort of a place."[36] Until something better came along French spent each day in the president's office, signing Pierce's name to land patents. He wrote, "I can sign 150 an hour, but probably do not sign over 100. There are now 10,000 ahead to be signed, & the commissioner informs me they intend to issue about 500 daily. Well, if I keep this office, I have a job before me and it is so intellectual!"[37]

Pierce may have felt the need to have a close friend nearby. His wife, who had always disdained politics and was not fond of Washington, D.C., was not able to offer much support, and his private secretary (Webster) was of a different generation, so having an old friend in the next office each day provided some relief. French seemed to sense this when he wrote to his brother, "But when Pierce comes in, and talks and laughs as in olden times, and jokes me about not writing his name elegant enough, and I tell him it is only envy, because my name is so much better looking than his, & c, & c., and he complains of the troubles and trials of his office, and tells me how he is annoyed by applications for office,—the wire edge wears off and I forget my degradation, if such it may be called."[38]

If French's presence lightened the president's burden, it did not eliminate the cloud of grief that hung closely over the White House. Jane had insisted that the state rooms be draped with mourning crape, and wore a heavy, black veil on the rare occasions when she left the White House.[39] Even the usually upbeat French was affected by it: "Twice, since I have been at the President's house, I have looked upon the portrait of poor little Benny, & for half an hour afterwards I could not speak to anyone—if I had attempted it I should have burst into tears, in spite of my manhood. It affects me strangely. Why should it? That that mild, innocent countenance, that beautiful forehead covered with fair hair smoothed down by the hand of a doting mother, should in a single instant pass from life to death, and in such a manner!—even now I can scarcely endure the thought."[40] One can only imagine Pierce's torment as he passed that portrait each day and faced his wife's grief and mourning each evening. But for French, the "degradation" of a menial job was only temporary. As promised, Pierce appointed him commissioner of public buildings in June. Assuming his new position on July 1, French found himself in a position similar to the president's, writing that now his doorbell rang from 6:00 a.m. to 10:00 p.m. each day as he attempted to "evade the hordes of office seekers."[41]

The unrelenting pressure of office seekers forced the members of Pierce's cabinet to attempt to avoid the crowds by finding "roundabout" routes from their offices to the White House and back to their boarding houses.[42] And the task did not end with the work day but carried over into the evening, as Pierce hosted small dinner parties each night to entertain and cajole party leaders who were in town to lobby for themselves or others. Jane reported that "one, two, three or four gentlemen dine here every day." She was present each evening, remarking, "I find it much less trying to meet perfect strangers than those who are in any way associated with the past. . . ." But she was concerned for her husband: "he needs more exercise—but tries to make sleep do in its stead—that is sleeping at night. . . ." This concern prompted her "to head on in the path of duty and necessity," despite wishing "to fly away sometimes . . . to freedom and quiet. . . ."[43] Fortunately, Abby Means, "always energetic and considerate and kind," was there to take on much of the hosting responsibility, relieving Jane of the need to do more than make an appearance each evening.[44]

Means left a description of one of these small dinner parties, noteworthy because it shows Pierce's persistence in finding solutions to his two most important appointments, other than his own cabinet: the positions of minister to Great Britain and collector of the Port of New York. Issues involving trade and fishing rights with Canada and a whole range of problems between the United States and Great Britain over Central America were immediately pressing on the new administration, requiring a strong, experienced representative in London. As much as two-thirds of the trade of the United States came through the port of New York, and the collector's office was the largest single government agency, employing between seven hundred and eight hundred workers, all political appointees. The selection of these two officials would determine much of the success or failure of Pierce's foreign policy and of his political intention to hold the various factions of his party together. At dinner on April 8 were the former secretary of state, James Buchanan, and Charles O'Conor, an Irish Catholic lawyer and representative of the "Hard" faction of the New York Democratic Party. Pierce's goal that evening was to convince Buchanan to take the post of minister to London and to elicit O'Conor's help in convincing the "Hards" in New York to accept Pierce's coalition slate of appointments for the key posts in the city.[45]

Means reported getting into a discussion with O'Conor that evening about the merits of public versus parochial schools. A Catholic council of bishops had recently urged public funds for Catholic schools in New York, as they opposed the use of the Protestant Bible exclusively taught in the public schools. Means argued in favor of all children attending public schools, while O'Conor, though labeling himself "a moderate Catholic," declared that "all denominations—should have separate institutions & thus insure religious education." Pierce was forced to intercede in the "spirited" discussion, declaring "that such a division of school money would strike a blow at union among men in political & secular affairs—& that the Catholics were now where they should be—at liberty under our laws to enjoy their own religion unmolested." Means reported that O'Conor "bowed & smiled for he had just received an office—& did not value his religion enough to contradict the President (just then)."[46] Pierce was in his usual position as peacemaker, but his effort to hold Protestants and Catholics together would prove as fruitless as his attempts to heal the breach among the Democrats of New York.

That breach dated back before the Mexican War and involved a host of state issues, particularly expenditures and patronage for the statewide canal system, but had become permanent with the presidential election of 1848, when free-soil Democrats bolted the party and supported Martin Van Buren for the presidency on the Free-Soil ticket. By 1852, with the Compromise of 1850 temporarily overcoming the antislavery agitation, the bolters, known as "Barnburners," sought to return to the Democratic party ranks. Blaming them for the defeat of the national and state tickets in 1848, the "Hardshells" or "Hunker" faction refused any contact with the Barnburners. The more moderate Democrats, known as the "Softshells" or "Softs," led by former governor and senator William L. Marcy, sought to reconcile all three groups and accepted the Barnburners back into the party. The result was an uneasy alliance in 1852, in which Pierce won New York and a Soft, Horatio Seymour, was elected governor.[47] But Pierce knew that the Hards sat on their hands during the presidential election and that his most active support came from the Barnburners led by "Prince" John Van Buren and former senator John A. Dix. This prompted Pierce's initial plan to make Dix secretary of state. The

Hards succeeded, because of their close ties to southern senators, in forcing Pierce to switch from Dix to the Soft leader, Marcy, for the key position in his cabinet, but now Pierce had to contend with the issue again as he attempted to select a slate of appointments at the state level.[48]

Marcy argued against attempting to reconcile all factions, but Pierce was determined to carry out his pledge to reward all wings of the party equally. With the help of his cabinet he proposed a slate for the nine offices in New York City requiring Senate confirmation.[49] Heading the slate was former senator Daniel Dickinson, the leader of the Hards as collector of the port. The second position in importance, that of sub-treasurer, was given to John A. Dix, a leader of the Barnburners. Of the nine positions, three went to each of the three factions of the Democratic Party in New York, with Charles O'Conor, Pierce's dinner guest on April 8, receiving the position of U.S. district attorney.[50] Though Marcy, writing to Governor Seymour, claimed to be opposed to the "theory" on which the appointments were made, he supported the final slate as less objectionable than it might have been.[51]

On April 1, the Senate confirmed all nine appointments, but for the first and only time during this special session insisted on a roll call vote on the Dix nomination. The reality that Pierce was determined to reward some who had bolted the party in 1848 was too much for southern and "old line" Democrats. They had threatened to not confirm Dix when Pierce was considering him for the cabinet, and now they wanted to issue a warning to the president not to go too far in rewarding free-soilers like Dix. Dix was confirmed by a vote of twenty-eight to eight, but a number of leading Democratic senators were absent, and among the negative votes were the Senate president, David Atchison of Missouri, and Senators Jesse Bright, Andrew Butler, James M. Mason and Thomas Rusk, all Democrats, from Indiana, South Carolina, Virginia, and Texas respectively.[52] A clear message was being sent, but Pierce was determined to press ahead with his plan.

The intransigent leader of the Hard faction, Daniel Dickinson, came to Washington to meet with Pierce. Upon learning that Pierce expected Dickinson to dispense the more than seven hundred positions in his department according to Pierce's formula, Dickinson promptly turned down the appointment.[53] Pierce next turned to another Hard, former state supreme court justice Greene C. Bronson, to be collector; unlike Dickinson, Bronson was a man of integrity, according to Marcy and others.[54] At the dinner on April 8, O'Conor was prevailed upon to return to New York to convince Bronson to accept the appointment, which the Senate had confirmed that day.[55] Bronson accepted, but all three factions waited anxiously to see if he could or would carry out Pierce's patronage plan.

The selection of John A. Dix for sub-treasurer in New York is significant, not just because he represented the Barnburners, but because it demonstrates Pierce's determination to have honest, competent administrators at all levels. For political reasons, Pierce believed he needed to include the Hards in his government, but he also knew their reputation for speculation and corruption in relation to the management of the state canal system. By placing a personal friend, a New Hampshire native, and man of impeccable honesty and reputation in charge of the money coming into the port of New York, Pierce was making more than a political statement. It was, undoubtedly, a message that Dickinson heard, and rather than be scrutinized in his actions by an honest subtreasurer, he chose to decline the position. Why Dix accepted is another matter. Disappointed at not being selected to the cabinet, he had received a promise from Pierce that he would be chosen as minister to France as soon as it was practicable for Pierce to make the appointment. He accepted the position in New York as a personal favor to Pierce, but with the understanding that it would only be temporary.[56] The Senate roll call vote on his confirmation should have alerted Dix, as it did Pierce, that choosing him for a top level diplomatic post would be a hard sell in the Senate. It is not surprising, therefore, that the position of minister to France was not included in any of the many diplomatic appointments made by Pierce during the first months of his administration. He was hoping that time, and Dix's graciously assuming a lesser position, would convince party leaders of his loyalty.

But the position of minister to Great Britain could not wait, and Pierce was determined to send James Buchanan to London. Mrs. Fillmore's death on March 30 (she had been ill at Willard's Hotel since moving out of the White House on March 4) caused the government to shut down for half a day, giving Pierce a much-needed break from cabinet meetings to address a personal letter to Buchanan offering him the post. Buchanan expressed interest and traveled the next week to Washington to meet with Pierce and Marcy.[57] After dinner at the White House on April 8, Pierce escorted Buchanan to his library in the family quarters for a frank discussion. Buchanan did not want the position if it was purely a gesture of reward for past services to the party, but only if he would be entrusted with considerable responsibility to carry out negotiations in London on all of the issues currently existing between the United States and Great Britain. Pierce assured him that this was his intention, and that Marcy concurred.[58]

The next day, Buchanan made the rounds of his friends in the District of Columbia, including Senator Bright and Postmaster General Campbell, who all urged him to accept the appointment. But he learned that day that the Senate, after exhausting its list of presidential nominations, had adjourned the special session. Buchanan assumed that Pierce had changed mind, as he had not sent his nomination to the Senate. Buchanan expressed this to Jefferson Davis on Sunday, April 11. Davis reminded Buchanan that it was not unusual for presidents to make appointments when the Senate was not in session, the appointee assuming his position immediately, with the Senate confirming when it reconvened. Buchanan was unwilling to leave for London without Senate confirmation, however, reminding Davis that other nominees had ventured overseas only to be rejected by the Senate. Davis, recognizing the logic of Buchanan's argument, immediately informed the president. On Monday morning, Pierce asked Buchanan to come to the White House, where the two men confirmed their earlier conversation about the post in London, and Pierce agreed to send Buchanan's name to the Senate that day if a quorum could be gathered. Enough senators (thirty-three) remained in Washington to reconvene, and Buchanan was confirmed that day.[59] Congress would not be in session again for nine months.

Though there were still hundreds of positions to fill, the pressure began to ease on the president by late April. His secretary, Sidney Webster, as gatekeeper to the president's office, suffered the most from the aggressive job seekers. He wrote, "I try hard to keep good natured, but it is an effort. The crowd however, say on the Avenue, that 'Webster is so cross that no one dares to address him twice.'"[60] French, still diligently signing the president's name to land patents, saw that "the President is getting rid of some of the pressure upon him, and often appears to me like that same Frank Pierce with whom, twenty years ago, I frolicked, and was merry & happy. . . . He appears happy & seems to bear the infliction of greatness as if he was created for the place he fills."[61]

The easing of the pressure from job seekers allowed the president to focus on other matters for the first time. He immediately set out to reform the way business was done in several executive departments. First was the attorney general's office. Congress had recently elevated the position to full cabinet rank, granting the attorney general an $8,000 salary equal to that of all the other members of the cabinet. With help from Marcy and Cushing, Pierce expanded the authority of the attorney general by assigning duties previously handled by the secretary of state to Cushing. By executive order, on April 6, 1853, the attorney general was given responsibility for the appointment and supervision of federal judges, district attorneys, and marshals.[62] With the added responsibility, Cushing decided not to engage in private law practice while serving in the cabinet, as others in his position had done. Explaining how he viewed the responsibilities and duties of his office, he wrote a lengthy paper that became a model for all future attorneys general.[63] With these strokes of a pen, Pierce created the modern Justice Department, though it would take another generation before Congress would get around to officially legislating its existence.

Another significant decision was transferring from the Department of the Interior to the War Department the responsibility for supervising the construction under way in Washington, D.C. Davis was put in charge of constructing the new wings and dome for the Capitol, the Washington Monument, and the aqueduct to carry fresh water to the city. He immediately chose Major C. Montgomery Meigs of the Army Corps of Engineers to supervise these projects, and Captain Thomas Jefferson Lee was put in charge of overseeing the renovations to the White House.[64] In April, the president along with Davis and members of Congress, including Senator Stephen A. Douglas of Illinois, traveled by steamer to the falls of the Potomac, where Pierce spoke briefly and turned over the first shovel of dirt for the new aqueduct.[65]

Pierce's emphasis on competence and integrity in the public service was put into practice with the promotion of Peter G. Washington, a career Treasury official, to the position of assistant secretary. Assistant Postmaster General Selah R. Hobbie, a Whig appointee to that position, was reappointed by Pierce for his effectiveness, as was the commissioner of the land office, John Wilson, another Whig. All three positions were traditionally political appointments, and, the land office job, particularly, was much sought after by Democrats.[66] By placing career bureaucrats in these key positions, Pierce was signaling that efficiency rather than politics and speculation would rule in his administration.

As the Pierce administration worked diligently at filling important government offices, word reached Washington on April 18 that another office had been vacated by the death of Vice President William R. King. The longtime senator from Alabama, close friend and ally of James Buchanan, had been nominated by the Democratic convention to placate the Buchanan wing of the party. Buchanan urged Pierce to seek King's counsel in selecting his cabinet, but Pierce ignored the advice. In fact, from the time of the convention in June, 1852, to King's death at his plantation in Selma, Alabama, on April 18, 1853, there was no communication of any kind between Pierce and King. King understood that he would have no role in the new administration, writing to Buchanan, "However kindly Genl. Pierce may speak and write concerning me, it is evident beyond all question that I am not one of those whom he takes into his confidence, for not a single line have I received from him since the nomination." In turn, King determined to have "as little intercourse with him as possible."[67]

By the winter of 1853, King was too ill from tuberculosis to worry about his future role in the Pierce administration. He left for Cuba in January, seeking relief, but by the time of Pierce's inauguration it was understood that he would never recover. A special act of Congress permitted the American consul in Cuba to swear King into office. The ceremony took place on March 24, the only time in U.S. history that a president or vice president took the oath of office on foreign soil.[68] King, too weak to stand unaided, was supported by Rep.

George Washington Jones of Tennessee. Newspapers in the United States reported the event: "The ceremony, although simple was very sad and impressive, and will never be forgotten by any who were present. To see an old man, on the very verge of the grave, clothed with honors which he cared not for, and invested with authority which he could never exercise, was truly touching. It was only by persuasion that Mr. King would go through with the ceremony, as he looked on it as an idle form, for he was conscious he would not live many weeks."[69]

Wishing to die at his home, King left Cuba on April 11, arriving at Pine Hills only to die the next day. For the second time in a month, the business of the government was shut down as Washington officials paid tribute to the vice president.[70] The office would remain vacant throughout the Pierce administration as there was no constitutional provision, at that time, for replacing the vice president. David Atchison of Missouri, president pro tem of the Senate, was next in line of succession for the remainder of the Thirty-third Congress.

On the surface, the new administration appeared to have gotten off to a successful start. During the first six weeks, all of the president's appointments had been confirmed by the Senate, and many of the key positions had been filled. But as the senators left Washington for home, cracks in the support for the new administration were evident to many close observers. Newspapers reported that individual senators were upset by their inability to get friends appointed to government positions. One report had Senator R. M. T. Hunter of Virginia storming out of Postmaster General Campbell's office shouting, "God damn you, who commands this concern," after Campbell's refusal to appoint Hunter's man to a postmaster position in Virginia. Hunter marched directly to the White House, where Pierce backed Campbell's decision.[71] The proadministration *Washington Union* was forced to defend the president's policy on patronage, claiming that Pierce was motivated by what was good for the country in "recognizing no distinction, and espousing no faction in the democratic party" and that by so doing, Pierce "manifests the catholic and comprehensive spirit which should animate the President of the United States."[72]

This may have been the ideal, but the reality was that patronage, not policy, fueled the "second party system." Because every issue of national significance, territorial expansion, railroads, and trade and tariffs divided the nation by geography and reopened the debate on slavery, politicians instinctively avoided strong policy positions. Since the issues in antebellum America could only divide and not unite national parties, the only thing that held them together was patronage.[73] Pierce understood this and attempted to open a broad umbrella under which men of various political distinctions could gather. He wanted to use the spoils of office to build a stronger, broader-based party. But the ability to deliver jobs to one's friends was so essential to a politician's success and power that Pierce's policy of opening opportunities for so many meant that individual political leaders would not be able to satisfy as many friends as they had anticipated. What was worse, the Pierce policy meant that rival factions in the same state would be given equal consideration, thus fueling bitterness on all sides. Add to this Pierce's pledge of good government, his insistence on competence and honesty in each appointee, and his selecting career bureaucrats regardless of party affiliation to key positions to monitor the activities of those in their departments, and political leaders saw not just a threat to their ability to award jobs to their friends but a limit on the opportunities for speculation, conflict of interest, and outright plunder that had become the expected rewards of people in public service.[74] It is no wonder that these first weeks of the new administration were viewed with alarm by many leaders of the Democratic Party and that newspapers were reporting by late spring "the most intense disappointment all over the country at Pierce's appointments" and predicting that "open rupture" was likely among the factions of the party.[75]

Even within the cabinet there was concern. Davis was upset that Pierce had awarded positions in Mississippi to his rivals, known as the "Union" party. He proposed to Cushing that the cabinet adopt the following policy on appointments: "That knowingly no man who is disposed to agitate against the institution of African slavery as it exists in some of the states of the Union, or who seeks or desires to destroy the Union of the states or who has avowed such sentiments has been or will be appointed to office."[76]

Davis's proposal went on to add that any appointee later found to hold such sentiments would be removed from office. Davis wrote at least four different drafts of this policy, but it was not formally announced by the administration, though all cabinet members supported the basic premise.[77] This shows, however, that the administration was concerned by the reaction to its initial round of patronage decisions. Newspapers in the North claimed that "nearly every appointment of any value has been given to the fire-eaters and disunionists, who opposed the Compromise of 1850 to the bitter end."[78] Southern papers, in turn, blasted the appointment of free-soilers, like Dix, as evidence that the administration was antislavery. Clearly, Pierce had made enemies within his own party by his independence from the "old guard" leaders in his policy on patronage. They would not forget and sought an opportunity to discipline the inexperienced president.

2

POLICIES, POLITICS, AND PUBLIC RELATIONS

JOBSEEKERS CONTINUED TO PRESS the president and his cabinet throughout the spring and summer of 1853. Amid all the demands for office, Pierce and his cabinet began to establish the policies that would guide the actions of the administration for the next four years. Pierce was committed to administrative change, and a reforming spirit dominated the cabinet proceedings. The cabinet met daily for the first six weeks, engaging in the give-and-take of filling offices, but regular meetings continued at least once a week for the next four years. At these meetings, Pierce took the lead, but each cabinet member shared freely his plans and policies and sought feedback and advice from the group. Pierce set the example of a hands-on management style that would characterize the leadership practices of all of his department heads. He worked hard, was in his office for long hours each day except Sundays, and frequently visited the various bureaus throughout the city, showing interest in the work in progress and, particularly, in the federal employees.[1] Just as he had done as a brigade commander in Mexico, Pierce liked to be with his men, encouraging and reassuring them of his support. This practice also reflects a physical restlessness in Pierce. He could not sit behind a desk for long and needed to be in motion and in the company of others.

Though the nation was at peace and the economy was booming, there were significant challenges facing the new administration in every department of government. Within weeks of taking office, each cabinet officer, with the approval of the president, had established a set of goals to guide his work and administrative systems to bring efficiency and uniformity to the activities of the employees of the executive branch.

The most wide-ranging challenges were faced by the State Department. William L. Marcy had no experience in foreign affairs and immediately agreed to reassign some of his department's responsibilities to the attorney general's office. He also created the office of assistant secretary and chose the experienced, energetic A. Dudley Mann for the position. For the next four years, foreign affairs and diplomatic crises would vie with domestic issues for the full attention of the administration and the nation.

Pierce's inaugural address had clearly set the goals of U.S. foreign policy: securing the national defense, enhancing trade throughout the world, expanding territory, and promoting democracy and freedom everywhere.[2] As it had been since independence was achieved, Great Britain was seen as the greatest obstacle to achieving American national goals, and Central America was the arena where the contest between the two nations would be played out over the next four years. Since the gold rush brought California into the Union in 1850, the need for improved communication and transportation with the West Coast became vital to the national defense and the economy. A trans-Isthmian canal or railroad across Central America was an immediate necessity, but Great Britain's presence in the area prevented a unilateral American solution. The Clayton-Bulwer Treaty of 1850 was meant to resolve the issue but proved insufficient due to ambiguous wording, and "unintelligible phrases." In essence, the treaty prevented any exclusive control over a future canal and declared against colonization of the area by either nation. But since the treaty was ratified, Britain had expanded its protectorate over the Mosquito Indians in Nicaragua, fortified Greytown at the mouth of the San Juan River (the most likely route for a canal), established a protectorate over a group of islands claimed by Honduras, and declared that the treaty did not apply to its colony in British Honduras (Belize). Thus, the Pierce administration inherited what H. C. Allen calls "probably the most persistently unpopular agreement ever made by the United States with a foreign government."[3] Marcy's first priority, then, was either to get the British to agree that the treaty meant what the United States thought it meant or, failing that, to negotiate a new treaty addressing all of the issues relating to British expansion of its influence in Central America.

Other matters pressing between the United States and Great Britain involved trade and fishing rights with Canada. Ever since Parliament repealed the Corn Laws in 1846, the Canadian economy had suffered, as it had lost its privileged position in the British market. Canada needed admission to American markets for its products. U.S. fishermen, in turn, wanted greater access to Canadian waters. A treaty of 1818 required U.S. fishermen to stay outside a three-mile limit of "Coasts, Bays, Creeks or Harbours" in British North America. The treaty had been loosely enforced until 1851, when the British navy began to patrol the coast, seeking violators. U.S. fishermen asked for protection from their government and threatened to arm themselves to prevent being seized by the British navy.[4] Pierce had barely assumed office when he began to hear from New Hampshire fishermen pleading for immediate help, as the new fishing season was about the begin.[5]

These issues with Great Britain had prompted Pierce to ask James Buchanan to accept the position of minister to London. Buchanan accepted with the understanding that he would be allowed to negotiate all of these issues in London. Pierce and Marcy agreed, at first, but within a few weeks began to have second thoughts. With New Englanders pressing for immediate help and British minister, John Crampton, offering to negotiate the Canadian issues separately with Marcy in Washington, Pierce decided to separate the Central American and Canadian issues. Buchanan would not arrive in England until the fall of 1853, and the opportunity existed to solve at least one set of problems before he could be settled in London.

After being confirmed by the Senate in April, Buchanan returned home to his Pennsylvania estate, Wheatland, to await his official instructions from Marcy. As weeks went by without any communication from Pierce or Marcy, Buchanan began to suspect that they had changed their minds about entrusting all negotiations to him. He returned to Washington in mid-May and met on three separate occasions with Pierce and several times with Marcy, from whom he learned that negotiations on the Canadian issues would likely take place in Washington, not in London.[6] Since Buchanan believed that the "great lever" of trade reciprocity with Canada was needed to force the British to make concessions in Central America, he began to question whether he should embark for England at all. In June, he wrote to Pierce, concluding that if the president had changed his mind on the fishing and reciprocity issues, "it would be vain for me to go to London to settle a question [about Central America] peculiarly distasteful to the British government, after they had obtained, at Washington, that which they so ardently desire."[7] Over the next month, Buchanan and Pierce engaged in a delicate dance, with Buchanan offering to withdraw as minister if it would not embarrass Pierce, who, in turn, was determined to have Buchanan in London, but on his terms, not Buchanan's.[8]

The relationship between Pierce, Marcy, and Buchanan was complex. Both Marcy and Buchanan had aspirations for the presidency and blamed each other for their failures to receive the party's nomination in 1852. Each believed that had the other released his delegates at a key moment in the Baltimore convention, the nomination would have been theirs, and each man now suspected the other of plotting for the nomination in 1856. Pierce's patronage policy also caused consternation to Buchanan. Almost none of the candidates he recommended for positions had been chosen. He could only conclude that Pierce was trying to build up his own party of public servants, loyal only to him, to secure his renomination in 1856, thus blocking Buchanan's bid one last time.[9] If this was Pierce's purpose, having a chief rival for the nomination in London, and out of the political scene, could only help his cause.

After several of his letters to Pierce went unanswered, Buchanan became more and more frustrated. On June 23, he wrote the president, "Be kind enough to permit me, in case your enlightened judgment has arrived at the conclusion that Washington, and not London, ought to be the seat of the negotiations, most respectfully to decline the mission."[10] Pierce finally responded to Buchanan's prodding on June 26, claiming Buchanan's earlier letters had been misplaced but justifying the decision to negotiate the fishery and reciprocity issues in Washington, due to "the threatening aspect of affairs on the coast in the provinces." He continued, "To suspend these negotiations at this moment, in the critical condition of our interests in that quarter, might, I fear, prove embarrassing, if not hazardous." Pierce claimed that only necessity had caused him to retreat from his earlier promise to allow Buchanan to negotiate all questions between the United States and Great Britain in London. Pierce added, "I need not say that your declination at this time would be embarrassing to me. . . ."[11] Buchanan replied that he understood why negotiations between Marcy and Crampton should not be broken off, but that he had agreed to go to London to negotiate "all questions or none" and, therefore, preferred not to go.[12]

Before hearing again from the president, Buchanan had an unexpected visitor, Assistant Secretary of State Mann, who presented Buchanan with his official instructions for the London mission, prepared by Marcy and approved by Pierce. The next day a letter arrived from the president claiming that "nothing, it is to be feared, but the prospect of a speedy adjustment [to the fishery question] will prevent actual collision" and urging Buchanan to accept the mission with the revised instructions.[13] Buchanan responded that Mann's visit had caused "some irritation," as he had decided not to accept the mission, but "to gratify your wishes . . . I shall take the question under reconsideration for a brief period." With the president planning a July trip north to attend the opening of the Crystal Palace exhibition in New York City, the first world's fair held in the United States, it was agreed the two would meet as Pierce passed through Philadelphia.[14] Pierce had Buchanan where he wanted him. By delaying and ignoring some of Buchanan's letters, Pierce and Marcy bought time to solidify their plans for negotiating on the British questions, and the delay made it more difficult for Buchanan to resign the commission without placing the president in an embarrassing position. As Pierce wrote, "What explanation could be given for it, I am unable to perceive."[15] Pierce and Buchanan each understood that resigning because he did not get all he wished for from the president would make Buchanan look peevish or petty in the eyes of the general public. Pierce would successfully employ his personal charm and persuasiveness to convince the conflicted Buchanan to accept the post when the two met in Philadelphia.

Relations with Great Britain would remain a priority for Pierce and Marcy, but other nations also posed problems for the United States. Mexico was a persistent concern. Despite the Treaty of Guadalupe Hidalgo, which ended the Mexican War, there were still boundary concerns in New Mexico, and Indian raids along the border caused complaints from residents of both nations. Two competing American firms had each claimed that the Mexican government granted them the exclusive right to build a canal or railroad across the Isthmus of Tehuantepec, and both wanted the U.S. government to intercede with Mexico on their behalf to honor their claims. The Mesilla Valley just south of the border of New Mexico appeared to be a promising route for a transcontinental railroad if the United States could acquire it from Mexico. In March 1853, word reached Washington that Santa Anna, president of Mexico during the Texas war for independence and the Mexican-American War, had returned to power and was in need of money. This presented a window of opportunity, and Pierce immediately appointed James Gadsden of South Carolina, a railroad promoter and longtime friend of Jefferson Davis, to be American minister to Mexico. Gadsden's instructions were to negotiate for the purchase of land from Mexico. A clause in the Treaty of Guadalupe Hidalgo made the United States responsible for protecting Mexican citizens from, and paying the damages caused by, Indian incursions along the border. Gadsden was instructed to get Mexico to release the United States from this responsibility.[16]

Americans had long had their eyes on Cuba as a potential territorial acquisition. Polk had offered to buy Cuba from Spain in the 1840s for $100 million.[17] Cuban planters were unhappy under Spanish control, and many Americans anticipated a revolution on the island. Adventurers or soldiers of fortune from the United States, known as filibusters, had attempted invasions of Cuba to foment revolution and bring about annexation by the United States. It would be a major goal of the Pierce administration to acquire the island. How this was to be accomplished was unclear, but Marcy's instructions to Pierre Soulé, the new minister to Spain, stated that the administration hoped Cuba would "release itself or be released" from Spanish control. Pierce was not ready yet to instruct Soulé to offer to purchase the island, but Soulé was to make it clear to Spain that the United States would not interfere with Spanish sovereignty so long as Spain did not try to transfer Cuba to any other power (Britain or France) or to make Cuba a "protectorate" of any other nation.[18]

The Pacific was of secondary but growing importance to the United States. Pierce and Marcy sent Robert McLane as minister to China with instructions to seek trade reciprocity with that nation.[19] Commodore Perry's fleet had been commissioned by the Fillmore administration to open up Japan to U.S. trade. Perry had left in November, 1852, and the Pierce administration, particularly Secretary of the Navy Dobbin, waited anxiously for news of his expedition.[20] The United States also had a growing interest in the Hawaiian, or Sandwich, Islands and was particularly concerned that no other nation, particularly Great Britain or France, attempt to annex them.

Even the excrement of sea birds, known as guano, was a matter of concern to Pierce and Marcy. Guano was a popular fertilizer found on uninhabited Pacific islands, and American businessmen were anxious to corner the market. Peru controlled some 50 million tons of the stuff but was charging a high price and restricting its exports to two hundred thousand tons per year. Marcy instructed the minister to Peru, John Randolph Clay, to negotiate with the Peruvian government for the "speedy removal of the obstacles to the free traffic in the Guano of Peru."[21] At the same time, enterprising Americans had discovered an uninhabited and unclaimed island in the Pacific, Saint Felix, and asked the administration to "please authorize U.S. citizens to visit the island to collect guano and protect them in doing this."[22] Pierce turned the matter over to Attorney General Cushing for a legal opinion.

The custom-bound, protocol-driven world of international relations and diplomacy did not lend itself to the reforming spirit of the Pierce administration, but Marcy did his part to change policies and procedures where possible. In June 1853, he issued three circulars to the heads of U.S. missions around the world. The most famous, known as the dress circular, declared that in keeping with our republican principles, each U.S. minister was encouraged to appear at court "as far as practicable, without impairing his usefullness to his country, . . . in the simple dress of an American citizen."[23] This seemingly innocuous directive was actually quite revolutionary in practice, as it was expected in the courts of Europe that diplomats would dress in the most elaborately decorated uniforms, resplendent with braids, sashes, swords, and hats of all types. American representatives, not used to that type of garb, had to create their own garish, monarchical-looking outfits, in order not to embarrass themselves in court. Now Marcy was instructing them to appear in a black coat, trousers, and a silk hat.

The two other circulars specified the hours that U.S. consulates were to be open for business, required that no uniforms be worn, and even declared that the consul's clerk was not to be referred to as "the chancellor." More significantly, the circulars ordered that all clerks and vice consuls must be Americans. Local residents, non-Americans, had frequently been employed in these lesser positions in U.S. consulates abroad. The goal was to make the foreign service more efficient and Americanized.[24]

If the State Department did not lend itself to broad reform and innovation, the Treasury Department did, and Secretary James Guthrie was the perfect instrument to bring it about. Henry Adams declared that with all of the government's money passing through the Treasury, it "is the natural point of control to be occupied by any statesman who aims at organization and reform."[25] Guthrie fit the bill. A successful banker and railroad promoter in Kentucky, he applied his business acumen to the federal government with absolute honesty and integrity. The least political of Pierce's cabinet officers, Guthrie became a ruthless reformer, unmoved by political considerations but supported by his president in nearly every instance. Guthrie was often arrogant and domineering and lacked many of the social graces that characterized politicians, causing him to be a controversial figure in the Pierce administration.[26] He inherited a huge government surplus from tariff revenue and public land sales. A large surplus in the treasury restricts the amount of money in circulation. Guthrie set about to reduce the surplus by buying back the national debt and purchasing silver bullion to coin more money, thus increasing the amount in circulation and further fueling economic growth.

He also proposed lowering the tariff to reduce government revenue and stimulate trade.[27]

The largest division of the Treasury Department was the custom service, but the department was also responsible for the revenue-cutter service, coast survey, lighthouse system, bureau of weights and measures, accounting system, and steamboat inspections. Guthrie inherited a department lacking in systems, control, and accountability. He discovered more than $100 million in unsettled accounts, dating back decades, in the offices of the auditors and comptrollers. Guthrie determined to settle as many as possible.[28] The Independent Treasury had been established in 1846 to keep government money safe and out of banks, but Guthrie found that the law had been ignored by the Whigs and that some of the government's money was not in the treasury, but remained in state and private banks, and $5 million was in the hands of agents who earned commissions by arranging the purchase of the public debt or in transferring the money from the treasury to a bank.[29] There was also general suspicion of fraud and corruption in the collector's offices, as there was no oversight to determine if the revenue turned in by the collector matched what was taken in at each port.

Guthrie set out to correct all of these problems. He withdrew government money from banks, including the politically connected and powerful Corcoran and Riggs Bank in Washington, which held $493,000 in federal deposits. Corcoran's biographer concludes, "After years of controversy and partial reform, the Independent Treasury was at last to be fully instituted."[30] On April 1, 1853, Guthrie sent a circular to all collectors of customs, urging them to "enter upon the task of reforming what has been amiss, and introducing a more energetic, vigilant, and economical system." He threatened to dismiss anyone not competent, and stated his goal "to infuse vigilance, fidelity, and economy into the public service."[31] To force this upon the collectors, Guthrie required them to submit monthly accounts rather than quarterly. He also established new standards for all clerks working within the department. A doctor's certificate was required to excuse an absence, no newspaper reading or unnecessary conversation were allowed on the job, and immediate dismissal was prescribed for anyone indulging in alcohol. He insisted that the public be treated with frankness, courtesy, and kindness and with "an accommodating spirit" by all clerks, "to conciliate . . . the confidence and respect of the people for the government and institutions of their country."[32]

Guthrie immediately ended a practice of the collector of the port of New York whereby half of the money collected in fines for violation of the tariff laws was kept and divided among the collector, naval officer, and surveyor of the port. The previous Whig collector had withheld some $60,000 from the treasury, and the new collector, Greene C. Bronson, was required to find and return that amount. About $20,000 per year in fines was collected at New York, and Bronson's decision to accept the position was based on the expectation of being able to supplement his salary. Guthrie's decision to end the practice, which he believed to be illegal, had serious political consequences, as it eliminated a key reason for the prodigal Hard faction in New York to support the new Democratic administration.[33]

Eliminating fraud and corruption was made even more difficult by the actions of the judicial system. Guthrie was unable to reclaim the $60,000 withheld in New York because a judge of the U.S. circuit court attached the money on a claim by the previous collector. Guthrie had to await a decision from the court in New York and was prepared to take the matter to the U.S. Supreme Court if necessary. In another case, Guthrie discovered that the former Whig collector in San Francisco, James Collier, had failed to turn over the revenue collected in that port and had lent the money to local enterprises. Newspapers reported the shortfall in the San Francisco office to be as much as $800,000. Guthrie had Collier indicted in San Francisco and arrested by the U.S. marshal there, only to have him freed by a writ of habeas corpus issued by a friendly judge in Collier's native state of Ohio. Guthrie discovered that he could not have Collier rearrested, as there was "no provision for an appeal from the decision of the State judge."[34] Thus, another corrupt official escaped justice.

Guthrie did have considerable success in other areas. He ended the practice of employing agents and brokers to handle treasury funds and reclaimed all but $100,000 of the millions held by agents and brokers when he took office. He instituted a rule that claims against the United States, once settled, could not be reexamined. Some claims by citizens or companies had been rejected only to be reintroduced with slightly different wording each year, in the hopes of eventually receiving a favorable ruling, taking up considerable time from the department staff. Guthrie also forbade the subletting of contracts. It had been common practice for bidders to sublet contracts awarded by the government, but this meant the work was being done by contractors not approved by the government and not under its direct supervision and that collusion between contractors was inflating bids. He also discontinued the employment of secret customs inspectors, hired in each port city, who were suspected of extorting hush money from shippers. In their place, he sent out from Washington inspectors to examine all books and accounts. Finally, in a cost-cutting measure, Guthrie asked Pierce to dismiss twenty-seven superfluous officers from the revenue-cutter service.[35] The cliché that "a new broom sweeps clean" characterizes Guthrie's first year in office. Is it any wonder that lobbyists complained about "the d—d obstinacy of Guthrie towards every little plan by which our pockets might be quietly and comfortably lined . . . and nobody . . . the wiser for it."[36]

A recent act of Congress created four levels of government clerks, with graduated pay for each level, based on the clerk's ability subject to examination. The new administration needed to determine the criteria and assign all of the seven hundred clerks employed in Washington to these four grades. Most of the clerks covered by the act were employed in the Treasury, Post Office and Interior departments, and Secretaries Guthrie, Campbell, and McClelland agreed upon similar procedures for examining the clerks. In each department a board of three examiners, including the supervisor of the office, would test each clerk on his ability to write an ordinary business letter and to do basic arithmetic. The exams took place during the late spring and early summer of 1853, and each secretary was able to report that he found most of the clerks in his department to be competent and assigned to one of the four classes, though the standards set were so high that not enough qualified for the two highest classes to fill all the designated positions.[37] An auditor in the Treasury Department later reported that the "rigid system of *examination*" had materially improved the efficiency and deportment of his clerks, who could now secure promotion based on performance, "not by political or personal favor."[38] Some thirty years before a civil service exam system was created by the Pendleton Act, the Pierce administration was examining and classifying many government employees.

Even more so than the Treasury Department, the Interior Department, which contained the Patent, Pension, and Land offices and the Bureau of Indian Affairs, was rife with corruption. The newest cabinet department, created by an act of Congress in 1849, was also lacking in standards and procedures. In fact, Congress had created the department without giving the secretary the authority to issue commissions directly to the heads of the four bureaus under his control. These had to be signed first by the secretary of state or treasury, the departments which had originally contained the four bureaus that now made up the Interior Department.[39] Robert McClelland, an officious, detail-oriented, and determined former congressman and governor from Michigan, was perfectly suited to create an orderly, systematic department, and he set to work immediately.

McClelland created a system for everything. Even the filling of patronage positions was systematized, with clerkships in his department being distributed among the states in proportion to their representation in Congress. McClelland urged this method upon the other cabinet officers: "In order to [get] a proper distribution, among the several States, of the appointments in my Department, I have the honor to request that you will furnish me a statement, showing the number of Clerks, from each State, in your Department, and their salaries, similar to the one which I have caused to be prepared in reference to this Department. . . ."[40] Congressmen had apparently recommended this system to exercise control over the selection process. The method became an almost permanent feature of the spoils system.[41] With the new examination system, the cabinet officers were still able to insure that all the clerks appointed were competent to do their jobs.

McClelland fostered accountability by creating standardized forms for all departments and frequently requested reports from his officials. The amount of paperwork and supervision was so great that it irritated holdover personnel such as William Easby, the commissioner of public buildings appointed by Fillmore. Absent supervision from above, Easby had established his own way of conducting business. Rather than leave his congressional appropriation in the treasury to be paid out for specific expenses, Easby withdrew the entire amount each year and kept the cash in the safe of a doctor who lived near the White House. Easby was not the only commissioner to handle government money this way. McClelland demanded that Easby justify his methods and accounts. Easby explained his practices, admitting that shortcuts had been employed. McClelland pressed for more particulars, even questioning the purchases of plants for the White House gardens and greenhouse and the amount of dirt he had observed being hauled to the South Grounds. Who was supervising this work? Easby had had enough. He walked out in June 1853, complaining that he could no longer tolerate McClelland's meddling.[42] It was to replace Easby that Pierce appointed his old friend, B. B. French, who also found it difficult to meet McClelland's taxing standards: "Yesterday I received a parcel of ridiculous questions from the Secretary of the Interior . . . I have written pages upon pages of reports to him since I have been in office on matters of the very smallest importance. . . ."[43]

McClelland reported on the corruption he had inherited in his department, writing that "numerous frauds have been committed under the pension laws," including "perjury and forgery." Some veterans were receiving military pensions as invalids "without any disability whatever." He complained that the laws placed a two-year limitation on prosecution for fraud from the time of the commission of the offense, not nearly enough time to uncover the evidence in many cases. Nevertheless, McClelland attained several prosecutions and convictions in his first months in office.[44]

In cracking down on corruption, McClelland was fortunate to have able commissioners working under him. George W. Manypenny of Ohio, commissioner of the Bureau of Indian Affairs, stands out as one of the most honest and diligent of Pierce's appointments. Manypenny reported that many of the Indian agents "appointed to reside with, and take care of these Indians, have not always been honest, faithful men." He complained that agents often worked with "avaricious traders and speculators" to defraud the Indians of their annuities.[45]

One glaring example of this type of fraud would hound Manypenny for years. Richard W. Thompson, a former Whig congressman from Indiana, had been appointed by the Taylor administration to be an agent to the Indians of the upper Midwest. In 1848 the Menominee tribe of Wisconsin had agreed to a treaty paying them $300,000 for some of their land. After accepting the treaty, the tribe learned that, due to an imprecise survey, they had in fact surrendered far more land than what they had been paid for. The chiefs hired Thompson to be their attorney to lobby in Washington for a revision of the treaty. In a clear conflict of interest, Thompson, already a government Indian agent, was able to negotiate a supplemental treaty with his own Whig administration, paying the tribe an additional $300,000. Thompson's fee was to be one-third of whatever amount the tribe received.[46] This treaty was pending in Congress when the Pierce administration took office.

Manypenny, suspicious of Thompson's activities, sent a special agent to negotiate a new treaty with the Menominee. On learning that an agent was on his way to negotiate with the chiefs, Thompson headed for the scene to intervene and protect his original treaty. He arrived too late. The chiefs had agreed to a new treaty paying them $150,000 for the additional land, the payments to begin in 1867, after the original treaty payments had been made to the tribe. There was no provision for Thompson. After Manypenny's agent left, however, Thompson convinced the chiefs to sign a special memorial asking that he be paid, up front, one-third of the new treaty amount. Manypenny denied Thompson's new claim, citing an act passed by Congress in 1852 stating that no attorney or agent could be paid out of Indian annuities.[47]

Thompson appealed to friendly senators to override Manypenny's denial of his claim. A lengthy Senate debate ensued. Through Manypenny, evidence was presented showing that the chiefs who agreed to Thompson's memorial could not read or write and did not know what they were signing. Thompson admitted to paying $10,000 to lobby in Washington for his claim. In a speech made to the tribe, Thompson stated that he had bribed a senator to get a favorable vote on the earlier revised treaty. It was also revealed that Thompson had a similar arrangement with the Shawnee, who were to pay him one-third of any money the tribe received, and to pay the trading company of W. G. and G. W. Ewing one-half. The Ewings and Thompson were related by marriage, and the Ewings were related to the Whig secretary of the interior, Thomas Ewing, who had approved all of their claims while in office. Manypenny also revealed that to prevent men like Thompson from getting their hands on Indian annuities, he had begun the practice of paying the annual amount per capita, rather than sending a lump sum payment to the chiefs. When Manypenny's paymaster was sent to distribute the money to the Menominee braves, he found Thompson and friends at the field acting in a menacing manner. The paymaster had to surround himself with thirteen bayonet-wielding soldiers to keep Thompson and company from seizing the money. It was learned that later that day Thompson's men got most of the braves drunk and took the money anyway.[48]

Faced with such damning evidence, the Senate refused to agree to Thompson's claim, but the vote was close, nineteen yeas to twenty-four nays.[49] Thompson was also pressuring Pierce with his claim and had enlisted the help of Pierce's close friend, B. B. French, who had known Representative Thompson when French was the assistant clerk of the House of Representatives. Pierce could not be moved, however, and French reported, "Dick Thompson's matter is stopped by the President . . . so the President has . . . stopped the payment! Just our d—nd luck!"[50]

McClelland backed Manypenny in changing the policies to prevent this type of fraud from occurring, including the per capita payment of the Indian annuities.[51] There was nothing to be gained politically by being efficient and honest in dealing with Indians, and, not surprisingly, these reforms lasted only as long as Pierce was in office. The Pierce administration had not heard the last of Thompson, who tenaciously continued to press his claim on future congresses. Manypenny's only consolation for his service as Indian commissioner was the reputation he attained "as one of the most prompt, faithful, business-like, and honest officers we have ever had in Government," according to Senator Stephen A. Douglas.[52]

Postmaster General James Campbell had his own unique set of problems. The mail service was supposed to operate on a paying basis, but Campbell faced a $2,000,000 deficit in his first year. The problem was in the expense of transporting the mail between twenty-three thousand post offices and overseas. Contracts were awarded to stagecoach lines and railroad and steamship companies, but with the nation expanding to the West Coast, the cost of transportation had risen from $2,900,000 in 1849 to $4,900,000 in 1853, nearly 75 percent of the total annual expense of operating the General Post Office. Unlike coach lines, which allowed several companies to operate along public roads so that competitive bidding for the mail contract kept costs low, railroads had no competition and could dictate their own price to the department. Thus, it cost the government twelve cents per mile to send the mail via railroad, compared to five cents per mile by stagecoach. Campbell concluded, "if they [the people] wish to continue to receive their letters and newspapers at a cheap rate of postage, they must not permit these companies to dictate to the Department their own terms."[53]

On taking office, Campbell began examining and checking the accounts of the postmasters. But he had only eighteen special agents in the field, half assigned to supervise the transportation of the mail and half dealing with depredations in the post offices. Considering the number of post offices and the distances involved in trying to monitor them, Campbell reported, "The whole system of accounting, . . . is so little calculated to protect and secure the public revenue that I cannot rest under the grave responsibility of permitting it to continue" without a "proper remedy."[54] Campbell would have his hands full for the next four years.

The War and Navy departments had the benefit of being administered by Jefferson Davis and James C. Dobbin, two of the most able and innovative secretaries to ever head these departments.[55] Each man inherited a similar set of conditions and problems. The American people had always feared large standing armies in peacetime, and Congress had kept the size of the army and navy to the bare minimum needed to protect U.S. shores. To Davis and Dobbin, the condition of the army and navy in 1853 was inadequate for this purpose and badly handicapped in promoting American interests around the world.

Davis administered an army of 10,500 officers and soldiers, of which 8,500 were stationed in "frontier departments." The authorized strength of the army was nearly 14,000, but it was plagued by frequent desertions, a low rate of reenlistment, and an inability to recruit new men, due to the low pay and lack of opportunities for promotion.[56] Davis set about to develop a sweeping set of proposals to reorganize the army, but these would have to wait, as he was beset with additional responsibilities that required his immediate attention. First was the assignment by the president to the War Department of the responsibility for supervising all of the construction underway in the capital: the refurbishment of the White House, the new wings and dome for the Capitol, the Washington Monument, and the aqueduct along the Potomac. Davis assigned this work to officers of the Army Corps of Engineers. Second was an act passed by Congress in early 1853, appropriating $150,000 for surveys to be made of potential transcontinental railroad routes. The secretary of war was required to have the surveys completed and a report ready for Congress by February 1854. Davis had to determine which routes to explore, and organize and outfit the expeditions to take advantage of the favorable weather through the mountains during the late spring and summer of 1853.[57]

Officers of the Corps of Topographical Engineers were chosen to lead the surveys, and Davis authorized four separate exploring parties to embark as soon as possible that spring. The northernmost survey, near the forty-seventh parallel, was assigned to the new governor of Washington Territory, Isaac Stevens, who was to be assisted by Captain George B. McClellan. Davis instructed Stevens's party to travel east from the Puget Sound through the Cascades, while McClellan's party began at Saint Paul, Minnesota, and proceeded through the Rocky Mountains to the Cascades. Captain Gunnison was assigned to lead the second survey along the thirty-eighth parallel through Utah to Sacramento. The third survey was assigned to Lieutenant Whipple along the thirty-fifth parallel from the Colorado River through Albuquerque and on to the Pacific. The final survey, under the leadership of Captain John Pope, was to explore a route along the thirty-second parallel from the Rio Grande along the Gila River in Mexican territory and on to the Pacific. By early summer all four expeditions were in the field.[58]

James C. Dobbin took over a navy of seventy-five hundred men and seventy ships, but the service was in deplorable condition. A small, spare widower, whose own health was precarious, Dobbin became "easily the most popular of the Pierce cabinet." He was both a man of vision and an able executive, whose tact and amiability won him many friends in Washington.[59] Dobbin found that only forty of the navy's ships were serviceable, and most of the rest were not worth repairing. With this limited capacity, the navy was to protect American interests around the world. At all times, five squadrons were at sea: the home squadron, the Brazil squadron, the Mediterranean squadron, the Pacific squadron, and the African squadron, which was assigned the duty of patrolling the coast of that continent to suppress the slave trade. A sixth, the East India squadron under Commodore Perry, was en route to Japan when Dobbin assumed office. The concerns expressed by New England fishermen prompted Pierce to order Dobbin to send a "special squadron" to patrol the fisheries of New Brunswick, Nova Scotia, and Newfoundland.[60]

Not only was the navy stretched thin around the world, but it was functioning with obsolete equipment. According to naval historians Harold and Margaret Sprout, "In 1853 the United States possessed not one vessel that could have stood up against any first class European warship."[61] Very few steamships were in use, and those the navy did have were side-wheelers unsuited to naval duty or war, as they could be easily disabled by an enemy, and they were expensive to operate, since they did not take to sail when their steam power was not needed. There were no steamers on duty with the African or the Pacific squadrons, and no steamers with more than ten guns.[62] A new type of steamship, powered by an underwater screw propeller instead of side wheels, had recently been invented by Captain John Ericsson. In the busy days before his inauguration, Pierce had been invited by then-Navy Secretary John P. Kennedy to tour Ericsson's new vessel. Kennedy wrote at the time, "We had Mr. President Fillmore and his elect successor, Mr. Pierce, Captain E. [Ericsson] and myself, and Mr. Everett [Secretary of State Edward], all riding together up and down on the piston—rather an amusing and rare inauguration of a new invention."[63] Pierce and Dobbin became converts to the new technology. Secretary Dobbin reported to Congress, "Steam is unquestionably the great agent to be used in the ocean, as well for purposes of war as of commerce."[64]

Ever since his term in the Senate, Pierce had advocated a larger and more modern military. His experience in the Mexican War added to his conviction that modern military science needed to be embraced and promoted.[65] As president, he fully supported the efforts of Davis and Dobbin to expand and modernize the army and navy. It was a difficult and thankless task. In both services promotion was based entirely on seniority, not merit. Many officers remained on active duty long past their time because there was no retirement system, and disabled officers also refused to leave the active list because there were few provisions for them. As Dobbin concluded, "The great evil of our present system is that neither merit, nor sea-service, nor gallantry, nor capacity, but *mere seniority of commission, regulates promotion and pay.*" Morale suffered when a gallant officer witnessed "the indolent, the imbecile, who have known no toils, and have never met the enemy, daily promoted over him."[66] Enlisted men, soldiers and seamen, came and went in alarming numbers. There was no incentive to remain in service, and with a growing economy, opportunities in civilian life were far more attractive than military service. Both the army and the navy needed complete reorganization. The Pierce administration was determined to take on the task.

As if the new administration did not have enough challenges, the internecine warfare within the Democratic Party made it virtually impossible for Pierce to solve many of the problems his administration had inherited. Within three months of his inauguration, open warfare was being waged against the president by Democratic leaders in New York, Pennsylvania, and in Pierce's home state, New Hampshire. The only issue was patronage, the motive was jealousy, and the only purpose was to seek revenge on the president who had failed to properly reward certain factions within the party. By June, former senator Daniel Dickinson of New York, who was leader of the Hard faction, newspaper editor and writer Francis J. Grund of Pennsylvania, and former congressman and editor Edmund Burke of New Hampshire were plotting the destruction of the Pierce administration. All three had supported Cass for the nomination in 1852, and none had received the hoped-for reward for backing Pierce after the Baltimore convention.

Dickinson had been offered the lucrative and powerful position of collector of the port of New York, but Pierce's insistence that the collector distribute the seven hundred positions in that office equally to all three factions of the state Democratic party caused Dickinson to turn down the job and seek revenge. In mid-May, reports from New York were reaching Pierce that the Hards were "unquestionably organizing under the direction of . . . Dickinson . . . & company an opposition to the administration." The writer wanted to "make the President understand what bad men they are who call themselves *Hardshells*. . . ." They were actively "denouncing the administration publicly . . . in the most hostile manner."[67] Dickinson's newspaper, the *Albany Argus*, declared "it is the 'Old Guard' of the National Democrats, upon which a truly National Administration must rely."[68]

Grund, a writer for the *Baltimore Sun* and *Philadelphia Public Ledger*, had hoped to be appointed editor of the *Washington Union*, the administration paper in the city or, failing that, to be selected to start an administration paper in New York City. Having been denied both positions, he declared his opposition to the administration in a letter to Caleb Cushing in April: "I have no longer any desire to act as a 'coefficient' to its [the administration's] second term."[69] He believed Cass's friends had been ignored, but his main complaint was that his fellow Pennsylvanian James Campbell, a Catholic, had been selected for the cabinet: "If Pierce has sold himself to the Irish Catholics, it is but proper that the Germanic protestants and Anti-Papists should show their hands and proclaim their hostility to Jesuitism in Church and State."[70]

Burke had a long association with Pierce and the New Hampshire Democratic Party. The two were both "radicals" in the initial opposition to railroads and corporations in the 1830s, and they served together in Congress. Burke was more of a Washington insider than Pierce, having remained in the capital after his third term in the House to serve under Polk as commissioner of patents, and then as assistant editor of the *Washington Union* during the Taylor and Fillmore administrations. Burke had been feeding at the trough of the spoils system for years and anticipated future rewards when his friend Pierce became president. But Burke had made an egregious error in the months leading up to the Baltimore convention. Among his Washington friends he had criticized Pierce when his name was first floated for the nomination. By the time Burke realized that

Pierce had a chance to win, his initial comments had reached Pierce and his friends in New Hampshire.[71] Burke worked hard for Pierce at the convention and claimed credit for the nomination, but the damage had been done. Pierce's friends did not trust Burke, and no role was assigned to him in the election campaign.[72]

Instead of campaigning for Pierce, Burke spent the summer of 1852 soliciting testimonials from politicians around the country that attested to his loyalty to Pierce and his service at the convention.[73] Burke still hoped to convince Pierce of his worthiness for a prominent position in the new administration and had his sight set on either his old position of commissioner of patents or the editorship of the *Washington Union.* Pierce's friends were not buying Burke's transparent attempts to ingratiate himself with the new president, and B. B. French observed, "I read his attempt to crawl out of a very tight place, in which he has very foolishly and very *unbecomingly* placed himself." Burke's effort reminded French of an old "epigram":

> He wires in, and wires out,
> until the people are in doubt
> whether *the snake* that made the track
> *was going South or coming back.*[74]

Needless to say, Burke was not offered a position in the new administration. Pierce may have known Burke too well. He had always been a harsh and uncompromising partisan, and his editorials in his newspaper, the *Newport Argus and Spectator,* were full of vitriol. Burke had also been carrying on a feud for years with William Butterfield, editor of the *New Hampshire Patriot,* Pierce's organ in Concord.[75] Burke was a ruthless political infighter who lacked Pierce's smoothness and willingness to compromise, and he was a loose cannon, as his earlier comments about Pierce had demonstrated. Pierce also may have questioned Burke's honesty and ethical conduct. As the former commissioner of patents, Burke had been hired as a lobbyist by those seeking patents. His standard arrangement was to receive $8 per diem for his time in Washington and $1,000 additional if successful. In one case, when his offer to lobby against the renewal of a patent on the Woodworth Planing Machine was rejected by a competing company, he offered his services to Woodworth to lobby for renewal and was hired.[76]

In April 1853, Burke met with Pierce in the White House.[77] What transpired between the two men is not recorded, but Burke returned to New Hampshire ready to undermine the president at the first opportunity. He began communicating with Dickinson and Grund and started a new newspaper in Concord, the *Old Guard*, to challenge Pierce's paper, the *New Hampshire Patriot*, and signal his intention to speak for those disaffected by Pierce's policy of rewarding all factions of the party.[78]

Burke's first opportunity to cause trouble for Pierce was the state Democratic convention in June 1853. At the gathering in Concord, a slate of candidates was nominated for the upcoming elections, but the sparks flew over a set of proposed resolutions to serve as the state party's platform. Burke had been chosen to chair the resolutions committee and arrived at the convention with a draft of a set of resolutions already prepared. They restated standard party positions, including support for the Compromise of 1850 and the Baltimore convention platform of 1852 and were unanimously endorsed by the committee. When the resolutions were read to the convention delegates, however, members of the Concord clique immediately objected to the fifth resolution: "That we encourage ourselves with the belief that our distinguished fellow citizen, now at the head of the Government of the United States, will not in his appointments over look the Old Guard of the Democratic party upon whom he must rely for successful support in all the emergencies which may arise in the progress of his administration."[79] Most delegates saw nothing objectionable in Burke's resolution, but those closest to Pierce knew what Burke was up to. Samuel H. Ayer, a young lawyer from Manchester, declared that the resolution was "a secret dagger at the heart of our own Frank Pierce": "It was an attempt to censure the administration for *not* appointing the old guard . . . It was an insinuation that Gen. Pierce had appointed secessionists, fanatics, abolitionists, factionists, to office. It would be so interpreted all over the country."[80] This was the last thing that most of the delegates intended to do, and the resolution was immediately withdrawn and replaced with one that endorsed "all the official acts of the administration."[81]

Having been exposed by Pierce's closest allies in Concord, Burke set out to defend his actions at the convention, claiming that the resolution was not an attack on the president, "and nobody would have imagined that it contained an assault on the administration, if it had not been pointed out by Ayers" of the Concord clique.[82] Burke's lengthy diatribe in his newspaper went on to attack the editor of the *Patriot* as a former "free-soiler" and Pierce's successor as chair of the state party as a former "Whig." He admitted, "I do not approve of the appointments to office of free-soilers, coalitionists, disunionists, or Whigs.... If the President has appointed a man to his cabinet who was but a short time since a leading federalist [Cushing], I say frankly that I do not approve of it." Burke claimed he was Pierce's only true friend, trying to protect him from those "who Iago like, ... used their positions to pour into his ears, along with their obsequious flattery and fulsome adulation, the envenomed poison which was to alienate him from his truest, longest tried and most devoted friends. In that they succeeded."[83] The *Patriot* countered that Burke was no friend to the Pierce administration and that his actions were "simply because that administration does not think proper to purchase Edmund Burke's support by giving him a lucrative office!" Burke had been heard to exclaim around town that "Pierce has treated him 'd——d mean.'"[84]

The war between Burke and Pierce's allies in New Hampshire waged openly and bitterly in the press over the next few months. Paul R. George, the older halfbrother of New Hampshire state party chair John H. George, correctly diagnosed the problem to Caleb Cushing in Washington: "While Gen. Pierce was here himself he was quick as lightening to detect a ... mischief making politician, he would snuff with a quick ear, as the deer will danger. All his men minded well. He would turn the trouble from the man intending to use it so that when the time came, the game would be blocked. Now there is no one, yet a Gen'l, to take the Gen'l's place."[85]

With Pierce in Washington, a vacuum was created in the leadership of the Democratic Party in New Hampshire. Pierce had left the Senate in 1842 to assume leadership of a divided state party. His political skills had kept that party united and victorious throughout the next ten years. As soon as Pierce returned to Washington, old feuds and jealousies resurfaced within the party in New Hampshire. Pierce was frustrated by Burke's actions and wrote to Senator Charles G. Atherton, "Did any man of sense ever make such an exhibition of himself." Pierce always claimed he had never said anything about Burke to anyone to justify his attack, but admitted "what my friends may have done it is not for me to say."[86] Always a conciliator, Pierce never initiated a political feud. His loyalty to his party and his kind and generous personality made it difficult for him to understand those who would hurt the party for personal reasons. Nevertheless, to the press and to political leaders, a president who could not command the united loyalty of his home state party was severely weakened. Though cheered on by Dickinson and Grund, Burke would gain nothing for himself by his actions. He never held elective or appointed office again at either the state or national level.

On July 11, 1853, Pierce left Washington, bound for New York City accompanied by cabinet secretaries Davis, Guthrie and Cushing. The stated purpose of the excursion was to attend the opening of the Crystal Palace. Political and diplomatic reasons also compelled Pierce's attendance. Queen Victoria had sent Earl and Lady Ellesmere, considered among the most popular and influential of the leading families of England, as her emissaries to the opening of the fair.[87] Pierce intended his gracious attention to the foreign visitors to pay dividends on the diplomatic front. He and Guthrie also needed to attend to political matters in New York, where collector Bronson was dragging his feet in making appointments according to Pierce's formula and Daniel Dickinson was openly hostile. The route through Baltimore, Philadelphia, and lesser cities and towns would be an opportunity for Pierce and company to be seen and to address the people, an opportunity denied him five months earlier when, because of Benny's recent death, the president-elect refused all public ceremonies during his trip to Washington.

Of course, Jane would stay behind in the White House. With the help of her companion, Abby Means, she had been writing letters to family friends and to Benny's former tutors and religious instructors, asking for personal reminiscences of her lost child. By summer she had received several replies attesting to the boy's great promise, his sensitivity, and religious devotion.[88] If these buoyed her spirits, it was not evident to visitors in the White House. Henry Watterson later recalled meeting Jane Pierce around this time. Henry was exactly Benny's age, and his father, former congressman Harvey Watterson, was an old and dear friend of Pierce. Henry recalled his introduction to Jane Pierce at the White House as "one of the most vivid memories and altogether the saddest episode of (his) childhood": "A lady in black took me in her arms and convulsively held me there, weeping as if her heart would break."[89] Jefferson Davis's young wife, Varina, also noted how Jane's normally dour exterior melted at the sight of young boys.[90] Her husband held his emotions in check in public, but Benny was never far from the president's thoughts. Pierce made certain that in his absence from Concord a suitable headstone was placed at the grave of his son and that the plot was attended to each week.[91]

On the eve of his departure for New York, the president and first lady attended the service at the First Presbyterian Church. A reporter happened upon the scene: "A handsome two-horse carriage, with driver and footman attired in plain blue dress, drove up, and a gentleman and lady—the latter dressed in deep mourning, and wearing a veil over her face—stepped out, and entered the church before me. . . . The pair passed in unnoticed, and took their seats in an ordinary pew in the center of the little church. The congregation was small and far from fashionable, and none seemed to be aware of, or if they were, to consider in any way remarkable the presence in their midst of the chief ruler of this mighty Republic and his amiable, but grief stricken consort."[92] That afternoon, as French would later report, Pierce and B. B. French took a ride in French's "buggy": "We rode three or four miles, and it did seem like going back twenty years." Pierce read excerpts from the speeches he had prepared to give on the trip, and French was impressed, predicting that "this tour, will add unfading laurels to his brow." Having worked in Pierce's office for several months, French had observed the president up close each day. French wrote his brother in New Hampshire, "I tell you that Frank Pierce *is* a great man—he is at least head and shoulders greater than I took him to be, before he became President. He is the best

President we have had since Jackson, and for the times, the very man we ought to have!"[93]

The president's party left the capital by train on Monday afternoon. At stops along the way many citizens climbed aboard to meet the president, so that by the time the regularly scheduled train reached Camden Street Station in Baltimore, it was filled beyond capacity. The station was so crowded with men, women, and children that Pierce had difficulty making his way through the terminal. Outside, the president mounted a beautiful white charger for the procession through the city. Pierce led the parade on horseback, surrounded by thousands of troops from militia units in full dress and followed by four barouches carrying the mayor and the members of Pierce's party. A crowd estimated at one hundred thousand lined the route, and as the president passed by, he was "again and again most enthusiastically cheered." The *Baltimore Sun* reported, "We never recollect gazing in this city upon such an immense multitude."[94]

At Barnum's City Hotel Pierce was escorted to a private parlor for a brief respite, but the crowd outside kept calling for him so "vociferously" that he came out to a stage, where the mayor welcomed him and Pierce spoke to the crowd. He remarked, "My heart is full, and it would be difficult to express the depth of feeling with which this cordial welcome has impressed me." His speech went on to praise the state of Maryland "where the banner of unbridled, unqualified religious toleration was first freely given to the breeze," and the city of Baltimore for its defense of Fort McHenry. He concluded that if Baltimore was not already known as "the Monument City" he would christen it "the City of the Star-Spangled Banner."[95] This would be the pattern of each of his speeches on the trip. He would praise the city or state with specific references to its historical or commercial achievements and make general but pointed remarks about ideals that mattered most to his administration: religious tolerance, free trade, open immigration, and preservation of the Union. At Baltimore the *Washington Union* reported, "His voice, loud, thrilling, and clear as a clarion, was heard at the extremist verge of the crowd."[96] Davis, Guthrie and Cushing followed the president with speeches of their own.

In the evening the president met with reporters from the city newspapers, attended a banquet at the hotel, and retired to his room at 10:00 p.m. suffering from the first symptoms of a cold. The next morning the party left Baltimore by train at 8:15 a.m., bound for Philadelphia. The president reached Wilmington just before noon, when another parade took him to city hall. In his speech he relayed a humorous incident that happened in the parade. While Pierce was riding in a carriage with the mayor, a man in the street was told "to get out of the way! He replied, 'the street that is broad enough to vote on, is broad enough for me to see the man I helped to make President.'" But the cold had settled into Pierce's throat, and he informed the crowd, "I regret extremely that in consequence of illness, the result of a sudden cold last night, it is not in my power to speak to you and your fellow-citizens as I would be glad to do."[97]

In midafternoon the president's party boarded the steamship *Indian Queen* for the trip up the Delaware River to Philadelphia. On board, former vice president George M. Dallas welcomed the president on behalf of the people of Philadelphia. Pierce replied that he had had "extreme doubt" about leaving Washington, due to the "absence from the peculiar field of my duty," but because of the response of the people, he said, "I am now satisfied that I came to the right conclusion." Once again, he cut his remarks short as "every word I utter, Mr. Dallas, is a sort of knife in my lungs."[98] The boat was welcomed in Philadelphia at 4:00 p.m. by the loud salute of the shore battery, and Pierce mounted a horse for another parade, this time to Independence Hall. A reporter wrote, "Throughout the whole route the President was received with cheers, waving of handkerchiefs, & c."[99]

James Buchanan viewed the parade from the second story window of Lebo's Commercial Hotel. He observed that Pierce "was on the right of General Robert Patterson, and being a good horseman, he appeared to much advantage on horseback." Pierce recognized Buchanan in the window and gestured to him.[100] John W. Forney later remarked that Pierce was "one of the most striking men that ever sat in a saddle."[101]

At Independence Hall, Pierce was welcomed by Mayor Charles Gilpin and managed to speak "at considerable length" of his "profoundest awe" at being in such a historic site. That evening a banquet was held at Merchants' Hotel. The ceremonies ran late, and it was nearly 9:00 p.m. when the party sat down to dinner. Buchanan was present, seated on the opposite side of Mayor Gilpin. Pierce leaned behind Gilpin and strongly urged Buchanan to accept the London mission. Buchanan refused to commit himself but agreed to meet with Pierce the next morning. The dinner did not break up until nearly midnight, with "the President cordially participating in the hilarity of the scene."[102]

At the dinner, Jefferson Davis made probably the most important speech of the trip. He addressed the issue of a transcontinental railroad. As a commercial and trade center, Philadelphia seemed the perfect place to float a trial balloon of possible federal government appropriation for the project. The Democratic Party had always opposed a federally funded system of internal improvements as unconstitutional. Davis claimed he would never waver from his constitutional principles simply for the purpose of expediency. To this, Pierce interjected that "he knew he would not." But Davis believed the constitution offered an opening, because a Pacific railroad was needed for the nation's defense. How else to move troops quickly across the continent, and the constitution clearly permitted federal expenditures for defense purposes.[103]

Pierce and Buchanan met early the next morning, July 13, before the president returned to Independence Hall at 9:00 a.m., where he stood for several hours, shaking hands with the citizens "who thronged" the hall "in great numbers." Several hundred were still in line at 11:00 a.m., when the president's party was forced to leave for the steamer to take them across the river to Camden to resume the journey to New York. Buchanan accompanied Pierce on the ship and finally agreed, after much coaxing and prodding, to accept the London mission. By the time the party reached Camden, Buchanan was in such good spirits, enjoying the company of Pierce, Guthrie, Davis, and Cushing, that he seemed reluctant to leave and was jokingly asked to come along to New York. Buchanan finally took the hint and departed as the president's party boarded the train that would taken them through New Jersey.[104]

The train proceeded through New Jersey with a major stop at

Trenton, where Pierce spoke of his father's military service in the Revolution. At Newark another large procession and ceremony was held. Once again Pierce's voice failed him, and he cut his remarks short, though claiming that "such a welcome as he had received was enough to make a dumb man speak."[105] Following another banquet in Newark, Pierce retired early, hoping to rest his voice for the culminating events of the trip in New York City.

The next morning, the *New York Herald* published an editorial, "A Word of Caution to the Hard Shells." Editor James Gordon Bennett had been critical of the administration's patronage policy, particularly as Pierce had failed to select Bennett for a diplomatic post. Nevertheless, the paper gave this warning: "We know they [Hards] are sorely disappointed and somewhat indignant concerning the distribution of the public plunder, and that it will be hard to restrain them from a public hint to the President of their displeasure on the very first opportunity. But we caution—yea, we conjure the hard-shells to remember that there is a time for everything, and that this Presidential dinner will not be the time for stirring up a disturbance in the family. . . . Have some compassion, also, for the President . . ."[106] Bennett need not have worried. There were no public demonstrations against the president by the Hards, but Pierce met with Hard ledgers at the Astor Hotel before he returned to Washington; no record exists of what was discussed.

Otherwise, the day was a success. The president's party crossed the Hudson on the steamer *Josephine* at 7:00 a.m., accompanied by a full salute from the batteries on Governor's Island. The river was full of ships "stretching on either side as far as the eye could reach" with colors flying "gorgeously in the sun, and men occupied every available place in the rigging and on the deck from which they could best do honor" to the president. With the Governor's Island band playing "Hail Columbia" and "The Star-Spangled Banner," Pierce landed at Castle Garden, where he was welcomed by Mayor Jacob Westervelt. Pierce acknowledged the welcome with his longest speech of the trip, commenting on the city's remarkable growth over the past thirty years. He credited immigration for much of the increase in population and stated, "How can we fail to welcome those who come to us from the gray old nations of Europe? Let them come! There is room enough for all . . ." Pierce criticized "all the schismatic organizations" that wanted to restrict immigration and that claimed that immigrants could not become real Americans. To Pierce, new arrivals ceased to be Europeans the moment they entered this country, and their contribution "destroys the claim that ours in a nation governed by men of one race alone. No single race of men can boast that to them alone is humanity indebted for such a country as this." Pierce also praised the great commercial and industrial progress of the city and advocated free trade as the best means of insuring continued prosperity.[107]

Following the ceremony, Pierce mounted a beautiful horse, Black Warrior, owned by an army major, to review the troops at Castle Garden. The horse was twenty-two years old and had served in Mexico, having been wounded twice in the same battles Pierce fought in. One reporter described the scene: "The President rode up and down the lines successively, making the tour of the Battery several times, and was enthusiastically received by the military and the people. He bowed very graciously to the troops in passing by, to some with more familiarity than others."[108]

The president's party reboarded the steamer *Josephine* at 11:30 a.m. for the short trip to lower Manhattan. Pierce was supposed to take a seat in a four-horse barouche for the procession up Broadway to the Crystal Palace, but the president insisted on being on horseback instead. The procession departed with Pierce leading the way riding the black stallion. This caused some confusion for the spectators, who had been informed that the president would be riding in a carriage. Since few had ever seen him, Pierce had already ridden past before many realized it was the president himself leading the parade. To add to the confusion, a violent rain storm suddenly struck, drenching the president and the troops riding and marching with him. Those in the barouches which followed were able to put the top up and remain relatively dry. The shower lasted nearly half an hour but was so localized, that those spectators above Fourteenth Street experienced no rain at all and were standing in the swirling dust as the president and party marched by dripping wet. The president's bedraggled appearance did not dim the crowd's enthusiasm, however, and as Pierce removed his flopping wet hat and bowed to the people along the way, he was showered with bouquets thrown by ladies from the windows above—some containing notes for the president.[109] Newspapers reported the crowd at nearly a million people.[110]

At 1:30 p.m. the procession arrived at Forty-Second Street and Sixth Avenue, the site of the Crystal Palace. Before going in, Pierce made a short stop at Mass and Villaman's Saloon on Sixth Avenue to dry off and "drank a glass of water, with just enough brandy to kill the insects." The crowd pressed against the windows of the saloon for a closer look at the president. Finally entering the Crystal Palace around 1:45, Pierce was met by some ten thousand people crammed into the hall and by many dignitaries on the stage. Among those in attendance were Governor Howell Cobb of Georgia; Governor Horatio Seymour of New York; Generals Winfield Scott, George Cadwalader, and John A. Quitman, who had served with Pierce in Mexico; and such old friends as Charles H. Peaslee, who had come down from Boston. The ceremony opening the Crystal Palace went on for several hours, with Pierce extolling the benefits of science in contributing to "our domestic comforts and our universal prosperity." His remarks were brief, and he thanked the crowd and croaked, "I have not the voice to address you more at length."[111]

Before heading for the Astor House, where the evening festivities would take place, Pierce made a brief detour to visit Earl and Lady Ellesmere, who had been unable to attend the festivities due to the illness of the earl. This departure from protocol was much appreciated by the British emissaries, who reportedly "feel very sensibly the high honor done them by the President—in his personal civilities and kind expressions." C. A. Davis wrote to Marcy, "They know and fully appreciate the departure the President chose to assume—from the usual course by calling on them personally." Davis added, "They seemed tickled amazingly by his personal kindness."[112]

At the Astor House, a banquet was followed by a visit by Pierce to the ladies' drawing room, escorted by George N. Sanders, who was recently appointed by Pierce as consul to London. Pierce paid his respects to Howell Cobb and family. At 11:00 p.m. a dance was held, followed by a light supper, though Pierce "looked excessively fatigued, . . . laboring under severe physical debility . . . from the arduous labors through which he [had] just passed in his journey from Washington."[113]

On Friday, July 15, Pierce returned to the harbor in the morning for a tour on board the *Josephine*, followed by a stop at the studio of Mathew Brady, who "took a splendid portrait [daguerreotype] of the President." He returned to the Astor House, where he received the citizens of New York for the rest of the afternoon. In the evening, it was back to the Crystal Palace for another banquet. Pierce made some brief remarks complimenting Sir Charles Lyell, regarded as the founder of modern geology, who was present, and then left before the speeches of Davis, Guthrie, and Cushing, to attend the opera at Castle Garden, where Madame Sontag was performing. Pierce was so exhausted that he left the performance early, receiving "three cheers" from the crowd of five thousand as he rose to leave.[114]

On Saturday, July 16, the president and his party, minus Cushing, who pressed on to Boston to speak at Harvard's commencement, left by train at 10:00 a.m. for Washington. They traveled straight through with no stops or ceremonies, reaching the capital at 9:00 p.m. the same day. Pierce went straight to bed to recover from his cold and fatigue.[115]

The reaction of the press to the president's trip was largely positive. According to the *New York Herald*, "Rest is a stranger to the man in high office." It was a "melancholy sight" to see Pierce "bowed down by fatigue . . . forced to respond to every shout!" The editorial continued, "The man is sacrificed to the system. Some portion of their applause may have been due to the talents and virtues of the man, but by far the greater portion was a mere testimony of the respect felt by all classes for the exalted station which he fills."[116] A Whig paper gave Pierce more credit: "Beyond all question, Mr. Pierce possesses the power of pleasing and moving his hearers. He is a *popular* speaker, and turns his public interviews with his fellow-citizens to good account; and he has the good sense also, in the main, to leave public affairs and public allusions out of his speeches."[117] Another paper concluded, "It was a proud moment to the President to see himself thus generously received by the huzzas, the eyes and hearts, of so many of his fellow-citizens. This sublime scene in his life he will never forget."[118]

The only highly critical comment from the trip came in a private letter from John W. Forney to James Buchanan. Forney had been with Pierce on most of the trip, but was a longtime friend and ally of Buchanan. Forney wrote, "Pierce has had a fine reception but I deeply, deeply, deplore his habits. He drinks deep. My heart bleeds for him for he is a gallant and a generous spirit. The place overshadows him. He is crushed by its great duties and he seeks refuge in. . . . His experience convinces me that a great mistake was made in putting him in at all."[119] To what, specifically, Forney is referring is not clear. Pierce did drink on the trip, as each banquet included toasts of wine or champagne, and Jane was not present to keep an eye on him, but he was also clearly suffering from a cold. Only Forney seemed to take exception to the president's behavior. Was he simply keeping his foot in Buchanan's camp, telling the old politician, who loved gossip, what he wanted to hear? B. B. French, who knew Pierce as well as anyone, never commented on his drinking, but French did label Forney "a drunkard and a most unprincipled & dishonest man."[120] Forney's opinion of Pierce changed drastically over the next few months, as he became a close adviser to the president. In his memoirs, written years later, Forney never referred to Pierce's drinking. Instead, Forney, by then a longtime Republican, described Pierce as "gallant, handsome, true-hearted, genial . . . one of the truest of my friends. I lay upon his grave the heartiest tribute of my unfading gratitude."[121] Time would determine if the goodwill generated by the trip and the proposals floated by the president and his cabinet, including the Pacific railroad and free trade, would bear fruit.

3

CRISES—FOREIGN AND DOMESTIC

WITH CONGRESS NOT IN session from April to December 1853, the Pierce administration was able to turn much of its attention to foreign policy. Several important diplomatic posts were still vacant when Congress adjourned. In the ensuing months Pierce and Marcy resorted to recess appointments, which would have to be confirmed when the Senate reconvened. Among the most noteworthy of these recess appointments was Governor Thomas H. Seymour of Connecticut, who served under Pierce in Mexico and was a hero of the storming of Chapultepec, chosen minister to Russia. To Portugal, Pierce sent John L. O'Sullivan, a former editor of the *Democratic Review*, who coined the phrase "Manifest Destiny." O'Sullivan was an unabashed spokesman for the expansionist goals of Young America. After his sister married a prominent Cuban planter, O'Sullivan lent his considerable influence in support of Cuban filibuster activity. As a consequence, he was twice indicted, in New York and New Orleans. Defended by fellow Barnburner John Van Buren, he was found not guilty in both cases. O'Sullivan was also a very close friend of Hawthorne's. August Belmont, New York agent of the Rothschild international banking firm, financier of the Pierce election campaign, son-in-law of Commodore Perry, and nephew-in-law of John Slidell, was selected to be chargé d' affaires in the Netherlands. George N. Sanders, another former editor of the *Democratic Review*, outspoken critic of "old fogies," and promoter of Young America, was chosen to be U.S. consul to London.[1]

Buchanan selected Dan Sickles to be his secretary of the legation in London. Pierce had also met Sickles and was impressed with the brilliant and charming young New York City politician.[2] Sickles, a member of the Hardshells, was already building a reputation as an unscrupulous politician with an unsavory personal life. His selection prompted considerable comment in his home state. Governor Horatio Seymour, a Softshell, was pleased to get Sickles out of the state assembly: "If there is any honorable way of getting him out of the country I hope it will be done as I regard him as the most able and efficient of the Hard Shells."[3] But Marcy's close friend J. Addison Thomas, who had been appointed to a lesser position in London was not happy at the prospect of closer contact with Sickles: "Of all bad appointments that were made this is the worst. It is especially disagreeable to me."[4] Hawthorne was already at his post and met his new counterparts in the fall, when their ship arrived at Liverpool. He could not resist recording in his journal his impressions of Sickles:

> A fine-looking, gentlemanly, intelligent young man, but, so I am told, very dissolute, and with some remarkably dark stains in his character. Unless belied, he has been kept by a prostitute, within a few years, and is now married to a woman whom he seduced. . . . Be that as it may, in aspect and address he does us credit.[5]

By the time Pierce returned from his New York trip, all of the important diplomatic posts had been assigned except for the mission to Paris. It had been Pierce's intention to appoint John A. Dix, who had done so much good work campaigning for Pierce in 1852, but Dix's former association with the Free Soil movement in 1848 made him anathema to the Hards in New York and their southern brethren in Congress. Dix had accepted the lesser position of subtreasurer in New York City in hopes of demonstrating his party loyalty, but Pierce, understanding the increasingly explosive political situation in New York, became convinced that Dix could never be confirmed by the Senate as minister to France. Dix attempted to further resurrect his reputation by issuing a series of letters to the southern press, defending himself as a loyal Democrat and no abolitionist, but these only made him appear, to his Barnburner friends, to be groveling to the slave power. Pierce hoped Dix would see the handwriting on the wall and release Pierce from his commitment, but Dix had already done this once regarding a cabinet post and was not about to make this decision easy for Pierce a second time.[6] It was October before the situation was resolved.

In his diplomatic appointments to Europe, Pierce had selected men who were associated with the expansionist Young America faction of the party. Except for Buchanan, they were all young, ambitious, aggressive, even impetuous, and they were Pierce's choices, not Marcy's.[7] But they could be controlled by the instructions they received from Pierce and Marcy, and the press was relatively complimentary in its reaction.

All the negative press regarding his domestic appointments, however, convinced Pierce of the need to have reliable, effective newspapers through which his administration could get its messages out to the public. The *Washington Union* had served this function for the Polk administration and continued under editor Thomas Ritchie and assistant editor Edmund Burke to espouse the Democratic cause during the Whig administration. But Ritchie had retired, the unreliable Burke was in New Hampshire, and the paper needed an infusion of new and talented editing. To be profitable, the paper relied on the printing contract awarded by Congress each session, and with this prospect in mind Pierce was able to convince former senator A. O. P. Nicholson of Tennessee to assume co-ownership of the *Union.*[8] Pierce had Nicholson install John W. Forney, chief clerk of the House, as one of the editors of the paper. Pierce's old friend and former congressman Harvey Watterson and Roger A. Pryor, a young and talented reporter from Virginia, were also added to the editorial staff of the paper. Attorney General Caleb Cushing also contributed editorials to the *Union* on a regular basis.[9] A further sign of trouble ahead for the administration was the launching of a new Democratic daily in Washington in September 1853. The *Washington Sentinel,* published by Beverly Tucker, was to be the mouthpiece of the southern Democratic position, and though its prospectus claimed it was the "friend and coadjutor" of the administration, it fully intended to be a "sentinel" against any antislavery backsliding by the president from New Hampshire.[10]

The New York trip convinced Pierce of the need for a loyal administration paper in that city. James Gordon Bennett, editor of the Democratic-leaning *New York Herald,* had already proven to be sympathetic to the Hard faction and was personally alienated from Pierce. Pierce asked John W. Forney to try to arrange financing to purchase and edit the *New York National Democrat* and turn it into an administration organ.[11] But Forney was unable to find the necessary financial backing, and the administration continued at a disadvantage in getting its message out in the nation's largest city.

The first international crisis of the Pierce administration involved a Hungarian national in far-off Smyrna, Turkey. Martin Koszta had participated in Louis Kossuth's revolutionary movement to free Hungary from Austrian control in 1848–49. With the failure of the revolution, Koszta fled to Turkey, which refused Austria's request to extradite Koszta and other Hungarian refugees. Eventually, Austria agreed to release its claim to Koszta on the condition that he never return to Hungary. Koszta made his way to the United States, where he lived for two years. On July 31, 1852, in New York City, Koszta took an oath renouncing his previous allegiance to Austria-Hungary and declaring his intention to become a citizen of the United States. He then returned to Smyrna on private business. On his arrival in Turkey, he presented himself at the U.S. consulate, producing the certificate of his intention to become a citizen, and was given a letter of safe conduct by the consul. Nevertheless, on learning of Koszta's presence in Turkey, the Austrian consul recruited what Marcy called fifteen local "desperados," who seized Koszta at a coffee shop, beat him, dragged him to "a den," threw him into a small boat, and carried him to an Austrian "brig-of-war," the *Husvar,* where he was kept in irons to be conveyed back to Austria by way of Trieste, Italy.[12]

The U.S. consul in Smyrna appealed to the Austrian consul and to the Turkish authorities for the release of Koszta. As Marcy later wrote, this proved "fruitless," but the consul also reported the situation to the U.S. chargé in Constantinople. By chance, the U.S. sloop-of-war *St. Louis,* of the U.S. Mediterranean squadron, was nearby, and chargé John P. Brown advised the American captain, David N. Ingraham, of the incident in Smyrna. The *St. Louis* arrived in Smyrna harbor on June 21, 1853, just as the *Husvar* was about to depart with

Koszta. Ingraham insisted on boarding the *Husvar* and speaking with Koszta. Convinced of Koszta's right to protection by the United States, Ingraham gave the captain of the *Husvar* three hours to release Koszta or be fired upon by the *St. Louis.* As an excited and expectant crowd gathered along the waterfront in Smyrna and awaited the start of a naval battle, the French consul intervened, offering to keep Koszta in the French consulate until the United States and Austria could agree on a satisfactory solution to the standoff.[13] Violence avoided, the dispute now entered its diplomatic phase.

News of the events in Smyrna did not reach the United States until the end of July. The story of the freedom-loving Koszta and the intrepid actions of Captain Ingraham won wide popular approval and editorial praise. Secretary of State Marcy and Attorney General Cushing were in Berkeley Springs,Virginia, at the time, commencing important negotiations with British minister Crampton on the fisheries and trade reciprocity matter with Canada.[14] It was not until August 10 that the full cabinet was able to gather to read over all of the dispatches from Captain Ingraham and U.S. officials in Turkey. The cabinet was unanimous in its decision to support all of the actions taken to protect Koszta and to resist any appeal from Austria. The official Austrian protest was presented to Marcy by the chargé in Washington, Chevalier Hulsemann, on August 29. The Austrian government demanded the deliverance of Koszta, claiming that he was still an Austrian subject who had merely declared his intention to become an American citizen. Thus, Ingraham's actions were a violation of international law, and Austria demanded the United States disavow the actions of its officials in Turkey and offer to Austria appropriate satisfaction for the outrage.[15]

Marcy immediately began working on the administration's answer. In its original draft, Marcy's reply covered more than seventy-five handwritten pages. He carefully related all of the facts in the case and demanded that Austria restore Koszta "to the same condition he was in before he was seized in the streets of Smyrna . . ."[16] Marcy's carefully worded argument was that Koszta was a refugee from oppression who had every right to choose to live in any country that would offer him "the fairest prospect of happiness." International law protects anyone who establishes domicile within a country regardless of citizenship. Koszta had followed all of the appropriate procedures on arriving in Turkey registering with our consul and receiving a letter of safe conduct according to the laws of Turkey, and, therefore, he was entitled to full protection. Marcy's paper praised the actions of Ingraham and strongly condemned "this outrage" by the Austrian consul at Smyrna for employing "lawless men" and "ruffians" in seizing and mistreating Koszta.[17]

Marcy's reply was given to Hulsemann on September 29 and printed in the nation's newspapers the next day. It was widely praised throughout the country and in Europe, where Lord Palmerston, the future British prime minister and a strong critic of the United States, told Buchanan it was "a very clever paper, very clever paper."[18] Marcy's "exposition of the significance of domicile as the basis for the right of diplomatic protection" was later endorsed by secretaries of state, international lawyers, and the U.S. Supreme Court.[19] On October 3, 1853, Austria released its claim to Koszta and dropped the matter entirely. Koszta was placed on a ship bound for the United States. The Austrian decision was not a direct result of Marcy's paper, which Austrian officials did not receive until weeks after Koszta's release, but was prompted by the determination of the Pierce administration to resist Austria's claim and by the fact that Austria's initial interest in Koszta was due to the suspicion that he knew something about the location of some crown jewels that were stolen by the revolutionaries. The jewels were found elsewhere while Koszta was in the custody of the French consul in Smyrna.[20] The Pierce administration and particularly Secretary of State Marcy could congratulate itself on the successful end to its first international crisis.

In an effort to avoid a similar clash with Great Britain, Pierce pushed for a settlement of the fisheries issue in Canada. The former secretary of state, Edward Everett, had tried to arrange a treaty with the British minister to Washington, John F. Crampton, during the last months of the Fillmore administration, but Fillmore had no interest in the project. Pierce knew that New England fishermen were arming themselves in case of interference by the British navy, which had begun patrolling the Atlantic coast off Canada. In May Pierce instructed Marcy to approach Crampton to resume negotiations, and in July he ordered Navy Secretary Dobbin to detach under

Commodore W. B. Shubrick a special a squadron to be stationed in Portsmouth, New Hampshire, for the "protection to such of our citizens as are there engaged in the fisheries."[21] This alarmed Crampton, who traveled to Halifax where he consulted with the British admiral, Sir George Seymour, urging caution in enforcing the laws related to U.S. fishermen in order to avoid a confrontation.[22]

Upon his return, Crampton met with Marcy at Berkeley Springs, Virginia, during the first week of August. Pierce had visited Berkeley Springs, a health resort along the Potomac northwest of Washington, in July after his New York trip, and Caleb Cushing was vacationing there away from the heat of the capital when Marcy and Crampton arrived. Marcy kept a diary of his dealings with Crampton over the next few days. The British seemed eager to give in to the United States on the fisheries issue, in return for a reciprocal trade agreement that would allow most of the products of Canada to enter the United States duty-free. Marcy and Crampton agreed on the first two articles of the treaty granting the U.S. fishermen free access to all the coastal waters and use of the shore for drying fish in the British North American provinces. In return, Canadian fishermen would have the same rights along the Atlantic coast of the United States.[23] It was the list of duty-free items that produced "the great difficulty in negotiating the Treaty . . ." Marcy balked at including coal from Nova Scotia in the agreement, as this would be opposed by senators from the coal-producing states of Pennsylvania, Maryland, and Virginia, imperiling ratification of a treaty. He also resisted a proposal that would allow Canadian-made ships to be registered in the United States, as this would be competition for U.S. shipbuilders. Crampton resisted including unrefined sugar on the list of items admitted into Canada from the United States, as this would interfere with British colonial trade policy.[24]

With these details still unresolved, the initial negotiations ended with Marcy and Crampton agreeing to resume discussions in Washington after reporting their progress to their superiors. Marcy asked former secretary of state Everett for his opinions on the issues still unresolved. Everett advised him to give in on the coal issue, but he advised Marcy, "You cannot admit their ships to registry."[25] Marcy also relied heavily on the expertise of Israel D. Andrews, former consul to Halifax, who had studied all aspects of Canadian government and economy. In 1850 Andrews had submitted a 775-page report to the secretary of the treasury on the "trade, commerce, and resources of the British North American colonies."[26] As consul, he had urged trade reciprocity on then-secretary of state Daniel Webster as a step toward eventual annexation of Canada by the United States: "The establishment of reciprocity would instantly allay all agitation—it would defer the question of annexation to a more distant day, while it would no less certainly ensure the ultimate accomplishment of this great measure, not by violent and dangerous disruption, but by breaking link by link the chains which link the colonies to the Mother Country, and by establishing that community of sympathies and interests between the two countries which would make annexation an inevitable political necessity."[27] Andrews's knowledge of Canada, his extensive contacts in the provinces, and his near obsession with forging closer ties between the United States and Canada would be fully utilized by the Pierce administration.

After consulting with the experts, Marcy addressed a note to Crampton and enclosed a draft of a treaty that did not include either the admission of coal to the free list or the registry of Canadian ships in the United States.[28] Crampton decided to submit Marcy's draft to Lord Clarendon, the British foreign secretary in London, for his advice. The process of ratifying a treaty, if one was concluded, was complicated, as it would need to pass the U.S. Senate, the British parliament, and the parliaments of each of the five Canadian provinces. Pierce was not willing to wait for the British government to act on the treaty. He saw the need to begin paving the way for future ratification. With this in mind, in September he appointed Israel D. Andrews special agent to "visit the North American colonies for the purpose of obtaining . . . all the information in your power relating to Trade and Commerce, and the present state of political feeling in the colonies, and the exact state of their relations with Great Britain and this country." Andrews was to lobby with Canadian officials and the press for the conclusion of a mutually acceptable treaty. They, in turn, might pressure Great Britain to expedite the treaty. Marcy instructed Andrews to use "discretion, vigilance, and constant application" in his "important and delicate" duties.[29]

The British government seemed in no hurry to conclude a treaty. In December Buchanan reported from London that he had had no success in pressing Lord Clarendon to act on Marcy's draft. He did note the arrival in London of Lord Elgin, governor-general of Canada, and hoped that his presence might influence the government.[30] When the Thirty-third Congress met in December 1853, Pierce and Marcy did not yet have a fisheries reciprocity treaty to present to the Senate, but they were determined to keep pressing the issue with Crampton in Washington, with Clarendon through Buchanan in London, and through the intense lobbying effort of special agent Andrews in the Canadian provinces.

At the same time Pierce and Marcy were deeply engaged in the Kozsta crisis and the Canadian reciprocity treaty, the Democratic Party in New York broke apart. Pierce's determination to keep the three factions, the Hardshells, the Softshells, and the Barnburners, under the broad umbrella of the national party by distributing patronage equally to each faction was doomed from the start because, as Mark Berger writes, the Hards were thoroughly "unscrupulous, often cynical, and totally devoid of principles, [and] they were in politics solely for the spoils of office."[31]

In the months following the appointment of Greene C. Bronson, a Hardshell, as collector of the port of New York, political leaders in that city and in Washington waited anxiously to see if he could or would follow Pierce's prescription by dividing the more than seven hundred positions in his office fairly among the three groups. Bronson was slow in making any appointments, but at first his political opponents made this assumption: "They cannot produce 25 incurable hard shells that are sober & honest enough for Bronson to appoint."[32] But as Bronson continually ignored the lists of acceptable candidates presented to him by the leaders of the Softs and Barnburners, Samuel J. Tilden advised Marcy that Bronson "is not following out the 'instructions' about which we heard so much when the collector was appointed & which were semi-officially set forth . . ."[33] Soft leader John Cochrane of Tammany Hall wrote directly to Pierce, "complaining of the course of the collector."[34]

The situation was complicated by events in Albany. The new governor, Horatio Seymour, a Soft, and a majority of the state assembly were determined to clean up corruption and focused their attention on Canal Commissioner Mather, a Hard, and his reported $9 million theft of state funds relating to canal contracts. Impeachment proceedings were brought against Mather by the assembly. The state senate tried Mather and debated his fate for three months before failing to achieve the two-thirds voted required to convict. Nevertheless, the arguments against Mather were published and distributed around the state. The Softs and Barnburners were consistently acting in concert, and this threatened the Hards' hold on state canal contracts and patronage.[35]

A decision by Secretary of the Treasury James Guthrie added fuel to the Hards' disenchantment with the administration. When Bronson accepted the collector's post, he could anticipate significant financial rewards from fees collected at the port. The reform-minded Guthrie ruled that the collector was not entitled to fees, only his salary. According to Governor Seymour, when Bronson agreed to the president's policy on appointments, he "supposed the place was worth twenty or twenty five thousand dollars. He *then* intended to carry out the policy of the Administration. The loss of the fees changed his feelings."[36]

Former senator Daniel Dickinson, the acknowledged leader of the Hard faction, tried to label the Softs and Barnburners as abolitionists in order to appeal for support from southern Democrats. But policy matters had no real connection to the motives of the Hards. Their policy of "rule or ruin" was motivated solely by their desire to get their hands into the state and national treasuries with "their wild schemes of plunder."[37] The realization that the Pierce administration was intractable on issues of speculation and corruption convinced Dickinson of the need to destroy the president. The state party convention held in Syracuse in September would be an opportunity for Dickinson to further this end.

Marcy anticipated trouble in Syracuse and advised his supporters, the Softs, to do whatever they could to keep the factions together in one party, but he wrote, "Our opponents—for so in truth they are . . . may give trouble at Syracuse." This was an understatement. The chairman of the state committee was a Hard. On the day of the convention, September 13, he abruptly changed the location of the gathering, but informed only the Hards of the new meeting place. The Softs and Barnburners showed up at the usual hall to find no one present. They searched around the city and found the Hards already convened at another hall with the doors locked. With their Tammany Hall allies, the Softs were able to break down the door, enter the hall, and with their numerical superiority in delegates elect the officers of the convention. The Hards then adjourned to a third location that evening, led by Canal Commissioner Mather,. Claiming they had been bullied and threatened by Irish thugs from Tammany Hall, the Hards nominated their own slate of candidates for the fall elections. The next day the Softs and Barnburners proceeded to nominate their slate and sent repeated invitations to the Hards to rejoin them. The Hards rejected these appeals. Both parties, for now there were two distinct Democratic parties in New York, passed similar sets of resolutions supporting the Baltimore platform, the Compromise of 1850, and the Fugitive Slave Act. The Hard convention did add a resolution copied directly from Edmund Burke's proposed resolutions in New Hampshire, advising the president to make his appointments only from "the Old Guard of the Democratic party."[38]

Less than a year after uniting to elect Pierce president, the New York Democratic Party had split in two, not over any national policy issues, but solely over the spoils of office. With the existence of two parties, which would Pierce's federal appointees in New York support? The answer came quickly. Tammany Hall held a rally to endorse the slate of candidates of the Union Democrats, the Soft and Barnburner party, and invited Collector Bronson and District Attorney O'Conor to address the rally. Bronson and O'Conor declined the invitations, claiming that the Hard faction was the real Democratic party in New York, and released letters to the press explaining their positions.[39]

The crisis in New York prompted Pierce to send Marcy to the state to survey the situation. Marcy wrote from New York to Attorney General Cushing, "I think that both Bronson and O'Conor should be removed, that B— should not be permitted to hold his position one day longer." According to Marcy, the longer Bronson remained in office the more the "bolters" could claim the "Pres. is changing his policy on appointments and is not displeased with Bronson's actions or the course of the 'bolters.'"[40]

Marcy's advice came a day late, as Pierce and Guthrie had already consulted on the matter with Pierce writing a draft of a letter for Guthrie to sign and present to Bronson. Critiquing his actions as collector, the letter took Bronson to task: "It has so happened that your appointments have been very generally made from that portion of the party to which you adhere. . . . the other portion of the party feel that they have not been fully recognized by you . . ." It reminded Bronson "that the President and his Cabinet, with entire unanimity, recognize that portion of the party as Democrats, distinctly avowing and firmly maintaining the principles of the Baltimore Platform, and entitled to be recognized by appointment to official stations in your department." The letter directed Bronson to "so recognize them in the way that will carry conviction with it."[41]

While awaiting Bronson's reaction to Guthrie's letter, which was published in the newspapers on October 3, Pierce announced the appointment of John Y. Mason of Virginia as minister to France on October 11.[42] This decision was in direct response to the New York situation and was meant to assure southern Democrats that in disciplining their Hard allies, Pierce was not signaling any antislavery sentiment. Mason, a former congressman and navy secretary in both the Tyler and Polk administrations, was an uninspired but safe choice. He was a close friend of Marcy's, and most significantly, he was not John A. Dix, the New York Barnburner who had long been rumored to be Pierce's choice for the position. In fact, on learning of Mason's appointment, Dix immediately resigned his position as subtreasurer in New York City.[43]

The president's rather mild rebuke of Bronson and the rejection of Dix caused consternation among the Barnburners. Their leader, John Van Buren, wrote anxiously to Marcy, demanding Bronson's removal from office. Van Buren reminded Marcy that he had loyally supported Pierce up till now, but Pierce had appointed Bronson, "whose mission has been to crucify my friends." Then, Van Buren continued, Pierce "promised Genl. Dix the mission to France," only to go back on his promise. Van Buren wrote, "The letter to Bronson by Guthrie (which I understand was written by the Prest.) was not what we wanted. We desired the President to say that Bronson had quit the party & to remove him for that cause." The delay in removing Bronson was only hurting the chances of the Soft-Barnburner party in the upcoming state elections, and Van Buren threatened, "I shall not hesitate to speak of the President's conduct as I think it deserves."[44]

In this confused situation, Guthrie arrived in New York on October 13, accompanied by his assistant secretary, Peter G. Washington, to have it out with Bronson.[45] This prompted Bronson, on October 17, to release his lengthy letter in answer to Guthrie's. His response was the height of insubordination. Bronson claimed he had never made any pledge to Pierce to follow any particular formula in making appointments. According to Bronson while Pierce claimed any Democrat who supported the Baltimore platform was eligible for office, the president expected Bronson to go back before the Baltimore convention to identify the various factions of the party that existed at that time and award them all equally. Bronson had signed no document pledging to do this. Besides, he said, the offices in question were in New York City, and the Hard faction had always been in a majority in that location and, therefore, were entitled to more offices. Bronson defended his decision to endorse the Hard party in the upcoming election and criticized the administration which he thought had "thrown its weight on the side of the freesoil ticket." He concluded, "This is, I believe, the first instance in which a member of the Cabinet has interfered with the discretion of a collector, marshal, postmaster, or any other government officer having patronage to bestow . . ." He denied the right of the secretary to interfere, stating, "The power of appointment is vested in the Collector alone."[46]

Bronson's defiant letter prompted his removal on October 22, 1853. In his letter (again probably written by Pierce) firing Bronson, Guthrie stated, "The concluding portion of your letter has left me no alternative but to lay the whole matter before the President, and take his direction concerning it. You assume that in relation to certain things you are to receive instructions from this Department, and in others, that you are to proceed without or contrary to such instructions. This cannot be admitted in any branch of the public service, for where the Department is not expressly empowered to give instructions to subordinates, it has the authority to do so, as inherent in the power to remove a refractory officer."[47] Guthrie concluded, "Those who are employed under you in the Custom House do, by the

Constitution and laws, derive their appointment and their authority as public officers from the Secretary of the Treasury alone." Guthrie continued, "What the language and temper of your letter would have rendered embarrassing, these unwarrantable assumptions, marked as they are by a manifest spirit of insubordination render impossible namely; your continuation in the office of the Collector of the District of New York."[48] That same day Heman J. Redfield, a Soft who had been serving as naval officer under Bronson, was named the new collector, subject to the Senate's confirmation. Redfield was Marcy's choice to replace Bronson.[49]

John Van Buren was satisfied: "The removal of Bronson is well received, as are the appointments. The delicate compliment to . . . myself cannot fail to be appreciated."[50] Others, while applauding the decision, feared it may have come too close to the state election to do much good. Henry J. Randall wrote to Marcy, "The removal of Bronson will greatly strengthen us, & it would have saved many now *committed* the other way, had it been done earlier."[51]

Pierce's effort to maintain a united party under a broad umbrella of tolerance and shared rewards had ended in failure in the cesspool that was New York state politics. The rest of the nation read of the goings on in New York with undoubted confusion as to what it all meant. Whether the public and the politicians alike understood the different factions in New York, they clearly perceived that Pierce had tried and failed to unite the party in the nation's largest state and that by October of his first year in office he was under vicious attack within his own party from a powerful faction claiming he was not an "Old Line" Democrat and was, very possibly, antislavery. Democratic newspapers that had been critical of Pierce's patronage policy seized on the Bronson case to defend the "National" Democrats, those "old line" regulars such as Dickinson and Burke. The *Washington Sentinel* called "the President's policy . . . one of the most glaring instances of unblushing and insolent demoralization that has ever presumed to offend the good sense of the American."[52] The *New York Herald*, now that editor James Gordon Bennett knew that he would not receive the position of minister to France that he coveted, called on Pierce to fire his entire cabinet, particularly Marcy, whom it blamed for the fiasco in New York.[53] The president could not allow the perception to stand that his administration was somehow hostile to regular Jacksonian Democratic principles.

Though it was little consolation at the time, the conflict with Bronson did establish one principle beyond question. Bronson's removal, and the reasons stated for it, put all federal employees on notice that they owed their positions solely to the approval of the president and his cabinet, not to the authority of any federally appointed local official who may have hired them, and that they could be removed from office for cause from Washington. New collector Redfield understood clearly and wrote Marcy, "I shall do nothing until I see you and the President. . . ."[54]

The Hards, by using the issue of slavery to justify a power grab, raised doubts about Pierce's views on the issue. The Massachusetts Democratic Party was also divided by the slavery issue. In September 1853, the "free" Democrats held their own state convention and passed resolutions opposed to the extension of slavery and the Fugitive Slave Act. One speaker attacked Attorney General Caleb Cushing, claiming he had once been a free-soiler and owed his position to previous support from the free-soil wing of the party. The regular Democrats followed with their own convention, endorsing the administration and defending Cushing.[55] During the campaign, local Democratic leaders in several counties formed coalitions of free and regular Democrats endorsing the same candidates for state offices. The situation might have been ignored by the Pierce administration had not one county chairman made a speech claiming that Bronson's removal was a signal that the administration was not opposed to coalitions between free-soilers and regular Democrats.[56] Cushing stepped in to correct this misconception.

On October 29, one week after Bronson was fired, Cushing sent a letter to R. Frothingham, an editor of the *Boston Post,* attacking the coalition movement in Massachusetts: "My judgment is that the Democrats who have participated in this, have done worse than to commit a fatal error. They have abandoned a principle which is fundamental. To support or vote for the Free Soilers of Massachusetts, is to give countenance and power to persons engaged avowedly in the persistent agitation of the Slavery question, and *therefore* hostile in the highest degree to the determined policy of the Administration."[57]

Speaking for the president, Cushing stated that Pierce's intention "is that the dangerous element of Abolitionism, under whatever guise or form it may present itself, *shall be crushed out*, so far as his administration is concerned."[58] In a conclusion that was likely intended more for Democrats around the nation than for those in Massachusetts, Cushing made this pledge in Pierce's name: "Depend upon it, no matter what consequences may impend over him, he will never allow it [the party] to be shaken by Abolitionists or factionists; but will set his face like flint as well against right-handed backslidings as against left-handed defections which may prejudice or embarrass the onward progress of the Republic."[59] The overly harsh tone of Cushing's "Ukase," as it was called, offended many in the North, but it accomplished its intended purpose. The letter, C. B. Fessenden wrote, "corrects the misapprehension of a good many democrats as to the policy of the administration; the removal of Judge Bronson having led them to regard the President as favoring the Coalition."[60] A son of former president Tyler concluded, "The country cannot now fail fully to comprehend the President's position *& the reason of his action*. It is made plain that the Adm. is on the Baltimore platform & cannot be broken from it."[61] But in the process of following a consistent policy against factionalism in New York and against free-soilism within the Democratic Party in Massachusetts, the Pierce administration had made more enemies than friends.

The state election results confirmed this, as the party went down to defeat in both Massachusetts and New York. The New York results were particularly discouraging, as the Whigs took control of the state assembly, and the total vote for the Hards equaled that of the Soft-Barnburner Union party. Governor Seymour, who now faced a hostile legislature, blamed Pierce: "The correspondence with Bronson hurt us badly. If he had been *promptly removed* the *rebellion* would have been checked at the beginning."[62] Tammany leader and future mayor Fernando Wood had a slightly different analysis of the results. Wood claimed that some forty thousand "Silver Grey" Whigs, the faction of that party opposed to antislavery agitation, crossed over to vote for the Hards. They chose, Wood said, "Dickinson over us & Van Buren—we are denounced as the 'Free-soil party.'"[63] Van Buren, in turn, blamed the strong proslavery resolutions of the Soft-Barnburner platform, policies he thought the voters had not supported, for the defeat of "our state ticket."[64] Only Dickinson was elated with the surprisingly strong showing of the Hards, writing to his colleague, Edmund Burke, in New Hampshire, "Pierce intended to 'crush out' myself from the moment he found himself elected. . . . there are some lessons ahead for him in the future."[65]

That fall the political news for Pierce was all bad. In New Hampshire, Burke continued his newspaper feud with Pierce's paper, the *Patriot.* Pierce took the high road until Burke began publishing extracts from personal letters from Pierce written before and immediately following the Baltimore convention, demonstrating what a close friend Pierce had been to Burke. Pierce had always destroyed personal letters, to the regret of historians, and assumed that others would do the same with his. In November he had his secretary, Sidney Webster, send Burke a curt letter asking for the return of Pierce's letters. Burke answered back, refusing to return the letters, as Pierce had allowed the *Washington Union* and his "friends at Concord to assail and misrepresent" him. Claiming he had "six important letters, at least," from Pierce, Burke promised, "I shall keep his letters to myself and use them at my discretion, and only in self-defence." The *Washington Sentinel* would be utilized as Burke's mouthpiece, as the feud between Burke and the Concord clique spread from New Hampshire to the national press.[66] There was nothing embarrassing in the letters, except that they did prove Burke's central role in helping Pierce achieve the nomination at Baltimore.

In October Pierce learned that Samuel H. Ayer, the young lawyer-politician who had so ably defended Pierce at the New Hampshire state party convention, had dropped dead at age thirty-five. In mid-November, Senator Charles G. Atherton died, equally suddenly, at age forty-nine. Atherton had already served in Congress for twelve years when Pierce personally arranged for his election to a full term in the Senate in 1852. The able, experienced, and highly respected Atherton was intended to be Pierce's floor leader in the Senate. The significance of Atherton's death is summed up in a letter from Henry F. French: "His death occurred yesterday, and it seems to me, one of the saddest events of this year of sad events. I regard it as a serious loss to this Administration. I thought when he was elected Senator, that New Hampshire had no other man, who could do so much for the President, and for New Hampshire, as he, and I see no living man to fill his place."[67] Without Atherton, and with all of the political opposition evident from within his own party, Pierce could only look with trepidation to the convening of the Thirty-third Congress in December 1853.

On the same day that Bronson was fired in New York, Pierce and Marcy sent out a new set of instructions to the U.S. minister to Mexico, James Gadsden. Throughout October, information from Mexico indicated that opposition to dictator Santa Anna was increasing and that his overthrow was likely. Having dealt with Santa Anna in the past and not knowing whom or what type of government might replace him, Pierce and Marcy wanted to conclude a treaty as soon as possible, to acquire additional land from Mexico and settle the border issues. Gadsden had arrived in Mexico City in early August and had proceeded cautiously in negotiating with Santa Anna's government, not wanting to give the impression that the United States was overanxious to buy land from Mexico as this might cause Santa Anna to attempt to hold the Pierce administration up for an exorbitant price. Marcy's instructions of October 22 ordered Gadsden to press for a quick resolution of the issues between the two nations.[68]

In Pierce's opinion, the Fillmore administration had made a mess of relations with Mexico. A survey team sent out by Fillmore to ascertain the exact boundary between the two countries had reported back a line some thirty miles north of what many thought was called for in the Treaty of Guadalupe Hidalgo. If the survey team's report was accepted some five thousand to six thousand square miles of land, three thousand American citizens, the town of El Paso, and a potentially viable railroad route would be in Mexico. The Senate Foreign Relations Committee rejected Fillmore's compromise boundary, but the question of the exact border between the two nations remained to be settled.[69] Fillmore's decision to accept a border so disadvantageous to U.S. interests was probably due to Indian problems in the border area. The Treaty of Guadalupe Hidalgo contained a provision (Article XI) making the United States responsible for controlling the Indians along the border and paying any claims of Mexican citizens for damage done by Indian raids. By 1853 Mexico was claiming $31 million in losses from 366 separate incidents in the past five years.

Army commander-in-chief, Winfield Scott told Fillmore it would require the presence of eight thousand troops at a cost of $10 million a year for the next ten to fifteen years to control the aggressive Apache, Comanche, and Kiowa tribes.[70]

Fillmore's administration had also complicated a controversial dispute between two American companies and the Mexican government. In 1842 a private company headed by U.S. citizen Don José de Garay, a land speculator, was granted the exclusive right to a railroad or canal route across the Isthmus of Tehuantepec. The Mexican government granted Garay 150 miles of land on each side of the proposed railroad route. Garay did nothing with the grant, however, and eventually sold it in 1849 to P. A. Hargous, who represented the New Orleans Company. One of the leading investors in the company was Judah P. Benjamin, a Louisiana Whig politician who was elected to the U.S. Senate in 1853. In 1851 the Mexican government annulled the Garay-Hargous grant. A second U.S. company, led by A. G. Sloo, also out of New Orleans, received the same grant from Mexico in February 1853. Fillmore's minister to Mexico, Alfred Conkling, signed a convention with the Mexican government, declaring the joint protection of the Sloo grant by both governments. Conkling's convention was signed on March 21, 1853, two weeks after Pierce took office but before he was able to replace Conkling with his own minister.[71] Each company was demanding intervention from Washington to force Mexico to honor their grant or to compensate them for it.

It was with these problems in mind that Marcy issued his initial instructions to the new U.S. minister, James Gadsden, on July 15, 1853. Gadsden was instructed to rescind the Conkling convention pledging U.S. protection of the Sloo grant and to take no action in support of the Garay-Hargous grant. He was to nullify with Mexico the Fillmore compromise boundary. Most importantly, Gadsden was instructed to offer to purchase land from Mexico south of the Gila River, a highly prized transcontinental railroad route, and to negotiate a settlement of the Mexican Indian-claims issue so as to abrogate Article XI, freeing the United States from future responsibility for protecting Mexico from Indians along the border.[72]

In October Pierce took a more direct role in the negotiations by personally drawing on a map six possible boundary lines and the price he was willing to pay for each option. Gadsden was to negotiate for the largest possible amount of land but was told, at the very least, to come away with a treaty granting the United States the Gila River area and the abrogation of Article XI. Pierce wanted more than just land from Mexico. He wanted a secure border based on natural boundaries, rivers or mountain ranges, and the first four of his proposed lines were drawn along such boundaries. The most ambitious option, line one, would have given the United States all of Lower California and the Mexican state of Sonora for $50 million. Each succeeding option was for less land and a lower price, down to option five, a line at 31° 48', the Gila River railroad route, for $15 million. Marcy's instructions, containing Pierce's personally drawn map, specifically stated that Gadsden was to focus his efforts on the boundary issue and the abrogation of Arcticle XI and that he was "not to complicate negotiations with any other issue," i.e., the claims of Garay or Sloo.[73]

A significant controversy developed over the means chosen by Pierce to convey these new instructions to Gadsden. Marcy later explained to Gadsden that he and Pierce were concerned about sending written instructions for fear that forces opposed to Santa Anna might intercept them. If it "became publicly known that such a cession was contemplated that that would not only defeat the object but overturn the existing government."[74] Therefore, Pierce decided to appoint a special agent to deliver the instructions verbally to Gadsden in Mexico. The man selected for the assignment was Charles L. Ward of Bradford, Pennsylvania, a longtime Democratic politician, friend to James Buchanan, member of the Democratic national committee in 1852, and delegate to the Baltimore convention. Pierce and Ward met several times at the White House in October to go over the instructions. Ward seemed eminently qualified for the secret mission, except for one fact: he was an agent for the Garay-Hargous claimants.[75] Pierce must have known of this connection but may have assumed that Ward's knowledge of Mexico, his loyalty to his party, and his being paid to convey a specific message from the president would override any self-serving motives. If so, Pierce was to be bitterly disappointed in Ward's actions on reaching Mexico.

When Ward met with Gadsden in Mexico City in November, he stated unequivocally that Pierce was personally directing that Gadsden seek recognition of the Garay-Hargous claim in any treaty negotiated with Mexico. Gadsden was incredulous at Ward's statement, as he had understood Pierce to be opposed to the federal government taking sides between a private U.S. company and a foreign government. Gadsden insisted that Ward write out for him the instructions he had received from Pierce and Marcy. Fortunately, a written copy of Marcy's instruction to Gadsden accompanied by Pierce's map survive, as does Gadsden's copy of what Ward wrote out for him in Mexico. Ward correctly copied out all of the instructions, including the details of Pierce's lines and border options, up to the statement that Gadsden was not to "complicate negotiations" with any other issue. Instead he added this in its place: "The President repeatedly stated in the most decided terms, that he had examined the claims of American citizens under the Grant made by Mexico to Don Jose de Garay, and fully concurred . . . that he was determined to support those claims in every proper form short of a declaration of war in regard to them alone. . . . It would manifestly be consonant with the views and wishes of the President of the United States, that such an adjustment should enter into the terms of the new treaty."[76] Gadsden wrote immediately to Marcy, complaining that the insistence on compensation for Garay might cause the negotiations to be "abandoned" by Mexico.[77] Marcy did not receive Gadsden's letter until mid-December, and he undoubtedly conferred with Pierce about what he had told Ward about the Garay grant. Marcy's reply to Gadsden of December 22 stated, "Ward was directed to inform you, not to embarrass your negotiations with it."[78]

This assurance from Marcy came too late, however, as Gadsden concluded a treaty with Mexico that was signed at the U.S. consulate on December 30, 1853. Ward had remained in Mexico City, lobbying behind Gadsden's back with government officials on behalf of the Garay-Hargous claimants. Infuriated by Ward's activities, Gadsden had other obstacles to overcome in concluding a treaty. In November William Walker sailed from San Francisco, accompanied by fifty soldiers of fortune, and invaded Mexican territory through Lower California, intending to detach Sonora from Mexico.[79]

Walker's was the first of many filibustering expeditions that the Pierce administration would have to contend with. In every case, the administration thwarted or at least impeded the efforts of the filibusters. Filibusters violated U.S. neutrality laws and interfered with normal relations between the United States and its Latin American neighbors, as well as the European powers, who all assumed that these paramilitary operations were at the very least acquiesced in, if not encouraged, by the administration. Pierce would not condone illegal activity, and he was supported in his condemnation of filibusters by the resolute and consistent enforcement actions of Attorney General Cushing, and army and navy secretaries Davis and Dobbin. The problems with enforcement of the law did not come from Washington but from local federal officials, who were subject to the intense public support of the filibusters that existed during the 1850s. The spirit of adventure, the belief in the Manifest Destiny of the United States, and a jingoistic impulse was rampant in the country at the time. In New York, San Francisco, and New Orleans, filibusters like Walker were able to find financiers and speculators ready and able to finance their illegal expeditions, and young men seeking adventure and fortune who were willing to volunteer to be soldiers in a dangerous game.[80]

William Walker, a former physician and journalist, became the most famous, or notorious, of the filibusters, but his first enterprise, launched from San Francisco in October 1853, was a foolish and ill-planned foray into Mexican territory. The planning drew the attention of federal officials in San Francisco, who attempted to prevent Walker from departing the harbor. Cushing directed U.S. attorney S. W. Inge to "use the utmost vigilance in the detection and prosecution" of filibusters.[81] Inge and the collector of the port informed Colonel Ethan Allen Hitchcock, commander of the army's department of the Pacific, of Walker's plans. Hitchcock sent a detachment of soldiers to board Walker's ship, the *Arrow*, and to confiscate all supplies. Someone had tipped off Walker, however, and the supplies had been transferred to another ship before Hitchcock's soldiers arrived. Walker then sailed away, sooner and with fewer men than he had anticipated, to begin his invasion. Hitchcock was suspicious that Inge was the culprit and that he had been "corrupted" by California's prosouthern and pro-filibustering senator William Gwin.[82] Marcy also suspected Inge of "tricks" in allowing Walker to escape, but Hitchcock's efforts were praised by the cabinet, and Davis promoted him to brigadier general on December 16, 1853.[83]

Walker's invasion occurred at a delicate time in the negotiations occurring in Mexico City, and Santa Anna protested loudly to Gadsden of the American invasion of northwestern Mexico. Walker briefly declared Lower California and Sonora to be an independent republic, and Gadsden alerted the United States naval commanders in the area to try to intercept Walker. By mid-February, Walker was back in the United States, facing prosecution by federal officials, having accomplished nothing more than to impede Gadsden's effort and to kill a few Mexicans.[84]

Under the circumstances, it is surprising Gadsden was able to conclude a treaty at all. Only Santa Anna's desperate need for money to keep himself in power explains his willingness to make an agreement, but he would consider only the smallest possible grant of territory to the United States, specifically Pierce's option number five, the Gila River railroad route. According to the treaty, the United States was to pay $15 million for the land. The treaty also included a $5 million settlement by the United States of Mexican citizens' claims arising out of the Indian raids, and attached to this amount was recognition of the Garay claim, with the United States assuming responsibility for settling with the claimants. Despite all his efforts, Ward had failed to get a separate $3 million payment to the Garay-Hargous claimants added to the treaty. Article XI was abrogated by the proposed treaty, and Gadsden agreed to Santa Anna's demand for inclusion of an article by which the United States and Mexico would work together to repel future attempts by filibusters.[85] Gadsden's treaty achieved the two main goals set down in the instructions of Pierce and Marcy, but how would the Pierce administration react to the articles relating to the Garay-Hargous claim and to filibustering? In early January, Gadsden wrote to Marcy, reporting completion of the treaty, and Ward set off for Washington to deliver a copy to Pierce and Marcy.[86]

Amid all of the political turmoil and the treaty negotiations with Great Britain and Mexico, Pierce set out to write his first annual message to Congress, to be delivered when the first session of the Thirty-third Congress convened in the first week of December 1853.

His cabinet members also completed reports of their department's activities during the first eight months of the Pierce administration. There was much to report, but considering the political condition of the time, there was much uncertainty as to the response of congressional leaders to all that had occurred since Congress last met in early April.

A few months earlier, John W. Forney had reported to Buchanan that he felt Pierce was not up to the job. In the intervening months, Forney had become an "intimate" adviser to the president. While believing that "a grievous mistake" was made in getting so involved in the political affairs in New York, Forney was optimistic about the future: "Pierce *will win.* He is able, popular, sincere, and a gentleman; and he attaches men to him warmly. Besides most of his secretaries (especially Campbell, Dobbin, and McClelland) are hard-working men, and these, at least, do not stop to interfere in other people's quarrels. . . . The Hards are wrong. . . ."[87]

4

KANSAS-NEBRASKA

THE FIRST SESSION OF the Thirty-third Congress convened at noon on Monday, December 5, 1853. The Democrats held huge majorities in each house, 37 to 22 in the Senate and 159 to 71 in the House of Representatives, but it was not a Congress distinguished by great men or strong leadership. The House reelected Linn Boyd of Kentucky as its Speaker. Boyd was "a ponderous compromiser" who was not viewed by his Kentucky colleague James Guthrie as being friendly to the administration. In the Senate, David Rice Atchison of Missouri returned as President pro tempore, and next in line for the presidency. Atchison was an imposing six foot two and ramrod straight, but he was intemperate in his language and in his drinking, and he was hostile to the Pierce administration because of its patronage policy. The Missouri Democratic Party was divided between the supporters of Atchison, who were proslavery, and those of former senator Thomas Hart Benton, who were free-soilers. Pierce's policy was to divide the spoils in Missouri equally among the two factions, but, predictably, he had incensed both groups. Atchison had been commiserating with Hard leader Daniel Dickinson in New York regarding their mutual dissatisfaction with the new president.[1]

None of the senators in the Thirty-third Congress were in office when Pierce left the Senate in 1842. The president had no close associations with any of the current members other than his New Hampshire colleague Moses Norris Jr., who was a loyal Democrat but not a strong or distinguished leader. Venerable Lewis Cass of Michigan was the most well known of the Democrats in the Senate, but the aging, obese former presidential candidate lacked energy and decisiveness.

Sam Houston of Texas was another senator of the old school who preferred whittling at his desk to taking an active part in the proceedings. Diminutive, rotund Stephen A. Douglas of Illinois was the most dynamic and aggressive Democrat. At forty, Douglas had his eyes on the White House and hoped to push through a legislative package that included territorial expansion, low tariffs, and a transcontinental railroad as his ticket to the nation's highest office. In establishing an effective working relationship with Senate Democrats, Pierce had counted on Charles G. Atherton, who had served a full term in the Senate, to be the administration's spokesperson. Atherton's death left Pierce without a reliable ally in the Senate.[2]

The opposition was led by William Seward, a calculating New York politician whose ambition for the White House was fostered by his close alliance with editor Thurlow Weed of the *Albany Evening Journal.* Charles Sumner of Massachusetts was a consistently outspoken antislavery advocate, as was Salmon P. Chase of Ohio, who called himself a Democrat but was shunned by his party for his abolitionist views.[3]

In the House, Pierce could count on his New Hampshire colleague, the professorial appearing Harry Hibbard, to speak for the president on any and all matters. Thirty-two-year-old John C. Breckinridge, a handsome, engaging representative from Kentucky, had become an administration favorite for his unabashed defense of the new president during his successful reelection campaign the previous summer. Alexander H. Stephens of Georgia, still nominally a Whig, was an experienced member and master of the House rules, who was inclined to support the administration. Among the Democratic members of the House, however, there were many who were not partial to Pierce. Thomas Hart Benton was returning to Washington after a two-year absence as a member from Saint Louis. Benton was determined to reclaim his lost Senate seat from Atchison and was willing to go to any lengths to weaken his rival in his home state of Missouri, even at the expense of the administration and his former friend and Washington messmate, Franklin Pierce. From New York came nearly a dozen Hard Democrats, including the notorious Irish politician Mike Walsh, future Tammany boss William Marcy Tweed and Francis B. Cutting, all determined to cause as much mischief as possible for the president. Lying in wait were abolitionists Gerrit Smith of New York and Joshua Giddings of Ohio, anxious to seize upon any issue to further their cause.[4]

Despite portents to the contrary, Pierce expressed confidence in the upcoming session of Congress: "*Faction* is powerless here, you would be surprised to see how perfectly so." He was also pleased with his first annual message, claiming he had given it his "best powers" and judging it "sound," but said, "the interest with which friends and foes have been looking for the message has naturally enough made me anxious."[5]

The message was read by the secretary of the Senate and by the clerk of the House on December 6, 1853.[6] Not until the Twentieth Century did presidents deliver the annual message in person. Pierce had relied on the detailed reports of his cabinet officers, which were also delivered to Congress, for much of the information in the message. He began by claiming, "We have still the most abundant cause for reverent thankfulness to God for an accumulation of signal mercies showered upon us as a nation." He proceeded to report on foreign relations, beginning with Great Britain. On the fisheries issue Pierce promised a "fair prospect of a favorable result" and reported that our minister to London was opening negotiations on Central America. Regarding Spain and Cuba, the president reported that no new filibustering expeditions had been launched during the past year, and he pledged, "All the means at my command will be vigorously exerted to repress" [future attempts]. The Kozsta case was summarized with Pierce defending the administration's support of Captain Ingraham and its rejection of Austria's demands. Commodore Perry was reported to have arrived in Japan, but no information had been received as to the success of his attempt to open up trade with the emperor. As to Mexico, Pierce said that negotiations on a treaty were under way, "but," he continued, "sufficient progress has not been made there to enable me to speak of the probable result." Guano found a place in the president's message, as Pierce reported much progress with Peru in resolving the dispute over U.S. efforts to engage in the free trade of the valuable fertilizer. The president concluded this section of his message by reporting the nation was "at peace with all foreign countries."[7]

Turning to domestic matters the president proclaimed, "The controversies which have agitated the country heretofore are passing away with the causes which produced them and the passions which they had awakened . . ." He noted that the peace that reigned at home and abroad offered an opportunity to adopt "a more comprehensive and unembarrassed line of policy and action as to the great material interests of the country." The nation's prosperity was evidenced by the fact that "ours is almost, if not absolutely, the solitary power of Christendom having a surplus revenue . . ." The fiscal year ending June 30, 1853, showed "a balance of $32,425,447 of receipts above expenditures." The administration had embarked on a policy of using the surplus to buy back the national debt and to propose a reduction in tariffs. Since Pierce assumed office, the debt had been reduced from $69,190,037 to $56,486,708. Pierce asked Congress to lower tariff duties and increase the number of articles on the "free list," to reduce the amount of money coming into the treasury.[8]

Pierce referred the Congress to the detailed reports of Davis and Dobbin on the condition of the army and navy and endorsed the recommendations made in those reports for "augmentation, or modification" of both services. He reported that more than 25 million acres of public lands had been disposed of within the last fiscal year, more than double the amount of the previous year; this included land sold to individuals, land warrants distributed to Mexican War veterans, and land grants made to the states. Pierce reported that the transcontinental railroad survey "parties are now in the field making explorations." He endorsed the need for a railroad as a more efficient and safer alternative to "either of the Isthmus routes" and pledged his administration "to aid by all constitutional means in the construction of a road which will unite by speedy transit the populations of the Pacific and Atlantic States." But he declared that the government should not undertake "to administer the affairs of a railroad, a canal, or other similar construction, and therefore that its connection with a work of this character should be incidental rather than primary."[9]

Pierce also recommended to Congress a reorganization of the federal judiciary, which at present was deemed "inadequate" to meet the needs of the newest states: Florida, Wisconsin, Iowa, Texas, and California. New circuit courts and district judges were needed, and Pierce offered to submit to Congress "a plan which [he was] prepared to recommend." The message concluded with a look to the future. Pierce renewed the pledge made in his inaugural address, "that this repose is to suffer no shock during my official term, if I have power to avert it, those who place me here may be assured." He projected that within fifty years the nation would embrace "more than 100,000,000 in population." National unity would be maintained with "the minimum of Federal government" and with a "wise economy" to protect against "corrupt and corrupting extravagance" caused by "insidious projects of private interest cloaked under public pretexts." He closed with the "hope" of "cordial cooperation . . . between members of the coordinate branches of the Government."[10]

Pierce has often been criticized on two counts—that he had no legislative agenda and that this vacuum in leadership led to the actions of more ambitious and unscrupulous politicians, like Douglas.[11] The first nine months of the administration show this charge to be untrue. Pierce had consistently, on the New York trip and in his annual message, endorsed a legislative package that included lower tariffs, reorganization and expansion of the army and navy, federal government involvement in the creation of a transcontinental railroad, reform of the federal judiciary, and reduction of the national debt. Pierce had a program. What he did not have was anyone in Congress to propose it or lead it to fruition, and the factionalism rampant within his own party made it difficult for him to push it through or to have his plan be given a fair hearing. Besides, Pierce's constitutional understanding was that the president should defer to Congress in domestic matters. When Pierce sought to offer leadership, it was toward a strong, aggressive foreign policy, while in domestic legislation he would try to influence, but not direct, the leaders of his own party in Congress.

In general, the press praised the message as "a strong State paper." Pierce was complimented for his "clear, plain, unpretending style" and "his graceful pen." The contents were seen as "temperate and judicious." The neutral *Baltimore Sun* concluded that the message was "characteristic of the author—plain, sensible, and thoroughly American."[12] Of course, there were critics, but Pierce's first annual message compares favorably with those of his contemporaries.

Factionalism emerged during the first days of the new Congress. On December 7, Harry Hibbard moved that the House consider the "election of the public printer." The *Washington Union*, the administration's paper, held the printing contract from both houses during the Thirty-second Congress. It was this lucrative incentive that induced former senator, A. O. P. Nicholson to enter into a partnership with Robert Armstrong to become co-owner of the paper. Throughout 1853 the *Union* had defended the actions of the administration against the attacks by Burke, Dickinson and the Hards in New York, Atchison from Missouri, and southerners who criticized Pierce's patronage policy. This had prompted the creation of a rival Democratic newspaper in the capital, the *Washington Sentinel.* Now the administration expected to reward the *Union* by the renewal of its contracts with Congress. Hibbard represented the president in nominating the *Union* to receive the House contract. Mike Walsh of the New York Hards nominated the *Sentinel.* The vote confirmed Pierce's choice, as the *Union* was selected, but twenty Democrats, mostly from New York, bolted the administration by voting for the *Sentinel.*[13]

The Senate waited until December 12 to elect its printer, and the administration did not fare as well as in the House. The *Washington Sentinel* of Beverly Tucker, "a violent pro-slavery, pro-southerner," was chosen through the combined effort of Whigs and disaffected Democrats by a vote of twenty-six to seventeen.[14] The individual votes were not recorded, but the press reported that among the Democrats who defected from the administration were Atchison, Jesse Bright of Indiana, Slidell of Louisiana, and both senators from Virginia, James M. Mason and Robert M. T. Hunter. In all, eight Democrats bolted the administration in sending a clear message of their discontent with Pierce and his patronage policies.[15] Even with large Democratic majorities in each house, Pierce could not count on the support of the congressional leaders within his own party.

With Congress in session the Washington social season was soon under way. A high point of every year was the president's New Year's levee. On Monday, January 2, Pierce and his cabinet welcomed the public to the newly redecorated White House. The diplomatic corps were received first, at 11:00 a.m. For the first hour Pierce greeted the foreign corps, including Crampton of Great Britain and Hulsemann of Austria, whho were dressed in their garish uniforms in many styles. At noon the "sovereign people" were allowed in, and for two hours Pierce stood shaking hands with all. The president "received those who called with his usual graceful and polished manner." B. B. French tried to count how many people were greeted by the president, and concluded that in all four thousand people shook hands with Pierce. Jane was not present.[16] The first anniversary of Benny's death was but a few days away, and she was still in mourning.[17]

On January 3, 1854, the Hards fired their next shot at Pierce in the House. Francis Cutting offered a resolution requiring the president to turn over all correspondence regarding the removal of Judge Bronson from the collector's office. Cutting claimed that implications had been made by the Pierce administration that Bronson was a "corrupt man" and that his firing was not simply the result of his insubordination. Cutting claimed to be defending "the character of an eminent citizen of my State" from the "calumny" committed against him. The proposed resolution offered the Hards the opportunity to level harsh criticism at Pierce from the floor of the House, but the president's allies prevailed, and the resolution was tabled by a vote of 104 to 66. The significance of the vote is that most southern Democrats voted against the Hard faction, indicating that the New Yorkers had failed to break up the support the president had counted on from that region.[18]

The resolution did prompt a discussion on the House floor as to the difference between the Hards and the Softs. Mike Walsh, an infamous Irish gang leader and drunkard, attempted to explain to the confused members in a colorful and entertaining speech that the Softs were a "despicable, and hollow-hearted set of hungry traitors" who had allied with "long-heeled Negroes." He said of the Softs that their "hearts and purposes were blacker than the faces of the poor dupes they were deluding in doing so." Walsh claimed that Pierce "seems egregiously to underrate and totally misunderstand the true character of the men with whom [he has] been so long and stupidly trifling." Walsh claimed to have no animus toward the president: "He is a very kind, agreeable man; and he is what the ladies would term a very polite, affable and pleasant gentleman—far more so, I am afraid, than it will ever be my lot to be considered. He has always treated me with marked kindness and seeming confidence; but since I have ascertained that this is generally his disposition to everybody, I must be compelled to take off an extraordinary discount for the compliment to myself. [Laughter.]"[19] Walsh concluded his speech by stating that the difference between the Hards and Softs was "the difference between an honest man and a rogue." To which William Smith of Alabama interjected, "I do not yet know whether the Soft is the rogue, or whether the Hard is the rogue." Smith remarked that the "absurdity of the political quarrel" made it "too sectional—I may say too factional—to disturb the harmony of the Democratic party throughout this country." Francis Cutting proceeded to make a lengthy speech recounting the history of the split in New York. For nearly three days the House debated the issue, before Charles Hughes of New York finally drew the matter to a close by stating that "the split in New York was a mere split for spoils, and he was surprised that his friends—the Hards—should lend themselves to such 'base uses.'"[20]

The mischief was not limited to the floor of the House. At the Jackson Day dinner in Washington, D.C., on January 8, 1854, several toasts were made that seemed critical of the president. John C. Breckinridge, who was emerging as the administration's chief spokesman in the House, rose to defend Pierce. In an effective, extemporaneous address he criticized the Hards for embarrassing the party with their petty attacks on the president for such a trifling matter as the spoils of office. To Breckinridge, Pierce had been true to the Baltimore platform and was deserving of united support from Democrats: "I am in favor of the union of the Democratic party. I believe it can exist, and believe it ought to exist."[21] Despite an intense effort, the Hards had failed to shake the president's support from most of the Democratic Party. Political insiders viewed the result as a clear victory for Pierce: "He has managed to kill off the 'Hards' in Congress and lobby, as dead as herrings."[22] But were they dead, or simply back in their "Hardshell"?

On January 19, special agent Charles L. Ward arrived in Washington to deliver Gadsden's treaty with Mexico to the president. Pierce was not at all happy with what he read. In a cabinet meeting held that day to discuss the treaty, Pierce recommended rejecting it outright and not submitting it to the Senate for confirmation. What upset the president was the article recognizing the government's responsibility to satisfy the claims of the Garay group. It was a matter of principle to Pierce that the federal government should not involve itself in the affairs of private businesses. Marcy had instructed Gadsden to not include this in his negotiations with Santa Anna's government, but special agent Ward had lobbied with Gadsden for the Garay group and had invoked the president's name as supportive of the claim. Pierce was also not pleased with the article which pledged the United States to work with Mexico to suppress filibustering expeditions. Though a strong opponent of this illegal activity, Pierce was concerned about making the United States responsible for defending Mexico's border. This could lead to the same kind of problems as the troublesome Article XI of the Treaty of Guadalupe Hidalgo which pledged the United States to take responsibility for Indian raids on both sides of the border. According to press reports, Cushing, Marcy, Davis, and Dobbin tried to temper the president's reaction by reminding Pierce that the treaty did give the U.S. enough land for a southern railroad and that it did free the United States from the responsibility of Article XI. By settling the boundary dispute, the treaty would end the threat of war with Mexico. The debate on whether to submit the treaty to the Senate went on in the cabinet for three weeks before a compromise was worked out.[23]

Pierce submitted the treaty to the Senate on February 10, with reservations expressed in three recommendations for changes. He rewrote the article on the claims of Mexican and American citizens, eliminating the Garay grant entirely, and he proposed changing the wording of the article on filibustering to a more general stipulation that the United States would "cheerfully cooperate" with Mexico in the suppression of unlawful invasions from both sides of the border.[24] The Senate would not get around to ratifying the treaty for some time due to a more serious matter that occupied the nation's attention and would prove to be the issue with which the Pierce administration is most identified. On January 23, Senator Stephen A. Douglas introduced a revised bill for the organization of the territories of Kansas and Nebraska.

A bill to organize the territory of Nebraska, the vast stretch of prairie between the Missouri River and the Rocky Mountains, had first been introduced by Representative Stephen A. Douglas in 1844. It had long been a goal of the ambitious Illinois politician to develop the Great Plains and to connect the two coasts by a transcontinental railroad: "It is utterly impossible to preserve that connection between the Atlantic and the Pacific, if you keep a wilderness of two thousand miles in extent between you."[25] But the region was a vast Indian reservation, and there was little interest in settling it until the 1850s. By 1852, however, petitions began arriving in Congress from residents of Iowa and Missouri asking for the organization of the Nebraska territory so that the fertile eastern region just beyond the Missouri River could be settled. County organizations as well as the state legislatures of Iowa and Missouri all endorsed the goal of opening up the territory to farmers.[26] A bill to create the Nebraska Territory, which would initiate Indian treaties to acquire the land, surveys to map and sell the land to settlers, and a territorial government to place the territory on the road to statehood, was considered during the final days of the Thirty-second Congress.[27]

The Senate failed to pass the bill due to the opposition of southern members, including Missouri's David Rice Atchison. The proposed territory was north of the 36° 30' line imposed by the Missouri Compromise of 1820, and, therefore, slavery was prohibited there. Many of the settlers seeking to move into Nebraska were slave owners from the western counties of Missouri, where slavery was well established and profitable. Atchison saw no advantage to his proslavery supporters in opening up a territory from which they were prohibited from settling with their slaves. In fact, he believed that the development of a free state to the west of Missouri would serve to weaken the institution in his home state which would eventually be surrounded on three sides by free land. Thomas Hart Benton, who was seeking Atchison's Senate seat, blamed the Senate president for blocking the bill and campaigned through the western counties of Missouri, asserting that as long as Atchison was in the Senate, the territory would never be opened.[28] By the time Atchison returned to Washington for the opening of the Thirty-third Congress in December 1853, he was determined to get a favorable bill through the Senate, which would enhance his prospects for reelection.[29]

Knowing that the new Congress would likely take up a bill to organize the territory, Interior Secretary McClelland inquired of the Commissioner of Indian Affairs George W. Manypenny as to the status of the land in the territory. Manypenny replied that no land in Nebraska was "in such condition that the white man [could] lawfully occupy it for settlement." Indian ownership had been established by treaty with the Kickapoo, Wyandotte, and other tribes. To pave the way for future treaty negotiations to purchase the lands, McClelland sent Manypenny on "a preliminary visit" to the region in September. This raised the hopes of white settlers that the territory was soon to be open to them.[30]

As the new Congress convened, the press predicted that a bill to organize the Nebraska territory would be one of the most controversial issues of the legislative session. Speculation was that an attempt would be made to circumvent the Missouri Compromise in some way to permit slavery in the territory, as the only means of getting the southern votes needed to pass a bill. The Compromise of 1850 had introduced the precedent of noninterference by Congress on the matter of slavery in the establishment of the territories of New Mexico and Utah. The question was left entirely up to the settlers even though Utah was north of the Missouri Compromise line. In December, the *New York Herald,* the *Richmond Enquirer*, and the *Albany Argus,* all staunch Democratic papers, conjectured that the Compromise of 1850 had, in effect, repealed the Missouri Compromise by "supersedure." The *Albany Argus* stated it best: "The Missouri Compromise undertook to provide on the part of Congress where slavery should and where it should not exist. The Compromise of 1850 established the precedent that without interference from Congress it should exist wherever the people of a State should have established it . . ."[31] Which concept would be applied to the Nebraska territory was to be the divisive question of the first session of the Thirty-third Congress.

On the first day of the session, Senator Augustus C. Dodge of Iowa reintroduced the Nebraska bill, and it was referred to Douglas's

Committee on the Territories. On January 4, 1854, Douglas reported the bill with a new section stating that "all questions pertaining to slavery in the territory were left to the decision of the people residing therein." The Missouri Compromise was not mentioned, but by implication the bill endorsed the concept of congressional noninterference with slavery in the territories.[32] Atchison had pressured Douglas to include this in the revised bill, but it was not entirely satisfactory to many southerners.

The political implications of the Nebraska bill were immediately apparent to politicians and to the press. Edmund Burke wrote to his old friend Douglas, "I am . . . glad that there is now a measure before Congress which will test the sincerity of the late Free soil Democrats whom Gen. Pierce has taken to his bosom."[33] Burke's paper in New Hampshire gloated that the Nebraska bill was a practical application of the Baltimore platform, and Softs, Barnburners, and those Democrats who endorsed the Wilmot Proviso had "now got to swallow the pill, or acknowledge their hypocrisy."[34] While many old-line Democrats, Atchison included, saw the bill as a test of Democratic orthodoxy, some in Congress did not think it went far enough in clarifying the status of slavery in the new territory.

Archibald Dixon of Kentucky, a proslavery Whig occupying Henry Clay's former seat in the Senate, offered an amendment to the bill on January 16 that stated, "The citizens of the several States and Territories shall be at liberty to take and hold their slaves within any Territory of the United States, or of the States to be formed there from . . ."[35] Douglas had been working behind the scenes to gather southern support for his bill. Dixon's amendment, coming from a Whig, was an outright repeal of the Missouri Compromise and could not be ignored. Many southerners, including Breckinridge, visited Dixon the next day to praise his amendment.[36]

Douglas was in danger of losing control of the contents of his own bill. On January 18, he met with Dixon to try to understand what was behind his strongly worded amendment. The two men went for a carriage ride, during which Dixon explained that unless the bill specifically repealed the Missouri Compromise, southerners could not take their slaves into the territory during the early stages of settlement. The concept of popular sovereignty by which settlers would sometime later vote to allow or reject slavery was meaningless if the Missouri Compromise prevented southerners from settling there in the beginning. Douglas saw the logic in Dixon's argument and reportedly stated, "By God, sir, you are right, and I will incorporate it in my bill, though I know it will raise a hell of a storm."[37]

On January 18, Douglas and Breckinridge asked Representative Philip Phillips of Alabama, a member of the House Committee on Territories, to prepare a Democratic amendment to the bill. Phillips proposed the following: "That the people of the Territory through their Territorial legislature may legislate upon the subject of slavery in any manner they may think proper not inconsistent with the Constitution of the United States, and all laws or parts of laws inconsistent with this authority or right shall, from and after the passage of this act, become inoperative, void and of no force and effect."[38] At Douglas's request Phillips carried his amendment to Atchison, who boarded with Southern senators Mason and Hunter of Virginia, Andrew P. Butler of South Carolina, and Rep. William Goode of Virginia. The group approved the draft.[39]

Dixon's amendment prompted a predictable response from antislavery forces, who were now fully alarmed by the bill. On January 17, the day after Dixon offered his amendment, Charles Sumner proposed one of his own, which "forever prohibited" slavery in any new territory.[40] When Senator Salmon P. Chase became convinced that Douglas was willing to accept the repeal of the Missouri Compromise in his bill, Chase began writing a manifesto against the bill to arouse the people of the North.[41]

The Pierce administration had not been consulted on the Nebraska bill. Having pledged his administration to preserve the "repose" on slavery following the Compromise of 1850, Pierce and his cabinet became concerned that the bill would create a firestorm of opposition in the North. The cabinet discussed the implications of Dixon's amendment on January 19, and Senator Cass called on Pierce to urge the president to reject repeal of the Missouri Compromise as destructive of party unity. As a result, the next day, January 20, the *Washington Union* ran an editorial, probably written by Cushing, denouncing both Dixon's and Sumner's amendments for needlessly stirring up the slavery issue. The editorial made Douglas realize he needed to inform the administration of the reasons why repeal of the Missouri Compromise could not be avoided. With Breckinridge as a liaison, he sent a copy of Phillips's amendment to the White House, and advised Pierce either to accept it or to write something more suitable.[42]

On Saturday, January 21, Pierce and the cabinet sent to Douglas a substitute amendment that read, "the rights of persons and property shall be subject only to the restrictions and limitations imposed by the Constitution of the United States and the acts giving governments, to be adjusted by the decision of the Supreme Court of the United States."[43] Their objection to a stronger amendment was that it would create an unnecessary uproar of opposition around the country. Believing the Missouri Compromise to be unconstitutional, Pierce and Cushing expected the Supreme Court would rule favorably on behalf of the slave interests in the matter, and this would buy time and free the administration of the responsibility for resurrecting the slavery controversy.[44]

Douglas and Breckinridge were both satisfied with Pierce's proposed amendment, but when Breckinridge reported it back to the residents of the boarding house at Ninth and F streets, Atchison and his colleagues rejected it, claiming it did not go far enough to repeal the Missouri Compromise.[45] The decisive moment in the life of the Nebraska bill had arrived. The bill was on the calendar of the Senate for Monday, January 23. Douglas was determined to present the final bill, with the united support of his party, on that day, otherwise it possibly would not pass during the current session of Congress. As Sunday, January 22, dawned, Douglas decided a face-to-face meeting with Pierce was necessary to hash out the final form of the bill in time for Monday's Senate session.

No transcript was kept of the fateful meeting at the White House on Sunday, January 22. We know that early that morning, Douglas, accompanied by "a number of members of the Senate, and Ho. Of Rep's," went to Jefferson Davis's home and explained to Davis the contents of the new bill, asking for his help in arranging a meeting with the president. Davis reminded his visitors that Pierce did not conduct business on Sunday, but they impressed him with the importance of securing the president's support for the bill that day.[46] Davis then traveled by carriage to the White House with Douglas and Atchison. The other participants—Breckinridge, Phillips, Hunter, Mason, Butler, Goode, and possibly Jesse Bright of Indiana—followed them on foot. At the White House, Davis went alone to the family quarters and explained to Pierce the purpose of the visit. Pierce then accompanied Davis to the library to meet with the Douglas delegation.[47]

Phillips later reported "being struck by the cold formality which seemed to prevail." Pierce was thinking of future antislavery agitation and the implications for his administration and of the Democratic party when he warned, "Gentlemen, you are entering a serious undertaking, and the ground should be well surveyed before the first step is taken."[48] The meeting lasted some two hours, during which Pierce was convinced of the need for the bill to effectively repeal the Missouri Compromise. He was concerned about the language such a repeal might take and, therefore, undertook to write out the draft of that portion of the bill himself. Pierce's draft, later seen in his own handwriting by his private secretary, read in part that the Missouri Compromise "was superseded by the principles of the legislation of 1850, commonly called the compromise measures, and is hereby declared inoperative and void." It concluded that the people of a territory were "perfectly free to form and regulate their domestic institutions in their own way."[49] The word "repeal" was not used, but this was simply a matter of semantics, as the meaning of the draft would be fully understood. The meeting concluded with Pierce asking the visitors to see Marcy, the cabinet member most opposed to the amendment, and inform him of the results. Breckinridge, Douglas, and several others stopped by Marcy's house, but the secretary of state was out and no further effort was made to see him that day.[50]

The next day, Douglas, confident of support from the president, introduced in the Senate his substitute bill, which created two territories, Kansas and Nebraska. The decision to divide the huge land mass in two was the result of pressure from Missouri and Iowa representatives and had nothing to do with the slavery article, but coupled with the repeal of the Missouri Compromise, it was attacked by northerners as a deal to create one slave and one free state, and this decision added to the opposition the bill would need to overcome.[51]

Why did Pierce go against his pledge to not do anything to upset the calm that prevailed in the country on the slavery issue? He later told friends that he fully understood what the reaction to the Kansas-Nebraska bill would be in the North.[52] To understand Pierce's decision, it is best to consider what the consequences would have been for his administration had he opposed the bill. The bill would have likely failed to pass. Pierce did not have much clout with the national party, but his opposition would have emboldened enough Democratic congressmen, particularly in the House, to bring about the defeat of the bill. If it had passed, he would have had either to sign or veto it. Any opposition to the bill from Pierce would result in certain retribution from Douglas and southern Democrats. There were a number of diplomatic appointments, made during the congressional recess, which had yet to be confirmed by the Senate. Redfield's appointment as collector of the port of New York was also still pending in the Senate. Southern senators would have undoubtedly punished the president, as they had done in selecting an official printer, by rejecting some or all of his appointments. Redfield's rejection would have destroyed the Soft and Barnburner coalition in New York and placed the Hards in the position that they coveted, allied with southern Democrats against the administration. This is certainly why Marcy, who was reluctant to agree to the repeal, went along with it when Pierce presented the fait accompli to his cabinet on Monday, January 23. Pierce's foreign policy goals would have been scuttled by his own party. Gadsden's treaty and the expected treaty with Great Britain on the fisheries and trade reciprocity matters would fail to receive the two-thirds vote needed to ratify. Pierce also would have faced resignations within his cabinet. Davis and Dobbin, though personally loyal to Pierce, would have been unable to withstand the pressure from their southern colleagues to remain in an administration that stood in the way of southern rights. The Democratic Party would have been ruptured by Pierce's decision, and the president would have been read out of that party by the old-line Democrats, who were unhappy with his patronage policy to begin with and would now have the confirmation they needed of Pierce's infidelity to party principles and untrustworthiness on the issue of slavery. Even before the Nebraska bill was introduced, politicians were speculating that Pierce could become another Tyler, a president without a party and with more than three years left in his administration.[53] The Kansas-Nebraska bill has been blamed for causing the collapse of the second party system and thus bringing on the Civil War. Failure of the bill to pass because of the actions of a Democratic president would have likely produced a similar result, with even more immediate and potentially violent consequences.

As it was, Pierce kept his cabinet together, demonstrated to party leaders his fidelity to the Baltimore platform, which endorsed the Compromise of 1850 and popular sovereignty, and prevented the rupture of his own party. He could still hope for better days if he, and the party, could ride out the storm that was coming. Besides, what had he really committed to? Pierce, along with Douglas, Cass, Phillips and others, did not believe that slavery could take root in the northern climate of Kansas and Nebraska. They had approved a principle, that southerners should have the same rights as all other Americans in their access to new territories, without giving away much in practice, and they were advocating leaving the matter in the hands of the people. What could be more democratic?[54] In the end, Pierce acted on his constitutional principles and on his loyalty to his party. These had always been the defining beliefs of his political career, and they explain his decision to support the Kansas-Nebraska bill. To do otherwise would have gone against all the lessons of Pierce's political career and everything he believed in or held sacred.

Once on board, Pierce did everything in his power to make the bill an administration measure and secure its passage. He wrote an editorial for the *Washington Union* which appeared on January 24, stating that the administration was "directly involved" in Douglas's bill. That day he met again at the White House with Atchison and Douglas to plan strategy for its passage. By Wednesday, January 25, Rep. Harry Hibbard of New Hampshire was writing to state party chairman John H. George in Concord, "The Nebraska bill as last modified by Douglas in the Senate is the thing for which all honest men are to go—it will probably pass by decided votes in both Houses."[55] The next day, Pierce received the first reward for his support, as Redfield was confirmed by the Senate.[56]

The opponents of the bill fired their first shot on January 23. Before Douglas's revised bill was even presented to the Senate, Salmon P. Chase had written his "Appeal of the Independent Democrats in

Congress to the People of the United States." The appeal was printed in the *National Era* on January 23 and defined the debate on the bill. In what was a "gross exaggeration" of the meaning and intent of the bill and its supporters, Chase's "Appeal" claimed the repeal of the Missouri Compromise was a violation of the "compact" between the North and the South on the slavery issue. Chase charged that the bill was a "bold scheme against American liberty" and that it was "an atrocious plot to exclude . . . free laborers from our own States, and convert it into a dreary region of despotism, inhabited by masters and slaves." Employing all of the invective that typified the abolition movement, Chase charged the bill as a "monstrous plot," a "violation of a sacred pledge," "a criminal betrayal," an "enormous crime" and attacked Pierce and Douglas as "servile demogogues" of the Slave Power who were intent on subjugating the nation "to the yoke of a slaveholding despotism."[57] The appeal, one of the most effective pieces of political propaganda ever written in the United States, aroused the attention and the anger of many in the North. As Amos A. Lawrence, the conservative "Cotton" Whig of Massachusetts and Pierce's cousin by marriage, wrote in his diary, "We went to bed one night, old-fashioned, conservative, compromise, Union Whigs, and waked up stark mad Abolitionists."[58] "Appeal of the Independent Democrats" also destroyed the Whig party. As Michael F. Holt states, "By exaggerating and impugning southern responsibility for the bill, by portraying it as a southern assault on the liberty and future economic prospects of northern whites," Chase had transformed the battle from a partisan struggle between Democrats and Whigs "into a sectional brawl."[59] Southern Whigs were left with no choice but to join with Democrats in defending their section from the attack of the Free Soilers, thus initiating a political realignment that brought on the Civil War.

Chases's "Appeal" also set the stage for the Senate debate on the bill, which began on January 30. Douglas opened the debates by defending himself from the charges made by Chase in his "Appeal." He asserted that "every man who is now assailing the principle of the bill under consideration . . . was opposed to the Missouri compromise in 1848" when they supported the Wilmot Proviso, which proposed to ban slavery in all territory acquired from Mexico, most of it south of the compromise line. If the Missouri Compromise was such a "solemn compact," why did they vote to annul it in 1848? Douglas stated that the Compromise of 1850, had already replaced the Missouri Compromise, and the popular sovereignty section of the Kansas-Nebraska bill was copied directly from the portion of the Compromise of 1850 which created the territory of New Mexico. Douglas said, "They say my bill annuls the Missouri compromise. If it does, it had already been done before by the act of 1850; for these words were copied from the act of 1850."[60] He denied that the intent of the bill was "to legislate slavery into these territories," but rather it was "to leave the people to do as they please. . . ." This was the same principle by which "New Hampshire became free, while South Carolina continued to hold slaves; Connecticut abolished slavery, while Georgia held on to it."[61] Douglas claimed that land and climate of Kansas and Nebraska were against slavery taking root in the new territory: "I do not believe there is a man in Congress who thinks it could be permanently a slaveholding country." The angry reaction to the bill was the result of the "falsification of the law and the facts" created by Chase, Sumner and the free-soilers: "This tornado has been raised by abolitionists, and abolitionists alone. They have made an impression upon the public mind. . . ."[62]

As the debate raged on in the Senate for the next month, Pierce worked diligently behind the scenes to gather support for the bill. He focused his attention on northern Democratic senators, whose constituencies had been aroused by the abolitionists. Pierce began with his own New Hampshire congressional delegation. A meeting in late January turned into a heated debate, as Senator Moses Norris Jr, speaking for the state's representatives, criticized the bill. Eventually, Norris voted for it, but only after several private meetings with the president.[63] Pierce also tried his charm on Senator Hannibal Hamlin of Maine, a longtime friend and supporter for the nomination in 1852. When charm and persuasion failed to sway Hamlin from opposition to the bill, Pierce attempted to buy his vote by offering greater control of state patronage. Nothing worked, however, and Hamlin left the White House still committed to voting against the bill.[64]

In case the private meetings with Pierce were not enough to convince Democrats in Congress that the president intended to use the full power of his office to reward the supporters and punish the opponents of the bill, on February 10 the *Washington Union* ran an editorial titled, "The Administration and the Nebraska Question." It stated that "the President has frankly and unreservedly expressed his conviction in favor of the principle of congressional non-intervention to all who have sought his opinions," and, according to the editorial, many had "sought the benefit of his consultations. . . ." The bill "cannot fail, when passed, to meet his ready approval."[65]

Predictably, threats to Democratic Party unity proved a greater obstacle to passage than the actions of the abolitionists or Whigs. Edmund Burke seized on the Kansas-Nebraska bill for the next phase of his slash-and-burn effort to destroy Pierce and his administration. Though claiming to be an "old guard" Democrat and an old friend of Douglas, nothing could deter Burke from causing mischief in New Hampshire and nationally. The March state elections in New Hampshire offered Burke his chance to weaken his own party. To inject Kansas-Nebraska into the state campaign, Burke wrote an editorial stating that the intent and purpose of the bill was "*unquestionably to revive and re-establish slavery over that whole region.*" The result would be that the slave states regained their "political preponderance in the Senate." Burke predicted that the debate on slavery created by the bill "will be more vehement and acrimonious than it has been on any previous occasion" and that the "free-soilers and coalitionists whom President Pierce has been hugging to his bosom, will . . . turn renegade a second time . . . in their hostility to the South . . ."[66] Burke's editorial was printed in newspapers around the nation.

Douglas was infuriated by the article and answered Burke in a letter that was also carried in the press. Restating his own claim that the "*true intent and meaning* of the act is *not* to legislate slavery into any Territory or State," Douglas correctly stated that Burke was writing "as a deadly enemy, under the hypocritical guise of friendship, for the purpose of furnishing aid and comfort to the northern whigs and abolitionists. . . ." He condemned Burke for his "unpardonable slander against every friend and supporter of the bill."[67] Burke's intent was to depict the Kansas-Nebraska bill in such an extreme proslavery position in New Hampshire that moderate Democrats would break from Pierce and the state party in the upcoming election.

As the national debate raged, opponents of the bill mobilized. Huge rallies were held at Faneuil Hall and elsewhere. In response to the call of the "Appeal of the Independent Democrats" for a response from the clergy, New England ministers sent a petition with over three thousand signatures to the Senate, which was presented to the Senate by Edward Everett of Massachusetts. The debate raged on in the Senate until an all-night session on March 3. Finally, at 5:00 a.m. Douglas was able to bring the bill up for a vote. It passed, thirty-seven to fourteen, a much larger majority than anyone had predicted. Only five Democrats, including Sam Houston of Texas and Hamlin of Maine, deserted the party to vote against the bill. Southern Whigs had joined with Democrats to provide the large margin of victory.[68] Pierce was undoubtedly pleased that his effort to impose party orthodoxy had prevailed, but he was uncomfortable in the role of enforcer. After the victory in the Senate, he offered the olive branch to Democrats who voted their conscience against the bill. An editorial in the *Union* announced that the administration did not regard them as enemies and would not punish anyone for his vote. Pierce's goal was always to hold his diverse party together, and his retreat must be viewed in this light.[69] The focus of the Kansas-Nebraska bill now moved to the House, where the battle resumed.

The nation looked with interest to see what result the Senate vote would have on the first election held since the issue had burst upon the political landscape. The result was mixed. On March 14, New Hampshire Democrats held on to the governorship and a small majority in the state legislature, but with a greatly reduced margin from the previous year. But the result was not the referendum on Kansas-Nebraska that Burke or the administration was hoping for. Despite the urging of Pierce to "take high and bold ground" in support of the bill, the state Democratic Party leadership had remained silent on the Kansas-Nebraska bill. Other issues, particularly temperance and nativism, influenced the voters. Though many claimed victory for Pierce and Douglas in the New Hampshire results, those closer to the scene understood that most of the successful Democratic legislative candidates were silently opposed to the bill.[70] This might have an impact when the legislature got around to choosing a successor to the late Senator Charles G. Atherton.

Pierce had been under pressure from within his own family to oppose the bill. Brothers-in-law Robert Aiken and Alpheus Spring Packard wrote letters urging him to "veto the abomination." Jane's cousin Amos A. Lawrence also exerted pressure on the president. What Jane thought of the matter is unclear. On the day the bill passed the Senate, she wrote to Packard, "My husband is in his usual health—I think he would tell you that his conscience upholds him in his present course—but I do not wish to talk for him—I earnestly desire that he may be guided by the 'wisdom that cometh from above.'"[71]

The winter of 1854 brought mixed news from Europe. All American ministers were finally at their posts, making their initial impressions at court and on the government in each host country. In Madrid, Pierre Soulé, already deeply suspect for his former revolutionary activity in France, immediately created a stir by getting into a duel with the French ambassador. At a ball hosted by the French ambassador, Marquis de Turgot, Soulé's son had overheard a member of the Spanish royal family, the Duke of Alba, make a critical comment about his mother's costume and corpulence. In December 1853, the younger Soulé fought a duel with swords with Alba, and Pierre Soulé challenged and shot Turgot in the leg in a duel with pistols. Turgot was hobbled for life by the injury.[72] The Democratic press in the United States tended to defend Soulé's actions: "The exhibition of a little American grit may do these lacqueys of despotism some good."[73] The administration chose to ignore the incident, as Marcy wrote, "I was content to pass it over as the President has done."[74]

While Soulé was making a splash in Spain, the other ministers were concerned about what to wear to court. Marcy's "dress circular" had prescribed wearing the "simple dress of an American citizen," but would this be viewed as disrespect to the host government? Buchanan, as minister to London, was the top-ranking diplomat and believed he had to set the right example for all the others. When he first broached the subject to the "master of court ceremonies" on his arrival in London in October, Buchanan was informed that he would not be received at court wearing civilian clothing. Buchanan set about looking for an alternative that would satisfy his hosts and not violate Marcy's directive. At one point he considered wearing a costume identical to that of America's first citizen, George Washington, but after examining portraits of the Father of his Country, Buhanan decided he would look ridiculous in such an outfit. The first opportunity to test Marcy's directive was the opening of Parliament in early February 1854, which was attended by the Queen and all of the diplomatic corps. Buchanan did not attend, not wanting to violate his invitation which required "full court dress." His absence was critically noted in the London press, and Buchanan decided he must attend the queen's levee in late February. Buchanan triumphantly reported to Marcy that he appeared "in the very dress which you have often seen me wear at the President's levees, with the exception of a very plain black-handled and black-hilted dress sword." The sword was added to "distinguish me from the upper court servants."[75] "As I approached the queen, an arch but benevolent smile lit up her countenance;—as much as to say, you are the first man who ever appeared before me at court in such a dress. I confess that I never felt more proud of being an American than when I stood in that brilliant circle, 'in the simple dress of an American citizen.'"[76]

August Belmont reported a similar triumph when he appeared at a royal ball at The Hague in simple evening clothes. The queen of Holland made a special point of singling Belmont out for attention, which included dancing a quadrille with him, "the only member of the diplomatic corps similarly honoured that evening."[77] In Spain Soulé compounded his initial bad impression by wearing an outlandish black velvet costume supposedly modeled after what Benjamin Franklin had worn at the French court of Louis XVI. An American observer noted it was a "fanciful resemblance" at best.[78]

In Paris timorous John Y. Mason attended a court ball at the Tuileries dressed in a conventional court costume. This angered the acting American chargé, Henry S. Sanford, who had been in Paris since 1849 and had worn simple dress to court on several occasions. He refused to accompany his boss, Mason, to the ball and wrote an angry letter to Marcy, complaining about Mason's failure to follow the dress circular. Marcy sent a mild letter of reproach to Mason.[79] Back in London, Dan Sickles, Buchanan's secretary of legation, insisted on wearing his New York State militia uniform to court. Modeled after the Austrian imperial guard the outfit caused Sickles to be "mistaken for a military attaché from Vienna."[80] Sickles had arrived in London without his seventeen-year-old bride and infant daughter, who were left behind in New York, but he was accompanied by the prostitute Fanny White. Sickles reportedly took Fanny to a royal reception at Buckingham Palace and introduced her to Queen Victoria and Prince Albert as Miss Julia Bennett of New York.[81]

The U.S. consul in London, George N. Sanders, caused considerable comment by openly courting the European revolutionaries living in that city. Sanders and Sickles sought to aide the exiles in fomenting a general uprising throughout Europe, and Sanders's London home became their virtual headquarters. It was there that the Hungarian Louis Kossuth met Italian Giuseppe Garibaldi for the first time.[82] On February 21, Sanders hosted a dinner party for Giuseppe Mazzini, Aleksandr Herzen of Russia, Kossuth, Garibaldi, and a half dozen other exiles. Buchanan was also in attendance as the guests drank to "a future alliance of America with a federation of the free peoples of Europe."[83] Buchanan wrote to Marcy that he had been very cautious in his remarks at the dinner. Though acknowledging that it would be "indiscreet . . . for me, as American minister, to invite any of them to my house, I should feel myself degraded as an American citizen to have refused the invitation of a friend [Sanders], simply because men who have suffered in the cause of liberty were to be present." Buchanan seemed to relish his friendships with his reckless, impetuous secretary and equally indiscreet consul. In an aside to Mrs. Sanders at the dinner party, Buchanan "asked her if she was not afraid the combustible materials about her would explode and blow us all up."[84]

Sanders was secretly engaging in illegal activity in fostering the revolutionaries, right under the nose of his superior, Buchanan, but this was not revealed until later in the year, by which time the ardor of the revolutionaries toward Sanders had lessened.[85] Mazzini had taken a stand against slavery, proclaiming, "Free men only can achieve the work of freedom," and Sanders insisted on assurances from the exiles that they "in no way desire to interfere with any domestic institution in the United States, especially . . . the subject of slavery . . ."[86] Sanders's goal of freeing Cuba from Spain and annexing it as a slave state was inconsistent with the beliefs of the European revolutionaries. Before all of this activity became public knowledge in the United States, Sanders's recess appointment had already been rejected by the Senate, which in February voted against his confirmation twenty-seven to ten.[87] Sanders had only himself to blame. His vicious attacks on the "old fogies" of the Democratic Party during the campaign of 1852, when he was editor of the *Democratic Review*, had alienated many. Now Cass, Houston, and the other "old fogies" got their revenge on Sanders, who would remain in London through the fall of 1854 before being replaced. By then Pierce, Marcy, and Buchanan would be suitably embarrassed by the actions of Sanders and Sickles.[88]

After passing the Kansas-Nebraska bill, the Senate finally got around to considering Gadsden's treaty on March 13. The Committee on Foreign Relations accepted Pierce's amendments to the treaty, except for the one eliminating the Garay-Hargous claim. The Senate debated the treaty in executive session to keep the still-secret treaty from public view. But this only permitted senators to openly pursue their personal interests, free from public scrutiny.[89] Over the next month senators debated not the merits of the treaty but the merits of the competing claims of the Garay and Sloo grantees. Senators lined up in various blocs, some favoring the Garay claimants, others the Sloo grant. Northern anti-Nebraska senators opposed the treaty, as it would add to the nation southern territory that might become slave, despite the desert climate, and it would aid in a southern railroad.[90]

When the senators became aware of the activity of special agent Ward, they asked Pierce to supply all correspondence related to Ward's dealings with the president and Gadsden. Pierce wrote back that in his meeting with Ward "at no time . . . was either the Garay grant or the convention entered into by Mr. Conkling [Sloo grant] alluded to otherwise than as subjects which might embarrass the negotiation of the treaty, and were consequently not included in the instructions."[91] Though Pierce regretted Ward's departure from "the instructions committed to him" and his failure to "convey . . . the correct import of remarks made by me," he nevertheless concluded, "I impute to him no design of misrepresentation."[92] How Pierce could excuse Ward's outrageous behavior in this manner is unclear, except that the Garay grantees were supported in the Senate by Douglas,

Mason, Slidell, and other leading Democrats. Pierce may have felt it prudent to state the facts, but not add to the controversy by leveling blame and alienating those same senators he had so recently appeased with his support of the Kansas-Nebraska bill.

In an effort to salvage the floundering treaty, Senator Thomas Rusk of Texas amended it further by reducing the amount of land to just enough for a railroad route. He also reduced the amount to be paid to Mexico from $15 million to $7 million. Rusk's version of the treaty made no mention of the private claims. In this form the treaty came up for a final vote on April 17 and was rejected, twenty-seven to seventeen, three votes short of the two-thirds required. Opposition came from the antislavery senators and the supporters of the Sloo grant.[93] The treaty appeared dead, and in fact Pierce declared that he would have rejected the Senate version with contempt. He charged that responsibility for war with Mexico would rest with the Senate for its failure to ratify the treaty with his amendments.[94] At the time the treaty was rejected, Gadsden was attending the Southern and Western Commercial Convention in Charleston, South Carolina. He addressed the convention on the importance of securing a southern railroad route to the Pacific. Gadsden assured the convention that Pierce was doing all he could to secure the land necessary for a route. The convention was attended by three southern senators, William Dawson of Georgia, James C. Jones of Tennessee, and Clement Clay of Alabama. Impressed with the strong advocacy of the convention delegates for a southern railroad route, the three returned to Washington determined to revive the Gadsden treaty. They proceeded to amend Rusk's version of the treaty by adding additional territory and increasing the compensation for Mexico to $10 million. To win the Sloo supporters, Dawson, Clay, Jones, and Rusk endorsed an amendment, offered by John Bell of Tennessee, promising protection by the United States of the work of the Sloo company. With these changes, the treaty was ratified on April 25 by a vote of thirty-three to twelve. Opposition came only from antislavery and anti-Nebraska senators of the North and two Democrats.[95]

Pierce was not happy with the much-altered treaty, particularly as it promised government intervention to protect the Sloo company in Mexico. He agreed to send it on to Santa Anna, without his recommendation, with assurance that he would sign it if Santa Anna approved the changes. Though pressured by the British minister in Mexico City to reject the treaty, as the insertion of the Sloo amendment might interfere with British plans for an Isthmian railroad, Santa Anna's need for money overcame his objections. Gadsden, back in Mexico, was particularly bitter at what had been done to his original treaty.[96] In the end, for many senators the recognition of the Garay-Hargous or the Sloo grant was more important than the acquisition of a railroad route or the peace with Mexico. Despite the effort by the Senate to keep the debate on the treaty out of the public eye, the press had a field day reporting inside information regarding the activities of the executive sessions. Confirming Pierce's good sense in trying to keep Sloo and Garay claims entirely out of it, the press reported that "filthy lucre" had been liberally dispensed to senators by both the Sloo and Garay agents, in the effort to win senatorial support.

As an early spring arrived in Washington, Pierce might have reflected on how the actions of the Thirty-third Congress had deflected his administration from pursuit of its stated goals. His pledge to not disturb the calm that existed in the country on the slavery issue had been destroyed by the Kansas-Nebraska bill; he had been disappointed in his attempt to acquire a vast new territory from Mexico; and any hope of lower tariffs, reform of the federal judiciary, reorganization of the army and navy, and the momentum for a transcontinental railroad had been pushed aside by the new issues and passions that had been aroused in the four months since Congress first convened. And the House had yet to consider the Kansas-Nebraska bill.

5

PARTY TESTS AND RECIPROCITY

PIERCE AND MARCY HAD been waiting for nearly six months for news from London on the fate of the fisheries reciprocity treaty. The British government seemed uninterested in the Marcy-Crampton *projet* of the treaty. As time went by, Marcy and Buchanan despaired of it ever being completed.[1] But Pierce was determined, and with another fishing season about to begin, he pressed his secretary of state to instruct Buchanan to insist on British consideration of the treaty. Pierce feared that New England fishermen, who the previous year had threatened to arm themselves to repel interference from the British navy, would actually do it if their expectations of a favorable treaty were frustrated. On March 11, 1854, Marcy sent a strong letter instructing Buchanan: "The President expects that you will avail yourself of any proper occasion . . . to impress upon Her Brittanic Majesty's ministers the importance of having all disputed questions as to Fisheries adjusted. . . ." Buchanan was to inform Lord Clarendon, British foreign minister, that "as soon as it is ascertained that the difficulties in relation to the fisheries cannot be arranged by negotiation this Government will prepare to sustain our fishermen in the assertion of all their rights on the coasts of the British Provinces; and these rights are regarded here to be more extensive than those conceded by Great Brit. or the Provinces."[2]

Marcy chose the right time to push the matter, for on March 28, 1854, Great Britain and France declared war on Russia. The Crimean War would tax the British military establishment and challenge British public opinion for the next two years, making it imperative that the government avoid any overt conflicts with the United

States. Buchanan immediately understood this and wrote to Marcy, "They cannot afford to go to war with us. In the present condition of England . . . it would be ruinous to them." Buchanan promised to have "another plain talk about the fisheries" with Lord Clarendon.[3]

Special agent Israel D. Andrews was also facing obstacles in his mission to win support for a treaty in the Canadian provinces. On April 3, he wrote Marcy, requesting money be placed in a special account for him to draw on in order to silence opponents of a treaty among Canadian politicians and the press. Though never using the word "bribe," Andrews clearly had this in mind. Marcy replied, "I have always been distrustful of attempts to change the public opinion of any community by such means as you refer to," but he promised, "I shall lay your communication before the President for his views upon the subject. . . ."[4]

Pierce's determination to achieve a favorable treaty is evident from his approval of Andrews's request for money. Authorizing clandestine activities in Canada was for Pierce a unique departure from his usually high legal and ethical standards and can only be explained by the priority he attached to a favorable treaty and his constitutional belief that the president has far more authority and leeway in dealing with foreign affairs than with domestic matters. Pierce had researched the matter and found precedents by previous presidents,which he wrote out in a memo titled, "Payments, out of the fund for Contingent Expenses of Foreign Inter-course settled on the Certificate of the President, 1826–1852."[5] In fact, Pierce did not wait for the mail to inform Andrews of his decision. He had Cushing telegraph Andrews of the special fund of $5,000 on April 12. Cushing advised Andrews, "The President is expecting you to produce results which I heartily trust may be the case."[6] In his follow-up letter to Andrews, Marcy wrote of Pierce, "He deems it to be his duty to use all proper means at his disposal to bring it [the treaty] to a successful conclusion." Andrews was to keep careful accounts of his expenditures or be prepared to explain them "to him [Pierce] confidentially."[7] Andrews interpreted Pierce's approval as giving him carte blanche, and he proceeded to apply far more grease to the wheels of Canadian politics and public opinion than Pierce, Marcy, or Cushing could ever imagine, or condone.

With the improved prospects of a treaty with Great Britain, the Pierce administration turned its attention to the House of Representatives for the second act of the drama that was the Kansas-Nebraska bill. The House took up the bill on March 21, when Douglas ally Rep. William A. Richardson of Illinois moved that the bill be referred to Richardson's own Committee on Territories. At this point, Francis Cutting, Hard spokesman, moved that the bill be referred instead to the Committee of the Whole. Cutting's proposal was another attempt at anti-Pierce mischief by the Hard faction from New York. Once Douglas's bill had become an administration measure, the Hards began plotting against it. By referring the bill to the Committee of the Whole, Cutting was placing it so far down the House calendar that it was unlikely to be acted upon at all during the present congressional session. Richardson condemned Cutting's motion for it "would be killing it by indirection," charging that this was the intent and that Cutting could not "disguise the fact." Richardson's anger was transparent as he attacked the Hards, claiming he had "no respect for those gentlemen . . . who profess to be for a measure, while they are using every effort by indirection to destroy it."[8] Cutting's motion was supported by all of the members from whatever party who were opposed to the bill and it passed by a vote of 110 to 95. By burying the bill in the House calendar, anti-Nebraska forces had won an important victory, and following the lopsided vote in the Senate, Cutting's actions encouraged the renewal of anti-Kansas-Nebraska agitation throughout the North.[9]

Cutting's motion prompted John C. Breckinridge, the administration's chief spokesman in the House, to attack the Hards. In a speech on March 27, Breckinridge claimed that his "sympathy and feelings" had always been with the Hard faction because of their fidelity to party doctrine: "Hence the bruise, hence the wound, hence the mortification which pervaded that part of the Hall friendly to the [Nebraska] bill . . . when they saw the gentleman from New York turn a sharp corner, turn his back upon his former course—enter into alliance with the enemies of the measure, Abolitionists and all, and play the leading part in a scheme which every man in the House with five grains of common sense must know was intended or calculated to smother it. . . . the act of the gentleman from New York was an act of hostility."[10] Cutting responded by calling Breckinridge a lackey of the Pierce administration and claimed Breckinridge's recent reelection in Kentucky had been aided by money sent to him by the Hards of New York. Breckinridge denied receiving any such money, and Cutting had to admit that his information was secondhand.[11] With Breckinridge attacking Cutting's motives and party loyalty and with Cutting questioning Breckinridge's honesty, the exchange produced the inevitable result. Cutting challenged Breckinridge to a duel, and the Kentuckian accepted. As the challenged party, Breckinridge had the choice of weapons; he chose rifles. At this point Cutting, who was an expert with pistols, began to get cold feet. Over the next few days political leaders from Benton to Pierce worked behind the scenes to effect a resolution short of violence. They succeeded, and on March 30 the dispute was amicably settled and a duel avoided, with both parties expressing regret.[12] But the Kansas-Nebraska bill remained buried in the House calendar. Democratic leaders had to come up with a plan to resurrect the bill during the current session of Congress.

Cutting's actions and the vote on his motion revealed to Pierce, Douglas, and other party leaders the difficulty they faced in trying to gather enough votes from northern Democratic representatives to pass the bill. Over the next six weeks, as the bill languished, Pierce and Douglas worked behind the scenes to win over individual Democratic representatives. The president had a powerful weapon at his disposal—patronage. Having used this means over the past year, unsuccessfully, to broaden the support for the Democratic Party, Pierce now used the promise of rewards to win back wavering votes in the House. With public opinion in much of the country strongly against the bill, any Democrat from the North who voted for it faced the likelihood of defeat in the next election. Benjamin B. French wrote in his journal, "I now prophesy that every Northern man who votes for it will find that he has sacrificed himself politically." There would need to be rewards for the sacrifice the president was asking individual representatives to make, but French predicted, "The power the President has over Congress is such that he can control the vote of the Senate and perhaps the House . . . but he cannot control the *people* of the Free states, and *that* he will ere long discover."[13]

French was deeply troubled by the path his friend had taken: "There never was so great a political blunder committed, as the bringing forward of this repeal measure at this time, in my opinion. It may be right in itself, . . . but the expediency of doing right under certain circumstances is questionable."[14] Pierce asked French to aid in the cause by writing a letter in support of the bill to friends in New Hampshire for publication in state papers. French declined but, in a letter of explanation to Pierce, stated that while he looked upon the bill "as unnecessary" he "nevertheless defended strenuously the principle."[15]

While French's support for Pierce was deeply shaken by the Kansas-Nebraska bill, he continued to admire much about his old friend. One winter evening, French was present at a meeting of the Agricultural Society at the Smithsonian Institution when Pierce entered and sat down to listen to the speaker. Following the lecture, Pierce rose, French wrote,

> and with a grace of manner which few men possess in a more eminent degree than Frank Pierce, he addressed the President (Mr. Wilder), thanking him for the invitation to be present, regretting that official engagements, probably not near so important as the business they were engaged in & certainly to him not so agreeable, demanded his presence elsewhere, & expressing a hope that their deliberations might result in great benefit to the country, he retired amid the enthusiastic cheers of the audience & the verbal expression all around the Hall of admiration at his manner & his remarks. It *was* Frank Pierce as I have seen him a hundred times—& although it was, no less, the President of the U.S., I forgot the President in the man—& a higher compliment I could not pay him."[16]

The Washington social season was in full swing, and despite the animosity engendered by the activities in Congress, Pierce continued to carry out his many social responsibilities. Among these was a weekly levee, or open house, at the White House throughout the winter months, during which Pierce stood and shook hands with the public. He was assisted by Jonah D. Hoover, marshal of the district, who inquired the name of each visitor and then introduced each one to the President. Hoover frequently misunderstood the names of strangers, "and they were rebaptized to their annoyance, but President Pierce, with winning cordiality, shook hands with each one, and put them directly as ease, chatting pleasantly until someone else came along . . ."[17]

B. B. French's son Frank, home from Harvard, recorded his impressions of one such levee on March 31, 1854, "the evening appointed for the last Levee" of the season:

> Uncle Henry and I concluded to call on Mr. Pierce, so we went up in an omnibus. The Marine Band were present and added much by their excellent performance. After checking our exteriors, we passed into the reception room, where stood the President receiving the company with his usual urbanity. He shook hands with us, asked me if I had a pleasant term at school. We went into the East Room, and it is really magnificent. The carpet is without a seam and of a beautiful pattern. The fresco painting, the whole room is one of the handsomest that I've seen. The company kept pouring in until the East Room, the hall, and smaller rooms were densely crowded."[18]

Pierce dropped by the French home one evening unannounced and young French recorded, "He walked up and back, looks quite well, and appeared with usual suavity of manners. I like this element of the General's character, his plain republican manner of private intercourse. Although I cannot agree with the Administration in all their acts, yet as a private citizen I have the greatest respect for Frank Pierce."[19]

White House dinners served both a social and a political function. Pierce often invited guests who were political antagonists, in hopes of bridging differences and keeping the political discourse civil. One such dinner was held on April 13, 1854, in the midst of the House debates on the Kansas-Nebraska bill. Amos A. Lawrence, Jane's cousin by marriage and an outspoken critic of the bill, was visiting from Massachusetts, probably intending to talk sense to the president. Pierce was equally intent on converting Lawrence to his views on the matter. Lawrence's journal described the evening:

> At 6 o'clock I went with Sarah to dine at the President's. The company consisted of 25 persons besides ourselves. The servants seemed to know who we were & ushered us into a handsome parlor where some of the guests were assembled. . . . Soon the President & Mrs. Pierce with Mrs. Means & Miss Mary Mason came in. They greeted us cordially, & the President introduced all the company to Mrs. Pierce. . . . Mrs. Pierce was handsomely dressed & appeared well, tho' somewhat sad, as she always does. Dinner was announced. Judge Douglas, Senator of Illinois (of Nebraska memory) took Mrs. Pierce, Gen. Shields (of Mexican War celebrity & now Senator) took Sarah & I had Mrs. Means. . . . The dining room was splendid; so was the dinner. All in good taste, & after the modest fashion: No meats on the table, nothing but flowers and fruits. . . . The President & Mrs. Pierce sat on opposite sides of the table, & appeared well.[20]

Whether any political talk went on between Pierce, Douglas, and Lawrence is not recorded, but time would prove that no one's views on the bill had changed. Though his administration was continuing to lose support from the general public, one longtime Washington observer later wrote, "President Pierce was the most popular man personally that ever occupied the President's chair."[21]

Lawrence spent more than a week as a guest at the White House in April 1854 and had an opportunity to assess the president's lifestyle and personal habits. He wrote of Pierce to his uncle, "He endeavours to be exemplary in his habits, & the stories to the contrary have no foundation. He never tastes wine or spirits on any occasion. He has prayers in his family every evening & reads them himself from Thornton's collection (given him by my father in 1847); he even asks the blessing before dinner, an uncommon thing in Washn. & he does it even at the state dinners where there are 30 persons. . . ."[22] Ida Russell, a Boston socialite visiting in Washington, gossiped to Cushing about the president's total abstinence from alcohol, but she believed it was "because he has a bad wife." To Russell, Jane Pierce had made the White House a cold and inhospitable place: "It is the meanest table that has been ever kept at the White House. She is sordid, vain, selfish, & egotistical. He would like to act his nature & be hospitable. She chooses to save money. . . . She watches him it is said with the most contemptible jealousy. She makes him sit at table with his glass turned down as a constant advertisement that he has weaknesses that he could not mend & to let the world know that his wife has a hard time taking care of him, instead of turning it up & resisting if that is best without placing him in a position degrading to his self-respect."[23]

Varina Davis, the young (twenty-eight-year-old) wife of the secretary of war, recalls a visit of the Pierces to the Davis summer house outside Washington offering further evidence of Jane's controlling nature. Pierce paced about with his hands in his pockets as he related a story about Hawthorne. Noticing Jane's critical gaze he spoke out: "No; I won't take them out of my pockets, Jennie! I am in the country, and I like to feel the comfort of it."[24] Jane had yet to make her first appearance at a public event, but she was no recluse. By the winter of 1854, she was viewed by contemporaries as directing the social life at the White House.

On May 3, 1854, Pierce issued the first veto of his administration. The bill titled "An act making a grant of public lands to the several States for the benefit of indigent insane persons," was the brainchild of philanthropist and reformer Dorothea Dix, who had been working tirelessly for nearly twenty years to improve the care of the mentally ill. By 1854, thanks to her efforts, at least a dozen states had built hospitals to care for the insane.[25] But she needed money to extend her work to other states. With the help of friendly congressmen, she created a plan whereby the federal government would grant 10 million acres of public land to the states, in proportion to the number of representatives from each. The states would then sell the land and invest the proceeds to create "a perpetual fund," the interest from which would be used for the care of institutionalized insane persons.[26] The bill had been considered during each of the previous three congressional sessions when it was reintroduced by Whigs William Bissell of

Illinois in the House and Solomon Foot of Vermont in the Senate in December 1853.[27]

Miss Dix was present in the capital throughout the session, lobbying with congressmen and the president for her bill. She first met with Pierce on December 7 and reported to her close friend Millard Fillmore that while the president expressed his "interest and good will," she found "his manner wavering and hurried." Pierce stated that he had not studied the matter, and Dix left the meeting disturbed by the president's "air of restless half uncertainty." Fillmore understood the reason: "My inference is that he is really and truly sympathetic with the object but he has not fully satisfied himself that as President he can constitutionally approve the measure."[28] In fact, Dix's bill was but one of a host of proposed legislation relating to the federal government's public land policy. Besides the Kansas-Nebraska bill, a homestead bill was working its way through Congress to provide free land to settlers, as were several bills to grant public lands to railroads. Dix's bill was caught up in the speculation as to how far Pierce would go in approving legislation relating to public lands.[29]

Dix was elated when the Senate passed the bill on March 8, 1854 by a vote of twenty-five to twelve. The House followed, approving the bill on April 19 by a vote of eighty-one to fifty-three.[30] She naïvely assumed that the large margin of victory meant that the bill might receive the president's signature or that there were enough votes to override a veto. Ominously, for the fate of her bill, twenty-five senators were absent, and the House barely managed a quorum on the day the bill was passed. Western Democrats apparently decided to allow the bill to pass, as one scholar has noted, "to preview Pierce's attitude toward their legislative priority, the homestead bill," while southern Democrats "used Dix's bill to sharpen their constitutional critique of federal initiatives in the public domain."[31] The fate of the Whig-sponsored bill and Miss Dix was now in the hands of the president.

Pierce discussed the bill with his cabinet, and Sidney Webster was overheard gossiping that the discussion became quite "excited."[32] If so, the leading proponent of the bill within the cabinet was likely James C. Dobbin, who as a state legislator in North Carolina had sponsored Dix's bill to create a state institution for the insane. While the bill was being debated in North Carolina, Dobbin's wife died, and Miss Dix had shown great personal concern and support for Dobbin during this difficult time.[33] But Davis and Cushing spoke strongly against the bill on constitutional grounds, and Pierce agreed.

In his lengthy veto message, Pierce admitted that he had "been compelled to resist the deep sympathies" of his "heart" in deciding against the bill, but his "deliberate conviction that a strict adherence to the terms and purposes of the federal compact" impelled him to veto it. Pierce stated, "If Congress has power to make provision for the indigent insane . . . it has the same power to provide for the indigent who are not insane, and thus transfer to the Federal Government the charge of all the poor in all the States." Pierce went on to say, "I cannot find any authority in the Constitution for making the Federal Government the great almoner of public charity throughout the United States. To do so would, in my judgment, be contrary to the letter and spirit of the Constitution and subversive of the whole theory upon which the Union of these States is founded." The founding fathers had clearly intended for public charity to be administered by the states. It would be "the beginning of the end" for the sovereignty of the individual states if this power was assumed by the federal government. He also declared that it made no constitutional difference, as some congressmen claimed, "whether the appropriation be in money or in land." According to Pierce, Congress did not have the power to dispose of the public land in this manner.[34]

Having denied the constitutionality of this particular bill, Pierce went on to offer guidelines for the constitutional disposal of the public domain. Comparing the federal government to a "prudent proprietor," Pierce stated that acts which would "enhance the sale value" of public land were acceptable. He offered two examples of past government actions of which he approved: the granting to the states of the "sixteenth sections" for the purposes of education and the "relinquishment of swamp lands to the States," which were then drained, "protecting the health of the inhabitants and at the same time enhancing the value of the remaining" government lands. Based on Pierce's constitutional interpretation, there must be "a national object" to legislation disposing of public lands.[35] Though not specifically mentioning grants to railroads or a homestead act, the message implied that these could receive Pierce's approval; at least, the *Washington Union* so stated in an editorial.[36]

Pierce's veto message succeeded, while the Kansas-Nebraska bill had failed, to unite Democrats around their perceived heritage of individual liberties, limited government, and states' rights. Senate debate on the veto message became a test of party fidelity, with Virginia's Hunter declaring, "We have an issue made upon principle," and westerners, specifically Douglas and Cass, endorsing the president's message as consistent with their need for land grants. Dix was devastated when the Senate voted to uphold the veto, twenty-six to twenty-one, on July 6. All leading Democrats, including Atchison, Bright, Butler, Cass, Douglas, Hunter, Mason, and Slidell, voted with their president, while some of Dix's supporters, including Foot, did not even show up to vote.[37] Dix blamed Pierce, declaring, "The poor weak President has by an unprecedented extremity of folly lacerated my life." She later referred to Pierce as "Judas the Younger," though her claim that he had promised to sign her bill is contradicted by her own correspondence.[38] With the *New York Tribune* declaring that Dix's "nervous system [was] completely prostrated" by the result, she fled to England in early September.[39] The need for Pierce to address the constitutionality of a homestead bill was precluded when the Senate substituted it with a graduation bill, which authorized the government to sell marginal lands at greatly reduced prices.

While exercising a measure of leadership within his party for his deftly crafted veto message, Pierce suffered abuse from the press for vetoing a bill that seemed to have considerable public support. During these hectic days, a friend of Dix wrote to Cushing that she was concerned because the youthful-looking and outgoing president she had met just a year earlier had aged and appeared tired and careworn, exhibiting "such a wreck of the good gifts he had been endowed with," and this after only a year in office. She was so distressed upon meeting the president following the Dix veto that she wrote, "I could not command my feelings & had to go immediately."[40]

By early May, supporters of the Kansas-Nebraska bill believed they had enough support lined up to resurrect the bill in the House. Pierce had been especially active writing editorials, meeting with representatives, and offering patronage. What specific inducements were offered is difficult to ascertain in most cases, but thirteen House members, who had originally voted for Cutting's motion to effectively kill the bill ultimately voted to pass it.[41] Twelve of the thirteen came from free states, and only one of those who switched was reelected. Pierce likely made a general promise to each representative that if he were defeated, he would be taken care of. Norman Eddy of Indiana, defeated for reelection in the fall of 1854, was immediately appointed by Pierce as attorney general of the Territory of Minnesota and later became a land agent in Kansas. Frederick W. Green of Ohio chose not to seek reelection and was appointed by Pierce to be clerk of the U.S. District Court in Cleveland, a position he held for the next twelve years. Andrew Stuart of Ohio lost his bid for reelection in 1854, but his company received the contract to carry the mail from Kansas to Santa Fe. John J. Taylor of New York was appointed by Pierce to be commissioner to settle the boundary dispute with Great Britain in the northwest, but he declined the appointment. Others who voted for the bill and in doing so sacrificed their reelection include Milton Latham of California, who was immediately named by Pierce collector of the port of San Francisco. Thomas A. Hendricks of Indiana was appointed commissioner of the General Land Office in Washington, and William W. Churchwell of Tennessee was appointed marshal for the district of east Tennessee.[42]

The press was aware of the horsetrading. The anti-Nebraska papers in New York were particularly vocal in condemning the "corruption" surrounding the bill's passage. Rumors were that Rep. Theodore Westbrook, one of Cutting's men who switched his vote, was offered the position of U.S. district attorney vacated by Hard leader Charles O'Conor. William Marcy Tweed supposedly sold his vote to Pierce on condition that a friend be made postmaster of Williamsburgh, New York. Reports were that Rep. George Houston of Alabama obtained offices for two nephews.[43] The specifics are difficult to confirm, but Pierce, Douglas, Davis, and Breckinridge were all reportedly active in soliciting support.

By using patronage to drive the bill through the House, Pierce was doing nothing more nor less than any president would have done. As the anti-Nebraska forces saw their votes slipping away, however, they equated politics as usual with the denial of the will of the people.

Pierce's old antagonist John P. Hale, who was effectively using opposition to the bill to resurrect his political career, said in a speech, "Let me ask you, my friends, if this is one of those minor questions which you are willing to trade off at the polls for a place in the Custom House? Are there not some things that are a little higher and holier than to be put in the political shambles for the market, and is not this one of those questions?"[44] Pierce's secretary, Sidney Webster, confirmed the large number of promises made by the president when he informed John H. George back in New Hampshire that it would be difficult to acquire a position overseas for George: "The President is, and will be more hereafter, embarrassed by inducements held out during the pendency of Nebraska, undoubtedly, I fear that will control him."[45]

Federal government employees in Washington were also feeling the pressure from Pierce to get behind the bill. Solicitor Frank L. Burt, who was suspected of anti-Nebraska leanings, believed Pierce's unexpected visit to his office was meant to "scare him." Another clerk was dismissed, allegedly "for insubordination," but opposition to the bill was the unstated reason. Paranoia was evident among anti-Nebraska federal employees, one writing, "I believe Pierce attends personally to all the little petty clerkships."[46] Pierce had employed all of the powers of his office to win over Democratic congressmen.

Believing they had a safe majority, administration forces, led by Richardson in the House, began on May 8 the laborious process of bringing the bill up for a final vote. First, Richardson moved that the House go into the committee of the whole. Then each of the eighteen bills ahead of the Kansas-Nebraska bill on the House calendar had to be laid aside. Eighteen roll call votes were taken, and the administration's majority held firm as each bill was successfully set aside. With the Kansas-Nebraska bill now under consideration, two weeks of debate and proposed amendments followed. Opponents of the bill, realizing they lacked the votes to defeat it, entered on a strategy of delay by offering amendments.[47] Throughout the debates, Douglas strolled about the House lobby arm in arm with Breckinridge as a show of unity. Davis was also much in evidence, keeping southern congressmen in line.[48]

In frustration at the delaying tactics, Alexander H. Stephens of

Georgia offered a unique solution to bring the bill to a final vote. House rule 119 stated that a motion to strike out the enacting clause of a bill had the effect of cutting off all further action and requiring an immediate vote on that motion. If this passed, the committee of the whole would then have to report the bill to the House for a final vote. All debate and amendments would be stopped. The motion to strike the enacting clause was passed, 103 to 22, opponents of the bill not understanding what was happening. Once they realized they had been tricked, they made repeated motions to adjourn. These were all defeated. The Senate bill was then substituted for the House bill and passed 113 to 100 at 11:00 p.m., to cheers from the galleries.[49]

It took a southern Whig to break the impasse, and Stephens basked in the glory: "When the signal guns upon Capitol Hill proclaimed the final passing of the Nebraska Bill I felt that the cup of my ambition was full."[50] But the victory was the result of intense effort on the part of Douglas, Breckinridge, Davis, and Pierce to use all the power of incumbency to keep the Democratic Party together. In the end, all but two of fifty-nine southern Democrats voted for the bill, while forty-four of eighty-six northern Democrats voted with the administration and against their constituents, in support of the bill. In light of the agitation the bill created in the North, it was a remarkable display of party discipline. It was the Whig party that had failed to hold together. Not one northern Whig voted for the bill, while twelve of nineteen southern Whigs endorsed it.[51] Pierce signed the bill into law on May 30.

In Boston, news of the passage of the bill brought Democratic office holders streaming out of the Custom House, dragging a cannon onto Boston Common to fire off a salute in celebration of the administration's victory. That same night, fugitive slave Anthony Burns was arrested in the city.[52] News of Burns's arrest quickly spread throughout Boston, giving anti-Nebraska and abolitionist leaders a cause to rally around. A meeting was held at Faneuil Hall on the evening of May 26, attended by nearly five thousand, who listened to inflammatory speeches by Wendell Phillips, Samuel G. Howe, Theodore Parker, and others. A portion of the crowd descended on the courthouse where Burns was being held, in an attempt to free the fugitive. The mob threw stones, breaking all of the windows, and tried to break down the doors. In the melee, a deputized federal marshal, James Bachelder, was stabbed and killed. The attempt to free Burns failed.[53]

To prevent any further mob action, Mayor J. V. C. Smith called in the state militia, and Pierce appointee U.S. Marshal Watson Freeman called in federal troops from nearby Fort Independence. Freeman telegraphed the president, "In consequence of an attack upon the court-house last night, for the purpose of rescuing a fugitive slave under arrest, and in which one of my own guards was killed, I have availed myself of the resources of the United States, placed under my control by letter from the War and Navy Departments in 1851, and now have two companies of troops from Fort Independence stationed in the court-house. Everything is now quiet. The attack was repulsed by my own guard."[54] Pierce wired back, "Your conduct is approved; the law must be executed."[55] He then asked Attorney General Cushing for advice on the authority that could be exercised by a federal marshal under these circumstances. Cushing's opinion, written quickly on May 27, was that the marshal had the authority to "summon the entire able-bodied force of his precinct, as a *posse commitatus.*" Cushing advised that Marshal Freeman had the right to call upon "any and all organized force, whether militia of the state, or officers, sailors, soldiers, and marines of the United States." Cushing also ruled that local and state judicial authorities had no right to issue a writ of habeas corpus to free a fugitive slave.[56] Cushing's opinion was entirely in line with the Fugitive Slave Act, but his strong policy statement left no doubt of the intention of the administration to enforce the law even in the face of a hostile public.

Thousands of Boston citizens gathered outside the courthouse for the Burns hearing on Monday, May 29, before Commissioner George Loring, another Pierce appointee, and U.S. District Attorney Benjamin H. Hallett, a longtime Pierce friend and political ally. Jefferson Davis sent the army's adjutant general, Colonel Samuel Cooper, to Boston with orders to use whatever force was necessary to maintain order.[57] On June 2 Mayor Smith placed the city under martial law in advance of Commissioner Loring's ruling: "On the law and facts of the case, I consider the claimant entitled to the certificate from one which he claims."[58] Burns was ordered turned over to his master. Hallett wired the president, "The Commissioner has granted the certificate. Fugitive will be removed today. Ample military and police force to effect it peacefully. All quiet. Law reigns. Col. Cooper's arrival opportune."[59]

At noon, some fifty thousand citizens lined the street as Burns was marched to the wharf to a waiting ship to take him back to Virginia. The procession was led by plumed cavalry on horseback, followed by a company of U.S. infantry; next was a company of U.S. marines, then Boston's "National Lancers," followed by the marshal's guard, and a horse-drawn field piece, manned by six members of the Fourth Artillery Regiment, and an additional platoon of marines. As the mounted lancers moved the surging crowd back, a witness described the scene of "a solitary black man walking down the middle of the busiest street in Boston on a Friday afternoon encased in a moving white army."[60] The steamer left the wharf at 3:20 p.m. The *Richmond Enquirer* reported, "We rejoice at the recapture of Burns, but a few more such victories and the South is undone."[61] The same could be said for the Pierce administration. Over the next few months District Attorney Hallett tried to convict the murderer of Bachelder, and the leading rioters. All were set free by the local courts.[62] The sentiments and intentions of the abolitionists is summed up in a letter written by Horace Mann, noted educator, who endorsed the Burns riot and lamented that only one man was killed: "It was folly not to kill enough to answer the purpose."[63]

Pierce's commitment to enforcing the law was unwavering and political considerations did not dissuade him. More slaves were returned by federal authorities during Pierce's administration than at any other time during the fourteen years that the law was in effect, and there were fewer slave rescues.[64] But the Burns case was a costly victory. The press estimated that enforcing the law in this case cost the government nearly $100,000, though Treasury Department records indicate that only $14,000 was actually paid.[65] Local and state authorities in the North continually placed obstacles in the way of enforcing the law. Nearly a dozen states passed personal liberty laws that challenged federal officials by making it difficult for them to carry out their duties, and local and state courts frequently granted writs of habeas corpus to free fugitives. One federal marshal, F. M. Wynkoop, who served under Pierce in Mexico, was jailed in Philadelphia for refusing to honor a writ of habeas corpus. Commissioner Loring was punished by the Massachusetts legislature with loss of his judgeship, and Harvard fired him from his teaching position. Despite the resolve of the administration, Burns was the last fugitive slave returned from New England.[66]

On the same day that the Burns riot took place in Boston, Lord Elgin, governor-general of Canada, arrived in Washington from London, carrying instructions from Lord Clarendon to finalize the fisheries reciprocity treaty. The British government agreed to give American fishermen free access to the coast and shore of Atlantic Canada and the Saint Lawrence River. In turn, Canadian fishermen would have the same rights along the Atlantic coast north of Virginia and in the Great Lakes. Tariffs on most raw materials would be eliminated, including those on furs, lumber, coal, and farm staples from Canada and tar, pitch, turpentine, rice, and unmanufactured tobacco from the United States. Buchanan had alerted Pierce and Marcy of the mission of Lord Elgin, but was unclear if he had the authority to conclude a treaty.[67]

Elgin and company arrived at an opportune time. The passage of the Kansas-Nebraska bill a few days earlier left many southern senators in a generous mood. They had been ambivalent, if not opposed, to improving relations with the free territories of Canada, but now saw a reason to reassure the North of their good intentions by agreeing to a reciprocity treaty. The passage of the Kansas-Nebraska bill and Elgin's arrival revived the social season in the capital. Over the next ten days Elgin and company dined at least once at the White House, and Marcy hosted them on several occasions. Elgin's secretary, Laurence Oliphant, wrote of late night parties at the homes of senators, where "Lord Elgin's faculty of brilliant repartee and racy anecdote especially delighted them . . ."[68]

Elgin also spent lavishly, plying the senators with food and drink. Along with the nightly entertaining, serious negotiations were taking place between Marcy and Elgin, resulting in a late-night session on June 5, when the final terms of the treaty were agreed upon. Around midnight Marcy and Elgin put their signatures to the document. Elgin's secretary, rather dramatically, recorded the scene: "There is something strangely mysterious and suggestive in the scratching of that midnight pen, for it may be scratching fortunes or ruin to millions. Then the venerable statesman takes up the pen to append his signature. His hand does not shake, though he is very old, and knows the abuse that is in store for him from members of Congress and an enlightened press.... So he gives his blessing and the treaty is signed."[69] By the time he wrote this description, Oliphant had been so indoctrinated in the party strife that persisted in Washington that he exaggerated the opposition Marcy and Pierce faced in ratifying the treaty. He described the dinner at the White House as "more senators and politics, and champagne, and Hard Shells and Soft Shells. I much prefer the marine soft-shell crab, with which I here made acquaintance for the first time, to the political one."[70] Pierce sent the treaty on to the Senate on June 19, and it was ratified by a vote of thirty-two to eleven on August 2. Because of the tariff implications, the House then passed an act carrying the treaty into effect as soon as it was ratified by Parliament and by the Canadian provincial legislatures.[71] Considering Elgin's public relations effort, one historian wrote that the reciprocity treaty was "floated" through the Congress "on champagne."[72] This remark ignores Pierce's persistence in pressing the issue with the British government and the considerable work done by special agent Israel D. Andrews. A mutual friend wrote to Pierce of Andrews, "I never saw anything nearer a man's heart than that Treaty was his."[73]

In May, Andrews reported to Marcy that he had already spent over $18,000 to win support for the treaty in Canada. He made a detailed list of his activities, including paying one member of the New Brunswick assembly $840. According to Andrews, W. H. Needham had sponsored a resolution opposed to the treaty. Following the payment by Andrews, he was now an enthusiastic supporter of it.[74] Another item on Andrews's list was a $3,900 "Contribution to Election Expenses for Gov't Candidate, etc...." P. F. Little, a member of the provincial assembly of Newfoundland, received $1,150. He proceeded to get himself appointed by the assembly as their delegate to meet Lord Elgin in Quebec and carry the terms of the treaty back to Newfoundland.[75] Andrews listed $4,218 "paid privately and by myself to officials, leading persons and the press..."[76] He also included "the sum of Three thousand Dollars, [which] will, if required, be the subject of personal explanation to the President or Secretary of State. The circumstances under which it was applied, are of so delicate a nature, that I do not conceive it judicious to make any explanation even in this confidential communication"[77]

Andrews returned to Washington for the Senate ratification effort. Marcy had finally agreed to include coal in the free list, and he called on Andrews to meet with senators from Virginia, Maryland, and Pennsylvania, "who may prove shaky on that point." Andrews overwhelmed them with statistics and his extensive knowledge of Canadian-American trade and won them over to the treaty.[78]

The treaty has been called the singular diplomatic success of the Pierce administration. It was the first reciprocity treaty ever concluded by this country. To Pierce, however, the key to the agreement was the access of New England fishermen to the Canadian coast. The treaty was to be in effect for ten years; following that time, a year's notice was required before the treaty could be abrogated.

Andrews returned to Canada to win ratification of the treaty in the provincial assemblies. He continued to spend lavishly, between $118,000 and $200,000, according the some estimates.[79] But he achieved success, as four of the five Canadian assemblies approved the treaty by December 1854. Shortly after, Pierce proclaimed that the treaty was in effect. Eventually, Newfoundland joined the other four provinces in ratifying the treaty, and Pierce issued a separate proclamation extending full benefits to that province.[80] In the first year after the treaty was operative, Canadian-American trade rose from $35 million to $57 million.[81] The popularity of the treaty proved to be short lived. Manufactured items had been excluded from the free list, and a growing protectionist movement in Canada resulted in higher tariffs on American manufactures. The Civil War also increased antagonism between the United States, Great Britain and Canada, causing the Republican administration to abrogate the treaty in 1866.[82]

For Andrews the news was even worse. Pierce and Marcy refused to approve most of his expenses. In September 1854, Marcy wrote to Andrews that "as they now stand, without further explanation and support by vouchers, they would undoubtedly be rejected" by the auditor of the Treasury Department.[83] In December, as Andrews was leaving Washington for Newfoundland, which was the lone holdout in ratifying the treaty, Pierce wrote to apologize for failing to approve his expenses: "It was a matter of sincere regret, that, I could not in the exercise of legal authority and just discretion embrace in the order of payment, all the items in your account for your expenses incurred and money actually paid." He, nevertheless, thanked Andrews: "I shall always entertain a high appreciation of the valuable services rendered by you in relation to the fishery question, and other matters, during the progress of the negotiations. . . . " And Pierce invited Andrews to stop in Concord on his way north "and visit our friend Revd. Henry Parker."[84]

Andrews would appeal his case to the government long after the Pierce administration had passed into history. In 1858 William Seward took up his case in the Senate. Andrews claimed expenses of $66,797.32, of which the government had paid him $14,012.38. Seward thus proposed Andrews be paid the balance of $52,784.94 upon the "principles of equity and justice."[85] Nothing was accomplished, so a year later Andrews appealed to Buchanan's secretary of state, Lewis Cass, "for adjustment" of his case.[86] There is no record of Andrews ever receiving any additional money from the United States, but the special agent was compensated by private individuals, including the Boston Board of Trade, which openly raised $53,000 to help Andrews settle his accounts.[87] What Pierce thought of Andrews's extravagance is unclear. It is curious that while Pierce saved very few personal papers from his administration, he did preserve all of the communication with Andrews. There was never any attempt by Pierce to hide Andrews's clandestine activities.[88]

The Canadian reciprocity treaty was widely praised in the press, but nothing could overcome the distress that the Kansas-Nebraska bill had caused the president or his closest friends. Hawthorne heard the criticisms as far away as Liverpool. His wife, Sophia, was particularly sensitive where Pierce was concerned. She wrote her father, who had reported to her the agitation the bill produced in New England,

> Such abuse of a good President as there is, is sickening. I hope those who vilify him for doing what he considers his duty have

> a quarter of his conscience and uprightness. He is a brave man. . . . He wrote Mr. Hawthorne that he had no hope of being popular during the first part of his administration at least. He can be neither bribed, bought, nor tempted in his political course; he will do what he thinks constitutional and right and find content in it. I wish our Senators had as good manners as the noble lords of Parliament. But we are perfect savages in manners as yet, and have no self-control, nor reverence.[89]

Another Pierce defender, Henry E. Parker, minister of Concord's South Congregational Church, suffered a personal humiliation because of his friendship with the president. He described what happened in a lengthy letter to Pierce. On the Sunday following the removal of Burns from Boston, Parker was scheduled to exchange pulpits with the minister of the Congregational Church in North Danvers, Massachusetts. That Sunday morning, a group of abolitionist members of the congregation met in the vestry before the service and voted to deny Parker the right to preach because of his association with Pierce. A deacon of the congregation visited Parker at the house where he was staying and informed him that their decision "was aimed not so much" at Parker as it was at Pierce. Parker wrote, "Their lash was not quite long enough to reach to Washington in any other way . . ." Parker admitted to being astonished at the unprecedented action, "this shutting of a N. E. church against an accredited minister not yet convicted of any crime." Parker asked for permission to address the group in the vestry. He explained to the group his reasons for not signing any of the petitions against the bill or the Burns case; "frankly acknowledging" his attachment to Pierce, he "gave them a few facts" relating to political matters, and "left them as courteously as I could without departing from my own self-respect. . . ." The deacon then followed Parker to the house where he was staying and invited him back to the church, saying that only a minority of the members were part of the committee and did not represent the sentiments of the congregation. Parker returned and reported, "I had a good congregation morning, afternoon, and evening: the crazy ones quietly staying away. I was treated cordially by those whose opinion I would care the most for, & even by the best of the abolitionists."

Parker admitted he would not have bothered Pierce with his troubles, except that the incident made the local papers and he was afraid the president would learn about it. Admitting that "under the present excitement here at the North my position will be somewhat odious," Parker went on to write, "The whole affair has made me feel more closely allied to yourself . . ." He also commented, "Hot-headed abolitionists have become lowered several pegs in my estimation."[90] Pierce, who always abhorred the politicization of religion, was undoubtedly incensed at Parker's treatment.

Politicians close to Pierce understood how the Kansas-Nebraska bill had overshadowed the president's own agenda. John A. Dix, no longer on friendly terms with Pierce after failing to get the mission to Paris, nevertheless, lamented that the repeal of the Missouri Compromise would weaken the administration: "I look to them with confidence for sound financial measures, and these are always of vital importance to good government."[91]

Rev. Parker, who had visited the Pierces at the White House, also understood the president's determination to reform the executive branch. He hoped that once the excitement over the Kansas-Nebraska bill had died down, "the country will soon see . . . the new life, exactness, efficiency & economy, infused into the Departments & Bureaus at Washington."[92] The more politically astute Paul R. George understood that honest, efficient administration was not enough: "no quiet, meritorious conduct" could overcome the "character and identity" that was attached to Pierce by "Nebraska." According to George, "Mr. Pierce must begin now to identify *his name* with a bold, dashing act." George recommended that Pierce "*take Cuba Bonaparte fashion* suddenly like a clap of thunder."[93] As spring gave way to the stifling heat of a Washington, D.C., summer and the lengthy congressional session dragged on, the Pierce administration prepared to take bold action regarding Cuba and other foreign problems.

6

CUBA

IN THE SPRING OF 1854, events in Cuba prompted the Pierce administration to initiate an aggressive attempt to acquire the island from Spain. United States interest in Cuba dates back to the Monroe administration. Then secretary of state John Quincy Adams declared that because of Cuba's strategic position, which allowed Cuba to command control of the Gulf of Mexico and the mouth of the Mississippi River, and the island's commercial importance as the world's leading producer of sugar, "the annexation of Cuba to our federal Republic will be indispensable to the continuance and integrity of the Union itself."[1] Later secretaries of state Clay, Van Buren, Buchanan, and Webster concurred regarding Cuba's importance to the United States.[2] Jefferson agreed that control of Cuba "would fill up the measure of our political well-being."[3] The Polk administration had offered Spain $100 million for the island.

Spain's oppressive and corrupt rule over Cuba tended to confirm the belief that the United States must ultimately control the island. Spain's dictatorial colonial policy, enforced by some forty thousand Spanish soldiers, drained the island of its wealth, through exorbitant taxes designed to prop up the financial crisis in the mother country. Creoles, native-born Cubans of Spanish descent, were denied any say over Cuban policies and were not allowed to hold office, but as land owners and planters, they had much at stake in the island's future. The economy, based on sugar, relied on slave labor. Creoles continued to import slaves from Africa long after the slave trade was banned. Spain's appointed captain-general required a bribe of $48 for each new slave brought into the island. By the 1840s the black population, slaves and free Negroes, far outnumbered whites, Creoles, and Spanish. Commercial relations with the United States were strained by the imposition of high tariffs, ranging from 50 to 175 percent on American imports. U.S. interest in Cuba was motivated as much by the desire to open up new markets for trade and shipping as it was to add new slave states. This explains the support annexationists received from commercial interests in New York City and New Orleans.[4]

Not surprisingly, Creole planters were ripe for revolution. Recognizing the difficulty in overcoming the tight military control of Spain, they sought help in the United States. In the late 1840s, Creole expatriates living in the United States formed the Order of the Lone Star, led by Narciso Lopez, to plan and execute a revolution. With headquarters in New Orleans and New York, the order approached U.S. military officers with the offer to lead the expedition in order to free Cuba. The expectation was that once a landing was made in Cuba, native Creoles would rally to the invaders. Among the military officers offered command of the filibuster expedition were Jefferson Davis, Robert E. Lee, William Worth, and John A. Quitman. All rejected the offers despite the prospect of up to $3 million in rewards from the well-financed Order of the Lone Star.[5]

Lopez led two unsuccessful filibuster invasions of Cuba in 1850 and 1851. The second invasion in August 1851, commanded by Col. William L. Crittenden, West Point graduate and nephew of then Attorney General John J. Crittenden, failed, as Spanish authorities rounded up nearly five hundred invaders, and executed Lopez, Crittenden, and fifty other Americans. In both invasions, local Creoles had failed to rally to the cause, and, in fact, had tipped off the Spanish authorities of the plans. In the United States the executions of Crittenden and the Americans caused rioting in New Orleans, during which the Spanish consulate was destroyed and the property of Spanish citizens set on fire. The involvement of prominent United States citizens in the filibuster led to indictments for violation of neutrality laws. Governor Quitman of Mississippi resigned his post to face trial in New Orleans. In New York, journalist John L. O'Sullivan, whose sister was married to a prominent Creole planter in Havana, was twice indicted. All those indicted were found innocent by sympathetic

U.S. juries or the charges were never pursued by federal officers in response to public sentiment in favor of the filibusters.[6]

The invasions raised considerable anxiety in Europe, where Great Britain and France looked on the prospect of U.S. annexation of Cuba with deep distress. In 1852 they proposed a tripartite agreement with the United States to agree to stay out of Cuban affairs. Though the Fillmore administration had no designs on Cuba and deplored the filibusters, Secretary of State Edward Everett rejected the proposed agreement, stating in a well-reasoned letter that the United States had legitimate interests in Cuba far more central to U.S. well-being than to that of England and France.[7] The fear of a tripartite agreement prompted a debate in the U.S. Senate on the subject of Cuban annexation, with Pierre Soulé, James M. Mason, and Lewis Cass the most outspoken advocates for future U.S. control of the island. John P. Hale of New Hampshire cuttingly offered that every argument in favor of annexation of Cuba also applied to Canada, yet none of the southern senators were proposing to annex our neighbor to the north.[8]

The Pierce administration assumed office with the active support of all those who favored an aggressive policy toward Cuba, and Pierce had acknowledged in his inaugural address that territorial expansion would be a goal. Cuba was understood by everyone to be the target of future U.S. expansion. In choosing the Senate's most outspoken advocate of Cuban annexation, Pierre Soulé, as minister to Madrid, Pierce signaled his future course. Alarmed at the appointment, the Spanish government immediately brought its minister in Washington, D.C., Calderon de la Barca, home to Madrid to serve as foreign minister to fend off Soulé's diplomatic agenda.[9]

Initially, Pierce and Marcy exercised caution in approaching Spain on the issue of Cuba. In his instructions to Soulé in July 1853, Marcy reassured Spain that it could "depend upon our maintaining our duty as a neutral nation towards her, however difficult it may be." He also instructed Soulé to make no proposition for the purchase of the island.[10] Despite these instructions, some historians have concluded that Pierce favored the filibusters, who were known to be reorganizing for another attempt to free the island from Spain. In the fall of 1852, the Order of the Lone Star was resurrected in New York, with

O'Sullivan playing a leading role. By the spring of 1853, the order had contracted with former Mexican War general John A. Quitman to lead the expedition for a future payment of $1 million once Cuba was freed from Spain.[11] As Quitman began to recruit and plan his invasion, Soulé was departing from New York for Madrid to the cheers of some five thousand who rallied at his hotel. Soulé's remarks to the crowd intimated that his mission was to free Cuba from Spain.[12] But a letter from the head of the Order of the Lone Star to Pierce in the summer of 1853 made it clear that the Creoles did not welcome future U.S. annexation. They intended Cuba to be free and for religious and cultural reasons were opposed to its ultimate political connection with the United States.[13]

There is no evidence that the Pierce administration was planning to support a filibuster invasion of Cuba with the expectation that, as in the case of Texas, the revolutionary government would then ask to be annexed by the United States. Rather, Pierce and Marcy were playing a waiting game, recognizing that any overt effort to acquire Cuba would upset the "repose" on the slavery issue that Pierce had promised to preserve and believing that diplomatic issues with Great Britain could best be resolved without adding Cuba to the mix of issues on the table. Political considerations, however, and the political war over patronage made it expedient for Pierce not to antagonize further his southern supporters. Besides, Pierce, Marcy, Davis, Cushing, Buchanan, and others in the administration sincerely believed Cuba must ultimately belong to the United States. How this was to be accomplished was unclear, but throughout 1853 and into 1854 there was no immediate need to act on the goal. In London, Buchanan reassured Lord Clarendon that the administration was opposed to filibustering to free Cuba but that if the Creoles revolted, there could be no stopping American citizens from assisting. The hope was that the Cubans would free themselves. Since Quitman was openly planning a filibuster to the island, his plans were well known to the administration, but his cautious, plodding progress offered no immediate threat that the invasion would occur any time soon.[14] Quitman believed his activity had the support or, at least, the acquiescence of the administration, but this belief did not come directly from Pierce or anyone in his cabinet. Those closest to Pierce insist that the administration was united in "condemning all these movements and in endeavoring to stop them."[15] Until the spring of 1854, therefore, the Pierce administration had not decided on a policy with regard to Cuba and Spain.

This all changed in the fall of 1853, when Spain sent a new captain-general to Cuba. Marques de la Pezuela was known to be opposed to slavery, and his stated policy, which was labeled "Africanization" in the United States, was designed to make the island undesirable to southern annexationists by suppressing the slave trade, importing more free Negroes and Asians to work the fields, and encouraging intermarriage between races. Instead of lessening interest in Cuba, Pezuela aroused the anxiety of southern politicians, who feared a future black republic in Cuba, similar to that in Haiti, which would threaten the existence of slavery in the United States.[16] This resulted in more pressure on the Pierce administration to act now.

The *Black Warrior* affair demonstrated Pezuela's new, more aggressive policy toward the United States. On February 28, 1854, the American steamer was detained, its cargo seized and its captain arrested in Havana harbor. The charge was the failure of the ship's captain to declare the cargo (nine hundred bails of cotton) and pay a fee to the royal treasury. The fact that the *Black Warrior* had already made the same trip at least seventeen times between New York and Mobile with a stop in Havana without ever having declared its cargo or paid the fee was of no consequence to the Pezuela administration. Previous port officials had an oral agreement with the captain, who was neither discharging nor taking on cargo at Havana, only passengers. Spanish officials refused to deal with Acting Consul William H. Robertson, who offered to have the ship's manifest revised and the fees paid.[17]

Pierce protested to the Spanish government about the "wanton injury of the Cuban authorities in the detention and seizure of the *Black Warrior*" and demanded "immediate indemnity for the injury which has thereby resulted to our citizens." In his report to the House on the incident, Pierce doubted that even in "so clear a case of wrong" could the Spanish government be counted on to act responsibly, as previous incidents of "aggression upon our commerce" and "insults to the national flag by Spanish authorities in Cuba" had resulted in "fruitless" negotiations for redress. He urged on Congress "the propriety of adopting such provisional measures as the exigency may seem to demand."[18] Marcy instructed Soulé, on March 17, to demand an indemnity of $300,000 from the Spanish government for the injuries sustained by Tyng and Company, owners of the *Black Warrior*.[19] On March 16, Spanish officials in Cuba released the ship after collecting a $6,000 fine from the owners.[20]

The *Black Warrior* affair demonstrated to Pierce that the new administration in Cuba was hostile to the United States. Information coming out of Cuba from the U.S. consul, Alexander M. Clayton, and special agent Charles W. Davis, who had been sent secretly by Pierce to the island to investigate the Africanization policy, revealed that Pezuela was proceeding with his reforms and that a Creole revolt was unlikely.[21] Quitman's filibuster to the island was gathering momentum and recruits, and filibusters planned to depart in the summer of 1854. Soulé was also reporting from Madrid that the government of Spain was in danger of collapsing under the weight of foreign debt and pressure from republican forces. To Pierce, the time seemed right for a new approach to Spain and a more aggressive attempt to acquire Cuba.[22]

The result was a new set of instructions to the U.S. minister in Spain, which were sent by Marcy on April 3, 1854, and authorized Soulé to begin negotiating for the purchase of Cuba at a price not to exceed $130 million. Marcy doubted that Spain would sell, and if his prediction proved true, Soulé was to proceed with "the next most desirable object which is to detach that island from the Spanish dominion and from all dependence on any European power." The ambiguous meaning of the word "detach" would plague Pierce and Marcy in the months ahead. They meant that the goal was Cuban independence if Spain refused to sell. This interpretation is confirmed by the next sentence in Soulé's instructions: "If Cuba were relieved from all transatlantic connection and at liberty to dispose of herself as her present interest and prospective welfare would dictate, she would undoubtedly relieve this government from all anxiety in regard to her future condition."[23] But Soulé would interpret the word "detach" differently.

With the decision made to attempt to purchase Cuba, the administration now set out to impede Quitman's filibuster. The need to take action was prompted on May 1 by the senator from Louisiana, John Slidell, who proposed a Senate resolution that would authorize the president "to suspend by proclamation" U.S. neutrality laws for a period of one year. Slidell's resolution was prompted by fears of Africanization in Cuba and the threat "of servile war" that might occur on the island. To Slidell, American interference was necessary and filibustering justified because, he said, "the price of present immunity from interference must be future emancipation [of slaves in Cuba]." The time was right for U.S. intervention, as Great Britain and France were occupied with war in Turkey and not likely to interfere to defend Spain.[24]

Once again a Democratic senator had acted without first communicating with the president. In fact, Slidell wrote to Buchanan, "There is probably not a member of the Senate, who does not consider his own individual opinion in every other respect entitled to quite as much consideration as that of the President. In other words he is the *de jure* not the *de facto* head of the party."[25] But Pierce was equally determined not to be dictated to by senators from his own party. On learning that Senator Mason's Committee of Foreign Relations was planning a favorable report on Slidell's resolution, Pierce summoned Mason, Slidell, Douglas, and others to the White House. He informed them of his determination to seek annexation of Cuba by purchase and his commitment to enforcing the neutrality laws against filibusters. Pierce read them a proclamation that he would issue the next day, May 31, condemning Quitman's planned expedition. Though Slidell protested vigorously, Pierce refused to postpone issuance of the proclamation. He advised the senators that any support of filibustering by them would only impede, not assist, his efforts to acquire Cuba by purchase.[26]

The proclamation of May 31 stated that a "military expedition for the invasion of the island of Cuba" was "derogatory to the character of this nation, and in violation of the obvious duties and obligations of faithful and patriotic citizens." Pierce went on to declare that "all private enterprises of a hostile character . . . against any foreign power . . . are forbidden. . . ." Promising "to prosecute with due energy all those who . . . presume thus to disregard the laws of the land and our treaty obligations," Pierce "charged" all law enforcement agencies, "civil and military," to "prevent any movement in conflict with law. . . ."[27] U.S. Navy Secretary Dobbin informed Mississippi representative A. G. Brown that "if the Filibusters do not spoil things the Island will be ours in twelve months."[28]

If the proclamation wasn't enough to take the wind out of Quitman's sails, the actions of the Pierce administration blocked the activity taking place in New Orleans. Pierce directed Marcy to telegraph the U.S. district attorney in New Orleans "to hold the filibusters in line."[29] Pierce's appointee to the Supreme Court, John A. Campbell, presiding over the U.S. Circuit Court in New Orleans, went even further, charging a grand jury to investigate whether a filibuster expedition was being planned in that city. Campbell instructed the jurors to consider bringing indictments against the organizers if they found the intent to break U.S. neutrality laws, even if no overt actions had yet occurred. Quitman and five associates were brought before the jurors but refused to answer most questions on the grounds of self-incrimination. The grand jury reported that the evidence of a filibuster had been greatly exaggerated in the press and that no further action should be taken by the courts. Faced once again with public opinion supporting illegal activity, the Pierce administration would not back down. Campbell, knowing he had the full support of the president, required Quitman and two others to post bond of $3,000 each as surety that they would not violate the neutrality laws for nine months. Quitman protested the high-handed actions of the judge in the local press but paid the bond and postponed further planning for the expedition until the following summer. Campbell, though a southerner from Alabama, was universally criticized for his actions by Slidell and other southern political leaders.[30] Having launched a new initiative with regard to Spain and Cuba and having successfully thwarted a filibuster expedition to the island, Pierce and Marcy now looked to U.S. ministers in Europe for diplomacy to achieve the goal of acquiring Cuba.

In the meantime, a new crisis broke out in Central America. In 1851 the British protectorate over the Mosquito Coast in Nicaragua had been extended to include the town of San Juan del Norte, at the mouth of the San Juan River; the town was declared a "free city" and

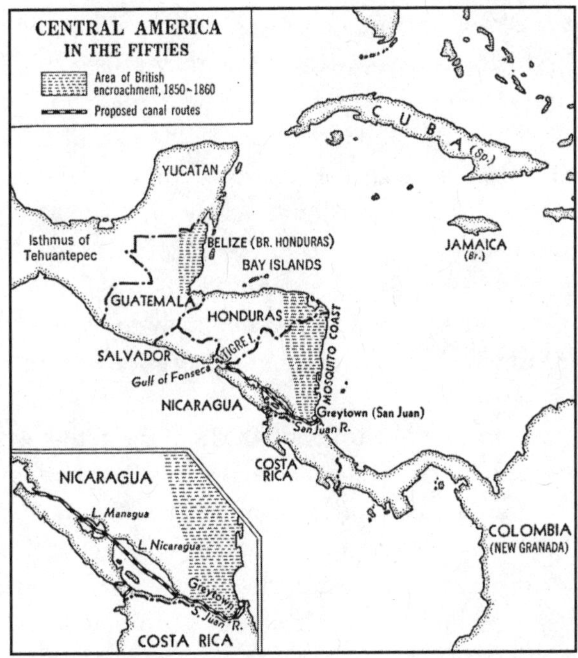

renamed Greytown. Immediately, trouble ensued between the officials of the town, backed by the British consul, and the officers of the Accessory Transit Company, owned by Cornelius Vanderbilt, which had the exclusive contract to convey passengers across the isthmus. The company erected its headquarters across the harbor from Greytown at Punta Arenas and refused attempts by the town officials to collect duties from the company's steamers heading up the river. Incidents occurred in which the lawless inhabitants of Greytown crossed the river to pillage the company's buildings. In the spring of 1854, company officials responded to one of these raids by chasing the thieves across the harbor and seizing one man. The next day armed men crossed from Greytown and kidnapped an employee of the company. As the standoff was reaching a climax, the river steamer *Routh* arrived with the American minister, Solon Borland, on board. To add to the tension, the steamer's captain had shot and killed a Negro crewman during an altercation. On learning of this outrage, thirty Jamaicans from Greytown rushed the steamer, attempting to board her to seize the captain. Borland intervened, brandished his gun, and threatened to shoot anyone boarding the ship. That night Borland entered Greytown to meet with U.S. commercial agent Joseph W. Fabens. A mob surrounded the house and demanded Borland submit to arrest. When Borland attempted to address the crowd, he was struck by a broken bottle and his face was cut. Only the intervention of a party of men from the Atlantic steamer *Northern Light* saved Borland from a worse fate, and he was escorted safely back to the ship. Previously, Borland had submitted his resignation as minister to Marcy, and he proceeded immediately to Washington, D.C., where he informed the secretary and the president of his treatment at Greytown.[31]

Pierce and Marcy had heard enough about the activities occurring in the lawless and, to them, illegal city and decided to demand satisfaction for the offense committed against the U.S. minister. On June 10, 1854, the United States man-of-war *Cyane* under Commander George N. Hollins, was dispatched to Greytown. Navy Secretary Dobbin ordered Hollins to consult with U.S. commercial agent Fabens to determine the facts of the incidents at Greytown. Dobbin directed that "these people be taught that the United States will not tolerate these outrages," but he added, "It is, however, very much to be hoped that you can effect the purposes of your visit without a resort to violence and destruction of property and loss of life."[32] Hollins reached Greytown on July 11 and found that Fabens had been unable to communicate with anyone in authority in the town, as all officials had fled and no government of any kind existed. The presence of the British war schooner *Bermuda* further emboldened the residents of Greytown to ignore any overtures from Hollins and Fabens.[33]

On July 12, his demands for satisfaction and compensation insolently ignored, Hollins gave notice that unless his demands were complied with within twenty-four hours, he would bombard the town. On the morning of the thirteenth, Hollins sent a steamer to safely transport any residents who wished to leave but found that most had fled during the night. Despite the protest of the British vice-consul and Lieutenant Jolly of the *Bermuda*, the bombardment of the town commenced at 9:00 a.m. After several hours of firing, Hollins sent a shore party into the town to burn what was left of Greytown. No lives were lost, though the shore party was fired upon, and all buildings in the town were completely destroyed, except that of a Frenchman who had cooperated with the Americans.[34]

News of Hollins's actions shocked Pierce and Marcy, who had not anticipated such a violent resolution of the problem. The administration determined, however, to sustain Hollins in all his acts, regardless of the protest that was expected from Great Britain. Marcy wrote to Buchanan in London, "The occurrence at Greytown is an embarrassing affair. The place merited chastisement, but the severity of the one inflicted exceeded our expectations. The Government will, however, I think, stand by Capt. Hollins."[35] Buchanan was left to deal with the British reaction.

Upon learning of the incident, Lord Clarendon "seized Buchanan by his coat-lapels" and declared that Hollins's actions were "without a parallel in the annals of modern times."[36] Buchanan advised the administration to admit that Hollins "exceeded his orders," as otherwise the incident would make it impossible for him to negotiate with the British on Central America, but Pierce was resolute and made no public statement on the Greytown affair until his annual message in December 1854.[37] In fact, Britain never made a formal protest, fearing it would only further antagonize American public opinion, and no damages were ever paid.[38]

Temperatures in Washington that summer hovered in the high nineties as Congress continued its lengthy session. The Greytown matter temporarily set aside, the Pierce administration turned once again to Cuba. Having determined on a policy of purchase, the question was how to induce Spain to sell. Back in the fall of 1852, the Jewish-born Austrian emigrant August Belmont had expressed a proposal that made its way to Buchanan, Marcy, and Pierce. With the Spanish government facing bankruptcy and its bonds nearly worthless, Belmont suggested that the Rothschilds, Barings, and other international banking firms that held the defaulted bonds could be induced to pressure the government in Spain to sell Cuba, if the money could be kept out of the hands of the profligate royal family and utilized to develop Spain's economy, including the building of railroads.[39] It was this proposal, in addition to the financial support he provided during the presidential campaign, that recommended Belmont to Pierce for a diplomatic post. Now in the Netherlands,

Belmont continued to discuss his plan with Buchanan, who wrote, "The present would seem to be a favorable moment for making the attempt."[40] Buchanan recognized that such an effort would need to be made behind the scenes to "the large capitalists of Europe" and would require delicate, secret negotiations.[41] This was just what our minister in Madrid, Pierre Soulé, was not noted for.

The impetuous, impatient Soulé had continued to antagonize the Spanish government by his actions. After having made a bad first impression by his duel with the French ambassador, Soulé had quietly carried out his initial instructions to not negotiate with Spain on Cuba. This ended with the *Black Warrior* affair. Armed with Pierce's message to Congress of March 15, documents relating to the incident, and Marcy's instruction to demand an indemnity of $300,000 from Spain, Soulé met with Calderon on April 9. Marcy had instructed Soulé to "obtain as early a reply as practicable to your demand. . . . A very few days it is believed will be sufficient for that purpose."[42] Soulé hardly needed prodding to take a hard line and followed up his meeting with Calderon with an impertinent and insulting letter that gave the foreign minister forty-eight hours to respond to the administration's demands before Soulé would conclude that Spain was upholding the conduct of its officials. He further exceeded Marcy's instructions by adding an additional demand that Spain dismiss or punish all persons involved in the *Black Warrior* matter. Calderon answered politely that he could not comply as he had only the American version of the story and had not received the facts of the case from his own officials in Cuba. In his response, Calderon charged that Soulé was using the *Black Warrior* matter as a "pretext for exciting estrangement, if not a quarrel, between two friendly powers."[43]

Calderon's answer to Pierce's demands came on May 7. Calderon concluded that there had been no insult to the U.S. flag and that the *Black Warrior* had already been returned to its owner and the $6,000 fine remitted. Spain's response reached Pierce and Marcy on June 2. They were appalled at the "misstatements" of fact, "evasion," and "disingenuous perverion of language" it contained. Marcy prepared a lengthy, carefully crafted presentation of the facts of the case and sent it off to Soulé on June 22, with instructions to read the letter to the Spanish foreign minister. The letter concluded by reassuring

Spain, "The President is unwilling to resort to any extreme measures to bring about a better state of things in respect to the island of Cuba. . . ."[44] This reflects the new policy of attempting to purchase the island as Marcy explained to Soulé in a separate letter with a line written by Pierce himself: "You are not expected to take any further steps in relation to the outrage upon the *Black Warrior*."[45] Soulé, ignoring his instructions, did not present the letter to Calderon.

After having taken such a strong stand with Calderon, Soulé was upset that the Pierce administration now instructed him to act cautiously on the matter. The political situation in Madrid convinced Soulé he was justified in ignoring Marcy's instruction to read the letter to Calderon. Insurrection broke out in the streets of Madrid during the first days of July, 1854, and by midmonth the government to which Calderon belonged had fallen. Soulé had been working with the republican forces in Spain to bring about the insurrection, even reporting to Marcy that a $300,000 gift to that faction could lead to a deal for Cuba.[46] But the republican faction failed, and the new government in Spain proved to be as monarchical as the previous administration, even exiling the queen mother, who was viewed as too sympathetic to the United States. A second attempt at revolution by the weak republican forces was quickly suppressed on August 28, and having acted so openly with the republicans, Soulé fled Madrid, closely followed by Spanish authorities. He reached Aulus in the French Pyrenees, where French police kept a close watch on his activities. Disappointed with the moderate policy of the Pierce administration, discredited with all those in authority in Spain, and fearful of returning to Madrid, Soulé prepared to resign as minister.[47]

In Washington, Pierce and Marcy had been struggling to devise an effective plan to bring about the purchase of Cuba. Belmont's proposal seemed to have the most to offer, but how should the United States present it to the Spanish government? At the meeting with Senators Mason, Slidell and Douglas on May 30, Pierce proposed that Congress approve the sending of a commission to Spain. This high-level task force would include former governor Howell Cobb of Georgia and former vice president George M. Dallas of Pennsylvania, who would join Soulé in negotiating with Spain. The highly respected commissioners would impress the Spanish government with the administration's determination and peaceful intent and would also keep Soulé from departing from his instructions.[48] Pierce informed Soulé of the plan, which was also endorsed by Buchanan and John Y. Mason in France, but the appointment of a commission required congressional action and was soon abandoned for lack of Senate support.[49]

On July 31, with Congress about to adjourn and news of the insurrection in Spain seeming to offer the opportunity of success on Cuba, Pierce persuaded James M. Mason to offer a resolution asking the president to report to the Senate on the state of negotiations with Spain. Pierce's message, already prepared, was delivered the same day. He reviewed the failure of negotiations to resolve the *Black Warrior* affair and reminded the senators of the real threat of filibuster activity toward Cuba, and, considering the unsettled nature of U.S. relations with Spain, he concluded, "I suggest to Congress the priority of adopting such provisional measures as the exigency may seem to demand."[50] Mason and Douglas planned to attach an appropriation of $10 million to the army bill, to give the administration flexibility in dealing with Spain during the upcoming four-month congressional recess, but there was not enough support in the Senate to pass it. Instead, the Senate passed a resolution offered by Slidell to approve of the president's policy on Cuba and Spain without making any recommendations or appropriating any money to help him.[51]

Congress adjourned on Monday, August 7, but not before receiving another veto from Pierce. The bill in question, a rivers and harbors bill titled, "An act making appropriations for the repair, preservation, and completion of certain public works heretofore commenced under the authority of law," was a classic case of pork barrel legislation. Some eighty-five projects totaling more than $2 million were lumped together in the same bill, many of which were only of local importance. Pierce had threatened to veto the bill. Attempts to amend it to give the president some discretion in the final approval of individual projects had failed, and his veto was read in the Congress on August 5.[52] Preoccupied with foreign affairs, Pierce had only time to pen a brief message stating that while certain projects "national in their character . . . would be compatible with my convictions of public duty to consent to; . . . it [the bill] embraces others which are merely local, and not, in my judgment, warranted by any safe or true construction of the Constitution." Pierce promised "to present to Congress at its next session a matured view of the whole subject" of internal improvements.[53]

Western and southern Democrats had allied with Whigs to pass the bill. They criticized Pierce, believing he raised constitutional objections to projects for the nation's interior while approving those along the coast. Democratic Rep. William A. Richardson of Illinois and Whig Rep. Lewis Campbell of Ohio threatened to form an alliance between western and southern Democrats and Whigs, to push through future internal improvement projects and overturn presidential vetoes.[54] Pierce had signed a bill to remove obstructions from the Cape Fear River in North Carolina because in rebuilding Fort Caswell on Oak Island the U. S. Army Corps of Engineers had damaged the river channel. Pierce believed that if the federal government caused harm, it was responsible for correcting the problem. This bill was for one project, not a whole smorgasbord of pet projects.[55] As usual, Pierce was entirely consistent in applying his constitutional principles to a political issue, but his veto blocked the opportunity for Democratic senators and representatives to deliver on promises to their constituents in an election year, and they did not leave Washington in a charitable frame of mind toward their president. Harry Hibbard, speaking in Pierce's defense, decried the "attempts at combinations of sectional elements for factious purposes . . . now being made in various quarters." To Hibbard and others, the problem was with the bill, "this mixture of evil with good," and not with the president.[56]

Pierce and his cabinet were on hand at the Capitol as Congress adjourned. Pierce signed some twenty-five bills passed in the final days of the lengthy and tumultuous session including army, navy, and post office appropriations bills. Many of the recommendations made in his annual address in December 1853 had been ignored by Congress, but Pierce had a few victories to savor. The army and navy would benefit from bills which increased the pay of soldiers and appropriated money for the construction of six steam frigates. The Gadsden and reciprocity treaties had been approved. His vetoes of the land grant bill for the insane and the pork barrel bill on rivers and harbors had been sustained, and the Kansas-Nebraska bill, though not his doing, would not have passed without his active support. As he left the Capitol at 2:00 p.m. that Saturday afternoon, one more indignity befell the president. While Pierce waited for his carriage in the Rotunda with James Campbell and Sidney Webster, an inebriated young man from South Carolina approached Pierce, shook his hand, and offered him a drink. Pierce declined, and turning to enter his carriage was struck by a hard-boiled egg, which knocked off his hat. The young man was detained and after Pierce departed, struggled with the police, stabbing himself in the leg with a pen knife in an apparent attempt at suicide. None of the South Carolina congressional delegation was willing to vouch for the young man, but Pierce decided not to prosecute and sent Cushing to the police station to have the arrested man released.[57]

Pierce was relieved to see congressmen and senators leaving town. Marcy expressed it best to Buchanan: "We are not sorry to be relieved from the presence of Congress for a few months. That body did not see fit to put at the disposal of the Executive extraordinary means for the adjustment of our difficulties with Spain."[58] With no help coming from the Senate, Pierce and his cabinet were left to their own devices. At this critical moment Dan Sickles arrived in Washington on August 8, sent from London by Buchanan to report on the situation in Europe. Sickles had recently visited Soulé and Mason in Madrid and Paris. Buchanan was anxious to be free of Sickles, who as a secretary was useless and undisciplined and had become an embarrassment because of his open support of the revolutionaries in London and his disrespect to the queen. This disrespect had been shown at a July 4 celebration hosted by expatriate Boston banker George Peabody. Sickles, attending the luncheon in his Twelfth Regiment uniform, was outraged by the presence of so many British guests, and by the huge portraits of Queen Victoria and Prince Albert, which dwarfed a small portrait of George Washington. There was no portrait of Pierce. When the ceremonies began, Sickles was further infuriated that the toast to the queen preceded that to the president. In protest, he refused to stand during Peabody's "exuberant toast to Queen Victoria." Dressed in his gaudy, colorful uniform, Sickles's action was obvious to all those in attendance and roundly condemned later by the British press.[59] Buchanan, fearing a possible duel between Sickles and Peabody, promptly dispatched the New Yorker to Washington.

Pierce invited Sickles to stay at the White House during his ten-day visit. At the president's request, Sickles penned a lengthy report, "On the State of Europe: Its Bearing upon the Policy of the United States." The two men spent much time together discussing European affairs, with Pierce giving Sickles the impression that the president would back drastic measures to attain Cuba. The result of Sickles visit was a new set of instructions for Soulé, written on August 16. Sickles was to deliver the instructions personally to Soulé, with copies for Mason and Buchanan. In place of a commission to deal with Spain, Pierce now proposed that Soulé, Mason, and Buchanan meet at some central location, Paris was suggested, "to consult together, to compare opinions as to what may be advisable, and to adopt measures for perfect concert of action in aid of [their] negotiations at Madrid." The meeting was Pierce's idea, as Marcy indicated in the opening of his letter to Soulé: "I am directed by the President to suggest to you a particular step from which he anticipates much advantage to the negotiations with which you are charged on the subject of Cuba."[60] In a personal letter to Buchanan, Pierce added, "Mr. Sickles visit at this time is, on several grounds, very opportune, and if he has participated in the pleasure he has conferred, he will have no occasion to regret it." Pierce added, "Mr. Sickles will return with dispatches for yourself, Mr. Mason, & Mr. Soulé, and will have much to communicate verbally with regard to home and other affairs."[61]

Buchanan was not enthusiastic about the proposed meeting. He wrote back to Pierce on September 1, "I can not for myself discover what benefit will result from a meeting between Mr. Soulé, Mr. Mason and myself. I perceive that you expect from it 'useful information and suggestions,' but it is impossible for me to devise any other plan for the acquisition of Cuba in which I could be useful than what I have already fully presented to you. We are willing to purchase, and our object is to induce them to sell."[62] To achieve this, Buchanan again referred Pierce to Belmont's plan, calling Belmont the "best agent" for the purpose.[63]

It is not clear what Pierce and Marcy thought would be accomplished by the meeting of the three ministers. They hoped that the more experienced and diplomatic Buchanan and the cautious and wary John Y. Mason would check the rashness of Soulé and place the negotiations with Spain on a more deliberate path, in line with Belmont's plan. They also knew that the British and the French intended to block any attempt by the United States to acquire Cuba. If Soulé was to have any success negotiating a purchase in Madrid, a careful plan was needed to coordinate diplomacy in London and Paris, to prevent interference by the world's two greatest powers.[64] The fact that the unpredictable Sickles was carrying not only Marcy's written instructions but also Sickles's verbal impressions of Pierce's sentiments on the matter further complicated the situation. Sickles and Soulé were of the same mind about Cuba, willing to take it by force if necessary.

Sickles may have been influenced in his views by a *Washington Union* editorial of July 26, which stated that if Spain would not sell Cuba the United States "should immediately abate and remove the nuisance" of Spanish control over the island.[65] The *Union* usually spoke for the administration but in this case may have expressed the views of its editor, John W. Forney, close ally of Buchanan, and not those of the president.[66] If Sickles believed Pierce endorsed this position, he was certainly mistaken, though it would not be the first time that a visitor to the president believed that the congenial Pierce was of a like mind when in fact the president's views and future actions proved otherwise. With the failure of the Senate to back the president's proposals regarding Spain, Pierce and Marcy fell upon the idea for a meeting in Europe as a last-resort attempt to bring some fresh ideas and energy to the process.

There was also a political motive. Slidell had been sabotaging Pierce's diplomatic efforts in the Senate throughout the congressional session. Marcy and Pierce were well aware that Slidell and Buchanan were in frequent communication regarding international affairs and domestic political matters and that Slidell was urging Buchanan to run for the presidency in 1856. By attaching Buchanan more directly and publicly to the administration's policy toward Cuba, Pierce and Marcy could counter some of Slidell's efforts to promote Buchanan. If the effort to purchase Cuba failed, as Marcy expected it would, Buchanan would share in the blame. This might weaken some of the ardor for Buchanan coming from southern politicians, who were beginning to view him as a more experienced and reliable alternative to Pierce.

Marcy's new instructions found Soulé in Aulus. With resignation his only alternative, Soulé seized on the new instructions and with Sickles's support began to plan the meeting with Mason and Buchanan. In the absence of Soulé from Madrid, the U.S. secretary of legation, Horatio J. Perry, began communicating directly with Marcy in September 1854. Perry, who had been at his post for five years and had married into a prominent Spanish family, was far more discerning in his understanding of the situation than Soulé was. Perry had been appalled at Soulé's conduct in Spain and informed Marcy, "The policy which Mr. Soulé has represented at this Court and urged with all his talent and all his resources is a complete and utter failure." Perry reported that Soulé was completely isolated in Spain without friend or influence, and that his policy of fomenting a republican revolution to free Cuba from Spain was "wholly erroneous:" "Mr. Soulé had not the power to do what he is supposed to have done. The importance given to his interposition is also exaggerated." Perry advised Marcy, "The peacable cession of the island of Cuba by Spain to us at this time is impossible. . . ."[67] Perry made contact with the new Spanish foreign minister and wrote to Soulé urging him not to return to Madrid. Soulé had taken with him all of the legation's papers, including Marcy's instructions of June 22 and 24, to prevent Perry from negotiating in his absence. Nevertheless, Perry reported that the new government in Spain was anxious to settle the *Black Warrior* matter; had recalled the officials in Cuba who carried out the affair, including Pezuela, the captain-general; and privately agreed that they had acted improperly. Perry was convinced that once the new Spanish administration felt more secure, the *Black Warrior* case would be amicably resolved.[68]

Perry had done more in a month than Soulé had accomplished in a year, but the matter of the acquisition of Cuba was still in Soulé's hands, based on the administration's instructions of August 16. Pierce and Marcy assumed the meeting between the three ministers would be conducted discreetly with a minimum of public attention. The close scrutiny that the notorious Soulé was attracting from both Spanish and French authorities made this kind of discretion impossible, as every move Soulé and Sickles made was reported in the press.[69] To add to the speculation in the press, a surprising number of prominent Americans were in Paris that fall, making it appear that something big was in the works. Assistant Secretary of State A. Dudley Mann was there, according to Marcy on private business, but Mann was determined to play a role in acquiring Cuba and wrote enthusiastically to Marcy, "The acquisition of Cuba will fill the measure of our country's glory!" He begged Marcy for instructions to serve in some capacity: "What an achievement for the President if we can obtain Cuba! What a future for our country." He continued, "The Union would be secure henceforth and forever."[70] When Soulé and Sickles reached Paris on September 23, Mann was there, reporting to Marcy, "Mr. Soulé is every inch a patriot. He is fidelity itself to his government. He has no sympathies for the Filibusteros in view of the purpose of the administration to purchase." Mann decided to postpone his return to Washington for a few weeks because of the pending meeting and wrote Marcy, "When I join you I want to salute you with the exclamation 'Cuba is ours, or as good as ours.'"[71]

John A. Dix was also in Paris at the same time as Mann, Soulé, and Sickles. All of France knew that Dix was Pierce's original choice for minister to Paris, so speculation was that he had some connection with the Cuba matter. In fact, Dix was on vacation, but the coincidence was too much for the Paris press.[72] John Van Buren was also there that fall, as was Lewis Cass, Jr., on private business. The U.S. minister to Italy was in Paris, escaping a cholera epidemic; John L. O'Sullivan arrived from Lisbon; and August Belmont from The Hague. The latter was the only one officially connected with the planning for the Cuba purchase.[73] After conferring with Belmont, Mason threw cold water on Belmont's plan, writing Marcy, "I venture to suggest, in very *strict confidence*, and with very kind feelings to Mr. Belmont, that it is not politic in my judgment to rely on the Rothschilds, on any confidential affairs of our country." Mason believed the international banking firms were too intimately connected with the monarchies of Europe to be trusted. Mason also reported that Soulé intended Sickles to act as secretary of the upcoming meeting "and share its confidence." Mason observed of Sickles, "I confess that I have not considered, that he is very discreet."[74]

With all the goings on in Paris, it is no wonder that Buchanan refused to meet there. He wrote to Marcy, "I deemed it of great importance that we should convene at a place where we would attract but little observation; but the 'Cat is now out of the bag,' & wherever we go we shall be watched & our meeting criticized. Indeed from the beginning no precautions have been used to secure secrecy."[75] Soulé suggested Basel in Switzerland, but that was too far for Buchanan, who proposed somewhere in Belgium.[76]

To add to the developing farce, George N. Sanders chose this moment, before he left Europe, to issue his parting shot for the revolutionaries. On October 4, a pamphlet appeared on the streets of Paris that was written by Sanders, U.S. consul in London, and addressed "To the People of France." Sanders called on the citizens of France to overthrow their repressive regime: "Well may Napoleon the Last! dread the expansive force so fearfully compressed!" He encouraged the French people: "America expects it of you. Strike! And though you fail a hundred times, we will applaud you at every trial! Strike!, and let those who lead be nerved by the knowledge that if overpowered and driven from France, America will ever welcome the men who fight for liberty."[77]

Sanders had also provided forged passports from the U.S. consulate in London to revolutionaries, allowing them to travel through Europe "as Bearer of Despatches" for the United States. Victor Frondé, a would-be French regicide, arrived in Lisbon in late August with a U.S. passport signed by Buchanan and asked our minister, John L. O'Sullivan, to forward to London a letter intended for another French revolutionary, Ledru-Rollin. Since Buchanan's name was on the passport and on the envelope presented by Frondé, O'Sullivan did forward the letter, but he also informed Marcy of his concern that a man of Frondé's reputation was carrying a U.S. passport.[78] Marcy was duly alarmed at this news and wrote Mason, in Paris, to warn the French government of the potential danger from Frondé. Marcy considered "it an act of duty to give warning to the persons against whom the mischief was directed."[79]

All of the communication from France concerned Pierce and Marcy. Marcy informed Mason that "there is no warrant" for Sickles to attend the conference: "The President talked pretty freely with S.

in my presence and probably more so when I was not by. He understandably thinks more of the man and much more of his discretion than I do. It was agreed that he should have no authority to speak for *us*—and the President has declared to me that he had no authority to speak for him."[80] Marcy also wrote to admonish Mann for his involvement: "The President is annoyed but probably less so than I am by the *éclat* which has been made about the conference. A grave charge of indiscretion in relation to this matter rests upon somebody. . . . In my judgment the chances of a good result are much diminished by the unfortunate notoriety which has been given to the movement."[81]

Marcy repeated these sentiments to Buchanan, and concluded sarcastically, "Your *secretary* [Sickles] and my *Assistant* [Mann] seem to have 'greatness thrust upon them,' for they are too discreet and modest to have done any thing to achieve greatness for themselves in this matter."[82]

The meeting finally convened at Ostend in Belgium on October 9. Sickles arrived with Soulé, but Buchanan wisely rejected Sickles's participation. The three ministers were pursued to Ostend by an excited and a persistent press and by French secret police. After three days in the public eye, the conference adjourned to Aix la Chapelle in Germany, where it was concluded with a report signed by the three ministers on October 18, 1854. Soulé had prepared in advance a complete set of notes for the report, probably after meeting with Belmont, but the final draft was written by Buchanan.[83]

As the meeting adjourned, Soulé and Buchanan traveled separately to London, and Mason returned to Paris. On October 20, the report, which became known as the "Ostend Manifesto," was sent by special messenger to Washington, accompanied by a private letter from Soulé to Pierce, which arrived on November 4.[84] The cabinet debated the contents of the document over the next week before Marcy composed the administration's response, which was sent to Soulé on November 13.

The misnamed Ostend Manifesto, which was not a declaration of national policy but simply a dispatch to the State Department, began by placing the onus for the document on Pierce: "The undersigned in compliance with the wish expressed by the President in the several confidential dispatches . . . addressed to us. . . ." This referred to

Marcy's instructions of April, which authorized purchase as the new policy but had used the word "detach" in stating the fallback position. The ministers completely ignored the issue of how to counter British and French influence on Spain and focused entirely on the reasons why Cuba was important to the United States and why Spain ought to sell it. It offered no new ideas or proposals for negotiating on the issue. Instead the ministers were preoccupied with the threat of Africanization of the island: "We should, however, be recreant to our duty, be unworthy of our gallant forefathers, and commit base treason against our posterity, should we permit Cuba to be Africanized, and become a second St. Domingo, with all its attendant horrors to the white race, and suffer the flames to extend to our own neighboring shores, seriously to endanger or actually to consume the fair fabric of our nation."[85] Despite concluding that "Cuba has become to us an unceasing danger and a permanent cause of anxiety and alarm," the manifesto stated a number of conditions and barriers to outright seizure of the island by the United States, including a filibuster. According to the manifesto, "the President [was] justly inflexible in his determination to execute the neutrality laws," but, the document continued, "should the Cubans themselves rise in revolt, . . . no human power could prevent citizens of the United States and liberal minded men of other countries from rushing to their assistance."[86] Buchanan had stated the same thing to Lord Clarendon in December 1853.

After listing the dangers to the United States of Cuba's continued attachment to Spain and the reasons why Spain should sell it to the United States, the ministers asked the questions that their meeting was intended, by Pierce and Marcy, to answer: "But, if Spain, dead to the voice of her own interests and actuated by stubborn pride, and a false sense of honor, should refuse to sell Cuba to the United States, then the question will arise: What ought to be the course of the American government under such circumstances? . . . Does Cuba, in the possession of Spain, seriously endanger the internal peace of our whole nation?"[87] This was their controversial conclusion: "Should this question be answered in the affirmative, then by every law, human and divine, we shall be justified in wresting it from Spain, if we possess the power; and this upon the very same principle that would justify an individual in tearing down the burning house of his neighbor, if there were no other means of preventing the flames from destroying his own home."[88] The manifesto concluded with one final caveat: "We forbear to enter into the question whether the present condition of the island would justify such a measure."[89]

The provocative statement "we shall be justified in wresting it from Spain" became the phrase that labeled the Ostend Manifesto in the eyes of the world and future generations as the classic example of the jingoistic, bellicose era of Manifest Destiny. It could be considered the high-water mark of that era: the point at which the reach of Young America exceeded the grasp of the United States. But the report also failed by not offering to the Pierce administration in Washington any new insight, information, or ideas as to how to negotiate a purchase with the Spanish government or to approach the British and French governments on the issue of Cuba. Maybe as our consul in Madrid stated to Marcy, "the peacable cession of the island of Cuba by Spain to us at this time [was] impossible, . . ." and when gathered together, the three ministers understood this, thus leaving nothing else to offer but the need to wrest it by force. Belmont, despairing of his plan ever succeeding, wrote Marcy and stated similar sentiments just prior to the Ostend meeting.[90]

Buchanan always defended the manifesto, writing, "I still believe we were right," and claiming that "the peaceful acquisition of Cuba" was its intent and that it had stated numerous conditions before any seizure was justified. But Soulé's letter, which accompanied the report, implied that the United States should inform the Spanish government "that if they did not agree to sell, we would take the Island by force," thus placing a more-aggressive interpretation on the report than was intended by Buchanan and Mason.[91] Faced with this, it is not surprising that Pierce and his cabinet rejected the lone recommendation of the manifesto.

Before this could be communicated, the French precipitated a brief international incident. On October 24, Soulé, having left London bound for Madrid, was denied permission to enter France by officials at Calais. Mason was informed that day by the French foreign minister that the government considered Soulé a threat to France because of his earlier duel with the ambassador at Madrid and his suspected communication with those planning to overthrow the French government. Mason also believed the recent conference had aroused French suspicion and a desire to prevent Soulé from carrying out whatever was planned there.[92]

Mason sent his secretary of legation, Donn Piatt, to England to get Soulé's version of the story firsthand. Mason then made a formal protest to the French foreign minister, Drouyn de Lhuys, on October 27. In the meantime, Soulé, Mason, and Buchanan had all sent dispatches to Marcy, describing the situation, with Buchanan claiming that "in modern times no such case [had] occurred" of a diplomat being denied the right to travel freely to his post. He concluded, "Napoleon couldn't seriously fear Mr. Soulé. I fear, therefore, that it is his settled purpose to treat the United States with indignity."[93] On November 1, the French government backed down, stating that they had no intention of preventing Soulé from traveling to his post in Madrid but restating their concern that his activities "have awakened . . . the attention of authorities invested with the duty of securing the public order of the country. . . ." The French government stated that Soulé was "free to pass through France," but not to tarry along the way.[94] Soulé departed London on November 3, anxious to receive the administration's response to the Ostend Manifesto.

That response came in a new letter of instructions from Marcy to Soulé, which was written on November 13. In it, Marcy restated that Pierce continued to believe the purchase of Cuba to be the only solution "which would with certainty place the relations of the two countries on the sure basis of enduring friendship." Soulé was instructed to begin negotiating for that purchase, but Marcy wrote, "[If] you have reason to believe that the men in power are averse to entertaining such a proposition, . . . It appears to the President that nothing could be gained and something might be lost by an attempt to push on a negotiation against such a general resistance."[95]

One can imagine Soulé's reaction as he read Marcy's next point. Stating that passages in the manifesto could be "construed" to mean that the ministers endorsed the idea of "cession or seizure," Marcy concluded that this could not have been their intent, for "to conclude that on the rejection of a proposition to cede seizure should ensue, would be to assume that self-preservation necessitates the acquisition of Cuba by the United States."[96] The failure of Spain to agree to our purchase of Cuba, according to Marcy, "would not, without a material change in the condition of the Island, involve imminent peril to the existence of our government."[97]

Once again, Marcy pushed Soulé to settle the *Black Warrior* matter and to read Marcy's letter of June 22 to the Spanish foreign minister. If purchase of Cuba was not possible, Soulé was to press the Spanish government for assurances that any future misconduct by its officials in Cuba would be quickly redressed. Marcy also instructed Soulé to decline any offer by Spain of arbitration on the issues separating the two nations, for "some of those claims are of such a character as self-respect would not permit us to submit to arbitrament in any form."[98] Though the wording of the letter to Soulé has been described as "roundabout and elusive," it was, nonetheless, "a sharp repudiation" of the manifesto's intention of "wresting" Cuba from Spain. There was also no reference made to Marcy's instructions of April 3, in which the word "detach" was used.[99]

The Pierce administration never had any intention of seizing Cuba by force or through filibuster. If the Cubans had freed themselves, or if Spain would have sold the island, the president would have welcomed the opportunity for annexation, but out of necessity Pierce had played out the game with the southern extremists and Young America, who had supported him in 1852. It was never possible to acquire Cuba in the 1850s. A filibuster would have been suicidal against Spanish forces on the island. The honor and pride of Spain and its dependence on Great Britain and France which deplored U.S. expansionism, all worked to prevent any peaceful cession of Spain's most valuable and strategic colony. Only Belmont's plan offered an outside chance of success, but the United States possessed no diplomat with the experience and skill to attempt it.

Secretary of War Davis blamed the Congress "that the executive was not promptly sustained . . . when he sent in his message in relation to Cuban affairs. . . ."[100] For political reasons Pierce and Marcy had to make the effort, but one senses that their hearts were never in the attempt, and they understood the practical reality that, short of war, Spain would never part with Cuba. The rejection of the Ostend report indicates that the Pierce administration had done all it intended to do regarding Cuba, but southern extremists were slower to accept the reality, and Quitman was still waiting for his bond to expire to resume planning his filibuster. As for Soulé, Marcy's letter of November 13 prompted his resignation, which was sent on December 17.[101] By February he was on his way back to the United States to defend in public his actions as minister to Spain.

Sickles and Sanders had already departed Europe by this time, leaving Buchanan the embarrassment of cleaning up the mess they had left behind in London. It was December before he realized how his trust had been abused by his rash young subordinates. He claimed not to have known anything about Frondé, but against State Department guidelines Buchanan had signed blank passports to be filled out by his staff. Marcy accepted Buchanan's explanation but was embarrassed by the misuse of the seal of the London Legation: "Sickles and Sanders have been entrusted with it. Sanders' letters have been sent under it, not only here, but to several countries of Europe. Our diplomatic character in Europe, which, I acknowledge with shame, is now miserably low, has been damaged by the Legation at London more perhaps than by any other, though Soulé has inflicted deep wounds on it. . . . The disrepute of this thing falls with the greatest weight upon my Department, and it is the result of the conduct of men who are my enemies and against whose appointment I made a strenuous opposition."[102] Assistant Secretary of State A. Dudley Mann also resigned on returning to Washington from his European sojourn, but he agreed to stay on until Marcy could find a qualified successor. Having finally freed itself of the colorful but undisciplined representatives of Young America, the administration could expect less turmoil emanating from Europe in the future.

The political fallout from the failed attempt to purchase Cuba was yet to occur. The Ostend report had been kept secret from the public; only the *New York Herald* had gotten wind of the contents and published a fairly accurate account of the conference in November 1854.[103] The public's attention to the matter, and that of Congress, would be aroused further by Soulé on his return to the United States.

7

REJECTION AT THE POLLS

When the Ostend Manifesto arrived in Washington in November 1854, the Pierce administration was absorbing the results of elections held in nineteen states between August and November. Seventeen of those states elected representatives for the Thirty-fourth Congress. The election cycle that began in August 1854 and ended with the new Congress in December 1855 has been called "the most labyrinthine, chaotic, and important off-year contests in all of American political history."[1] Pierce may not have appreciated the historic significance of the results, but one thing was clear: his administration had been harshly rejected by the voters, particularly in the free states.

Pierce fully expected the election contests to be fought over the Kansas-Nebraska Act, and he urged Democrats around the nation not to waiver in holding that banner high before the voters. But the elections took a surprising turn with the sudden emergence of a virulent fever of anti-Catholicism and anti-immigrant sentiment embodied in the Know-Nothing movement, which swept much of the nation in 1854, complicating the political process and clouding the meaning of the results. What the voters wanted may have been muddied, but it was clearly not what the Pierce administration was offering. In all of the thirteen northern states that voted between August and November 1854, none had a traditional two-party, Whig-versus-Democrat, contest. In every state, coalitions of anti-Nebraska men, free-soilers, Whigs, independent Democrats, Know-Nothings, and temperance advocates combined in some form to oppose the traditional Democratic Party. These coalitions varied from state to state and called themselves different names. In Michigan and Wisconsin the opposition took the name "Republican," while in Ohio and Indiana they called themselves "People's" movements. In the Northeast the "Know-Nothing" or "American party" designation was more commonly used. In some cases (Michigan, Ohio, Wisconsin) anti-Nebraska, or free-soilism was the dominant issue. In others (Massachusetts, Pennsylvania) Know-Nothing sentiment was strongest. And in a few states (Maine and New York) temperance was the main issue. In every free state, however, the Democrats suffered devastating losses.[2]

The Know-Nothings, officially "The Order of the Star-Spangled Banner," had formed in 1849 in New York as a secret organization for Protestants opposed to the impact immigrant Catholics were having on American society. In 1852 the Order reorganized under the leadership of James W. Barber and began to open chapters throughout the nation. The Know-Nothings affected local elections by identifying candidates who agreed with their goals and voting for them as a bloc. The society's secret grips, passwords, signs, phrases of recognition, and initiation ritual permitted members from different chapters to communicate without identifying themselves to the general public. Nevertheless, the press began to suspect the presence of the organization. Horace Greeley's *New York Tribune* was the first to use the name "Know-Nothings," possibly because of the stonewalling by suspected members when questioned about their political activities. The Order appealed to the many Americans, brought up on Protestant teaching against popery and troubled by, or fearful of, the changes they were witnessing in their communities from the five million immigrants, mostly Catholics, who had entered the country in the past decade, bringing with them poverty, crime, intemperance, and, most significantly, competition for jobs.[3]

The movement reached a fever pitch in late 1853 due, in part, to the visit to the United States of the papal nuncio, Monsignor Gaetano Bedini, who was sent to settle some conflicts existing within the church in America. His tour of the states was marred by demonstrations and threats on his life. The opposition grew so dangerous that Bedini cut short his visit and fled to Canada.[4] Pierce had contributed to the movement by appointing James Campbell, a Catholic, to his cabinet. This was viewed by some as evidence that the president was under the influence of the pope. In response, when the voters in Campbell's hometown of Philadelphia next went to the polls in the spring of 1854, they elected a Know-Nothing for mayor. A few weeks later Washington, D.C., also elected a Know-Nothing mayor, despite administration opposition. The residents of the nation's capital had first demonstrated their hatred of Catholics a few months earlier. Pope Pius IX had sent a block of Italian marble to be used for the Washington Monument as a gift to the United States. An angry mob broke into the shed where the marble was stored and threw it into the Potomac.[5] The victories in the local elections in Philadelphia and Washington were followed by a Know-Nothing convention in New York City in June 1854, with delegates from thirteen states.[6] This signaled to the nation that the secret organization had "become a material fact."[7] In the weeks following the convention, anti-Catholic riots occurred in Brooklyn, Newark, and Manchester, New Hampshire.[8] The Know-Nothings had emerged from the shadows to prey upon the discontent and the prejudices of the voters. From Washington, James Campbell, alarmed by the events in Philadelphia and elsewhere, reported to Buchanan the administration's first impressions of the Know-Nothings: "This order is one of the most dangerous that has ever arrived in the politics of our Country—a secret society, bound together by the most horrible oaths—they swear never to vote for a foreigner or a Catholic to any office. It is a Whig device to catch Democratic votes and unfortunately for us, they have caught too many. My impression is, that its existence will be but temporary, but for a year or so, may do us harm."[9]

As the off-year election campaign was taking this unanticipated turn, the Pierce administration was fully engaged in the final weeks of the congressional session and in the diplomatic initiatives related to the Greytown affair and Cuba. The constant pressures did not prevent Pierce from enjoying some aspects of the social life in the capital. He and Jane had become close to Jefferson Davis and his young wife, Varina, and their infant son Samuel. The Pierces visited the Davis home frequently, and Franklin was known to walk over from the White House, unannounced, late in the evening. Jane was so fond of little Sam that Varina allowed her to take him on rides in her carriage several times. In June, precocious Sam became ill, possibly from measles, and died on June 13, just shy of his second birthday. Pierce was present at the funeral two days later in the Davis home, but Jane was too overcome to attend.[10] Later that summer, the Pierces invited the still-grieving parents to join them for a week's vacation at Capon Springs, Virginia. Both Jane and Varina reported that the time away from Washington did their busy husbands much good.[11]

The summer months also included weekly concerts by the marine band on the South Lawn at the White House. At these evening events, which were open to the public, Pierce often made an appearance, mingling with the crowd and even escorting interested guests on an impromptu brief tour of the White House.[12] In the fall Varina Davis's mother arrived for a lengthy stay in Washington. Mrs. Howell reported to her family back in Mississippi, "No one has been more kind to me than Mr. and Mrs. Pierce. The society here is really delightful."[13] In November Elizabeth Schuyler Hamilton, widow of Alexander Hamilton, died in Washington at age ninety-eight, fifty years after her husband's death in the duel with Aaron Burr. Her son, James A. Hamilton, sent a letter with a lock of his mother's hair to Jane Pierce, thanking the Pierces "for their kindness and attention to his sainted mother" and referring to Mrs. Hamilton as Jane's "excellent friend."[14] During this, her second year in the White House, Jane had ventured out more and participated some in the visiting that was an expected part of the social routine of life in the capital.

During the fall election campaigns, Pierce did his best to support Democratic candidates around the nation. The Kansas-Nebraska Act had tied him closely to the fortunes of Senator Stephen A. Douglas, who had embarked on a crusade in the summer to defend the bill to the voters of the North. Douglas had begun his defense of popular sovereignty with two speeches in New York in June, and a major address in Philadelphia in Independence Square on July 4. His views on the imposition of religion into the political process by Protestant clergy were identical to Pierce's. At Philadelphia Douglas connected the Know-Nothings to the anti-Nebraska movement, condemning the nativists: "To proscribe a man in this country on account of his birthplace or religious faith is subversive of all our ideas and principles of civil and religious freedom. It is revolting to our sense of justice and right."[15] Douglas saw firsthand that the combination of anti-Nebraska, nativist, and anti-Catholic feelings was causing the disintegration of the Democratic Party throughout the Northeast.

At the end of the congressional session in early August, Douglas embarked for Illinois to attempt to save his party and his reputation in the upcoming state election. Along the way he encountered angry crowds and demonstrations, particularly in Ohio, causing Douglas to remark, "I could travel from Boston to Chicago by the light of my own effigy."[16] The climax occurred at an address in Chicago on September 1 in front of North Market Hall. Douglas had been warned that he might face an angry mob. Not only was anti-Nebraska sentiment strong in northern Illinois, but Douglas was also criticized by the Chicago press for voting against the rivers and harbors bill, which Pierce had vetoed. For two hours that night, Douglas attempted to address the crowd, but was shouted down by the angry mob, which also hurled "missiles" onto the platform. Frustrated in his attempt to speak above the din, Douglas lost his temper, shaking his fist at the crowd. Eventually, he gave up the effort and returned to his hotel, followed by hostile demonstrators.[17] The press around the country condemned Douglas's treatment, criticizing the Know-Nothing and abolitionist movements for denying, "by mob violence, the privilege of free speech to those who differ with them in matters of public policy."[18] While shaken by the experience in Chicago, Douglas was buoyed by the reaction of the national press and wrote to John C. Breckinridge, "The Chicago mob has done us much good & we know what use to make of it."[19] With renewed determination, he proceeded to campaign around the state in an attempt to reverse the tide running against the Democrats.

Back in Washington, Pierce was alarmed by Douglas's treatment and did his best to bolster Douglas's chances. He responded immediately to Douglas's request for patronage, writing, "The change has been made at DeKalb as you desire." Pierce also tried to encourage Douglas to press on with his aggressive defense of the Kansas-Nebraska Act: "Neither justice nor sound policy point to forbearance toward men of unsound principles and known to be opposed to our true Union-loving patriotic friends. A bold manly correct fight is the only one which holds out any promise of success."[20] Pierce asked

Douglas, "What are the prospects in Illinois and Indiana[?]" and reported, "Our information from Pennsylvania would seem to leave no reason to doubt of the success of our ticket. But with the 'Know Nothing' element pervading the community it is impossible to predict with any certainty."[21]

Pierce had imposed himself into the governor's race in Pennsylvania. The state nominating convention had totally ignored Kansas-Nebraska in passing its platform for the statewide campaign, and Governor William Bigler, running for reelection, had said nothing about the issue during the summer months, despite the Democratic state committee's endorsement of the law. Bigler was a close friend of Postmaster General Campbell, making the governor vulnerable to anti-Catholic forces, and had flip-flopped on the temperance issue. Pierce urged Bigler to get behind the Kansas-Nebraska bill. Bigler finally announced his support for repeal of the Missouri Compromise in late August. This caused Democratic congressman David Wilmot, the state's leading free-soiler, to endorse Bigler's opponent, Whig James Pollock. Pollock also joined a Know-Nothing lodge that summer, thus winning the endorsement of both the free-soil and nativist elements in Pennsylvania. He was already committed to the temperance cause.[22] Why Pierce was optimistic about Pennsylvania is difficult to fathom.

In New York the situation was even more confused. In July Pierce appointed John McKeon as U.S. district attorney for the city to replace Charles O'Conor. This brought down on Pierce renewed criticism from Softs and Barnburners, as McKeon was labeled a Hard. Marcy had urged Pierce to appoint L. R. Shepard, a leader of Tammany Hall who was also supported by Governor Horatio Seymour. Why Pierce ignored this advice is conjecture, but McKeon's reputation as a Hard was due to his outspoken hostility toward Tammany Hall. Marcy wrote, "He has denounced the institution so often that those who love it hate him."[23] McKeon had also endorsed the Kansas-Nebraska Act. Pierce had known McKeon when the two were in Congress together years before and knew that he was no friend of Dickinson or Bronson. Having failed a year earlier to appease all factions with his appointments, Pierce chose a man he knew to be able and honest rather than make a purely political appointment from the dunghill that was Tammany Hall. McKeon would prove to be a most effective, determined, and loyal district attorney, but the appointment brought down on Pierce renewed criticism from New York. Tammany Hall, which had supported Pierce in the past, condemned the decision: "We deeply deplore the appointment of John McKeon . . . which contributes seriously to impair the confidence heretofore reposed in the President and the administration."[24]

McKeon's appointment was also an embarrassment to Marcy, whose advice on New York politics had been rejected yet again. Marcy had pleaded with Pierce not to appoint McKeon: "I do so with apology for taking any further step in a matter which has given you, as well as myself, too much trouble."[25] To Governor Seymour, Marcy wrote, "I am deeply mortified as a man can be at the appointment of McKeon. What may be the consequences of my course in this matter I cannot now tell. I have pressed my advocacy of Mr. Shepard—and more particularly—my opposition to McKeon very far. I fear too far and probably have given some cause of dissatisfaction without intending it."[26] But while not understanding why Pierce chose McKeon, Marcy still tried to defend the president to the governor: "Except in matters of appt. in New York, I have no matter of complaint, no cause for dissatisfaction. In other respects he has treated me with great personal kindness and I should be guilty of ingratitude not to acknowledge it on all proper occasions. You can hardly realize the difficulty of his position. I hope you will act considerately in regard to the Administration."[27] Seymour was unforgiving, however, answering Marcy, "You know my opinion of the President. I think he is a fool who aspires to be a knave." Seymour threatened not to accept his party's renomination for governor, stating, "if I am a candidate I anticipate a blow from Washington."[28]

Within a few weeks, however, Seymour was back in the race and pleading for help from the administration. He asked Pierce to make key appointments of "custom house and post office agents" around the state. Pierce had offered some advice, to which Seymour replied, "I will carry out the suggestions of the President in a short time."[29]

Seymour needed all the help he could get. As Michael F. Holt has noted, "Know-Nothingism was spreading like wildfire across the state," and prohibitionism was the "dominant sentiment" of upstate voters. In 1853 the state legislature had passed a prohibition bill similar to the Maine Law, but Seymour had vetoed it. The Whigs seized on the issue by nominating temperance leader Myron H. Clark for governor.[30] The Hards chose former customs collector Greene C. Bronson as their candidate and cynically, considering the Democratic Party's traditional support from Catholic and immigrant voters, attempted to infiltrate the Know-Nothing lodges to gain the movement's support for Bronson. Hard leader Daniel Dickinson explained to Edmund Burke in New Hampshire that the goal was to destroy the administration: "The manner employed are of no sort of consequence—the evil justified any thing but crime."[31] Burke needed no prompting. He had already published an editorial in his newspaper in Concord that praised the Know-Nothing movement, and he began to try to influence the movement for his benefit in the upcoming election in New Hampshire in March 1855.[32]

But the Know-Nothings rejected the opportunistic efforts of the Hards and in October nominated their own candidate for governor, Daniel Ullman. With four candidates in the race, New York attorney George Templeton Strong recorded in his journal, "We may well have a memorable row here before the fall elections are over, and perhaps a religious war within the next decade, if this awful vague, mysterious, new element of Know-Nothingism is as potent as its friends and political wooers seem to think it is."[33]

In the final days of the race, Pierce was completely engaged, sending post office agents from Washington into New York to make certain that all postal employees in the hundreds of offices throughout the state knew which candidate (Seymour) was endorsed by the administration. The effort nearly paid off. Seymour came in a close second to Clark, losing by only 309 votes of the nearly 500,000 cast. Bronson and the Hards finished a dismal fourth with only 7 percent of the vote, while the Know-Nothing candidate scored a close third with 26 percent.[34] Characteristically, Seymour blamed Pierce for his defeat: "The unfriendly spirit of the President had been felt so uniformly that I could not fail to detect it. At the late election I could have at any time called out ten thousand additional votes for myself by an expression of hostility to the National Administration, but I stood as its friend. . . ."[35]

Election results in Pennsylvania defied the president's previous optimism, as Bigler went down to a crushing defeat. In Illinois, Douglas's courageous campaign managed to salvage several congressional races, but the majority in the new legislature was anti-Nebraska, thus ensuring an antiadministration senator would replace Douglas's colleague and Pierce's Mexican War associate Gen. James Shields. For the future of the Pierce administration, the major impact of the fall election results was in the make-up of the Thirty-fourth Congress. In New York Democrats won twenty-two of thirty-three House seats in 1852. In the fall election of 1854 they won only six of thirty-three seats.[36] In Pennsylvania proadministration Democrats won only four of twenty-five seats in 1854.[37] In Ohio all twenty-one seats went to anti-Nebraska "Peoples" candidates. Massachusetts had the most shocking result. The Know-Nothings, running as an independent party separate from the Whigs, free-soilers, and Democrats, elected the governor in a four-way race with 63 percent of the total vote. They also elected 100 percent of the members of the state senate and 376 of the 378 members of the lower house. In the congressional races, all eleven of the state's representatives had voted against the Kansas-Nebraska bill, but only two were reelected, and those two had joined the Know-Nothing movement.[38] In all, Democrats in the free states lost two-thirds of the House seats they occupied during the Thirty-third Congress. With more than a dozen states yet to vote in 1855, the Democratic Party was destined to be a minority party in the Thirty-fourth Congress. The party system of Democrats versus Whigs crumbled in the elections of 1854, and the Pierce administration was the most immediate casualty of the voter revolution.[39] The results were not simply a repudiation of the Pierce administration and the Kansas-Nebraska Act but reflected broader social and economic changes occurring in the country that were beyond the control or responsibility of a president.

The election results around the nation were pleasing to Edmund Burke in New Hampshire. He called a convention of anti-Pierce Democrats, which met in Concord in October. Claiming that "the administration has become a corpse," Burke pushed through a resolution endorsing Sam Houston as his faction's choice for president in 1856.[40] Other party leaders did not relish the demise of the Pierce administration the way Burke did, but they saw just as clearly that the party would need to offer a new man in the next election. Former governor Howell Cobb of Georgia wrote to Buchanan in London, urging him to run, declaring, "You have been absent from the country during this bitter Nebraska contest and are not therefore complicated with it personally." The party could not afford to take a chance again with "a speculative candidacy" and needed "a man whose position and character as a statesman shall be known and appreciated."[41]

When the second session of the Thirty-third Congress convened on December 4, 1854, most of the members knew that they were lameducks, having already been defeated for reelection to the Thirty-fourth Congress. The short session of Congress, which lasted into March, was less productive of major legislation than the previous session and also far less contentious, but for the Pierce administration there were several significant accomplishments.

Pierce's second annual message was read in both houses on the first day of the session. The president reported that the economy remained strong in spite of the dreadful drought that had plagued farmers during the past summer. The nation was at peace with all countries, but the Crimean War had renewed the longstanding U.S. insistence that neutral shipping rights be respected by warring parties. Pierce reported that Great Britain and France had agreed with the U.S. demand that "free ships make free goods, except in the case of contraband of war, . . . but as a mere concession for the time being." Pierce and Marcy were pushing for a convention of nations to make this a permanent fixture of international law. Progress had been stalled, however, by the king of Prussia, who, acting on behalf of Great Britain and France, had insisted on an article renouncing privateering. Pierce informed Congress that the United States could never agree to this, as our small navy required the United States to employ privateers in time of war. To Pierce, foregoing "a resort to privateers in the case of war" was equated with agreeing "not to accept volunteers for operations on land."[42] The president went on to give a lengthy explanation and defense of the actions of the navy in the Greytown affair. Pierce made no mention of the meeting at Ostend or the attempt to purchase Cuba from Spain.

Turning to domestic matters, Pierce reported that the federal budget remained in a surplus condition during the past year, with more than over $20 million in receipts over expenditures. This had made possible further reduction of the federal debt, and once again Pierce stated, "I therefore renew my recommendation for a reduction of the duties on imports."[43] Reform of the executive departments remained a priority. Pierce reported that fraud had occurred in four customs offices, Oswego, Toledo, Sandusky, and Milwaukee, during the Fillmore administration, costing the government $198,000. In prosecuting these cases, the administration was handicapped by inadequate laws. No laws prevented federal officials from taking all of the office records with them upon leaving office; in fact, they were considered the private property of the office holder. There was not even a law making it a felony "to make false entries in the books or return false accounts." Pierce asked Congress "to change the laws . . . to the protection of the Government."[44]

Pierce renewed his call upon Congress to increase the size of the army, specifically by adding four new regiments. He reported that the large number of "incursions of predatory bands" made it necessary "to provide for increasing the military force employed in the Territory inhabited by the Indians."[45] The president reported that the pay increase for the rank and file of the army "has had beneficial results, not only in facilitating enlistments, but in obvious improvements in the class of men who enter the service." He called on Congress to make a similar increase in pay for officers. He also proposed the establishment of a retired list for officers in both the army and the navy and asked Congress to consider creating a retired list for one year, to determine the impact on the service.[46] Pierce fully endorsed the reports of Davis and Dobbin calling for major reorganization of the army and navy.[47]

There was no specific mention in the message of the two most controversial subjects of the preceding year: the Kansas-Nebraska Act and the enforcement of the Fugitive Slave Act. Pierce alluded to both, however, along with the Know-Nothing movement, in his lengthy closing statement which began,

> We have to maintain inviolate the great doctrine of the inherent right of popular self-government; to reconcile the largest liberty

> of the individual citizen with complete security of the public order; to render cheerful obedience to the laws of the land, to unite in enforcing their execution, and to frown indignantly on all combinations to resist them; to harmonize a sincere and ardent devotion to the institutions of religious toleration; to preserve the rights of all by causing each to respect those of the other; to carry forward every social improvement to the uttermost limit of human perfectibility, by the free action of mind upon mind, not by the obtrusive intervention of misapplied force....[48]

When Pierce had vetoed the rivers and harbors bill the previous August, he had promised Congress a more-thorough explanation of his views on internal improvements. In his report of December 30, 1854, Pierce traced the history of internal improvements and explained which types were constitutional. To receive federal government funds, projects were to be national in scope or to "have reference to military or naval purposes." Projects solely "intended to promote the revenue from commerce" constituted to Pierce "a perpetual admonition of reserve and caution." To avoid future vetoes, Pierce suggested that Congress separate each proposed improvement into a separate bill. He also advised that when states or cities sought federal support for local improvements, they should cede the land in question to the federal government, as had been done in the early days of the republic for the construction of forts and lighthouses. According to Pierce, Congress had the authority to appropriate money for the improvement of federal government lands but not land that was owned by a state.[49]

The reports of his cabinet officers also revealed the progress being made in meeting the administration's goal of executive reform. Guthrie announced that he had assigned William M. Gouge, a longtime Jackson-era official and architect of the Independent Treasury, as a special agent to inspect the accounts of all customs offices and that Gouge had completed much of that task. Gouge reported that facilities (buildings or vaults) to secure government money safely from fire and theft did not exist in many locations, causing public officers to deposit the government's money in local banks or private safes. Gouge was also assigned to supervise the steamboat inspectors, a new government agency, and reported that he had urged them to be less timid in reporting violations. Pierce endorsed Guthrie's request that steamboat captains be made liable to the same laws and standards as railroad engineers.[50] Guthrie reported that the new system of monthly accounts by customs collectors had "been adhered to and fully carried out." He also announced that the examination system for clerks had resulted in "great improvement in that force."[51]

Interior Secretary McClelland continued to bemoan the pension laws. As a congressman and senator, Pierce had also criticized the problem of old claims for pensions receiving support from congressmen without proper evidence. McClelland reported, "The evil is of so absurd a character, . . . as to be exceedingly annoying and mortifying, as well as unjust." He proposed that by "cutting off all arrearages of pensions, the great evil of the system may be remedied." McClelland continued to complain that the two-year statute of limitations for "prosecutions for perjury and forgery committed in pension and land warrant cases" allowed many "criminals" to escape justice. Nevertheless, his department had issued thirty indictments over the past year: "Eleven have been convicted, nine fled and forfeited their recognizance, one died, one committed suicide, two have eluded the officers, and six await trial."[52]

Only the General Post Office continued to run a significant deficit, but Postmaster General Campbell had reduced it by $360,000 during the past year, despite the increase in expenses for railroad mail service about which Campbell reported, "This Government is paying much more . . . than it is worth." The government paid far more than the prices paid for similar railroad mail service in England, France, Germany, and Canada.[53]

The Washington social season began with the president's New Year's levee. Jane's appearance, her first at a public White House reception, was the subject of much notoriety. Benjamin B. French recorded, "Mrs. Pierce wore black except for her headdress which was white. She looked better than usual."[54] The wife of Senator Clement Clay of Alabama remembered Jane, in her "first public appearance at the White House, clad in black velvet and diamonds, her natural pallor being thereby greatly accentuated," and noted that "a universal sympathy was awakened for her."[55] Abby Means was more than usually concerned for Jane's emotional health, as the levee occurred each year around the anniversary of Benny's death. Means wrote to Jane's sister that Jane approached "this season with much sadness": I can always sympathise with her when she mourns without apining—but this feeling makes me tremble lest a worse sorrow may come. The fatigue of 'receiving'—& the two large dinner parties—your dear sister has borne extremely well, & has enjoyed the success of the dinner parties & the many compliments paid to the house which it is said was never so comfortable or so handsome."[56] At the levee, French recorded, "Such a multitude . . . I have seldom—I am not sure as ever—witnessed. Many thousands shook the hand of their Chief." French continued, "No man dresses more appropriately on all occasions than Gen. Pierce. Yesterday he wore a suit of plain but rich black, & wore, as he ever has since the death of his boy, black gloves. . . . The General looks to me, as if the cares & troubles of his office wore upon him; still he appears cheerful, and is affable."[57]

Abby Means wrote, "Our dear President is the life of the house & retains his faculty for sleeping away his cares."[58] Pierce enjoyed the social and ceremonial responsibilities of his position. In January 1855, some four thousand veterans of the War of 1812 converged on Washington for the fortieth anniversary of the Battle of New Orleans and the end of the war. On January 8, Pierce invited them all into the White House for a reception. Nearly two thousand men crammed into the East Room, a visitor from New Hampshire wrote home describing the scene: "Gen. Pierce received them and addressed them in a brief but beautiful speech that was eloquent and highly pleasing to those who listened. His conclusion was beautiful indeed. 'Officers & soldiers you are in your own house. I am your tenant, you are the power, I am your humble servant. In the name of your grateful country I honor & thank you for the noble services you have rendered her in the days of her peril and may that country whom you have so well served reward you in your declining years, and God bless you all.'"[59] It was difficult for those who met Pierce at these events to perceive how unpopular he was becoming around the country. The New Hampshire man concluded, "Pierce is very popular here and will come out right in the end. He is bold honest and fearless and patriotic and history will do him justice."[60] Jane recognized the pressures on her husband that the public did not see, writing to a relative at this time, "My husband is now about as well as usual altho. thin and feeling pressing need of more exercise than he is able to take—his life is a most busy one, and which he feels the great weight of care and responsibility. He bears up with a stout heart."[61]

A highlight of the winter season was the arrival in the capital of Commodore Perry and gifts sent by the government of Japan. The treaty negotiated by Perry had arrived months before and was immediately ratified by the Senate. Perry and his flagship the *Mississippi* returned to the United States by way of Europe. Perry had met with his son-in-law, August Belmont, at The Hague and with Buchanan and Hawthorne in England. Hawthorne turned down Perry's invitation to write up the expedition for publication. Perry finally reached the United States in January, more than two years after his departure. Pierce hosted a state dinner in his honor, and Congress rewarded the commodore with a $20,000 bonus and agreed to pay for the publication of a narrative of the Japan expedition.[62]

The gifts, which arrived that month by a separate ship, caused a sensation. Pierce kept many at the White House and invited the public to view them, while others were displayed at the U. S. Patent Office. Eventually, most of the gifts ended up at the Smithsonian. French wrote, "Some of the things are magnificent. . . ."[63] Among the gifts were four tiny dogs of a rare breed unknown in the West. Pierce showed up at the Davis home one day and announced that he was presenting them with a dog. Davis asked what he could do with a dog in the city, to which Pierce replied, "Oh, if it crowds your big house, you can put it in a tea-saucer." Jefferson Davis became very fond of his new pet "Bonin," but to Varina the dog was so small it became the scourge of the house. Visitors and servants frequently had to somersault over the animal to avoid stepping on it. When Varina threatened to banish "Bonin," Davis responded that he "would build a house for myself and my dog." The Davises kept the dog until they left Washington at the start of the Civil War.[64]

As much as Pierce may have enjoyed the social responsibilities of his office, they were a considerable drain on his salary. During the years 1854 and 1855, for which Pierce's personal records survive, he wrote checks to William H. Snow, White House steward, totaling

$8,560. These payments included Snow's salary and all the expenses related to food and entertaining. This did not include the expense of heating the White House, which cost the president between $1,200 and $1,500 a year, and the salaries of his secretary, bodyguard, and servants. Congress paid only the salary of the doorman and his assistant until Pierce's final year in office, when they picked up the cost of heating the White House.[65] Nevertheless, the president was frugal with his personal finances and managed to save a considerable portion of his $25,000 salary.

In February, a personal matter added to the concerns of the president. The wife of the late senator Charles G. Atherton suddenly appeared in Washington, demanding an audience with Pierce. Atherton and Pierce had been political allies and friends for years before the senator's sudden death in November 1853, and Atherton was distantly related to Jane. His will contained a surprise bequest of $8,000 to Pierce, along with an "unopened paper" that was to be delivered to Pierce by the executor (a Dr. Spalding) of Atherton's estate. In asking to see Pierce in private, Anne Atherton wrote, "I wish to be informed, unreservedly, upon the subject involving the eight thousand dollar legacy bequeathed to you by Mr. Atherton's will. I had borne a widows-heart ten days less than thirteen months, ere I was told that that [money] was not for you. . . . You can conceive that I am in deep affliction. . . . Do treat me on this subject with frankness and let my visit be confidential. . . . I may sometimes feel that it is best as it is, but 'ignorance is bliss'—in comparison."[66]

The nature of the bequest to Pierce has only recently come to light. Charles G. Atherton was the father of a Flora Atherton, born out of wedlock, in Washington, D.C., in 1849. The letter and bequest to Pierce was almost certainly Atherton's acknowledgment of his paternity and his direction that Pierce utilize the $8,000 to see to the needs of the child. All this was to be kept secret from Anne Atherton. How she found out about it is unclear, but Charles Atherton certainly did not plan to die at such an early age and did not foresee that the man he was entrusting with this responsibility would be president of the United States at the time and not just a lawyer practicing in New Hampshire. While it is conjecture, Pierce, in his overly taxed and sensitive position, would have needed to assign the task of distributing the money and looking out for the child to someone else, thus breaking confidence on the matter, the knowledge of which eventually made its way back to the grieving widow.[67] How Pierce explained the meaning of the bequest to Anne Atherton that Saturday morning at the White House is not known, but Anne described her feelings following the meeting in a letter to the president:

> Alas, this is the one drop too much in my basinful cup of sorrow! . . . I am not what I seemed, on Saturday morning. I was palsied with the variety and depth of my emotions as I met you. And, all the time I was with Mrs. Pierce, I felt as though the blood had left its natural channels. Never did I expect to be brought to this.
>
> I cannot harbor a shadow of unkindness to anyone; much less to you in whose success in life both Mr. Atherton and myself were so much interested. I will confess frankly to you, however, that I was deeply wounded to know, that the expressed wishes he had sealed by his dying breath were not regarded by you as a sacred confidential trust. . . . No one but you need to have known the contents of what Dr. Spalding bore you. . . . And I should have been spared the sorrow and rankling in my heart, the deep shadow on my pathway.[68]

It is noteworthy that Jane was included in the meeting and that Pierce kept Anne Atherton's letters. One wonders how much Pierce knew of Atherton's other life before his death.

The second session of the Thirty-third Congress produced important legislation recommended by the Pierce administration. Davis's request for four additional regiments, two cavalry and two infantry, which Pierce had endorsed in his annual message, was passed without partisan rancor or debate.[69] Dobbin also succeeded in getting his retirement board for the Navy. Congress passed "a bill to promote the efficiency of the navy" by lopsided majorities.[70] The president was to appoint a board made up of five captains, five commanders, and five lieutenants. The board would then compile a list of all naval officers "incapable of performing promptly and efficiently all their duty both ashore and afloat." If the officer was physically unable to perform his duties, he was placed on a reserve list with reduced pay and no chance for promotion. Officers who were to "blame" for their own inefficiencies were dropped from the service.[71]

The board was quickly established and in December 1855 reported 201 officers incapable of performing their duties. It recommended to the president that forty-nine be dismissed, that eighty-one be retired on furlough pay, and that seventy-one be retired on leave of absence pay.[72] Pierce approved the entire list and the officers were removed from active service. This produced a firestorm of criticism as individual officers appealed the decisions to Congress and to the press. Charges of "conspiracy, favoritism," and self-promotion were leveled against the board. Before Pierce left office, Congress caved in to the pressure, granting every officer dropped from service a review of his case before a court of inquiry, and promising every officer not later reinstated one year's salary. The retired list survived, however, and in 1860 seventy officers remained on the list.[73] Despite the controversy surrounding the retirement board, the navy benefited greatly by eliminating deadwood at the top and opening up promotion to deserving officers. Admiral Alfred Thayer Mahan later concluded, "It would be difficult to exaggerate the benefit of this measure to the nation. . . ."[74]

Congress passed another bill that was close to Pierce's heart. "A bill for the establishment of a board for the investigation of claims against the United States" was designed to place individual claims before a court of three judges appointed by the president.[75] This would eliminate the practice of citizens bringing claims before the Congress,where decisions were often based on flimsy evidence or self-interest. Pierce had long complained of abuses of the system, fraud, and the waste of government money that resulted. He tapped New Hampshire Superior Court Judge John J. Gilchrist to head the three-judge U. S. Court of Claims. Despite the best efforts of the honest and efficient judges, the new court suffered a fate similar to the navy retirement board. The court was not part of the judicial system, but reported directly to Congress. Approval by Congress of the court's decision in a case was conclusive, "putting an end to repeated hearings on the same case."[76] But the old abuses crept back in as Congress overruled the Court on some cases, rewarding or denying claims as they had in the past. Eventually, Congress amended the law to give the court of claims the powers it needed.[77]

Another piece of reform legislation was less pleasing to the administration. "A bill to remodel the diplomatic and consular systems of the United States" was designed to bring more uniformity to the diplomatic service. The bill abolished the title "chargé d'affaires, raising all to the rank of minister plenipotentiary. It also raised the salaries of all ministers but eliminated the expenses known as "outfit" that each previously could claim and required all missions to have a secretary of legation, whose salary also had to be paid out of the minister's salary. The salary of consuls was also raised, but they were no longer able to supplement their income with fees.[78] Marcy had sought reform, but the final bill did not please him. On learning of the new law, U.S. ministers and consuls abroad bombarded Marcy with complaints. The added expense of paying the salary of a secretary, the rent for their offices, and the elimination of "outfit" and of fees more than offset the salary increase.[79] Marcy admitted to John Y. Mason in Paris that he was upset: "I hardly trust myself to speak, even in a confidential way, my sentiments upon the Diplomatic & Consular Act. There are some provisions in it I like, but many—very many—I dislike . . . as a whole it is the crudest piece of legislation that I have ever known, and I am mortified to be assured that it found favor in congress and escaped strangling because I was there regarded its putative father."[80] Nathaniel Hawthorne complained directly to Pierce about the act, which would eliminate the lucrative fees that had attracted him initially to the position as consul at Liverpool: "For Heaven's sake do not let the next session pass without having this matter amended."[81]

Pierce did better than that. He asked Cushing for advice on whether the president had the prerogative, under his appointment power, to ignore certain provisions of the law. Cushing responded positively in two lengthy opinions addressed to Marcy. He claimed that the law did not require the president to replace the chargé d'affaires with ministers but only designated salaries to the ministers if he did replace the chargés d' affaires. According to Cushing, the "Act *invites* the President to make new appointments—it does not require it."[82] According to Cushing, the president has constitutional discretion that cannot be overridden by statute. In a second opinion, Cushing advised that the law pertaining to consuls was also not applicable, as the Constitution, not Congress, created the position of consul. Cushing also advised that the act did not abolish all fees, only those specifically mentioned.[83] Armed with this legal advice, Pierce proceeded to ignore most of the provisions of the act until Congress got around to amending it.

In his letter complaining about the consular bill, Hawthorne apologized to Pierce for not writing more often: "I am sure, my dear General, that you will not impute it to any forgetfulness or lack of affection, that I so seldom write you, but to tell the truth, it is not quite so easy to write to the President of the United States as it used to be to write to Frank Pierce. By the by, we shall be on good terms again, and for my part, I don't care how soon."[84]

Hawthorne offered support for all the criticism Pierce had been subjected to over the Kansas-Nebraska Act: "What a storm you have had to face! And how like a man you have faced it! I long to talk over these matter with you by the fireside, after the events of your government shall have become history."[85]

The Congress failed to pass other reform measures pressed by the administration. "A bill to establish a department of law" was intended to prescribe certain duties to the attorney general and to give him supervisory authority over violations of law occurring in the Treasury Department. The bill was debated but postponed without action.[86] "A bill to modify and amend the judicial system of the United States" was Cushing's plan to create eleven circuit courts to meet the needs of the expanding nation. The plan would have eliminated the requirement that Supreme Court justices preside in person over a circuit court, which would instead be headed by new circuit court judges.[87] The bill also received a respectful hearing in the Senate. Objection to removing the circuit court responsibility from a Supreme Court justice was based on the belief "that he may imbibe something of the spirit of popular jurisprudence" by traveling each year to his circuit court.[88] The bill was postponed until the Thirty-fourth Congress. Cushing also wrote a draft of "a bill for the further Regulation of the Executive Department," intended to more clearly define the responsibilities of federal officials, including Treasury Department auditors, the solicitor, and clerks in the various departments.[89] This bill was sent on to Senator Stephen Adams of the Committee on Reform and Retrenchment but was not introduced during this session of Congress. The Supreme Court did give the Pierce administration some needed support in this area with its ruling in the case of *Ring v. Maxwell.* The court ruled that fines collected at the ports "are not distributable" to customs office employees and that all money "shall be paid directly into the treasury." Cushing had personally argued the government's case before the court.[90]

Pierce vetoed two bills passed during this session of Congress. The "French Spoliation" bill appropriated $5 million to settle claims made by American citizens against the government of France for damages done to our shipping during the undeclared naval war in the 1790s. In his veto message Pierce laboriously presented the history of these claims and the treaty with France of 1803, by which that nation set aside 20 million francs to settle all claims of American citizens. By 1809 all legitimate claims had been paid, and Pierce wondered how Congress could now determine that any valid claims still existed: "What remains? And for what is five millions appropriated?" Pierce stated that no "new facts, not known or not accessible during the Administration of Mr. Jefferson, Mr. Madison, or Mr. Monroe" had been discovered. His conclusion was that "the United States have in the most ample and the completest manner discharged their duty toward such of their citizens as may have been at any time aggrieved by acts of the French Government, so also France has honorably discharged herself of all obligations in the premises toward the United States."[91] The bill was simply one more example of profligate politicians trying to extort money from the treasury and place it into the hands of their friends. The House sustained Pierce's veto, but the vote of 113 to 86 was close to the two-thirds needed to overturn it.[92]

The other veto was for an even more egregious assault on the treasury. A steamship company owned by E. K. Collins had the exclusive contract to carry the mail between New York and Liverpool. In 1847 Congress had contracted to lend Collins the money to build five steamships, which he would sell to the United States in time of need for use by the navy. Collins would use the ships to carry the mail and receive $385,000 per year for the service. By 1852 Collins had built only four of the ships, but Congress renewed the contract and more than doubled the compensation to Collins, to $858,000 per annum, but with the condition that the contract could be canceled after six months' notice. Investors in the Collins Line, including Washington banker W. W. Corcoran, organized a massive lobbying campaign to pass the renewal bill. Among the lobbyists employed by the company were Edmund Burke, B. B. French, and Francis J. Grund. Thousands of dollars in bribes were dispensed to congressmen in the process.[93]

An extension of the contract was passed in March 1855, without the cancellation clause, following a similar lobbying effort. Pierce's veto message reported that during the four years prior to 1855, Collins had received $2,620,000 from the federal government, not including the loan to build the ships, while the government had taken in only $734,000 in receipts from postage on mail to England. Add to this the "large receipts from transportation of passengers and merchandise" that Collins earned from the ships, and Pierce concluded "that the privileges bestowed upon the contractors are without corresponding advantages to the Government. . . ." To Pierce, signing the bill "would be to deprive commercial enterprise of the benefits of free competition and to establish a monopoly in violation of the soundest principles of public policy and of doubtful compatibility with the Constitution."[94] The veto message must have shamed some members of Congress, as the House failed to overturn it by a large margin, seventy-five to ninety-eight.[95]

Pierce's close friend B. B. French was one of those hired by Collins to lobby for the bill. With Pierce's veto, French worried about whether he would ever receive his money, writing, "I received a letter from Latham [Rep. Milton Latham, Cal.] today, he says he has got nothing yet from Collins—that they behave very badly. He says as soon as he gets anything, I shall hear from him. I believe in Latham yet, and wish everyone, *especially Senator J* [James C. Jones of Tenn.]—were as honest as I think he is. I have not heard one word from that Senator yet!"[96]

In the last days of the congressional session, the Ostend Manifesto was finally exposed to the light of public attention. Pierre Soulé had arrived back in the United States in late February 1855 and immediately embarked on a personal campaign to defend his actions and attack Marcy and the Pierce administration for its failure to back

Soulé in his attempt to acquire Cuba. The House passed a resolution requesting the president to submit all correspondence related to the Ostend meeting and the Cuba situation.[97] In reviewing the correspondence prior to submitting it to Congress, Pierce and cabinet had edited out the instructions to Soulé which included the words "to detach." In the form submitted by the Pierce administration, "The Ostend Correspondence" was published in the newspapers. Marcy wrote to John Van Buren, "I had doubts as to the propriety of sending it to the Congress, but Mr. Soulé deserved it and wished parts of it included which had been marked for omission."[98]

B. B. French saw through the "Ostend Correspondence," writing, "If ever there was such a display of 'backing and filling,' as our President and Gov. Marcy have made about that, I have never seen it. Poor Soulé—was completely humbugged by them, and if Marcy and the President did not set a trap for Buchanan, Mason, and Soulé, as deliberately as ever Benny did for 3 mice, then I am no judge of trap setting, and they, like three ninnies, went and put each 'their foot right in it.' . . . It really is rich. But it goes to show the weakness of men, even though they be in high places![99]

Soulé also carried on a feud with his former consul, claiming Horatio Perry had undermined his attempts to negotiate with the Spanish government. From Madrid, Perry tried to defend himself by writing letters to the press in the United States. One of these letters, addressed to Pierce, was printed in the *National Intelligencer* seven days before it was received by the president. Perry claimed to not know how the letter got to the press and not to the president, but Pierce would not tolerate such "a disrespectful irregularity" and fired Perry. Marcy explained to Perry, "The President had seen with surprise and regret a letter, in a newspaper, from you addressed to him, touching upon and to some extent discussing our relations with the government to which you are accredited. So far as I am aware, this is a step without a precedent, it is certainly very unusual and manifestly improper."[100]

In the meantime, Soulé had been replaced by former Iowa senator Augustus C. Dodge. Pierce had first offered the post to John C. Breckinridge, who had been gerrymandered out of his congressional district by the Whig legislature in Kentucky, but he declined.[101]

By the summer, Soulé was back in New Orleans and rumored to be collaborating with A. Dudley Mann on an expose of Soulé's mission. The book was never written, and Soulé never blamed the president for his failure abroad: "General Pierce, I am sure, with some two or three other members of his cabinet, was ever right, both in his head and in his heart." But he did conclude, [Pierce] "has been lacking in firmness, and that has destroyed him."[102]

It was during this session that Jefferson Davis finally presented his report on the Pacific railroad surveys. Instead of helping settle the controversy as to which was the best route, the report only further confused the matter. All the routes were judged practicable, and the estimated cost to build each was similar, but Davis recommended the most southerly route along the thirty-second parallel because it was the least mountainous and snow was not an obstacle.[103] For political reasons, Davis was biased in favor of the southerly route, but his report accurately reflected the findings of each of the survey parties. The failure of the surveys to clearly designate a best route and the sectional controversy surrounding any attempt to select one made the construction of a Pacific railroad at this time impossible. But the thirteen-volume, *Pacific Railroad Reports* was, as William H. Goetzmann has noted, "a monumental achievement," an "encyclopedia of western experience."[104]

The Thirty-third Congress adjourned on March 3, 1855. Pierce turned his attention to the state elections in New Hampshire in mid-March. After the results of the fall elections around the nation, Pierce understood the odds were against a Democratic victory. He wrote to the state party chair, John H. George, in January, "It is, I am well aware, to be a desperate battle, but if you win the field it will be the most decisive and the most important triumph ever achieved in N.H."[105] He offered to send Senator Cass, former governor Joseph Lane of Oregon, and former Gov. Horatio Seymour of New York to New Hampshire to speak. Seymour had made the offer after Pierce had agreed to appoint a friend, John Miller, as secretary of the legation at Peru. Pierce informed Marcy, "I should incline to comply with the Governor's wishes."[106] But Miller's nomination was quickly withdrawn from the Senate when Pierce learned that Miller had been an outspoken opponent of the Kansas-Nebraska bill. Once again Marcy tried to mollify Seymour, who was outraged by Pierce's change of mind. Marcy explained that while Pierce had determined "not to discriminate, for that cause alone, between democrats," Miller had used "exceptionable means" against the bill, organizing opposition in his county, cooperating with Whigs, and making violent speeches, in which he declared that "Douglas ought to be hung" and that he was fit only to be "a negro driver." Marcy concluded that Seymour's recommendation of Miller "was unsatisfactory—and . . . truly—offensive."[107]

Pierce had all he could do to hold his state party in line. Democratic Governor Nathaniel Baker and editor William Butterfield had flirted with the Know-Nothing movement, but it was Edmund Burke who successfully manipulated the Know-Nothings into nominating Ralph Metcalf, a Democrat, for governor. The coalition of Free-Soilers, temperance advocates, Burke's Hunker Democrats, and Know-Nothings offered the voters a substantial change.[108] John P. Hale campaigned for the coalition in hopes of winning back his senate seat but did not join a Know-Nothing lodge. State Democrats were reluctant to defend Catholicism and the Kansas-Nebraska Act before the angry electorate, instead accusing Metcalf of hypocrisy for once considering an offer to be a commissioner for the enforcement of the Fugitive Slave Act.[109]

At one point, Pierce sent $2,000 raised in Washington and $1,000 raised at the customs office in New York to help in the campaign.[110] But before election day he realized the hopelessness of the Democratic cause. Sidney Webster wrote to George about the prospects of Burke or Hale becoming the next senator from New Hampshire: "My God! Just think of that mass of encrusted corruption being a U.S. Senator from N.H. for six years. You and I may as well adjourn from public life . . . going to Vancouver Island."[111] Pierce thanked George for making the good fight: "I am naturally anxious about the result . . . in N.H., but tell my friends that if after a contest, conducted with the ability, honor & courage which this has been, we are defeated, such defeat under such circumstances will never disturb me for a moment. If you could have carried the state with the aid of any one of the *isms* by a majority of 20,000 and would have consented to do so—I should in my feelings have sounded the depth of humiliation."[112]

The defeat was monumental. Know-Nothings elected the governor, all three congressional seats, ten of twelve state senate seats, and three-fifths of the seats in the state house of representatives.[113] When the legislature met in June, John P. Hale was selected to return to the U.S. Senate to complete the term of Pierce's late friend Atherton. One Democrat, defeated for the state legislature, wrote to Cushing, "I should have joined the Know-Nothings when invited."[114]

One who did join the Know-Nothings was Benjamin Brown French, Pierce's close friend of more than twenty-five years. French had joined the secret order in Washington briefly in 1854 before quitting and had written anonymous editorials for a Massachusetts newspaper, endorsing the Know-Nothing campaign of a relative, who was elected lieutenant governor. Pierce had taken a strong stand insisting than anyone showing sympathy for the Know-Nothing cause must be dismissed from any federal government office. He wrote to one postmaster, "If there are persons in your office who sympathize with a political party hostile to the Democratic Party—you should know them and neither employ nor trust them. . . . Have they been Know-Nothings. Do they sympathize with that political organization. Is your chief clerk a Whig with Know-Nothing sympathies . . . If you cannot answer these questions with confidence & satisfactorily changes will be made. . . . Answer me promptly and in full."[115] Eventually, rumors of French's activity reached Pierce, who demanded an explanation. At first French denied his connection to the movement, but additional facts reached Pierce, who confronted French: "Well, Major they have got you now!" French responded, "Yes, they have so," and offered Pierce his resignation. Pierce accepted it saying, "Well, Major, I think it will be better for both of us, under the circumstances that you be, for the present, out of office. . . ."[116] French had become increasingly disillusioned with the Pierce administration since the Kansas-Nebraska bill, had always believed he had not been properly rewarded for his service in the campaign of 1852, and had failed to profit personally from his attempts to lobby Pierce on behalf of the Thompson Indian claim and the Collins steamship bill. Several weeks after his resignation, French visited Pierce again at the White House: "We had a long talk & he gave evidence in his conversation that he at least remained my warm friend. We conversed on various matters,

& I have no doubt from what he said that he has some expectation of being renominated for the next term. He cannot again be elected under any circumstances!"[117]

8

TROUBLE IN THE TERRITORIES

THE KNOW-NOTHING MOVEMENT crested in the spring of 1855. Pierce's former congressional crony, drinking buddy, and presidential supporter Henry A. Wise was elected governor of Virginia in May. Wise had waged a vigorous campaign against the Know-Nothings, successfully labeling them abolitionists in disguise. The connection between northern Know-Nothings and the antislavery movement effectively discredited the movement in much of the South. The administration placed great significance on Wise's success. Marcy wrote to Buchanan, "The news has just reached us that Wise has been elected Governor of Virginia. It was an exciting and furious contest, and is justly regarded as a great triumph for the democratic party."[1] Buchanan, whose own presidential hopes rested on the strength of his party, had "awaited the result with the most anxious solicitude." He was almost gleeful at the news: "I know not when I have been so much gratified as at the news of Wise's election."[2] The election in Virginia was closely followed by more good news from Maine, where the Democrats united with the small remnants of the Whig Party to defeat a coalition of Know-Nothings, abolitionists, and temperance advocates.[3] To Pierce it seemed that sanity was returning to the political world.

Throughout the second half of Pierce's term of office, his administration was plagued by problems in the territories. Utah was a particular focus of the president's attention from the fall of 1854 through the spring of 1855. Mormon leader Brigham Young had been appointed territorial governor by President Fillmore in 1850. Young thus occupied a unique position in U.S. history, combining both political and spiritual power in one man: an actual theocracy. Since Mormons made up the entire white population of the territory, except for a few appointed federal officers, Young's dual role did not attract much notoriety, at first. In August 1852, however, Young the religious leader officially endorsed plural marriages.[4] The presence of polygamy among the Mormons had been one of the reasons they had been persecuted in the East. Now the press took notice of a federal official sanctioning the practice.

Young, as did most territorial governors, served a dual role as superintendent of Indian affairs for his territory. In August 1853, following several Indian raids, Young proclaimed the Utah Indians were "in a state of open and declared *war* with the white settlers," and called out the militia.[5] At this time, Captain John W. Gunnison arrived in the territory, leading one of Jefferson Davis's Pacific railway survey teams. Gunnison, a New Hampshire native, had served in Utah a few years prior to this and knew the territory, the governor, and the Indians. He had written a book about the Mormons, which, though sympathetic to them, was condemned by Young. Before leaving Washington, D.C., Gunnison had asked Commissioner of Indian Affairs George Manypenny for gifts to give to the Utah Indians, who had "been represented as hostile."[6] Gunnison's party arrived in Utah in late August 1853 and proceeded to explore remote canyons and valleys south of Salt Lake City. Young was always wary of the federal government, and though he knew of the location of Gunnison's party, he never attempted to inform the American soldiers of his recently declared war on the Utah Indians. On October 25, 1853, after dividing his party, Gunnison was massacred with seven of his soldiers by Indians near the Sevier River in southwest Utah.[7] On learning of the massacre Young sent out a party to investigate.

At first, Jefferson Davis complimented Young for his initial "account of the massacre" and for recovering the records of the survey, "which were of special value."[8] But in a more complete report, Young concluded that the massacre was not related to the problems with the Utah Indians but was the result of a party of emigrants to California attacking "peaceful" Indians who had visited their camp. These Indians were looking for revenge when Gunnison's party arrived. Considering these "facts," Young hoped "the Indians in our borders may not be censured unjustly."[9] Months went by and Young made no effort to bring the Indians involved in the massacre to justice. Surviving officers of Gunnison's party wrote of their suspicions of collusion between Young, who wanted to impede federal government activity in Utah, and the Indians who had attacked Gunnison.[10] Pierce and Davis decided to send the army in to investigate. In April, 1854, Col. Edward J. Steptoe was ordered to reconnoiter a military road to California and to bring supplies, horses, and mules to the army in Washington territory. Davis added to this assignment in May, directing Steptoe to detour into Utah to investigate the massacre and to demand the Indians surrender the perpetrators or to "take their chiefs or head men as hostages until they were surrendered."[11]

Steptoe was a close friend of Pierce. They had served together in the Mexican War, and Steptoe was a witness to the dispute between Pierce and Captain Magruder at the Aztec Club in Mexico City, which later led to charges of cowardice being leveled at Pierce during the presidential campaign. Steptoe had met with Pierce in Boston during the campaign and wrote a defense of the candidate, which was published in the newspapers. On learning of Benny's death, Steptoe, then stationed in Rhode Island, had rushed to Pierce's side, remaining with him through the funeral. Steptoe, accompanied by 175 soldiers, 150 civilian employees, and nearly 1,000 horses and mules, arrived in Utah on August 31, 1854. He made such a good impression on Young and the Mormons that territorial judge John Kinney, a Pierce appointee, wrote to the president on October 1, recommending that Steptoe be appointed territorial governor, for the colonel was "much esteemed by the Mormons."[12] Young's four-year commission as governor was about to expire that fall, and there was great anxiety in Utah as to whether he would be reappointed. Kinney advised that a change was "much needed, and would be cheerfully submitted to by the people of the valley."[13]

Steptoe decided to winter in Utah and pursue the guilty Indians when the snows kept them more confined. In the meantime, on December 13, Pierce nominated Steptoe to be territorial governor, and the Senate unanimously confirmed the appointment on December 21.[14] It was not at all certain, however, that Steptoe would accept the appointment, as it would require him to give up his military career. The press speculated that Pierce knew Steptoe would not accept, and that the appointment was simply a clever maneuver by the president to appear to act in removing the controversial Young while, in fact, allowing him to remain in office, thus avoiding trouble from the Mormons if Young was forced out: "The Brigadier President has more shrewdness in some matters than he has credit for by the public generally. He appoints Col. Steptoe, knowing full well that the gallant Colonel will not accept the appointment and that Brigham Young will hold on to his office until some other person shall supersede him."[15] Before learning of his appointment as governor, Steptoe and other leading men of the territory signed a petition recommending that Young be reappointed governor.[16] When Steptoe learned of his appointment in February, 1855, he wrote a personal letter to Sidney Webster, explaining his indecision about whether to accept. Expressing his loyalty to Pierce—"There are few things indeed that I would not attempt at least, if only to gratify him"—Steptoe explained that the personal and professional sacrifice might be too great and that "so much—too much—would be expected of the Governor to check Ploggammy [polygamy] when in fact, he could not exert the least influence in the matter."[17]

Through negotiation rather than force, Steptoe convinced the Utah chiefs to turn over eight braves involved in the Gunnison massacre. The Mormon grand jury indicted only three. When they were tried in March 1855, Judge Kinney directed the jury to find the Indians guilty of first-degree murder or release them. Instead, the jury convicted them of manslaughter. Kinney reluctantly accepted the jury's verdict and sentenced the convicted Indians to three years in prison. A few days after the trial, the Mormons allowed the Indians to escape.[18] Federal officials in Utah were appalled by the results of the trial. It was clear that Young had tampered with the jury in his effort to convince the Indians that he was more powerful than the United States government and that their future protection was in his hands. Nevertheless, Steptoe wrote, "These Savages have undoubtedly learned from Dr. Hunt and myself . . . *for the first time* what relation they hold to the Government, and that to *it alone* they must look for encouragement in well-doing, or chastisement for mischief."[19]

If the trial results did not convince Steptoe to decline his appointment as governor, the deteriorating relations between his soldiers and the Mormon population certainly did. During the winter there were several fights or near riots between drunken soldiers and citizens in Salt Lake City. As a result, Steptoe moved his force out of the city to a camp some forty miles to the south, where his horses and mules were grazing. This led to a different problem. In town, the randy soldiers had connected with many opportunistic, flirtatious young Mormon girls and wives who were anxious to be free of the restrictions and polygamy imposed on them by the Mormon community. As many as one hundred young women ran away from home to follow their soldier boyfriends and to seek asylum in the army camp. This "underground railroad" caused great consternation among the Mormon leaders, who demanded the return of their daughters or wives. Steptoe was happy to leave on April 29, 1855, writing to the Adjutant General, "I am truly gratified at being able so early to leave for the growing ill feeling of the inhabitants toward the troops—very fully reciprocated by the latter—gave me constant uneasiness."[20] He proceeded on to California, accompanied by horses, mules, soldiers, civilian employees, and the Mormon women. The press back east was titillated by the situation. The *New York Herald* reported, "The Mormon women are ripe for rebellion," and advised Pierce to "send out to the Great Salt Lake a fresh detachment of young and good looking soldiers."[21] Brigham Young claimed to be happy to be free of women who "wish to go to California to whore it . . .", but if U.S. soldiers returned to Utah and acted in a similar manner, he said, "So help me God, we will slay them!"[22] Young remained in office as Pierce exerted a policy of benign neglect regarding Utah for the remainder of his presidency.

Minnesota offered the president a different and even more perplexing set of problems. In 1853 a number of important politicians became investors in a land speculation venture at Superior City, Wisconsin, at the western end of Lake Superior next to Duluth, Minnesota. The investors in the six-thousand-acre tract were led by Minnesota's territorial representative in Congress, Henry M. Rice, and included senators Stephen A. Douglas, Jesse Bright, and R. M. T. Hunter, and representatives John C. Breckinridge, William A. Richardson, John L. Dawson, William W. Boyce, William Aiken, Horace Walbridge, and John McQueen. Other important investors were John W. Forney, editor of the *Washington Union* and chief clerk of the House; Robert J. Walker, former treasury secretary; and W. W. Corcoran, powerful Washington banker. Corcoran acted as trustee for the politicians in order to keep their names off the public record.[23] Their shares quickly escalated in value when, in 1854, the territorial legislature chartered the Minnesota and Northwestern Railway Company, which proposed to run a railroad from Superior City through Saint Paul to the Iowa line near Dubuque.[24] Breckinridge reported that just the prospect of a railroad caused his half share to jump in value from $1,250 to more than $10,000.[25]

The congressmen hoped to further enhance their investment by passing a bill to make the new railroad eligible for federal land grants. Rice introduced the bill, which easily passed the Senate but failed in the House, where competing Midwestern railroad interests lobbied friendly representatives against the bill. The rumors that so many congressmen would personally profit from the railroad also had an impact on the debate, though Rice virtuously denied any personal interest in the proposed railroad. Minnesota's territorial governor, Willis A. Gorman, a Mexican War officer and close friend of Pierce, traveled to the capital to lobby against Rice's group. Gorman had been appointed by Pierce over the objections of his home-state senator, Indiana's powerful, combative, and prodigal Jesse Bright. The appointment earned the president Bright's unwavering enmity. Gorman had set an independent course as governor, steering clear of the vested interests of Indian traders and land speculators in Minnesota. He succeeded in getting the Congress to pass a second bill, which allowed federal land grants to "future" railroads in Minnesota but not to any company already "constituted or organized." This eliminated the conflict of interest so evident in the first bill while allowing other railroad plans to proceed. In this form the bill received Pierce's signature.

After the bill had been passed and signed, someone changed two words in the printing of the new act, which completely altered its intent. The word "future" was omitted, and the phrase "constituted or organized" was changed to "constituted and organized." The Minnesota and Northwestern Railway Company was incorporated but had yet to be organized, thus it was made eligible for land grants after all.[26] Rep. Elihu B. Washburne of Illinois noticed the alteration and proposed an investigation to discover who was to blame. Washburne was an opponent of the Illinois Central Railroad faction, which was known to be allied with the Minnesota and Northwestern.[27] John C. Breckinridge, one of the investors in the scheme, was chosen to head the special investigation committee, which, not surprisingly, concluded that no intentional deception had occurred. In testifying before the committee, Rice and Forney both lied by stating they had no personal stake in the bill. In fact, Forney had been paid $2,500 to make the alterations in the law. Though the committee recommended only that the original wording should be restored, the Senate repealed the law and the land grant on the last day of the congressional session. Breckinridge's committee had tried to cover up the wrongdoing, but Forney's role was widely suspected. A resolution in the House to fire Forney attained only eighteen votes. The Pierce administration tried to administer the final blow to the Minnesota and Northwestern scheme. After the law was repealed, Interior Secretary McClelland, with Pierce's approval, placed the land that had been set aside for the railroad on the market, making it available to settlers.[28]

The scene now shifts to Minnesota. Rice believed that Congress had illegally repealed the altered bill and that the original land grant to his railroad company was valid. He decided to test the constitutionality of the repeal act in court. To do this, he bribed the federal district attorney, John E. Warren, to bring suit against the Minnesota and Northwestern for trespass for cutting trees on federal land. The district court ruled for the railroad, claiming that title to the land was ceded to the territory by an act that Congress had later repealed and ruling that the land belonged to the railroad. Warren then appealed the case to the U.S. Supreme Court. Warren's payoff was that he was hired as real estate agent to sell the land along the railroad route. Pierce and Cushing were incensed that Warren was involving the administration in a scheme to benefit the railroad. In fact, Warren had acted independently, without communicating in any way with his superiors in Washington. On December 30, 1854, Cushing fired Warren for violating department rules by initiating a suit without approval from Washington. In a lengthy report to Pierce, Cushing explained that Warren was motivated by "private interests." In anticipation of the Supreme Court case, the railroad hired prominent New York attorneys, including Greene C. Bronson, the Hard faction leader recently fired by Pierce from the position of collector of the port of New York. But the Pierce administration refused to allow the case to go forward because the federal government could not be sued without its approval.[29]

Inevitably, Pierce became personally enmeshed in this tangled web of speculation and special interest. Rice, back in Washington for the second session of the Thirty-third Congress, proceeded to lobby Pierce to fire Governor Gorman, who was opposing the railroad company in Minnesota. Rice claimed that Gorman was ruining the party in the territory and was personally corrupt in his dealings with the Indians in his dual role as superintendent of Indian affairs in the territory.[30] Pierce promised that if Gorman was corrupt, he would be removed. Pierce had wanted to do something for Breckinridge, who had been such a loyal defender of the administration in Congress, going so far as to promise the position to the young Kentuckian if Gorman was replaced. But Pierce insisted that Gorman was entitled to an impartial investigation. He sent treasury official J. Ross Browne to Minnesota on the pretext of examining land sales in the territory. Browne's report, which was received by Pierce at the end of March 1855, exonerated Gorman of any misconduct and sharply criticized his accusers. Commissioner of Indian Affairs George W. Manypenny had also informed Pierce that he had "not found any reason" for doubting Gorman's honesty in his dealings with the Indians.[31]

During a four-hour meeting with Pierce on April 11, 1855, Douglas and Rice exerted all their influence and pressure to manipulate the president into firing Gorman. But Pierce refused, citing Browne's report. When the conversation became heated, Pierce informed his visitors that Browne had found evidence that Rice, not Gorman, was the one who was guilty of land fraud. Pierce did promise to investigate the matter further and sent his own secretary, Sidney Webster, on a six-week tour of the Midwest, with stops in Saint Paul and

Superior.[32] Webster also found nothing, and Gorman remained in office until 1857, "leaving a name untarnished by any stain of dishonor. . . ."[33] Rice was furious with Pierce, writing to Breckinridge that the president was "a miserable weak squirt."[34] Forney, $2,500 richer, was more forgiving, writing to Breckinridge that Pierce was "full of kindness" despite his inability to make Breckinridge governor of the territory.[35] The entire experience soured Pierce on federal land grants for railroads, a sentiment he had expressed in his annual message in December 1854.[36]

Pierce was often labeled as "weak" by those who asked him to endorse their schemes or personal interests. But this charge hardly bares scrutiny. Pierce had nothing to gain by supporting Gorman, a man with no influence outside Minnesota and relatively little in it. Pierce had stood up to the leaders of his own party, rejecting their efforts to profit personally from their own legislative actions. He needed the support of these men for his administration to accomplish anything, yet he was unwilling to compromise his principles to maintain that support. Throughout his term in office, Pierce was surrounded by powerful politicians whose ethical standards were beneath his own. When lobbied by them to make decisions that went against his principles, Pierce invariably tried to use his sympathetic nature and charm to cajole them while delaying making a final decision that he knew would disappoint and anger them. To deny their requests was to risk losing the support of powerful members of his own party. So he delayed and bought time, which was misunderstood as concurrence. When forced to decide, he always fell back on his principles and his constitutional duty, but it had to be a painful process to reject men whose support he so desperately needed. His weakness was not want of character or ethics but too much sensitivity in trying to avoid hurt feelings and the political consequences of rejecting the machinations of influential people. In Washington, Pierce was supported by department heads of his own choosing, men like McClelland and Manypenny, who shared his ethical standards.

The situations in Utah and Minnesota were annoyances and distractions, but Pierce's reputation was most affected by the trouble that erupted in Kansas Territory. In the spring of 1854, in anticipation of the passage of the Kansas-Nebraska bill, Indian Commissioner

Manypenny negotiated treaties with Indian tribes in the area west of the Missouri River.[37] Past government policy had been to remove Indians entirely as new lands were opened for white settlement, but Manypenny knew that many of the Indians in eastern Kansas had been removed previously from the East and had been promised their new lands "as long as the grass grew or water run."[38] As one historian has noted, Manypenny "stands out as one of the few commissioners who truly sought to protect and improve Indian welfare, no matter what the consequences."[39] He determined not to use trickery in negotiating with the Indians in Kansas, and to secure for them a significant portion of the land so that they would not have to be removed. Manypenny planned that the land reserved for the tribes would eventually be distributed in two-hundred-acre lots to individual Indians. He expected that, in time, these Indians, surrounded as they would be by white settlers, would adapt to farming ways "and their complete civilization [would be] effected."[40]

Manypenny's naïve but well-intentioned policy complicated the settlement of Kansas. Land ceded by the Indians to the government became part of the public domain to be distributed through land sales by the General Land Office. Land that remained part of the Indian reserves or allotments, twenty-eight percent of the total area of Kansas, was to be administered by the Office of Indian Affairs. The law stated that sales of these lands to whites could not be made below market price and required the approval of the Indian commissioner.[41] To complicate the situation Congress did not get around to ratifying the Indian treaties until the late summer of 1854 and did not authorize the surveying of the lands in the public domain until November 1854. Thus, when Congress opened the new territory to settlers on May 30, 1854, "not an acre of land was legally open to them and they were subject to heavy penalties for invasion of the [Indian] reserves."[42]

The Pierce administration had ample evidence to anticipate future problems in Kansas. Secretary of War Davis was petitioned by settlers from Virginia who asked permission to spend the winter of 1854 in Fort Leavenworth, so they would be ready to stake their claims when spring weather broke. Davis denied the request and advised the settlers to "take up temporary residence in Independence or

Westport, Missouri."[43] When these settlers did cross into Kansas in June 1854, they staked claims to lands that were not yet in the public domain and had not been surveyed. They expected the policy of pre-emption to apply. This policy permitted "squatters," who lived on and improved public land, to buy the land at a reduced price when the government opened the land for sale. These squatters soon learned that their right to the land was not certain. A Missourian who represented a squatter association explained the situation to Attorney General Cushing and asked for his opinion:

> They put up good houses and had their families comfortably fixed and expect to pre-empt the quarter section of land upon which they live. They are told, that to entitle them to pre-empt, they must make new improvements, *since* the extinguishment of the Indian title; or that strangers who come upon the same quarter section and make improvements since the extinguishment of Indian title, will have the right to pre-empt their land, and turn them out of their homes. Will you be kind enough to let us know if that is your construction and, understanding of the spirit of the law."[44]

Cushing replied that after a careful "exploration of the duties of the Atty. Genl." he was "not authorized to give opinion in such a case."[45] Pierce's choice for chief justice of the supreme court of the territory of Kansas, Samuel D. Lecompte, also anticipated land issues dominating his court and asked Cushing to send him any opinions by [himself] or others on these matters, writing, "Controversies in relation to titles will be, at once, the first, in time and importance, to demand adjustment."[46]

If land title controversies were not enough of a forewarning of future difficulties in Kansas, the words coming from the mouths of leading politicians regarding the popular sovereignty aspect of the Kansas-Nebraska Act should have brought fear into the hearts of any official charged with enforcing the law in the territory. In May 1854, before Pierce even signed the bill, Senator Seward of New York threw down the gauntlet to the South: "Come on then, gentlemen of the Slave States. Since there is no escaping your challenge, I accept it on behalf of the cause of freedom. We will engage in competition for the virgin soil of Kansas, and God give the victory to the side which is stronger in numbers as it is in right."[47] To guarantee that the "numbers" in Kansas were on the side of freedom, Eli Thayer, a schoolmaster from Worcester, Massachusetts, formed an organization to help settlers from New England move to the territory. In April 1854, before the Kansas-Nebraska bill was even passed, the Massachusetts legislature approved a bill incorporating the Massachusetts Emigrant Aid Company, which was authorized to issue stock up to $5 million. In June, Amos A. Lawrence, Jane Pierce's cousin by marriage, became the treasurer of the company and its financial benefactor. Soon the society merged with a similar group from New York, forming the New England Emigrant Aid Company. The threat of this much money backing up free-state settlers was alarming to the South, even though the reality was that the company always struggled to keep its head above water financially and managed to assist fewer than two thousand New Englanders to move to Kansas over the next five years.[48]

Believing that the North had fired the first shots in the war for Kansas, the South, predictably, responded with a vengeance. David Rice Atchison of Missouri, president pro tempore of the U.S. Senate, was determined that Kansas would be a slave state. He raised the stakes by claiming that the future of slavery in Missouri and across the South was dependent upon spreading the institution into Kansas: "If we win we carry slavery to the Pacific Ocean, if we fail we lose Missouri, Arkansas, and Texas and all the territories. The game must be played boldly . . ."[49] Atchison was ready to lead the effort from his base in western Missouri. He described in graphic terms to Jefferson Davis what it would take:

> We will have difficulty with the Negro theives in Kansas, they are resolved they say to Keep the slave holders out, and our people are resolved to go in and take their "*niggers*" with them, now the men who are hired by the Boston Abolitionists, to settle and Abolitionise Kansas will not hesitate, to steal our slaves, takeing this for granted, I on the 21st of this month advised in a public speech the squatters, in Kansas and the people of Missouri, to give a horse theif, robber, or homicide a fair trial, but to hang

> a Negro theif or Abolitionist, without Judge of Jury, this sentiment met with almost universal applause, and I could with difficulty Keep the *"Plebs"* from hanging two gentlemen who called a Cow, *"Keow."*
>
> We will before six months rolls around, have the Devil to play in Kansas and this State, we are organizing, to meet their Organization we will be compelled, to shoot, burn & hang, but the thing will be soon over, we intend to *"Mormonise"* the Abolitionists.[50]

Atchison remained in Missouri to lead the crusade, absenting himself from the second session of the Thirty-third Congress, and hoped to ride the issue to reelection to the Senate.

All of this posturing took place before federal officials took up their positions in Kansas. Until October 1854, only Indian agent John W. Whitfield was present, representing the administration. Pierce chose a geographically balanced ticket of territorial officers. For governor he selected Andrew H. Reeder of Easton, Pennsylvania. Reeder was recommended by Postmaster General Campbell and John W. Forney, who both believed the appointment would help the Democratic Party in northeast Pennsylvania. The ruddy, stoutly built forty-seven-old lawyer had never held public office before, but he apparently also received the endorsement of Jefferson Davis, whose wife was acquainted with Mrs. Reeder.[51] Chief Justice Lecompte was from Maryland and would be assisted by Associate Justices Rush Elmore of Alabama and Saunders W. Johnston of Ohio. Daniel Woodson of Arkansas was appointed territorial secretary.[52]

On the day of his arrival in Kansas, Reeder invested $1,000 in the land company of H. Miles Moore, a free-state settler who was speculating in land far to the west of the initial settlements in the territory. Whatever else happened during his tenure, Reeder was determined to profit financially from the experience. He then resisted the call of the early settlers and proslavery leaders for the immediate election of a territorial legislature. Instead, he ordered the election of a delegate to Congress to be held on November 29, 1854.[53] Had the legislature been elected that fall, it would certainly have been dominated by proslavery supporters. Reeder probably believed that there were not enough settlers yet in the territory to justify a legislature, but the early election of a proslavery legislature would have discouraged free-state settlers from venturing into Kansas. Reeder's personal interests required the influx of free-state settlers to increase the market for his land. His known land speculation with free-state emigrants, coupled with his initial decisions relating to elections, demonstrated to the proslavery side that Reeder was not impartial.

The congressional enabling act that created the territorial government defined legal voters as "residents" of the territory. Reeder defined residency as "the actual dwelling or inhabiting in the Territory to the exclusion of any other present domicile or home, coupled with the present *bona fide* intention of remaining permanently for the same purpose," but he prescribed no term of residency.[54] Some Missourians crossed back and forth into Kansas, staking a claim to land but preferring the comforts of an established home until the following spring. Others were speculating in land and had no intention of giving up their residence in Missouri, but all intended to protect their claims by voting in Kansas. On election day these "residents" were joined by hundreds of other fully armed "ruffians" who marched to the polling places, determined to elect the proslavery candidate, J. W. Whitfield, who received 2,258 of the nearly 3,000 votes cast, easily defeating two other candidates. In spite of reports of massive voter fraud and intimidation of election judges and free-state voters, Reeder let the results stand without comment or objection.[55] Whitfield would have likely won an honest election, as most legal residents of the territory had moved in from Missouri, but the precedent had been established that voter fraud and intimidation was to be the favored tactic of the proslavery supporters.

Reeder set March 30, 1855, as the date for the election of a territorial legislature. Proslavery elements feared that this late date would give free-state settlers too much time to arrive in the territory. Reeder's priority continued to be his own financial interests. Along with Judges Rush Elmore and Saunders W. Johnston, District Attorney Andrew J. Isaacs, and antislavery leaders Charles Robinson, Thomas Ewing, and Samuel C. Pomeroy, Reeder and company negotiated for the purchase of twenty-three-hundred acres of land to be set aside for half-breed Indians. The contract was made with French

Canadian traders who had married descendants of the half-breeds, and the transaction completely bypassed the local Indian agent, who was required by law to be present and to approve of any sale of Indian lands. In November 1854, Indian agents in Kansas reported the group's actions to the Indian commissioner. In January Manypenny refused to authorize the sale of these lands, claiming the group was cheating the half-breeds by paying less than market price. Reeder's name did not appear on the contracts, but his involvement in the scheme was known to everyone. Manypenny made a formal report to Pierce, who refused to authorize the land sale. Reeder claimed the half-breeds had every right to sell, and continued to press his case for the purchase, but historian Paul Wallace Gates, who spent a career studying western land policy, labeled Reeder's activities "obviously fraudulent."[56] The land in question was located some 125 miles west of the Missouri line, far removed from the initial settlements. To make the land more valuable, Reeder determined to locate the capital of Kansas on this land, calling it Pawnee. His personal stake in this site was some 360 acres. Chief Justice Lecompte, one of the few territorial officials not involved in this scheme, warned Cushing of the prospect. The territorial enabling act gave the governor discretion in the location of a temporary capital, but to Lecompte, "The policy of locating the Capital at a point so remote to the west as Pawnee, [was] very questionable." He warned Cushing that this would not "engage the sympathies of the great mass of the population" who were living "between the Missouri line and a meridian eighty miles east of the proposed place."[57]

The arrival in Kansas of the first wave of settlers from the free-states added to the confusion and caused the first violence to occur. Many of these new settlers came from the Midwest, not from the Northeast. Squatters from Missouri often claimed land by placing a few logs as a foundation for a cabin or a series of stakes in the ground before returning home. They intended either to return the following year or, more likely, to speculate in the land and remain residents of Missouri. Newly arrived immigrants, mostly from the free-states, finding the best lands not occupied by actual settlers, appropriated the land to themselves and established their homes. This claim jumping, which occurred on a large scale, was tied to the slavery issue, as groups of proslavery or antislavery people attempted to defend their claims or drive off rival claimants. These conflicts often escalated into destruction of property, theft, and murder, all done in the name of "higher law" or "southern rights," but with land ownership the underlying goal.[58] Even before the election of the territorial legislature, the proslavery *Squatter Sovereign* newspaper proclaimed, "It is a historical fact that almost all the contentions which result in bloodshed in the settlement of a new country, have their origin in some dispute over land claims . . ."[59] Lecompte asked Cushing for some remedy "to protect the public lands, until they are brought into market." He "suggested that every bona fide settler shall be constituted . . . a sort of agent for the government & authorized to prevent the depradations of others."[60]

In this fluid situation, Reeder attempted to take a census of actual settlers, in preparation for the March 30 election of the territorial legislature. Reeder used the census as an excuse to travel about the territory and scout out more land for his own speculation. He also returned to the lands he had attempted to purchase from the half-breeds, to have them sign affidavits attesting to their competency to sell their land without the presence of the Indian agent, an act that Reeder hoped would meet Manypenny's objections to the sales. An eyewitness to one of these encounters wrote Manypenny, "We had quite an amusing affair here . . . for two or three days. . . ." Reeder, accompanied by Justices Johnston and Elmore, swore in a local man as justice of the peace to approve the affidavits. They then had each Frenchman who had married a half-breed wife sign his paper. On approaching

> Po Jim, a very black half breed Kaw, Jim refused to sign his paper saying he had already signed three papers & got no money yet. The Governor then told Jim that in case he refused to sign that paper he . . . would keep both the land and the money too. That raised the *dander* of Jim & he told the Governor to keep it all as he expected he intended to do anyhow, and go to *hell* with it, for he would not sign any more of his d___d papers. This caused the Governor to make an appeal to Jim's sympathies. He told Jim that if he refuse to sign this paper it would ruin both him the Governor & Jim too, but no go, Jim was inexorable & refused

> to sign the affidavit. The Governor then refused to pay the Ferryman his charge—a quarrel ensued & the Ferryman refused to cross him back & we left.[61]

This witness claimed that when Reeder initially approached the half-breeds, he misled them by claiming that only the governor could purchase their lands. The witness also claimed that an agent of Reeder had "purchased a section or two from two little girls about 8 & 10 years old—pieces of the original reserve. He had these little children to sign the deed." Reeder then appointed this same man to be the justice of the peace so that he could attest to the validity of the sales.[62]

The fact that the census was taken in mid-February, when the snow was deep, and that Reeder had failed to give advance notice of the census meant that many Missourians who claimed land were not in the territory to be counted. His five-month delay in authorizing the election to allow free-state settlers to arrive, his land speculation with antislavery leaders, the unannounced census, and his intention to locate the capital far removed from the Missouri line made it clear to proslavery elements that Reeder was not objective in his administration of the territory. On the eve of the election the *Squatter Sovereign* railed at the governor for banning the sale of liquor on election day: "Perhaps the Governor regards the sale of liquor, as he does slavery, as a 'moral, social, and political evil,' and finds the 'Higher Law' power to prohibit the sale of liquor, and to destroy the property of the Grocer and Merchant, as he does the right to prohibit slavery, and steal his neighbors negroes! . . . But in sober earnest does this *man* imagine himself a Monarch." The paper promised "to expose the gross assumption of power, and neglect of duty on the part of Gov. Reeder, ever since he has been in Kansas."[63]

The same paper advised that residency was not a requirement for voting: "By the Kansas act, every man in the Territory on the day of the election is a legal voter, if he have not fixed a day for his return to some other home."[64] Missourians took this interpretation to heart and poured into the territory on the days immediately preceding the election. As many as eight hundred a day ferried across the Missouri River in the three days before the voting.[65] Nearly a thousand descended on the antislavery settlement at Lawrence (named for its benefactor, Amos A. Lawrence), marching to a drumbeat, with banners flying and two fieldpieces to back up their intention to vote. The local election judges withdrew under threat of violence, turning over the poll book. In other locations judges were ordered to turn over the ballot box or be killed. In most locations free-state settlers were too intimidated to vote. Senator Atchison, who had encouraged Missouri voting and was in the territory on election day, exulted in the result: "The pro slavery ticket prevailed everywhere as far as heard from, by overwhelming majorities. We had at least 7,000 men in the territory on the day of the election and one third of them will remain there."[66]

Reeder's imprecise census had counted 2,905 eligible voters in Kansas. On March 30, 6,307 ballots were cast. Thirty-six proslavery legislators along with three free-soilers had been elected. There had been no bloodshed, "though much cocking of revolvers" had been employed by the insurgents. New England Emigrant Aid Company agent S. C. Pomeroy reported, "Missourians in great numbers came over. More than 5,000—not all voted."[67] The question was what would Reeder do about the results? Free-state leader Charles Robinson wrote to Amos A. Lawrence in Massachusetts, "The election is *awful* & will no doubt be set aside. So says the Gov. although his life is threatened if he don't comply with the Missourians demands. I, with others, will act as his body guard tomorrow as that is the day they have set to assassinate him."[68] No attempt to kill Reeder occurred, but he may have been intimidated enough to certify most of the election results, setting aside the vote in only six districts and ordering new elections there on May 22. Importing voters (Charles Robinson had also brought into Kansas nearly one hundred free-state voters on election day) and committing fraud was typical of U.S. elections at that time, particularly in the territories and in eastern cities. The proslavery forces might have won an honest election in this early period of Kansas settlement if there had been a consensus as to what was fair. But by ensuring their victory with blatant voter fraud and threats of violence, the Missourians had gone too far.[69]

Reeder was in a precarious position. Proslavery interests were demanding his ouster and Missourians had threatened his life, while his land speculation scheme and dispute with Manypenny had been presented to the president and to the Congress.[70] In mid-April 1855, Reeder fled east, seeking assurances of support from the president and from the press. His first stop was in his home town of Easton, Pennsylvania, where on April 30 he made a speech that recounted the recent election frauds and criticized the Missouri ruffians for subverting the democratic process and the principle of popular sovereignty. Reeder reached Washington on May 4, and spent the next two weeks in the capital, meeting frequently with Pierce and members of his cabinet.[71]

Pierce was placed in an untenable position. He had Manypenny's very recent account of Reeder's land speculation, which the governor acknowledged but defended as legal. The Indian commissioner had written to Reeder, "I had no idea that the most material of the charges (the speculation of Territorial Officials in these half-breed lands) would have been so soon admitted and that, too, under the signature of one of them, the Governor of the Territory himself, candidly confessing the truth. Still less, Sir, did I expect that whilst making this confession on behalf of yourself and Associated speculators you would have had the boldness and bad taste to attempt a defense of the morality and propriety of the Acts!"[72] Pierce would have certainly fired Reeder immediately on receiving Manypenny's most recent report if not for the grossly illegal activity of the Missourians in the elections in Kansas. Public opinion in the North was so aroused by the activity in Kansas that Pierce's dismissal of Reeder for land speculation would be viewed as simply a pretext to get rid of an obstacle to the designs of the proslavery forces there. Pierce was under enormous pressure from both sides. Besides Reeder, who was seeking approval of his course in Kansas, Pierce also had to contend with David Atchison, who had traveled to Washington to demand the governor's removal. Within his own family, Pierce was pressured to support Reeder. Amos A. Lawrence had written the president, praising Reeder for declining "to be used as an agent of this illegal combination" and urging "the Government to sustain him in the position in which he [was] placed in the performance of his duty."[73] Lawrence's stepmother, Jane Pierce's aunt and an outspoken Whig, was staying at the White House that spring and was accompanied for a time by Lawrence's brother, William Lawrence, and his business partner, Robert M. Mason, who reported that Pierce was upset that Amos "was mixed up in that business."[74] In mid-May Amos traveled to Washington to meet with Reeder and with the president. Amos reported that he was "well satisfied" by his discussion with Reeder and that the president and his cabinet were "all right on that question & determined to support their agent."[75]

In his frequent and intensive discussions with Reeder over the two-week period, Pierce expressed outrage at the actions of the Missourians in Kansas and appeared, to Reeder, to be supportive, though Pierce did take the governor to task for his land speculation and for his speech in Easton, which was too one-sided for the president's liking. According to Reeder, Pierce "stated that this Kansas matter had given him more harassing anxiety than anything that had happened since the loss of his son; that it haunted him day and night, and was the great overshadowing trouble of his administration."[76] The fact that Reeder had certified most of the election results, despite the reports of massive voter fraud, was also a problem. It should have been clear to Reeder that Pierce wanted him to resign, especially when the president drafted a resignation letter for Reeder. In it, Pierce recommended that Reeder submit a report in which he narrate the course of events in Kansas, including the "interposition of Emigrant Aid Society to *force* a solution on one side," which was followed by the "reactionary interposition of citizens of Missouri to *force* a solution on the other side." Reeder was then to explain his actions in administering the law and "his necessary antagonism to all foreign interference from any of the States." Pierce, next, instructed Reeder to "explain and vindicate himself from specific charges." Regarding the recent election, Reeder was to explain that since he had certified most of the election results, even the subsequent "inflammation of the public mind" regarding the matter did not eliminate the "difficulty of suggesting any means by which the President can interpose in election frauds or votes." Finally, Pierce asked Reeder to conclude with his "readiness to return but in view of excitement & prejudice if appointment of another person would seem to be for the public interest ready to resign so that completion of the organization of the Gov. of the Territory may be conducted by a new man. . . . " Pierce continued with this instruction: "In this connection put distinctly considerations of personal dignity & duty."[77]

Despite the intense negotiation, Reeder refused to resign, and Pierce would not fire him. Pierce was not getting definitive advice from his cabinet on the Reeder situation, as reflected by Marcy's letter to Buchanan: "The condition of things in Kansas is very unpropitious. I confess I cannot see a favorable issue to the difficulties which have there arisen. If Governor Reeder goes back to the Territory, as I think he will, there is some reason to fear that he will be ill-treated, and his authority condemned. To supersede him I am quite sure would produce consequences as mischievous as the worst effects which would attend his return."[78] While Reeder was in Washington, more information about his land purchases was arriving at the Indian Office from agents in Kansas.[79] This new information gave Pierce a way out of the situation. Reeder would be allowed to return to Kansas, but Marcy and Cushing would launch an official investigation into Manypenny's charges against the governor. Cushing addressed letters to Reeder, Justices Johnston and Elmore, and District Attorney Isaacs, stating, "These transactions being apparently in violation of acts of Congress and of regulations of the Departments the President feels embarrassed to see how, consistently with his convictions of duty, he can allow the present official relations to the Territory of yourself, or of either of the other gentlemen named to continue, unless the impressions, which now rest upon his mind, shall be removed by satisfactory explanations."[80] Reeder returned to Kansas in time for the opening of the legislative session in early July. The legislature convened at Pawnee, Reeder's chosen capital, despite the fact that the building provided for them lacked ventilation and that housing was inadequate. Faced with meeting out of doors in the stifling heat while living in tents or sleeping in wagons, the mostly proslavery legislators were in no mood to compromise with Reeder. In the four days that they stayed at Pawnee, they invalidated the elections of most of the free-soil members and then voted to move the capital to Shawnee Mission on the Missouri border near Fort Leavenworth. After overriding Reeder's veto, the legislature reconvened at its new location in mid-July.[81]

Reeder then proceeded to veto all the acts of the legislature. Regarding a bill to incorporate a ferry across the Missouri River,

Reeder first noted that he saw "nothing in the bill itself to prevent [his] sanction of it," but, according to Reeder, "since the legislature [was] meeting in an unlawful place," all of its acts were illegal.[82] In turn, the legislature overrode all of Reeder's vetoes, adopted the Missouri law code, and enacted a strict slave code, which included two years at hard labor for writing or circulating anti-slavery material and the death penalty for inciting a slave rebellion.[83] The animosity between Reeder and the legislature was so pronounced that at one point proslavery leader Benjamin Stringfellow challenged the governor to a duel. When Reeder declined, Stringfellow knocked him down, and the two men wrestled to the floor, each man drawing his pistol before witnesses intervened.[84]

The situation was deteriorating to the point that free-state leaders asked the New England Emigrant Aid Company to supply them with weapons: "I wish we had a couple of hundred of Sharp's rifles for the purpose of protection. Government has left us without protection, and we are a prey to a set of heartless wretches a thousand times more devilish than the arch fiend himself."[85] Charles Robinson wrote to Amos A. Lawrence, "There is a loud talk of *war* . . . and if I believed half I hear I should suppose that I could not possibly live 24 hours."[86] Lawrence was distressed by the news from Kansas and by the change in attitude of the administration toward Reeder. Lawrence wrote to Pierce's brother-in-law, Professor Packard, "It is with reluctance that I conclude that the settlers must protect their own liberty by force of arms."[87] Lawrence proceeded to send Sharp's rifles, the most modern weapon available, to the Emigrant Aid Company officials in Kansas.

Lawrence wrote another lengthy letter to President Pierce, defending Reeder's land speculation. Admitting he did not know "what the law is to which you refer in Mr. Marcy's communication to Gov. Reeder," Lawrence concluded that "it must have become obsolete or nearly so from nonobservance & from not having been enforced in other cases. It is well known that for many years it has been the practice of Govt & army officers who are sent to the Territories to invest money for themselves & for their friends in lands & without any concealment."[88] Concluding that the charges against Reeder "are as unjust as they are untrue," Lawrence went on to explain "The Govt has kept so far aloof as to force the settlers to the conclusion that if they wd. be safe they must defend themselves: & therefore many persons here who refused at first (myself among them) have rendered them assistance by furnishing them means of defence."[89]

Lawrence may have been accurate in describing the land speculation of government officials in other territories, but Reeder's "obviously fraudulent activities" involved Indian reserves and half-breed allotments and came under a different set of laws and the supervision of the implacable Manypenny. Indian agent Clarke's letter of May 8 had charged that Reeder had continued to speculate in Indian reserves even after Manypenny had denied his initial purchase of the half-breed lands. Reeder's reply to the charges was addressed to Marcy on June 26. Pierce was not satisfied and, in Marcy's absence (the Secretary was vacationing at Old Point Comfort, Virginia), had the acting secretary of state dismiss Reeder in the president's name: "After due consideration of the explanations which you offer in regard to your purchase of Kansas half-breed lands, and the facts in the case as reported to him and communicated to you by the Department of the Interior, he finds nothing in these explanations to remove the impressions which he had previously entertained of the character of the transactions."[90] Among the additional charges was that Reeder had undergone "to lay out new Cities on military or other reservations" and "had summoned the Legislative Assembly . . . to meet at one of the places referred to" while the purchases "were undergoing official investigation within that Territory." Reeder had offered no explanations to these additional charges.[91] Reeder's removal was followed immediately by the firings of his partners in speculation, Justices Elmore and Johnston and District Attorney Isaacs.[92]

Two days before Pierce fired Reeder, the Kansas legislature had sent a memorial to the president, demanding Reeder's removal. The memorial had no impact on Pierce's decision, as it arrived in Washington days after Reeder was removed, but its focus on Reeder's land speculation attests to its central role in the governor's downfall. The legislators charged that Reeder had begun his illegal speculation from his first day in the territory, had continued it even after being informed it was illegal by his superiors in Washington, and had used the excuse of preparing for a census to travel the territory for the purpose of "speculation, for he was known to be a large shareholder in many of the various town companies throughout the territory." The legislature blamed Reeder for "setting an example of insubordination," which had touched off the subsequent events in the territory.[93]

When Reeder was fired, Jefferson Davis was also out of town, attending to political matters in his home state of Mississippi. While there he countered claims that he had induced Pierce to fire Reeder. In a letter to a friend he wrote, "No fair man can ascribe the action of the President [in removing Reeder] to an unworthy pursuit of popularity; and I hope indeed, confidentially trust, that my fellow citizens of Mississippi will appreciate the Executive who, regardless of consequences, moves steadily, firmly and quietly on to the full discharge of his duty."[94]

The actions of what they called the "bogus" legislature and the dismissal of Reeder caused the free-state leaders to decide that they must resist the territorial government. They met first in late August at Big Springs, where Reeder, openly committed to the free-state cause and his own investments, offered a resolution that the Free-State Party ignore the territorial legislature and create its own. Free-state leaders also proposed to elect their own representative to Congress and nominated Reeder for that post. Another resolution that passed prohibited the emigration of free blacks to Kansas. One member later recalled that the free-state men's "hatred of slavery was not as strong as their hatred of Negroes."[95] They then boycotted the territorial legislature's election for a representative to Congress, which reelected Whitfield, and a week later held their own election, in which Reeder was chosen without opposition as the Free-State Party's representative.[96]

In the meantime, Pierce was considering a replacement for Reeder. After consultation with Senators Douglas and Mason on August 10, Pierce announced the appointment of Wilson Shannon the next day. Unlike Reeder, Shannon had considerable political experience, as the former governor of Ohio, representative in Congress, and minister to Mexico. Manypenny's endorsement of his Ohio political ally must have reassured Pierce that Shannon would avoid illegal land speculation. Shannon had also voted for the Kansas-Nebraska bill during his one term in the House. Maintaining geographic balance in his territorial officials, Pierce chose I. M. Burrell of Pennsylvania and Sterling G. Cato of Alabama for the vacant judgeships in the territory.[97]

The news from Kansas that free-state settlers were planning to establish their own government caused Lawrence some anxiety. Writing to Charles Robinson, he admitted that at first he thought the plan to set up a "Free-state" was "just the thing," but with Pierce's appointment of the experienced Shannon, Lawrence feared putting the free-state cause "in collision with the United States."[98] Lawrence knew the president well enough to know how Pierce would react to any extralegal political movement. Nevertheless, in October 1855 the "Free-state" movement proceeded to hold at Topeka a convention in which the delegates created the "free and independent . . . *State of Kansas*." The Topeka constitution was ratified by free-state voters in December.[99] In his journal, Lawrence wrote, "I have never encouraged the project of establishing a State organization before Kansas is admitted to the Union, foreseeing that it would probably lead to a collision with the U. States Government, but the Topeka Convention was called and a free Constitution was formed and now we must do the best we can to help it along."[100] The battle lines had been drawn in Kansas. Two alternative governments existed: "The regularly constituted but fraudulently elected proslavery territorial government, and the illegal, unauthorized, Topeka free-state government."[101] Governor Shannon and the Pierce administration would have to deal with the consequences. With many new congressmen elected for their outspoken hostility to the Kansas-Nebraska Act heading to Washington for the opening of the Thirty-fourth Congress in December 1855, the already tempestuous political climate would become even more chaotic and violent.

9

FILIBUSTERS, RECRUITMENT

ALONG WITH THE mounting contentiousness, chaos, and violence in Kansas the craze of filibustering, unique to the 1850s, was reaching its high point in 1855 and adding to the legal, political, and diplomatic pressures on the Pierce administration. Though Cuba was still a target of the filibusters, Central America became the scene of their most aggressive and temporarily successful venture. The pitifully weak and inept governments in the region created a vacuum of power that almost invited intervention. With the United States and Great Britain in a diplomatic standoff over policy in the region, American adventurers viewed the local conditions as ideal for their schemes of glory and plunder.

The most ambitious of these schemes at the beginning of 1855 was the Central American Land and Mining Company, headed by Colonel Henry L. Kinney. Kinney claimed to have received a large grant of land in Mosquitia, that part of Nicaragua that was set aside for the Indians and that was under British protection. He was openly seeking settlers to join his company and move to Nicaragua. At first the Pierce administration did not know what to make of Kinney's enterprise. Was his land grant legitimate, and were his aims peaceful? Marcy's initial investigation of Kinney's project failed to uncover any illegality, and Marcy stated in the *Union* that the government had no right to interfere in a peaceful migration.[1]

This seeming endorsement emboldened Kinney to become more aggressive in his planning. From his headquarters at the National Hotel in Washington, D.C., he was reported to be examining weapons for use in his expedition. He claimed to have over seven hundred emigrants ready to sail from Baltimore at the end of January. These reports caused Pierce and Marcy to become more assertive in examining Kinney's intentions. They called Kinney to the White House and found him to be evasive regarding the location of his land grants. On January 27, Marcy demanded that Kinney provide a letter outlining all of the particulars of his enterprise. Kinney's response, written the next day, was still vague as to where he was going, but he announced his purpose "to establish municipal regulations for the immediate government of the colonists."[2] This statement was Kinney's undoing, as it alerted the Pierce administration of his hostile purpose of replacing local government with his own.

On February 7, the *Union* published another opinion from Marcy, warning that Kinney's stated purpose would "be in contravention of our neutrality laws, and all those engaged in it [would] subject themselves to severe penalties."[3] He also warned that if the emigrants got in trouble with the Indians, the British, or the Nicaraguan authorities, the United States government would not protect them.[4] This effectively put a stop to Kinney's public recruiting and delayed his departure, but his planning for a scaled-down expedition went on. When Kinney was discovered recruiting in New York, Attorney General Cushing had District Attorney John McKeon indict Kinney on April 27 on a charge of fitting out a military expedition against the republic of Nicaragua. Joseph W. Fabens, U.S. commercial agent in Central America, who had become secretary of the company, was called to Washington to explain his involvement to Marcy. In the meantime, Fabens was also indicted in New York. He was arrested in Washington by the U.S. marshal and returned to New York. Marcy removed Fabens from his position as commercial agent.[5]

Knowing that juries rarely convicted filibusters, Kinney and Fabens demanded an immediate trial. McKeon asked for a postponement to gather up his witnesses. The judge refused the postponement and, when McKeon insisted he was not ready to proceed, discharged Kinney and Fabens on their own recognizance. They traveled to Philadelphia, where Kinney immediately began recruiting, only to be indicted again by U.S. Attorney James C. Van Dyke. Kinney's attorney, former vice president George M. Dallas, managed to get Kinney freed on a bail of $4,500.[6] Kinney returned to New York where he planned to slip away in the steamer *United States*, which was bound for Nicaragua. Federal authorities were one step ahead of him, however, and on May 25, 1855, Pierce directed McKeon and Captain Charles Boarman of the navy to detain the *United States* and seize Kinney.[7]

Three navy warships and a revenue cutter blockaded the *United States* in New York harbor for the next six weeks. Kinney and Fabens failed to show up for the start of their trial in New York on June 5. They were both arrested the following day, but the trial was again postponed, and they were once again released on bail. Fabens and Fletcher Webster, Daniel Webster's son and an investor in Kinney's enterprise, traveled to Washington to lobby with Pierce for release of the *United States*. In the meantime, unbeknownst to Fabens, Kinney slipped away in the dead of night on the schooner *Emma* with about twenty-five men.[8] Fabens wrote to Kinney that he had returned to New York "in season for court, presented myself & could not get a trial—of course—yesterday being the last day of the term, I was discharged in full, so ends that farce." He reported, "[Fletcher] Webster & I have been in Washington for a week, Pierce—poor devil is frightened half out of his boots. He trembles for himself & for his brave companions in arms."[9] As usual, Pierce was caught between his desire to please close associates who were investing in a scheme and his understanding of the law. Fabens eventually made his way to Greytown, where he met up with Kinney and his scaled-down expedition which ultimately failed to accomplish anything. With Kinney and Fabens both gone, Pierce ordered the release of the *United States* on July 12.[10] The ship's captain had sent to Congress a memorial containing more than eight thousand signatures, demanding damages be paid by the government for income lost while his ship was detained.[11]

The Pierce administration had broken up another filibuster, but as usual the president paid a price for enforcing the laws. One of his own officials (Fabens) was an officer of the company; his good friend Fletcher Webster lobbied Pierce to approve the enterprise; his own secretary, Sidney Webster, was rumored to be an investor in the scheme, as was A. O. P. Nicholson, publisher of the *Union*; another friend and political supporter, George M. Dallas was the attorney for the filibusters; and Kinney had the enthusiastic support of southern Democrats and the Hard faction in New York. But Pierce never wavered in his determination to enforce the neutrality laws. When Marcy requested a special appropriation of $500 from a contingency fund to help McKeon in the "prosecution of the suit of the United States vs. Kinney," Pierce scribbled at the bottom of the note, "Let the advance be made as requested."[12] Knowing that the public sympathized with the lawbreakers, and that convictions in court were impossible, federal district attorneys used indictments and postponements as a delaying tactic. Since ship captains were happy to convey filibusters for a price, the navy had to be called out to intercept ships suspected of transporting lawbreakers, but this also delayed legitimate passengers and cargo. In all, preventing filibusters was an unpopular, expensive, and thankless task that gained the administration no credit, even in diplomatic circles, where the involvement of so many men close to the administration was seen as evidence of its collusion in the enterprise. Lord Clarendon, British foreign minister, reported to Prime Minister Palmerston that Kinney had been "of course operating under secret instruction" from Washington. Nicaragua's minister to Washington "bypassed the president entirely" and appealed to former Whig secretary of state John M. Clayton, now a U.S. senator, for help in stopping Kinney's expedition.[13]

It was one thing to stop filibuster expeditions from the East Coast, but communication being what it was, stopping similar expeditions leaving the West Coast was even more difficult. Thus, while Kinney's plan was being thwarted in Washington, New York, and Philadelphia, William Walker, leader of the failed filibuster to Sonora in 1853, was able to slip away from federal officials and sail from San Francisco in late May 1855 with fifty-seven men bound for the west coast of Nicaragua. Walker took advantage of the civil war going on in Nicaragua to obtain a contract from one of the warring parties, the Liberals, to bring in Americans to settle, become naturalized, and fight on the Liberal side. At first the Pierce administration did not view the Walker expedition with as much alarm as it did Kinney's more grandiose plans, but the charismatic Walker was soon reinforced by more Americans, many of them miners crossing the isthmus bound for the California gold fields, and his forces began to have an impact on the civil war in Nicaragua.[14]

John A. Quitman, whose plans for a filibuster to Cuba had been postponed a year earlier due to the actions of the Pierce administration and Supreme Court Justice Campbell, was determined to launch his expedition in the spring of 1855. The failure of the Ostend meeting to make any progress toward acquisition of the island made Quitman's supporters more determined than ever to proceed. But the obstacles in his way were even more formidable in the winter of 1855, as the Pierce administration was working closely with Spanish authorities to foil Quitman's plans.

Based on intelligence provided by the Spanish consul in New York, in late January the steamer *Massachusetts* was seized by U.S. revenue officers and marshals off the coast of New Jersey. The ship was loaded with weapons, ammunition, and provisions bound for Quitman in New Orleans. Officials confiscated the cargo, effectively disrupting the New York branch of Quitman's enterprise. Faced with the overt opposition of the Pierce administration, Quitman traveled to Washington to lobby with friendly congressmen and senators to pressure the administration to back off. He induced Senator Albert G. Brown of Mississippi, a political opponent of Jefferson Davis, to sponsor a bill to repeal sections of the neutrality laws. Senator Slidell's resolution in 1854 to allow the president to temporarily suspend the neutrality laws had failed, and Brown found the going even tougher in 1855. The new Spanish administration in Cuba had backed away from the "Africanization" policy, and with the threat of the abolition of slavery on the island lessened, many southern politicians no longer viewed Cuba as a priority. Brown's bill, introduced on March 3, was never voted on.[15]

Convinced of the imminence of Quitman's invasion, Spanish officials in Cuba imposed a blockade of its coast. On March 6, the U.S. mail steamship *El Dorado* was stopped, boarded, and searched by a Spanish navy corvette eight miles off the coast. The Pierce administration protested the action, claiming the *El Dorado* was outside Cuban territorial waters. Marcy's strongly worded letter warned the Spanish minister that the United States would resist any searches of American commercial vessels, as it had previously when the British navy attempted to search American ships off the coast of Africa in enforcing treaties against the slave trade. Pierce instructed Navy secretary Dobbin to dispatch vessels to Havana as a show of strength to back up Marcy's letter.[16]

Quite by accident, Pierce ran into Quitman one day in March during one of the president's frequent walks along Pennsylvania Avenue. The two talked about Cuba, and Pierce invited Quitman to continue the discussion at the White House. When Quitman arrived a few days later for his appointment, he was surprised to find Marcy and Spanish minister to the United States, L. A. del Cueta, along with the president. They shared with Quitman details of the military buildup in Cuba. This information and Pierce's determination to prevent the expedition finally convinced Quitman of the hopelessness of his enterprise. He traveled back to New Orleans and formally presented his resignation to the Cuban junta on April 29.[17] Though Pierce had failed to acquire Cuba, an impossibility in any case short of conquest, he had finally convinced the Spanish government of his peaceful intentions. Spanish authorities canceled their blockade of the Cuban coast. Pierce's actions in preventing a filibuster of the island had also saved the lives of dozens of Americans who would have certainly perished had they managed to reach Cuba.

As if Pierce did not have enough crises to deal with in 1855, an entirely unnecessary internal conflict within the administration required the president's careful scrutiny and personal diplomacy. The relationship between Secretary of War Jefferson Davis and the commanding General of the Army, Winfield Scott, was doomed from the start. Not only did Pierce inherit Scott, his defeated opponent in 1852, as American commanding general, but his secretary of war had a personal grudge against the vain, pedantic, and contentious Scott. Davis had been briefly married to General Zachary Taylor's daughter in the 1830s before her untimely death. During the Mexican War he had served under his former father-in-law and developed both admiration and affection for Taylor. He came to share Taylor's hatred of Scott, whom Davis believed had stripped Taylor's army of its strength and built up his own army for the Mexico City campaign to claim all the credit and glory for himself. After the war, Scott lobbied "with almost indecent eagerness" for promotion to lieutenant general, a rank that had been held by only one other American, George Washington. As a senator Davis had outspokenly opposed Scott's promotion.[18]

Adding to the potential for conflict between Davis and Scott was the nebulous relationship between the offices of secretary of war and commanding general. As Allan Peskin notes, "The office of commanding general . . . was an anomaly. Its authority was undefined by statute, and its functions had been shaped more by accidents of personality and circumstance than by conscious design. Its creation had been something of an afterthought, and its utility was often questioned by a skeptical Congress."[19] Scott's first action following Pierce's inauguration in March 1853 was to move his headquarters from Washington to New York City. He had previously relocated to New York during the Taylor administration but had returned under Fillmore. Despite the distance between them, both physical and personal, Davis was determined to rein in his commanding general. He wanted Scott to understand that the chain of command ran from the president through the secretary of war to the commanding general and that Scott could not bypass the secretary of war in exercising his authority. In May 1853 Davis had rejected Scott's travel vouchers, which totaled $577.60, because the trips had not been authorized by his "proper superiors."[20] Scott claimed he had no superior officers, but Davis was determined to demonstrate that the military was under civilian control. Scott continued to press his claim to the expenses for the next two years.[21]

Davis next challenged Scott's Mexican War accounts, claiming that the commanding general must return over $6,000 in cash he had retained from the money sent for him to carry out his duties in Mexico. Scott claimed the money was his according to "the laws and usages of war."[22] Scott and Davis pressed the case in person to the president, who appeared sympathetic to each in turn. This matter was left also undecided until 1855.[23]

This increasingly bitter feud reached extraordinary levels of petulance and vindictiveness after Scott finally was awarded the rank of lieutenant general by Congress in March 1855. Pierce sent the nomination to the Senate in February: "For eminent services in the late war with Mexico, I nominate Major-General Winfield Scott, . . . to be Lieutenant-General by brevet . . . to take rank as such from March 29, 1847, the day on which the United States forces under his command captured Vera Cruz and the Castle of San Juan de Ulua."[24]

The Senate quickly confirmed the promotion. But even the generous nomination by his political adversary in 1852 did not mollify Scott. He had been lobbying on his own behalf in Washington throughout the winter, but Pierce, always conscious of symbols, waited until Washington's birthday to send in the nomination. According to George Templeton Strong, "General Scott took the President's delay in sending in his name to the Senate for the new office of lieutenant-general in high dudgeon, and went back to Baltimore on the 21st, not understanding that it was intended to pay him a sort of compliment by selecting the 22nd as the date of the nomination."[25]

The day after his promotion was confirmed, Scott submitted a bill to the paymaster general for $26,661.72 of back pay. Davis, claiming the promotion was intended to be honorary, rejected the claim. Davis also argued that the rank of lieutenant-general had been repealed in 1802 and, therefore, there was no pay scale attached to the revived rank. Scott argued that the pay scale existing the last time there was a lieutenant-general was revived by his promotion. On April 26, 1855, Davis wrote that he had "referred to the Attorney General" Scott's "claim for brevet pay as lieutenant general" and invited Scott to make his own case directly Cushing.[26] Both men submitted massive briefs to Cushing, Scott's totaling thirty-three printed pages with six attachments and eight endorsements, including several from former attorneys general. It would take Cushing several months to wade through all of the arguments and produce an equally detailed and carefully reasoned decision.[27]

It may seem that Davis was consumed by the conflict with Scott, but in reality the spring and summer of 1855 was his most creative and forward-looking period as secretary of war. In April, with the Crimean War raging, he convinced Pierce to authorize a three-man commission to travel to Europe to observe the military forces of England, France, Prussia, Austria, and Russia. Davis's detailed instructions directed Majors R. Delafield, A. Mordecai, and Captain George B. McClellan to study every aspect of the European armies, including organization, weapons, tactics, training, equipment, and transportation.[28] One military historian termed the trip "the most ambitious military mission of the ante-bellum era," while another expert in military intelligence claims, "This was the first time . . . that military officers were detached from service to perform intelligence collection missions abroad in peace time."[29] Each of the three officers produced a detailed report of the mission, and McClellan returned with a saddle later adopted for use by the U.S. cavalry. He also translated the complete Russian manual.[30]

In May, Davis assigned Major Henry C. Wayne of the quartermaster's office to special duty. In November 1853 Wayne had recommended to Davis the use of camels by the army to transport supplies in the arid southwest: "By the use of the Camel, we can double the average of our daily journeys at a first cost not beyond that now incurred with a diminishing expenditure for teamsters & c, and almost nothing for forage & by the aid of the Dromedary we shall be able to traverse long distances in a short time.[31]

In 1855, Davis ordered Wayne to proceed to the Levant, where he was to acquire camels, and then to return to Texas, where Wayne was placed in charge of training them for use. A navy ship, captained by Lieutenant David Dixon Porter, was assigned to carry Wayne and the camels. The expedition was gone for nearly a year, but returned with thirty-three camels to Indianola, Texas, in May 1856. Wayne immediately sent one camel into the town to transport hay back to the camp. The curious residents watched as the kneeling animal was loaded with four bales of hay weighing 1,256 pounds. The camel then rose easily and walked off with its load. The initial success of the experiment prompted Davis to order Porter back to the Middle East for more camels. Porter returned to Texas with forty-one animals in February 1857. While Davis's successor tried to continue the program, the experiment ended with the Civil War. Pierce did get some new socks from the project. A Mrs. Mary A. Sharkey of Victoria, Texas, observed the camels marching through her town and managed to collect enough hair from the shedding animals to spin into yarn, from which she knitted the president a pair of socks. These were mailed to Major Wayne, who passed them through the secretary of war's office and on to the president.[32]

The correspondence between Scott and Davis became even more

heated in July, when Davis learned that Scott had granted General Ethan Allen Hitchcock a four-month leave from his post at Fort Pierre without consulting the secretary of war. Davis complained that Hitchcock could not be spared "on the eve of a campaign against the Indians" in the region.[33] Scott took offense at Davis's letter claiming the secretary of war should only "speak in the name of the President." He continued, "In the very dogmatic letter before me I do not perceive the slightest allusion to the wishes or instructions of the constitutional commander-in-chief."[34] Davis answered, "The President speaks and acts through the heads of the several Departments . . . the Secretary is in legal contemplation the act of the President, and as such claims to be respected and obeyed."

He ordered Scott to "revoke" the leave of absence and added, "I leave unnoticed the exhibition of peevish temper in your reply . . ."[35] Scott replied that Davis was attempting "to goad" Scott "into some perilous attitude of official opposition" and that Davis's "partisan hostility" was "thinking to entrap" him.[36] Davis fired back that Scott's correspondence was "the most memorable example on the records of this Department of a vain controversialist, defeated, and a false accuser exposed." He went on in the next twenty-seven pages to outline all of Scott's failings.[37] It was Scott's turn to escalate the conflict by attacking Davis for his "spleen and vengeance" and labeling his previous letter "savage and scurrilous."[38] Scott's letter addressed all of the issues between them at equally great length. Considering the volume of correspondence, it is a wonder than any other work got done during the summer and fall of 1855.

Finally, in late August Cushing submitted his opinion on Scott's claim for the "pay and emoluments" of a lieutenant-general. In forty printed pages, which analyzed all of the legal precedents and included references to Roman law and English practices, Cushing agreed with Scott that the pay of the rank of lieutenant general had been "revived" by Scott's new rank.[39] Before giving in, Davis appealed directly to Pierce. In another lengthy summation of his arguments he concluded, "It appears to me that the Attorney General . . . has too hastily taken it for granted that the lieutenant generalship was the only office established by the statute, that the pay was attached to it, and that the office has been revived."[40] Despite Davis's final plea, Pierce decided Scott "is entitled to the pay and allowances of his brevet rank since March 29, 1847."[41] Pierce did eliminate most of the perquisites Scott had been claiming, awarding the general a total of $10,465.67.[42] Pierce also directed Davis to pay Scott the money for the travel vouchers. In addition, Pierce ruled on Scott's Mexican War accounts, writing to Davis, "In the settlement of General Scott's account he is hereby authorized to retain the entire sum of six thousand one hundred and forty nine dollars and eighty six cent."[43]

In a separate opinion, Cushing concluded in Davis's favor regarding orders given to General Scott, stating that "the direction of the President is to be presumed in all instructions and orders issued from the competent Department" and all such orders "are valid and lawful, without containing express reference to the direction of the President."[44]

Davis was not satisfied with this partial victory and threatened to resign. According to Varina Davis, Pierce walked over one evening and convinced Davis to stay on by accepting full responsibility for the decisions. Though Pierce had been eminently fair to Scott, even risking the resignation of his good friend Davis to rule in Scott's favor, the vindictive general later called Pierce "the meanest creature that ever aspired to be President."[45] Scott and Davis continued the ludicrous bickering, with Davis accusing Scott of "querulousness, insubordination, greed of lucre and want of truth." He declared that Scott's reputation had been "clouded by grovelling vices" and criticized his "petulance, characteristic egotism and recklessness of accusation," to which Scott replied, "Compassion is always due to an enraged imbecile, who lays about him in blows which hurt only himself, or who, at the worst, seeks to stifle his opponent by the dint of naughty words."[46] In December 1856 Congress added the final embarrassment by calling for all the correspondence and publishing it in a 254-page volume for the entire country to read.[47]

Relations with Great Britain continued to deteriorate throughout 1855. The president pressed Marcy and Buchanan to settle the disagreements over Central America, where British claims to the Bay Islands, Mosquitia, Greytown, and Belize violated U.S. interpretation of the Clayton-Bulwer Treaty. The British administration, however, rejected the U.S. interpretation of the treaty, and Buchanan had made no progress pressing the matter in London. The Crimean War added to the growing difficulties between the two nations. The British had been fighting the war with volunteer troops. The fall of Sevastopol in October 1854, despite the gallant charge of the Light Brigade at Balaklava, had depressed public opinion in Great Britain and France regarding the war, and the number of men volunteering to serve decreased. In response, on December 23, 1854, Parliament passed the Foreign Enlistment Act. British consul at Philadelphia, George B. Mathews, suggested recruiting in the United States, but John Crampton, British minister to Washington, was not enthusiastic about the prospect. He understood that U.S. neutrality laws, which the British condemned Pierce for not enforcing in Latin America, were an obstacle to successful recruiting in the United States.[48]

Nevertheless, Crampton followed his instructions from foreign minister Lord Clarendon and promised "to make the experiment on a moderate scale, and without any risk of being charged with a violation of the Neutrality Laws of the United States."[49] Those laws prohibited "hiring or retaining" recruits within the United States for service in foreign armies without the formal approval of the government. Crampton had taken the precaution of consulting with his Washington attorney, J. Mandeville Carlisle, who had advised that men could be conveyed to a foreign location where the actual enlistment would take place. Crampton proceeded to communicate with the governor of Nova Scotia, who agreed to set up an enlistment station in Halifax. The governor also sent Joseph Howe to Washington to coordinate the recruitment within the United States. Howe, in turn, selected agents in major cities to establish recruiting offices from which men would be shipped to Halifax, where they would enlist, with their passage paid by the British government.[50] Crampton was impressed with Howe, calling him "a sharp and active man who seems well qualified for the work we have in hand," and reported to Clarendon on March 12, 1855, "I am hard at work on the subject of recruitment."[51]

Howe proved more aggressive and less circumspect than Crampton, however, and within weeks his agents had attracted the attention of the U.S. government by their open advertising for men. On March 22, Marcy was shocked to learn from New York district attorney

John McKeon that handbills offering bounties for enlistment into the British army to natives of the British Isles and Germany had been circulating in New York and that a "passage office" had been established on Pearl Street.[52] Marcy turned the matter over to Attorney General Cushing, who advised McKeon, "Any such enlistment is contrary to law." Cushing had consulted with Pierce: "He has accordingly directed me to address you at once in order to prevent delay, and to desire you to take proper and lawful steps in your discretion to bring to punishment all persons engaged in such enlistments within your District."[53] Cushing followed this with a similar letter to district attorney Van Dyke in Philadelphia.[54]

Marcy and Crampton met on March 23, with the British minister assuring the secretary of state that he disapproved of the recruiting and had addressed a letter to his consul in New York to stop all such activity. Marcy impressed upon Crampton that the neutrality laws would be strictly enforced.[55] But the recruiting went on, only more secretly, over the next few months. Crampton had been advised by Clarendon "to have no concealment" from Marcy on the matter, and Crampton misled his own foreign minister by assuring him, "I am upon a perfectly good understanding with Mr. Marcy on this subject."[56] In May Crampton went a step further by traveling to Halifax to personally take over the recruiting project from Howe. Crampton sent his chargé d'affaires to Marcy's house to assure Marcy that the trip was intended to prevent any violations of U.S. neutrality laws and to present Marcy with a copy of Lord Clarendon's most recent instructions on the subject.[57] But Marcy was increasingly alarmed by reports that recruiting was continuing, and in late May he confidentially addressed Buchanan in London on the subject for the first time writing, "It is now no longer a matter of doubt that British agents have been engaged, with the approval of their Government, in recruiting soldiers for its army in the Crimea within the limits of the United States. . . . Great Britain has agents employed in violating our laws within our own borders."[58]

Adding to the confusion over interpretation of the neutrality laws was a ruling by U.S. Circuit Court Judge Kane in Philadelphia. On May 22, in a preliminary hearing to determine if recruiting agents should be held for trial, Kane stated that while enlistment carried out in the United States was a violation of the law, conversations to promote enlistment and paying someone to travel to Halifax were not.[59] Kane's ruling emboldened Crampton to think that he was successfully avoiding violating the law. Over the next few months, Crampton's activities continued. In all, he disbursed £5250 from his secret service account to pay his agents, who secured several hundred men and transported them to Halifax.[60]

In June Marcy formally instructed Buchanan to address Clarendon on the recruiting issue. Marcy asked Buchanan to assert that recruiting was more than just a violation of the neutrality laws, as it demonstrated lack of "respect for our obligations of neutrality" and was against "the comity due to us as a friendly power": "The President will be much pleased to learn that her Majesty's government has not authorized the proceedings herein complained of; and has condemned the conduct of her officials engaged therein, called them to account, and taken most decisive measures to put a stop to the illegal and disrespectful procedure."[61] As soon as he received Marcy's directive, Buchanan met with Clarendon, who assured him that there was no intention to violate U.S. neutrality laws and that Clarendon had sent an envoy to Halifax "to put an end to all such attempts."[62] On June 22, Clarendon sent an official dispatch to Crampton, ordering him to abandon the project entirely.[63] On July 16, Crampton responded, "With regard to the recruitment, I have put a stop to all fresh measures for carrying it on or enlarging it. . . ." But he also wrote that he was allowing several agents to complete the work they had already commenced.[64] Marcy was aware of the continued activity and wrote to Buchanan that despite Clarendon's assurances, recruiting was continuing as aggressively as ever.[65] Crampton finally put an end to all recruiting on August 7, upon learning that Clarendon had given Buchanan a copy of the instructions Clarendon had sent to Crampton on June 22.[66]

In the course of the investigation into the actions of British recruiting agents, Henry Hertz in Philadelphia and Max F. O. Strobel in New York, Crampton's central role in directing the entire project finally came to the attention of the administration. Hertz, particularly, made a sweeping confession of his own activities and of the fact that he was hired and directed throughout by Crampton.[67] Marcy had left

Washington on July 21, to vacation at Old Point Comfort, Virginia. Pierce and his wife planned to join Marcy there in early August after the president had taken care of matters in Kansas by dismissing governor Reeder and selecting his replacement.[68] In Marcy's absence, Cushing presented Pierce with affidavits and other documents from Hertz and Strobel that incriminated Crampton.[69] On receiving the information about Crampton's direct involvement in recruiting, Pierce wrote to Marcy, "It is quite possible that I shall be compelled to abandon the trip altogether."[70] The next day he asked Marcy to return to Washington "on account of certain intelligence, which has been received connected with [his] Department." Fearing this curt message might alarm the secretary of state, Pierce followed it a few hours later with another, "I am sorry to interrupt your sojourn at Old Point, but trust you will regard it only as an *interruption* not a termination of your visit. It is quite probable that I may go back with you but circumstances attending the subject which requires your presence make it desirable that our interview should take place here. Mrs. Pierce is decidedly better and we still adhere to the purpose of visiting "Old Point." The matter which induces me to ask your return, I ought perhaps to say is not one to perplex or awaken solicitude tho' it is certainly important & may demand prompt action."[71]

Marcy found the evidence against Crampton convincing. Cushing also presented the president with a legal opinion on the subject of recruitment. His broad analysis of the subject made it clear why Crampton's actions and those of the British Government were so insulting to the United States:

> All which it concerns foreign governments to know is, whether we, as a government, permit such enlistments. It is bound to ask permission of us before coming into our territory to raise troops for its own service. It has no business to inquire whether there be statutes on the subject or not. Least of all has it the right to take notice of the statutes only to see how it may devise means to evade them. Instead of this, it is bound, not only by every consideration of international comity, but of the strictest international law, to respect the sovereignty and regard the public policy of the United States."[72]

Cushing concluded that Great Britain had "committed an act of usurpation against the sovereign rights of the United States" and that all those involved, including consuls, were "indictable as malefactors by statute" and that the foreign minister could be expelled for his actions in abetting recruitment.[73]

Marcy addressed a letter to Crampton, informing him of the evidence of recruiting and of the minister's direct involvement in the illegal activity. Marcy concluded his letter with a personal comment regarding Crampton's involvement: "This part of the case gave me much pain."[74]

With a diplomatic crisis looming with Great Britain in mid-August, Pierce and his wife, accompanied by his secretary, Sidney Webster, and the marshal for the district, Jonah D. Hoover, finally embarked for a much-needed rest. Instead of Old Point Comfort, they traveled to Warm Springs and White Sulphur Springs in Virginia. On arriving at Warm Springs, the exhausted president came down with a fever and chills, which he called the "ague," or malaria, which had recurred from a bout he had the previous fall. The symptoms ran their predictable course and caused Pierce to extend his stay to nearly two weeks. The president's itinerary included receptions and speeches at Warm Springs, hosted by Senator Mason and Rep. John S. Barbour; at White Sulphur Springs hosted by former president Tyler; and on the way back at Charlottesville.[75] Pierce visited Jefferson's home, Monticello, and entertained a group of friends at his hotel one evening in Charlottesville. Among the guests was Sara Pryor, the wife of Roger A. Pryor, a young journalist and editor for the *Washington Union* whom Pierce had recently appointed a special commissioner to Greece. For family reasons Sara Pryor had been unable to accompany her husband, and Pierce made a point of telling her "all [she] wished to know of the exile far away in Greece." He also presented Mrs. Pryor "with two gorgeous volumes, bound sumptuously in green morocco, and inscribed, from my 'friend Franklin Pierce,' in his own fine handwriting." Sara Pryor then played the piano "at his request . . . he sitting the while beside the piano." She wrote in her memoirs of Pierce's "captivating voice and manner. Surely its source was in genuine kindness of heart."[76]

The cabinet met on September 2 immediately following Pierce's return to the capital. The developing diplomatic crisis with Great Britain dominated the discussion. Marcy was directed to write another letter to Crampton and to advise Buchanan of the evidence of the British minister's involvement in recruiting. During the summer, Buchanan had resigned as minister to Great Britain, pending Pierce's appointment of his successor. He had hoped to return to the United States in the fall to tend to his own presidential ambitions, but considering the mounting tension between the two countries, Pierce appealed to Buchanan to stay on: "Whatever the result of negotiations may be, touching this embarrassing subject, I deem it very important that you 'see it out.' I have been reluctant to urge you to remain at London beyond Sept. 30th, but shall never fail to appreciate the high considerations which have prompted your determination."[77] On receiving Marcy's detailed letter outlining the evidence against him, Crampton was noncommittal, replying only that he was referring the matter to his government in London.[78]

The trial of British recruiting agent Henry Hertz and an accomplice began in Philadelphia on September 21. Cushing advised District Attorney Van Dyke to present evidence that the instructions sent from the British foreign office required their consuls to violate the "spirit" of the neutrality laws if not the letter of the laws but that these instructions still "violate[d] the sovereign rights of the United States." By carrying out these instructions, each consul "abused his Consular functions by the violation of his international duty to the United States."[79]

The trial lasted a week and resulted in the conviction of Hertz and the acquittal of his accomplice. At the close of the trial Van Dyke was permitted to read into the transcript two letters from Cushing, which stated that the trials had been authorized by the president and referred to British officials as "malefactors."[80] Cushing had used the trial successfully to implicate the British government in the recruiting scheme.

From London, Clarendon continued to deny any government involvement in illegal recruiting and objected strongly to the language used by Cushing in his letters read at the trial, calling it "most insulting."[81] In Washington, Crampton was throwing up a smoke screen to counter the accusations against him. He officially charged that the United States was overlooking the actions of Russian sympathizers who were arming a ship in New York harbor for use as a privateer in the Crimean War against Great Britain. Cushing had District Attorney McKeon look into the matter: "The allegation against the vessel was improbable on its face; but, determined as the President is not to suffer any of the belligerent powers to trespass on the neutral rights of the United States, it was deemed proper to investigate the case, out of respect for the British Minister . . ."[82] McKeon's investigation showed that the bark *Maury* was preparing for the China trade, and a few guns had been added to fend off pirates. Cushing concluded "that the suspicions of the British consul as to the character and destination of the *Maury* were wholly erroneous; and justice to her owners and freighters require[d] that the libel against her be dismissed."[83]

No sooner had this matter been resolved than Crampton charged that Irish immigrants in New York were planning "an expedition for the military invasion of Ireland." Once again Cushing passed the accusation along to McKeon: "While it is difficult to believe that such intention is entertained by any persons in the United States . . . it seems proper that the subject should have your consideration."[84] McKeon found nothing other than a group of Irish immigrants who were unhappy with life in the United States and were planning to return home.

Lord Clarendon supported Crampton and exerted additional pressure on the United States by increasing the British naval fleet in the Caribbean. Buchanan reported on November 7 that there were twenty-five naval vessels carrying 712 guns in the area, compared with sixteen ships with 310 guns only a month before.[85] He asked Clarendon for an explanation and was told that the increase was to protect against privateers and Irish nationals leaving the U.S. to fight against Great Britain. Marcy did not accept this explanation, charging that the real reason was "to influence our action in regard to the offenders, official and unofficial, in the British recruiting scheme." British actions only made Pierce more determined to press on the British government U.S. demands for satisfaction regarding the matter, and he was determined to get an answer before the Congress met in December.[86] Clarendon's official answer sent on November 16, again stated that "no offence to the United States was offered or contemplated" and that the recruitment had ended "months ago"; in addition, Clarendon asserted, "If it can be shown that there are persons now in the foreign legion who have been enlisted, or hired, in violation of the United States law, as well as of British law, her Majesty's government will be prepared to offer them their discharge."[87] Marcy called Clarendon's responses "very laconic, but certainly a very unsatisfactory answer to the demand of redress by this government for a violation of its laws and an affront to the sovereign rights of this country."[88] Historian H. Barrett Learned concluded that Clarendon's letter "gave neither credence nor consideration to the more glaring facts in the situation. To President Pierce and his advisers it seemed illusory and unsatisfactory."[89] In a separate meeting Clarendon did inform Buchanan that the British navy had withdrawn four ships sent out to America and that more would soon be recalled.[90] How would Pierce answer the less-than-satisfactory British response? With all of the evidence against Crampton and the British consuls in New York, Philadelphia, and Cincinnati and the convictions of British agents in Philadelphia and New York, the administration had only one viable option: the dismissal of Crampton and the consuls. But Pierce and Marcy would proceed cautiously before exercising it.

In November, with the presidential election a year away, Pierce decided to seek reelection. It was not an easy decision for him to make an open race for renomination. In 1852, though his supporters had worked tirelessly behind the scenes to gain his nomination, Pierce had been able to remain in the background, appearing not to be grasping for the office but willing to accept it if the party and the country needed him. To gain the presidency in 1856, he would need to be more aggressive. The contentious political climate over Kansas and Know-Nothingism, and his own patronage policies made it unlikely that his own party would draft him again to run. But in the fall of 1855 there were signs that the Democratic Party was rebounding from the disastrous state and congressional elections of the previous fall. In June the Know-Nothings had met in convention in Philadelphia to formalize themselves as a national party and prepare for a presidential run in 1856. The slavery issue divided the convention, however, and the antislavery forces led by Senator Henry Wilson of Massachusetts bolted the party.[91] The Republican Party absorbed the antislavery nativists and emerged as the most powerful threat to the Democrats.

In the last of the elections for members of the Thirty-fourth Congress, Democrats gained seats in North Carolina, Tennessee, and Alabama. In September the coalition of Democrats and Whigs won in Maine, defeating the previously dominant Maine Liquor Law Party and its Know-Nothing allies. B. B. French, no longer an office holder in the Pierce administration, ran into the president one day during one of his frequent walks and found Pierce positively buoyant over the results in Maine, claiming it "an Administration triumph." He viewed the victory as a referendum on the Kansas issue, and predicted "that Connecticut, N.H. N.J. Ill. Inda. Iowa, and he thought Michigan would follow." French "told him [that he] doubted his premises," as French believed local issues were the greatest factor in Maine, but Pierce predicted that "in 18 months Democracy would be again firmly in the ascendant and all over the Union, & the Constitution and Union would stand firmer than ever."[92] Another positive sign was the defection of a Whig senator, Archibald Dixon of Kentucky, to the Democratic Party in the fall of 1855. Dixon was soon joined by two former Whigs, Senator Robert Toombs and Representative Alexander H. Stephens of Georgia.[93]

John W. Forney had speculated as early as August "that Pierce is a candidate," but it wasn't until around November 1 that he discussed the matter with his cabinet. They were unanimously in favor of his seeking a second term.[94] The campaign for the nomination began with the New Hampshire State Democratic Convention in mid-November. Sidney Webster began corresponding with state party chair John H. George and the editor of the *New Hampshire Patriot,* William Butterfield, to be ready for the convention by preparing resolutions, endorsing Pierce's policies as president, proposing his renomination, and selecting delegates to the convention in Cincinnati who would pledge to vote for Pierce.[95] Harry Hibbard was assigned to prepare the resolutions and to present them at the convention. With additional help from Charles H. Peaslee, working out of the customs house in Boston, the old team from 1852 resurrected its mastery of the state Democratic Party. The three hundred delegates at the state convention unanimously and enthusiastically endorsed all the actions of the Pierce administration, including popular sovereignty, and pledged all of its delegates to the national convention to vote as a unit for the president's renomination.[96] The absence of Edmund Burke, who was temporarily allied with the Know-Nothing governor, added to the harmony within the state party. Webster was pleased with the results, writing to George, "What a fine convention you must have had! . . . The resolutions reported cover the whole ground. . . . Everything looks well." Democratic conventions in Massachusetts and Vermont also endorsed Pierce's renomination.[97] Webster predicted, "To my mind there is no reasonable doubt presented of the renomination of General Pierce."[98]

But while Pierce had entered the contest, he continued to resist resorting to the usual methods of achieving the nomination. John W. Forney, editor of the *Washington Union* and a longtime friend of Buchanan, met with Pierce in November to offer his resignation, fearing that his known support of the president's chief rival for the nomination might embarrass Pierce. Forney reported to Buchanan that Pierce had refused to accept his resignation, "in his frank and generous way," stating, "All I ask at your hands is that you give me, as I know you will, the benefit of fair treatment. I am irrevocably in the field. You may rely on it I never will take a nomination if it is to be had by conflict with others." Forney concluded, "he can be so beyond most men."[99] Webster was aware of Pierce's meeting with Forney and wrote to George that "the President has released him [Forney] fully so far as Penna. is concerned" but that Forney would stay on at the *Union*. Webster explained Pierce's thinking:

> General P, while he is a candidate for renomination is not the antagonist of any other candidate. He desires a nomination, only when the convention at Cincinnati consider that he is the best and most available candidate. His purpose is to treat every candidate for the succession, and the friends of every candidate, *who sustains his administration and its measures*, with the kindness and consideration which by his position he owes to every man in the democratic family. In Pennsylvania he is the friend of Buchanan and Dallas. In Virginia he treats Mr. Hunter and Mr.

> Wise as alike entitled to his confidence and esteem. And he does so because he supposes them all devoted to the measures of his administration. In a word he has no quarrel with anybody who is a democrat; his *friends* can conduct and will conduct the canvass as they see fit.[100]

Compared to most politicians Pierce was remarkably humble and self-effacing. He had never had to grasp for nomination to elective office in New Hampshire, nor had he ever forced himself on the voters. Even the presidency came to him without much outward effort on his part. While he could be ruthless in purging his party of men like Hale, Atwood, and Burke, or his administration of Know-Nothing sympathizers like his old friend B. B. French, he would never use similar methods to advance his own personal agenda. Even to make known his intention to seek renomination was a departure from his usual practice, but to not run would weaken his administration further, as a lame duck president has little influence on events. He still had too much to accomplish and nearly a year and a half left in his term, but as always he placed the unity of his party above his personal ambitions. Pierce desired the affirmation of his administration that renomination would offer but understood that it would be meaningless if it divided the party.

10

CONGRESS AND KANSAS IN CHAOS

If Pierce thought his political prospects looked promising in November, the events of the next few months destroyed any hope of renomination. Filibuster activity in Nicaragua intensified, the conflicts with Great Britain over Central America and British recruiting in the United States worsened, and a hostile Congress convened at the start of the presidential election year, determined to do everything possible to impede the plans of an incumbent president. But it was events in Kansas that galvanized the attention of the public and overwhelmed all other issues in determining the fate of the Pierce administration.

The Thirty-fourth Congress assembled on December 3, 1855. The Democratic Party continued to control the Senate, but the new House was made up of 102 Republicans, 43 Whigs/Know-Nothings, and 79 Democrats, compared with 154 in the previous Congress.[1] Gone were reliable supporters of the president, including John C. Breckinridge of Kentucky and Harry Hibbard of New Hampshire. In fact, the entire New Hampshire delegation, both senators and all three representatives, were elected by the anti-Nebraska/Know-Nothing fusion party. Pierce had his annual message ready to deliver to the Congress, but the House was unable to receive it because the members could not organize and elect a Speaker. With Chief Clerk John W. Forney presiding, the representatives voted 133 times over the next two months in an unprecedented and futile effort to elect a Speaker. Each of the three parties stubbornly refused to give in and trade its votes to give any candidate the required majority.[2] In the meantime, the House could conduct no business, while a restless president tried to tackle the problems facing the nation without a functioning Congress.

On December 4, Pierce confided his concerns about the new Congress to his brother, Henry: "The message is completed but when I shall receive notice that Congress is ready to receive it seems very doubtful. The discordant elements in the House of Representatives do not find it easy to *fuse.* Know-Nothingism & abolitionism seem likely to furnish a practical illustration of their entire incompetency to conduct public affairs."[3] Following the death of Pierce's older half-sister Elizabeth McNeil in April 1855, Henry was now his only surviving sibling, and Pierce began to reach out more to his youngest brother, with whom he had never been particularly close.[4]

With the House unable to organize, the Senate was also hamstrung in its ability to carry on normal activity, but this did not stop one of its newest members, John P. Hale of New Hampshire, returning from a two-year absence and political exile in New York, from taking every opportunity to agitate the Kansas situation and ridicule his former friend and mentor, Franklin Pierce. On December 5, Hale offered a resolution requiring the president to "inform the Senate whether he has received any evidence of . . . resistance to the execution of the laws in Kansas as to require the introduction of military force for the restoration or preservation of law and order in that Territory. . . ."[5] When reminded by other senators that it was unprecedented to ask the president to communicate with the Senate before his annual message had been received, Hale withdrew his resolution, but with the sarcastic comment that it was "entirely new" to him that "the country [was] waiting with great anxiety for the [president's] message. (Laughter)."[6]

Hale's resolution was in response to news reports from Kansas of what was exaggeratedly referred to as the "Wakarusa War." The new governor of the territory, Wilson Shannon, had arrived at his post in mid-September. Whereas former governor Reeder had immediately allied himself with the free-state speculators in the territory, Shannon was accused of siding with the proslavery cause. On his way to the territory he had made a speech in Westport, Missouri, reportedly stating that the institutions of Kansas should "harmonize" with those of its slave state neighbor, Missouri. Shannon denied that the speech had anything to do with slavery: "I said nothing on the subject of slavery; on the contrary, I remarked that that was a question I would not discuss."[7] The antislavery eastern press seized on the speech to attack the new governor and undermine his ability to work with both sides in Kansas.[8]

In the succeeding weeks the Free-State Party successfully organized, ratifying its Topeka constitution, which banned free blacks from entering the territory, and organizing a Free-state militia armed with some $43,000 in weapons, bought with funds raised in New England. The Free-State Party had signaled its intention to achieve its ends by the threat of violence.[9] In response, the proslavery side formed the Law and Order Party, which met in convention in Leavenworth in mid-November, with Governor Shannon presiding. The convention claimed the Topeka movement to be treasonable and rebellious.[10]

Despite all the posturing over slavery, it was a land claim dispute that resulted in the first death in what the eastern abolitionists exaggeratedly named "bleeding Kansas." A free-soil settler, Branson, and a proslavery settler, Coleman, had been quarrelling over their claims since 1854. Branson had given some of the disputed land to a man named Dow. Coleman encountered Dow at a blacksmith shop one day in November 1855, an argument ensued, and Coleman shot and killed Dow. Coleman, claiming self-defense, fled to Missouri, but a free-state posse led by Branson was determined to seek revenge. They burned down Coleman's empty house and the homes of two other proslavery settlers and intimidated witnesses who backed up Coleman's self-defense claim. Douglas County Sheriff Samuel J. Jones set out with his own posse and arrested Branson. But a free-state

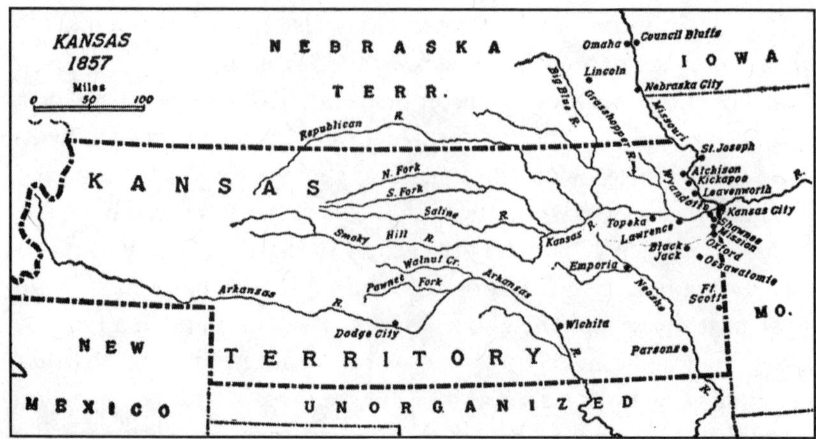

posse intercepted Jones's posse, freed Branson, and escorted him safely to Lawrence. Jones had acted with restraint, letting Branson be taken rather than start a war, but he did notify Governor Shannon of the incident. Shannon called out the militia and asked Colonel Edwin Sumner at Fort Leavenworth for military assistance. Sumner, a cousin of Massachusetts antislavery senator Charles Sumner, refused to comply without orders from the president.[11] On December 1, Shannon telegraphed the president, "I desire authority to call on the United States forces at Leavenworth to preserve the peace of this Territory, to protect the Sheriff of Douglas county, and enable him to execute the legal process in his hands." Shannon claimed that "an armed force of 1,000 men, with all the implements of war . . . are at Lawrence."[12] Pierce wired back on December 3, "All the power vested in the Executive will be exerted to preserve order and enforce the laws. On the receipt of your letter the preliminary measures necessary to be taken before calling out troops will be promptly executed, and you will be fully advised."[13] Pierce was unwilling to commit troops without a written request, but Shannon could not wait. His call for the militia had resulted in nearly two thousand men, mostly from Missouri, massing along the Wakarusa River, bent on burning Lawrence. Uncertain of his ability to control his own militia, Shannon began a series of meetings with the leaders in Lawrence and of the Missouri forces, to avoid bloodshed. The problem was confounded by the murder of a free-state man who had tried to run the blockade surrounding Lawrence and the fact that Branson had fled Lawrence at the insistence of the Free-State Party leaders. With the help of former senator David Atchison and a grandson of Daniel Boone, Shannon negotiated an agreement, signed on December 8, in which the Lawrence leaders denied any complicity in Branson's case and affirmed their willingness to aid in legal action against criminals. The agreement avoided any pledge to recognize the validity of the laws of what the Free-State leaders called the "bogus" legislature.[14] Shannon then ordered his militia to disband and return to their homes, but fearing they would not leave, he also signed a paper authorizing the Free State leaders to raise a militia to defend Lawrence from attack. In fact, the Missourians did leave peacefully, but Shannon's document was later used by the Free-State Party in claiming their revolutionary military force had the authorization of the governor. The immediate crisis over, the leaders of both sides, including Sheriff Jones, attended a ball at the Free-State Hotel in Lawrence.[15] Back east, free-state propaganda reported the "Wakarusa War" as a victory that furthered the legitimacy of the Topeka movement. Shannon wrote to Pierce of his "forebodings as to the future," insisting that only U.S. troops could be relied on to preserve the peace.[16]

While the turmoil in Kansas was escalating, the Pierce administration was receiving disturbing information about the situation in Nicaragua. The administration's determined effort to stop filibuster activity had hindered Kinney's planned incursion into the country, but the resourceful William Walker, referred to by southern journalists as "the grey-eyed man of destiny," had slipped away from U.S. authorities in San Francisco and reached Nicaragua with a small band of men. In early October, Walker's forces, which had grown significantly, helped the Liberals defeat the Legitimists at Virgin Bay. A week later the capital, Granada, was taken, the Legitimist leader was executed, and Walker was installed as commander in chief of the army in a coalition government. Walker's dominant role in the new government was clear from dispatches that Marcy received from the U.S. minister to Central America, John H. Wheeler. Equally disturbing to Pierce and Marcy was Wheeler's enthusiastic support of the new government and his apparent involvement in negotiations to set up the coalition.[17]

In November Marcy sent a dispatch to Wheeler, chastising him for "improperly interfering in the conflict between the contending parties" and ordering him not to "intermeddle in the concerns of any of the parties." According to Marcy, the president would not recognize the "*de facto* Government" that had been established by "a band of foreign adventurers" and that did not represent the will of the native people.[18] Marcy also tried to assure the Costa Rican minister that the U.S. was not supporting the incursion into Nicaragua by American citizens.[19] Pierce backed up Marcy's assurances by issuing a proclamation on December 8, stating that evidence had been received that persons were being recruited within the United States "to participate in military operations within the State of Nicaragua." Pierce warned "all persons against connecting themselves with any such enterprise" and charged all officers of the government to enforce the nation's neutrality laws.[20]

In mid-December, Parker H. French, a disreputable former California legislator, arrived in Washington, sent by Walker's government as Nicaragua's official envoy to the United States. Marcy refused to receive French, who then traveled to New York City to recruit men for service in Nicaragua. Marcy alerted Cushing, who advised the U.S. district attorney, John McKeon, "It appears that Col. Parker H. French is concerned in the engagement at New York of persons and of arms for transmission to Nicaragua." Cushing urged McKeon to be vigilant, stating that French's claim to diplomatic status "cannot be a cloak for infringement of our laws."[21] Cushing also sent instructions to district attorneys in eighteen other U.S. port cities, stating that by the direction of "the President" they were "to detect and defeat" all efforts "to recruit men for the invasion of . . . Nicaragua" and "to detain any vessels fitted out to carry on the undertaking."[22] McKeon found evidence that filibusters were about to embark from New York on the *Northern Light,* a steamer owned by the Accessory Transit Company, the U.S. firm that had the exclusive contract to transport people and supplies across Nicaragua and that was supporting Walker's government.[23]

On December 24, Pierce ordered McKeon and Captain Bigelow of the U.S. Navy to detain the ship.[24] McKeon directed U.S. marshals to board the steamer and order the captain to delay his departure. McKeon then visited the office of the Accessory Transit Company and read the president's dispatch to French and Joseph L. White, a director of the company, who argued vociferously that "he did not care a d——n for the President of the United States or his despatches."[25] McKeon then proceeded to the navy yard to coordinate plans with Captain Bigelow, who sent a revenue cutter with an armed force to board the *Northern Light* and two steamers to block the harbor in case the ship had already left the wharf. Defying the four U.S. marshals on board the *Northern Light,* Captain Edward L. Tinklepaugh set the steamer on its way, to the cheers of the crowd, estimated at eight hundred, which had gathered on the dock to witness the confrontation. McKeon had just arrived and shouted to the captain, "This vessel must not go. I am the District Attorney of the United States, and have the authority of the President to detain her." To which some in the crowd shouted, "Throw him off the dock." McKeon called back, "Americans, will you not sustain your own laws?"[26]

The revenue cutter intercepted the *Northern Light* off Ellis Island as it headed toward Sandy Hook and open water. The cutter fired a blank cartridge across the ship's bow. The *Northern Light* ignored this warning and kept on her course, but the cutter then fired a ball, which hit the ship. At this point the *Northern Light* stopped, was boarded by officers of the revenue cutter, and brought to the New Jersey shore, where it was anchored under the guns of the cutter.[27] In the meantime, McKeon's assistant district attorney was proceeding at Brooklyn City Hall to obtain arrest warrants against those involved in the filibuster activity. The Accessory Transit Company's president, Cornelius Vanderbilt, tried to intervene, but arrived after the judge had left for the day. That night Joseph L. White and Captain Tinklepaugh visited McKeon at his home to apologize for their rash actions, claiming ignorance of the presence of filibusters on board the *Northern Light.* They asked permission to disembark over one hundred of the detained passengers, who were in the process of "breaking in the cabin doors and causing all sorts of mischief." McKeon agreed to allow the passengers to leave the ship, as his goal of "breaking up the expedition" had been achieved, but he did inform White and Tinklepaugh that they would be arrested the next day for "defiance of the law." At 6:00 p.m. McKeon telegraphed Cushing, "Northern Light brought back." Pierce telegraphed that night, complimenting McKeon and Captain Bigelow and directing them to "omit no measure and spare no effort to vindicate the law."[28]

On Christmas Day, McKeon sent a full report to Cushing stating, "The movement of the President so prompt and decided is affirmed by every respectable man I meet. It is a glorious vindication of the Law. . . . All praise is due to the Captain of the Revenue cutter."[29] Pierce agreed to release the *Northern Light* after the Accessory Transit Company provided $100,000 in security. McKeon presented the evidence to a grand jury, which indicted twelve of the leaders of the expedition for violating the neutrality laws. He had ten of them in custody by January 15.[30] Being under indictment, and discredited in the press after the Pierce administration exposed his criminal past,

Parker H. French fled the country. White and Tinklepaugh were tried later that year and acquitted.[31]

On January 9, another of the Accessory Transit Company's ships, *The Star of the West,* was detained by order of the president, and five filibusters were arrested.[32] Many on board had tickets and claimed to be laborers employed by the Transit Company to build a new pier in Nicaragua but were really intending to join Walker's army. Once again a large crowd gathered at the dock and hooted and jeered McKeon's effort to search the ship and hissed at references to Pierce. Since most of the passengers possessed legitimate documents, McKeon allowed the ship to depart, to the cheers of the crowd. In February McKeon presented Vanderbilt with evidence that filibusters intended to embark on the next trip of *The Star of the West* and threatened to seize the ship. To avoid this fate, Vanderbilt finally promised that his vessels would no longer carry filibusters to Nicaragua.[33]

Pierce had waited for four weeks for the House to organize so that he could deliver his annual message. On December 31, with no sign that the stalemate was near resolution, he took the unprecedented step of sending his message to Congress. His motive in doing so was to place his detailed explanation of the administration's position on the Central American dispute with Great Britain before the public prior to the opening of Parliament in late January. Buchanan had been urging Pierce to do this for over a year as the British press and public were ignorant of the American position; Buchanan believed that if they understood it, public pressure would be exerted on the Palmerston government to settle the matter on U.S. terms. As the month dragged on without a presidential message, Buchanan expressed his frustration: "I regret that the difficulties in the organization of the House have prevented me from receiving a copy of the President's Message. . . . The British public expect a pretty strong expression of opinion in that document on the Central American question; and I am persuaded this will do good."[34] As the days passed with no message, Marcy wrote Buchanan, "I presume that you will be as much disappointed as we are that the Message has not yet seen the light."[35] On December 28, Buchanan was still pleading for it: "I expect the President's Message with much anxiety on Monday."[36]

The message was read in the Senate on December 31, 1855, and released to the press, but the House, in its still unorganized condition, refused to receive it. Pierce more than fulfilled Buchanan's hopes for a message focused largely on foreign affairs. Pierce meticulously outlined the U.S. position on the meaning of the Clayton-Bulwer Treaty of 1850, which was the point of contention between the two nations. The Treaty "covenanted that 'neither will ever' 'occupy, or fortify, or colonize, or assume or exercise any dominion over Nicaragua, Costa Rica, the Mosquito Coast, or any party of Central America,'" yet, in spite of this wording Great Britain continued to exercise "large authority" over the Mosquito Coast, had claimed "Balize as her absolute domain," and "had formally colonized" the Bay Islands, which rightfully belonged to Honduras.[37] Pierce stated "that the two Governments differ widely and irreconcilably as to the construction" of the treaty. The British claimed that the treaty was "prospective only and did not require Great Britain to abandon" any possessions held prior to its ratification, but Pierce charged that other than "Balize," Great Britain did not possess these areas prior to the treaty and that her interpretation made "the treaty therefore practically null so far as regards our rights." The president warned, "This international difficulty can not long remain undetermined without involving in serious danger the friendly relations which it is in the interest as well as the duty of both countries to cherish and preserve."[38]

Pierce then turned to the recruitment crisis, restating the various applications of the neutrality laws and concluding, "The very attempt to do it without . . . consent is an attack on the national sovereignty. . . . It is difficult to understand how it should have been supposed that troops could be raised here by Great Britain without violations of the municipal law."[39] The fact that recruiting had "been conducted under the supervision and by the regular cooperation of British officers, civil and military. . . . impelled [Pierce] to present the case to the British Government in order to secure not only cessation of the wrong, but its reparation." He promised further communication with Congress on this matter, "in due time."[40]

Pierce went on to review relations with Spain, Cuba, and other nations, and then turned to domestic matters. The treasury remained in surplus, and $10 million of the national debt had been redeemed during the past year. Pierce repeated from his two prior messages to

Congress his recommendation to endorse Davis's plans for "reorganization of the Army" and the creation of a retired list, as had been established the previous year for the navy.[41]

Regarding the situation in Kansas, the president reported, "There have been acts prejudicial to good order, but as yet none have occurred under circumstances to justify the interposition of the Federal Executive. That could only be in case of obstruction to Federal law or of organized resistance to Territorial law, assuming the character of insurrection, which, if it should occur, it would be my duty promptly to overcome and suppress."[42] Pierce expressed the hope that intervention by the federal executive would "be prevented by the sound sense of the people of the Territory," if they were allowed to exercise their rights "without interference on the part of the citizens of any of the States."[43]

The remainder of the annual message was a lengthy lecture by Pierce on the dangers of sectional conflict and agitation of the slavery question. He reviewed the creation of the Union and the Constitution by the founding fathers and their "wise" determination to engage "in no extravagant scheme of social change" regarding "the subject races, whether Indians or Africans." Pierce reminded the Congress that the Constitution was one of limited powers, and checks and balances and that the founding fathers had left internal domestic matters "wholly" the authority of the individual states. He warned, "If one State ceases to respect the rights of another and obtrusively intermeddles with its local interests . . . we are no longer united, friendly States, but distracted hostile ones. . . ." He continued, "While the "Southern States confine their attention to their own affairs . . . too many inhabitants of the [Northern States] are permanently organized in associations to inflict injury on the former by wrongful acts . . ." These "political agitators" were now practicing "aggression" on the "political organization of the new Territories. . . ."[44]

Warming to his theme, Pierce affirmed the propriety of popular sovereignty as "natural and legitimate" and criticized those who "denounce and condemn it." He warned that states would be impelled "to meet extremes with extremes" and concluded that "sectional agitation now prevailing in some of the States" was "impracticable" and "unconstitutional," and would "end calamitously" with "disunion and civil war. . ."

> Disunion for what? If the passionate rage of fanaticism and partisan spirit did not force the fact upon our attention, it would be difficult to believe that any considerable portion of the people of this enlightened country could have so surrendered themselves to a fanatical devotion to the supposed interests of the relatively few Africans in the United States as totally to abandon and disregard the interests of the 25,000,000 Americans; to trample under foot the injunctions of moral and constitutional obligation, and to engage in plans of vindictive hostility against those who are associated with them in the enjoyment of the common heritage of our national institutions.[45]

Pierce predicted, "The storm of frenzy and faction must inevitably dash itself in vain against the unshaken rock of the Constitution. I shall never doubt it. I know that the Union is stronger a thousand times than all the wild and chimerical schemes of social change which are generated one after another in the unstable minds of visionary sophists and interested agitators."[46]

The message achieved its foreign policy objective. Buchanan wrote from London that the Central American "questions" in the message were "well and ably stated" and that the "President's Message has received great commendation among enlightened people in this country."[47] After conferring with Lord Clarendon, Buchanan concluded, "From present appearances the Central American questions can lead to no serious difficulties with England. Public opinion would seem to be nearly altogether in favor of our construction of the Treaty."[48]

Democratic senators and the party press also praised the message. Even Amos A. Lawrence wrote in his diary, "The message well written."[49] Pierce's former friend B. B. French wrote that despite the "uproar that ensued" in the House over the timing of it, Pierce had "succeeded in getting his Message before the Country" and that the message was "generally a good one," though it would make Pierce "still more unpopular at the North." French noted, "He is almost as unpopular as possible now!"[50]

The message did, in fact, anger many opponents in Congress and in the North. John P. Hale spoke for them in a speech delivered in the

Residents of the White House

Franklin Pierce, 1853, and Jane Pierce

The White House, ca. 1846 (the earliest known photograph of the White House)

Abigail Kent Means, Jane's childhood friend, aunt by marriage, part-time White House hostess

Pierce Cabinet

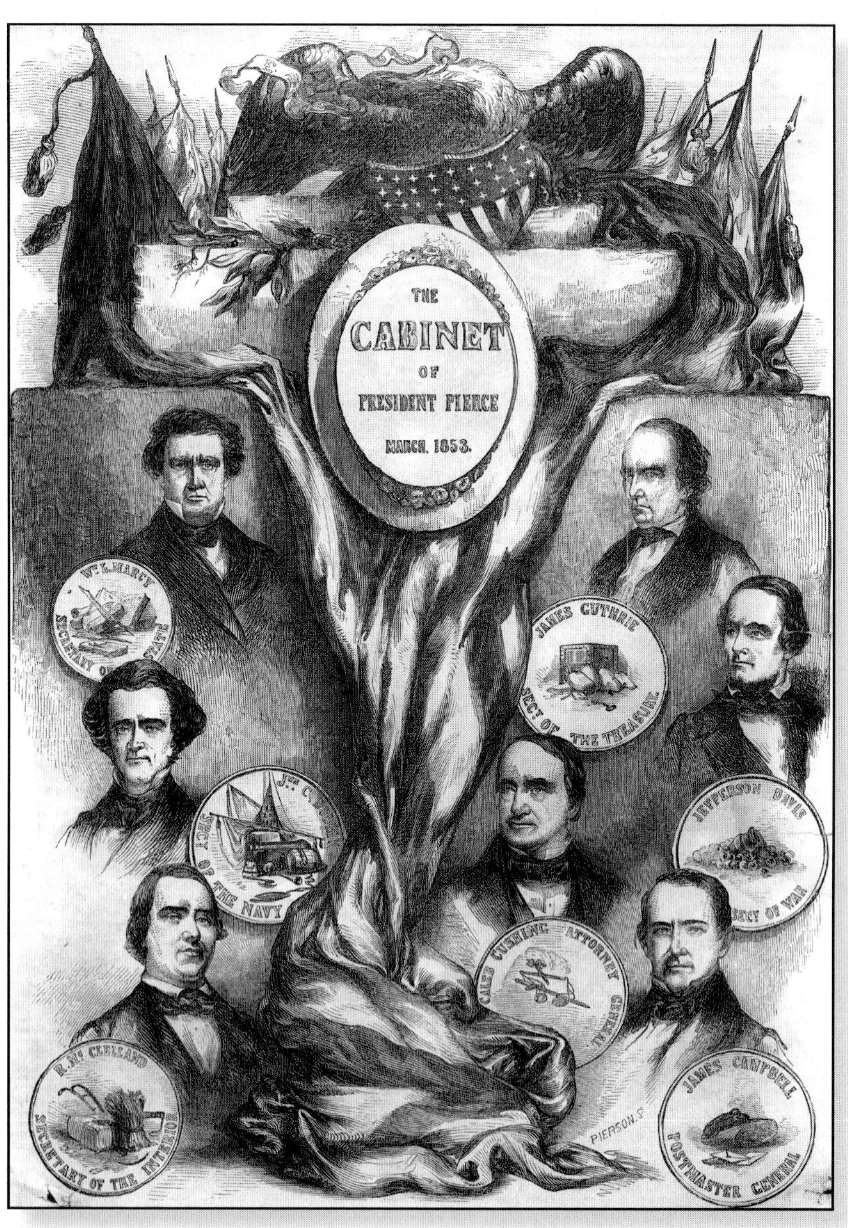

Clockwise from upper left: Secretary of State William L. Marcy, Secretary of Treasury James Guthrie, Secretary of War Jefferson Davis, Postmaster General James Campbell, Attorney General Caleb Cushing, Secretary of Interior Robert McClelland, Secretary of Navy James C. Dobbin

Pierce Administration Diplomatic Corps

Pierre Soulé,
Minister to Spain

August Belmont,
Minister to the Hague

John Y. Mason,
Minister to France

Daniel Sickles,
Secretary of the London Legation
in his Civil War uniform

New York Democratic Party Leaders

Governor Horatio Seymour, Softshell ally of Marcy

Former Senator John A. Dix, Barnburner

Former Senator Daniel Dickinson, Hardshell

Rep. Francis B. Cutting, Hardshell leader in 33rd Congress

Sen. David Rice Atchison, Missouri, Senate President Pro-tempore, 33rd Congress

Rep. John C. Breckinridge, Kentucky

Sen. R. M. T. Hunter, Virginia

Sen. James M. Mason, Virginia

Congressional Proponents of Kansas–Nebraska Bill

Sen. Stephen A. Douglas, Illinois

Sen. Archibald Dixon, Kentucky

Rep. Philip Phillips, Alabama

Rep. Alexander H. Stephens, Georgia

Pierce Antagonists

Edmund Burke, New Hampshire politician, editor

Sen. John P. Hale, Republican from New Hampshire

Richard W. Thompson, former U.S. Representative, Indian Agent

Alfred O. P. Nicholson, former Senator, co-owner of Washington Union

John W. Forney, Chief Clerk of the House, Editor of the Washington Union

Mrs. Jefferson (Varina Howell) Davis

Mrs. Roger A. (Sara Agnes Rice) Pryor

Mrs. John C. (Jesse Benton) Frémont

Dorothea Dix

Governors of Kansas Territory

Andrew H. Reeder

John W. Geary

Buchanan Campaign Managers

Sen. John Slidell, Louisiana

Sen. Jesse David Bright, Indiana, President Pro-tempore of the 34th Congress

Anti-Buchanan broadside showing Buchanan riding on the back of President Pierce and others in support of slavery

North Branch, October 5, 1861.

R. M. C. Esqr

× × × ×

Presdt P— in his passage has drawn many brave and influential men to the League. P— y. of the L.C.S. — & sent a line to Dr F (by H— the Mormon Elder, who as you perhaps know is just across the line from Port H— The league is doing nobly in M., I. & Wis. He is cautious but in common with others is gradually preparin the minds of the people for a great change. He expresses a fear that any attempt to draf men will produce a premature outbreak. I think his fear is well founded. A member of the League in Genesee who passed through the woods on his way with despatch to Dr. F.— told that any attempt to draft our friends there would bring on an open rupture. I think our ~~friends there would bring on~~ leaders should look to this as no doubt they will

× × ×

Yours in the cause

∗ ⊐ < ∧ ʒ // ⊡

Copy of hoax letter forwarded to Pierce by Secretary of State William H. Seward (left)

*Col. Edward E. Cross,
New Hampshire Fifth
Regiment of Volunteers*

*Col. Thomas J. Whipple,
New Hampshire Fourth
Regiment of Volunteers*

*Rep. Clement L. Vallandigham,
Ohio Copperhead*

*Rep. Samuel S. Cox,
Ohio*

Fifty-two South Main Street, Concord. Pierce died in this house he rented from Willard Williams. The house was destroyed by fire in 1981.

Pierce cottage at Little Boar's Head

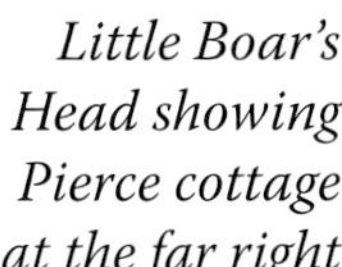

Little Boar's Head showing Pierce cottage at the far right

Franklin Pierce, ca. 1861

Senate on January 3, a speech that his biographer characterized as a "rancorous" and "savage and quite uncharacteristic personal attack."[51] Hale first stated that the message should not have been received by the Senate as it "was irregularly sent," before the Congress was fully organized. He assigned political motives to Pierce's sending the message at this time, claiming that it was intended to influence southern state political conventions scheduled to meet in January to select delegates to the national convention but that it was a "desperate" move, as Pierce had "no more chance of . . . being renominated, than there is of one of our pages receiving that honor."[52] Hale mocked the president's focus on Central America: "There is a central place in the United States—not Central America . . . —called Kansas, about which the people of this country are thinking vastly more at this time than they are about Central America down in the land of filibusters. . . . "[53] Hale charged the president with aiding the proslavery side in that territory by not sending in troops to prevent acts of violence. According to Hale, employing the army was what "great military" presidents like Washington, Jackson, and Taylor would have done: "God knows they could not say it of this President. [Laughter in the galleries.]"[54]

Hale concluded by attacking Pierce's "lectures on slavery" as an attempt to "stigmatize" those who opposed slavery as "enemies of the Constitution": "When he does it he comes down from the high place which God, in his wrath for the punishment of our national sins, and for the humiliation of our national pride, has permitted him to occupy. I say he comes down from that high place into the arena of a vulgar demagogue, and strips himself of everything which should clothe with dignity the office of President of the United States. I deny the issue; I hurl it back in his face; I tell him, when he undertakes to designate these men as enemies of the Constitution, he abuses and defames men whose shoe-latchets he is not worthy to untie."[55] Hale was called by the *Washington Union* "a low man, and a low demagogue," for his "wild and angry assertions" and the "violence and vituperation" of his speech. To add to the indignity to the president, Hale showed up at a White House levee in mid-January, accompanied by several ladies. While Pierce graciously greeted Hale's guests, the usually amiable and forgiving president turned his back on the senator, an action which drew considerable comment in the national press.[56]

Pierce has been criticized by historians for his failure to exercise "constructive statesmanship" and for evading his responsibilities regarding Kansas.[57] His third annual message is cited as the best evidence of his failure in not enforcing the Kansas-Nebraska Act by setting aside the fraudulent elections and calling for new ones supervised by U.S. troops. Though the message was delivered on December 31, it had been written before Congress convened and before the "Wakarusa War" took place. Despite the Wakarusa incident, there had been little violence in Kansas, and Pierce reasoned that with winter setting in, further violence over the next few months was unlikely, and he wanted to confer with Governor Shannon, who was confident enough in the temporary peace to leave the territory and travel to Washington to confer with the administration on the situation.[58] Stephen A. Douglas, sponsor of the Kansas-Nebraska Act and chairman of the Senate Committee on Territories, was seriously ill and would not return to Washington until mid-February. Pierce had previously conferred with Douglas on Kansas matters and needed his leadership in the Senate if the president were to offer any new proposals.[59] Finally, the decision to redeploy the U.S. Army to the territory was a serious matter. The few hundred soldiers stationed at Fort Leavenworth were hardly sufficient to patrol the huge territory, and moving additional forces to the area would require reducing the already overstretched U.S. Army in places where real fighting was actually taking place—the Pacific Northwest, the upper Midwest, and the Texas border, where Indian wars were in progress. With the House temporarily dysfunctional, Pierce could anticipate no new appropriations to pay for any enlargement of the federal government's role in Kansas. His decision not to offer constructive proposals in the annual message was a tactical one, based on practical considerations and his strongly held opinion that the president did not have the constitutional authority to interfere in local matters. Instead, he hoped the strength of his words would convince the public that agitation of the slavery issue could produce nothing but conflict and violence. Pierce had been saying the same thing for over twenty years, ever since the antislavery cause had become a political reality in New Hampshire in 1835. These were his honest opinions and beliefs regarding antislavery agitation. The message was not intended to aid his renomination bid by appealing to potential southern delegates, as Hale charged; rather, its timing was meant to convince Parliament of the merits of the administration's interpretation of the Clayton-Bulwer Treaty; in this it succeeded.

The Pierce administration continued to be preoccupied with British affairs. Following Lord Clarendon's unsatisfactory response of November 16 to the evidence presented about British recruiting, Marcy and Pierce had been cautiously considering their options. The result was a dispatch that Marcy sent to Buchanan on January 3, 1856, with instructions to read it to Clarendon. Of the dispatch, Marcy wrote, "The manner I am quite sure will please Ld. Clarendon but I presume the matter will not. I really believe he does not know how offensively British officers have behaved in this recruiting business—but he had the means of knowing all about it . . . It should have been investigated."[60] The carefully worded dispatch, in twenty-three printed pages, laid out all of the facts of British recruiting in the United States. Marcy focused on errors of fact in Clarendon's answer to the charges. Most significant of these was Clarendon's claim that he had stopped the recruiting in March 1855, as soon as he learned of it. Marcy presented evidence that the recruiting had gone on, at an increased level, until late July. He also implied that British minister John Crampton had lied to Clarendon by reporting Crampton had "confidential communication" with Marcy before starting the recruitment project. Finally, Marcy criticized the British government for not fully investigating the matter when it was first presented by the United States. He contrasted British lack of response to the immediate investigation launched by the United States to the absurd British charge that the *Maury* was being outfitted as a Russian privateer. Marcy was able to document "several hundred cases" in which recruiting agents had induced citizens or foreigners living in the United States to enter into the British service in violation of U.S. laws. As a result of the failure of the British government to immediately stop the recruiting and to take action to redress the wrongs committed against the United States, Pierce directed Buchanan to demand the recall of Crampton and the removal of the British consuls in New York, Philadelphia, and Cincinnati.[61]

Marcy's dispatch exonerated the British government of any intention to violate U.S. neutrality laws and placed the blame for the recruiting scheme on its overzealous representatives in the United States. This was in response to Clarendon's complaints about the "tone of hostility" he sensed in previous communications on the matter, and Buchanan praised the "excellent" tone of Marcy's letter but predicted "its conclusion" would "startle this Government."[62] When Buchanan read Clarendon the dispatch requesting the recalls, the British foreign minister was taken "by surprise, and he replied with emotion, 'We will not do it!' "[63] Clarendon defended Crampton's conduct and blamed Attorney General Cushing for his biased prosecution of the matter, which was "calculated to inflame the American people against England."[64] To the press, the British government claimed the recall request was done "for mere electioneering purposes" by the Pierce administration. Buchanan complained to Clarendon of the injustice done to the president and assured him that the dispatch was the work of Pierce and Marcy, not Cushing. Buchanan reported that Clarendon "agreed . . . that such charges against President Pierce were unjust and unbecoming, and he was sorry they had ever been made . . ."[65] Clarendon asked for time to prepare a formal answer to the recall request, and Buchanan assured him that the Pierce administration would not act by dismissing the British officers before receiving Clarendon's official response.[66]

Buchanan observed that relations between the United States and Great Britain seemed "to be approaching a diplomatic, if not a belligerent rupture." He continued, "I deem it almost certain that as soon as the news shall arrive in this country that you have sent Mr. Crampton his passports, I shall receive mine from Lord Clarendon." While not expecting war to come of it, Buchanan wrote, "The news that you have sent Mr. Crampton his passports will, beyond all question, produce an intense sensation throughout England. This will doubtless be followed . . . by my dismissal: and I shall be made the peace offering—a most willing victim so far as I am personally concerned." He warned that British pride was "mortified" by the failure to produce a military victory in the Crimean War, and war with the United States could result "if they attach this wounded pride to Crampton's dismissal."[67] But it would not be Buchanan who would deal with the consequences. In late January, Pierce finally honored Buchanan's request to return home by appointing former vice president George M. Dallas as minister to Great Britain.[68] Buchanan prepared to return to the United States in the early spring, to contest for the presidential nomination.

Events in Kansas soon prompted decisive action on the part of the president. On January 15, the Free-State Party held its elections for governor and the legislature. Charles Robinson, a friend of Amos A. Lawrence and an officer of the Emigrant Aid Society, was elected governor by a large majority of the 1,700 free-state voters. Though the election was largely ignored by the proslavery side, one free-state man was killed by a group calling itself the Kickapoo Rangers from Missouri.[69] Fearing that the formal organization of their "revolutionary" government would provoke a massive retaliation by the legitimate territorial government and its Missouri supporters, Robinson and militia leader James H. Lane sent Pierce two letters, on January 21 and 23, asking for protection by federal troops to prevent an invasion from Missouri and requesting a proclamation by the president that would order the Missouri forces to disperse.[70] Before receiving these requests, Pierce had already prepared a lengthy message to Congress on the situation in Kansas.

The message asked the Congress to appropriate funds to execute the laws and maintain order in Kansas. Pierce reviewed the history of the organization of the territory, placing much of the blame for the trouble on former governor Reeder for arriving late to his post; failing to order a census immediately; delaying the election of a legislature until March 30, 1855; and not convening the territorial legislature until July 1855, more than six months after the meeting of the first Nebraska legislature. Thus, Kansas was left "without a complete government, without any territorial legislative authority, without local law, and, of course, without the ordinary guaranties of peace and public order" for over a year after the territory was formed by the act of Congress. Reeder compounded these failings by diverting his attention to illegal land speculation, setting "an example of the violation of law," a violation that required his removal.[71]

Pierce went on to condemn the influence of "propagandist" organizations for interfering in the settlement of the territory and for the "extremely irritating and offensive" language of their press. This propaganda prompted the "intense indignation" of neighboring Missouri but did not justify "the illegal and reprehensible countermovements which ensued."[72] Admitting that "illegal votes" and "fraud and violence" occurred in the elections in Kansas, Pierce criticized Reeder for certifying most of the results, thereby giving "complete legality to the first legislative assembly of the Territory." Consequently, "whatever irregularities may have occurred" Pierce concluded that it was "too late now to raise that question." He continued, "For all present purposes the legislative body thus constituted and elected was the legitimate authority of the Territory."[73]

According to Pierce, Reeder then incited the new legislature by attempting to locate the capital "unlawfully on land within a military reservation," and when the members protested, he proceeded to veto all of the legislature's laws. The governor's actions encouraged those opposed to the legislature, "merely a party of the inhabitants," to take the "revolutionary" step of calling a convention, writing a constitution, electing officials, and declaring a state government.

Pierce concluded that his constitutional duty required "him to take care that the laws of the United States be faithfully executed" and to put down any "insurrection." He directed territorial officials to call on the military, the militias of neighboring states, or the "*posse comitatus*." Pierce also declared, "If the Territory be invaded by the citizens of other States, whether for the purpose of deciding elections or any other, and the local authorities find themselves unable to repel or withstand it, they will be entitled to . . . the aid of the General Government."[74] Pierce asserted, "Interference on the one hand to procure the abolition or prohibition of slave labor . . . has produced mischievous interference on the other for its maintenance or introduction. One wrong begets another." Pierce then reiterated the belief, stated by many during the debates on the Kansas-Nebraska bill, that the territory could not long sustain slavery, if not for the outside interference: "Climate, soil, production, hopes of rapid advancement . . . would have quietly determined the question which is at this time of such disturbing character."[75]

Predicting that "disorders" would "continue to occur there, with increasing tendency to violence," Pierce proposed a law be enacted to authorize the territory to become a state as soon as its population was of "sufficient number." Since the population at the time was less than a third of the required ninety-three thousand, this would leave the territorial government in control for the foreseeable future and short-circuit the Free-State Party's effort to achieve immediate admission based on its Topeka constitution.[76]

Since the House was still in stalemate over the election of a speaker, the arrival of Pierce's secretary, Sidney Webster, on the floor of the chamber to deliver the message to the clerk prompted "screeches and screams" from the Republican members, who proceeded "bawling and halloing like a parcel of wild Comanche Indians" to prevent the message from being received. Despite much "swearing" and amid "great commotion and confusion," Clerk Forney was able to restore order, upon which Alexander H. Stephens moved that the message be received and read. Both motions passed, a surprising development, as the House had previously refused to receive the annual message.[77] Republicans saw a political motive in the message: an appeal to southern Know-Nothings to induce them to break away from their candidates for speaker and support the Democrat. If this was the intention of the message, it failed, as the House finally voted on February 2 to elect a speaker by plurality rather than majority vote. Nathaniel P. Banks of Massachusetts, a Republican who had formerly been a Know-Nothing, was elected by a scant three-vote margin.[78]

Pierce followed his message on Kansas with a proclamation of February 11, 1856, which was drafted by Cushing and commanded "all persons engaged in unlawful combinations against the constitutional authority of the Territory of Kansas . . . to disperse and retire peaceably to their respective abodes . . ." He warned all persons attempting insurrection or "aggressive intrusion" in the territory that the U.S. Army would support the "local militia" in protecting "the persons, property, and civil rights of all peaceable and law-abiding inhabitants of the Territory." Pierce advised "the good citizens" of Kansas to "repulse" the "agitators" and "disorganizers" and "to testify their attachment to their country."[79] After conferring with Pierce and his cabinet, Governor Shannon was ordered back to Kansas, with authorization to employ the federal troops at Fort Leavenworth, "but only if he should find a resort to it unavoidable in order to insure the due execution of the laws and to preserve the public peace."[80] Secretary of War Davis instructed Colonels Sumner and Cooke in Kansas to support the governor, with this admonition: "You will exercise much caution to avoid, if possible, collision with even insurgent citizens; and will endeavor to suppress resistance to the laws and constituted authorities by that moral force which, happily, in our country, is ordinarily sufficient to secure respect to the laws of the land. . . ."[81] Davis then urged the president to ask Congress "for an early appropriation of three millions of dollars for increasing the military efficiency of the country, to be applied, at the discretion of the President" to the situation in Kansas.[82] Pierce also considered sending a two-man commission, a northerner and a southerner, to Kansas to attempt pacification of the conflict. Marcy tried to convince former governor Horatio Seymour of New York to serve, but Seymour declined, writing, "I am satisfied it [the commission] will do more harm than good."[83] The idea was dropped.

In Kansas, the Free-State government was inaugurated on March 4 at Topeka, with the convening of its legislature and the inaugural address of its governor, Charles Robinson. Sheriff Jones was present, observing the proceedings, and many members expected to be arrested for treason. In his address, Robinson justified the revolutionary movement but pledged "not a finger should be raised against the Federal authority until there shall be no hope of relief but in revolution."[84] Proceeding with caution, the legislature decided against passing any laws until Congress acted on its application for statehood; the legislature then adjourned until July 4. Governor Shannon had also acted with restraint by not breaking up the illegal gathering. All sides, including the Pierce administration, looked to the now fully organized Congress for action.

John P. Hale responded to Pierce's message and proclamation with another tirade in the Senate. While previously condemning Pierce for not sending troops to Kansas, Hale now charged the president with sending "his myrmidons to shoot down the free inhabitants of Kansas. . . ." He continued, "Let him fire." Senator James C. Jones of Tennessee objected to the "offensive" language of Hale's attack and concluded that the New Hampshire senator's recent return to Congress was a case of the Devil taking care of his own. Hale agreed: "Sir, you know who brought me back here. It was the President of the United States, and nobody else who has done it. If it had not been for the course which the President of the United States took upon this very subject—if it had not been for the manner in which he outraged public sentiment in his native State, so that he has not got a single friend from that State in either House to say, "God bless him!" I should not have been here. That is the devil who took care of me—the President of the United States."[85] Jones responded with sarcasm that if Hale was "indebted" to the President for his senatorial seat, Hale was "the most ungrateful wretch that ever disgraced the American Senate. [Laughter and applause in the galleries.]"[86]

Pierce's recommendations from his message on Kansas had been referred to the Senate Committee on Territories where chairman Stephen A. Douglas, finally back in his seat after a lengthy absence due to illness, set about preparing a report and a bill to enable the territory to make the steps needed for statehood. The report was read in the Senate on March 12. It closely "followed Pierce's reasoning" by blaming the Emigrant Aid Society for initiating the trouble in Kansas, and arousing the retaliatory actions of the Missourians. The report condemned the revolutionary Topeka statehood movement as an attempt to overthrow the legitimate territorial government. Though it was a "manifestly one-sided" report, Douglas did condemn both sides for the foreign intervention in Kansas.[87] A minority report was presented by Jacob Collamer, a Republican from Vermont. This equally one-sided report justified the actions of the free-state movement and proposed the immediate admission of Kansas under the Topeka constitution.[88]

Douglas's bill was presented on March 17. The bill would move the territory in steps toward statehood by first requiring a census. When the population reached ninety-three thousand, the legislature was to provide for a convention of delegates, elected by residents who had lived in the territory for a minimum of six months, to write a constitution and create a state government. The bill assumed the legitimacy of the territorial government. Since Kansas did not meet the population requirement, the territorial government would be sustained for the immediate future.[89] The bill closely followed Pierce's recommendation, but was unacceptable to Republicans and those who supported the free-state movement. Senator Seward offered a substitute bill which would admit Kansas immediately under the Topeka constitution.[90] Rancorous debate on the Kansas bills began on March

20 and dragged on into the spring. At one point, Douglas chided the Topeka government, which was supported by "the especial friends of the negro," for banning free blacks from the territory: "If the negro be free, you will not let him come! If he be a slave, you will not let him stay!" In a speech in April, Seward compared Pierce to George III for attempting to put down those who resisted tyranny.[91] With the Senate controlled by Democrats and the House by Republicans, no bill was likely to pass both houses. In a presidential election year, the Republican Party, which arose in response to the Kansas-Nebraska bill, could only benefit by allowing Kansas to bleed.

The Republican-dominated House did create a special committee to investigate election fraud in Kansas. The three members, Republicans William A. Howard of Michigan and John Sherman of Ohio and Democrat Mordecai Oliver of Missouri, set out immediately for the territory, backed by a special appropriation of $10,000 to defray their expenses.[92] While in Kansas, the committee members took volumes of testimony and became embroiled in the events that erupted that spring. The House also contested the seat of Kansas territorial delegate J. W. Whitfield, who had been elected by the proslavery voters. The Republicans attempted to unseat Whitfield and replace him with former governor Reeder chosen by a free-state election. But even some Republicans balked at seating the "irregularly" elected Reeder. Whitfield reported from Washington in March, "I must confess Reeder & his army of Ab.[olitionists] give me some trouble. I have thrown him twice & I think will give him another toss. I feel certain they have despaired of his getting a seat & only hope to send the election back."[93]

In this acrimonious climate, being unable to count on supportive action from a divided Congress, Pierce saw his political fortunes declining. Buchanan, who had the advantage of absence from the United States throughout the Kansas-Nebraska debacle, was gaining support for the presidential nomination. John Slidell, a leader of Buchanan's campaign, predicted that the delegates at the convention would desert Pierce "for a man who can win. . . ." Slidell continued, "They know that Pierce cannot."[94] On March 28, John W. Forney, who had served the Pierce administration as editor of the *Washington Union*, resigned from the paper to return to Pennsylvania and lead the Buchanan effort in his home state.[95] Others clung loyally, if unenthusiastically, to the president. Senator Robert Toombs of Georgia wrote in February, "Pierce is anxious for the nomination, is fighting Buck hard. As things now stand I rather incline to think we cannot do much better than to run him."[96]

The March state election in New Hampshire was another blow to Pierce, as the Democrats failed to regain the governorship and the legislature. Hard leader Daniel Dickinson of New York rejoiced to the turncoat Edmund Burke: "I had noted the defeat of Piercedom in your election and was exceedingly glad of it. It was indispensable to the course of political decency and common morality. The means to gain such an end are comparatively of little consequence. I conclude there is no danger of Pierce's renomination at Cincinnati."[97] The election had been extremely close, however, and Sidney Webster remained optimistic: "The result has not prejudiced Genl. P in my judgment, anywhere, and in many localities I think it has aided his prospects. Mr. Buchanan's friends are making earnest efforts to accomplish his nomination. . . . They are full of zeal, of efficiency, and are well disciplined—better perhaps than those of any other candidate. I have no belief, however, that B will come within even a long distance of a nomination. None whatever. Nearly all well informed politicians here, of all parties, admit that General Pierce will have a majority of the convention on the first ballot."[98] Pierce was more realistic. The results in New Hampshire prompted him to summon his brother Henry to Washington: "You ought to come on every account, but I desire to see you especially to converse about plans for life when my labors here shall come to a close—having reference to you as well as myself. The Democracy of N.H. have done nobly—all that men could do. They will carry the State next Fall I think beyond question."[99]

Election year politics and partisan hostility did not prevent Pierce from carrying out his social responsibilities during the winter of 1856. As was customary, the president invited every senator and representative to dine with him sometime during the first session of Congress. The weekly dinners, composed of about twenty guests each, must have been a strain on Jane, who was usually present, but the president was always a gracious host. Jane's twenty-year-old niece, Mary

E. Aiken, visited the White House that winter and reported on one of the dinners:

> Yesterday we had the last of the Congressional dinners. It was just the very last picking and a real Know-Nothing set. There were only six ladies besides ourselves and they were very common looking people—one or two pleasant ones but that was all. I had one of the most agreeable, a Mr. [Gilchrist] Porter of Missouri who was a most monstrous talker and entertained me with an account of his wife and "four little responsibilities" at home. The gentleman who sat at my right was absolutely unbearable. I did not speak to him once. My man had a dark silk handkerchief, shoveled his food in with his knife and informed me that I had no appetite but he would eat enough for both. It was a french dinner and looked very nice . . . the servants were intensely amused with some of the people. Alonzo and Edward [White House servants] could not keep it to themselves. One man took a veal cutlet up in his fingers and eat it . . .[100]

A further glimpse into life in the Pierce White House is provided by Jonathan P. Cilley, the son of Pierce's former college friend, who had been a congressman from Maine and who had been slain in the notorious duel in 1838. "Prin," as the younger Cilley was known, visited Washington that winter and reminded everyone of his late father. Pierce had once offered young Cilley a place at West Point, but Prin chose to attend Bowdoin instead. In 1855 Pierce had sent Cilley $100 to help with his college expenses, but the young man had returned the money, as he did not need the financial aid. Arriving in the capital in January 1856, Cilley first called on B. B. French, another old friend of his father, and then proceeded to the White House to meet the president. Writing to his sister, Cilley reported that Pierce received him "very cordially." Cilley continued, "He invited me to come and stay in his mansion . . . I could not resist—and at half past nine my baggage—Uncle Burley's old valise with a rope tied around it for a lock—was at the door."[101]

Pierce "conversed very pleasantly with" the young man "for an hour or more." Cilley wrote, "He showed me my room himself giving me all the little anecdotes a stranger would require. It was a beautiful room, opposite his own." The next morning, Sunday, a snow storm was "raging," but Pierce insisted on attending church. Cilley wrote, "We walked arm in arm down Pennsylvania Avenue—would you not have smiled to have seen us?" Cilley reported, "Mrs. Pierce is quite unwell." He added, "I have not seen Mrs. Pierce and probably will not as she seldom leaves her room." That evening he concluded his letter to his sister, "in the President's private office." He wrote, "Pres. Pierce not far from me by the side of the fire."[102]

On April 11, Governor Shannon reported to Marcy that since the Topeka legislature had adjourned in March, the territory had been peaceful. Shannon did not anticipate an invasion from Missouri but was concerned about the weapons being smuggled into Kansas. He confessed that he had "misgivings" about the future.[103]

The Pierce administration pursued an aggressive policy in relation to Great Britain and against filibusters. But the president earned no credit from the voters for these consistent and determined actions. The nation's attention was focused on events in Kansas. Pierce tried to steer a middle ground in the troubled territory. Though the governor was authorized to use the army to put down insurrection or invasion from Missouri, federal troops were not to be used to interfere with the peaceful activities of the "revolutionary" Free-State movement. For a change, Pierce was working in concert with the congressional leaders of the Democratic Party. They hoped to pass legislation to delay the question of statehood, support the territorial government, and allow popular sovereignty to work via the peaceful settlement of the territory. Pierce expected that this would lead to a free state, but one that voted Democratic. But the Republican majority in the House was equally determined to foment as much trouble as possible to keep the issue before the voters of the North and to reap the rewards in the presidential election, and no one in Washington controlled the actions of the competing forces in Kansas.

11

MORE CRISES AND A CONVENTION

DURING A LULL BETWEEN crises, Pierce celebrated one of the signal successes of his administration: the construction of six new steam frigates for the navy. Admiral Mahan later described these powerful vessels as "the nucleus of the fighting force" of the navy, and "the most formidable ships of this class afloat, or as yet designed." Intended for use on the high seas against a foreign enemy, the huge, unwieldy frigates proved of little value during the Civil War, when naval operations were confined along the southern coast and shallow ports, but foreign navies immediately copied the "thoroughly up-to-date" steamers.[1] The first of the ships, the *Merrimac*, was launched in April 1856. Pierce and Secretary of the Navy Dobbin toured the ship at Annapolis on April 19. The night before, the president took the train to Annapolis, where he spoke at a reception held at the Maryland State House. Later that evening, Pierce and Dobbin attended a ball in the president's honor at the Naval Academy. The next morning, he was presented to the entire school of 120 midshipmen who demonstrated their skills with guns and mortars by firing at targets as much as three or four miles out in the bay. At noon the president's party, along with congressmen and ladies, toured the *Merrimac*. Captain Pendergast thrilled his guests by having the crew of more than five hundred sailors simulate a battle by racing to their posts, firing the powerful 84- and 120-pound guns, and preparing to board the imaginary enemy ship with boarding pikes and cutlasses. Following the battle exercise, the guests assembled in the captain's cabin for refreshments. By evening, Pierce, long an advocate for modernization of the military, was back in Washington, after following one of the most personally satisfying and enjoyable days of his administration.[2]

April also saw the renewal of the ongoing controversy between the Pierce administration and former Whig congressman and Indian agent Richard W. Thompson. Since the beginning of his administration, Pierce, Interior Secretary McClelland, and Indian Commissioner Manypenny had resisted Thompson's claim to one-third of all money appropriated to the Menominee Indians of Wisconsin for serving as their attorney during treaty negotiations. Senate hearings had been held at Thompson's insistence, bribes amounting to over $10,000 had been paid by Thompson to congressmen and lobbyists, but the effort had failed to produce congressional approval of his claim. The victory for the administration was shortlived. Thompson had influential and unscrupulous friends in Washington. On the last day of the Thirty-third Congress, March 3, 1855, Senator Bright tacked on a twenty-seventh section to "the civil and diplomatic appropriations bill," granting Thompson one-half of the more than $80,000 that he claimed, with this caveat: "Provided, that the same be paid with the consent of the Menomonies."[3] Pierce, who waited at the Capitol to sign last-minute bills, may not have been aware of the additional section, but he could hardly veto such a major general appropriations bill at the moment Congress adjourned without hamstringing his administration, and he may have been satisfied by the caveat that Thompson would not receive his money until the Indians had an opportunity to reconsider.

On March 7, 1855, Thompson applied to the Treasury Department for the money. Objections were raised immediately by the Pierce administration. Treasury Secretary Guthrie claimed the payment to Thompson would violate provisions of the treaty with the Menominee and asked Attorney General Cushing for an opinion as to whether an act of Congress could alter a treaty.[4] Interior Secretary McClelland and Indian Commissioner Manypenny also appealed to Cushing, claiming that Thompson's original agreement with the Menominee was signed by only one-third of the chiefs, without a government agent or interpreter present, as required by law, to determine if the illiterate chiefs understood what they were signing.[5]

Cushing's opinion of May 21, 1855, did not answer all of the constitutional issues. Stating that the "Indians are the wards of the United States, and the President is their Great Father," Cushing determined that no contracts could be made by them without the president's approval and that Congress had overstepped its authority by granting Thompson his money. But in his investigation of the matter, Cushing uncovered a more egregious problem. From the time the "civil and diplomatic bill" was passed until it was printed, a change had taken place in the wording of the twenty-seventh section. The condition, "provided, that the same be paid with the consent of the Menomonies," was missing from the printed bill. As the law read, Thompson was entitled to his money without conditions. Altering the wording of bills after they had been passed was a habitual problem with the Thirty-third Congress, and blame may be assigned to the Senate president pro tem, Jesse Bright, a friend of Thompson's from Indiana, and to Chief Clerk John W. Forney, who both had a financial stake in Thompson's claim.[6] Cushing concluded, "Where the law as it stands written manifests error, the President may suspend the execution of it until he shall have opportunity to consult Congress on the subject."[7]

Faced with another lengthy delay in receiving his money, Thompson met with Cushing and proposed to Pierce that the original intent of the bill be carried out and that the Menominee be asked to reconsider Thompson's claim to money from their treaty. That summer, Guthrie sent Treasury Department troubleshooter Samuel Clarke to Wisconsin. On September 7, 1855, a meeting was held in which Clarke and Thompson both addressed the chiefs, as did Indian superintendent Dr. Huebschmann, representing the Bureau of Indian Affairs. On September 10, the Menominee chiefs voted unanimously not to consent to pay Thompson. Guthrie reported this decision to Pierce.[8] Thompson went back on his word to accept the decision of the chiefs, claiming that the meeting had not been fairly conducted and that Clarke and Huebschmann had prejudiced the chiefs against him in advance. Clarke and Huebschmann, in turn, accused Thompson's friends of pressuring the chiefs on his behalf. Thompson appealed his case to the new Thirty-fourth Congress. On March 6, 1856, the Senate passed a resolution requiring the president to provide all information relative to the Thompson claim. On April 10, the Pierce administration submitted 319 pages of letters and testimony, which was assigned to the Senate Committee on Indian Affairs.[9] On May 19, the committee issued a one-sentence recommendation that no further action be taken, thus allowing the president's decision on the matter to stand.[10] The continuing effort of the Pierce administration to protect the treasury from fraud and corruption was an exhausting and thankless task, and Thompson wasn't done yet. He still had Senate president pro tem Jesse Bright on his side.

In May the many-headed hydra of unresolved issues, filibusters and Nicaragua, British recruitment and Central America, Congress and internal improvements, and the violence and politics of Kansas combined to destroy the Pierce administration on the eve of the Democratic convention. Public opinion in the United States had always favored Walker's filibuster in Nicaragua. By the spring of 1856, his government tenaciously clung to power, and Walker had appealed his case to the American people through a newspaper editorial claiming that if he was a filibuster than so were Lafayette, DeKalb, and Steuben, who had left their homelands to assist the United States in its quest for independence.[11] Though directed by Cushing to intercept filibusters headed for Nicaragua, U.S. attorneys in San Francisco and New Orleans, burned by past failed prosecutions and influenced by local opinion, looked the other way as vessels openly embarked with recruits for Walker. In April, 208 men departed from New Orleans as bands played and newspapers reported the event.[12]

Pierce was reluctant to recognize Walker's de facto regime, but ignoring it left the United States powerless to influence events in Nicaragua. Walker was feuding with Vanderbilt and revoked the exclusive contract of the Accessory Transit Company to transport passengers and supplies across the isthmus. Following civil unrest in Panama, American citizens had no safe alternate route to reach California. Great Britain, fearful of losing its control of Greytown and the Mosquito coast in Nicaragua, was encouraging other Central American nations to intervene there. Costa Rica invaded Nicaragua in April after securing an offer of arms from Great Britain.[13] To Pierce, failure to recognize Walker's government risked the unintended consequence of aiding Great Britain in extending its power and influence in Central America.

Secretary of State Marcy remained unconvinced of the wisdom of recognizing Walker. He wrote to the U.S. minister in London, George

M. Dallas, in late April: "We are a good deal perplexed with the present status of Central America. Walker's govt has its partisans, but I am not one of them. I have yet seen nothing which would justify the recognition of it."[14] Walker made a second attempt at achieving recognition in May by sending a new representative to Washington, the respected Father Augustin Vijil, the curate of Granada. Pierce decided to receive Vijil against Marcy's advice: "We have had under discussion a very difficult matter—the recognition of the Rivas-Walker govt. The President has determined to take that step—I advised against it, but it is determined. . . ."[15] Marcy understood that the actions of Great Britain had forced Pierce's hand, "had she acted as she ought to have done in the whole Central American question things would not have come to this pass."[16] He later wrote, "The public mind in England seems to be moved by the recognition of the Government of Nicaragua. This act which I regarded as premature (though it seems that I was in arrears of public opinion in this country) was precipitated by the conduct of the British Government in furnishing aid to Costa Rica . . . to crush out the only existing authority in Nicaragua." The United States could not allow Great Britain "to obtain complete ascendancy in all the States of Central America."[17]

Pierce explained his reasons for recognizing Walker's government in a message to Congress on May 15, 1856. In justifying his action, he focused almost entirely on Great Britain's history of meddling in Central American affairs and its violations of the Clayton-Bulwer Treaty. The message implied no approval of Walker's regime: "It is the established policy of the United States to recognize all governments without question of their source or their organization, or of the means by which the governing persons attain their power, provided there be a government *de facto* accepted by the people of the country. . . ."[18] He acknowledged the disruption of "the interoceanic communication by the way of Nicaragua" as an additional reason to resume "diplomatic intercourse" to protect the property and passage of American citizens in that country.[19]

Pierce wrote the message himself without the aid of Marcy. He regretted that his decision did not have Marcy's support, and late one night after finishing the message he sent a note to his secretary of state: "Altho' I cannot have what would have offered me great relief, the approbation of your judgment in relation to the reception of the minister from Nicaragua it is pleasant to believe that I can have your advice as my friend in all matters connected with myself or our Country, and to know that I can never fail to appreciate a friendship so generous and true, as that which has been exemplified by you in all our intercourse."[20]

Although the timing of the recognition was determined by Vijil's arrival in Washington, the press saw a political connection. Buchanan arrived back in the United States on April 23 to an enthusiastic public reception and parade in New York.[21] This began a carefully orchestrated procession through eastern cities, organized by the managers of his presidential campaign. The public parades in Philadelphia and elsewhere demonstrated that Buchanan's presidential fortunes were rising at the expense of those of the president. Buchanan reached Washington on May 12, the same day that Pierce wrote his message to Congress recognizing Nicaragua. Marcy acknowledged in a letter to Dallas the connection between the two events but declared that Buchanan had "not yet got a two thirds or even a majority vote.[22] The recognition of Walker's government appealed to public opinion and may have, momentarily, diverted attention from Buchanan's triumphal procession, but Pierce's main reason for doing it was his determined and consistent effort to force the British government to acknowledge and respect the United States' right to a sphere of influence in Central America.

Predictably, the recognition of Walker's government was praised by the Democratic press and attacked by the opposition. In New York a rally was held on May 23, attended by twenty thousands, to celebrate the event. Senator Cass addressed the meeting by letter, praising Walker: "He who does not sympathize with such an enterprise has little in common with me." Governor Rodman Price of New Jersey and Tammany leader Isaiah Rynders, the notorious Irish gang leader and longtime endorser of filibusters, spoke at the meeting.[23] That same week, however, news from Kansas overshadowed the Nicaraguan situation and prevented Pierce from gaining any advantage from his decision to recognize Walker's government.

Spring weather brought renewed turmoil to Kansas. In mid-April, Sheriff Jones returned to Lawrence to arrest men who had helped

Branson escape in December. A crowd of free-state citizens surrounded the sheriff, preventing him from making any arrests. The next day, Jones returned with a small posse and again was repulsed by an angry mob. Jones then appealed for help from Governor Shannon, whose instructions from the president were to call on the military for help only when duly constituted authority was resisted. Shannon asked Colonel Sumner for assistance, and the colonel ordered a lieutenant and ten dragoons to accompany Sheriff Jones to Lawrence. In the presence of the U.S. Army the Lawrence citizens backed off, and Jones was able to make six arrests. That night, while camped outside of Lawrence with the soldiers guarding his prisoners, Jones was shot in the back by a sniper.[24] The sheriff recovered from his wound, but his shooting was widely reported in the press and incited Missourians to take to the field once again.

In early May, territorial chief justice Lecompte convened a grand jury, which indicted all of the leaders of the Free-State government for treason. The federal marshal was sent to Lawrence to make arrests. Reeder, Lane and others escaped from the territory, but the Free-State governor Robinson was captured and held at Leavenworth. The congressional investigating committee, taking testimony in Lawrence, was witness to many of the events in April and early May and sent reports to the East, some of which were carried by Mrs. Robinson who hid them in her clothing.[25]

In mid-May the federal marshal returned to Lawrence to make more arrests, accompanied by the recovering Sheriff Jones and a posse of five hundred to seven hundred men organized without Governor Shannon's knowledge. The citizens of Lawrence called on Colonel Sumner for protection. He forwarded the request to Governor Shannon, who denied it, stating that only the marshal and a small posse were in the area. Shannon was increasingly out of touch with events in the territory. He had failed to temper Justice Lecompte's sweeping indictments, was rumored by the free-state press to be perpetually drunk, and was providing inaccurate reports to the administration.[26]

On May 21, Jones led his posse with five artillery pieces into Lawrence. The free-state newspaper office was destroyed, as was the Free State Hotel, a fortresslike structure that had withstood the artillery barrage but was set on fire. Former senator Atchison was present and tried to prevent the worst of the destruction. The loss of property was severe, but the citizens of Lawrence were spared. The only casualty was a member of the posse who was struck by falling debris.[27]

The distance and time required for letters and reports to reach Washington left Pierce in the dark about the situation. As initial reports of the "sack of Lawrence" reached him, Pierce telegraphed frantically to Shannon for information. Pierce asked, "Has military force been found necessary to maintain civil government in Kansas?" Colonel Sumner had reported by letter to Secretary of War Davis the denial by Governor Shannon of his request to send troops to protect Lawrence. Pierce advised Shannon, "His [Colonel Sumner's] suggestion strikes me as wise and prudent":

> My knowledge of the facts is imperfect; but with the force of Colonel Sumner at hand, I perceive no occasion for the posse, armed or unarmed, which the Marshal is said to have assembled at Lecompton. The instructions issued to yourself and Colonel Sumner during your last visit to this city must be efficiently executed. Sufficient power was committed to you, and you must use it. Obedience to the laws and consequent security to the Citizens of Kansas are the primary objects. You must repress lawless violence in whatever form it may manifest itself.[28]

Two weeks later, Pierce continued to appeal for information,

> Were my dispatches of May 23d received by yourself or Colonel Sumner? If they were, why have they not been acknowledged? Confused and contradictory accounts continue to reach me of scenes of disorder and violence in Kansas. If the civil authorities, sustained by the military force under the command of Colonels Sumner and Cooke placed at your disposal, are not sufficient to maintain order and afford protection to peaceable and law-abiding citizens, you should have advised me at once. I hardly need repeat the instructions so often given. Maintain the laws firmly and impartially, and take care that no good citizen has just ground to complain of the want of protection.[29]

The exaggerated reports of the burning of Lawrence were a propaganda victory for the free-state cause. Three days after the attack on Lawrence, in retaliation, the free-state murderer John Brown led his own posse and hacked to death five proslavery settlers in the middle of the night at their settlement along the Pottawatomie Creek. All of the victims were poor settlers, none of whom owned slaves, but Brown justified their killing as "doing God's service."[30] The visiting members of the Republican-controlled House investigating committee took voluminous testimony regarding the invasion of Lawrence but refused to hear testimony about Brown's Pottawatomie Massacre.[31]

As Lawrence was burning, the Senate was debating the Kansas bills of Douglas and Seward. On May 20, Senator Charles Sumner of Massachusetts, in support of Seward's bill to admit Kansas immediately as a free state, made a highly provocative but carefully prepared and rehearsed speech in which he personally insulted other senators. Attacking Douglas, Sumner declared, his "tongue . . . fills the Senate with its offensive odor." His most vulgar references were to the elderly, courtly, South Carolina senator Andrew P. Butler, who had a speech impediment. Sumner referred to the "incoherent phrases, discharged with the loose expectorations of his speech. . . ." Sumner continued, "The Senator touches nothing that he does not disfigure. . . . He cannot ope his mouth, but out there flies a blunder."[32] Senator Cass called the speech "the most un-American and un-patriotic that ever grated on the ears of the members of this high body." Douglas speculated, "Is it his object to provoke some of us to kick him as we would a dog in the street, that he may get sympathy upon the just chastisement?" Three days later, Sumner got his wish. To avenge the honor of his uncle, Senator Butler, Rep. Preston Brooks entered the Senate chamber and brutally beat Sumner over the head with his cane. The bleeding senator was led away to martyrdom in the northern press and a lengthy absence from the Senate. Brooks became a hero to the South, receiving numerous gifts of replacement canes, including one engraved with the phrase "Hit Him Again."[33]

Congress provided Pierce with an additional problem during the crisis-filled month of May. Three internal improvement bills, one to improve navigation at the mouth of the Mississippi River and two to deepen the channels of the Saint Clair flats and Saint Marys River in Michigan, reached the president.[34] Though the bills totaled less than $500,000 in appropriations, Pierce vetoed all three. His brief veto messages repeated his constitutional objections to any "general system of internal improvements" intended purely for commercial purposes. Since the improvements "would serve no valuable purpose as contributing to the common defense," his constitutional scruples required him to veto the three bills.[35] The bills had been sponsored by Democratic Senators Cass of Michigan and Slidell and Benjamin of Louisiana. Senator Mason of Virginia wrote that the vetoes "tend[ed] to exasperate feeling and render his nomination . . . more doubtful."[36] Pierce had never compromised his principles to gain personal political advantage and he wasn't about to start in the final days leading up to the Cincinnati convention.

The conclusion to the British recruiting controversy also occurred in late May. The Pierce administration had waited patiently since December for an answer from the British government to the U.S. request for the recall of British minister Crampton and the consuls at New York, Philadelphia, and Cincinnati for their involvement in the recruiting scandal. The answer from British foreign minister Lord Clarendon was finally received in Washington on May 17. As expected, the British government refused to recall its officers in the United States and denied any intent to violate U.S. neutrality laws. Despite the conciliatory tone of the letter and a vague apology that any U.S. laws had been broken, the letter accepted Crampton's version of the events without question and continued to repeat errors of fact.[37] There was no alternative left to the president, and Marcy informed Dallas in London on May 19, "Mr. Crampton will get his passport. . . ." Charging that Clarendon's letter was "got up for home consumption" and was "full of errors," Marcy advised Dallas that the deed would not be done until "a reply to Lord C's last" could be written, which would "require a week or ten days for preparing."[38]

Marcy was assisted in writing the reply by Pierce and Attorney General Cushing, who submitted a lengthy report to the president to correct "the palpable errors of statement" concerning Cushing that were contained in Clarendon's letter.[39] Marcy's reply of May 27 accepted the British government's assurance that it had not intended to violate U.S. laws, but stated that the weight of evidence against

Crampton and the consuls was too strong to be ignored. The letter concluded, "The President, out of consideration to the interests of both countries, could take no other action than reluctantly to dismiss the British minister and revoke the exequaturs of Messrs. Mathew, Rowcroft, and Barclay."[40] The dismissal of the four British officers occurred the following day, and the Pierce administration braced itself, once again, to await the reaction from London.[41] Marcy was hopeful, however, that the British government would not retaliate. He wrote to Dallas, "I think the grounds on which the dismissal of Mr. Crampton & the other consuls is played will cause the Ministry to hesitate in sending your passport to you," but he urged Dallas to be prepared in case he was dismissed: "You are at liberty to retire to the Continent & select such place as will be agreeable to you so long as convenient for speedy communication with this government."[42]

Marcy's letter was generally praised in the press, but the timing of the dismissals, less than a week before the Cincinnati convention, prompted charges that Pierce was risking the possibility of war with England in a desperate attempt to win political support within his party.[43] The sequence of letters between Marcy and Lord Clarendon disproves this charge, and, in later years, even Jefferson Davis's wife Varina felt the need to defend Pierce's action: "The President was personally partial to Mr. Crampton, and it is difficult to perceive how, except from an irresponsible writer, ignorant of the truth, the Administration of President Pierce could have been accused of a desire to derive 'popularity,' or a new 'tenure of office,' from involving England and America in a war."[44]

It is hard to imagine that Pierce had time for political strategizing during the hectic weeks before the convention, but his campaign managers, Charles H. Peaslee, John H. George, Harry Hibbard, and Charles G. Greene, who was editor of the *Boston Post*, all veterans of his 1852 campaign, arrived in Washington around May 21 to meet with the president before moving on to Cincinnati.[45] Accepting that no candidate had a clear majority of delegates entering the convention, Pierce's team forged an uneasy alliance with the supporters of Stephen A. Douglas. Pierce and Buchanan had the most delegates, with Douglas a distant third. By agreeing to have some of his delegates support Pierce in the early balloting, Douglas hoped to block

Buchanan. Pierce's delegates would then switch to Douglas in later balloting if the president's support proved inadequate to gain the nomination.[46]

Pierce was realistic about his chances. He could count on the votes of New Hampshire, Massachusetts, Vermont, Rhode Island, Kentucky, and all the states of the deep South except Louisiana. The key states would be New York and Virginia. Pierce was backed by the Softs in New York, led by former governor Horatio Seymour, surrogate for Marcy. The now permanent division between the Hards and Softs had resulted in two separate state conventions, each selecting a full slate of delegates to the national convention. While the Softs maintained a two-to-one voting majority over the Hards in the state, Daniel Dickinson was determined to get the Hard slate recognized by the convention as the true representatives of the Democratic Party in New York. In Virginia, Senators Hunter and Mason supported Pierce, but the delegation was led by Governor Henry A. Wise, whose switch from Buchanan to Pierce at the 1852 convention had started the ball rolling for the dark horse nominee. Wise was backing Buchanan again in 1856, and the Virginia delegation's decision to adopt the unit rule would place all of the state's votes in Buchanan's column, at least in the early balloting.[47]

In late May, Pierce received a letter from Jane's sister, Mary Aiken, expressing anxiety for his well-being, considering the pressures he was under from the violence in Kansas, the reports of possible war with Great Britain, and the concern over his renomination. Pierce tried to reassure her: "My steps have all been taken very deliberately." He continued, "There will be no war with England and you will hereafter admit that my action has been wise and patriotic." As for Kansas, he wrote, "I deplore some passing events as you do, but if men in high position will deliberately manufacture causes, it is vain to try to avert consequences." He tried to reassure Mary regarding his political future:

> I beg you not be anxious for me. I am inclined to think, that you will be glad to have me express the opinion which I now entertain, that I shall not be renominated. The vote for me will be earnest, true and of a character to satisfy my pride—but Mr.

> Buchanan & Mr. Douglas will be able to prevent a ⅔ vote. While they may defeat me, there is little probability that either can secure his own nomination. You would be surprised to know with how much indifference I contemplate the result so far as it is calculated to affect me personally. I am weary of incipient labor but in good health and good heart. Dear Jane is also pretty well and somewhat anxious and troubled as you are.[48]

Pierce may have expressed indifference, but he was most desirous of preventing Buchanan's nomination, backed as Buchanan was by all of Pierce's bitterest foes within the party. Leading the Buchanan effort were the unscrupulous bully and western speculator Senator Jesse Bright of Indiana and the shrewd, calculating filibuster advocate Senator John Slidell of Louisiana.[49] They made their way to Cincinnati to personally direct Buchanan's convention forces and were joined there by other Buchanan stalwarts, including Washington banker and financier of speculation and congressional bribery W. W. Corcoran and New York Hard leaders Daniel Dickinson and Dan Sickles. Henry M. Rice, of the Superior land deal, was tentatively backing Douglas but was ready to switch to Buchanan at the first opportunity.[50]

The first national convention held west of the Appalachian Mountains opened in Cincinnati on Monday, June 2, with a near riot, as rival delegations from Missouri and New York overpowered the guards and forced their way into the hall. Order was quickly restored, and the strength of Buchanan's well-organized campaign was immediately demonstrated by the election of a Buchaneer, John E. Ward of Georgia, as permanent chairman. With control of the chair, the Buchanan strategy was set in motion. A platform was adopted first, which included a popular sovereignty resolution designed to appease Douglas. Ward looked the other way as Buchanan's managers circulated through the delegations, promising government jobs to those who had failed to obtain them from Pierce.[51] These efforts still seemed inadequate to Ward, who wrote on June 3, "Buchanan in my opinion will *not* be nominated, but I doubt if either of the others will be."[52] But Slidell and John W. Forney had been working on Douglas for weeks, trying to weaken his alliance with Pierce, the understanding being that at age forty-three the Illinois senator should step aside for the elderly Buchanan and then receive the party's endorsement in 1860. That evening Douglas, accurately assessing his chances, wired his campaign manager, Rep. William A. Richardson, advising, "If the withdrawal of my name will contribute to the harmony of our Party . . . I hope you will not hesitate to take the step."[53]

The decisive moment for Pierce came on Thursday morning, June 5, with the report of the credentials committee. The majority report proposed the seating of only the Soft delegation of New York, but a minority report recommended both groups be seated and the state's thirty-five votes be divided equally among the Hards and Softs. By a narrow margin the minority report was adopted by a convention vote, and the Hards finally achieved their revenge on Pierce.[54] With this the president's chances of leading on the first ballot disappeared. That afternoon the balloting began. Buchanan led the first ballot with 135; Pierce had 122, Douglas 33, and Cass 5. Thirteen more ballots took place that day with Pierce's support withering throughout the afternoon and evening. By the fourteenth ballot the president was still second but with only 79 votes to 152 for Buchanan. As expected, with the dimming of Pierce's chances, his delegates began moving toward Douglas, who ended the day with sixty-three votes.[55]

In Washington, Pierce was kept informed of the balloting by telegraph. On Thursday night, with his support slipping away, he wired his managers to withdraw his name from nomination in the morning. The expectation was that most of his support would go to Douglas and that Buchanan could still be stopped. On Friday morning, Harry Hibbard of the New Hampshire delegation withdrew the president's name. Douglas's support rose to 121 votes on the sixteenth ballot, but Buchanan was still leading with 168. Douglas wired Richardson to withdraw his candidacy, and Buchanan was unanimously selected on the seventeenth ballot.[56] The convention proceeded to select John C. Breckinridge of Kentucky for vice president. Breckinridge had loyally kept his delegation in line for Pierce and then for Douglas throughout the balloting, and his selection was seen as a peace offering to the supporters of the defeated candidates.[57] In a further effort at unity, the convention delegates unanimously passed a resolution praising the Pierce administration: "In the face of the most determined opposition it has maintained the laws, enforced economy, fostered progress, and infused integrity and vigor into every department of the government. . . . It has signally improved our treaty relations, extending the field of commercial enterprise and vindicated the rights of American Citizens abroad. . . . and has at all times been faithful to the constitution."[58]

Though Pierce had kept faith with the Democratic Party's platform and principles, party leaders knew that he could not win reelection. Buchanan, because he had been out of the country for the entire Kansas controversy and could carry his home state of Pennsylvania, gave the party its best chance for victory in 1856. Pierce became the only elected president who sought reelection to be denied renomination by his party.

Pierce effectively hid his disappointment in the days and weeks ahead. On Saturday night, June 7, after the convention had adjourned in Cincinnati, an enthusiastic rally was held in Washington endorsing the Buchanan-Breckinridge ticket. The five thousand in attendance were addressed by Senators Cass and Douglas. At 10:00 p.m., led by the Marine Band, the throng marched to the White House to "serenade" the president. As the band played "Hail to the Chief," Pierce appeared in a window over the portico, to the enthusiastic cheers of the crowd. He stated, "The preference of the convention is the preference in this crisis of every friend who cares more for the country than for himself." He pledged his support of the ticket for "the prosperity of the republic." He continued, "The perpetuity of this blessed Union, depends essentially upon the vindication and maintenance of the principles declared by the recent convention."[59] Marcy reported on the convention to Dallas in London: "The President bears his disappointment manfully. He has now I believe less confidence in the faith of men than he had. If delegates had redeemed their voluntary pledges to him and his friends, the result would have been different. The President was less hopeful as the day for the meeting of the convention approached."[60]

Outside of the administration there was little sympathy for Pierce. One of the few who regretted the convention's decision was Senator Clement Clay of Alabama, who wrote on June 7, "Pierce was my choice above all men in the South, North, East, or West. If we could keep him in office for four years longer, the tariff would be brought down to a purely revenue standard, the Democratic Party put upon the true constitutional anti-internal improvement platform, the backbone of abolition broken, or badly strained, and the Government fixed in the old republican tack."[61] Other southern politicians doubted Pierce's antiabolition credentials. Alexander H. Stephens of Georgia blamed Pierce's defeat on the president's having "shot down all the true friends of the Kansas Bill in the Northern States two years ago—not with gunpowder . . . but with executive patronage by putting . . . enemies in power over their necks and heads." Stephens continued, "Many of our best friends at the North were *hostile* to Pierce, and to my knowledge they had reason to be." Stephens also wrote, "When he [Pierce] sent Reeder to Kansas his design or that of his Cabinet I am clearly of opinion was to make Kansas a free State."[62] From New Hampshire, Edmund Burke echoed Stephens's assessment in a congratulatory letter to Buchanan: "You will pardon me for saying, that during the last three years many of the best democrats of this state and of the North [who] fought the battle against abolitionism without flinching have been under the prosecution from 'the powers that be.'"[63]

Equally unsympathetic, if for the opposite reason, was attorney George Templeton Strong of New York, who wrote in his journal, "Pierce is served right. The South used him sufficiently and has thrown him away, enjoyed the fruits of his treason and kicked him out of the doors. He'll find cold comfort at home when he goes there; his neighbors have just been hanging him and Brooks [Preston, who attacked Sumner] in effigy . . . he cannot make himself more infamous than he is already by any new exhibitions of baseness."[64] John P. Hale was just as harsh in writing to his wife, "I do not know but I am prejudiced, perhaps I am, but, upon the coolest reflection which I can bestow upon the subject, it appears to me that no man in modern times has inflicted such serious injury upon his country as Franklin Pierce."[65]

Another former friend of Pierce, B. B. French, though highly critical of the administration for overturning the Missouri Compromise, believed the president had been brought down by Buchanan and his friends: "He and his understrappers have been laboring the whole of Pierce's term to compass his defeat & Buchanan's elevation. I have seen it all, and deprecated and denounced it, and I hope most sincerely that the mean, contemptible, underhanded game they have played to betray Pierce, while they pretended to be his friends, will not result in their triumph."[66] Thus, Pierce's reward for attempting to steer a principled course guided by integrity, the law, and the Constitution was the contempt of fellow Democrats, most of his countrymen, and an early retirement.

With eight months left in his administration, the president's work was not done. Reaction from England to the recognition of Walker's government in Nicaragua and to the dismissal of the British minister and consuls was encouraging. The British press was critical of the recognition of Walker, but less so than anticipated. Most gratifying to Pierce was the reaction to Marcy's letter explaining the dismissal of Crampton. On June 11, Dallas read the letter to Lord Clarendon, who responded that "he was obviously much gratified by its tone and import . . ." and praised its "clearness," and "a spirit so candid and conciliatory." Clarendon pledged "to reach an adjustment of the whole difficulty."[67] The London press condemned the British government's role in the recruiting and demanded publication of all pertinent documents. On June 16, in the House of Commons, Tory leader Benjamin Disraeli made a seminal address on U.S.-British relations, stating, "It would be wise if Britain would at last recognize that the United States, like all the great countries of Europe, have a policy, and that they have a right to have a policy."[68] The prime minister, Lord Palmerston, influenced by the negative reaction to his government's role in recruiting, announced that Dallas would not be removed and that friendly relations with the United States would be maintained.[69] Dallas reported to Marcy that after three years of pressure by the United States, Lord Clarendon was finally ready to begin serious negotiations to resolve the Central American disputes.[70]

The consistently strong stand of the Pierce administration against any and all acts and policies of the British government that infringed upon U.S. neutral rights or U.S. interests in the Western Hemisphere had produced a turning point in U.S.-British relations. The change was "impressive," as it revealed an increasing "sense of justice" of U.S. foreign policy by the British government.[71] From his post in Liverpool, Nathaniel Hawthorne understood the significance of the change and Pierce's role in bringing it about:

> Frank has brought us safely and honorably through a great crisis: and England begins now to understand her own position and ours, and will never again assume the tone which hither to she has always held toward us. I am sorry Frank has not been nominated if he wished it. Otherwise I am glad he is out of the scrape.[72]

From Congress Pierce received one humiliation after another throughout the summer of 1856. The three vetoed internal improvement bills were all overturned in both the Senate and the House in early July.[73] These were the first presidential vetoes to be overridden since the Tyler administration. Richard W. Thompson's claim on the Menominee treaty money came up again in late July. The president pro tem of the Senate, Jesse Bright, one of Buchanan's campaign managers, introduced a resolution to pay Thompson the $40,000 called for by the "civil and diplomatic appropriations bill" of the previous year. Bright's motive was both political and personal. Thompson, a former Whig congressman, was now a leader of the Know-Nothing (Native American) Party in Indiana. Bright, who had previously lent Thompson $3,000 to enable him to press his claim for the treaty money, wanted Thompson's assurance that he would "prevent the consummation of a coalition in Indiana between his party and the Republicans, thus insuring a Democratic victory in a crucial state."[74] Senators representing the states in which the Menominee lived, Cass and Stuart of Michigan and Dodge of Wisconsin, argued vociferously against Thompson's claim, questioning his veracity, reminding the Senate of the administration's voluminous evidence against paying the claim, and decrying the impact that paying Thompson would have on the tribe. The Menominee would lose two years of its annual annuity from the treaty, and this would be taken from a peaceful tribe whose "hands were never stained with the blood of the white man."[75] Bright chose a day, August 8, when no important business was on the Senate calendar to bring his resolution to a vote. With many senators, including Cass, Stuart, and Dodge, absent and with barely a quorum, Bright's resolution passed, eighteen to sixteen.[76] In defiance of the Senate's vote, the administration continued to withhold the money from Thompson for the remainder of Pierce's time in office.

In Kansas, the burning of Lawrence and the Pottawatomie murders touched off four months of guerilla warfare. Small companies of armed men roamed the territory, engaging in brief skirmishes, shooting, burning, and terrorizing settlers in the name of liberty or protection of their rights. The territorial militia was completely ineffective. At one point, a militia unit led by a deputy U.S. marshal was surrounded and captured by John Brown and his men. Governor Shannon directed Colonels Cooke and Sumner to intercept the illegal military companies of both sides and order them to disperse. Sumner disbanded several hundred Missourians, only to have them scatter across the countryside and reassemble.[77] Southerners patrolled the Missouri River, turning back free-state recruits and stealing their weapons and supplies. That summer, the fifteen-year-old son of Maine Senator William Pitt Fessenden, ran away from home to fight for the free-state cause, only to be intercepted by Missourians at the river and gently sent on his way back home.[78] Governor Shannon was increasingly ineffective. He could not control the Missourians and had no credibility with the free-staters. Governor Robinson's wife, Sara, after one encounter with Shannon, noted his "look of utter weariness, of inability to do any thing, or incapacity to know what to do." Colonel Sumner did assume custody of "governor" Robinson and the other prisoners being held for treason, keeping them under military guard in a comfortable tent prison near Lecompton.[79]

In Washington, Pierce and his cabinet were hamstrung by poor communication with Shannon and Sumner. It took eight days for Pierce's telegrams to reach the governor, and the president was forced to send messengers to carry duplicate copies of his orders to Shannon. The full reports of Shannon and Sumner recounting the details of the burning of Lawrence and the Pottawatomie Massacre did not reach the president and the War Department until June 19, nearly a month after the events.[80] Election-year politics and the exaggerated press reports of the violence in Kansas influenced an increasingly restive Congress. On June 10, Senator John J. Crittenden of Kentucky proposed a resolution that General Winfield Scott be sent to Kansas. Senator Mason of Virginia reminded the senators that this would be interfering with the president's role as commander in chief: "He, and he alone can direct the military force. . . ."[81]

The Republican Party and its presidential candidate, John C. Frémont, having endorsed the admission of Kansas as a free state, expected to ride the issue into the White House in November. Finding a means to quiet the situation in Kansas was essential to the Democratic Party and its candidate, James Buchanan. On June 23, Senator Robert Toombs proposed a bill calling for immediate statehood for Kansas by bypassing the population requirement. The Toombs bill provided for five commissioners appointed by the president to conduct a new census in Kansas in preparation for the election of delegates to a constitutional convention. The convention delegates would be elected on the same day as the national presidential election in November, thus discouraging Missourians from crossing into Kansas, and the three-month residency requirement for voters would discourage last-minute migration. The federally appointed commissioners would monitor the entire process, which would be independent of both the "bogus" territorial legislature and the insurrectionary Topeka government.[82]

Douglas's Committee on Territories reported the Toombs bill to the Senate on June 30, and the debate began immediately. Hale was suspicious of allowing Pierce to select the commissioners. Cass had spoken with the president about this and assured Hale that "if the Commissioners are selected under the bill by the Executive, they will be selected impartially from the different shades of party in the country, and the best men that can be got." Hale responded that "the terms 'partial' and 'impartial' are comparative terms, and what the President of the United States might consider very impartial and upright and fair, might not look so to everybody."[83] On July 3, the Senate passed the Toombs bill by a vote of thirty-three to thirteen, but the bill did not fare so well in the House, where the Republican majority set it aside without a vote.[84] Douglas correctly assessed the political reasons in an angry speech: "All these gentlemen want is to get up murder and bloodshed in Kansas for political effect. They do not mean that there shall be peace until after the presidential election.... Their capital for the presidential election is blood. We may as well talk plainly. An angel from heaven could not write a bill to restore peace in Kansas that would be acceptable to the Abolition Republican party previous to the presidential election."[85] The House members were more interested in the report of the special three-member investigating committee, which had returned from Kansas. On July 2, the "Howard Report" was printed. The nearly twelve hundred pages of testimony from dozens of witnesses detailed the election fraud and violence in the territory. Not surprisingly, the two Republican members concluded that the territorial legislature was fraudulently elected and that the free-state Topeka Constitution accurately represented the will of the majority of residents of Kansas. The committee's Democratic member submitted a minority report, declaring that the election frauds had occurred in only five of the eighteen elections districts in Kansas; therefore, the territorial legislature was legitimate.[86]

Not anticipating any help from Congress, Pierce did his best to restore order in the territory. On June 27, he assigned General Persifor F. Smith, an old friend from the Mexican War, to become commander in the West, with headquarters at Fort Leavenworth. Pierce conferred with Smith, a fellow Democrat, in Washington, impressing on him the need to be fair and impartial in his actions, to deprive the Republicans of their campaign issue. Smith did not reach the territory until July 7.[87] In the meantime, the free-state legislature was scheduled to convene at Topeka on July 4. Governor Shannon had left the territory in late June for St. Louis, justifying his absence to Pierce by claiming, "There are not at this time, on either side, any armed bodies of men in the Territory, so far as I am advised."[88] Shannon had assigned to Colonel Sumner the responsibility of dispersing the illegal legislature. On July 4, Sumner, accompanied by the territorial secretary of state, Daniel H. Woodson, and two hundred dragoons, mounted the speaker's platform in the legislative hall in Topeka and ordered the legislature "to disperse." If they did not, Sumner declared, "I shall use the whole force under my command to carry out my orders." The members did not resist.[89]

The dismissal of the peacefully assembled legislature was condemned by the eastern press and by many in Congress. Though Sumner later defended his action by claiming the Topeka legislature was "insurrectionary" under the terms of the president's proclamation of February, 1856, Secretary of War Davis criticized Sumner for not using other, less heavy-handed means to achieve the legislature's adjournment.[90] Davis had been assuring the president throughout the spring and summer that military officers in Kansas had been instructed to use force only "in suppressing insurrection or . . . aggression against the organized government of the territory, or armed resistance to the execution of the laws."[91] Free-State governor Robinson later confirmed the actions of Pierce and Davis in directing the military to restore order impartially: "Take it all in all, the conduct of the army during the Kansas conflict, even though under the direction of Jefferson Davis, Secretary of War, is worthy of all praise, with the single exception of the dispersion of the Legislature, and this was afterward disapproved even by Secretary Davis and the President."[92]

But the dispersal of the Topeka legislature was an excuse for the Republicans in the House to make political capital. This amendment was added to the routine army appropriations bill: "that no part of the military force of the United States . . . shall be employed in aid of the enforcement of any enactment of the body claiming to be the Territorial Legislature of Kansas."[93] The Pierce administration had consistently denied that the army had ever been used to aid the territorial legislature in enforcing its acts, and the Democrats in the Senate refused to agree to the House amendment, but as the adjournment of Congress drew near, the stalemate threatened to paralyze the army.[94]

Pierce was also under pressure to release Governor Robinson and fellow prisoners held in Kansas for treason. In the House, resolutions were offered that questioned the legitimacy of the laws of the "bogus" legislature under which the arrests were made.[95] In spite of the fact that the prisoners were held in comfortable quarters under the protection of the army and that they were permitted to have their wives with them and to have free access to visitors, the prisoners still faced possible execution.[96] Amos A. Lawrence was among those urging the president to release the prisoners. In July he sent S. C. Pomeroy, an agent of the Emigrant Aid Company who had recently fled Kansas, to meet with Pierce to inform him firsthand of the situation in the territory and to plead on behalf of the prisoners. Lawrence advised Pomeroy, "I believe Mr. Pierce's father was in the battle of Bunker Hill. Perhaps you can bring that in to claim a kindred spirit in him (The spirit is there, but keeping a long sleep)."[97]

The wretched July heat in the capital had brought on a bout of the malaria that Pierce suffered from each summer during his administration, but after several postponements caused by his illness, Pierce had a long, private meeting with Pomeroy on July 24. Pomeroy reported to Lawrence that Pierce promised to remove Governor Shannon: "He has been waiting to hear from Persifer Smith . . . I am still sure we shall have a new Governor, though many of our people laugh that I should believe in the President's promises." As to the prisoners and the treason charge, Pomeroy was not so optimistic, reporting how Pierce mentioned "disobedience to law and *punishment* as the necessary consequence." Pomeroy continued, "He was very severe upon the 'unauthorized' Free state movement." The conversation became animated on this point, Pomeroy reporting, "*Both of us got hot*—and *showed some passion*. I content myself by feeling that I did not show more than he did."[98]

Pomeroy also noted that Pierce was "very anxious" for the Toombs bill to pass.[99] That bill, which had earlier been rejected by the House, was resurrected in late July, when Douglas tried to substitute it for a House bill that would admit Kansas as a free state under the Topeka Constitution. The Senate again passed the Toombs bill, and Pierce lobbied hard with House members to accept it. His focus was on Know-Nothing members, who held the balance of power in the House. Pierce asked Amos A. Lawrence, the former Whig who was now a member of the American (Know-Nothing) Party, for help in convincing his party's House members to vote for the bill. Pierce assured Lawrence that he would select a politically balanced and impartial set of commissioners to enforce a fair election in Kansas. Lawrence urged his friends in Congress to support the bill, claiming Pierce had shared with him the names of the men he would select, but that Lawrence could not divulge them.[100] The effort was in vain, as the House again refused to even vote on the Toombs bill.

On July 27, Pierce appointed John W. Geary of Pennsylvania to be the new governor of Kansas. An imposing presence at six feet five and a half inches, the thirty-seven-year-old Geary had scaled the fortress of Chapultepec in the Mexican War, held several political posts in California territory, and was operating a mine in Virginia at the time of his appointment.[101] A decisive man of action with frontier experience, Geary was the antithesis of Shannon. Geary met with Pierce and was promised the full support of the administration. As a lifelong Democrat, Geary was just as anxious as the president to quiet the situation in the territory prior to the presidential election. The new governor waited in Washington before heading west, anticipating any action of the Congress regarding Kansas.

The stalemate in Congress persisted to the end of the session. The House would vote only for a Kansas bill that recognized the Topeka Constitution, and the Senate persisted in the Toombs bill, which Douglas called the "only, fair, just and equitable" settlement.[102] The House also refused to pass the army appropriation bill without the amendment forbidding the military to be used to enforce the laws of the territorial legislature. The Senate refused to vote for the army appropriation *with* this amendment. Republicans in the House proposed a deal to eliminate the amendment in exchange for release of the prisoners in Kansas, but Pierce would not consider it, and Congress adjourned on August 18 without passing Kansas legislation and, most significantly, without approving the army appropriation.[103]

Acting decisively, Pierce called Congress into special session on August 21, declaring, "If requisite funds be not speedily provided, the Executive will no longer be able to furnish the transportation, equipments, and munitions which are essential to the effectiveness of a military force in the field. With no provision for the pay of troops the contracts of enlistment would be broken and the Army must in effect be disbanded, the consequences of which would be so disastrous as to demand all possible efforts to avert the calamity."[104] Pierce had already closed the armories, putting civilian employees temporarily out of work. Indian wars in Washington, Oregon, and the western plains would have to be suspended and the settlers left defenseless. There was no mention of the situation in Kansas.[105]

The special session of Congress met from August 21 to August 30, when finally a few American Party members, including those friendly to Lawrence, voted 101 to 98 to "strike out" the amendment restricting the use of the army in Kansas.[106] Pierce had his appropriation for the army but little else from the Thirty-fourth Congress. The congressmen quickly fled the capital, returning home to participate in the presidential campaign. With Governor Geary making his way to

Kansas and Pierce's friend General Persifor Smith commanding the army there, the president could venture the hope that peace would come to the territory in time to influence the presidential election. For the first time since the nominating convention, Pierce could begin to plan for his and Jane's future after the expiration of his term as president.

12

CLOSING THE BOOK ON THE PIERCE ADMINISTRATION

THROUGHOUT THE SUMMER OF 1856 there was a noticeable coolness between members of the Pierce administration and the Buchanan campaign. Pierce's generous concession speech in Washington had gone completely unacknowledged by the candidate. Breckinridge, in contrast, had written a heartfelt thank you to Pierce, who answered, "My brief remarks to which you allude were in tone and spirit what my friends had a right to expect of me, but unworthy of any special commendation." To the president, a Democratic victory in November was a necessity: "I consider the continuance of the Union as directly involved in the result." The emergence of an entirely sectional party (the Republican Party and its candidate John C. Frémont) with a chance of winning the presidency increasingly alarmed Pierce: "The question between sectionalism and nationalism has never been so distinctly presented before and this aspect of the contest is evidently impressing itself upon the minds of all thoughtful, reflecting men." If Pierce felt personally detached from Buchanan, he took solace in having a friend on the ticket: "I need not express the great gratification which your nomination affords me. You will regard me always as your friend. Should any particular act occur to you as likely to be useful on my part, in promoting the general result I am sure your friendship will not fail to suggest it."[1]

Buchanan's closest advisors warned the candidate that the president felt slighted by his lack of attention. After a conversation in Washington with John H. George of New Hampshire, Rep. Howell Cobb of Georgia wrote to Buchanan in mid-July, "The President is far from being pleased with the present state of things. He thinks that the support of himself and friends is not sought in the election. He refers to the fact that while Breckinridge wrote him a handsome letter on receiving his speech made here, that he has never received either from yourself or any friend of yours the slightest evidence of any appreciation of that act. In a word I fear that the President and his cabinet are *sore* and unless something is done to conciliate their feelings we shall receive less aid from that quarter than we ought to have."[2] Cobb also noted the continuing feud between Pierce supporters and Edmund Burke in New Hampshire: "Perhaps another idea has entered their heads and that is that Burke and other enemies of the President being now very active for you are to be put ahead of them in the counsels and favors of your administration."[3]

Buchanan acknowledged his error: "It would have been 'comme il faut' if I had written a letter of thanks to the President, Gen. Cass and Mr. Douglas for their noble speeches, . . . I wish I had done so; but the truth is that my house was filled with company to such a degree that I had no time to put pen to paper at that moment, and I did not suppose either of these gentlemen would doubt my gratitude for their truly generous conduct."[4] Buchanan added, "I have too good an opinion of the President to suppose for a moment that he would require a request from me to induce him to employ all proper exertions to render the Democratic cause triumphant."[5]

In the weeks ahead Cobb continued to press Buchanan to write to Pierce or Marcy or find some way to acknowledge their effort. An opportunity presented itself in August. Secretary of the Navy Dobbin had been actively campaigning for the party in North Carolina. He reported to Buchanan on August 13 of the party's victory in the state elections, a reliable predictor of how the state would vote in the presidential election in November.[6] Buchanan sent his congratulations to Dobbin and added, "I am glad to learn that the President enjoys good health, not withstanding the fatigue, trouble, and responsibility incident to his position. I concur with you in opinion as to the character of his manly and excellent address on the receipt of the intelligence from Cincinnati. It was no more than what might have been expected from him by all who knew him."[7] Dobbin almost certainly shared this letter with Pierce. But Buchanan may have undone the impact of this letter by his criticism of Pierce for calling the special session of Congress. Marcy explained to the candidate that the president had no choice, considering "the situation of the country," but Buchanan wrote back, "I should have been sorely tempted had I been the President to let the Black Republicans bear the consequences of their outrageous conduct in refusing to pass the Army Bill without the Proviso. This would beyond question have decided the fate of the Presidential election in our favor, & thus have prevented the danger to the Constitution & the Union which would exist should Frémont be elected."[8] Buchanan may have been willing to risk the safety of American settlers on the frontier and in Kansas for the sake of his political success, but Pierce would never do so.

The Douglas camp was equally offended by Buchanan's failure to acknowledge their support. In the fall, Buchanan finally wrote to the Illinois senator thanking him for contributing money to the campaign from the sale of some of Douglas's own land. His letter only added insult to injury, as Buchanan addressed it to "The Hon. Samuel A. Douglas."[9]

Pierce understood that the best thing he could do for the Democratic cause in November was to reduce the violence in Kansas. His administration did all it could to accomplish that goal. August was the most violent month to date in that unhappy territory. Jim Lane's free-state army of four hundred entered Kansas from Nebraska in late July. Along with John Brown's vicious guerrillas, the free-state forces created havoc. The southern town of Osawatomie was looted and burned on August 7. Franklin fell on August 12, with six proslavery defenders killed. On the sixteenth a Missouri guerrilla band led by Henry C. Titus was routed and thirty-five men captured outside of Lawrence.[10] On the nineteenth Lane's force threatened to overrun the territorial capital at Lecompton, but Lt. Col. Philip St. George Cooke and his dragoons arrived in time. Cooke lectured Lane into marching off. Pierce received a telegram which read, "Lecompton not taken—defended by citizens and troops. . . ."[11]

Governor Shannon, aware that his replacement was on his way to Kansas, tried one last time to arrange a truce. Accompanied by an Army company, he visited Lawrence but refused to call out the territorial militia, which he had been unable to control in the past. Being unnerved by the presence of some eight hundred armed free-state men in Lawrence and having his life threatened by proslavery leaders for his refusal to authorize the use of the militia, Shannon fled the territory on August 21.[12] The acting governor, Secretary of State Daniel Woodson, armed with information supplied to him by Shannon and urged on by Atchison, declared the territory in a state of rebellion and called out the militia. Once again Missourians stormed into Kansas. Proslavery forces swept back into Osawatomie on August 30.[13]

On September 1, 1856, Woodson requested Colonel Cooke, commander of the six hundred U.S. dragoons in the area, to move his troops into the free-state capital, Topeka, to "disarm all the insurrectionists or aggressive invaders against the organized government of the Territory . . . [and] level to the ground all their breastworks, forts or fortifications."[14] Cooke denied the acting governor's request, quoting Pierce's instructions, "It is only when an armed resistance is offered to the laws and against the peace and quiet of the Territory and under such circumstance a requisition for a military force is made upon the commanding officer [General Smith] by the authority specified in his instructions that he is empowered to act."[15] General Smith's instructions to Cooke on August 28 stated, "But it will not be within the provision of the troops to interfere with persons who may have come from a distance to give protection to their friends, or others, and who may be behaving themselves in a peaceful and lawful manner. And further, 'to make every exertion in my power, within the force under my orders to preserve the peace and prevent bloodshed.'"[16] In denying Woodson's request, Cooke concluded, "No specification of resistance by the people of Topeka is made in your request. . . . It is simply a call upon me to make war upon the town of Topeka."[17]

Under careful instruction from the Pierce administration, the army continued to act impartially, protecting both free-state and proslavery citizens. The escalation in violence, however, prompted General Smith to ask Secretary of War Davis for more troops. Davis's response of September 3 directed Smith to take command of the territorial militia and if necessary to draw on militias from Kentucky or Illinois (Pierce having received assurances from governors of these states of their availability). Davis reminded Smith, "You will, therefore, energetically employ all means within your reach to restore the supremacy of law, always endeavoring to carry out your present purpose to prevent the unnecessary effusion of blood."[18]

Governor Geary finally arrived in Kansas on September 9, fully informed of the situation he was inheriting, as he had met former governor Shannon along the way. He delivered his inaugural address at Lecompton on September 12, calling on all parties for restraint. "Will you not suspend fratricidal strife? Will you not cease to regard each other as enemies . . . ? Let us banish all outside influences from our deliberations. . . . Let us all begin anew."[19] His first act as governor was to disband the volunteer militias and to create a new territorial militia made up of "all free male citizens" of the territory, pro and antislavery settlers alike.[20] Geary, accompanied by U.S. troops, arrived in Lawrence on September 15 and ordered the Missouri militia surrounding the town to disperse. He also met there with Charles Robinson, just released from captivity, and earned the free-state governor's trust. Geary ordered the army, under Col. James A. Harvey, to find and disperse Lane's free-state militia. Harvey disarmed more than one hundred and the rest fled into Nebraska. By mid-October Geary was able to make a tour of the territory, being saluted by all parties for his impartial actions in bringing peace to Kansas.[21]

From Washington, Pierce did what he could to assist his new governor. Republicans and the northern press had been demanding the release of Robinson and the other free-state officials held in Kansas on charges of treason. Pierce conferred with Cushing, who had the indictments forwarded to Washington. With the change of venue, territorial justice Lecompte released the prisoners on bail.[22] Amos A. Lawrence took credit for the action. He had drafted a letter that Mrs. Robinson copied, begging for her husband's release. The letter was given to Lawrence's stepmother, Jane Pierce's aunt, who forwarded it to Jane Pierce "with the request that she wd. read it to her husband." Lawrence later wrote, "She read it, then gave it to him [Pierce] & he read it." Pierce then wrote to Lawrence's brother "that he had given such instructions as wd. gratify him & his friends here" and especially Lawrence's stepmother, "whose good opinion [Pierce] valued more than that of all the politicians."[23] Lawrence urged Mrs. Robinson to visit Pierce in Washington and "to treat him with all the respect which the *office* demands, if not more."[24] Pierce may have been happy to let Lawrence take the credit for his humanitarian gesture, but the release of the prisoners was in the works before Mrs. Robinson's letter reached the White House, and it was intended by Pierce to strengthen Geary's hand in dealing with the free-state leaders in Kansas.

Having finally found the right governor and commanding officer to restore order in Kansas, Pierce was able to look to his own future. He decided to travel to New Hampshire in the fall to find a place to live after March 4. Sidney Webster and Josiah Minot, whom Pierce had appointed to a position in the Treasury Department, informed party leaders in Concord that the president would be visiting sometime after September 20. The exact date of the visit was uncertain, as it depended on events in Washington and in Kansas, but Webster advised John H. George, "A large, a tremendous reception is *vital*, and yet secresy is equally so."[25]

George saw the potential benefit of the president's visit to the state party's chances in the November election. Ignoring Webster's request that the visit "be kept *secret*" until the last minute, George called a public meeting in Concord on September 22 to plan for the reception of the president. The announcement of the meeting was signed by four Democrats and four Republicans, including the mayor of Concord.[26] On the night of the meeting, however, hundreds of Republicans stormed the hall, shouted down the speakers, hissed and booed at any mention of Pierce, and forced through a resolution: "That it is inexpedient for us, as citizens of Concord, to make any arrangements for giving President Pierce a public reception at this time."[27] Those supporting the president's visit met privately later that night and renewed their plans for his reception.

Reports of the insult from the citizens of his hometown prompted an angry response from Pierce in a letter to William Butterfield, editor of the *New Hampshire Patriot*: "It has not hither to appeared to me that I could definitely say that I would be at Concord in the early part of October, but the action on the part of the *disunionists* leaves me no ground of choice—I shall reach Concord in the forenoon train of Thursday, October 2nd."[28] George reported on September 25 that sixty people had already contributed money to defray the expenses of the president's reception.[29] Pierce left Washington on September 30, accompanied only by Sidney Webster, Jonah D. Hoover, and General Alexander Anderson of Tennessee, and traveled by train through Baltimore, Philadelphia, and Trenton and on to New York, where he spent the night. There were no large receptions or parades along the route, as there had been on his trip to New York in the summer of 1853. The next day, he traveled through Springfield and Worcester, Massachusetts, receiving delegations at each town, and spent the night in Hollis, New Hampshire, at the home of a friend, J. H. Cutter.[30]

The reception in Concord turned out to be everything Pierce could have hoped. On a beautiful fall day he was met by a huge crowd at the station when his train arrived at 11:30 a.m. on October 2. Mounting "a splendid bay," Pierce rode in a procession through the city streets, accompanied by marching bands from New Hampshire and Massachusetts, military units in full dress, and leading citizens in fancy carriages. Along the route, buildings and homes were decorated with signs welcoming the president home. The parade reached the State House grounds, where Pierce was introduced to the crowd by his former law clerk and law partner, John H. George. Pierce thanked the crowd and the "personal friends of different political parties" surrounding him on the podium. He reminded his listeners that his visit was of a personal nature and that he had "no new sentiments or opinions upon leading political topics" to discuss. He then proceeded to defend his actions as president, stating, "I am quite sure that no honest and intelligent citizen of New Hampshire will doubt that my public conduct has been controlled by none other than high and patriotic motives." Still angry at those who would have denied him a friendly welcome, Pierce challenged the crowd, "Are comparative strangers to the people of New Hampshire, men who have not a personal acquaintance with one hundred of the assemblage now present, men who have never sacrificed for their country, in their whole lives, one hour of ease—who never encountered, and never expect to encounter, the slightest degree of danger for its honor and its right, to dictate when and under what circumstances it is proper for me to breathe my native air, and tread my native soil? I have answered this question today by my presence, and you have answered it by meeting me here."

He "lamented" the sectional divisiveness in a nation at peace and prosperous, saying, "There is a sectional spirit in the land, counseling hatred and all uncharitableness . . . which threatens, at this moment, to rock the Union to the centre." But he claimed to be "no alarmist" and reiterated his "hope and faith in this Constitution and in the permanence of the institutions which it upholds. . . ." Pierce stated that he was looking forward to being "at home again," among the "sons of New Hampshire," concluding, "I claim to be your brother."[31]

Following the speech, the president moved inside the State House, where he shook hands with "thousands" of people. After several hours he was escorted across the street to the Eagle Hotel, where he received more visitors. At one point, the large crowd gathered outside the hotel and called him to the balcony, where he again thanked them for the warm welcome. That night, at a levee at Depot Hall, Pierce greeted the ladies of Concord. The festivities ended with an impressive display of fireworks, and the many visitors from out of town headed home on the special trains that had brought them earlier in the day. The friendly *New Hampshire Patriot* estimated the crowd at forty thousand, while the hostile press concluded only eight thousand people were present. The antislavery *Independent Democrat* described the event as the "coldest kind of civilities" and mocked Pierce, claiming he spent two hours "dyeing his hair which has grown to be 'grey as a badger'. . . ."[32] After reading the press accounts of Pierce's welcome home, Marcy exulted in a letter to Dallas in London, "His reception . . . was truly a most brilliant affair,—second only to the Coronation of Alexander 2d."[33]

The next day Pierce traveled to Hillsborough by carriage with his brother Henry. There Pierce stayed at the family homestead, now owned and occupied by his niece, Fanny McNeil. Saturday he traveled to Andover, Massachusetts, to stay with Jane's sister, Mrs. John Aiken, and spend the Sabbath. The president must have been pleased and "somewhat amused" that among those greeting him after church in Andover was Calvin Ellis Stowe, ardent abolitionist and husband of Harriet Beecher Stowe; he had been a classmate of Pierce's at Bowdoin. Pierce returned to Concord on Monday and visited Portsmouth on Wednesday before departing for Washington on the navy ship *Wabash*, which landed at Annapolis on October 17.[34] There were no unpleasant incidents throughout his visit. Republicans apparently decided to ignore Pierce entirely following the negative publicity accorded their disruptive behavior at the planning meeting. Democrats were prepared for anything, however, and Albert R. Hatch, in inviting Pierce to Portsmouth, promised, "If a single rascal dares raise hand or voice against him, our boys will 'deal seriously' with him."[35] Pierce made no decision about buying a home in New Hampshire but looked at property around Concord and Portsmouth.

Pierce was not the only member of his administration to travel during the presidential campaign. James Campbell spent much of his time that fall in his hometown of Philadelphia, shoring up the Irish Catholic vote for Buchanan. McClelland visited Michigan and reported that he was "exceedingly anxious" about the party's prospects there.[36] James Dobbin was back in North Carolina trying to recuperate from a bout with tuberculosis that would ultimately prove fatal. He confessed, "I feel a little gloomy about the approaching election." Dobbins felt that Buchanan was not as strong a candidate in the South as Pierce would have been: "Mr. Pierce's popularity in the South is even beyond my expectation. His nomination in my opinion would have prevented even the *formation* of a ticket for Fillmore [American Party candidate] in any state south of Virginia. Still Mr. Buchanan will be well sustained."[37]

All eyes were on Pennsylvania, where the state election took place in mid-October, some three weeks prior to the presidential canvass. Buchanan needed to win a large northern state to add to his expected dominance in the South in order to secure a majority of the electoral votes. The Democrats prevailed in Pennsylvania by a narrow margin, and McClelland shared the feelings of the entire Pierce administration in his letter to John W. Forney, who managed Buchanan's campaign in the Keystone State: "Permit me to congratulate you on your most signal success under all the circumstances, it is the most important triumph, which in my judgment, has ever been obtained by our party. The result settles the Presidential question, and saves the Union."[38]

Following the Pennsylvania state election, the presidential vote was anticlimactic. Buchanan won the Electoral College (Buchanan 174, Frémont 114, Fillmore 8) but failed to win a majority of the popular vote (Buchanan 45 percent, Frémont 34 percent, Fillmore 21 percent). Democrats also won back control of the House of Representatives, following the disaster of the fall of 1854. The results in New Hampshire surprised and disappointed Pierce, however. After his gratifying reception in October, he had predicted a Democratic victory in the state. On election day over 90 percent of eligible voters turned out. Frémont won New Hampshire by nearly six thousand votes. Recent voting analysis shows that one-sixth of those who voted for Pierce in 1852 had switched to Frémont in 1856. The Republicans had also attracted many first time voters to the polls by effectively combining antislavery and anti-Catholic sentiment.[39] Pierce wrote to Buchanan, "I congratulate my country and congratulate you." But he admitted his "mortification at the result in New Hampshire." Pierce blamed the result in his home state on "a perverted and desecrated pulpit."[40] A Massachusetts Democrat described the Republican sweep in the northeast as: "This mania has swept over New England & New York like the witchcraft scourge of 1692."[41] The president's consolation was that the Democrats remained in control of the federal government, but the realignment of voters in New Hampshire permanently placed Pierce and his friends in the minority party at home.

Relations with Great Britain continued to improve that fall. Pierce had helped Marcy prepare revised instructions for Dallas regarding the Central American issues.[42] Dallas and Clarendon met during the summer and by late August had completed a draft of a treaty, which the cabinet considered in late September. Marcy then sent Dallas a dispatch with several alterations of the proposed treaty, which Lord Clarendon accepted. By November the revised treaty was ready to be presented to the U.S. Senate for ratification. The Dallas-Clarendon convention addressed all of the issues that had grown out of the disputed Clayton-Bulwer Treaty of 1850. The Mosquito Indians were to be assigned to a reservation within Nicaragua (rather than remain under British protection) and were to be paid for their past land grants; Greytown was also to become a free port with self-government under Nicaraguan sovereignty; boundary disputes in the area would be arbitrated by the United States and Great Britain; and the Bay Islands would become a free territory within Honduras. In return for Great Britain's giving up its protectorates over the Mosquitoes, Greytown, and the Bay Islands, the United States agreed to exempt Belize from the Clayton-Bulwer Treaty, allowing it to remain a British colony.[43]

While the treaty seemed to be a fair settlement, the continuing crisis in Nicaragua threatened to derail the treaty's ratification in the Senate. William Walker's shaky regime was crumbling by late summer. He had split with his Nicaraguan allies, removing any claim that his government had local support. Besides a civil war within Nicaragua, the nation was being invaded by armies from its Central American neighbors. In late September, when Walker sent a new minister to Washington, the Pierce administration refused to receive him. Marcy also recalled the U.S. minister to Central America, Joseph Wheeler, who had been much too supportive of Walker's enterprise from the start to please Pierce and Marcy.[44] In an attempt to help shore up Walker's government, one of his leading investors, Pierre Soulé, traveled to Nicaragua that fall. Soulé convinced Walker to declare that slavery was legal in Nicaragua, a decision that Wheeler heartily endorsed and so wrote the administration in Washington. Wheeler's recall letter had already been sent, and this final violation of his instructions prompted an angry dressing down from Marcy when Wheeler reached Washington in November.[45]

The withdrawal of the administration's recognition of Walker angered the filibuster's many powerful friends in the United States, including most southern senators. They took out their frustration on the Dallas-Clarendon Treaty, claiming that while it assigned jurisdiction of the disputed areas to Nicaragua and Honduras, the British would likely maintain informal control of these areas. Marcy reported to Dallas that he was doubtful the Senate would approve the treaty: "Your Treaty does everything for the honor and interest of the nation, and for the independence and safety of the Central American States, in all future time: but these sages think nothing done, because Walker is not patted on the back! Well, if the spirit of fillibusterism can't see beyond the tip of its nose, and, like Abolitionism, it increases in force, we shall ultimately have, I suppose, to submit to our 'blind guides,' and let them lead us to calamities which they have not the sagacity to provide against. . . ."[46]

Pierce had used the recognition of Walker's government as leverage to force the British to the bargaining table on Central America.

With that accomplished and with Walker demonstrating the true intent of his enterprise, Pierce severed all connection with the filibuster regime. Walker's supporters in the United States redoubled their efforts to prop up his fading government. In December a major effort was undertaken in New York to raise money, supplies, and recruits for Walker. A large gathering of Walker's friends was addressed by the Irish gang and Tammany Hall leader Captain Isaiah Rynders, who had a minor post in the Pierce administration as assistant surveyor of the port of New York. Rynders called Pierce "a small potato Jackson" and Marcy "a white-livered dough face" for failing to support Walker. The *New York Times* editorialized, "President Pierce and Mr. Marcy will be made sensible that the 4th of March [inauguration day] is not far off, when they find that one of their own employees can venture to take part in a meeting where they are so roundly abused."[47] The meeting helped raise several thousands of dollars for the purchase of supplies and some three hundred recruits for Walker. These were to depart from New York on the steamer *Tennessee* on December 24, 1856. District Attorney McKeon had kept Cushing informed of the activity and was directed by the attorney general to do what he could to stop the ship. For the second consecutive Christmas Eve, McKeon had two revenue cutters ready to help him, and a large crowd gathered at the dock, expecting to witness a confrontation. The filibusters had learned from previous experience, however, and most of the recruits for Walker had legitimate tickets, and the supplies did not include weapons. McKeon reluctantly permitted the *Tennessee* to sail. McKeon's vigilance had prevented at least one hundred other recruits, who did not have tickets, from departing on the *Tennessee*. The ship never reached Nicaragua, however. A storm damaged the shaft, the ship put in at Norfolk, most of the recruits scattered, and only about forty ever reached Nicaragua.[48] Walker's luck had run out. By spring 1857, he was forced to flee back to the United States.

The third session of the Thirty-fourth Congress convened on December 1, 1856, and Pierce's fourth and final annual message was read to the members of both houses the next day. Holding nothing back, the president congratulated the people on the recent presidential election, claiming that the result "emphatically condemned the idea of organizing in these United States mere geographical parties. . . ." Though never mentioning the name "Republican," he accused that party of being "inflamed with desire to change the domestic institutions of existing States." Pierce stated that their goal was the abolition of slavery, asserting, "The only path to its accomplishment is through burning cities, and ravaged fields, and slaughtered populations." The president further accused the Republicans of endeavoring "to prepare the people of the United States for civil war by doing everything in their power to deprive the Constitution and the laws of moral authority . . . ": "Ardently attached to liberty in the abstract, they do not stop to consider practically how the objects they would attain can be accomplished, nor to reflect that, even if the evil were as great as they deem it, they have no remedy to apply, and that it can be only aggravated by their violence and unconstitutional action."[49] Acknowledging the good intentions of the people who supported the Republican Party, Pierce believed that they would "shrink with unaffected horror" from the knowledge of what was to come. He continued, "But they have entered into a path which leads nowhere unless it be to civil war and disunion, and which has no other possible outlet."[50]

Pierce then traced the history of antislavery agitation up to the Kansas-Nebraska Act. He defended the repeal of the Missouri Compromise: "All the repeal did was to relieve the statute book of an objectionable enactment, unconstitutional in effect and injurious in terms to a large portion of the States." He challenged the belief of many that slave and free labor could not exist in the same territory, asking if slavery had "such irresistibly superior vitality" that it would supplant free labor everywhere it was permitted, despite the "climate, soil, . . . moral and natural obstacles" and "the more numerous population of the Northern States?"[51]

Pierce congratulated his administration on "the peaceful condition of things in Kansas," crediting "the wisdom and energy of the present executive of Kansas and the prudence, firmness, and vigilance of the military officers on duty there" for restoring tranquility "without one drop of blood having been shed . . . by forces of the United States."[52] Pierce continued to blame outsiders for inflaming the situation in the territory and for exaggerating the violence "for purposes of political agitation elsewhere." He restated that the election frauds committed in Kansas "were beyond the sphere of action of the Executive," claiming he had no more right to interfere there than to correct "irregularities" that frequently occurred in elections in the states: "The President of the United States has not power to interpose in elections, to see to their freedom, to convass their votes, or to pass upon their legality in the Territories any more than in the States." The people were ultimately the "guardians of their own rights" and they would remedy "in due season" any "unwise legislation" that might result from fraudulent elections. Once again, Pierce criticized the attempt in Kansas "to remedy unwise legislation by resort to revolution . . . inasmuch as existing legal institutions afford more prompt and efficacious means for redress of wrong." Now that the territory was peaceful, Pierce believed that "calm reflection and wise legislation" would prevail.[53] Pierce's reasoning anticipated Douglas's Freeport Doctrine by implying that even if slavery were established by statute in a territory, it could not survive if the will of the people prevented its enforcement.

Turning to other matters, Pierce reported on the sound condition of the treasury. The budget remained in surplus, allowing a further reduction of the national debt by $12 million during the past year. Since Pierce had taken office, the national debt had been reduced by $45 million, leaving a debt of $30 million. Customs receipts totaled $64 million during the past year, far more income than the government needed to operate, and Pierce once again called on Congress to reduce tariffs to bring the total receipts down to around $50 million per year.[54] Pierce referred Congress to the report of Jefferson Davis and endorsed his call for a reorganization of the army. With the six new frigates "now afloat," the navy showed "the most gratifying evidences of increased vigor," but Pierce urged "a still further increase of our naval forces."[55]

As to foreign affairs, Pierce reported on the improved relations with Great Britain and recommended to the Senate the treaty recently negotiated by Dallas, which addressed all of the issues between the two nations in Central America. He focused most of the rest of his message on two matters involving freedom of the seas, a long-held goal of the United States. For four hundred years Denmark had collected a fee for all ships passing through the Danish Sound. Believing this violated international law, Pierce and Marcy had notified Denmark that after April 1856 they would terminate the treaty to pay the fee. This prompted an international conference at Copenhagen between European nations. Pierce reported in his annual message that he expected a favorable result from the conference. In the spring of 1857, a treaty was concluded that ended the practice of paying passage fees, with each nation granting Denmark a one-time payment for permanent maintenance of the channel, buoys and lighthouses.[56] Historian Charles E. Hill concluded, "The United States had added one more contribution to the freedom of the seas."[57]

The second issue involved the rights of the ships of neutral nations in wartime. The Crimean War had renewed the call of the United States that free ships make free goods. In 1856 the Paris peace conference took up the issue. The United States was not represented at the Congress of Paris, not being a belligerent in the war, but the Pierce administration was asked to endorse its agreement on neutral shipping. Pierce explained in his annual message that he and Marcy had refused to comply because the agreement outlawed privateering. This would prevent a nation without a large navy from arming private merchant ships in times of war. The alternative was to build a large navy, which the United States was reluctant to do; therefore, the right to arm private ships in wartime needed to be protected. Pierce and Marcy proposed an amendment to the agreement to correct this problem, but it was not endorsed by the European nations.[58]

Pierce closed his last message by pointing to "the administrative condition" of the departments of the executive branch. He complimented "the intelligence and the integrity" of all departments and "the beneficial effects of that on the general welfare." Reform of the executive branch had been a major goal of his administration, and the president could point with pride to his successes in this area. Even though the United States was "actually at peace at home and abroad," Pierce cautioned that the growing strength of the nation presented new challenges, including the need to exert "calmness and conscious dignity" in foreign affairs and "to guard against the shock of discontents" in U.S. domestic relations. He would leave office contemplating "the spectacle of amicable and respectful relations between ours and all other governments and the establishment of constitutional order and tranquillity throughout the Union."[59]

The message was vigorously condemned by Republicans in Congress and in the press. The partisan attack by the president on a political party made the message "a very extraordinary and unprecedented one," according to John P. Hale: "The message is an arraignment of a vast majority of the people of eleven States of this Union. . . . I deny it totally."[60] Senator Wade of Ohio accused Pierce of "departing at all events from good taste, even if he had a constitutional right to do so. . . . He assailed the motives of one half of the people of this Union."[61] Fessenden of Maine declared that Pierce "studiously misrepresented the facts. Fessenden continued, "He has sedulously endeavoured to fix upon a very large portion of the people of this country accusations which he knows to be applicable to but few."[62] Democratic senators Brown, Butler, Mason, and Rusk defended the speech, claiming that Pierce had accurately represented the Republican Party's and the abolitionists' actions in interfering with the domestic institutions of the southern states.[63]

The press was equally divided in its reaction. The *New York Evening Post* stated, "This is the first example of gross indecorum of which any President has been guilty in any message addressed to the National Legislature." The *New York Times* called the message "insulting, impertinent, and silly."[64] Pierce had his defenders, however, among them the *Boston Post*, which praised the message for discussing "the slavery question with point, frankness, and boldness giving no quarter to the anti-nationalists." The Washington *National Intelligencer* concluded, "The remarks of the President on the principles and structure of the government, the supremacy of the constitution, and the correlative rights and duties of the States, are enlightened, just and forcible."[65] Historians have tended to attack the message as the bitter diatribe of a small, angry man lashing out at his enemies, but Pierce had been saying the same thing for years. Several of the statements in the message had appeared previously, nearly verbatim, in his earlier speeches, dating back to his debate with John P. Hale in 1845. Pierce was nothing if not consistent, and the message, though strident out of frustration, was his prophetic final warning to the nation of what was to come. It may have been impolitic to use the occasion of his final message for such a partisan attack, but Pierce's honesty always trumped his political sensitivity. He could not leave the national stage without forcibly stating his views.[66]

While Pierce boasted in his message of the peace that prevailed in Kansas, Governor Geary was struggling to keep the relative tranquility from unraveling. In November, 1856, General Smith reported to the adjutant general in Washington that the "disorders" in the territory had been suppressed: "The laws have again been put in operation, and the administration of justice revived. Deserted farms are again occupied, fences rebuilt, fields put under cultivation, and the ruins of houses destroyed by fire, replaced by more durable habitations; roads are covered with travelers, unarmed and secure. . . ."[67] With that, he moved his troops into winter quarters at Fort Leavenworth, leaving the governor only a small company of infantry at Tecumseh and a company of dragoons near Lecompton.[68]

Governor Geary turned his attention from marauding militias to his own territorial administration. He had complained to Pierce that most of the territorial officials he had inherited were so strongly identified with the proslavery party as to be ineffective and biased in carrying out their duties. He particularly quarreled with Chief Justice Samuel Lecompte. Their dispute came to a head in November, when Geary ordered the arrest of Charles Hays, a proslavery militiaman accused of killing a free-state settler. Lecompte promptly freed Hays on bail, the bond supplied by Sheriff Jones. An outraged Geary ordered Hays rearrested, only to have Lecompte free him a second time on a writ of habeas corpus. Geary wrote to Pierce, requesting the removal of Lecompte, U.S. Marshal Donaldson, and Indian Agent Clark.[69] Pierce agreed to the removals, and Donaldson and Clark were promptly replaced, but Lecompte's replacement required Senate approval. Fearing he would have difficulty gaining confirmation from the Senate for replacement of a proslavery southerner, Pierce tried to make a recess appointment in the days before Congress convened. Pierce wrote two telegrams under the signature of the treasury secretary, Guthrie, requesting that vice president-elect Breckinridge ask James O. Harrison of Kentucky to accept the position. Breckinridge's telegraphic reply that Harrison would accept arrived too late, however, as Congress had already convened. Guthrie wrote to Breckinridge, explaining what had happened: "The question of removal [of Lecompte] is yet an open one, but had your telegraph been recd. on Saturday, the removal would have taken place and Mr. Harrison appointed to office. . . . Now the nomination would go to the Senate and have to await their action before the commission could be offered."[70] Lecompte remained in office, as the Senate never considered Harrison's appointment. Once again, Pierce had been blocked by a Senate controlled by his own party.

Geary thanked Pierce for removing Donaldson and Clark: "The censure which has been heaped upon your administration for mismanagement in Kansas affairs is not attributed to you, but is the consequence of the criminal complicity of public officers, some of whom you have removed the moment you were clearly satisfied of their true position."[71] Though stating he was not the "vindicator" of the actions of the free-state men, Geary wrote, "I do say that the men holding official position have never given you that impartial information on the subject so necessary to form correct conclusions, which your high position so imperatively demanded."[72] He informed Pierce that territorial representative John Whitfield had written from Washington of a meeting with the president in which Pierce stated "that all the odium brought on your Administration was the dire result of Clark, Whitfield, Atchison, Stringfellow and others' indiscreet action. Why Whitfield would write thus, when he owes no seat to you, . . . I know not, but I am sure that he never penned a greater truth."[73] Pierce wrote a supportive letter to Geary, which was delivered by the new U.S. marshal, in which he advised the governor, "Be so just and true to the right that no man can challenge your impartiality." In accepting Pierce's advice, Geary wrote, "I have known and will continue to know 'no party, no section, nothing but Kansas and my country.'"[74]

Geary's attempt to follow the president's advice brought him the contempt of the proslavery legislature. Believing that the free-state movement would die quietly if it were not provoked, Geary determined to ignore the Topeka legislature when it convened in early January. A deputy marshal, acting without the governor's knowledge, arrested twelve members and brought them to Lecompton. When the territorial legislature met in mid-January, Geary's effort to moderate its laws produced only modest results. The legislature passed a bill providing for a constitutional convention to meet in September. Geary vetoed the bill, because, he believed the territory was not ready for statehood and because the bill did not provide for submission of the constitution to the voters and restricted voting for delegates to only those living in the territory prior to March 15. This was unfair to free-state settlers planning to move into Kansas that spring. The legislature overrode Geary's veto.[75]

Opposition to Geary reached a dangerous level in February. Geary had blocked the appointment of William T. Sherrard for sheriff of Douglas County. Sherrard confronted Geary, spat in his face, and threatened to kill him. To prevent trouble from Sherrard's many proslavery friends, Geary asked General Smith to send "two additional companies of dragoons" to report to the governor "with the least possible delay."[76] The next night, Sherrard disrupted a pro-Geary meeting, fired on one of Geary's defenders, and was, in turn, shot and killed.[77] General Smith turned down the governor's request for additional troops, using the same argument made when acting governor Woodson had asked for help in putting down the free-state militia the previous September. Smith reminded Geary that the army was to be employed to suppress insurrection, or "to repress combinations to obstruct the execution of the laws, too strong for the civil power." Smith continued, "Insults or probable breaches of the peace do not authorize the employment of the troops." Smith reported to Geary that there had been no disturbances near Leavenworth, and stated, "I can hear of none from various inhabitants."[78]

Geary also felt threatened by the action of Chief Justice Lecompte, who had written a lengthy defense of his decision to free Hays the previous fall. Lecompte sent his report to his home-state senator, James A. Pearce of Maryland, who passed it on to Pierce, who turned it over to Marcy. Lecompte plausibly demonstrated that his acceptance of bail for Hays was consistent with judicial practice in similar cases, that the bail was sufficiently high to secure Hays's presence at trial, and that Lecompte had acted within his legal authority. Marcy sent a copy of Lecompte's report to Geary, asking him to "explain discrepancies" between his report and Lecompte's. Geary, offended by Marcy's curt letter, refused to comply: "I have simply to state that 'what I have written I have written,' and that I have nothing further to add, alter, or amend, on that subject." He asked Marcy to publish his report and Lecompte's "for the inspection of the country."[79]

Uncertain of his future in Kansas, Geary wrote to president-elect Buchanan, apprising him of the situation in the territory and offering to remain as governor if "it should please" Buchanan to "approve" Geary's policy and to provide him with "faithful officers willing to perform their duties . . . [and] a sufficient military force. . . ." Though pleading with Buchanan, stating, "I need to know my situation," Geary waited in vain for a reply.[80] On inauguration day he submitted his resignation and left the territory on March 12, 1857.[81]

Pierce's commitment to impartial administration of the territory under the law was not accepted by either side. When the proslavery forces had the advantage, the free-state element broke the laws to create an insurrectionary government, with full support from antislavery politicians and abolitionists in the North. Amos A. Lawrence met murderous John Brown for the first time in January 1857 and referred to him in his diary as "the old Kanzas hero."[82] Later, when an impartial administration appeared to aid the more numerous free-state settlers, the Lecompton legislature did everything it could to impede the governor's effort to keep the peace in the territory, with full support from southern politicians in Washington. Predisposed to believe the worst about abolitionists from his own personal experience, Pierce too readily accepted the actions of the officials he had appointed to the territory, naïvely accepting that they were executing legal authority. When he learned the truth, that they were just as guilty of fraud and atrocity as the free-state forces, he tried to impose what he had always endorsed, impartial administration of the laws in Kansas. Southern politicians now turned their hostility toward the outgoing president, claiming, "He has all along done everything in his power to bring it [Kansas] in as a free state . . ."[83] Senator Toombs of Georgia agreed: "I am certain Pierce for the last six months has done all he could to make Kansas a free state."[84] Pierce had done no such thing. He was philosophically committed to the concept of popular sovereignty and had been willing from the start to accept whatever result its application produced in Kansas. In fact, he expected the territory, because of its climate and the more numerous northern settlers, to ultimately become a free state, even if proslavery forces had the upper hand at first. The violence in Kansas was never as bad as the exaggerated reports in the press. One recent study assigns directly to the political conflict a total of fifty-six violent deaths in Kansas, and most of those occurred in a single month, August 1856. In comparison, 583 violent deaths occurred in California in a single year, 1855. But the violence in Kansas was exaggerated for political purposes by both proslavery and antislavery forces around the nation.[85] Attempting to impartially uphold the law, Pierce was criticized by both sides, but for the final six months of his term, the policies of the Pierce administration had brought peace to the territory.

The waning days of the Pierce administration were not idle ones. On January 18, a ferocious blizzard, one of the worst storms ever to hit Washington, crippled the city. Jefferson Davis's wife, Varina, was desperately ill following the birth of a daughter on the sixteenth. Pierce, unable to get news of Varina's condition due to the storm, braved the six foot snow drifts and set out on foot to the Davis home. It took the president over an hour to walk the several blocks from the White House, and he sank up to his waist several times in the snow. He explained to Davis that he came himself rather than send a servant, as he did not think anyone else could have made it through the deep snow.[86] In her memoirs the grateful Varina described Pierce: "Chivalrous, generous, amiable, true to his faith, frank and bold in the declaration of his opinions, he never deceived anyone. And, if treachery had ever come near him, it would have stood abashed in the presence of his truth, his manliness, and his confiding simplicity."[87]

Marcy spent his final days in office waiting anxiously for news from the Senate on the ratification of the Dallas-Clarendon Treaty, but he was not optimistic. He wrote Dallas in London that opposition to the treaty was "too formidable . . . to be overcome." Because the Senate debated the treaty in executive session, Marcy was not clear what the objections to it were, but he sensed that the "friends of the new admin" were not anxious "to get rid of the C.A. [Central American] embroglio by having the Treaty passed."[88] Buchanan arrived in Washington in early February to select his cabinet. Pierce entertained the president-elect at the White House. Marcy was present and left the dinner more convinced than ever that Buchanan was "opposed" to the treaty, which he had been unable to accomplish during his tenure in London.[89] In fact, the Senate took no action on the treaty until after the close of the Pierce administration. In mid-March the new Senate ratified the treaty, but with so many amendments that the British government refused to approve it.[90]

Attorney General Cushing was particularly active during these final months. Davis had learned that army doctors were unable to use the new anesthesia, ether, without paying the discoverer, Dr. Morton, who had patented it. Davis asked the president for advice, and Pierce turned the matter over to Cushing for a legal opinion. On December 24, 1856, Cushing wrote, "The discovery that a particular natural substance will, . . . produce assigned physiological or pathological effect on the human body, is not a thing patentable by existing laws."[91] Cushing declared that only the invention of "specific instruments or methods of . . . application" could be patented. His opinion, sustained by future court decisions, applied to many future discoveries, to the benefit of humanity.[92]

The Pierce administration's war on filibusters continued to the end. The often-postponed trial of Joseph Fabens, former U.S. commercial agent in Central America and partner in Kinney's Nicaraguan land scheme, finally resumed in February in New York. Fabens's attorney produced an envelope "under the frank of the President" into evidence, trying to implicate Pierce in Kinney's scheme. McKeon objected, won a delay from the judge, and telegraphed Cushing asking for advice as to how to proceed, not wanting to embarrass the president.[93] Cushing spoke to Pierce, who drafted his own reply to McKeon: "If Mr. Fabens has an envelope with the President's frank upon it, such envelope did not contain a letter by him nor any letter written with his knowledge—and that he can have no possible wish as to the production or non production of any letter or other paper in the pending trial except such as may arise from a desire that the facts in the case may fully and truly appear."[94] Cushing added in his instructions to McKeon that Pierce had "not and never had, interest in any land grants or property whatsoever, in Central America" and that McKeon was to challenge any implication "on this point." Cushing also wrote, "You are therefore instructed . . . to continue to proceed, as you have done in such cases without fear or favor, in the impartial performance of your whole duty as well to the people as to the government of the United States."[95] The envelope had contained a letter from Pierce's secretary, Sidney Webster, who was an investor in Kinney's scheme through his cousin, Fletcher Webster, son of Daniel Webster.[96] The ubiquitous filibuster movement had reached to the White House, but Pierce and Cushing remained an isolated island of integrity in a sea of illegal speculation and foolish adventurism.

Two days before leaving office Cushing issued a highly controversial opinion. The postmaster at Yazoo City, Mississippi, was refusing to deliver a copy of the abolitionist *Cincinnati Gazette*. Postmaster General Campbell asked Cushing for his legal opinion on the matter. Cushing answered that the postmaster was "not required by law to become, knowingly, the enforced agent or instrument of enemies of the public peace, to disseminate, in their behalf . . . printed matter, the design and tendency of which" were "to promote insurrection in such State."[97] This censuring of the mail and the press added to the growing conviction in the North that even the most basic constitutional rights were being sacrificed in defense of slavery.

There was nothing left for Pierce but to await the final action of Congress on several of his recommendations for legislation. On February 21 he signed a bill to increase the pay of army officers, something he and Davis had been proposing for four years. The Senate debate on the bill offered New Hampshire's gadfly Republican senator one last opportunity to lash out at his former college mate, close friend, and political mentor. In opposing the bill, Hale went a step further, stating, "I would abolish this whole Army which has been so vaunted and boasted of." Hale extolled the founding fathers for their hostility to "any standing army" and accused that institution of producing several bad presidents: "I think I should be doing no violence to history if I were to say that the specimen of a President we now have . . . such as he is, owes his position to his connection with this standing army of ours. . . . I think the whole Army is a nuisance."[98]

On the last day of the Thirty-fourth Congress, March 3, Pierce and other members of his cabinet waited in the vice president's office at the Capitol to sign last-minute bills. He was pleased to pen his signature to a naval appropriations bill, which not only increased the size of the navy from seventy-five hundred seamen to eighty-five hundred but also authorized the building of six new sloops of war.[99] The steam sloops, smaller than the new frigates, would be effectively utilized during the Civil War, particularly in winning the victory at New Orleans and in gaining control of the Mississippi.[100]

Another bill that met with Pierce's approval called for the secretary of the navy to authorize the use of two ships for the purpose of laying the transatlantic telegraph cable from Newfoundland to Ireland. The bill was the work of Cyrus Field and Peter Cooper, who had formed a company in New York for the purpose. Field then traveled to London, where he attracted local investors and received Parliament's approval of a contract to assist in laying the cable and paying an annual fee for its use. Field lobbied with Pierce by letter and in person during the winter of 1856–57 to support a similar bill in Congress.[101] The bill, introduced by Republican Senator Seward of New York, was opposed by many southern Democrats, particularly Butler and Hunter, who claimed it was unconstitutional and gave greater benefits to Great Britain, which would control both ends of the cable, than to the United States.[102] Cushing answered the constitutional objection by declaring that the arrangement was the same as the postal contracts granted by the government to transportation companies to carry the mail.[103] The bill passed both houses of Congress in late February, and Cyrus Field was standing by Pierce's side at the Capitol on March 3 when the president signed it into law. U. S. Navy Secretary Dobbin had anticipated the passage of the bill and had delayed the placement of guns on the deck of the largest of the new steam frigates, *Niagara*, anticipating that its deck would need to be clear for use in the peaceful enterprise.[104]

The final act of Congress was the passage of a tariff reduction bill, long a goal of the Pierce administration. Guthrie had urged that Congress remove the tariff on raw materials and reduce it on other items. The final bill added hundreds of raw materials to the free list and reduced the tariff on many other goods from 30 percent to 20 percent. It was the closest the United States had been to free trade since the protection movement began in 1815.[105]

From the time of Buchanan's election it had been clear that the president-elect would not retain any member of Pierce's cabinet. By inauguration day only Davis's future was certain. The Mississippi legislature had chosen him for the U.S. Senate seat in the new Congress, which would convene the day after Buchanan took the oath of office. The uncertainty included the president, who had yet to find a permanent home in New Hampshire, despite frequent correspondence with friends in Concord and Portsmouth.[106] Relatives worried about the impact of the transition on Jane's health. Abby Means wrote on March 2 to Jane's sister, "I have heard from dear Jane—she thought herself stronger. I thought much of her yesterday—her last Sabbath in a place of power and trust that had almost seemed like home."[107]

On March 3, Pierce was presented with a letter signed by all the members of his cabinet: "We have witnessed with satisfaction and respect the untiring devotion to the public service,—the ardent zeal for the good of the country,—the purity of purpose,—and the scrupulous observance of constitutional principle,—which have been manifested by you at all times, and in all circumstances."[108] Acknowledging that the nature of the position made the president "peculiarly subject amid the prejudices and pressures of the hour, to encounter blames," the letter continued, "We, who have seen you most, and with the fullest opportunities of appreciation, know well, how conscientiously you have discharged the high trust devolved upon you, and we confidently believe that, as time rolls on, the voice of impartial history will ratify our attestation of the integrity and patriotism of your exercise of the executive power of the United States."[109] The letter went on to thank Pierce: We . . . express our grateful sense of dignified courtesy and considerate candor which have uniformly marked your deportment towards us . . . This . . . has efficiently contributed to maintain a unity of administration, few examples of which recur in the annals of the Republic."[110] The Pierce administration remains the only time in U.S. history that no changes occurred in a cabinet over a full four-year term.

The morning of the inauguration, a final meeting was held and Pierce presented a letter thanking his cabinet for their "daily intercourse, happily undisturbed by any element of discord. . . ." He accepted full responsibility for the more-controversial decisions of his administration: "These were matters which alone could be determined by my own conscience and judgment, and in the responsibility of which no one could participate." But he vigorously defended the record of his administration:

> You may I think recur, with just pride, to the condition of the country during the four years now about to close. It has concededly been a period of general prosperity; defalcations on the part of federal officers have been almost entirely unknown; the public treasury, with more than twenty millions of dollars constantly in hand, has been free from the touch of fraud or peculation; long standing foreign questions have been amicably and advantageously adjusted; valuable additions have been made to our already vast domain; and peace has been maintained with all the nations of the earth, without compromise of right or a stain upon the national honor.[111]

Before the final cabinet meeting, Davis had stopped by for a private farewell. He reported that Pierce was emotional, stating, "I can scarcely bear the parting from you who have been strength and solace to me for four anxious years and never failed me."[112]

Four years earlier Pierce had moved into a White House that was left a mess by the Fillmore family, who had moved out that day. Always thoughtful, Pierce and Jane moved out a day early to allow the executive mansion to be readied for its new occupant. The Pierces moved in with the Marcys and planned to remain there in consideration of Jane's precarious health until the weather improved for their long journey north. One final indignity befell Pierce on inauguration day. The president was to be picked up at the White House and taken to the National Hotel to join the president-elect in the ride to the Capitol, but no carriage arrived. When the noon hour passed, Pierce called for his own carriage and made his way to the hotel, where he joined Buchanan in the open barouche for the procession down Pennsylvania Avenue. The warm spring weather, in contrast to the cold snowy day four years earlier, added to the festivities. Following the ceremony, Pierce returned with the new president to the White House and left Buchanan at the front door.[113] Amos A. Lawrence wrote in his diary that day a valedictory to the presidency of his cousin by marriage: "President Pierce goes out of office today, I do not envy him his reputation. If he has acted honestly he may not suffer from remorse, but his policy seems to me to have been anything but honest or judicious in many respects, especially in his action with those who brought out the Missouri Compromise Repeal."[114]

In other times the Pierce administration might have been celebrated for its accomplishments. It had honestly and effectively managed a growing treasury. It had reformed and efficiently administered all executive departments. It had aggressively pursued U.S. interests abroad, achieving success and gaining the respect of European powers without risking war. It had impartially enforced the laws and had strictly interpreted the Constitution, in the process obstructing the schemes of self-aggrandizing politicians, speculators, and filibusters. It had modernized the Army and the Navy, and expanded U.S. territory. But only one issue mattered, and by supporting the Kansas-Nebraska bill, the Pierce administration had precipitated a political crisis over slavery that could not be resolved except by civil war. The peace that Pierce inherited on the slavery issue following the Compromise of 1850 was illusory, at best, considering the determination of abolitionists to upset it. Therefore, any forward-looking proposal—for example, the annexation of Cuba or Nicaragua, a Pacific Railroad bill, a larger grant of land from Mexico, even a homestead bill—could have provoked a reaction similar to that touched off by the Kansas bill. Pierce was not to blame for slavery, and no president or statesman could solve the issue or even maintain the "repose" for long, not with moralistic abolitionists and ultrasensitive southerners ready to seize on any issue to press for the "higher law" or for their "rights." By the 1850s sectional peace could not be maintained as long as slavery existed, slavery could not be abolished without changing the Constitution, and constitutional amendments could not be approved as long as the slave states remained in the Union.

Historians have indicted Pierce for failure to lead the policies of his own administration, which they claim were controlled by the more dynamic and aggressive members of his cabinet, particularly Cushing, Davis, and Marcy.[115] This conclusion does not bare close scrutiny. All of the important policy or political decisions of the Pierce administration were entirely consistent with his constitutional philosophy and past political positions. Pierce did listen to advice from his very able cabinet and was often slow to assume a position, even vacillating at times, but he inevitably adopted a policy that was in keeping with his political instincts, legal understanding, and personal integrity.

In fact, Pierce ruled against his most influential cabinet advisers on some critical decisions. His support for outright repeal of the Missouri

Compromise went against prior advice from Cushing and Marcy. If he listened to Davis in making this decision, he ruled against his secretary of war in the very personal matter of his dispute with General Scott, following Cushing's carefully reasoned legal opinion. Cushing was overruled on several matters. He had long opposed free trade, had represented clients with claims against France, and opposed the recognition of Walker's government in Nicaragua. Pierce's decision to recognize Walker's government also went against the advice of Marcy, and Pierce consistently rejected the secretary of state's recommendations on patronage issues in New York and in the appointments of ministers and consuls.

Pierce provided leadership in important areas. The Canadian fishing rights and reciprocity treaty is the best example of an issue pressed from start to finish by Pierce's initiative and persistence. His personal interest in expanding and modernizing the army and navy dates to his time in Congress, as did his opposition to a general system of internal improvements and his distrust of government consideration of old claims and pensions. His vetoes were all matters of personal conviction, not influenced by political considerations or by his cabinet, and he set the standard for reform, efficiency, and frugality that was carried out in all departments. Pierce did employ Cushing as the administration's mouthpiece in writing editorials for the *Union*, and in helping prepare veto messages, proclamations, and annual messages. In this way Cushing was first among equals in his influence on Pierce, but this was as much a function of his not having a large bureaucracy to manage, unlike Davis and Marcy, as it was his having considerable learning, broad legal talent, and prodigious energy. Claims that Cushing was a "prime minister" or Pierce's "Richelieu" are highly exaggerated.[116] There is no example of Cushing ever convincing Pierce to take a position that was not consistent with the president's own legal or political opinions. Pierce was no one's puppet, and, in fact, none of his cabinet officers ever claimed that he had been anything but the leader of his own administration.

13

TRAVELS AND TRAVAILS OF AN EX-PRESIDENT

BECAUSE OF JANE'S "FEEBLE" condition, the Pierces remained in Washington for three weeks after Buchanan's inauguration.[1] It must have been an uncomfortable time for the former president, as the Buchanan administration was giving every indication of distancing itself from the policies and practices of it predecessor. The only consolation for Pierce was the selection of his friend Isaac Toucey to be secretary of the navy. Buchanan dithered for months before choosing the former Connecticut senator and attorney general over Nathan Clifford of Maine for the New England spot in the cabinet. To Marcy, it was "a decision of character," and Buchanan's waffling between the two men was, Marcy said, "the most remarkable instance of indecision that ever fell under my observation." Based on "character" and "fitness," the choice should have been obvious.[2] With Toucey safely in the cabinet, Pierce was at least spared the embarrassment of seeing his outspoken enemy, Edmund Burke, in the new administration. Toucey would have influence over any appointments from New England, and he shared Pierce's distrust of Burke. Nathan Clifford informed Burke, "We lost all."[3]

Buchanan's patronage policy was an unprecedented application of the "spoils system." His intention was to strengthen his own political base by purging the executive branch of any holdover Pierce appointees. Never before had a president, succeeding a member of his own party, initiated such a sweeping policy. Marcy was appalled by the "Iron Rule" that all those holding positions were "to be dropped and new appts. made."[4] The former secretary of state was quoted in the

New York Herald, "Well, they have it that I am the author of the office seeker's doctrine, that 'to the victors belong the spoils,' but I certainly should never recommend the policy of pillaging my own camp."[5] *Washington Union* co-owner and editor, A. O. P. Nicholson found Buchanan's animosity towards Pierce supporters repulsive: "Mr. Buchanan's hatred is as bitter as it is careless towards every Pierce man, & he never appoints a man til he asks whether he supported his *nomination*—not his election only."[6]

Buchanan's "hatred" extended to his vice president. Breckinridge, a former supporter of Pierce and Douglas, was refused a private meeting with Buchanan in the days following the inauguration and never met privately with the president nor was consulted in any way for the next three and a half years. He thus became one of the most ignored vice presidents in U.S. history.[7]

In favoring the Hard faction in New York, Buchanan signaled a change in policies as well as personnel. Marcy, upset that his followers were ignored by the new president, wrote that "a worse cast" could not have been made. The all important position of collector of the port was given to "a stupid fellow," who Marcy feared "wont cheat himself but has hardly sufficient capacity to prevent others from doing so." George N. Sanders, who had disgraced himself as consul to London, was named navy agent in New York. Marcy declared it "shocking," a "wonderment" that Sanders received any position at all, let alone "one where the opportunity and temptation for frauds" was "the greatest." The selection of Hards to the important positions in New York threatened a departure from Pierce's commitment to efficiency and honesty in all government offices and also reversed the previous administration's policy towards filibusters. Buchanan chose Isaiah Rynders, Irish gang leader and outspoken supporter of William Walker, to the federal government's chief law enforcement office in the city. Marcy could only record in his journal, "Rynders for Marshal!!! . . . Low vilany seems to be current. . . . What are we coming to—or rather what have we come to!!"[8] To Marcy even Know-Nothings were "better liked" by the administration than "Pierce-men," who were "hunted down like wild beasts."[9] Chief Justice Roger B. Taney commiserated with Pierce. Though suffering from intense criticism himself for the Dred Scott decision, Taney wrote that he "deeply regret[ed]" the new administration's patronage policy: "The principle adopted by the present administration . . . will, I fear, do great mischief."[10]

Pierce said and wrote nothing about Buchanan's actions, but in light of the vehemence with which Marcy was scratching away at his journal while the former president was staying at the Marcy home, the two men must have had some pointed discussions about the new president. The Kansas policy of the Pierce administration was also a subject of criticism in the press during the days following the inauguration. Geary's resignation was blamed by Republican newspapers on the failure of the Pierce administration to support the governor's enlightened policies. In his farewell address in Lecompton on March 12, Geary had blamed the "wicked passions . . . of many lawless, reckless and desperate men" for the troubles there, and praised the army and General Persifor F. Smith for his "many valuable services."[11] Nevertheless, the antislavery press interpreted the speech as critical of the Pierce administration. Geary arrived in Washington and met privately with both Pierce and Marcy. He denied ever uttering "one word of complaint" or feeling "one sentiment of dissatisfaction at the conduct of the late admn. towards him," and, in fact, said that he had received "all the support that had been promised to him."[12] Buchanan's patronage policy must have made it clear to Geary that he would not have been kept on or received any support from the new administration.

It was a relief to Pierce to finally depart Washington by train for Philadelphia on March 25. Marcy wrote that while Pierce was there, Marcy's "house was thronged by his numerous warm hearted friends anxious to pay their kind respects to him and his most excellent Lady": "I venture to say no occupants of the White House ever left Washington with such deep feelings of affection from the people of this city. I do not think there is more than one man in all the Old North State that can fairly pretend to enter into competition with Genl. Pierce [in] the art of winning hearts."[13] The Pierces settled in to the La Pierre House in Philadelphia, where they remained for the next six weeks. Jane was being treated there by Dr. Meigs, who had been recommended by former postmaster general James Campbell, whose wife, in the final stages of tuberculosis, was also under the doctor's care. After a few days in Philadelphia, Pierce wrote, "Mrs. Pierce has been improving ever since we left Washington and is now sitting in the parlour bright and cheerful."[14] He reported to Marcy, "We are passing the time very quietly and comfortably . . . but not without noting the absence of many things, which were so agreeable under your hospitable roof." Pierce dined in Philadelphia with former president Martin Van Buren at Mayor Gilpin's house and remarked that though he had not seen Van Buren in eighteen years, he was "struck by his freshness and unchanged exterior" and "perceived no diminution of sprightliness or vigor."[15]

Marcy found himself alone in Washington, the last holdover from the Pierce cabinet. He continued to be a sounding board for all those removed from office. One visitor was George W. Manypenny, former commissioner of Indian affairs, who reported that the Buchanan administration had finally paid Richard W. Thompson the money he had been claiming from the Menominee Indian treaty. The Pierce administration had blocked the payment for four years, and Marcy lamented, "His claim agt. the (Menominies) is founded in fraud. The manner in which it was paid shows that the Treasury has passed into *loose hands*. The payt. was a very indiscreet act and I think the case will make some noise."[16] In fact, the press did pick up on the matter when the *New York Herald* published a letter from a Senate clerk criticizing the payment to Thompson. The letter writer, George C. Herrick, was then physically assaulted by an official of the Treasury Department newly appointed to office by Buchanan.[17] Marcy, unaware that the payment to Thompson was a payback for his political activity in Indiana during the recent presidential campaign, was incredulous: "Why should they have so promptly have taken up a case already overruled?—and as it was a transaction in relation to Indian affairs, why was the gentleman (Manypenney) at the head of Indian bureau passed by unconsulted or noticed in relation to it.?"[18] When a letter from Manypenny finally caught up with the former president later that spring, Pierce could only reply, "After all I fear that our efforts to protect the Treasury against fraud and speculation have accomplished little except delay."[19]

After his initial optimism, Pierce was reporting in May that his wife's health had not really improved. But as the weather warmed, she was able to occasionally ride horseback and enjoy the "fresh foliage and blossoms." Marcy had finally left Washington and stopped in Philadelphia to visit with the Pierces on his way to New York.[20] They followed him to the city, arriving on May 20, and spent the next week at the home of former senator and governor Hamilton Fish. While in the city Pierce had his picture taken by Mathew Brady and dined with Marcy, historian George Bancroft, and former Pierce administration officials Heman J. Redfield and Charles O'Conor.[21]

The deliberate procession northward found Pierce in Boston in late May. He had dropped Jane off in Andover to stay with the Aikens. On May 27, the former president made his first public address since leaving the White House. Pierce spoke at an Order of Cincinnati convention at Faneuil Hall. In a typical speech he lectured his audience about the importance of respecting the rights of others by faithfully upholding all of the provisions of the Constitution. Only in this way could the Union, which had brought such benefit to the human race, be preserved.[22]

Jefferson Davis wrote from Mississippi, praising the speech. He had been forced to defend the Pierce administration at the state Democratic Party convention. A resolution had been proposed censured the new governor of Kansas, Robert J. Walker, who on arriving in the territory had pledged that any constitution drafted to achieve statehood must be ratified by the voters. The resolution charged that this was a continuation of Pierce's policy of appointing only free-state supporters to offices in Kansas and was part of a larger design by Pierce and Buchanan to make the territory a free state. Davis succeeded in preventing the passage of the resolution by reading portions of Pierce's Faneuil Hall address and remarking that he would not speak to Pierce's "personal preferences" regarding slavery but that it was a "slanderous falsehood" to charge bias in Pierce's "using . . . executive functions to aid the free-soilers in Kanzas."[23]

Pierce finally reached New Hampshire in early June. Still seeking a permanent home, he moved into the family homestead in Hillsborough temporarily while Jane remained in Andover. Later in the summer, Jane joined her husband at the Rockingham House in Portsmouth, where they remained near the ocean through the fall. What was intended to be a restful summer was interrupted by tragedy. Marcy died suddenly on July 4 while staying at a resort near Saratoga Springs. The seventy-year-old former governor, senator and secretary of state had recorded in his journal throughout June that he was experiencing a "walloping" and "palpitation of the heart" and had drawn up his will but still planned a trip to Europe in August. Pierce and Cushing had promised to see him off. Instead, Pierce traveled to Albany, where he joined Van Buren at Marcy's funeral.[24] Cushing wrote that news of Marcy's death was "like a stroke of electricity." Cushing was in Washington at the time, defending former treasury secretary Guthrie from a lawsuit brought by the ubiquitous Richard W. Thompson. Guthrie lamented to Pierce that Marcy "did not get to write the history" of the Pierce administration. Guthrie continued, "I hope for your own sake and the good of the country you will."[25] B. B. French recalled that Pierce had been the subject of his last conversation with Marcy: "You were the subject of our remarks—when he said to me, 'you and the General will sit before the fire, smoke your pipes, and talk over old times and enjoy yourselves long after I'm gone."[26] Pierce best summed up the loss, writing, "He was a great man and true patriot, and I found in him not merely a wise advisor but at all times a firm and confiding friend."[27]

More bad news arrived in August. Pierce's navy secretary, James C. Dobbin, and Jane's faithful companion Abby Means both died on the same day, and Mrs. Campbell's death occurred a few days later.[28] The letter informing Pierce of Means's death failed to reach him in time to attend her funeral. He wrote to Jane's sister of the coincidence of his two close friends dying on the same day: "They saw a good deal of each other in Washington. They had many points of sympathy and each understood the other thoroughly. In many respects they were alike—alike in their quick comprehension of character which was very remarkable in both. Alike in mental activity—in the admirable balance of their faculties and in their calm fortitude sustained by Christian graces."[29]

Before leaving Washington, Pierce had invested $6,000 with General James Shields in Minnesota lands. Shields, a friend from the Mexican War, had been a senator from Illinois, who moved to Minnesota territory after his senate term expired. It is noteworthy that Pierce waited until he had left office to begin speculating in western lands. Later that summer Shields informed Pierce that he had purchased an additional 170 acres for the former president along the Mississippi River near Faribault, but Pierce sent his own agent to look over the property and on his advice decided not to complete the purchase.[30]

In his quest to buy property in the Portsmouth area that summer, Pierce met Clement March of Greenland, New Hampshire. March's older brother Charles, a journalist, had once studied law in Pierce's office and had visited the president in Washington. A warm friendship developed between Pierce and forty-one-year-old Clement, which March described frequently in his diary. In October Pierce and March attended the state fair in Concord. Pierce had been invited to enter his beautiful stallion, Union, in the fair but had declined.[31] He did accept an invitation to speak, however, addressing the fear that so many young people were leaving the state and moving west. Based on what he had seen at the fair, Pierce pronounced that the state's economy was healthy and its future bright.[32] That night at the Eagle Hotel, Pierce, March, and two other companions played cards (shoemaker's loo and brag) until 5:00 a.m. March won $70, with Pierce the big loser. March noted, "Brandy and Champagne were imbibed to a considerable extent." After only an hour's sleep, the party was up early, "walked about the town, breakfasted" and were back at the fair grounds by 11:00 a.m., where they witnessed a balloon ascent.[33] Removed from the scrutiny of the Washington press and from his wife, Pierce returned to his former habits.

Over the next few weeks, March spent much time with Pierce and peppered him with questions about his administration and earlier life and career. Pierce shared the fact that "he always had a presentiment that he would be President. But he was too wise to let any one know of his thoughts, or to make any apparent efforts towards its attainment." He described his first court case—"a complete failure"—his quarrel with Isaac Hill, and his friendship with Webster. Pierce recited "the remarks he made at the famous dinner at Franklin," credited Webster with making him president, and told "all he knew" of his nomination for president. Pierce declared that he fully expected "the hostility he would encounter" for the repeal of the Missouri Compromise but had always believed it unconstitutional. March concluded that Pierce "was a firm believer in an over-ruling Providence, and impute[d] to that source all his success." March "found the General a very sociable, agreeable and interesting companion, and formed quite an attachment for him." March also declared that "by my intercourse with the President I have been improved in political and social knowledge."[34]

The friendship encompassed more than just reminiscence and political gossip. March describes "the greatest frolic of my life" with Pierce in Boston on Friday night, October 23:

> The General and I dined at the Tremont at 1 o'clock, a glass of brandy and water before, a pint of champagne at dinner, went to the Fair Grounds and returned to the Tremont at 5, drank brandy and water till 7½, supped at Parker's on broiled oysters beefsteak and Pomy's Claret, went to the Theatre, and saw Fanny Kemble and her daughter in a private box by mistake, returned to Parker's and drank some very old brandy in his private room, went back to the Theatre and took possession of our "proscenium box," then again to Parker's and had raw oysters and a bottle of Stein Wine, then to the General's room, drank two pint bottles of Champagne, took a stroll about the Streets, and made a call in Fruit Street, where we disbursed some thirty dollars, and at 4 o'clock repaired to our rooms at the Tremont.

March awoke with a headache.[35] His description of the evening is suggestive for what it does not say. While describing in detail the men's activities prior to the "call in Fruit Street," the author does not explain for what purpose they "disbursed some thirty dollars" in the early morning hours. Fruit Street was located in the notorious Hill district of the West End, a neighborhood of dance halls, gambling houses, and brothels. Their all night "frolic" may have involved more than just drinking, eating, and theater going.[36]

It was through his friendship with March that Pierce decided to travel with Jane to Madeira, the Portuguese islands off the coast of Morocco, to spend the winter. Her health made avoiding the New England winter a necessity, and Pierce had initially thought of Cuba as the most healthful destination, but March's uncle, John Howard

March, was U.S. consul at Funchal, the capital city of Madeira. This would also be a convenient stepping off point for a tour of the continent in the spring.[37] Pierce friend and navy secretary Isaac Toucey arranged for the president's free passage on the navy steamer *Powhatan*, which would depart from Norfolk in early December. Clement March met Pierce and Jane in New York City in mid-November as they began their trip. The two men walked about the city on November 21, stopping by Brady's studio to see Pierce's picture, which had been taken on his visit to the city the previous spring.[38]

Before departing, Pierce wrote a letter to Caleb Cushing, thanking him for his vigorous defense of the administration at a speech in Faneuil Hall on October 27. Cushing had attacked the Republican Party for seeking "the equality of Africans and Americans" despite the fact "that the two races are unequal by nature . . ." He defended the repeal of the Missouri Compromise and predicted that popular sovereignty would work in Kansas because free labor was superior to slave labor and would ultimately prevail. Cushing decried the "exaggerated" reports of violence and fraud in Kansas, claiming that the troubles there were "not half so grave as the troubles in British India."[39] In his letter, Pierce praised Cushing's defense of Marcy and recalled the unanimity of opinion within the cabinet "in favor of the direct repeal of the Missouri compromise."[40] In the six months since the close of the Pierce administration, Marcy, Davis, and Cushing had all publicly come to its defense.

The loyalty of Pierce's cabinet was unquestioned, as was their individual administrative talent and integrity while in office, but former senator Augustus C. Dodge, whom Pierce appointed minister to Madrid, offered what may have been the best assessment of their impact on his administration when he wrote Pierce, "I personally liked very much every member of your cabinet and think no President or country was ever blessed with one more pure, upright and patriotic. They were the most indifferent men to what we familiarly call 'popularity' that I met with in station. . . . you possessed all those qualities and I know from observation that you could please a man better when refusing him his request—than most of your excellent associates could when granting it. Had they possessed an iota of your talent for making friends your renomination and reelection would have been a fixed fact which not all of the disappointed and venal place seekers in America could have prevented."[41] But this was now in the past, and Pierce looked forward to turning his back on the contentiousness that ruled American politics; he also looked forward to having a lengthy respite abroad.

While in Norfolk, Pierce and Jane visited with some orphans from a yellow fever epidemic and the former president "went to see several invalids." Pierce's party, which included Jane's maid Minnie and two horses one of which was a gift from Marcy to Jane, boarded the *Powhatan* on December 8. The voyage to Madeira took nearly three weeks, as the steamer was idled for four days off the coast of Virginia, waiting for delivery of a valve. Jane praised the accommodations and the attentions of Captain Pearson, with whom the couple dined each day, but spent most of her time in the cabin or seated on deck with her "wadded jacket and grey mantilla—and a bottle of hot water" to warm her feet. Her husband, on the other hand, paced about the deck, conversing with everyone and never missing the nightly drills of the sailors and marines. Before disembarking at Madeira, Pierce "made a little farewell speech to the whole company of the ship," after which the band played, and the ship's guns fired a salute to the former president.[42]

The Pierces settled into their host John March's "quinta," where they remained for the next six months. The beautiful mountain scenery, lush flowers and fruits, and warm climate had the desired effect. Pierce lost the cough that had nagged him since before leaving Norfolk, and Jane reported gaining some "flesh" lost during the long ocean voyage. She was soon out riding on horseback, "over very steep rough paths, two men at the side of the very fine horses which Mr. P. had from the States." She rode between four and eight miles most days, "full tilt," according to her husband, who frequently went off on his own for longer rides over the mountains.[43] When they learned of her activities, Jane's relatives back in New England expressed surprise: "I couldn't help exclaiming at the idea of Aunt Jane's riding . . . on horseback. She must be a *little* better than she was in Andover. . . ."[44] In late February, Jane confirmed this to her sister, Mary Aiken: "This is an easy quiet regular life and (thanks to Mr.

March) I could not be better situated in regard to comfort & convenience—and also in other respects—for my husband is well and quietly enjoys all—which is much for *me* but after all dear Mary—I can not be an available member of society with such inability—and infirmity as I have. . . . If I could only continue as well as I am just now I should feel that I ought to be well contented."[45] The prospect of a tour of the continent prompted the Pierces to take up French lessons. Jane reported, "Mr. P. quite engaged with his French—which I enjoy seeing him so interested in—as he has begun, seems (in the true spirit of a conqueror) determined to master it." But, Jane found the lessons frustrating: "I am sorry to find that my imperfect hearing is a great obstacle to my using French—as it is difficult for me to understand *my own* language—conversation of course with a foreign one."[46] They continued studying the language throughout their trip, being tutored as often as three times a week.[47]

Though far removed from the political battles in Washington, Pierce retained a lively interest in any news from the states. Mail was infrequently received in Madeira, but Pierce was kept informed by letters from Sidney Webster, John H. George, Robert McClelland, and Caleb Cushing, of the political war being waged within the Democratic Party. Buchanan and Douglas had split over the president's determination to accept the proslavery Lecompton Constitution without full ratification by the voters of Kansas. Douglas viewed this decision as a flagrant violation of popular sovereignty and a violation of the president's word. Governor Walker of Kansas resigned in protest of Buchanan's decision, and Douglas's outspoken criticism of the president brought threats of banishment from the party.[48] Buchanan's old friend and supporter John W. Forney also broke with the president, charging, "The Kansas catastrophe of the administration has utterly demoralized our organization."[49] McClelland "regretted that Mr. Buchanan so quickly discarded the policy" that Pierce had been "pursuing in regard to Kansas."[50] From afar, Pierce sarcastically reflected on Buchanan's plight:

> Considering the promise of what large experience and statesmanship, at the helm, were to accomplish—the change for the better—the palpable improvement, which was to be at once

> apparent—at home and abroad—the establishment of fraternal relationships at least among the wings of our party—North, South, East, West—softs & hards. The complication of affairs, just at this point of time is quite notable, and one can but be struck by the readiness with which Democrats both in & out of Congress have arrayed themselves on different sides of prominent questions. Oddly enough, it sounds to hear Mr. Douglas within the first three weeks of the session, discussing the question whether he is in or out of the party, and whether the Executive intends to read him out or not.[51]

Cushing wrote from Washington, where he was arguing cases before the Supreme Court, "The Senators & Representatives in Congress console me every day with their reminiscences of comparative respect and regard for you and your Cabinet." Cushing and Pierce's former secretary, Sidney Webster, had formed a law partnership with offices in New York and Boston.[52]

In June 1858, the Pierces left Madeira for Europe. They stopped first in Lisbon, where old friend John L. O'Sullivan was still serving as minister. Then it was on to Cadiz by steamer, then to Valencia, Seville, and Gibraltar. They spent a few days in each city before traveling to Marseilles, Lyons, and Geneva, spending the rest of the summer in Switzerland. At each stop, Pierce made side trips to all the important historic or scenic places, walking as much as eleven miles a day while in Switzerland, but Jane often stayed behind in the hotel as she was "still unable to make long stages."[53] Pierce wrote to John H. George, "I am without any definite plans, as I was when I left home—leaving my movements to be determined entirely by the state of Mrs. Pierce's health and what may seem to promise most for its restoration. She is decidedly better than when we left the states. . . . She has been able to enjoy a good deal."[54] The death of George's young daughter, his second child to die within a year, reminded Pierce of his own family tragedies: "Great sorrows make another link between us. As you visit the graves, & a part of your own children you will be sure of my sympathies, and you will meet my thoughts as you pause at the small enclosure, which contains *all* of mine."[55] Jane's thoughts were never far from her lost children. She traveled with Benny's Bible and a locket containing locks of his hair. She wrote, "It is soothing my dear sister when you speak of my child's picture—does it not seem to say, as he did in my dreams 'I'm nicely Mother, just as well as I want to be'—precious ones all! God grant that we may meet them in glory, when the ever changing scenes of this life are over—indeed it seems more and more to me like a moving panorama."[56] Pierce had engaged a servant, Gustave, "respectful unselfish & devoted," who remained with them for most of the time in Europe, while Minnie was described by Jane as "useful, but not as useful as she might be."[57]

While in Geneva, Samuel F. B. Morse called on the Pierces. He had been feted at a dinner in Paris at the successful installation of the transatlantic cable, but the celebrations on both sides of the Atlantic proved to be premature, as the cable laid by Cyrus Field using the navy steam frigate, *Niagara*, which was built by the Pierce administration, soon failed. Jane wrote her sister, "The telegraph I see is not likely to bring your message to me very soon . . . when it really begins to work—will our country people rejoice again then—or make this suffice."[58]

In the fall the travelers moved on to Italy. They spent eight weeks in Florence, a week in Naples, and several months on the Island of Capri. The weather in "sunny Italy" disappointed, however, as both Frank and Jane complained in their letters of the nearly constant rain they experienced from October through January.[59]

In February 1859, the long-anticipated reunion with Hawthorne occurred when the Pierces arrived in Rome. The writer had resigned as consul to Liverpool in February 1857 but remained at his post until his successor arrived in October. The Hawthorne family then traveled about Europe before settling down in Rome in the fall of 1858.[60]

The meeting with Hawthorne proved another opportunity for Pierce to offer his old friend assistance. Hawthorne's teenage daughter Una, his oldest child, had been seriously ill for months, suffering from malaria. By the time Pierce arrived, her condition was critical. Thirteen-year-old Julian Hawthorne recalled Pierce's first visit: "I recollect the first evening Pierce came to our house, and sat in the little parlor in the dusk, listening to the story of Una's illness. 'Poor child! poor Child! he said occasionally, in a low voice. His sympathy was like something palpable,—strong, warm and comforting.

He said very little, but it was impossible not to feel how much he cared. He knew of his own experience what it was to lose children."[61] Pierce took Hawthorne on long walks around the city, visiting his friend as often as three times a day to check on Una and offer support. Hawthorne, who had not seen Pierce in nearly six years, wrote, "He is singularly little changed; the more I see him, the more I get him back, just such as he was in our youth. This morning his face, air, and smile, were so wonderfully like himself of old, that at least thirty years were annihilated. . . . He is a most singular character, so frank, so true, so immediate, so subtle, so simple, so complicated."[62] Sophia Hawthorne noted that Pierce "wrapped [her husband] round with the most soothing care," and after Una was out of danger Hawthorne concluded, "Never having had any trouble before, that pierced into my very vitals, I did not know what comfort there might be in the manly sympathy of a friend, but Pierce has undergone so great a sorrow of his own, and has so large and kindly a heart, and is so tender and strong that he really did us good, and I shall always love him better for the recollection of those dark days."[63] Hawthorne saw that the friendship was unbreakable: "We have passed all the turning-off places, and may hope to go on together still the same dear friends, as long as we live."[64] Pierce wrote to their mutual friend, Horatio Bridge, that Hawthorne was "entirely unchanged in heart & genius." Pierce continued, "Can anything better be said of any man?"[65]

The two families made plans to meet up again in London in the fall and return to the states on the same ship, but Hawthorne was offered £600 for his next book by a British publishing house, and Pierce encouraged him, "in view of Una's rather delicate health," to accept the offer and remain in England until the spring of 1860.[66]

In the spring of 1859, the Pierces moved on to Vienna by way of Venice, where they were somewhat alarmed and inconvenienced by a war that broke out between Sardinia and Austria. Troops were seen everywhere on their trip to Vienna, and they were delayed in leaving the city by the fact that "the cars" were "entirely devoted to the troops." Jane was also "quite disabled" and unable to see much of the city. The couple eventually moved on to Bavaria, where Jane's health continued to deteriorate so that she was forced to see a physician. She weighed only eighty-five pounds. "It seems very sad to me . . . to go back to the old state of trouble & weakness—after knowing the comfort of being more or less better of it." But she continued to report to her family on their activities and was amused by her husband's futile attempts at fishing in the streams around Schwabach: "Everything forgotten for the one idea—trout . . . he is just himself and nobody else—as ever."[67]

In June they moved on to Paris by way of Brussels. They found many friends in Paris, including Charles March and Thomas H. Seymour, on his way home after serving as minister to Russia in the Pierce administration, but considering her health, Jane wrote, "My husband warns everybody off. . . ."[68] Their last stop was London, where they arrived in mid-July. Pierce attended a session of the House of Commons.[69] Throughout their tour the Pierces had traveled modestly and unceremoniously, not expecting and not recording any meetings with heads of state, the pope, or even Queen Victoria. The itinerants sailed for home in mid-August, arriving at Norfolk on September 7. Buchanan invited them to stay at the White House on the way back to New England, but the Pierces bypassed Washington entirely and, on September 11, reached Andover for a reunion with Jane's family.[70]

The unpopularity of the Buchanan administration, which had failed to bring Kansas into the Union as a slave state under the Lecompton Constitution and which was rocked by scandals and corruption in New York City and in the Bureau of Indian Affairs, raised questions as to whether Pierce would be a candidate for the Democratic nomination at the Charleston convention in the spring of 1860. James D. B. DeBow, editor of *DeBow's American Review,* wrote to McClelland: "The contrast presented by the present administration & the one with which you were associated is too striking not to attract notice. It makes me so sad as it does others. Would to God we could have another Pierce dynasty indeed I would bring back every member of that cabinet but Cushing! Alas, however things as you say are indeed out of joint."[71] Pierce was also Jefferson Davis's first choice for 1860, but the former president had written from London that he was not interested. Davis, claiming that Pierce was "preferred above all others" in Mississippi, urged him to keep the door open: "I hope you will not obstruct the wish of your friends, should circumstances indicate it, to use your name for the nomination."[72]

In contrast to his feelings in 1852, Pierce was not willing to allow his friends to act for him. In late September, he wrote a supporter from Alabama, "I feel . . . that my public life is closed and have not a single lingering desire that it should be otherwise. This and more my friends at the North understand. They know that it would annoy me if I believed that my name would come before the Charleston Convention under any possible combination of circumstances. Although some of my warm personal friends have been elected delegates in Maine and Massachusetts and more probably will be in New England, I have reason to believe that they will regard my wishes in this relation."[73] He insisted the same thing to Clement March, who recorded in his diary a conversation with Pierce: "He dined with me, and conversed much about the Consul, Madeira, Europe, and American politics. He persists that he has no desire, and would not consent, to be President again."[74] Pierce's decisiveness seemed to have the desired effect, and speculation about his possible candidacy subsided.

In the fall of 1859 Pierce resumed his search for property to buy in New Hampshire. Clement March continued to show him farms in the Portsmouth area, but ultimately Pierce purchased sixty acres in Concord on Pleasant Street about a mile west of downtown. There was no house on the property, so the Pierces moved into rented quarters on South Main Street until a suitable home could be built on the farmland.[75]

March accompanied Pierce to Concord on October 12 to look over the property. They drove to the site with Pierce's "beautiful horse," Union. Later, at the Eagle Hotel they "played cards all night." On this occasion, Pierce and his partner, John H. George, were the big winners. In the morning they left at 5:30 a.m. by train for Nashua to attend the state fair, "to witness a ploughing match."[76]

A few days later, on October 16, 1859, John Brown and associates raided the federal arsenal at Harpers Ferry in a misguided attempt to incite a slave uprising. An alarmed nation observed anxiously the trial and awaited the execution on December 2. Governor Henry Wise of Virginia called out the state militia. With more than fifty thousand Virginians under arms, the nation appeared on the brink of civil war. Though northern abolitionists, including Emerson, claimed that Brown's action would "make the gallows glorious like the cross," most northerners condemned the violence. Following Brown's execution, Union rallies were held in many northern cities. Pierce was invited to address two of them, one at Faneuil Hall on December 7 and the other in New York City. He declined both invitations, but sent letters instead which were read at the meetings. The occasion offered Pierce the opportunity to reiterate his long-held view of the abolitionists and the danger inherent in their fanaticism: "Let us act calmly and deliberately, without passion and without acrimony. Let us take no hasty or narrow view of the causes which have produced the dangers we would meet and if possible, avert. It is not the recent invasion of Virginia, which should awaken our strongest apprehensions, but the teachings still vehemently persisted in, from which it springs, with the inevitable necessity which evolves the effect from the cause. . . . Those who boldly approve and applaud the acts of treason and murder perpetrated within the limits of Virginia are not the most dangerous enemies of the Constitution and the Union." To Pierce the real danger lay with "subtle, crafty men [abolitionists], who passing by duties and obligations habitually appeal to sectional prejudices and passions, by denouncing the institutions of the people of the South and thus influence the Northern mind to the pitch of resistance to the clear provisions of the fundamental law." Pierce denied that there was an "irrepressible conflict" between the North and the South. Fifty years of fighting side by side during the Revolution and later establishing the Constitution and the strong Union demonstrated that the differences between the sections were not insurmountable.[77] But to his brother Henry, Pierce expressed his apprehensions about the future of the nation. He observed, "Orders for merchandize and for various articles of manufacture are being constantly countermanded by the Southern people, social intercourse between the North and the South and business arrangements also are being seriously disturbed—and if the interruption becomes more complete, political relations cannot long be maintained."[78]

The Pierces decided to spend the winter of 1860 at Nassau in the Bahamas. On the eve of his departure from New York in January,

Pierce addressed a letter to Jefferson Davis: "Nothing but the state of Mrs. Pierces' health would induce me to leave the country now although it is quite likely that my presence at home would be of little service." He urged Davis to be the party's "standard bearer in 1860" and reminded him that the "exasperated" people of the South still had many friends in the North. Pierce warned against secession: "I have never believed that the disruption of the Union can occur without blood, and if through the madness of northern abolitionism that dire calamity must come, the fighting will not be along Mason and Dixon's line merely. It [will] be within our own borders in our own streets between the two classes of citizens of whom I have referred. Those who defy law and scout Constitutional obligations will, if we ever reach the arbitrament of arms, find occupation enough at home."[79] This letter would be used against Pierce in the future.

That same night Pierce wrote a letter to John H. George, who was running for Congress from New Hampshire and had asked his mentor for advice as to how to deal with the slavery question in his campaign. The former president, writing at 3:00 a.m. and being "too weary" to write at length, offered this advice: "It will not be useful to discuss the question of the rightfulness of slavery as an abstract proposition. Upon this point we may perhaps be said to have expressed our opinion years ago by abolishing it. Treat of it as it exists under our Constitution and our Constitutional theory of state rights. The doctrine of the equality of races is untrue and absurd. If slavery were abolished throughout the United States tomorrow, N.H. would not admit the doctrine but would legislate against it."[80]

Presidential election year politics engaged Pierce's attention throughout the five months he and Jane spent in Nassau. George kept him informed of the campaign for the state election in March, reporting that Protestant ministers were using the pulpit to attack the Democrats on the slavery issue by stating that "no religious man" could "do otherwise than vote the republican ticket."[81] Pierce, who was always sensitive on the issue of a politicized ministry replied angrily, "The cant heresy and treason fulminated from many of our New England Pulpits Sunday after Sunday on the approach of every general election is really appalling.... The great mass of Union loving Constitution revering men in N.H. have paid their money for the opportunity of listening to treason, rather than for the privilege of gospel instruction."[82] The New Hampshire state election was a hopeless cause, so Pierce focused his attention on the upcoming national convention in Charleston. His former law partner and treasury department official Josiah Minot was the state party chairman, and Pierce advised him to bring a united delegation to the national convention: "I hope our delegation will vote as a unit and having decided upon the candidate to whom they will give their preference vote for him steadily & as long as there may be hope of his nomination. . . ."[83] Pierce did not state a preference for any particular candidate, as he was always willing to support any Democrat nominated by a united party. The New Hampshire delegation joined many other northern states in supporting Stephen A. Douglas at Charleston.[84]

Douglas's candidacy posed a serious problem for the southern delegates. The failure of popular sovereignty to produce a slave-state Kansas; Douglas's Freeport Doctrine, which asserted that despite the Dred Scott decision, the people could eliminate slavery in a territory by failing to pass laws for its enforcement; and John Brown's raid all caused southern leaders to demand a platform that included a territorial slave code enforced by the federal government. Douglas supporters knew that such a plank would doom his candidacy in the North, while southerners understood that running under Douglas's "squatter sovereignty" banner would doom the party in the South. In April at the Charleston convention, chaired by Caleb Cushing, Douglas won the platform fight, but some southern delegations walked out in protest. The convention dragged on for ten days before adjourning without nominating a candidate. The remaining delegates agreed to reconvene the convention in Baltimore on June 18.[85]

The Pierces returned from Nassau in mid-May and settled into the Clarendon Hotel in New York, where Jane was to undergo medical treatment. From Nassau, Jane reported her weight had increased to nearly one hundred pounds, but her health was not improved, and she agreed to the "pretty powerful remedies" prescribed by Dr. Peaslee.[86] While in New York, Pierce attended the wedding of his former secretary, Sidney Webster, to the daughter of Hamilton Fish.[87] But Pierce was preoccupied with the state of his party. He had long believed that a national, united Democratic Party was essential to the preservation of the Union. Now the party seemed on the verge of collapse. From his hotel in New York he met and communicated by mail with party leaders, hoping to find a solution to keep the party together at Baltimore.

The Republican convention met in May. Lincoln's nomination surprised many who had expected Seward to be chosen. Pierce was advised, "In putting up Lincoln they get rid of the odium which attaches to Seward without giving up Seward's views!"[88] The Republicans had seized their opportunity to win the presidency; could the Democrats block them? Discussing options if Douglas could not be nominated, John W. Forney, a Douglas supporter, wrote to Pierce, "I will go for you." He reveled in the failures of the Buchanan administration: "The very devil is to pay, but thank God his 'general' representative on earth, Old Buck, is to have his desserts, and you some revenge by the contrast between the Heaven of your administration and the Hell of his!"[89] Davis also wrote Pierce that southern delegates "would gladly unite upon you," but the former president was having none of such talk, and on June 7 he met in his hotel room with Cushing and M. W. Cluskey, a Democratic propagandist from Washington; Pierce urged his former attorney general to consider accepting the nomination. Cushing was adamant in refusing to have his name brought before the Baltimore convention.[90] Pierce met with other New England delegates as they passed through New York on the way to Baltimore. It was clear that "the Douglas men" hoped "to force him through," while Davis warned that southern delegates would "support any sound man," but they would "not vote for a 'squatter sovereignty' candidate any more than for a 'free-soiler.'"[91]

Cushing presided again at the Baltimore convention, but not for long. The Douglas delegates, in order to insure his nomination, were determined to deny seats to those who had bolted the convention in Charleston. When the credentials committee report was approved, which refused to reseat the delegates from Alabama and Louisiana, Virginia led a walkout, which was followed by delegations from North Carolina, Tennessee, and some from Maryland, California, and Oregon. The next day, following a futile night of negotiation, Kentucky, Missouri, and Arkansas followed previous delegations out of the convention, and Cushing dramatically left the podium and walked out. He was followed out the door by Pierce's longtime friend and delegate from Massachusetts, Benjamin F. Butler, who was protesting the convention's refusal to seat B. F. Hallett, former national party chairman and U.S. attorney in Massachusetts during the Pierce administration. Hallett, a Breckinridge supporter, wrote to Pierce, describing his treatment by the Douglas-dominated credentials committee, which influenced the former president's future course in regard to the nominations. What was left of the Baltimore convention proceeded to nominate Douglas, while the bolters, just over one-third of the total delegates, met in a separate hall and nominated John C. Breckinridge.[92]

Pierce privately expressed his support for Breckinridge. He declared that the actions of the credentials committee in denying Hallett and others their seats was a violation of party practice and "usage" and was intended to break up the convention; thus, the people were not bound by the nomination. But he continued to urge caution: "At all events it is no time for crimination and recrimination."[93] The impact on the party in New Hampshire also concerned Pierce. Most of his friends, including Albert R. Hatch and John H. George, supported Breckinridge, but the delegation from the state had voted for Douglas throughout the two conventions. Pierce feared that the state party would split into two sets of electors, one for Douglas and one for Breckinridge. He wrote to Hatch, "I am utterly opposed to any organization outside that of the party as it now exists." He was opposed to any factions running an independent ticket: "If any foolish factious men wish to run as an independent ticket they must not be countenanced unless we are compelled to do it."[94] Pierce agreed with Hatch that "an overwhelming majority of Dems in this state" would "support Douglas. . . ." Pierce continued, "Any separate action on the part of the friends of Mr. B[reckinridge] must be ineffectual, and by dividing the Party tend to perpetuate its defeat."[95]

All of the resources of the Buchanan administration were placed in support of Breckinridge, including the use of federal patronage to support his campaign. In New York, Pennsylvania, and other states postmasters and other officials who were friendly to Douglas were replaced with Breckinridge supporters. This chance to settle old scores posed another problem for Pierce. Edmund Burke seized upon the opportunity to write to Isaac I. Stevens, Breckinridge's campaign chairman, to complain about the lack of open support for Breckinridge coming from administration officials in New Hampshire. Burke advised "as absolutely indispensable" the removal of postmasters at Concord, Manchester, Nashua, and Newport, men who were all friends of Pierce. Before acting, Stevens, who had served as governor of Washington Territory under Pierce, wrote to his former boss for advice.[96] Burke's demand infuriated Pierce, who answered, "I can hardly conceive a degree of madness which would suggest the removal of the Postmasters. . . ." He stated that none of the postmasters were "noisy partisans," and he did not know who they supported but that their removals would "subserve the interests of the extreme friends of Judge Douglass in N.H." Pierce correctly assigned Burke's letter to "maliciousness and unaccountable folly" and concluded, "I cannot conceive what the very bad & unprincipled man who writes you means unless it be to do all possible mischief here and bring deserved condemnation upon the administration—I earnestly hope that his wicked purposes may not be accomplished."[97] Stevens agreed, and Pierce had temporarily fended off one more effort by Burke to break up the party in New Hampshire.

Burke wasn't finished. He established a pro-Breckinridge newspaper in Concord, and when the Democrats refused to place any Breckinridge candidates on the electoral ticket, he organized a convention to select a separate slate of electors pledged to the vice president. Despite his personal preference for Breckinridge, Pierce continued to oppose any attempt to divide the state's Democratic voters, writing in October that he was "so decidedly against the nomination of an independent electoral ticket in this state" that he was unable to "favor it in any way."[98] The regular state Democratic Party organization and press continued to support Douglas.

That summer and fall, state elections in Missouri, Kentucky, Maine, Vermont, Pennsylvania, Indiana, and Ohio all pointed to a Lincoln Electoral College triumph in November. With the national Democratic Party vote divided between Douglas and Breckinridge and with former Whig John Bell running on the Constitutional Union Party ticket in the border states, Lincoln could easily win state after state with only a plurality of the votes. In desperation, Democrats looked for a way to unite the opposition against the Republicans. James Campbell, writing from Philadelphia, proposed that Pierce offer himself as a candidate if Douglas and Breckinridge would agree to drop out of the race. Pierce had another idea: "My belief is that if Mr. Breckinridge & Mr. Douglass would voluntarily withdraw, and concur in the nomination of Mr. Guthrie & Gov. Seymour of New York it is not too late to retrieve our fortunes and defeat sectionalism. . . . I could not consent to be a candidate. It would be unwise for the party, *and absolutely out of the question for myself.*"[99] Campbell tried this idea out in Pennsylvania, but Douglas's campaign manager there, John W. Forney, refused to consider it. Campbell reported to Pierce, "I very much fear that nothing can be done. The state will go for Lincoln."[100]

Lincoln's sweeping victory in the North made a reality of all of Pierce's fears for the nation. In New Hampshire, the Republican ticket won in every county, though the Democratic Party held together well, and Breckinridge received only three percent of the vote. What would the slave states do in response to the election of a president who was not even on the ballot in nine southern states? Pierce knew that secession was likely, even as the Republican press tried to reassure northerners that the South was only playing a game of bluff: "The declarations 'no danger' 'no secession' reminds me of the story of the man who thought there would not be much of a shower when he stood by the ark with the waters of the flood at his hips."[101]

14

THE CIVIL WAR YEARS

PIERCE FULLY UNDERSTOOD THE danger to the Union posed by Lincoln's election. He knew the mind of the southern leaders far better than most politicians in the North. A few weeks after the election, he put his thoughts on paper in a draft of a letter that was never sent. Charging that the crisis was the result of "the heresies" that "swept over the North," he declared, "I have never desired to survive the wreck of the Union." According to Pierce, the election of Lincoln was "beyond all doubt Constitutional," but Pierce knew it would have consequences: "The people of the Southern States look beyond it to see, if they can, what it implies." They saw it as an endorsement of northern resistance to slavery, of personal liberty laws, and of Lincoln's own claim: "We cannot go on as we are, but must in the end be all free or all slave states." Lincoln's election was the fulfillment of Seward's prediction of an "irrepressible conflict." He believed it was "vain" to try to talk the South out of secession: "How can I urge the men of the South to take a view I should not take if I were there, a view which I do not take as a northern man with all I have at stake here." Pierce believed only "action, immediate action" by the North to repeal all acts that "have nullified the Constitution" could save the Union, but he saw no hope of that happening.[1]

In fact, throughout the intervening four months between Lincoln's election and his inauguration, the Republicans treated talk of secession, as Richard Carwardine has noted, "As little more than hot-air threats of unrepresentative fire-eaters, whose proposed secession ordinances would surely fail." Lincoln "consistently misjudged" the determination of the southern states and, even after seven states had voted secession, continued to believe this was simply to strengthen their bargaining position with the new administration.[2] Pierce knew better and over the next few months did what he could in a vain attempt to halt the inevitable march toward civil war.

Pierce's anxiety for the nation may have helped bring on a severe lung and throat infection which kept him incapacitated for much of December and January. He described it to John H. George as the worst illness he had suffered from in more than twenty years.[3] But that did not prevent him from expressing his views on the impending crisis. In late November, Interior Secretary Jacob Thompson wrote Pierce, asking for advice. Pierce answered, "To my mind one thing is clear—no wise man can under existing circumstances dream of coercion. The first blow struck in that direction will be a blow fatal even to hope."[4] The letter was read to Buchanan and his cabinet.[5]

In December, Supreme Court Justice John A. Campbell, Pierce's only selection to the nation's highest court, asked Pierce to travel to Campbell's home state of Alabama in the company of Senator Benjamin Fitzpatrick to address that state's secession convention on January 7. Campbell had cleared his proposal with President Buchanan.[6] Pierce declined to go, citing his health, but wrote an open letter to the people of Alabama, which was widely published. In it he urged delay to give the people of the North a chance to correct their errors and repeal the personal liberty laws. He appealed to Alabama "to arrest the progress of disintegration": "I think our brethren of the South, warm hearted chivalrous men as they are, should remember in their highest exasperation, how steady true and unfaltering has been the defence of their rights, on the part of hundreds of thousands of the people of the northern States; and how warmly in the hearts of those hundreds of thousands still glow fraternal regard. I do not see how the South can overlook these facts."[7] He did not propose that the state delay "for any considerable period"; but he continued, "In the name of our Common inheritance, Common religion, and Common blood . . . you ought not—must not—imperil everything most important to you as to us, by inconsiderate haste, by precipitate steps which it may be impossible to retrace." He urged the South to allow some time "for the casting out of fanaticism, and the enthronement of reason." He concluded, "If we cannot live together in peace, then in peace and on just terms, let us separate." [8]

In thanking Pierce for his letter, Campbell reported that Buchanan's "mind" seemed to have "lost its power of comprehending a complicated situation." Campbell continued, "He is nervous & hysterical, & I think completely unmanned." The president was listening to too many "counsellors" who were making "confusion of confusions." To Campbell, "the imbecility of the administration & the general opinion of its infidelity and corruption" had greatly exacerbated the secession crisis.[9] Cushing was one of those "counsellors" whom Buchanan had called to Washington to give him guidance. Cushing reported to Pierce of the "utter helplessness" of the situation: "The town is utterly depopulated; the President is embarrassed with insoluble questions; Congress is paralyzed by party spirit; and everybody seems to despair of any help from *man*, though many are looking vaguely for they know not what near interposition of Providence." [10]

In January South Carolina cut off supplies and mail to Fort Sumter. In an effort to resupply and reinforce Major Anderson, Buchanan decided to send an unarmed merchant steamer, *Star of the West*, to the Fort. The administration intended the mission to be secret, but it was widely publicized in the papers, and shore batteries drove the ship away. After the steamer had left for Charleston, Major Anderson reported that he was in no immediate danger and did not need relief, but this information reached Washington too late to recall the ship. As a consequence of this fiasco, the two remaining southern members of Buchanan's cabinet resigned.[11] Pierce was in Boston at the time, under the care of Dr. Hoffendahl for his lung and throat infection. He wrote to Jane, "I cannot conceive of a more idle, foolish, ill advised, criminal thing than the sending of the Star of the West to Charleston under existing circumstances. I wish it might turn out to be nothing more than 'fuss & feathers.' But will not the first act of war the useless sending of this steamer, and the first hostile gun never breath and blaze along the whole Southern line calling men to arms. . . ." [12]

Within days, Alabama, Mississippi, and Florida seceded. Pierce's close friends Clement Clay and Jefferson Davis, announced their resignations from the Senate. Each wrote a sincere letter to their friend, the former president. Davis wrote from his desk in the Senate chamber, "I leave immediately for Mississippi and know not what may devolve upon me after my return. Civil war has only horror for me, but whatever circumstances demand shall be met as a duty and I trust be so discharged that you will not be ashamed of our former connection or cease to be my friend."[13] Pierce expressed his feelings to his minister, Rev. Henry Parker, who had met Clay and Davis on his several trips to Washington during the Pierce administration: "They were all sincere, union loving men and feel, with their constituents, that they have been driven out by long continued aggression and vituperative assault, on the part of those from whom they had a right to expect fair dealing, if not paternal regard."[14]

The fact of secession prompted some moderates to face the reality of civil war. In Congress, Senator John J. Crittenden proposed a series of constitutional amendments to address the concerns of the South regarding the future protection of slavery. Former president Tyler chaired a peace convention in Washington, in which James Guthrie played a major role as chair of the resolutions committee. A total of 132 delegates from twenty-one states participated in the hopeless effort to avert war. Lincoln briefly considered Guthrie for a place in the cabinet, in hopes of reassuring the border states.[15] Amos A. Lawrence, attending the peace convention, proposed that the former presidents come to Washington "to exert their influence in favor of the Union." To Pierce he wrote, "There is no one whose opinions would be more favorably recd. & would be more effective than yours."[16]

The irony of Lawrence's invitation, considering his role in stirring up trouble in Kansas, must have struck Pierce, who, nevertheless, wrote back politely, "I would go to Washington at once, if I thought I could be of the least service." But Pierce went on to say, "I have, as yet, seen no point for effective interposition." He reminded Lawrence of their long-standing disagreement on the causes of the trouble: "I have never been able to see how a successful appeal could be made to the South, without first placing ourselves right."[17] All of these last-minute efforts to avert trouble failed to achieve anything, and the Lincoln administration was inaugurated on March 4.

The firing on Fort Sumter on April 12, 1861, brought a new challenge to Pierce and to all northern Democrats. With the headlines blazing, "*War Exists*," northerners rallied to the defense of the nation. The *New Hampshire Patriot* urged caution and reprinted Pierce's letter to the people of Alabama: "If we cannot live together in peace, then in peace and on just terms let us separate." Blaming the Lincoln administration for precipitating hostilities, the *Patriot* continued to recommend "negotiation and compromise *without* war."[18] But with South Carolina firing the first shots at American troops and with rumors rampant that Washington was about to be attacked, northerners of all political persuasions rallied to defend the flag.

In Concord a citizen's meeting was held on April 20, which was attended by Republicans and Democrats alike, including Pierce's close friends John H. George and Rev. Parker, who both addressed the assembly. The gathering adopted a resolution:

> That in the present crisis we, as American citizens and as citizens of the State of New Hampshire, acknowledge our fealty to our National and State Governments, to the Constitution of the United States and of the State of New Hampshire, and that we will support them in every required capacity.[19]

Pierce was in Massachusetts when the meeting was called and did not arrive back in Concord until the following afternoon. That evening he addressed "a large crowd" from the balcony of the Eagle Hotel. Declaring that the resolution passed the night before received his "cordial approval," he explained, "The question has resolved itself into one of patriotism and stern duty." He continued to hope, "so long as fratricidal strife [was] not more fully developed than at present," for a peaceful resolution, saying, "I do not believe that aggression by arms is a suitable or possible remedy for existing evils." In the event of "a war of aggression" being "waged against the National Capital and the North," Pierce urged unity: "I would advise you to stand together with one mind and heart." Pierce concluded his speech, which was frequently interrupted by "vociferous cheers and applause" with these words: "I would not live in a State, the rights and honor of which I was not prepared to defend at all hazards, and to the last extremity."[20]

The speech was misunderstood as endorsing the administration's policy of forcing the southern states to return to the Union. What Pierce was supporting was a defensive war, if the North was invaded. As the threat of an attack on Washington diminished, Pierce explained to friends, like former Connecticut governor Thomas H. Seymour, that he had not changed his mind and would never support a war of subjugation. Pierce continued to strive to avert all-out war and wrote to former president Van Buren in April, suggesting a meeting of former presidents to propose some kind of resolution. Van Buren was not enthusiastic, however, and the effort never materialized.[21]

Many Democrats openly endorsed the administration's policy of restoration of the Union by force. Stephen A. Douglas had supported Lincoln since the election, even holding the new president's hat as he stood beside Lincoln during his inaugural address. Douglas traveled throughout the North, until his death in June, rallying citizens to the cause, as did New York Hard leader Daniel Dickinson and Soft leader John A. Dix, a New Hampshire native, who was commissioned a major general. Opportunistic newspaper editor John W. Forney placed his *Philadelphia Press* firmly behind the administration and soon became Lincoln's "favorite editor."[22] Benjamin F. Butler, another native of the Granite State, joined up as brigadier general of a volunteer regiment in Massachusetts, ignoring Pierce's advice not to take part in the war.[23] Thomas J. Whipple, who had served under Pierce in Mexico, became lieutenant colonel of the First New Hampshire Regiment of Volunteers. Thomas O'Neill, Pierce's orderly in Mexico and bodyguard as president, joined a Massachusetts regiment, and Rev. Parker signed on as chaplain to New Hampshire's Second Regiment.[24] Eventually, Caleb Cushing migrated to the Republican Party. But Pierce was unwavering, and when Jane mailed him an address by General Robert Patterson that endorsed the war, he responded, "I know him, and know that he can do, what I cannot do—bow to the storm. My purpose, dearest, is irrevocably taken. I will never justify, sustain or in any way or to any extent uphold this cruel, heartless, aimless, unnecessary war. Madness and imbecility are in the ascendant, I shall not succumb to them. Come what may, I have no opinion to retract—no line of action to change."[25] Clement March recommended to the governor that Pierce be made brigadier general of the New Hampshire forces, but following another of their all-night sessions "conversing chiefly on the condition of the country," Pierce convinced March that the former president was "opposed to the subjugation and destruction of the South, and in favor of a peaceable separation of the States." Attesting to Pierce's continuing influence over his state party, March concluded, "The democratic party of New Hampshire will henceforth oppose the prosecution of the War, and leave the Republican party to do the fighting."[26]

What strengthened Pierce's determination to oppose an aggressive war of conquest was Lincoln's decision, on April 27, 1861, to suspend the privilege of the writ of habeas corpus along the transportation routes between New York and Washington. Volunteer troops had been blocked and attacked on their way to the nation's capital by prosecession rioters in Baltimore, resulting in several deaths and prompting Lincoln to take executive action. But Pierce's literal interpretation of the Constitution was that only Congress may suspend the writ of habeas corpus. Chief Justice Taney's ruling to this effect, on May 26, in *Ex parte Merryman*, received the former president's full endorsement. Lincoln ignored Taney's ruling, and Merryman remained imprisoned. Pierce wrote his old friend, Taney, expressing his support, and the chief justice replied, predicting "a reign of terror . . . ruinous to the victors as well as the vanquished."[27]

Throughout his political career Pierce had assigned to the opposition party, whether Federalist, Whig or Republican, centralizing tendencies and a willingness to expand the power of the executive and restrict the freedoms of the average citizen. He had always deplored the excuse of "state necessity" to justify such expansion of power. The Civil War would become the ultimate nightmare to a civil libertarian like Pierce, as Lincoln, supported by a willing Congress, ultimately extended the suspension of the writ of habeas corpus throughout the nation and imposed martial law, enforced by military commanders and military trials of civilians, in the North. Pierce believed that martial law could be imposed in the vicinity of military action but not in areas far removed from the fighting where civil courts were functioning.[28]

The "suspension of the Constitution" was to be a major theme of the New Hampshire Democratic Party's attack on Republicans over the next few years. The *Patriot* editorialized, "If the vital principles and guarantees of the Constitution are to be disregarded and destroyed . . . it matters little to our people whether that is done by open rebellion under the lead of Jefferson Davis, or by the arbitrary use of usurped power under the direction of Abraham Lincoln." The Democratic press had other reservations about Lincoln's intent, as the *Patriot* warned, "If the war is to end slavery, then it is a party war, and an unconstitutional war."[29] To the Republican press, the opposition was expressing "treasonable sentiments" in questioning the actions of the president in a time of national emergency: "There are traitors abroad." Many in New Hampshire and around the nation were threatening to punish them for speaking out.[30]

Every partisan activity was liable to be condemned as treasonous. During the state legislature's session in June, the Democrats united in opposition to a million-dollar loan bill to support the New Hampshire volunteer regiments. The Democrats declared that the bill was twice as much as was required and gave the governor far too much discretionary power over the use of the money without proper oversight. The bill passed, but Republicans claimed the opposition came "as near treason as can be," and Henry F. French charged, "Pierce is at the bottom of it."[31]

The disastrous Union defeat at Bull Run in July 1861 increased the tension between the parties in New Hampshire. The ninety-day volunteer troops, including the New Hampshire First Regiment, returned home shortly after the humiliating battle. The press analyzed the defeat concluding that the troops were poorly prepared and ill led. The Democratic papers were particularly critical. Edmund Burke's *Democratic Standard* of Concord referred to "This Vile War!" and the battle as "a total rout, and a disgraceful, ignominious fight." Always trying to out-Pierce Pierce among state Democrats, Burke had taken the most extreme antiwar position, declaring Jefferson Davis a "patriot" and attacking "Lincoln's mob, robbers and murderers."[32] For months there had been threats to shut down Burke's paper. On August 8, a mob, including some of the troops home from the front, destroyed the office and attacked the editor, Brackett Palmer, who fired on the rioters as they forced their way into his office. Two rioters were slightly wounded. The *Patriot*, though expressing no love for Burke or the *Democratic Standard*, denounced the lawless action, supported as it was by "very respectable" citizens of Concord and ignored by the police, who stood by and watched. The *Patriot* declared that "the right of freedom of thought, opinion and speech" was at stake.[33]

A few days later, another Democratic newspaper in Haverhill, Massachusetts, was attacked, its editor dragged through the streets, tarred, and feathered. The "summer of rage" saw numerous Democratic papers destroyed by mobs or shut down by local, state, or federal officials.[34] Republican newspapers, seeing a chance to permanently hamstring the Democratic Party, condemned the violence but fomented it by frequent charges of treason against the opposition press. Pierce was under threat as well. The *Statesman* reported that he was meeting with Cushing and that the two were communicating by mail with friends in the South. At one point, rumors circulated that Pierce had been arrested and was being held by federal authorities at Fort Lafayette in New York.[35]

Pierce had planned to spend his usual late-summer vacation on the New Hampshire coast but suddenly changed his mind and left the state in late August for a three-week trip to the Midwest. The purpose of the trip has never been clear. He may have needed to check on investments in Michigan, where his niece's husband was in the lumber business and where family members owned land. It may have been, as the *Patriot* explained, a fishing trip on Lake Huron, or, very probably, Pierce just needed to get away from the tense atmosphere of New Hampshire and the threats of violence or possible arrest. In a brief address at Lafayette, Indiana, on the way home, Pierce stated that the trip was "the fulfillment of a long and cherished purpose to visit the Great West."[36]

Pierce may have intended his trip as an escape from the dangerous political climate in New Hampshire, but his movements were being closely monitored by the Lincoln administration. On September 2, Henry McFarland, editor of Concord's *New Hampshire Statesman*, wrote a letter to Secretary of War Simon Cameron: "Ex President Pierce is at Louisville, Ky. There is a very general suspicion here that his mission there is not one friendly to the government." McFarland advised, "If the government has any way to observe his motions I hope it will do so. . . ."[37] Cameron passed the letter on to President Lincoln, who seemed unconcerned: "I think it will be well that P. is away from the N.H. people. He will do less harm anywhere else; and by *when* he has gone, his neighbors will understand him better."[38]

Secretary of State William Seward, whom Lincoln had placed in charge of internal security, was also made aware of Pierce's activities, by an anonymous letter written from New York on September 17, which declared that Pierce and Clement March were "traitors" who were "aiding and abetting secretly and covertly the leaders of the Southern rebellion."[39]

Pierce visited with his former treasury secretary, James Guthrie, in Louisville before moving on to Michigan. Pierce's presence in Detroit attracted attention at a time when the local press was on its own witch hunt for traitors. Pierce was staying with former interior secretary Robert McClelland when Detroit's Democratic mayor, James G. Berret, was arrested by federal officials for antiwar activity. To local Democrats, Pierce expressed his outrage at the denial of Berret's constitutional rights, and his opinions reached the Republican press.[40] The *Detroit Tribune* editorialized, "While in this city, he was closeted with a select circle who are known to be doubtful in their loyalty. . . . Our opinion is Franklin Pierce is a prowling traitor spy." The *Detroit Free Press* responded, defending Pierce: "We have seen or heard of nothing and know of nothing that he has either said or done upon which to ground any such charge. . . ."[41]

The attacks on leading Democrats in the newspapers prompted an antiwar Democrat in the frontier settlement of North Branch, Michigan, to take action. Dr. Guy S. Hopkins decided "to play a practical joke upon the Detroit press" by sending an anonymous letter, dated October 5, 1861, full of strange symbols, initials, and references to a secret society plotting to overthrow the government. Hopkins presumed this letter would be a lesson to "the treason-seeking presses," whose ultimate embarrassment at being taken in by the hoax might serve "to quiet their howls."[42] The press's speculation on the purpose of Pierce's visit prompted Hopkins to include in his letter this line: "Presdt. P____ in his passage has drawn many brave and influential men to the League." The Detroit postmaster intercepted the letter (proof that the mail was censored by Republican officials) and turned it over to a federal marshal, who forwarded it to the State Department. Shortly after writing the letter, Hopkins, a known secession sympathizer, was arrested by federal authorities, transported to Fort Lafayette in New York, and held there without charges, along with other civilian prisoners of the military. Not knowing what offense he had committed, Hopkins wrote a letter, on November 29, to Secretary of State Seward, confessing to authorship of the hoax letter and assuring the secretary that it was all a practical joke.[43]

Pierce was oblivious to all of this until just before Christmas, when he received a brief note from the State Department, under Seward's signature, but in the handwriting of a longtime department clerk known to Pierce, with an extract from the hoax letter and asking for "any explanation upon the subject" that Pierce could "offer."[44] Pierce was offended, both by the aspersion implied in the letter and by the manner in which it was sent to him. He fired back a long response on December 24, 1861: "It is not easy to conceive how any person could give credence to, or entertain for a moment, the idea that I am now, or have ever been connected with a 'secret league,' or with *any* league, the object of which was, or is, the overthrow of the government of my country."[45]

Declaring the extract to be "incoherent and meaningless," Pierce expressed astonishment that it should have been passed along to him for "explanation." He stated that only "the gravity of the insinuation" and the fact that it came from such a "high official source" and would "hold a place upon the files of the Department of State" required him to reply. He concluded, "My loyalty will never be successfully impugned so long as I enjoy the constitutional rights which pertain to every citizen of the republic, and especially the inestimable right to be informed of the nature and cause of accusation, and to be confronted face to face with my accusers."[46]

Seward answered Pierce's letter with an apology for not having written the first letter himself and claimed that it was intended to "render" Pierce "a service" by informing the former president of the existence of the anonymous letter. Seward stated that the letter writer had been detected and confessed his authorship.[47] Pierce was not appeased by Seward's rather lame apology and closed their correspondence with another letter, in which he charged, "I failed to discover in your official note, a desire to render me a service." He continued to be offended by the fact that he had been treated "with as little consideration as a note of rebuke might have been addressed to a delinquent Clerk of one of the Departments." He was further angered by the fact that Seward had information about the hoax letter, particularly who authored it, that he had not initially passed on to Pierce. He assumed that Seward must know more about why the author of the letter used Pierce's name that Seward was still not revealing.[48]

There the matter rested for several months, though Pierce did inform several of his close friends, including Senator James Pearce of Maryland and Robert McClelland, of the correspondence with Seward to let them "understand upon what kind of evidence one's loyalty" could, "in these times . . . be questioned."[49] McClelland, whose initials were also used in Hopkins's letter, claimed that he too had been falsely accused: "I have been charged with belonging to the Knights of the Golden Circle, an order of which I know nothing, and to which I am an entire stranger."[50]

Pierce's ever-evolving attitude toward the war is evident from a letter of Nathaniel Hawthorne written in February 1862: "Frank Pierce came here and spent a night, a week or two since; we drank a bottle of arrack together, and mingled our tears and condolements for the state of the country. Pierce is truly patriotic, and thinks there is nothing left for us but to fight it out; but I should be sorry to take his opinion implicitly as regards our chances in the future. He is bigoted to the Union, and sees nothing but ruin without it; whereas, I, (if we can only put the boundary far enough south) should not much regret an ultimate separation."[51] And Pierce demonstrated empathy for President Lincoln at this time. On learning of the death of Lincoln's son, Willie, in late February, Pierce penned a letter of sympathy to the president, reminding Lincoln that Pierce knew what it was to lose a child while in a position of great responsibility and pressure. It is doubtful if Lincoln ever saw the letter; at least, no reply exists.[52]

The hoax letter and resulting correspondence with the State Department remained confidential until March 1862, when the

Detroit Tribune published the anonymous letter under the headline "Curious Document." Newspapers around the nation picked up the story; Pierce read it in the *Boston Journal* of March 22 in an article entitled "Treasonable Plot in Michigan."[53] Sidney Webster had shown copies of the full correspondence between Pierce and Seward to his friends in New York and reported, "A few friends—among them Gov. Fish, Mrs. Marcy, . . . Ex-President Van Buren, Gov. Hunt, Gov. Seymour, Robert McLane—have seen the correspondence in my hands. All condemn Seward and pronounce your letter *perfect*." In the same letter, Webster advised Pierce to make the correspondence public.[54] Pierce wrote Senator Milton Latham of California, who, on March 26, 1862, offered to the Senate a resolution requesting Seward to turn over all correspondence related to the initial letter.[55] Seward did so on March 31 but curiously omitted Pierce's final letter of January 7, which Latham noted in a Senate speech of April 2; he then read the letter into the Senate record.[56]

The publication of the documents embarrassed Seward and was viewed by many as a victory for Pierce and the Democrats.[57] Among those who congratulated the former president on the exchange with Seward was Clement L. Vallandigham of Ohio, the leading Copperhead in Congress, who wrote, "In common with every just man in the land, I am indignant at the insult & outrage offered to you by Seward. But it has resulted in his disgrace & your vindication. Your letter extorts praise even from enemies."[58] The response of the press was most gratifying. The Republican *New York Times* called the charges against Pierce "utterly false." John W. Forney's *Philadelphia Press* declared the "most complete vindication of Ex-President Pierce" and editorialized, "Franklin Pierce is too brave, generous and unselfish to have ever allowed any man or party to seduce him from his loyalty to his flag and country." Forney, though now backing the Lincoln administration, was always personally fond of Pierce. The former president also learned from friends in New York that even his archenemy, James Gordon Bennett of the *New York Herald* bestowed on Pierce "the palm of victory," though in a back-handed manner: "Poor Pierce, in this matter, has enveloped himself in the first positive blaze of glory by which he has ever been surrounded."[59]

For Pierce, who was always sensitive on the issue of the restriction of civil liberties, the experience hardened his attitude toward the war and the administration. It also made Pierce a lightning rod for those who had suffered even more serious harm from the administration's policies. Over the next few years Pierce frequently received letters from officers removed from the army without cause, except for the suspicion that they were associated with the Democrats. One of these was General Fitz-John Porter, a New Hampshire native, who was court-martialed and cashiered for his failings at the second battle of Bull Run and who sought Pierce's help in his appeal.[60] Sidney Webster's brother was consistently passed over for promotion, despite a stellar record, presumably because of his association with Pierce.[61] New Hampshire's gallant Col. Edward Cross of the Fifth Regiment, was bitter at being denied brigadier general's rank because of his past political associations.[62] Paul R. George, half brother of John H. George and former quartermaster of Cushing's regiment in Mexico, was rejected for a commission as division quartermaster in Benjamin Butler's army, even after George had fitted out the expedition to New Orleans.[63] Lieutenant Andrew J. Edgerly of the Fourth Regiment of New Hampshire Volunteers was discharged from service after voting for the Democrats in the state election of 1863.[64]

Pierce was likely most affected by the fate of his former Mexican War officer Thomas J. Whipple, who had campaigned so effectively for Pierce in 1852. Whipple had volunteered at the start of the Civil War and was second in command of the First New Hampshire Volunteers. When the regiment returned to New Hampshire after ninety days, he immediately recruited and commanded the Fourth Regiment of Volunteers. Colonel Whipple returned to New Hampshire in the summer of 1862 and recruited a third regiment, the Twelfth Regiment of New Hampshire Volunteers. In three days the brilliant orator convinced more than a thousand recruits to sign up at a time when the war was becoming increasingly unpopular. Despite his past record, Whipple was rejected by Republican Governor Nathaniel S. Berry for a commission to lead the regiment. The recruits, expecting to serve under the popular and dynamic colonel, made a "long and bitter" protest of the governor's decision, sending "scores" of "petitions and remonstrances," and many threatened "never to leave the state until Col. Whipple should lead them," but the governor was unmoved. Thirty-five years later, the author of the regiment's history recorded, "A scar . . . still remains."[65] For partisan reasons another prowar Democrat with extensive military experience was needlessly sidelined for the duration of the war. The knowledge of the treatment of these men, along with more frequent correspondence from Copperhead congressmen Vallandigham and Samuel S. Cox of Ohio, added to Pierce's growing bitterness.[66]

Pierce was also disillusioned by the lack of response from ordinary voters. When Secretary of War Stanton, now in charge of internal security, declared martial law across the nation on August 8, 1862, Pierce wrote angrily to John H. George:

> Our people have bowed so tamely to the march of glaring usurpation, that I suppose they will scarcely murmur at the late order of Mr. Stanton, placing the rights of citizens, freedom of opinion, freedom of speech, personal liberty, primarily in the keeping of the Marshalls, superintendents or chiefs of police of any town, City or District and then turning them over to the tender mercies of a military commission. Is not this the worst form of despotism? Martial Law declared throughout the land, with the additional appendage of a band of prejudiced, passionate, irresponsible, abolition office holders, constituted as a special corps of accusers! What ideas must this Secretary have of the unlimited and unrestrained *Central power* when he assumes thus to impose duties upon and give instructions to "Superintendents or chiefs of police of any town City or district"? Let there be no more talk of Sovereign States, of Constitutional Rights—of trial by Jury—of legal protection for persons & property.[67]

Except for the bitterness reflected in his letters, Pierce kept a low profile following the interaction with Seward and the administration. He was not by nature a crusader and had no intention of leading a public campaign against the administration. Instead, he focused more of his time on personal and business matters. Though not practicing law during these years, he did advise a former client, E. B. Bigelow, the Boston carpet manufacturer, in his efforts to renew six patents on power looms.[68] Pierce also tried to resurrect a family business, a plumbago, or graphite, mine on Sunapee Mountain in the town of Goshen, New Hampshire. The property had been in the Pierce family since the 1820s and periodically efforts were made to extract the graphite, which was used as a lubricant for the blacking of iron pots and pans and as lead in pencils. In 1862 Pierce formed the Plumbago Company, sold shares to such friends as Clement March and J. D. Hoover, involved his brother Henry in the operation, mined the graphite using steam power, and sold the lead to the Dixon Crucible Company, maker of Ticonderoga pencils, and to others. The initial effort was successful, and Hoover expressed his delight at the first year's profit report.[69] The effort was shortlived, however, and the mine shut down when Joseph Dixon reported he could not use the lead because it was a different quality than what his machines were able to refine. Years after Pierce's death the Dixon Crucible Company did buy the property from Pierce's heirs.[70]

Setting up Henry in the Plumbago Company was one more attempt by Pierce to assist his brother financially. Henry was a respected attorney in Hillsborough, had served in the state legislature, and for nineteen consecutive years was elected moderator of the town meeting, but he was always in debt. In his letters Pierce frequently scolded Henry about his profligacy in financial matters, and Pierce did not confine his opinion of his brother's habits to their personal correspondence. To one of Henry's creditors Pierce wrote, "You know how annoying this settling and paying 'nearly all up' but leaving something to dangle behind is to me and my brother knows it too. I am determined that he should be out of debt. Even against his will and then if he is determined to keep on in his slip-shod, dilatory way, he must start anew and show that he has no appreciation of what is due to himself or me."[71] The relationship between the brothers was frequently strained, with Pierce acting as the strict and impatient father, and Henry the irresponsible child, even though the two men were only a few years apart in age. Pierce's distrust of his brother may account for the former president's frequent trips to Hillsborough. He was away from Jane frequently during the war years. She spent much of her time with the Aikens in Andover, Massachusetts, while Pierce moved about between their rented home in Concord and Andover, Boston, Hillsborough, Lowell, and Rye Beach. His plan to build a house on the property on Pleasant Street in Concord was never realized, but he did see to the farming operations on the sixty-acre site.

As the Civil War dragged on and the Lincoln administration moved inexorably toward making it a war of emancipation as well as a war of restoration of the Union, Pierce's frustration and bitterness spilled over into his correspondence. In his writings made prior to the Civil War, one searches in vain through all of his speeches and letters for any indication of his racial beliefs. Pierce had always discussed slavery as a constitutional right of state sovereignty and, secondarily, as a reality that defied practical solution short of civil war, though he admitted the institution was morally offensive. Race played no part in his public statements against abolitionists. But the Emancipation Proclamation brought forth his deep-seated race prejudice in a letter to John H. George:

> The last proclamation of the President caps the climax of folly & wickedness. . . . Mr. Lincoln has been and is to the extent of his limited ability and narrow intelligence their [abolitionists] willing instrument for all the evil which has thus far been brought upon the country. But what will the world say of a proclamation emanating from the President of the United States not only in defiance of the fundamental law of the Country for the upholding of which he ought to have been willing to shed his own blood, but in defiance of all law human & Divine which invited the black race in six entire states and in parts of several others to use and with all the barbaric features which must be inseparable from a successful servile insurrection to slay & devastate without regard to age or sex, without any condition of restraint except that the homes smouldering in ashes shall be the homes of the descendants of men whose fathers fought with our fathers the battles of the Revolution, . . . Yes and one other, that the women and children brutally violated & slaughtered shall be *white women & children.*[72]

Pierce was always a defender of the social status quo, and that included belief in the superiority of the white race. Lincoln had expressed similar racial beliefs in his debates with Douglas in 1858.

In fact, Lincoln coupled his Emancipation Proclamation with a proposal to Congress for the colonization of freed blacks outside the United States.[73] But Lincoln was a pragmatist, while Pierce remained rigidly inflexible once he had established a position. What caused Pierce's racism to come to the surface was the victory of his bitter enemies, the abolitionists, including the evangelical Protestant crusaders whom he had always characterized as inherently intolerant and ultimately destructive of the people's freedom. His belief in law and order was also deeply disturbed by the sense that Lincoln was issuing the proclamation in an attempt to stir up chaos and a race war between masters and slaves.

The rhetoric of the 1863 winter election campaign in New Hampshire reflects Pierce's growing bitterness. While not taking a public role in any of the election campaigns during the war, Pierce's views were incorporated into the speeches of his closest party associates, John H. George and Josiah Minot. George, waging another unsuccessful campaign for Congress, reportedly stated, "President Lincoln is a knave, an imbecile, a usurper, and a tyrant, who curses the country with his Administration. . . ." In criticizing emancipation, George referred to the "poor, miserable, ignorant, lousy negro. . . ." Pierce would never have spoken this way, but a contemporary described George as "gruff, opinionated, domineering and overbearing, a fighter who never compromised." Minot, state party chairman, was quoted as being "personally opposed to Abolition, and in favor of the perpetuity of Slavery."[74] The party organization remained strong and aggressive throughout the war, with traditional Democratic voters clinging tenaciously to their party despite its increasingly extreme positions. Prowar Democrats, few in number in New Hampshire, were unable to mount a credible third party, or Union, campaign in 1863. Their gubernatorial candidate won only seven percent of the vote, but this was enough to deny the election to the Democrat, who won a plurality, but lost in the state legislature.[75]

The combination of emancipation and conscription raised the political debate to new levels of animosity. Democrats increasingly appealed to the racism of the voters by raising the specter of African-Americans moving north and competing for jobs.[76] The futility of the fighting and the unpopularity of the draft added to the prospects for success of the opposition party. General Burnside's arrest of Vallandigham in May 1863, his trial and conviction by a military commission for "publicly expressing . . . sympathy" for the enemy and "declaring disloyal sentiments," and his ultimate banishment to the South, made Vallandignam a cause célèbre to the Democrats. While Vallandigham had repeatedly criticized the "wicked, cruel, and unnecessary war," he had never advocated violation of the law, draft resistance, or desertion. Nevertheless, Lincoln defended the arrest, charging Vallandigham with discouraging enlistments and encouraging desertion. Protests occurred around the North to demand Vallandigham's release, but Lincoln feared he would be blamed "for making too few arrests rather than too many." Responding to the Albany Resolves, orchestrated by Governor Seymour, Lincoln argued famously, "Must I shoot a simple-minded soldier boy who deserts while I must not touch a hair of a wiley agitator who induces him to desert?"[77]

Pierce was incensed by the violations of Vallandigham's constitutional rights, and closer to home, he was personally affected by letters from Col. Edward Cross, wounded eleven times in battle, yet denied promotion. Cross wrote, "I find that everything I said or done as a democrat is known here . . ."[78] Cross charged, "The Army is full of Abolition spies, under the guise of tract distributors, State Agents—chaplains & Sanitary Commission Agents. The correspondents of the Abolition papers are also among the most malignant spies of the administration. Every opinion an officer privately expresses in social conversation is liable to appear against him when he least expects it. All the 2d & 3d rate officers, the Sneaks, the Malingers, the *Cowards*, have found this out, & cover their deficiencies by the cloak of Abolitionism. That is why so many of this lot are coming up to be Colonels, Generals &."[79] In this highly charged atmosphere, Pierce agreed to be the keynote speaker at a state Democratic Party rally held in Concord on July 4, 1863. It was the first time he had spoken in New Hampshire since the address from the balcony of the Eagle Hotel in April, 1861. He was urged by Sidney Webster not to do it, for fear that Pierce might suffer the same fate as Vallandigham, but Clement March recorded that Pierce was "unterrified."[80] Hawthorne, understanding the danger to his friend, traveled to Concord for the event, to lend moral support.

An estimated twenty-five thousand people heard Pierce's speech, during which he read a section of Lincoln's letter defending the arrest of Vallandigham. Lincoln had expanded his condemnation to "the man who stands by and says nothing when the peril of his government is discussed . . . [or] talks for his country with 'buts' and 'ifs' and 'ands.'"[81] Pierce replied to this, "Who, I ask, has clothed the President with power to dictate to any one of us when we must or when we may speak, or be silent upon any subject, and especially in relation to the conduct of any public servant? By what right does he presume to prescribe a formula of language for your lips or mine?"[82] Pierce decried the restrictions on civil liberties: "True it is, that any of you, that I, may be the next victim of unconstitutional, arbitrary, irresponsible power. But we, nevertheless, are free men, and we resolve to live, or if it must be, to die, such."[83] He echoed Vallandigham in describing "this fearful, fruitless, fatal civil war," but as to how to end the conflict, Pierce could only offer reliance "upon moral force, and not upon any of the coercive instrumentalities of military power." He urged the people to defend their own liberties: "What if the ballot box is sealed? . . . My reply is, you will take care of yourselves with or without arms. . . ."[84]

Pierce was followed to the podium by numerous speakers including Rep. Daniel Voorhees, a Copperhead from Indiana. The five-hour rally ended just as news of the great Union victory at Gettysburg was filtering through the crowd. Pierce closed the gathering by sponsoring a collection for the sick and wounded soldiers, pledging fifty dollars himself. He had often given to this cause in the past. Pierce was unaware until later that day of the death of his friend Colonel Cross, who had been killed at Gettysburg on July 2.[85]

The opposition press was caustic in describing the event as a "treasonable orgy" and mocking Pierce, who they claimed spoke with "shattered nerves" and could barely "bring the glass of water to his lips" because of his "hydrophobic repugnance manifested towards Adam's ale." The news of the victories at Gettysburg and Vicksburg proved "a wet blanket" for the Democrats, who spoke "*treason*, who complain[ed] of the Government as arbitrary and despotic."[86] Pierce had confined his remarks entirely to the violations of the Constitution and the hopelessness of the conflict and did not mention emancipation or appeal to racism in his speech.

Pierce immediately turned his attention to another cause, the relief of the Rev. Nathan Lord, president of Dartmouth College, who was forced out of office by the board of trustees for his views on slavery. Lord had been president of the college for thirty-five years, resurrecting the institution from the aftermath of the Dartmouth College case. He had opened the school to black students, one of the few such institutions to accept them. But he had a theological disagreement with abolitionists, believing they misrepresented the Bible in their attacks on slavery, which his literal interpretation concluded authorized the institution, but only as a punishment for sin. Lord had confined his views to theological papers, but the board, made up by the 1860s of many Republican abolitionists, including former congressman Amos Tuck, censured him at a meeting on July 24, 1863, prompting Lord's resignation.[87]

Pierce admired Lord, whom he characterized as "the only clergyman of eminence . . . of his denomination [Congregational] in New England, who has firmly withstood the on-slaught of abolitionism." Pierce described the seventy-year-old as a "brave, conscientious old man!"[88] Lord's resignation had practical consequences, as he had never been paid more than $1,600 a year and as he had at his own expense educated his twelve children, including eight sons, whom he had put through Dartmouth. The resignation left him potentially destitute, and Pierce spearheaded a drive to raise money for an annuity. He solicited donations within and outside New Hampshire, collecting more than $3,000 in the state and a similar amount from more distant alumni. Lord was comfortably fixed with a $1,200 annual annuity, and he and his sons expressed their undying gratitude to Pierce for the effort.[89]

Pierce's spirits were lifted later that summer by Hawthorne's determination to dedicate his last book, *Our Old Home*, to his old friend, "as a slight memorial of a college friendship, prolonged through manhood, and retaining all of its vitality in our autumnal years."[90] The reaction to Hawthorne's dedication demonstrates Pierce's standing in New England following his July 4 speech. Publisher James T. Fields had tried to get Hawthorne to eliminate the dedication, fearing it would hurt sales of the book, but Hawthorne was intransigent: "My long and intimate personal relations with Pierce render the dedication altogether proper, especially as regards this book, which would have had no existence without his kindness; and if he is so exceedingly unpopular that his name is enough to sink the volume, there is so much the more need that an old friend should stand by him."[91] When Hawthorne's sister-in-law, Elizabeth Palmer Peabody, called Pierce a traitor, the author grew stronger in his defense: "A traitor? Why, he is the only loyal man in the country, North or South! Everybody else has outgrown the old faith in the Union, or got outside of it in one way or another; but Pierce retains it in all the simplicity with which he inherited it from his father. It has been the principle and is the explanation (and the apology, if any is needed) of his whole public life."[92]

When the book, duly dedicated to Pierce, was published, it produced the reaction Fields had predicted. Harriet Beecher Stowe wrote Fields, "Do tell me if our friend Hawthorne praises that arch-traitor Pierce in his preface and your loyal firm publishes it. I never read the preface, and have not yet seen the book, but they say so here, and I can scarcely believe it of you, if I can of him. . . . What! Patronize such a traitor to our faces! I can scarce believe it."[93]

Emerson reportedly cut out the dedication page.[94] But others saw beyond the politics to recognize the importance of the friendship. Publisher Fields wrote in his diary, "It is a beautiful incident in Hawthorne's life, the determination, at all hazards, to dedicate this book to his friend." Hawthorne even brought Pierce to meet Fields, who had to admit, "He is at least a most courteous gentleman and interesting man, kindly and thoughtful."[95] Fields's wife pointed out the potential sacrifice the always financially strapped Hawthorne was making: "He will dedicate the volume to Franklin Pierce, the Democrat—a most unpopular thing just now, but friendship of the purest stimulates him, and the ruin in prospect for his book because of this resolve does not move him from his purpose. Such adherence is indeed noble. Hawthorne requires all that popularity can give him in a pecuniary way for the support of his family."[96] In the end, the book sold well despite the dedication.

Jane Pierce wrote to Hawthorne from Pigeon's Cove along the Massachusetts coast, where the Pierces spent a late summer vacation, thanking him for the dedication: "The added interest of the preface and the warm assurance of a friendship which has on both sides been so constant so affectionate and so true gives it [the book] a hold upon my regard of which even the *Scarlet Letter* and *Marble Fawn* are destitute."[97] That was one of the last letters Jane would write. Her long struggle with poor health, more specifically with tuberculosis, ended with her death in Andover on December 2, 1863 at age fifty-seven. Despite her continuously precarious health, her death seemed to surprise her family. A niece put it best: "I was not prepared to hear so soon of dear Aunt Jane's death. She had so often been very feeble & afterward been restored to nearly her former health that I looked for better tidings. . . . I still thought I should see her again."[98]

Hawthorne was by his friend's side for the funeral in Andover and the burial in Concord at the Old North Cemetery. He was quite unnerved by the experience, especially viewing Jane's body: "It was like a carven image laid in its richly embossed enclosure, and there was a remote expression about it as if the whole had nothing to do with things present." He reported that Pierce was "overwhelmed with grief," but his solicitude to Hawthorne was evident at the graveside on a typical December day in New Hampshire when Pierce "though completely overcome with his own sorrow, turned and drew up the collar of Hawthorne's coat to shield him from the bitter cold."[99]

A complete understanding of the thirty-year marriage is not possible, because Pierce kept none of his wife's letters. Whether he discarded them along the way, as he tended to do with other personal letters, or all at once after her death is not clear, but none survive. The few surviving letters of Frank's to Jane show his constant affection and tender concern with her health but also reveal that he did discuss politics with her. Whether she responded in kind and, if so, disagreed in any way with her husband's positions is not known. It is also not clear what she knew about his other life and activities when he was away from her. Did she nag him about his drinking? Was her strict religious morality offended by his card playing and gambling? From the numerous letters that survive from Jane to her family, she seems completely devoted to her husband, missing him when he was away, never criticizing him in any way, and appearing to delight in his energy, sociability, and catholic interests, even if rarely participating herself.

A few years after her death, Pierce, responding to a request from an author who was preparing a book on presidential wives, described Jane: "Mrs. Pierce's life, as far as she could make it so, was one of retirement. She very rarely participated in gay amusements, and never enjoyed what is somewhat called fashionable society. Her natural endowments were of a high order, recognized by all persons with whom she was, to any considerable extent, associated. She inherited a judgment singularly clear and correct, and taste almost unerring. She was carefully and thoroughly educated, and moved all her life, prior to her marriage, very quietly in a circle of relatives and intimate friends of rare culture and refinement." This rather objective assessment begs the question, what attracted Frank to Jane in the first place? The always intrusive Clement March was forward enough to ask the former president "how he came to marry such an invalid?" March wrote down Pierce's response: "I could take better care of her than anyone else was the reply."[100]

Within weeks of his wife's death, Pierce unwittingly became a central issue in the state election campaign. The letter he had written to Jefferson Davis on January 6, 1860, had been recovered by Union soldiers when they raided Davis's plantation in Mississippi in August 1863. The extent of the partisanship of the military during the war is evident from the fact that Captain William H. Gibbs of the Fifteenth Illinois sent a copy of the letter to Concord's *Independent Democrat*, the state's most influential Republican newspaper, advising, "You can make such use of it as you may deem proper."[101] In his letter, Pierce predicted that if civil war should come, it would "not be along Mason and Dixon's line merely" but would take place "within our own borders, in our own streets, . . ."[102] To the *Independent Democrat*, this was proof that Pierce was part of a "conspiracy" with southern leaders "to forward their wicked scheme of Rebellion" by assuring them of support in the North. The paper charged that the state Democratic Party continued to be "manipulated and controlled by Pierce and his pliant tools to the sole purpose of Treason. . . ."[103] Though Pierce hid in the background, the press claimed he dictated to his "henchmen," John H. George, Josiah Minot, Albert R. Hatch, and Edmund Burke, now prominently restored to the party's good graces.[104] Pamphlets and broadsides were printed and distributed, declaring Pierce "Chief Sachem of the 'Knights of the Golden Circle' in New Hampshire" and, through his endorsement of Vallandigham, "the eulogist of political crimes and errors, and the open and secret patron of disloyalty and treason."[105]

To answer these charges, Minot published four of Pierce's letters written between December 7, 1859, and January 6, 1860, immediately preceding the letter to Davis, in a pamphlet, "The Record of a Month." The letters give a more complete picture of Pierce's thinking during the period of excitement following John Brown's raid, including Pierce's call for calm, his denial that there was an "irrepressible conflict," and his advocacy of law and the Constitution. Minot wrote that because of "his domestic bereavement," Pierce declined to defend himself from the charges made by the opposition press, but Minot's pamphlet clearly demonstrated the fallaciousness of the charges made by the *Independent Democrat.*[106] The pamphlet was praised by Pierce's friends, and Governor Horatio Seymour of New York invited the former president to Albany for a political strategy session, but the further damage to Pierce's already tarnished reputation was evident on election day, March 8, 1864, when the hostile *Independent Democrat* reported that Pierce slipped quietly into town, was "shunned" by his neighbors at the polls, and "skedaddled" immediately by train after casting his ballot.[107] The Republicans swept to victory in both the gubernatorial and legislative races.[108]

The personal abuse Pierce experienced at this time was observed by Jessie Benton Frémont, daughter of Thomas Hart Benton and wife of General John C. Frémont; she had had a crush on Pierce as a young girl in Washington and encountered him in the Boston train depot. She became aware of the former president's presence by overhearing passengers speaking harshly about him as she moved between trains: "It was a chase and a push to catch up with him in the crowded station, where, hand in hand, with a thousand home memories crowding on me, I spoke with him for the last time."[109]

Still recovering from his wife's death and his political and personal humiliation, Pierce endured yet another loss. Hawthorne had grown noticeably feeble in the winter of 1864. By the spring, sensing that he was dying, he chose to spend his final days with Pierce. Sophia Hawthorne clung to the hope that a trip with Pierce would restore her husband's health. She wrote to Pierce, "I would not trust him in any hands now excepting just such gentle and tender hands as yours." She acknowledged her husband's frail condition: "He really needs to be aided in getting in and out of carriages, because his eyes are so affected by this weakness, and his steps are so uncertain." She recalled how much Pierce had helped when Una was sick in Rome: "How singular it is that you should be the guard angelic of Mr. Hawthorne again as once before." Sophia concluded, "God bless you dear General Pierce for your aid in this strait."[110]

In spite of Sophia's description of his condition, Pierce was not prepared for the wasted figure he met in Boston in early May. He brought Hawthorne back to Concord to await better weather before departing by carriage in mid-May for Dixville Notch. By the third day, they had reached the Pemigewasset House in Plymouth. Along the way, Hawthorne asked Pierce if he had read the account of Thackeray's death, remarking what a "boon" it would be to pass away without a struggle. That night, Hawthorne fell asleep around 10:00 p.m., and Pierce left the door to their adjoining rooms open so that he could look in on his friend during the night. At 3:00 a.m., Pierce noticed that the usually restless Hawthorne was lying in the same position he had been earlier. Pierce wrote, "Hastening softly to his bedside, I could not perceive that he breathed, although no change had come over his features. I seized his wrist, but found no pulse; ran my hand down upon his bare side, but the great, generous, brave heart beat no more. The boon of which he spoke in the afternoon had, before morning's dawn been graciously granted to him."[111] In going through Hawthorne's effects, Pierce found a picture of himself in the author's pocket book.

The former president accompanied the body home and sat with Sophia Hawthorne and the children at the funeral in Salem, Massachusetts, as Hawthorne's literary colleagues, Emerson and Longfellow included, served as pallbearers. The Sleepy Hollow

Cemetery in Concord, Massachusetts, was swirling with apple blossoms in the spring breeze as Hawthorne's casket was laid in the grave. Pierce picked up a handful of the blossoms and sprinkled them over the casket before turning to leave his friend of nearly forty-five years. To Horatio Bridge, Pierce wrote, "I need not tell you how lonely I am, and how full of sorrow."[112] Over the next few years, Pierce reread all of Hawthorne's books, appreciating his friend's genius all the more upon reflection.[113]

Pierce's anguish over the course of events and the loss of his friend was interrupted by a three-week vacation trip in late July and early August with young Julian Hawthorne. Pierce used the trip to counsel Julian to remain in school at Harvard and offered him financial assistance. They visited the Pemigewasset House and Lake Winnipesaukee before reaching the seaside at Rye. Pierce and Hawthorne swam naked in the surf. Julian marveled at his sixty-year-old companion's fitness and recalled, "His chest was impressive, and the great muscles of his arms and legs. . . ." In turn, Pierce described the strapping eighteen year-old as a veritable "Hercules in form and strength," and predicted the young man's future success though he knew not in what field of endeavor.[114]

One day, Pierce and Julian Hawthorne sailed to Appledore in the Isles of Shoals. Joining them on the "little smack" was historian James Parton, who reported his conversation with Pierce to General Benjamin F. Butler in New York. According to Parton, Pierce "spoke darkly of private information that much encouraged him to think" that "a truce and a negotiation would result in re-union." At the time there was much speculation concerning a conference that had occurred in Canada between Clement Vallandigham and two "commissioners" sent by Jefferson Davis, Clement Clay and Jacob Thompson, both former friends of Pierce. Horace Greeley claimed that the commissioners were authorized to negotiate a peace and urged Lincoln to invite them to Washington. Whether Pierce had any direct knowledge of the events in Canada is not known, but Parton suspected he did. Nevertheless, he judged Pierce "a very agreeable and companionable man," and "understood Gen. Pierce to go for *No disruption of the Union on any terms. . . .*"[115] If Parton accurately reported

Pierce's views, it is certain that the former president had not communicated with the Confederate "commissioners," for their instructions required them to negotiate only for "the independence of the Confederate States," and Lincoln refused to negotiate for anything less than reunification and emancipation of the slaves.[116]

Nearly ten years of continuous losses and declining fortunes did not dim Pierce's enthusiasm for politics. The presidential election of 1864 engaged his interest, though more than ever from a position behind the scenes. At the approach of the Democratic National Convention in Chicago in late August, he addressed a delegate from New York with his prediction that General McClellan would be nominated, though Pierce also approved of Governor Seymour of New York or old friend James Guthrie. As always, Pierce was more concerned with the platform than the candidate, and he emphasized that while the restoration of the Union remained the goal, the policy of the administration, "the emancipation, confiscation, subjugation, devastation theory" had failed and that reason and negotiation must be offered as the alternative.[117] Pierce's consistent criticism of the Lincoln administration and strong public defense of civil liberties and the Constitution caused some Democrats to view Pierce as a potential nominee. Cushing, still nominally a Democrat, had written to friends, recommending Pierce be nominated as a compromise candidate who could unite the war and peace Democrats.[118]

Pierce stayed up all night during a visit with Clement March, writing letters to delegates and expressing his concern that Lincoln might cancel or postpone the election. These fears were aroused by reports that the administration was sending three thousand troops to Chicago to be present during the Democratic convention. One of the letters went to Richard Spofford, a delegate from Massachusetts. Pierce assigned Spofford the task of withdrawing Pierce's name if it should be placed in nomination at the convention, noting, "How painful it would be to me to have my wishes in this relation disregarded by my friends in any part of the country." He urged unity and harmony, but considering the Lincoln administration's history of usurping the rights of the people, and the intimidation of thousands of troops in Chicago, Pierce wanted the convention to declare "that the approaching election shall be a *free* election . . . with no military presence to overawe the unarmed citizen."[119] In conversations with Clement March, Pierce "counsel[ed] resistance by arms to Military interference with the election."[120]

On the first day of the Chicago convention, Pierce was placed in nomination, "to great applause," by seventy-six-year-old Kentucky delegate Charles A. Wickliffe, a former congressman, governor, and U.S. postmaster general. Spofford immediately urged withdrawal of the nomination, citing "both written and verbal instructions" from Pierce. Wickliffe explained that he had not consulted in advance with any of the delegates from New Hampshire but had nominated Pierce because he was "a man of experience in matters of statesmanship and great purity of character, who was unstained as a politician and as a man." In obedience to Pierce's wishes, Wickliffe, "though unwillingly," withdrew the nomination, to further cheers from the delegates.[121]

As expected, McClellan was nominated by the convention. Pierce's letter to Spofford was published in the newspapers, bringing down on Pierce further criticism for expressing his "apprehension that bayonets will attempt to control the judgment of the voters." The *New York Tribune* charged, "Mr. Pierce ought to know that there is no danger of this whatsoever; and if he does not, he must be deeper in dotage than anyone supposed."[122] What the Lincoln administration might have done had it faced certain defeat at the polls can only be conjectured. The initial promise of a McClellan victory in the national election ended with the success of the Union army in the South. The fall of Atlanta in September was the turning point. From then on, Union victory seemed inevitable, and Lincoln was easily reelected. The policies that Pierce had so criticized had succeeded in restoring the Union.

As the war came to an end, Pierce was living quietly in Concord, where he had spent the winter struggling once again with a "heavy cold and wearing cough."[123] The announcement of Lincoln's death on April 15 drove many citizens into the street, for what purpose they seemed uncertain, but after mingling for a while, they began to march to the homes of those residents who were not displaying the flag. Around 9:00 p.m. a mob estimated at between two and four hundred arrived at Pierce's door step and called him out. He inquired, "What is your desire?" and when told, "We wish to hear some words from you on this sad occasion," Pierce spoke to them:

> "I wish I could address to you words of solace. But that can hardly be done. The magnitude of the calamity, in all its aspects, is overwhelming. If your hearts are oppressed by events more calculated to awaken profound sorrow and regret than any which have hitherto occurred in our history, mine mingles its deepest regrets and sorrows with yours.[124]

He continued on expressing his "warm, outgushing sympathy" and deploring "the great crime and deep stain," when one person in the crowd shouted, "Where is your flag?" This touched a nerve, and Pierce became more animated:

> It is not necessary for me to show my devotion for the stars and stripes by any special exhibition, or upon the demand of any man or body of men. My ancestors followed it through the Revolution.... My brothers followed it in the war of 1812; and I left my family, in the Spring of 1847, among you, to follow its fortunes and maintain it upon a foreign soil. But this you all know. If the period during which I have served our State and country in various situations, commencing more than thirty-five years ago, have left the question of my devotion to the flag, the Constitution and the Union in doubt, it is too late now to remove it, by any such exhibition as the enquiry suggests. Besides to remove such doubts from minds where they may have been cultivated by a spirit of domination and partisan rancor, if such a thing were possible, would be of no consequence to you, and is certainly of none to me. The malicious questionings would return to reassert their supremacy and pursue the work of injustice.... I have never found or felt that violence or passion was ultimately productive of beneficent results.[125]

Pierce closed his remarks by thanking the crowd, which had listened "with absolute quiet," for their "silent attention"; he bid them "Good night!" and received "three cheers" from the mob, which "retired quietly as though there had been no scene of excitement in the city."[126] Throughout the war, Pierce had sacrificed his reputation by courageously defending civil liberties and speaking out against the policies of the Lincoln administration. This extemporaneous speech, so typical and so consistent with his lifelong beliefs and with no regrets of his past actions, demonstrates that Pierce was resigned to becoming a martyr to his vision of the Union and the Constitution.

15

FINAL YEARS

ROMANCE ENTERED THE LIFE of Franklin Pierce in the spring and summer of 1865. The identity of the woman is not known. As usual, Pierce kept no personal letters, but a neighbor in Concord recorded in his journal on May 15, "Franklin Pierce . . . called at my house with a lady. . . . It is rumored that he is soon to be married."[1] J. D. Hoover, in a letter to Howell Cobb, catching up on news with southern friends now that the war was over, reported that Pierce had "lost his wife" and that he was "said to be looking for another."[2] Hoover remained one of Pierce's most faithful friends to the end, visiting the former president in New Hampshire on several occasions and naming his only child Franklin Pierce Hoover. Hoover's frequent letters to Pierce always refer to the lad as, "Pierce Boy."[3] Hoover was wrong, however, in predicting a new marriage for Pierce as the former president was destined to spend his final years alone.

It was the fate of another old friend, Jefferson Davis, that most concerned Pierce. Davis was being held in solitary confinement at Fortress Monroe, under the threat of being tried for treason and for alleged complicity in the Lincoln assassination conspiracy. To the prison physician, Davis expressed the hope that Pierce would serve as his counsel, but Charles O'Conor, a brilliant trial lawyer who had served in the Pierce administration as district attorney in New York, volunteered his services and became Davis's lawyer.[4] Pierce communicated frequently with O'Conor, at first to improve the conditions under which Davis was held and, ultimately, to have him released.[5] Caleb Cushing, Jeremiah Black (Buchanan's attorney general), Horace Greeley, and Francis P. Blair joined Pierce in pressuring the government on Davis's behalf. The effort paid off. In the summer of 1866,

Pierce heard from a friend of Davis that "his treatment" was "much mitigated." Davis's wife, Varina, and their baby were living with him in a four-room apartment, he had "the liberty of the fort during the day," and he was only locked up at night. But the threat of a trial still loomed.[6]

Pierce almost certainly contributed money as well as influence in helping Davis. The former president was always generous to his friends and family. He paid for Julian Hawthorne's tuition at Harvard, and Pierce paid all of the expenses, "board, tuition . . . and all necessary books" for the education of his nephews, Kirk and Frank, the sons of his brother Henry, who was still in debt and unable to afford it himself. Pierce even sent "a turkey, a goose, and 2 chickens" to Kirk at school one Christmas for him to share with his friends "for a gentleman's dinner."[7] Frank graduated from Princeton, but Julian flunked out of Harvard in the fall of 1865. He was soon studying with a tutor in hopes of reenrolling.[8] Years later, Julian expressed his appreciation and fondness for Pierce: "There was a winning, irresistible magnetism in the presence of this man. Except my father, there was no man in whose company I liked to be so much as in his. . . . His voice, his look, his gestures, his gait, the spiritual sphere of him, were delightful to me. . . . He was a good, conscientious, patriotic, strong man, and gentle and tender as a woman. He had the old-fashioned ways, the courtesy, and the personal dignity which are not often seen nowadays. His physical frame was immensely powerful and athletic, but life used him hard, and he was far from considerate of himself. . . ."[9]

Pierce's drinking contributed to a severe attack of "bilious fever" in November 1865. He was so ill that there were fears for his life. On learning of the severity of his illness, Sophia Hawthorne dispatched Julian to Concord to be of service, but the crisis had passed, and after a day spent reading to Pierce, Julian returned home, reporting that Pierce was "very weak, and unable to sit up, and fearfully wasted, but not 'blue.'"[10] A few days later, Pierce was able to write to Horatio Bridge, "I suppose that my condition was very critical at one stage of the illness. But the worst is over now. The disease is apparently mastered and within the last few days I have been gaining strength as rapidly probably as is desirable."[11]

Confronted by his own mortality, Pierce was shocked into making some changes in his life. His first act was to be baptized at St. Paul's Episcopal Church in Concord on December 3, 1865. Pierce wrote to John Aiken, "I have neither consulted nor conversed with any of my friends upon the subject with the exception of the Rector, Dr. Eames. You and my dear Sister will pray that my conviction of sin be deep, that its heinousness be ever before me—that my faith may be firm and abiding and that my life may be humble, watchful & consistent. It is a great step—a great change—involving the assumption of great responsibilities."[12] John Aiken had frequently urged Pierce to "join us," meaning Jane's family, in the Congregational Church, but despite Pierce's deep religious faith, which conformed to Calvinist belief in preordained fate, personal depravity, and retribution for sins, Pierce was never comfortable with the evangelism and political activism regarding abolitionism of the Congregational ministers. The Episcopal Church had stubbornly and consistently avoided secular and political matters in its preaching throughout the period leading up to the Civil War. Not surprisingly, with local Congregational, Baptist, and Methodist ministers railing against the sin of slavery and attacking the Democratic Party Sunday after Sunday, many party leaders in Concord found their way to Dr. Eames's church. By the time Pierce joined them, St. Paul's congregation included all of his personal and political friends, William Butterfield, editor of the *Patriot*; John H. George; Josiah Minot; and the family of the late Isaac Hill. Pierce's confirmation took place on March 6, 1866.[13]

The Episcopal Church's abstention from the political debate over slavery had consequences. With leading Democrats joining the congregation, St. Paul's and its rector, Dr. Eames, were suspected of disloyalty by the Republican press. When the war broke out, delegates at the annual Episcopal Diocesan Convention, held in Concord in May 1861, refused to consider a resolution of support for the Lincoln administration and its policies. Dr. Eames reminded the convention delegates that "matters of State" had "always been kept from our Convention." But the failure of the convention to issue a strong resolution of support for the war brought down upon the Episcopal Church in New Hampshire the full force of the opposition press. The *Congregational Journal* attacked the church as the only religious denomination that had failed "to express loyalty to the Government under which it lives," while Concord's leading Republican paper went a step further warning, "It is not *safe* for any church or pulpit to be far behind the holy enthusiasm of a patriotic people."[14] St. Paul's remained a refuge for Democrats throughout the war. Following his confirmation, Pierce participated actively in the church. He rented two pews, attended corporation meetings, was twice chosen a delegate to the annual diocesan convention, and offered the resolution to increase the salary of Dr. Eames.[15]

The "heinous" sins Pierce committed refer to his personal life rather than to any of his political acts, which he never retracted or regretted. Drinking was certainly one of those sins, and Clement March reported in January 1866, "The General seems in good health and spirits, and does not make use of stimulating spirits, as I do." The two men had lengthy conversations about religion, with Pierce trying to convert his friend, who recorded, "We agree very much in opinion—and I hope to be able to join the church conscientiously."[16]

His health restored, both physically and spiritually, Pierce embarked on a new project. He purchased eighty-four acres on the coast at Little Boar's Head in North Hampton, New Hampshire, and built a small two-story cottage on the rocky coastline, right at the water's edge. He farmed the land, reveling in the "ploughing" and planting at the property on Little Boar's Head and on his sixty-acre plot in Concord. His cottage was always open to guests, with nephews and nieces visiting him each summer where he spent four or five months of the year. Pierce, remembering his youth on the farm in Hillsborough, had always viewed farming as the most honorable of occupations, and he was able during his last years to refer to himself as an "old farmer."[17]

Pierce retained his interest in politics. President Andrew Johnson, a Jacksonian Democrat before Lincoln tapped him as vice president, was soon battling with radical Republicans over Reconstruction policy. Johnson's plan was to restore the southern states to the Union as quickly as possible by granting amnesty and pardon to all who fought for the Confederacy, with the exception of officials and wealthy planters, who would be required to apply in person to the president. Johnson would allow the southern states to decide on the political rights of the freedmen. Radical Republicans wanted to punish the southern states and insisted upon full voting rights for blacks.[18] Pierce endorsed Johnson's plan for Reconstruction, and as the battle in Washington became more heated, he sent a brief letter to the president, thanking Johnson for his "brave devotion to the Constitution and the Union."[19]

Pierce also praised a speech in the Senate by Thomas Hendricks of Indiana, whom Pierce had once appointed commissioner of the U. S. General Land Office. The speech had criticized a bill to enlarge the powers of the Freedmen's Bureau. Hendricks answered that the bill was part "of a series to enslave the men of the South, and to break down the plain rights of the States everywhere in the Union." Hendricks believed that if Johnson could "stand firm," the voters were certain to reject the radical program "upon two questions": "1st. the [southern] states shall come in and 2nd the Negro shall not be made our political equal."[20]

Pierce's letter to the president was part of a broader effort by leading Democrats to encourage Johnson to break from the Republican Party and return to his roots. Pierce communicated with Robert McClelland; James Guthrie, now a senator from Kentucky; and Senator James Dixon of Connecticut, who viewed Johnson's battle with the Radical-Republicans as an opportunity to revive the Democratic Party by winning over the president.[21] With this goal in mind, Edmund Burke headed for Washington in the summer of 1866 to meet with Johnson and assure him of the full support of New Hampshire's Democrats. Pierce wrote Burke a letter of introduction, referring to him as "one of our most prominent citizens and a firm supporter of the policy of Prest. Johnson." Burke reported that Johnson agreed to use his patronage to help Democrats in New Hampshire and encouraged the state party to send delegates to a convention in Philadelphia in August to endorse the president's policies.[22] Burke headed the delegation from New Hampshire, but the convention occurred just after a bloody race riot in New Orleans in which thirty African Americans were killed, demonstrating to many that Johnson's conciliatory policy toward the South would not work. Johnson never intended switching to the Democratic Party; instead he hoped to create a Union Party of Democrats and conservative Republicans. This became evident in New Hampshire through his inconsistent patronage appointments, which did little to aid the state party.[23] On a personal level, it is difficult to understand the reconciliation of Pierce with Burke, who had been such a caustic critic and such a divisive factor in the party for so many years, but Burke's views on the Civil War were consistent with those of party leaders, and Pierce never seemed to hold a grudge for long, always putting the success of his party ahead of his own feelings.

In May 1867, Pierce traveled south to visit with Jefferson Davis, still a prisoner at Fortress Monroe in Old Point Comfort, Virginia. Davis's first court appearance was scheduled for May 13. On May 8, Pierce arrived at the fort by steamer from Baltimore, carrying "a small carpet sack in his hand," which probably contained his own plan for Davis's defense. But Pierce had failed to inform government officials in advance of his visit, and the guard refused to admit him to the prison. Pierce was forced to check into the same Hygeia Hotel that he and Marcy had visited on summer breaks from the White House. Later that day, General Henry S. Burton, commander of the fort, arrived and escorted Pierce to the prison. His meeting with Davis lasted into the evening. Following the visit, Davis wrote Pierce a brief note of appreciation: "Given on this day made bright by a visit of my beloved friend and ever honored chief."[24]

On May 13, the military turned Davis over to civilian authorities in Richmond. Davis was then indicted for treason, and O'Conor announced that he was ready for trial, but the government's attorney refused to proceed, and Davis was freed on $100,000 bond. Horace Greeley was present and had helped arrange Davis's bond.[25] Pierce, having just arrived back in New Hampshire after visiting with Sidney Webster in New York, addressed a letter to Varina Davis, inviting the family to stay at his cottage at Little Boar's Head: "I would not influence your husband with regard to his movements, but I am strongly impressed with the convictions, that his state of health, if no other consideration, should settle the question of his remaining at the North during the summer months now near at hand. My cottage at Little Boar's Head will be ready to receive all your family by the middle of August. The latter part of that month and the whole of Sept. is usually delightful there. The place will be quiet as could be desired. . . ."[26] He sent Davis a "package of books" and Varina a photograph of Jane "taken during the last year of her life when she was very feeble."[27] But the Davises had decided to live in Canada, where their older children were attending school, and he and Pierce would not meet again.

While spending most of his time between his rented home in Concord and the cottage at Little Boar's Head, Pierce made frequent visits to Jane's sister and her husband, Mary and John Aiken, in Andover, Massachusetts. Pierce also took an annual trip to the White Mountains, always staying at the Pemigewassett House, where the manager described Pierce to friends of Hawthorne, who made the pilgrimage to the hallowed site, "If one didn't know anything about his politics, it would be said of him that he was one of the best of men. There is nobody who comes to this house of more uniform and unfailing gentlemanliness than he."[28]

But Pierce was drinking again. In August 1867 his nephew John McNeil found him very ill and alone (with no company other than that of his housekeeper) at the cottage. McNeil reported Pierce's condition to Clement March who wrote that Pierce's illness was "from effects of drinking." March continued, "All had left him." Over the next few weeks, March visited Pierce several times and recorded, "The General is not in so bad a way as he [his nephew] anticipated—but has had a hard time. His visitors have not all gone—and do not know the cause of his illness [drinking]."[29]

Pierce rallied once again and by the spring of 1868 was writing, "I am enjoying excellent health and find a plenty of objects to occupy my time." He was busy "removing the rocks and ploughing the seashore lot" in preparation for "setting out trees, shrubbery & plants—repairing and renovating the old farm house—arranging drive ways etc."[30] And his interest in politics was revived by the impeachment trial of President Johnson and the upcoming presidential election. He wrote to J. D. Hoover about the impeachment: "But it seems from all I hear and read that the questions of President Johnson's guilt or innocence is not the matter to be passed upon. He is, more or less, in the way and is to be displaced. Not because such displacement will be warranted by law or fact, justice or reason, but upon 'the plea of state necessity' under which the hand of the tyrant upon the bell-rope has so often, in other lands, and in these later years, shame to say, in ours, struck down the shield of freemen by ringing the knell of 'the great writ of liberty.'"[31] Johnson was acquitted in mid-May. Later that summer, Pierce was able to personally thank Senator James W. Grimes of Iowa, one of seven Republican senators who sacrificed their political future by voting for acquittal. Grimes and his wife visited with Pierce at Little Boar's Head after vacationing at the Isles of Shoals. Pierce later sent them "stereoscopic views" of his cottage, and Mrs. Grimes thanked Pierce for his "many attentions & constant kindness."[32]

The upcoming presidential election also engaged Pierce's attention. He was impressed with the quality of the potential candidates for the Democratic nomination: "You know how highly I estimate the culture, powers, and elevated characteristics of Mr. [George] Pendleton, Gov. Seymour, Mr. Hendricks, and Mr. [James] Doolittle. I think I must also have spoken to you during the late Civil War of Genl. [Winfield Scott] Hancock. I knew him well twenty years ago and had the pleasure of meeting him with the late gallant General Reno on one occasion since the Mexican Campaign of 1847–48. By their dashing intrepidity, knowledge and large manhood they attracted universal confidence and in an unusual degree the warm regard of officers and men."[33] Other visitors that summer included B. B. French and his son Frank, who stopped by the cottage after walking along the shore. French wrote in his journal, "We found him in bed suffering with neuralgia in his left shoulder and arm. As soon as it was made known to him that we were there, he sent for us to come to his chamber, which we did, and were most kindly & cordially welcomed. I have not seen him before since he left Washington, and was surprised to see how well he bears his age. He does not look a day older than when he left the Presidential chair."[34]

Pierce's appearance belied his declining health, however, and that fall found him suffering once again. He confessed to Horatio Bridge, "I do not spring up readily from my serious illness . . . [and] have not much strength now." Pierce concluded, "Does it occur to you, Bridge, that we are rightly classed among the old men now?" The former president sensed the end was near: "I do not, my dear friend, look upon it gloomily, but sometimes when I seem to be gathering up vigor so slowly I doubt if I take into account, fully enough, my protracted and severe illness, or the fact that nearly sixty-four years of pretty strenuous life have passed over my head. I am driving out more or less, daily, and can repeat, with more or less comfort, 'Thou art my God, my time is in Thy hand.'"[35] His strength returned for a few months in the winter and spring of 1869. He reported, "I ride out or take a little walk daily when the weather is fine." Pierce had known the new president during the Mexican War and expressed optimism about his administration: "I indulge a pretty decided hope that Genl Grant will exert his best powers to bring our country back to cordial Union, reduce the public debt and make integrity and economy the general rule, instead of the exception."[36]

In May, Pierce felt well enough to take a final trip to Baltimore for the Order of Cincinnati Convention. This fraternity of descendants of Revolutionary War veterans held a special place in Pierce's heart, as it connected him with his roots—his father, who had provided the guiding principles of his life. Pierce paid homage to that legacy in his final speech to the delegates, during which he made reference to the Howards of Baltimore, patriots who had been imprisoned during the Revolution by the British: "If the Howards were disloyal, I was disloyal too, tho' I do not believe that I ever saw a day when I would not have made any possible, personal sacrifice to maintain the Constitution of my country and the Union based upon it. The opinions or perhaps it would be better to say the convictions which have controlled me may have been matters neither of merit or demerit. Some men are so constituted that they do not incline to bow before a storm. At all events, I was not educated in the school where it has been taught that the great work of the fathers was 'a covenant' or a 'league' with anything evil. Other lessons were taught at my father's fireside."[37]

Pierce was soon back at his cottage by the sea, where he wrote his nephew, "I have been upon my land all day and am too tired to say much. . . ." But he did congratulate young Frank on his upcoming graduation from Princeton, though his nephew had written that his rank in class was lower than he had expected and he hoped that his benefactor would not be disappointed. Pierce answered, "I am not disturbed by your disappointment. I have done what pleased me and you have done your best."[38]

That summer the final illness set in. On July 30, Clement March was reporting, "General Pierce is very ill." A few weeks later, March wrote, "I saw Gen. Pierce, who still drinks." March returned a few days later, reporting that Pierce was "physically very weak."[39] Horatio Bridge visited Little Boar's Head and found Pierce "too weak to leave his bed" and "sadly emaciated." Bridge remembered that as he prepared to leave, Pierce "raised himself from his pillow" and, in Bridge's words, "embraced me like a brother."[40] This time the condition was dropsy, an accumulation of fluids in the body, probably caused by liver failure, for a time accompanied by a chronic case of hiccups. In late September, Pierce returned to Concord; his abdomen was distended and he weighed less than one hundred pounds. Two local physicians examined him and informed him of the seriousness of his condition. Pierce replied, "I think so myself, and I am convinced I shall not recover."[41]

A death watcher, Mrs. Seth Hopkins, was hired to care for the dying patient. She moved into the house on South Main Street that Pierce had rented for years from Willard Williams. By October 7, Pierce was in and out of consciousness but still responded to his doctors and the Williams family, who gathered by his side. But he was in great discomfort and agony from the toxic fluid buildup, and around 9:00 p.m. that night it was clear that he no longer recognized the five people by his bedside. At 4:35 a.m., on Friday, October 8, after thrashing about for several hours, Pierce relaxed, opened his eyes, looked around the room, and died. No members of Pierce's family were present at his death.[42]

President Grant proclaimed the day of the funeral, Monday, October 11, a day of mourning in Washington, where all government business was suspended, buildings were draped in mourning, and navy yards around the country directed to fire a salute to the former president at noon.[43] In Concord, where the members of the local bar association had assumed responsibility for the arrangements, the mayor suspended all business between 11:00 a.m. and 2:00 p.m. on the day of the funeral, and the public schools were closed. At 10:00 a.m. that morning, Pierce's body was taken from the Williams residence and moved to the State House, led by a procession of twelve carriages. A large crowd waited in front of the Capitol, where public viewing took place in Doric Hall between 11:30 and 12:30. Men and women, many of them simple farmers or old acquaintances of Pierce, reportedly "wept as they gazed upon the well remembered features." Pierce appeared natural, and many commented on "his mass of curly black hair, somewhat tinged by age, but which was still combed on a deep slant over his wide forehead."[44]

At 1:00 p.m. the funeral commenced at St. Paul's Church, across the street from the Capitol. The Reverend Dr. Eames presided and preached the sermon. Among the hymns was Pierce's favorite, "While Thee I Seek, Protecting Power," sung to the tune of "Old Brattle Street." At 2:00 p.m., the funeral procession proceeded to the Old North Cemetery. The number of mourners around the grave, within the Minot enclosure, was considerably greater than the number who were able to crowd into the church for the funeral. The brief seven minute graveside service ended with Pierce's casket being lowered slowly into the grave, next to Jane and their two children.[45] Present for the services were Pierce's brother Henry; the Aikens from Andover; Pierce's former secretary, Sidney Webster; former marshal of the District of Columbia, J. D. Hoover; and Charles Levi Woodbury, son of Pierce's mentor, Levi Woodbury.[46] Clement March was also present for the "solemn and impressive" services and recorded in his journal that when he learned of Pierce's death, he felt ill and "drank about half a bottle of whiskey."[47] In Washington, former friend B. B. French wrote in his journal, "He had many of the best qualities that adorn human nature. 'De mortuis nil nisi bonum [Of the dead say nothing but good].'"[48] Daniel Voorhees, congressman and future senator from Indiana, offered a more generous tribute in a letter to John H. George. Referring to Pierce as "the gallant gentleman, the high soul," Voorhees continued, "He had more ways to charm, more ways to endear himself than any man I ever met in the journey of life. His mere presence inspired all that was good and noble and pure in the hearts of others and rebuked every unworthy thought or sentiment. You and I will never look upon his like again, as he appeared to us. Blessings upon his memory, and rest for his warm and loving, but wearied heart."[49]

EPILOGUE

PIERCE LEFT AN ESTATE of $72,386.01, equal to around $2 million today, most of it in bank and railroad stocks, notes, bonds, and other accounts. His real estate was valued at $13,000 in nine different properties. Bequests of money went to thirty-four people mostly relatives. Pierce's brother Henry received $7,000, but considering their ongoing conflict over Henry's poor financial management, Pierce pointedly left $8,000 to Henry's wife, Susan. Henry's oldest son, Kirk, received $10,000, and his younger son, Frank Hawthorne Pierce, was left the bulk of the estate after everything else had been paid, probably $20,000. The children of Pierce's closest friends, Nathaniel Hawthorne, John H. George, and Josiah Minot, also were left between $200 and $500 each. Pierce's landlady, Mrs. Sarah A. Williams, received $1,800 and her daughter $500. Pierce's most treasured possessions, swords, canes, pictures, saddles, horses, were divided among eighteen friends, including Sidney Webster, Josiah Minot, John H. George, Jonah D. Hoover, Clement March, Thomas H. Seymour, and Thomas J. Whipple. At the time of Pierce's death, all of his real estate except one small lot in Washington, D.C., was in New Hampshire.[1]

Franklin Pierce was a product of the Granite State. He admired the independent small farmers who eked out a living from its hardscrabble lands as well as the artisans, shopkeepers, and merchants who made up the small-town life he knew so well. He was raised on the participatory democracy of northern New England: the annual town meeting, the frequent elections, short terms for office holders, and regular rotation in office. In these communities public office was seen as a duty, an obligation, as one was called to serve by one's neighbors, not as the fulfillment of personal ambition or the opportunity to pursue self-interest or self-aggrandizement. This sense of duty or calling was ingrained in Pierce by his father and his Hillsborough upbringing, before Jacksonian Democracy emerged to put a party label around the creed of limited government, state sovereignty, local control, strict interpretation of the Constitution, nationalism, and respect for the common man. Pierce was a true Jeffersonian, and as the Democratic Party seemed to lose its focus on these ideals in the 1840s and 1850s, he retained his commitment to its creed.

This heritage provided the source of Pierce's values and his political philosophy, but it does not explain everything about him. Nathaniel Hawthorne, a brilliant student of human nature, found his friend infinitely interesting, "so simple, so complicated." Hawthorne acknowledged "the simplicity" with which Pierce "inherited" his "faith in the Union" from his father, referring to it as the principle of Pierce's whole public life.[2] But Pierce's life was complicated by forces beyond his control, which led to insecurities and rigidity in his thinking. The source of this aspect of his personality was a combination of circumstances, including his mother's mental instability and probable alcoholism, the deaths of several of his siblings in their early years, his own inherited weakness for alcohol, the chronic ill health and mental depression of his wife, the deaths of all three of their children, and his inability to find comfort or support in religion or the church. Add to this a sensitive, compassionate nature, which was attested to by all who knew him, friend and foe alike, and it is apparent that Pierce clung to a few simple truths to bring order and predictability to his personal and public life.

Among these was a resistance to drastic change. Pierce referred to the Constitution and the law for the source of most of his political positions. According to Pierce, law and order was the base upon which the nation had to rely to fulfill its destiny. While Pierce maintained a fervent belief in progress, accepting changes such as territorial expansion, a rapidly increasing population fed by immigration, technological breakthroughs, industrial and commercial growth, as the inevitable product of our enlightened democratic system, he drew the line at a social revolution forced on a reluctant populace by those who viewed their particular cause as more important than the peace of the community. This accounts for his consistent opposition to the "isms" of his day, prohibitionism, nativism, anti-Catholicism, and abolitionism. In each crusade he saw a radical minority willing to go beyond the law to achieve its goal. The personal abuse he took from temperance crusaders and abolitionists at a relatively formative period in his political career steeled his sensitive nature, preventing him from being able to feel the injustice felt by others.

Pierce did not oppose abolition because he loved slavery but because he viewed the movement as destructive of the Union and the Constitution, which was the source of the people's liberty. The liberty of white people, of course, is implied, as Pierce was unable to foresee any benefit to either the white or black race from emancipation. What he did foresee was the violence of civil war, the growth of a potentially oppressive central government, the expansion of executive power in violation of the Constitution, and the disruption of the nation's progress. What he did not understand was that ultimately the existence of slavery undermined the principles upon which the nation was founded in a fundamental way. It is worth noting that in all of Pierce's references to the Union and the Constitution he never mentions the Declaration of Independence and its pledge that all men are created equal, an idealism that was too ethereal for Pierce.

While modern sensibilities are offended by Pierce's racism, there was precious little that he could have done as president to improve the lot of black Americans. Before the Civil War, slavery was protected by the Constitution and the laws. As president, Pierce pledged to uphold the Constitution and enforce the laws. Any variance from this by a Democratic president would have produced a volcanic reaction and likely brought on the dissolution of the party and the Union five years sooner than it actually occurred. The Civil War was the culmination of all of Pierce's fears for the nation, as Lincoln violated constitutional rights and exercised vast powers, including executive emancipation, to bring about a social revolution. As Pierce's bitterness over the course of events increased, his resistance to change and his racism came more to the surface. While Pierce never resorted to racial vulgarities in his speeches or letters, his close associates within the Democratic party in New Hampshire did appeal to race prejudice in statewide campaigns during and after the Civil War, apparently without any admonishment from Pierce.

His conventional, nineteenth-century views on race seem to have carried over to gender as well. Pierce was always popular with women. Memoirs of female contemporaries, Varina Davis, Jessie Benton Frémont, Mrs. Clement Clay, Mrs. Roger Pryor, all attest to Pierce's charm, his kindness, his genteel manners, and his sincerity. But while Pierce attracted the attention of women, he seems to have had few close relationships with any other than his oldest sister, Elizabeth, and his wife, Jane. He admitted that what attracted him to Jane was her need for protection. To Pierce, a woman's role was the conventional one of wife, helpmate, and mother. On the one occasion when Pierce was confronted by a strong-willed female political activist, Dorothea Dix, his patronizing manner left her confused, and her later bitterness at Pierce was, at least in part, caused by his failure to share his constitutional concerns with her. But if he confined women to a conventional role, Pierce was more influenced by his wife than he might have admitted. Jane's moral and religious strength, combined with her physical disability, kept her husband close and his drinking under control, at least when in her presence. Since he was rarely apart from his wife during his administration, Jane's influence was significant. But it was also obvious to contemporaries, adding to Pierce's reputation as weak and indecisive. Pierce preferred the company of men and shared many of the nineteenth-century pursuits that characterized manliness. He was an accomplished horseman and an avid fisherman, and he enjoyed working in the fields, hunting, card playing, gambling, cigars, and drinking. To his male companions, Pierce was always an interesting, an engaging and a loyal friend.

Pierce's reputation for weakness may have been influenced as well by his approach to politics and public office. While personally ambitious, Pierce was never ruthless in his pursuit of office or power. He always put his party and his patriotism ahead of his personal ambition. He looked to the founding fathers for his model of public service and refused to force himself upon his party or the electorate. This self-effacing approach to political office was coupled with absolute honesty, integrity, and a strong ethical sense in his conduct of public affairs. But surrounded as he was by more grasping, ruthless, and unscrupulous politicians Pierce appeared vacillating and insecure as he courageously tried to steer a nationalistic course that was legal and ethical.

Pierce's personal and political failings have relegated him to a lesser position among the political leaders of his era, but, on balance, he contributed to many of the positive movements of his time. He always defended the rights and liberties of the common man and supported the westward movement and the territorial expansion of the nation, even putting his life on the line in Mexico and sacrificing his administration to open up the Kansas and Nebraska territories. He was an uncompromising spokesman for open immigration and the rapid assimilation of new citizens and defended freedom of religion at a time when it was most imperiled by the Know-Nothing movement. He advanced U.S. commercial interests overseas by improving trade and neutral rights and supported scientific advancement and its application to the military, transportation, and communication. His outspoken opposition to abolitionists was due, in part, to their association with other causes—temperance, nativism, and anti-Catholicism—which Pierce equated with intolerance and an evangelical Protestant religious agenda that he thought threatened the liberties of American citizens.

In fact, Pierce's public life is relevant today, as he took unequivocal positions on many issues that still resonate. In his time Pierce addressed such current issues as the control of immigration, the imposition of religious agendas into the political process, the proper role of the federal government in people's lives, the assumption of vast power by the executive in times of national emergency, the limits of dissent and the place of the Bill of Rights in wartime, and America's role in defending and spreading democracy around the world.

History has accorded to the Pierce administration a share of the blame for policies that incited the slavery issue, hastened the collapse of the second party system, and brought on the Civil War. Early in his political career, Pierce was labeled a "doughface" by his abolitionist enemies. This characterization of a northern politician who followed a southern agenda has stuck to Pierce ever since. It is both an inaccurate and unfair judgment. Pierce was always a nationalist attempting to find a middle ground to keep the Union together. If the Kansas-Nebraska Act and the enforcement of the Fugitive Slave Act angered northerners, Pierce's determination to prevent filibusters, his opposition to acquiring Cuba or Mexican territory by force, and his impartial use of the army in Kansas went against the wishes of southern Democrats. Pierce had to deal with the political system as he found it, with fifteen slave states and their representatives exercising the inordinate amount of power that the Constitution, with its three-fifths clause, gave them. The alternative to attempting to steer a moderate course was the breakup of the Union, the Civil War and the deaths of more than six hundred thousand Americans. Pierce should not be blamed for attempting throughout his political career to avoid this fate. In fact, the nation was better served than it realized, then or since, by a president who was so politically honest, so unmoved by schemes and corruption, so determined to enforce the law at all cost, so intractable in his interpretation of the Constitution, so determined to promote the nation's interests abroad, and so unmotivated by personal ambition as to resist making decisions based solely on expediency or self-interest. In the divisive political climate of the 1850s, Pierce's consistent legal and ethical conduct kept the nation on a course of prosperity and growth. Slavery was not a problem that could be solved within the antebellum political system. The Pierce administration's honest, efficient, legalistic, nationalistic stewardship was the best the nation could have hoped for at the time. Hawthorne may have had the life and career of Franklin Pierce in mind when he observed that to be American is "a text of deep and varied meaning."[3]

NOTES

Note: *To reflect each writer's voice and the flavor of historical documents, original materials are quoted with their original spelling, misspellings, and punctuation intact.*

Chapter 1: *Launching an Administration*

1. Allan Nevins, *Ordeal of the Union,* vol. 2, *A House Dividing, 1852–1857* (New York: Charles Scribner's Sons, 1947), 52; William Seale, *The President's House: A History* (Washington, D.C.: White House Historical Association and the National Geographic Society, 1986), 1: 310, 315.

2. Seale, *The President's House,* 1: 316.

3. B. B. French wrote in his journal in August 1854, "this has shown itself the meanest House of Representatives I ever knew—they even refused fuel and a furnace keeper to the President's House! The U.S. has built a furnace that burns an immense quantity of fuel, warming the entire mansion with heat from steam, and requiring the constant attention of one man, and have thus saddled upon the President an expense of some 12 or 1,500 dollars per year. . . ." Benjamin Brown French, *Witness to the Young Republic: A Yankee's Journal, 1828–1870,* eds. Donald B. Cole and John J. McDonough (Hanover, N.H.: University Press of New England, 1989), 212; Wilhelmus Bogart Bryan, *A History of the National Capital,* (New York: MacMillan, 1916), 2: 584; Amy LaFollette Jensen, *The White House and Its Thirty-Three Families* (New York: McGraw-Hill, 1958), 70.

4. Nevins, *Ordeal of the Union: A House Dividing,* 53.

5. Ibid.

6. Leonard D. White, *The Jacksonians: A Study in Administrative History, 1829–1861* (New York: MacMillan, 1954), 156.

7. Seale, *The President's House,* 1: 314–18; William Ryan and Desmond Guinness, *The White House: An Architectural History* (New York: MacMillan, 1980), 134; Betty Boyd Caroli, *Inside the White House* (New York: Canopy Books, 1992), 80–81. Capitol architect, Thomas U. Walter, wrote on June 29, 1853, "We have the President's house turned inside out, and will make it look more like a President's house than it ever has done before." Seale, *The President's House,* 1: 318.

8. Seale, *The President's House,* 1: 310, 324; Ryan and Guinness, *The White House,* 134.

9. *Washington National Intelligencer*, April 28, 1853 (hereafter cited as *National Intelligencer*).

10. Hudson Strode, *Jefferson Davis: American Patriot, 1808–1861* (New York: Harcourt, Brace, 1955), 1: 250–51.

11. *Journal of the Executive Proceedings of the Senate,* vol. ix, 33rd Congress, special session, vol. 9, 46–52.

12. Personal journal of Henry E. Parker, March 8, 1854, in "The Letters of Henry E. Parker," owned by Lawrence Brown of Albany, Georgia; available online at www.freepages.genealogy.rootsweb.com/~henryeparker/.

13. Sidney Webster, *Franklin Pierce and His Administration* (New York: D. Appleton, 1892), 39.

14. Nathaniel Hawthorne's most recent biographer uses the word "obtuse" to describe Pierce's honesty, in Brenda Wineapple, *Hawthorne: A Life* (New York: Alfred A. Knopf, 2003), 48–49; Webster, *Franklin Pierce and His Administration*, 38.

15. James A. Richardson, ed., *A Compilation of the Messages and Papers of the Presidents*, vol. 5 (Washington, D.C.: Government Printing Office, 1897), 200–201.

16. Mark W. Summers, *The Plundering Generation: Corruption and the Crisis of the Union, 1849–1861* (New York: Oxford University Press, 1987), 194–195.

17. Franklin Pierce to Caleb Cushing, May, 1853, Caleb Cushing Papers, Library of Congress (hereafter cited as Cushing Papers).

18. White, *The Jacksonians*, 398; *National Intelligencer*, May 24, 1853; Ivor Debenham Spencer, *The Victor and the Spoils: A Life of William L. Marcy* (Providence, R.I.: Brown University Press, 1959), 227–228; Dorothy G. Fowler, *The Cabinet Politician: The Postmasters-General, 1829–1909* (New York: Columbia University Press, 1943), 83.

19. White, *The Jacksonians*, 68, 72–73.

20. *New Hampshire Patriot*, March 30, April 6, 1853; *Journal of the Executive Proceedings of the Senate*, 33rd Congress, special session, vol. 9, 88.

21. Tony Freyer, "Campbell, John Archibald," *Oxford Companion to the Supreme Court of the United States*, ed. Kermit L. Hall, and others (New York: Oxford University Press, 1992), 116–17; Martin Siegel, *The Supreme Court in American Life*, vol. 3, *The Taney Court, 1836–1864*, (New York: Associated Faculty Press, 1987), 292–94; *Journal of the Executive Proceedings of the Senate*, 33rd Congress, special session, vol. 9, 88. Fillmore had previously nominated Edward A. Bradford of Louisiana (August 16, 1852), George E. Badger of North Carolina (January 10, 1853), and William C. Micou of Louisiana (February 24, 1853) for the seat on the Court. Congress took no action on Bradford and Micou and postponed indefinitely a decision on Badger. Siegel, *The Taney Court*, III, 52–54.

22. William L. Marcy to James Buchanan, March 5, 1853, and James Buchanan to William L. Marcy, March 8, 1853, in William L. Marcy Papers, Library of Congress (hereafter cited as Marcy Papers); Spencer, *The Victor and the Spoils*, 224.

23. Richardson, *A Compilation of the Messages*, 5: 198–99.

24. H. Barrett Learned, "William Learned Marcy," *The American Secretaries of State and Their Diplomacy*, ed. Samuel Flagg Bemis (New York: Pageant Books Company, 1958), 6: 169, 174.

25. Spencer, *The Victor and the Spoils*, 225; Frank Lawrence Owsley, "A. Dudley Mann," *Dictionary of American Biography*, (New York: Charles Scribner's Sons, 1933), 12: 239; *New Hampshire Patriot*, March 30, 1853; Learned, "William Learned Marcy," 175; *Journal of the Executive Proceedings of the Senate*, 33rd Congress, special session, vol. 9: 103, 109, 160.

26. *New Hampshire Patriot,* April 13, 1853; *Journal of the Executive Proceedings of the Senate,* vol. 9: 157, 159.

27. Nathaniel Hawthorne to Horatio Bridge, October 13, 1852, in *Selected Letters of Nathaniel Hawthorne,* ed. Joel Myerson (Columbus: Ohio State University Press, 2002), 166–167; *Journal of the Executive Proceedings of the Senate,* 33rd Congress, special session, vol. 9: 99, 109.

28. Edwin Haviland Miller, *Salem Is My Dwelling Place: A Life of Nathaniel Hawthorne* (Iowa City: University of Iowa Press, 1991), 391–392; James R. Mellow, *Nathaniel Hawthorne in His Times* (Baltimore: Johns Hopkins University Press, 1980), 428.

29. Mellow, *Nathaniel Hawthorne,* 428.

30. French, *Witness to the Young Republic,* 233.

31. Ibid., 234–235.

32. Ibid.; John W. Forney to Franklin Pierce, March 7, 1853, and John W. Forney to William L. Marcy, March 13, 1853, both in the John W. Forney Papers, Library of Congress.

33. French, *Witness to the Young Republic,* 236–237.

34. Ibid.

35. B. B. French to Henry F. French, April 9, 1853, French Family Papers, New Hampshire Historical Society, Concord (hereafter cited as French papers).

36. Henry F. French to B. B. French, April 22, *1853,* French Papers.

37. French, *Witness to the Young Republic,* 238.

38. B. B. French to Henry F. French, April 17, 1853, French Papers.

39. Seale, *The President's House,* 1: 307.

40. French, *Witness to the Young Republic,* 239.

41. Ibid., 240.

42. *National Intelligencer,* April 28, 1853.

43. Jane Pierce to Mary Aiken, May 31, 1853, Pierce-Aiken Papers, Library of Congress.

44. Ibid.

45. Abigail Kent Means to Mrs. Noyes, April 18, 1853, Abigail Kent Means Papers, Library of Congress (hereafter cited as Means Papers); George Ticknor Curtis, *Life of James Buchanan* (New York: Harper and Brothers, 1883), 2: 76–77; Roy Franklin Nichols, *The Democratic Machine, 1850–1854* (New York: Columbia University Press, 1923), 192–93; Summers, *The Plundering Generation,* 196–97.

46. Means to Noyes, April 18, 1853, Means Papers.

47. Summers, *The Plundering Generation,* 196–198.

48. Nathaniel G. Upham to Franklin Pierce, October 20, 1852, and Martin Van Buren to Franklin Pierce, October 18, 1852, both in Pierce Papers; John A. Dix, *Memoirs of John Adams Dix,* (New York: Harper and Brothers, 1883), 1: 272.

49. Spencer, *The Victor and the Spoils,* 227.

50. *New Hampshire Patriot,* April 6, 1853; *Journal of the Executive Proceedings of the Senate,* 33rd Congress, special session, vol. 9, 118.

51. William L. Marcy to Horatio Seymour, April 10, 1853, Marcy Papers.

52. Nichols, *The Democratic Machine*, 192; *Journal of the Executive Proceedings of the Senate*, 33rd Congress, special session, vol. 9, 118.

53. *New Hampshire Patriot*, April 13, 1853; Samuel J. Tilden to William L. Marcy, April 7, 1853, Marcy Papers; Nichols, *The Democratic Machine*, 192.

54. Charles O'Conor to Robert McClelland, April 13, 1853, Robert McClelland Papers, Library of Congress (hereafter cited as McClelland Papers); J. Addison Thomas to William L. Marcy, April 9, 1853, Marcy Papers.

55. Charles O'Conor to Robert McClelland, April 13, 1853, McClelland Papers; J. A. Thomas to William L. Marcy, April 14, 1853, Marcy Papers.

56. Summers, *The Plundering Generation*, 196; Dix, *Memoirs*, 1: 273–74.

57. Mrs. Fillmore became ill with pneumonia following the Pierce inaugural, where she sat in the cold and snow. With her husband and two children by her side, she died at Willard's Hotel. During her final illness, Pierce had offered to send a White House servant, Abby, who had previously attended Mrs. Fillmore, to help out, but the former president politely declined the offer: "We have two excellent nurses, and fortunately, neither myself, nor the rest of my family has anything to do but wait upon her." Millard Fillmore to Franklin Pierce, Monday, March 28, 1853, Pierce Papers. For more on Mrs. Fillmore's final illness, see Margaret Brown Klapthor, *The First Ladies* (Washington, D.C.: White House Historical Association, 1975), 35. Franklin Pierce to James Buchanan, March 30, 1853, and James Buchanan to Franklin Pierce, April 2, 1853, both in John Bassett Moore, ed., *The Works of James Buchanan*, (Philadelphia: J. B. Lippincott, 1909), 8: 504–5.

58. Curtis, *Life of James Buchanan*, vol. 2, 76–77,

59. Ibid., 78–79; *Journal of the Executive Proceedings of the Senate*, 33rd Congress, special session, vol. 9, 166.

60. Sidney Webster to John H. George, March 15, 1853, George Family Papers, New Hampshire Historical Society, Concord.

61. French, *Witness to the Young Republic*, 238.

62. Executive Order, Department of State, April 14, 1853, copy in Caleb Cushing Papers, Library of Congress.

63. "Office and Duties of the Attorney General," March 8, 1854, in C.C. Andrews, ed., *Official Opinions of the Attorneys General of the United States: Advising the Presidents and Heads of Departments in Relation to Their Official Duties* (Washington, D.C.: Robert Farnham, 1856; reprinted 1944), 6: 326–55; Claude M. Fuess, *The Life of Caleb Cushing* (New York: Harcourt Brace, 1923), 2: 136–37; Henry Bassett Learned, *The President's Cabinet* (New Haven: Yale University Press, 1912), 176–81.

64. Executive Order, Franklin Pierce to Jefferson Davis, March 23, 1853, in Letters Sent to the President by the Secretary of War, RG105, M127, National Archives; Seale, *The President's House*, 1: 315; Jefferson Davis to Captain Montgomery C. Meigs, April 4, 1853, in Jefferson Davis, *Jefferson Davis, Constitutionalist: His Letters, Papers, and Speeches*, Dunbar Rowland, ed. (New York: J. J. Little and Ives, 1923), 2: 194–95.

65. Nevins, *Ordeal of the Union, A House Dividing*, 53.

66. White, *The Jacksonians*, 197; Nichols, *The Democratic Machine*, 191.

67. William R. King to James Buchanan, December 13, 1852, Buchanan Papers, Historical Society of Pennsylvania, Phildadelphia.

68. *Congressional Globe*, 32nd Congress, 2nd session, 787, 1020; John Milton Martin, "William Rufus King: Southern Moderate" (Ph.D. dis., University of North Carolina at Chapel Hill, 1955), 357–58.

69. *National Intelligencer*, April 8, 1853.

70. *Washington Union*, April 19, 20, 21, 1853; *National Intelligencer*, April 20, 1853.

71. *New Hampshire Independent Democrat*, March 31, 1853 (hereafter cited as *Independent Democrat*).

72. *Washington Union*, April 12, 1853.

73. Richard P. McCormick, *The Second American Party System: Party Formation in the Jackson Era* (Chapel Hill: University of North Carolina Press, 1966), 13–15, 30, 349–53.

74. Summers, *The Plundering Generation*, 194–97.

75. *Independent Democrat*, March 31, 1853, and May 26, 1853.

76. Davis complained to Cushing that before the Baltimore convention "States rights Democrats" outnumbered "Union" Democrats in Mississippi "4 or 5 to one," but since both groups united to support Pierce at the convention and during the campaign, the "Union" Democrats were now claiming and receiving half of the patronage jobs in the state. Jefferson Davis to Caleb Cushing, June 18, 1853, Cushing Papers; Fowler, *The Cabinet Politician*, 84.

77. Davis to Cushing, June 18, 1853, Cushing Papers.

78. *Independent Democrat*, May 26, 1853.

Chapter 2: *Policies, Politics, and Public Relations*

1. "The President Visited Some of the Departments this Morning in his Usual Quiet and Unceremonious Way." *Washington National Intelligencer*, July 30, 1853; Frank L. Burr to Gideon Welles, March 6, 1854, Gideon Welles Papers, Library of Congress; Leonard D. White, *The Jacksonians: A Study in Administrative History, 1829–1861* (New York: MacMillan, 1954), 70.

2. James A. Richardson, ed., *A Compilation of the Messages and Papers of the Presidents*, (Washington, D.C.: Government Printing Office, 1897), 5: 197–203.

3. H. C. Allen, *Great Britain and the United States: A History of Anglo-American Relations, 1783–1952* (New York: St. Martin's Press, 1955), 429; H. Barrett Learned, "William Learned Marcy," *The American Secretaries of State and Their Diplomacy*, Samuel Flagg Bemis, ed. (New York: Pageant Book Company, 1958), 6: 250–51. Thomas A. Bailey also refers to the Clayton-Bulwer Treaty as "the most persistently unpopular pact ever concluded by the United States." See Thomas A. Bailey, *A Diplomatic History of the American People* (New York: F. S. Crofts, 1940), 292.

4. Charles C. Tansill, *The Canadian Reciprocity Treaty of 1854* (Baltimore: Johns Hopkins University, 1922), 52–55; Learned, "William Learned Marcy," *The American Secretaries of State*, 6: 276–80.

5. Albert R. Hatch to Franklin Pierce, April 14, 1853, Pierce Papers, New Hampshire Historical Society, Concord (hereafter cited as Pierce Papers).

6. Buchanan left a detailed account of the events that transpired before his departure for London. See "The Mission to London" in George Ticknor Curtis, *Life of James Buchanan*, vol. II, (New York: Harper and Brothers, 1883), 2: 76–93.

7. James Buchanan to Franklin Pierce, June 14, 1853, in John Bassett Moore, ed., *The Works of James Buchanan*, (Philadelphia: J. B. Lippincott, 1909), 9: 2–4; and Curtis, *Life of James Buchanan*, 2: 83–84.

8. Curtis, *Life of James Buchanan*, 2: 76–93.

9. Buchanan to John W. Forney, December 13, 1853, in Moore, *The Works of James Buchanan*, 9: 111–12; Curtis, *Life of James Buchanan*, 2: 80.

10. Buchanan to Pierce, June 23, 1853, in Moore, *The Works of James Buchanan*, 9: 4–5; Curtis, *Life of James Buchanan*, 2: 84–85.

11. Pierce to Buchanan, June 26, 1853, in Moore, *The Works of James Buchanan*, 9: 6; Curtis, *Life of James Buchanan*, 2: 86.

12. Buchanan to Pierce, June 29,1853, in Moore, *The Works of James Buchanan*, 9: 7–9; Curtis, *Life of James Buchanan*, 2: 87–89.

13. Pierce to Buchanan, July 3, 1853, in Moore, *The Works of James Buchanan*, 9: 10; Curtis, *Life of James Buchanan*, 2: 89–90.

14. Buchanan to Pierce, July 7, 1853, in Moore, *The Works of James Buchanan*, 9: 11; Curtis, *Life of James Buchanan*, 2: 90.

15. Pierce to Buchanan, July 3, 1853, in Moore, *The Works of James Buchanan*, 9: 10; Curtis, *Life of James Buchanan*, 2: 90.

16. Paul Neff Garber, *The Gadsden Treaty* (Philadelphia: Press of the University of Pennsylvania; reprint by Paul Smith, 1959 edition), 3–63; Learned, "William Learned Marcy," 6: 274.

17. Basil Rauch, *American Interest in Cuba, 1848–1855* (New York: Columbia University Press, 1948), 48–80.

18. Rauch, *American Interest in Cuba*, 262–263; William L. Marcy to Pierre Soulé, Diplomatic Instructions, July 23, 1853, Marcy Papers, Library of Congress (hereafter cited as Marcy Papers).

19. *Journal of the Executive Proceedings of the Senate*, 33rd Congress, 1st session, vol. 9, 167; Marcy to Humphrey Marshall, June 7, 1853, Diplomatic Instructions to Minister Marshall and to Robert M. McLane, Marcy Papers, LC.

20. Arthur C. Walworth, *Black Ships Off Japan: The Story of Commodore Perry's Expedition* (Hamden, Conn.: Archon Books, 1966), 21–32. Before departing, Perry insisted on "large discretionary powers" in conducting his mission. "It is plain therefore that stern necessity makes it imperative on the United States to secure 'peacably if we can, forcibly if we must' [a trade agreement with Japan]." He continued, "I must be governed by circumstances as they may transpire, and which cannot be foreseen. . . ." Matthew C. Perry to the Secretary of the Navy [John P. Kennedy], November 11, 1852, copy in Despatches from Special Agents of the Department of State, RG59, M37, National Archives.

21. Marcy to John Randolph Clay, August 30, 1853, diplomatic instructions, Marcy Papers.

22. A. C. Benson and A. M. Frank to Franklin Pierce, May 3, 1853, Caleb Cushing Papers, Library of Congress (hereafter cited as Cushing Papers).

23. Ivor Debenham Spencer, *The Victor and the Spoils: A Life of William L. Marcy* (Providence, R.I.: Brown University Press, 1959), 234.

24. Ibid., 235; John A. Dix to Marcy, June 13, 1853, Marcy Papers.

25. Henry Adams, *The Life of Albert Gallatin* (Philadelphia: J. B. Lippincott, 1880), 267.

26. Robert Spencer Cotterill, "James Guthrie," *Dictionary of American Biography*, (New York: Charles Scribner's Sons, 1932), 8: 60–62.

27. Report of the Secretary of the Treasury, December 6, 1853, *Congressional Globe*, 33rd Congress, 1st session, appendix, 2.

28. Ibid., 4.

29. Ibid., 3; White, *The Jacksonians*, 184; Mark W. Summers, *The Plundering Generation: Corruption and the Crisis of the Union, 1849–1861* (New York: Oxford University Press, 1987), 194–195.

30. Henry Cohen, *Business and Politics in America from the Age of Jackson to the Civil War: The Career Biography of W. W. Corcoran* (Westport, Conn.: Greenwood Publishing, 1971), 93–94.

31. *Senate Executive Documents*, April 1, 1853, 33rd Congress, 1st session, vol. 2, 111; White, *The Jacksonians*, 185.

32. Report of the Secretary of the Treasury, December 6, 1853, *Congressional Globe*, 33:1, Appendix, 3; *Senate Executive Documents*, October 1, 1853, 33rd Congress, 1st session, vol. 2, 355; White, *The Jacksonians*, 185.

33. Report of the Secretary of the Treasury, December 6, 1853, *Congressional Globe*, 33rd Congress, 1st session, appendix, 3.

34. Ibid., 6; *New Hampshire Daily Patriot*, June 17, 1853; *New Hampshire State Capital Reporter*, July 29, 1853.

35. Report of the Secretary of the Treasury, December 6, 1853, *Congressional Globe*, 33rd Congress, 1st session, appendix, 1–6.

36. Summers, *The Plundering Generation*, 195. Pierce's own appointees had difficulty getting paid from the Treasury for their expenses. See B. F. Hallett to John H. George, January 9, 1854, John Hatch George Papers, New Hampshire Historical Society, Concord (hereafter cited as George Papers).

37. Report of the Secretary of the Treasury, December 6, 1853, *Congressional Globe*, 33rd Congress, 1st session, appendix, 5; Report of the Secretary of the Interior, December 5, 1853, *Congressional Globe*, 33rd Congress, 1st session, appendix, 23–27; White, *The Jacksonians*, 371–34.

38. *Senate Executive Document*, November 19, 1853, 33rd Congress, 1st session, vol. 2, 138; White, *The Jacksonians*, 374.

39. Report of the Secretary of the Interior, December 5, 1853, *Congressional Globe*, 33rd Congress, 1st session, appendix, 27.

40. Letter Book. Miscellaneous, No. 1, August 27, 1853, Department of the Interior, National Archives.

41. *Washington National Intelligencer,* May 24, 1853; White, *The Jacksonians,* 398.

42. William Seale, *The President's House: A History* (Washington, D.C.: White House Historical Association and the National Geographic, 1986), 1: 321–22.

43. Benjamin Brown French, *Witness to the Young Republic: A Yankee's Journal, 1828–1870,* ed. Donald B. Cole and John J. McDonough, (Hanover, N.H.: University Press of New England, 1989), 249–50.

44. Report of the Secretary of the Interior, December 5, 1853, *Congressional Globe,* 33rd Congress, 1st session, appendix, 23.

45. Annual Report of the Commissioner of Indian Affairs, December, 1853, *Congressional Globe,* 33rd Congress, 1st session, appendix, 27.

46. *Congressional Globe,* 33rd Congress, 2nd session, 702.

47. Ibid., 699–706.

48. Ibid., 705, 720–24; Summers, *The Plundering Generation,* 156–57.

49. *Congressional Globe,* 33rd Congress, 2nd session, 728.

50. B. B. French to Henry F. French, April 1, 1855, French Papers.

51. Report of the Secretary of the Interior, December 5, 1853, *Congressional Globe,* 33rd Congress, 1st session, appendix, 25.

52. Franklin Pierce to George Manypenny, July 17, 1857; Jacob Thompson to George Manypenny, January 28, 1858; both in Library of Congress; Manypenny Papers, *Congressional Globe,* 33rd Congress, 2nd session, 730; Summers, *The Plundering Generation,* 156–157.

53. Report of the Postmaster General, December 1, 1853, *Congressional Globe,* 33rd Congress, 1st session, appendix, 7.

54. Ibid., 9

55. White, *The Jacksonians,* 231–50.

56. Report of the Secretary of War, December 1, 1853, *Congressional Globe,* 33rd Congress, 1st session, appendix, 29.

57. Ibid., 32–34; William H. Goetzmann, *Army Exploration in the American West, 1803–1863* (New Haven, Conn.: Yale University Press, 1959), 275.

58. Report of the Secretary of War, December 1, 1853, *Congressional Globe,* 33rd Congress, 1st session, appendix, 32–34; Davis's instructions to Isaac Stevens and Lieutenant Whipple are found in Jefferson Davis, *Jefferson Davis Constitutionalist: His Letters, Papers, and Speeches,* ed. Dunbar Rowland, (New York: J. J. Little and Ives, 1923), 2: 199–201, 223–26.

59. Report of the Secretary of the Navy, December 5, 1853, *Congressional Globe,* 33rd Congress, 1st session, appendix, 15; J. G. de R. Hamilton, "James C. Dobbin," *Dictionary of American Biography* (New York: Charles Scribner's Sons, 1930), 5: 335–36.

60. Report of the Secretary of the Navy, December 5, 1853, *Congressional Globe,* 33rd Congress, 1st session, appendix, 13–14.

61. Harold and Margaret Sprout, *The Rise of American Naval Power, 1776–1918* (Princeton, N.J.: Princeton University Press, 1939), 138.

62. Report of the Secretary of the Navy, December 5, 1853, *Congressional Globe,* 33rd Congress, 1st session, appendix, 15.

63. Henry T. Tuckerman, *The Life of John Pendleton Kennedy* (New York: G. P. Putnam's Sons, 1871), 224.

64. Report of the Secretary of the Navy, December 5, 1853, *Congressional Globe,* 33rd Congress, 1st session, appendix, 15.

65. See Pierce's speeches in the Senate, *Congressional Globe,* 25th Congress, 2nd session, appendix 488–92; 26th Congress, 1st session, 109; 27th Congress, 1st session, 258; and "Reception of General Pierce," *New Hampshire Patriot,* special edition, January 28, 1848.

66. Report of the Secretary of the Navy, December 5, 1853, *Congressional Globe,* 33rd Congress, 1st session, appendix, 17.

67. J. Addison Thomas to William L. Marcy, May 17, 1853, Marcy Papers.

68. *Albany Argus* article quoted in the *New Hampshire State Capital Reporter,* July 8, 1853.

69. Francis J. Grund to Caleb Cushing, April 9, 1853, Cushing Papers.

70. Francis J. Grund to Edmund Burke, August 17, 1853, Edmund Burke Papers, Library of Congress (hereafter cited as Burke Papers).

71. Sidney Webster to John H. George, February 22, 1852, and March 18 and March 25, 1852; and A. G. Allen to George, March 23, 1852; all in George Papers.

72. Edmund Burke to Franklin Pierce, June 8 and June 24, 1852; Franklin Pierce to Edmund Burke, June 14, 1852; both in Pierce Papers.

73. J. W. Bradbury to Edmund Burke, July 20, 1852; Benjamin F. Hallett to Edmund Burke, August 28, 1852; Gideon Pillow to Edmund Burke, September 4, 1852; B. B. French to Edmund Burke, September 17, 1852; all in Burke Papers.

74. B. B. French to Caleb Cushing, January 31, 1853, Cushing Papers.

75. Franklin Pierce to Edmund Burke, June 14, 1852, Pierce Papers.

76. *New Hampshire Daily Patriot,* July 2, 1853, quoting Edmund Burke's letter to Munn and Co., December 25, 1851; White, *The Jacksonians,* 416.

77. *New Hampshire State Capital Reporter,* August 13, 1853.

78. *New Hampshire State Capital Reporter,* January 4, 1853, June 14, 1853; The *Old Guard* merged with the *State Capital Reporter* on August 27, 1853; Francis J. Grund to Edmund Burke, August 17, 1853, and Daniel Dickinson to Edmund Burke, September 25, 1853 in Burke Papers.

79. *New Hampshire Independent Democrat,* June 16, 1853; *New Hampshire State Capital Reporter,* June 14, 1853.

80. *New Hampshire Independent Democrat,* June 16, 1853.

81. Ibid.

82. *Newport (N.H.) Argus and Spectator,* June 17, 1853.

83. Ibid.

84. *New Hampshire Daily Patriot,* June 22, 1853.

85. Paul R. George to Caleb Cushing, June 30, 1853, Cushing Papers.

86. Franklin Pierce to Charles G. Atherton, October 29, 1853, Pierce Papers.

87. Theodore Sedgwick, President, New York Crystal Palace for the Exhibition of the Industry of all Nations, to William L. Marcy, May 9, 1853; C. A. Davis to William L. Marcy, July 19, 1853; both in Marcy Papers.

88. Asa Wilgus to Abby Means, July 29, 1853; D. Lancaster to Jane Pierce, November 30, 1853; both in Pierce Papers. Wilgus wrote, "I say to you in truth and sincerity, that in a long and busy life, I never met with any human being, save my own immediate family, who inspired me with so much love and affection as did this little boy." Lancaster concluded, "You may well be thankful that you had such a son, as certainly I am that I once had such a scholar."

89. Henry Watterson, *"Marse Henry": An Autobiography* (New York: George H. Daron, 1919), 1: 32–33.

90. Varina Davis, *Jefferson Davis, Ex-President of the Confederate States: A Memoir by His Wife,* (New York: Belford Company Publishers, 1890), 1: 534–36.

91. Josiah Minot to Franklin Pierce, April 29, 1853, Pierce Papers.

92. *New York Herald,* July 12, 1853.

93. B. B. French to Henry F. French, July 10, 1853, French Papers, New Hampshire Historical Society, Concord.

94. *Baltimore Sun*, July 12, 1853.

95. Ibid.

96. *Washington Union,* July 13, 1853.

97. *Baltimore Sun,* July 13, 1853; *Philadelphia Public Ledger,* July 13, 1853.

98. *Philadelphia Public Ledger*, July 13, 1853.

99. Ibid.

100. Curtis, *Life of James Buchanan,* 2: 91.

101. John W. Forney, *Anecdotes of Public Men* (New York: Harper and Brothers, 1889), 2: 418–19.

102. Curtis, *Life of James Buchanan,* 2: 91; Franklin Pierce, Philadelphia speech, draft, July 1853, Pierce Papers.

103. *Philadelphia Public Ledger*, July 13, 1853; Lynda Lasswell Crist, ed., *The Papers of Jefferson Davis,* (Baton Rouge: Louisiana State University Press, 1985), 5: 29–34.

104. Curtis, *Life of James Buchanan,* 2: 92; *Philadelphia Public Ledger,* July 14, 1853.

105. *New York Herald,* July 14, 1853.

106. *New York Herald*, July 14, 1853.

107. *New York Herald,* July 15, 1853; Franklin Pierce, New York speech, draft, July, 1853, Pierce Papers.

108. *New York Herald*, July 15, 1853.

109. Ibid.

110. *Baltimore Sun,* July 16, 1853.

111. *New York Herald,* July 15, 1853.

112. *New York Herald,* July 16, 1853; C.A. Davis to William L. Marcy, July 19, 1853, Marcy Papers.

113. *New York Herald,* July 15, 1853.

114. *New York Herald,* July 16, 1853; *Baltimore Sun,* July 18, 1853.

115. *Baltimore Sun,* July 18, 1853; *Washington Union,* July 17, 1853.

116. *New York Herald,* July 16, 1853.

117. *New York Commercial Advertiser* quoted in *Washington Union,* July 19, 1853.

118. *The Pennsylvanian* quoted in the *Washington Union,* July 21, 1853.

119. Roy F. Nichols, *Franklin Pierce: Young Hickory of the Granite Hills,* rev. ed. (Philadelphia: University of Pennsylvania Press, 1931; revised 1969), 283–84.

120. French, *Witness to the Young Republic,* 255.

121. Forney, *Anecdotes of Public Men,* 2: 418–19.

Chapter 3: *Crises—Foreign and Domestic*

1. *Journal of the Executive Proceedings of the Senate,* vol. ix, 33rd Congress, 1st Session, 167, 220, 241; Edward L. Widmer, *Young America: The Flowering of Democracy in New York City* (New York: Oxford University Press, 1999), 185–189.

2. Franklin Pierce to James Buchanan, July 27, 1853, Buchanan to Pierce, July 29, 1853, Pierce to Buchanan, July 31, 1853 in John Bassett Moore, ed. *The Works of James Buchanan,* vol. IX (Philadelphia: J. B. Lippincott, 1909), 30–31.

3. Horatio Seymour to William L. Marcy, July 25, 1853, William L. Marcy Papers, Library of Congress.

4. J. Addison Thomas to Marcy, August 8, 1853, Marcy Papers, L.C.

5. James R. Mellows, *Nathaniel Hawthorne in His Times* (Baltimore: The Johns Hopkins University Press, 1980), 432.

6. John A. Dix to Robert McClelland, September 23, 1853, Robert McClelland Papers, Library of Congress; Morgan Dix, *Memoirs of John Adams Dix,* vol. I (New York: Harper and Brothers, 1883), 273–278.

7. Ivor Debenham Spencer, *The Victor and the Spoils, A Life of William L. Marcy* (Providence: Brown University Press, 1959), 228–231.

8. Wilhelmus Bogart Bryan, *A History of the National Capital,* vol. 2 (New York: MacMillan, 1916), 418–425; Leonard D. White, *The Jacksonians: A Study in Administrative History, 1829–1861* (New York: MacMillan, 1954), 285–288.

9. John W. Forney, *Anecdotes of Public Men,* vol. II (New York: Harper and Brothers, 1889), 420; Sara A. R. (Mrs. Roger A.) Pryor, *Reminiscences of Peace and War* (New York: MacMillan, 1904), 15; Henry Watterson, *"Marse Henry": An Autobiography,* vol. 1 (New York: George H. Daron, 1919), 53.

10. Washington *National Intelligencer,* July 30, 1853; *New York Herald,* July 30, 1853; Bryan, *A History of the National Capital,* vol. 2, 424.

11. *New York Herald,* July 30, 1853.

12. "Draft of a Letter from William L. Marcy to Mr. Hulseman, Charge," September, 1853, Marcy Papers, L.C.; *New York Herald,* August 5, August 8, 1853.

13. Ibid.

14. *New York Herald,* August 5, August 8, 1853; Marcy's Diary, August 1, 1853, Marcy Papers, L.C.; Charles C. Tansill, *The Canadian Reciprocity Treaty of 1854* (Baltimore: Johns Hopkins University, 1922), 56–58.

15. *New York Herald,* August 10, 1853: H. Barrett Learned, "William L. Marcy," *The American Secretaries of State and Their Diplomacy,* Samuel Flagg Bemis, ed., vol. VI (New York: Pageant Books, 1958), 271.

16. "Draft of a Letter from William L. Marcy to Mr. Hulseman, Charge," September, 1853, Marcy Papers, L.C.

17. Ibid.

18. *Washington Union,* October 6, 1853; Spencer, *The Victor and the Spoils,* 269.

19. Learned, "William L. Marcy," *The American Secretaries of State,* VI, 271–273.

20. *Washington Union,* October 8, 1853; Spencer, *The Victor and the Spoils,* 269.

21. Albert R. Hatch to Pierce, April 4, 1853, Pierce Papers, NHHS; Learned, "William L. Marcy," *The American Secretaries of State,* VI, 276; Tansill, *The Canadian Reciprocity Treaty,* 54–55.

22. John F. Crampton to Marcy, July 3, 1853, Marcy Papers, L.C.

23. Diary of William Marcy, August 1–4, 1853, Marcy Papers, L.C.

24. Ibid.

25. Edward Everett to Marcy, August 15, 1853, Marcy Papers, L.C.

26. Tansill, *The Canadian Reciprocity Treaty,* 61.

27. Israel D. Andrews to Daniel Webster, July 9, 1851, Despatches from the Special Agents of the State Department, RG 59, M37, vol. 16, National Archives.

28. Tansill, *The Canadian Reciprocity Treaty,* 62.

29. "Instructions to Israel D. Andrews" from William L. Marcy, September 12, 1853, Pierce Papers, NHHS.

30. James Buchanan to Marcy, December 22, 1853, Marcy Papers, L.C.

31. Mark L. Berger, *The Revolution in the New York State Party System, 1840–1860* (Port Washington, N.Y.: Kennikat Press, 1973), 31.

32. John Van Buren to Marcy, May 21, 1853, Marcy Papers, L.C.

33. Samuel J. Tilden to Marcy, June 21, 1853, Marcy Papers, L.C.

34. John Cochrane to Marcy, June 29, 1853, Marcy Papers, L.C.

35. Mark W. Summers, *The Plundering Generation: Corruption and the Crisis of the Union, 1849–1861* (New York: Oxford University Press, 1987), 196–198; Stewart Mitchell, *Horatio Seymour of New York* (Cambridge, MA: Harvard University Press, 1938), 149–150.

36. Horatio Seymour to Marcy, October 17, 1853, Marcy Papers, L.C.

37. Berger, *The Revolution in the New York State Party System,* 31; Seymour to Marcy, October 17, 1853, Marcy Papers, L.C.

38. Marcy to Dean Richmond, September 4, 1853, J. A. Thomas to Marcy, September 13, 1853, Marcy Papers, L.C.; New Hampshire *State Capital Reporter,* September 20, 1853; James Maurice to Edmund Burke, September 15, 1853, Burke Papers, L.C.

39. *Washington Union,* September 27, 1853.

40. Marcy to Caleb Cushing, October 1, 1853, Cushing Papers, L.C.

41. James Guthrie to Greene C. Bronson, September 30, 1853, printed in *Washington Union,* October 3, 1853.

42. *Journal of the Executive Proceedings of the Senate,* 33rd Congress, 1st session, vol. 9, 167.

43. Dix, *Memoirs of John Adams Dix,* 1: 277–78.

44. John Van Buren to William L. Marcy, October 15, 17, 1853, Marcy Papers.

45. Roy F. Nichols, *The Democratic Machine, 1850–1854* (New York: Columbia University, 1923), 211.

46. Greene C. Bronson to James Guthrie, October 17, 1853, printed in *Washington Union,* October 20, 1853.

47. James Guthrie to Greene C. Bronson, October 22, 1853, printed in *Washington Union,* October 23, 1853.

48. Ibid.

49. Ibid., William L. Marcy to Caleb Cushing, October 1, 1853, Marcy Papers.

50. John Van Buren to William L. Marcy, October 24, 1853, Marcy Papers.

51. Henry J. Randall to William L. Marcy, October 24, 1853, Marcy Papers.

52. *Washington Sentinel* printed in *New Hampshire State Capital Reporter,* October 28, 1853.

53. *New York Herald,* October 18, 1853.

54. White, *The Jacksonians,* 178; Heman J. Redfield to William L. Marcy, November 1, 1853, Marcy Papers.

55. Claude M. Fuess, *The Life of Caleb Cushing* (New York: Harcourt Brace, 1923), 2: 139–40; Nichols, *The Democratic Machine,* 216.

56. Ibid.

57. Fuess, *The Life of Caleb Cushing,* vol. II, 139–40.

58. Ibid.

59. Ibid.

60. C. B. H. Fessenden to Caleb Cushing, November 2, 1853, Cushing Papers.

61. Robert Tyler to Cushing, November 2, 1853, Cushing Papers.

62. Horatio Seymour to William L. Marcy, November 11, 1853, Marcy Papers.

63. Fernando Wood to William L. Marcy, November 24, 1853, Marcy Papers.

64. Ibid.

65. Daniel Dickinson to Edmund Burke, December 3, 1853, Burke Papers.

66. Sidney Webster to Edmund Burke, November 9, 1853; and Edmund Burke to Sidney Webster, November 18, 1853; both in Burke Papers; *New Hampshire State Capital Reporter*, October 29, 1853.

67. Henry F. French to B. B. French, November 16, 1853, French Family Papers, New Hampshire Historical Society, Concord; Paul R. George to Caleb Cushing, November 16, 1853, Cushing Papers.

68. Memorandum of Instructions, William L. Marcy to James Gadsden, October 22, 1853, Despatches from Special Agents, RG59, M37, vol. 19; Paul Neff Garber, *The Gadsden Treaty* (Philadelphia: Press of the University of Pennsylvania; reprinted by Peter Smith), 90–91.

69. Garber, *The Gadsden Treaty,* 15–18; Mike Dunning, "Manifest Destiny and the Trans-Mississippi South: Natural Laws and the Extension of Slavery into Mexico," *Journal of Popular Culture* 35, no. 2 (Fall 2001): 123.

70. Garber, *The Gadsden Treaty,* 28–37.

71. Ibid., 43–54, 59–60; Ana R. Suarez, "The Precious, the Priceless Right of Way across the Isthmus of Tehuantepec," *Journal of Popular Culture* 35, no. 2 (Fall 2001): 156; Marcela Terrazas, "The Regional Conflict, the Contractors, and the Construction Projects of a Road to the Pacific at the End of the War between Mexico and the United States," *Journal of Popular Culture* 35, no. 2 (Fall 2001): 162.

72. "Instructions," William L. Marcy to James Gadsden, July 15, 1853, Despatches from Special Agents of the Department of State, RG59, M37, vol. 19.

73. Memorandum of Instructions, William L. Marcy to James Gadsden, October 22, 1853, Despatches, RG59, M37, vol. 19.

74. William L. Marcy to James Gadsden, January 6, 1853, Marcy Papers.

75. Garber, *The Gadsden Treaty*, 90–92, 94; Terrazas, "The Regional Conflict, the Contractors," 164–65.

76. C. L. Ward to James Gadsden, November 14, 1853, Despatches from Special Agents, RG59, M37, vol. 19, N.A.

77. James Gadsden to William L. Marcy, November 20, 1853, Despatches from Special Agents, RG59, M37, vol. 19, N.A.

78. William L. Marcy to James Gadsden, December 22, 1853, Despatches from Special Agents, RG59, M37, vol. 19, N.A.

79. C. L. Ward to William L. Marcy, December 4, 1853, Despatches from Special Agents, RG59, M37, vol. 19, N.A.; William O. Scroggs, *Filibusters and Financiers: The Story of William Walker and His Associates* (New York: MacMillan, 1916; reprinted by Russell and Russell, 1969), 49–50; Albert Z. Carr, *The World and William Walker* (Westport, Conn.: Greenwood Press, 1963; reprinted 1975), 73–89.

80. For a complete account of filibusters and their role in the politics of the 1850s, see Robert E. May, *Manifest Destiny's Underworld: Filibusters in Antebellum America* (Chapel Hill: University of North Carolina, 2002).

81. Ibid., 132–33; Caleb Cushing to Samuel W. Inge, January 16, 1854; and Samuel W. Inge to Caleb Cushing, March 16, 1854; both in *Senate Executive Document*, 68, 34th Congress, 1st Session, vol. 68, 7–8.

82. May, *Manifest Destiny's Underworld*, 133; Diary of Ethan Allen Hitchcock, October 9, 1853, in Ethan Allen Hitchcock, *Fifty Years in Camp and Field: Diary of Major-General Ethan Allen Hitchcock, U.S.A.*, ed. W. A. Croffut (New York: G. P. Putnam's Sons, 1909), 401–03; Scroggs, *Filibusters and Financiers*, 50.

83. Bradford Ripley Alden to Ethan Allen Hitchcock, January 17, 1854, Ethan Allen Hitchcock Papers, Library of Congress; Hitchcock, *Fifty Years in Camp and Field*, 401; May, *Manifest Destiny's Underworld*, 133.

84. James C. Dobbin to Commodore Dulany, December 19, 1853, January 3, 1854, in K. Jack Bauer, ed., *The New American State Papers: Naval Affairs* (Wilmington, Del.: Scholarly Resources, 1981), 2: 159–162; Scroggs, *Filibusters and Financiers*, 51. On his arrival back in San Francisco, Walker was promptly arraigned in federal court for violation of neutrality laws. See, Carr, *The World and William Walker*, 90–91.

85. Garber, *The Gadsden Treaty*, 101–105.

86. James Gadsden to William L. Marcy, January 7, 1854, Marcy Papers.

87. John W. Forney to James Buchanan, November 21, 1853, Buchanan Papers, Historical Society of Pennsylvania, Philadelphia.

Chapter 4: *Kansas-Nebraska*

1. *Congressional Globe* 33rd Congress, 1st session, 33:1, 1–2; Roy Nichols, *Franklin Pierce: Young Hickory of the Granite Hills*, rev. ed. (Philadelphia: University of Pennsylvania, 1931; revised 1969), 307; William E. Parrish, *David Rice Atchison of Missouri: Border Politician* (Columbia: University of Missouri Press, 1961), 134–38; James A. Rawley, *Race and Politics: 'Bleeding Kansas' and the Coming of the Civil War* (Philadelphia: J. B. Lippincott, 1969), 28.

2. William Carl Klunder, *Lewis Cass and the Politics of Moderation* (Kent, Ohio: Kent State University Press, 1996), 260; Robert W. Johannsen, *Stephen A. Douglas* (New York: Oxford University Press, 1973), 388–90; Frank L. Burt to Gideon Welles, January 15, 1854, Gideon Welles Papers, Library of Congress (hereafter cited as Welles Papers).

3. See Frederic Bancroft, *The Life of William H. Seward* (New York: Harper and Brothers, 1900); Frederick J. Blue, *Salmon P. Chase: A Life in Politics* (Kent, Ohio: Kent State University Press, 1987).

4. George S. Hale, "Harry Hibbard, A Memoir," *The Grafton and Coos Bar Association* (1895–1896) 3: 103–07; William C. Davis, *Breckinridge: Statesman, Soldier, Symbol* (Baton Rouge: Louisiana State University Press, 1974), 92, 97; Rudolph Von Abele, *Alexander H. Stephens* (New York: Alfred A. Knopf, 1946), 144; Samuel Treat to Caleb Cushing, December 18, 1853, Cushing Papers, Library of Congress (hereafter cited as Cushing Papers). Treat wrote from Saint Louis, "Benton is to oppose the administration—whether covertly or openly, will depend on circumstances."

5. Franklin Pierce to John L. O'Sullivan, December 5, 1853, John L. O'Sullivan Papers, Massachusetts Historical Society, Boston.

6. *Congressional Globe* 33rd Congress, 1st session, 5, 8–12.

7. James D. Richardson, ed., *A Compilation of the Messages and Papers of the Presidents, 1789–1897* (Washington, D.C.: Government Printing Office, 1897), 5: 207–12.

8. Ibid., 212–14.

9. Ibid., 215–21.

10. Ibid., 218, 224–25.

11. Allan Nevins, *Ordeal of the Union*, vol. 2, *A House Dividing, 1852–1857* (New York: Charles Scribner's Sons, 1947), 77; Michael F. Holt, *The Rise and Fall of the American Whig Party* (New York: Oxford University Press, 1999), 804; Johannsen, *Steven A. Douglas*, 390.

12. *Daily Wisconsin, New Orleans Courier, Charleston (S.C.) Courier, Baltimore Sun,* all quoted in *New Hampshire Patriot,* January 4, 1854.

13. *Congressional Globe*, 33rd Congress, 1st session, 1, 15.

14. *Congressional Globe,* 33rd Congress, 1st session, 28; Nevins, *Ordeal of the Union,* II, 75.

15. Parrish, *David Rice Atchison*, 139.

16. Benjamin Brown French, *Witness to the Young Republic: A Yankee's Journal, 1828–1870*, ed. Donald B. Cole and John J. McDonough (Hanover, N.H.: University Press of New England, 1989), 241–42.

17. On the anniversary of Benny's death, brother-in-law John Aiken wrote to Franklin Pierce, "The affliction through which you were called to pass was one of terrible severity. The Grace of God could alone bear one up under so crushing a might. Both you & dear Jane have, I trust, found that Grace sufficient to sustain you." John Aiken to Frank Pierce, January 7, 1854, Pierce Papers, New Hampshire Historical Society, Concord.

18. *Congressional Globe*, 33rd Congress, 1st session, 113, 121–22.

19. *Congressional Globe*, 33rd Congress, 1st session, 190–91; Mark L. Berger, *The Revolution in the New York State Party System, 1840–1860* (Port Washington, N.Y.: Kennikat Press, 1973), 26.

20. *Congressional Globe*, 33rd Congress, 1st session, 191–94.

21. *Washington Union*, January 11, 12, 1854; John Payne to John C. Breckinridge, January 19, 1854, John C. Breckinridge Papers, Library of Congress (hereafter cited as Breckinridge Papers); Davis, *Breckinridge*, 99–100.

22. Frank L. Burt to Gideon Welles, January 15, 1854, Welles Papers.

23. Paul Neff Garber, *The Gadsden Treaty* (Philadephia: Press of the University of Pennsylvania; reprinted by Peter Smith, 1959), 115–16; *New York Herald*, February 9, 1854; *Journal of the Executive Proceedings of the Senate*, 33rd Congress, 1st session, vol. 9, 235–36.

24. Richardson, ed., *A Compilation of the Messages*, 5, 229–31; *Journal of the Executive Proceedings of the Senate*, 33rd Congress, 1st session, vol. 9, 238–39.

25. Johannsen, *Stephen A. Douglas*, 390–91.

26. Johannsen, *Stephen A. Douglas*, 395; P. Orman Ray, *The Repeal of the Missouri Compromise: Its Origin and Authorship* (Cleveland, Ohio: Arthur H. Clark, 1909), 163–65.

27. *Congressional Globe*, 32nd Congress, 2nd session, 543.

28. Ray, *The Repeal of the Missouri Compromise*, 115–16; Parrish, *David Rice Atchison*, 141–50; Nicole Etcheson, *Bleeding Kansas: Contested Liberty in the Civil War Era* (Lawrence: University Press of Kansas, 2004), 11–12.

29. Ray, *The Repeal of the Missouri Compromise*, 198.

30. Ibid., 127, 155–57.

31. *Albany Argus*, December 14, 1853; *Richmond Enquirer*, December 23, 1853; *New York Herald*, January 2, 1854.

32. *Congressional Globe*, 33rd Congress, 1st session, 44, 115.

33. Johannsen, *Stephen A. Douglas*, 409.

34. *New Hampshire State Capital Reporter*, January 21, 1854.

35. *Congressional Globe*, 33rd Congress, 1st session, 175.

36. Davis, *Breckinridge*, 104.

37. Susan Bullitt Dixon (Mrs. Archibald Dixon), *The True History of the Missouri*

Compromise and Its Repeal (Cincinnati: Robert Blacke Company, 1899), 445; Johannsen, *Stephen A. Douglas,* 411–13.

38. Philip Phillips, "A Summary of the Principal Events in My Life," June 10–20, 1876, in Philip Phillips Papers, Library of Congress; Henry Barrett Learned, "The Relation of Philip Phillips to the Repeal of the Missouri Compromise," *Mississippi Valley Historical Review* 8 (March, 1922): 310.

39. Phillips, "A Summary of the Principal Events of My Life."

40. *Congressional Globe,* 33rd Congress, 1st session, 186.

41. Salmon P. Chase to E. S. Hamlin, January 22, 1854, in "Diary and Correspondence of Salmon P. Chase," *Annual Report of the American Historical Association* 2 (1902): 255.

42. *Washington Union,* January 20, 1854; Johannsen, *Stephen A. Douglas,* 413–17; Davis, *Breckinridge,* 105.

43. Ray, *The Repeal of the Missouri Compromise,* 213.

44. Sidney Webster, *Franklin Pierce and His Administration* (New York: D. Appleton, 1892), 59–62.

45. Davis, *Breckinridge,* 106; *New York Herald,* January 24, 1854.

46. Jefferson Davis to Mrs. Archibald Dixon, September 27, 1879 in Dixon, *The True History of the Missouri Compromise,* 457–59.

47. Phillips, "A Summary of the Principal Events of My Life."

48. Ibid.

49. John C. Breckinridge to Robert J. Breckinridge, March 8, 1854, Breckinridge Papers; Joseph Robinson to John H. George, January 24, 1854, George Papers, New Hampshire Historical Society, Concord (hereafter cited as George Papers); *Congressional Globe,* 33rd Congress, 1st session, 239.

50. Davis, *Breckinridge,* 106; Johannsen, *Stephen A. Douglas,* 414.

51. *Congressional Globe,* 33rd Congress, 1st session, 239; Johannsen, *Stephen A. Douglas,* 417.

52. Diary of Clement March, October 16, 1857, Center for Southwest Research, University of New Mexico, Albuquerque.

53. Gideon Welles to John S. Williams, October, 1853, Welles Papers. In this letter Welles writes, "I am apprehensive that we may all be disappointed in our President. He is *no* Jackson, that is certain. If he does not prove a Tyler, I shall be thankful."

54. Webster, *Franklin Pierce and His Administration,* 63; Phillips, "A Summary of the Principal Events of My Life"; Frank B. Woodford, *Lewis Cass: The Last Jeffersonian* (New Brunswick, N.J.: Rutgers University Press, 1950), 300; Klunder, *Lewis Cass,* 267.

55. *Washington Union,* January 24, 1854; Joseph Robinson to John H. George, January 24, 1854, and Harry Hibbard to George, January 25, 1854, George Papers.

56. *Journal of the Executive Proceedings of the Senate,* 33rd Congress, 1st session, vol. 9, 217; Heman J. Redfield to William L. Marcy, February 2, 1854, Marcy Papers, Library of Congress (hereafter cited as Marcy Papers.)

57. Blue, *Salmon P. Chase,* 93; Johannsen, *Stephen A. Douglas,* 417; Nevins, *Ordeal of the Union: A House Dividing,* 112.

58. Thomas H. O'Connor, *Lords of the Loom: The Cotton Whigs and the Coming of the Civil War* (New York: Charles Scribner's Sons, 1968), 98.

59. Michael F. Holt, *The Rise and Fall of the American Whig Party* (New York: Oxford University Press, 1999), 815.

60. *Congressional Globe,* 33rd Congress, 1st session, appendix 37–41.

61. Ibid., 43.

62. Ibid., 45–46.

63. French, *Witness to the Young Republic,* 244; Franklin Pierce to Moses Norris Jr., February 3, 1854, Pierce Papers, Library of Congress.

64. H. Draper Hunt, *Hannibal Hamlin of Maine: Lincoln's First Vice President* (Syracuse, N.Y.: Syracuse University Press, 1969), 81–82.

65. *Washington Union,* February 10, 1854.

66. *New Hampshire State Capital Reporter,* February 14, 18, 1854.

67. *New Hampshire Patriot,* February 22, 1854.

68. *Congressional Globe,* 33rd Congress, 1st session, 532.

69. *Washington Union,* March 3, 1854.

70. Lex Renda, *Running on the Record: Civil War Era Politics in New Hampshire* (Charlottesville: University Press of Virginia, 1997), 46–48; Isaac O. Barnes to Caleb Cushing, March 15, 1854; J. H. Wright to Caleb Cushing, March 18, 1854; Charles March to Caleb Cushing, March 16, 1854; all in Caleb Cushing Papers. March wrote, "many elected as regular democrats will prove strongly anti-Nebraska."

71. Alpheus S. Packard to John Aiken, February 26, 1854, Means-Aikens Papers, Library of Congress; Jane Pierce to Alpheus S. Packard, March 4, 1854, Pierce File, Bowdoin College Library.

72. Nevins, *Ordeal of the Union: A House Dividing,* 2: 68; James Buchanan to William L. Marcy, March 3, 1854, Marcy Papers.

73. *New Hampshire State Capital Reporter,* January 14, 1854.

74. William L. Marcy to J. A. Thomas, [April] 1854, Marcy Papers.

75. James Buchanan to William L. Marcy, October 28, 1853, February 18, 1854, James Buchanan to Harriett Lane, February 21, 1854; both in George Ticknor Curtis, *Life of James Buchanan* (New York: Harper and Brothers, 1883), 2: 107–14; James Buchanan to William L. Marcy, February 24, 1854, Marcy Papers.

76. James Buchanan to Harriett Lane, February 24, 1854, in Curtis, *Life of James Buchanan,* 2: 114.

77. H. Barrett Learned, "William Learned Marcy," *The American Secretaries of State and Their Diplomacy,* ed. Samuel Flagg Bemis (New York: Pageant Book Company, 1958), 6: 265.

78. Ibid., 267.

79. Ibid., 269.

80. Thomas Keneally, *American Scoundrel: The Life of the Notorious Civil War General Dan Sickles* (New York: Doubleday, 2002), 36.

81. Ibid., 2–3.

82. Merle Curti, "Young America," *American Historical Review* 32 (October, 1926): 48.

83. Basil Rauch, *American Interest in Cuba, 1848–1855* (New York: Columbia University Press, 1948), 283.

84. James Buchanan to William L. Marcy, February 24, 1854, Marcy Papers.

85. James Buchanan to William L. Marcy, December 22, 1854, Marcy Papers; Curti, "Young America," 48.

86. George N. Sanders to Louis Kossuth and others, June 2, 1854, copy in Cushing Papers.

87. Curti, "Young America," 52.

88. Marcy to J. A. Thomas, [April?] 1854, Marcy Papers.

89. *Congressional Globe,* 33rd Congress, 1st session, 883, 924, 985. Executive sessions were called on March 13, April 10, 17, and 25.

90. Garber, *The Gadsden Treaty,* 117–18; *Congressional Globe,* 33rd Congress, 1st session, appendix, 27; Marcela Terrazas, "The Regional Conflict, the Contractors, and the Construction Projects of a Road to the Pacific at the End of the War between Mexico and the United States," *Journal of Popular Culture* 35, no. 2 (Fall 2001): 164–65.

91. Richardson, ed., *A Compilation of Messages,* 5: 236–37; Garber, *The Gadsden Treaty,* 122–23.

92. Ibid.

93. Garber, *The Gadsden Treaty,* 124–25.

94. Ibid., 128.

95. Garber, *The Gadsden Treaty,* 128–30; *Journal of the Executive Proceedings of the Senate,* 33rd Congress, 1st session, vol. 9, 309–11.

96. Garber, *The Gadsden Treaty,* 130.

97. *New York Tribune,* May 2, 1854; Terrazas, "The Regional Conflict, the Contractors," 167–68.

Chapter 5: *Party Tests and Reciprocity*

1. James Buchanan to William L. Marcy, December 22, 1853, January 28, 1854, Marcy Papers, Library of Congress (hereafter cited as Marcy Papers).

2. William L. Marcy to James Buchanan, March 11, 1854, Marcy Papers.

3. James Buchanan to William L. Marcy, March 31, 1854, Marcy Papers.

4. Israel D. Andrews to William L. Marcy, April 3, 1854; William L. Marcy to Israel D. Andrews, April 10, 1854, Despatches of the Special Agents of the Department of State, RG 59, M37, vol. 16, National Archives (hereafter cited as Despatches of the Special Agents).

5. "Payments, out of the fund for Contingent Expenses of Foreign Inter-course settled on the Certificate of the President, 1826–1852," n.d., Pierce Papers, Library of Congress (hereafter cited as Pierce papers); Ivor Debenham Spencer, *The Victor and the Spoils: A Life of William L. Marcy* (Providence, R.I.: Brown University Press, 1959), 252.

6. Caleb Cushing to Israel D. Andrews, telegram, April 12, 1854, Despatches of the Special Agents, RG 039, M37, vol. 16.

7. William L. Marcy to Israel D. Andrews, April 15, 1854, Marcy Papers.

8. *Congressional Globe,* 33rd Congress, 1st session, 701; Leonard L. Richards, *The Slave Power: The Free North and Southern Domination, 1780–1860* (Baton Rouge: Louisiana State University Press, 2000), 185–86.

9. *Congressional Globe,* 33rd Congress, 1st session, 703; Mark L. Berger, *The Revolution in the New York Party Systems, 1840–1860* (Port Washington, N.Y.: Kennikat Press, 1973), 29; Richards, *The Slave Power,* 185–186.

10. *Congressional Globe,* 33rd Congress, 1st session, 763.

11. Ibid., 759–63.

12.Berger, *The Revolution in the New York Party Systems* 29–30; William C. Davis, *Breckinridge: Statesman, Soldier, Symbol* (Baton Rouge: Louisiana State University Press, 1974), 115–18; Frank L. Burt to Gideon Welles, March 30, 1854, Gideon Welles Papers, Library of Congress (hereafter cited as Welles Papers).

13. Benjamin B. French, *Witness to the Young Republic: A Yankee's Journal, 1828–1870,* ed. Donald B. Cole and John J. McDonough (Hanover, N.H.: University Press of New England, 1989), 249.

14. Ibid.

15. Benjamin B. French to Franklin Pierce, March 27, 1854, in French, *Witness to the Young Republic,* 261–62.

16. French, *Witness to the Young Republic,* 245–47.

17. Ben Perley Poore, *Perley's Reminiscences of Sixty Years in the National Metropolis,* I (Philadelphia: Hubbard Brothers, 1886), 1: 470.

18. Amos Tuck French, ed., *Exeter and Harvard Eighty Years Ago: Journal and Letters of F. O. French, '57* (Chester, N.H.: Privately printed, 1932), 61. Frank French was named after Francis Ormand Jon Smith, former congressman from Maine and partner with B. B. French in a telegraph company. B. B. French, Smith, and Pierce had roomed in the same boarding house in Washington when Pierce and Smith were in Congress and French was the assistant clerk of the House in the 1830s.

19. Ibid., 67.

20. Diary of Amos A. Lawrence, April 13, 1854, Amos A. Lawrence Diaries, Massachusetts Historical Society, Boston.

21. Perley Poore, *Perley's Reminiscences of Sixty Years,* 1: 495.

22. Amos A. Lawrence to Giles Richards, April 21, 1854, Amos A. Lawrence Papers, Massachusetts Historical Society, Boston.

23. Ida Russell to Caleb Cushing, May 4, 1854, Cushing Papers, Library of Congress (hereafter cited as Cushing Papers).

24. Varina Davis, *Jefferson Davis, Ex-President of the Confederate States of America; A Memoir by His Wife* (New York: Belford Company, 1890), 1: 559.

25. Allan Nevins, *Ordeal of the Union,* vol. 2, *A House Dividing, 1852–1857* (New York: Charles Scribner's Sons, 1947), 122.

26. James D. Richardson, ed., *A Compilation of the Messages and Papers of the Presidents, 1789–1897* (Washington D.C.: Government Printing Office, 1897), 5: 248.

27. *Congressional Globe,* 33rd Congress, 1st session, 45, 67, 73.

28. Dorothea Dix to Millard Fillmore, December 8, 1853, and Millard Fillmore to Dorothea Dix, December 20, 1853, quoted in Thomas J. Brown, *Dorothea Dix: New England Reformer* (Cambridge, Mass.: Harvard University Press, 1998), 200; David Gollaher, *Voice for the Mad: The Life of Dorothea Dix* (New York: The Free Press, 1995), 321.

29. Brown, *Dorothea Dix*, 205.

30. *Congressional Globe,* 33rd Congress, 1st session, 572, 954.

31. Brown, *Dorothea Dix*, 205.

32. Ida Russell to Caleb Cushing, May 4, 1854, Cushing Papers.

33. Dorothy Clarke Wilson, *Stranger and Traveler: The Story of Dorothea Dix, American Reformer* (Boston: Little, Brown, 1975), 198.

34. Richardson, ed., *A Compilation of the Messages and Papers of the Presidents,* 5: 247–53.

35. Ibid., 254–255.

36. *Washington Union,* May 27, 1854.

37. *Congressional Globe,* 33rd Congress, 1st session, 1604, 1621.

38. Gollaher, *Voice for the Mad*, 331; Brown, *Dorothea Dix*, 215.

39. *New York Tribune*, September 11, 1854.

40. Ida Russell to Caleb Cushing, May 4, 1854, Cushing Papers.

41. *Congressional Globe,* 33rd Congress, 1st session, 703, 1254.

42. *Biographical Directory of the American Congress, 1774–1927* (Washington, D.C.: Government Printing Office, 1928), 933, 1031, 1583, 1600, 1206, 1087, 810; Paul Wallace Gates, "A Fragment of Kansas Land History: The Disposal of the Christian Indian Tract," *Kansas Historical Quarterly* 6, no. 3 (August 1937): 236.

43. Mark W. Summers, *The Plundering Generation: Corruption and the Crisis of the Union, 1849–1861* (New York: Oxford University Press, 1987), 210–12; Richards, *The Slave Power*, 187.

44. Summers, *The Plundering Generation*, 212.

45. Sidney Webster to John H. George, June 5, 1854, John H. George Papers, Library of Congress.

46. John S. Williams to Gideon Welles, March 20, 1854, Welles Papers.

47. *Congressional Globe,* 33rd Congress, 1st session, 1128–32.

48. Davis, *Breckinridge,* 118.

49. *Congressional Globe,* 33rd Congress, 1st session, 1241–48.

50. Rudolph Von Abele, *Alexander H. Stephens* (New York: Alfred A. Knopf, 1946), 145.

51. *Congressional Globe,* 33rd Congress, 1st session, 1254.

52. Albert J. Von Frank, *The Trials of Anthony Burns: Freedom and Slavery in Emerson's Boston* (Cambridge: Harvard University Press, 1998), xviii.

53. *National Intelligencer*, May 29, 1854.

54. Ibid.

55. Ibid.

56. Caleb Cushing, "Extradition of Fugitives from Service," in C. C. Andrews, ed.

Official Opinions of the Attorneys General of the United States: Advising the Presidents and Heads of Departments in Relation to Their Official Duties (Washington, Robert Farnham, 1856), 6: 466–74; John M. Belohlavek, *Broken Glass: Caleb Cushing and the Shattering of the Union* (Kent, Ohio: Kent State University Press, 2005), 273–74.

57. Jefferson Davis to Samuel Cooper, May 31, 1854, in Jefferson Davis, *Jefferson Davis Constitutionalist: His Letters, Papers, and Speeches,* ed. Dunbar Rowland, (New York: J. J. Little and Ives, 1923), 2: 360–61.

58. Von Frank, *The Trials of Anthony Burns,* 203.

59. Ibid., 206.

60. Ibid., 213.

61. *Richmond Enquirer,* June 2, 1854.

62. Stanley W. Campbell, *The Slave Catchers: Enforcement of the Fugitive Slave Law, 1850–1860* (Chapel Hill: University of North Carolina Press, 1968), 131.

63. Horace Mann to Theodore Parker, June 5, 1854, in Mary Mann, *Life of Horace Mann* (Boston: Walker, Fuller, 1865), 461.

64. Campbell, *The Slave Catchers,* 103–107.

65. Ibid., 130; B. F. Hallett to Caleb Cushing, 1854, Cushing Papers. Hallett complained to Cushing about the delay that occurred before the government paid those involved in enforcing the law in the Burns case: "The money has got to be paid, the accounts are fairly adjusted and legally vouched, and the credit of its payment as an honorable and popular act the President & Cabinet depends much on its promptness. Do judge it."

66. Campbell, *The Slave Catchers,* 137, 171–75; Belohlavek, *Broken Glass,* 274, 291.

67. James Buchanan to William L. Marcy, May, 1854, Marcy Papers.

68. Laurence Oliphant, *Episodes in a Life of Adventure* (London: William Blackwood and Sons 1887), 49.

69. Ibid., 54–55.

70. Ibid., 48.

71. *Journal of the Executive Proceedings of the Senate,* 33rd Congress, 1st session, vol. 9, 376.

72. Frederick E. Haynes, "The Reciprocity Treaty with Canada of 1854," *Publications of American Economic Association* 7, no. 6, 17–18, quoted in Charles C. Tansill, *The Canadian Reciprocity Treaty of 1854* (Baltimore: Johns Hopkins University, 1922), 73–74.

73. Draft of a letter from Henry E. Parker to Franklin Pierce, October 16, 1854, in "The Letters of Henry Elijah Parker," courtesy of Lawrence Brown of Albany, Georgia, available online at www.freepages.genealogy.rootsweb.com/henryeparker/.

74. Israel D. Andrews to William L. Marcy, May, 1854, Pierce Papers; also in Despatches of the Special Agents, RG59, M37, vol. 16.

75. Ibid.

76. Ibid.

77. Ibid.

78. William L. Marcy to Israel D. Andrews, June 9, 1854, and William L. Marcy to

R. M. T. Hunter, July 20, 1854; both in Despatches of the Special Agents, RG59, M37, vol. 16.

79. Nevins, *Ordeal of the Union, A House Dividing,* 377; Spencer, *The Victor and the Spoils*, 308.

80. Richardson, *A Compilation of the Messages*, 5: 325–26, 389–90.

81. H. C. Allen, *Great Britain and the United States: A History of Anglo-American Relations, 1783–1952* (New York: St. Martin's Press, 1955), 450.

82. Tansill, *The Canadian Reciprocity Treaty of 1854*, 81.

83. William L. Marcy to Israel D. Andrews, September 16, 1854, Despatches of the Special Agents, RG59, M37, vol. 16.

84. Franklin Pierce to Israel D. Andrews, December 4, 1854, Despatches of the Special Agents, RG59, M37, vol. 16.

85. "Senate proceedings of June 1, 1858 in relation to the adjustment of the accounts of I. D. Andrews," in Despatches of the Special, RG59, M37, vol. 17.

86. Ibid.

87. Enoch Train, Sam Lawrence, and others to Franklin Pierce, March 31, 1856, Pierce Papers. The committee appointed by the Boston Board of Trade reported to Pierce that Andrews "has been taken to jail on one suit, and held to bail on several others for these debts" from his expenses relating to the treaty. They wrote to Pierce, asking for his support to get Congress to appropriate money to compensate Andrews. Calling the treaty, "one of the most valuable to the Commercial and industrial interests of the county ever made by the Government," the committee offered "to contribute its quota towards relieving him [Andrews] temporarily from his present embarrassment." Spencer, *The Victor and the Spoils*, 308.

88. There are eleven items, most of them receipts, from or to Andrews between September 1853 and November 1854 in the Pierce Papers.

89. Sophia Hawthorne to her father, April 14, 1854, in Rose Hawthorne Lathrop, *Memories of Hawthorne* (Boston: Houghton, Mifflin, 1897), 271.

90. Draft of a letter from Henry E. Parker to Franklin Pierce, June 15, 1854, in "Letters of Henry E. Parker."

91. John A. Dix, *Memoirs of John Adams Dix* (New York: Harper and Brothers, 1883), 1: 285.

92. Draft of a letter from Henry E. Parker to Franklin Pierce, October 16, 1854, in "Letters of Henry E. Parker."

93. Paul R. George to Caleb Cushing, July 22, 1854, Cushing Papers.

Chapter 6: *Cuba*

1. Basil Rauch, *American Interest in Cuba, 1848–1855* (New York: Columbia University Press, 1948), 24.

2. Allan Nevins, *Ordeal of the Union*, vol. 2, *A House Dividing, 1852–1857* (New York: Charles Scribner's Sons, 1947), 347; Sidney Webster, "Mr. Marcy, the Cuban Question and the Ostend Manifesto," *Political Science Quarterly* 8 (March 1897): 1.

3. Rauch, *American Interest in Cuba*, 24.

4. Rauch, *American Interest in Cuba*, 25, 35, 181; Edward S. Wallace, *Destiny and Glory* (New York: Coward-McCann, 1957), 54.

5. Rauch, *American Interest in Cuba*, 76; Wallace, *Destiny and Glory*, 56–57.

6. Rauch, *American Interest in Cuba*, 100–161; Wallace, *Destiny and Glory*, 61–98; Robert E. May, *John A. Quitman: Old South Crusader* (Baton Rouge: Louisiana State University, 1985), 275.

7. Samuel Flagg Bemis, *A Diplomatic History of the United States* (New York: Holt, Rinehart and Winston, 1955), 318.

8. *Congressional Globe*, 33rd Congress, 2nd session, 97–99, 109–10, 123–45, 300, appendix 100–02; Rauch, *American Interest in Cuba*, 242–52.

9. Wallace, *Destiny and Glory*, 130.

10. William L. Marcy to Pierre Soulé, July 23, 1853, Marcy Papers Library of Congress (herafter cited as Marcy Papers); see also, William R. Manning, ed., *Diplomatic Correspondence of the United States, Inter-American Affairs, 1831–1860*, vol. XI—Spain (Washington, D.C.: Carnegie Endowment for International Peace, 1939), 11: 160–166.

11. Rauch, *American Interest in Cuba*, 262–69; May, *John A. Quitman*, 275.

12. *New York Herald*, August 6, 1853; *National Intelligencer*, August 9, 1853.

13. Rauch, *American Interest in Cuba*, 265.

14. James Buchanan to William L. Marcy, November 1, 1853, in James Buchanan, *The Works of James Buchanan*, ed. John Bassett Moore (Philadelphia: J. B. Lippincott, 1909), 9: 84–85; May, *John A. Quitman*, 275–81; Rauch, *American Interest in Cuba*, 273–275.

15. Webster, "Mr. Marcy, the Cuban Question and the Ostend Manifesto," 14–15.

16. Rauch, *American Interest in Cuba*, 275.

17. Ibid., 279; Henry Lorenzo Jones, "The Black Warrior Affair," *American Historical Review* 12 (January 1907): 281–88.

18. *Congressional Globe*, 33rd Congress, 1st session, 601; James A. Richardson, ed., *A Compilation of the Messages and Papers of the Presidents* (Washington, D.C.: Government Printing Office, 1897), 235–236.

19. William L. Marcy to Pierre Soulé, March 17, 1854, Marcy Papers.

20. Rauch, *American Interest in Cuba*, 279; Jones, "The Black Warrior Affair," 288.

21. Alexander M. Clayton to Jefferson Davis, December 17, 1853, in Jefferson Davis, *Jefferson Davis, Constitutionalist: His Letters, Papers, and Speeches*, ed. Dunbar Rowland (New York: J. J. Little and Ives, 1923), 2: 333–34.

22. Rauch, *American Interest in Cuba*, 278.

23. William L. Marcy to Pierre Soulé, April 3, 1854, Marcy Papers.

24. *Congressional Globe*, 33rd Congress, 1st session, 1021–1025.

25. John Slidell to James Buchanan, January 14, 1854, quoted in Louis Martin Sears, *John Slidell* (Durham, N.C.: Duke University Press, 1925), 107.

26. May, *John A. Quitman*, 283–84; Rauch, *American Interest in Cuba*, 286–87.

27. Richardson, *A Compilation of the Messages*, 5: 272–73.

28. Rauch, *American Interest in Cuba,* 287.

29. Ivor Debenham Spencer, *The Victor and the Spoils: A Life of William L. Marcy* (Providence, R.I.: Brown University Press, 1959), 323.

30. May, *John A. Quitman,* 285–86; Rauch, *American Interest in Cuba,* 287.

31. William O. Scroggs, *Filibusters and Financiers: The Story of William Walker and His Associates* (New York: MacMillan, 1916, reprinted by Russell and Russell, 1916, 74–75; Nevins, *Ordeal of the Union: A House Dividing,* 2: 364–66.

32. James C. Dobbin, "Orders to Visit Greytown," June 10, 1854, in K. Jack Bauer, ed., *The New American State Papers, Naval Affairs, 1789–1860,* vol. 2, *Diplomatic Activities* (Wilmington, Del.: Scholarly Resources, 1981), 227.

33. George N. Hollins, "Report of Bombardment of Greytown," July 26, 1854 in Bauer, *The New American State Papers, Diplomatic Activities,* 231–33.

34. Ibid.

35. William L. Marcy to James Buchanan, August 8, 1854, Marcy Papers; also found in Buchanan, *The Works of James Buchanan,* 9: 243–44.

36. Nevins, *Ordeal of the Union: A House Dividing,* 367.

37. James Buchanan to William L. Marcy, August 18, 1854, and August 25, 1854, in Buchanan, *The Works of James Buchanan,* 9: 244–48, 249–50.

38. Spencer, *The Victor and the Spoils,* 316–17; H. C. Allen, *Great Britain and the United States: A History of Anglo-American Relations, 1783–1952* (New York: St. Martin's Press, 1955), 435–36.

39. W. J. Staples to William L. Marcy, November 26, 1852; James Buchanan to William L. Marcy, March 8, 1853; both in Marcy Papers; Irving Katz, *August Belmont: A Political Biography* (New York: Columbia University Press, 1968), 24.

40. James Buchanan to John Slidell, May 23, 1854, in Buchanan, *The Works of James Buchanan,* 9: 200–02.

41. Ibid.

42. William L. Marcy to Pierre Soulé, March 17, 1854, in Manning, *Diplomatic Correspondence,* 11: 174–75; Amos A. Ettinger, *The Mission to Spain of Pierre Soulé, 1853–1855: A Study in the Cuban Diplomacy of the United States* (New Haven, Conn.: Yale University Press, 1932), 227–33.

43. Ettinger, *The Mission to Spain of Pierre Soulé,* 260–61; H. Barrett Learned, "William Learned Marcy," in Samuel Flagg Bemis, ed., *The American Secretaries of State and Their Diplomacy,* (New York: Pageant Book Company, 1958), 6: 196–97.

44. William L. Marcy to Pierre Soulé, June 22, 1854, Marcy Papers; see also Manning, *Diplomatic Correspondence,* 11: 180, 189; Ettinger, *The Mission to Spain of Pierre Soulé,* 269, 276–77.

45. Note in Franklin Pierce's handwriting in Marcy Papers, n.d.; William L. Marcy to Pierre Soulé, June 22, 1854, in Manning, *Diplomatic Correspondence,* 11: 189.

46. Pierre Soulé to William L. Marcy, July 15, 1854, Department of State, Diplomatic Despatches: Spain, vol. 39, National Archives; Learned, "William Learned Marcy," 6: 200; Spencer, *The Victor and the Spoils,* 324; Ettinger, *The Mission to Spain of Pierre Soulé,* 293–95.

47. Pierre Soulé to William L. Marcy, August 18, 1854; Horatio Perry to William L. Marcy, September 6, 1854; John Y. Mason to Marcy, September 25, 1854; all in Marcy Papers; Learned, "William Learned Marcy," 6: 200; Ettinger, *The Mission to Spain of Pierre Soulé*, 304–06; Katz, *August Belmont*, 42.

48. William L. Marcy to Pierre Soulé, June 24, 1854, in Manning, *Diplomatic Correspondence*, 11, 190–91; see also Spencer, *The Victor and the Spoils*, 323; Ettinger, *The Mission to Spain of Pierre Soulé*, 279–81; Philip Shriver Klein, *President James Buchanan: A Biography* (University Park: Pennsylvania State University Press, 1962), 236.

49. John Y. Mason to William L. Marcy, July 23, 1854, Marcy Papers; James Buchanan to William L. Marcy, July 11, 1854, in Buchanan, *The Works of James Buchanan*, 9: 212; Ettinger, *The Mission to Spain of Pierre Soulé*, 279–81.

50. Franklin Pierce, "Message to the Senate and House," July 31,1854, original copy in Pierce Papers, Library of Congress.

51. *Congressional Globe*, 33rd Congress, 1st session, 2040, 2178.

52. Ibid., 1145–46, 1152–65. Senator Judah P. Benjamin of Louisiana suggested dividing the bill into "distinct improvements" so that Pierce could "examine into the expediency and constitutionality of each improvement as presented." To Benjamin the fact that the president was "called upon to approve or disapprove the whole of them *en masse*" was unfair. Benjamin commented that the president might approve nine-tenths of the projects but would have to veto the entire bill because Congress "[deprived] the President of an opportunity of exercising his fair executive discretion upon the subject." *Congressional Globe*, 33rd Congress, 1st session, July 28 and 29, 1854, 1152, 1164.

53. Richardson, *A Compilation of Messages*, 5: 256–57.

54. Richardson, a close associate of Douglas, attacked Pierce in a speech on August 5: "I do not care what the President may think upon this, or that, or any other subject. The policy of the Government which allows appropriations to the seaboard, and claims them to be constitutional, and yet denies them to the interior, is wrong and unjust, and I condemn it." *Congressional Globe*, 33rd Congress, 1st session, 2223.

55. *Congressional Globe*, 33rd Congress, 1st session, 1654.

56. *Congressional Globe*, 33rd Congress, 1st session, 2222.

57. *Baltimore Sun*, August 7, 1854; *New Hampshire State Capital Reporter and Old Guard*, August 12, 1854.

58. William L. Marcy to James Buchanan, August 8, 1854 in Buchanan, *The Works of James Buchanan*, 9: 243–44.

59. Thomas Keneally, *American Scoundrel: The Life of the Notorious Civil War General Dan Sickles* (New York: Doubleday, 2002), 41–42; Klein, *President James Buchanan*, 236–37; "Account of July 4, Dinner," an article from a copy of the *Boston Post*, in Marcy Papers.

60. Kenneally, *American Scoundrel*, 44; William L. Marcy to Pierre Soulé, August 16, 1854, Marcy Papers; see also Manning, *Diplomatic Correspondence*, 11: 193–94.

61. Franklin Pierce to James Buchanan, August 12, 1854, in Buchanan, *The Works of James Buchanan*, 9: 243.

62. James Buchanan to Franklin Pierce, September 1, 1854 in Buchanan, *The Works of James Buchanan*, 9: 251.

63. Ibid.

64, Webster, "Mr. Marcy, the Cuban Question, and the Ostend Manifesto," 22.

65. *Washington Union*, July 26, 1854.

66. Sidney Webster, Pierce's personal secretary, later claimed that the *Union* was never a reliable spokesman for the administration. Its editorial staff frequently took positions that caused the administration problems because of the impression that the views expressed in the paper reflected those of Pierce and his cabinet. Webster, "Mr. Marcy, the Cuban Question, and the Ostend Manifesto," 25.

67. Horatio J. Perry to William L. Marcy, September 6, 1854, Marcy Papers.

68. Horatio J. Perry to William L. Marcy, September 21, 1854, Marcy Papers; Ettinger, *The Mission to Spain of Pierre Soulé*, 283–84.

69. John Y. Mason to William L. Marcy, September 25, 1854, Marcy Papers.

70. A. Dudley Mann to William L. Marcy, August 24, August 31, September 4, 1854, Marcy Papers.

71. A. Dudley Mann to William L. Marcy, October 2, 1854, Marcy Papers.

72. John Y. Mason to William L. Marcy, September 25, 1854, Marcy Papers.

73. Ibid.; Spencer, *The Victor and the Spoils*, 328; Nevins, *Ordeal of the Union, A House Dividing*, 319; Ettinger, *The Mission to Spain of Pierre Soulé*, 349.

74. John Y. Mason to William L. Marcy, September 25, 1854, Marcy Papers.

75. James Buchanan to William L. Marcy, October 3, 1854, Marcy Papers.

76. Ibid.

77. George N. Sanders, "To the People of France," October 4,1854, copy in Marcy Papers.

78. William L. Marcy to John Y. Mason, September 20, 1854, and October 13, 1854, Marcy Papers; Ettinger, *The Mission to Spain of Pierre Soulé*, 324–28.

79. William L. Marcy to John Y. Mason, September 30, 1854, Marcy Papers.

80. William L. Marcy to John Y. Mason, October 13, 1854, Marcy Papers.

81. William L. Marcy to A. Dudley Mann, October 18, 1854, Marcy Papers.

82. William L. Marcy to James Buchanan, October 19, 1854, Marcy Papers.

83. Klein, *President James Buchanan*, 239; Katz, *August Belmont*, 43–44.

84. Learned, "William Learned Marcy," 6: 204–205.

85. "The Ostend Report," Buchanan, *The Works of James Buchanan*, 9: 260–66; also printed in *House Executive Documents*, 33rd Congress, 2nd session, 127–32.

86. "The Ostend Report," in Buchanan, *The Works of James Buchanan*, 9: 264.

87. Ibid., 265.

88. Ibid.

89. Ibid., 266.

90. Ibid.; Katz, *August Belmont*, 43.

91. James Buchanan to William L. Marcy, December 8, 1854, Marcy Papers.

92. Learned, "William Learned Marcy," 6: 205–06.

93. James Buchanan to William L. Marcy, October 25, 1854, Marcy Papers.

94. John Y. Mason to William L. Marcy, November 9, 1854, Marcy Papers; Learned, "William Learned Marcy," 6: 207.

95. William L. Marcy to Pierre Soulé, November 13, 1854, Marcy Papers; see also Manning, *Diplomatic Correspondence*, 11: 196–97.

96. William L. Marcy to Pierre Soulé, November 13, 1854, Marcy Papers.

97. Ibid.

98. Ibid.

99. Learned, "William L. Marcy," 6: 211.

100. Jefferson Davis to Thomas J. Hudson, November 25, 1855, in Jefferson Davis, *The Papers of Jefferson Davis*, ed. Linda Lasswell Crist, (Baton Rouge: Louisiana State University Press, 1985), 5: 138. Davis made this claim on more than one occasion, including a speech in Vicksburg on June 6, 1855; see "Speech at Vicksburg," ibid., 108–10.

101. Pierre Soulé to William L. Marcy, December 17, 1854, Marcy Papers.

102. William L. Marcy to James Buchanan, December 11, 1854, and James Buchanan to William L. Marcy, December 22, 1854, Marcy Papers; William L. Marcy to J. Addison Thomas, December 2, 1854, Marcy Papers; see also Ettinger, *The Mission to Spain of Pierre Soulé*, 330–33. For Buchanan's explanation of the Frondé and Sanders matter, see James Buchanan to John L. O'Sullivan, December 5, 1855, and James Buchanan to John Y. Mason, December 18, 1855, Buchanan Papers, Historical Society of Pennsylvania, Philadelphia.

103. *New York Herald*, November 18, 1854.

Chapter 7: *Rejection at the Polls*

1. Michael F. Holt, *The Rise and Fall of the American Whig Party* (New York: Oxford University Press, 1999), 838.

2. Ibid., 837–908; William E. Gienapp, *The Origins of the Republican Party, 1852–1856* (New York: Oxford University Press, 1987), 98–162; Tyler Anbinder, *Nativism and Slavery: The Northern Know Nothings and the Politics of the 1850s* (New York: Oxford University Press, 1992), 53–87.

3. Ray Allen Billington, *The Protestant Crusade, 1800–1860* (Chicago: Quadrangle Books, 1964), 380–87; Humphrey Desmond, *The Know Nothing Party* (Washington, D.C.: New Century Press, 1904), 7, 52–53; Anbinder, *Nativism and Slavery*, 4, 21.

4. Billington, *The Protestant Crusade*, 300–302; Desmond, *The Know Nothing Party*, 71–73; Anbinder, *Nativism and Slavery*, 27–30.

5. Billington, *The Protestant Crusade*, 314.

6. Ibid., 384.

7. George Templeton Strong, *The Diary of George Templeton Strong*, ed. Allan Nevins and Milton Halsey Thomas (New York: MacMillan, 1952), 2: 176.

8. Allan Nevins, *Ordeal of the Union*, vol. 2, *A House Dividing, 1852–1857* (New York: Charles Scribner's Sons, 1947), 332; Desmond, *The Know Nothing Party*, 75; *New Hampshire State Capital Reporter*, July 8, 1854; Peter Haebler, "Nativist Riots in

Manchester: An Episode of Know-Nothingism in New Hampshire," *Historical New Hampshire* 39, nos. 3 and 4 (Fall/Winter, 1984), 122–138.

9. James Campbell to James Buchanan, June 15, 1854, quoted in Dorothy G. Fowler, *The Cabinet Politician: The Postmasters General, 1829–1909* (New York: Columbia University Press, 1943), 82.

10. William J. Cooper Jr., *Jefferson Davis, American* (New York: Alfred A. Knopf, 2000), 261–62; Varina Davis, *Jefferson Davis, Ex-President of the Confederate States of America: A Memoir by His Wife* (New York: Belford Company Publishers, 1890), 1: 534–35.

11. Varina Davis, *Jefferson Davis*, 1:, 536; Jane Pierce to Mrs. A. S. Packard, September 1854, Pierce Papers, Bowdoin College Library.

12. Wilhelmus Bogart Bryan, *A History of the National Capital* (New York: MacMillan, 1916), 2: 276; Betty Boyd Caroli, *Inside the White House* (New York: Canopy Press, 1992), 180.

13. Hudson Strode, *Jefferson Davis: American Patriot, 1808–1861* (New York: Harcourt, Brace, 1955), 1: 270.

14. James A. Hamilton to Franklin Pierce, November 9, 1854, Pierce Papers, New Hampshire Historical Society, Concord.

15. Robert W. Johannsen, *Stephen A. Douglas* (New York: Oxford University Press, 1973), 446.

16. Ibid., 451.

17. Ibid., 453–54; Granville D. Davis, "Douglas and the Chicago Mob," *American Historical Review* 54 (April 1949): 553–56; *New York Herald*, September 5, 1854.

18. Johannsen, *Stephen A. Douglas*, 454; *New York Herald*, September 5, 6, 1854; *New York Tribune*, September 5, 1854; *National Intelligencer*, September 13, 1854.

19. Stephen A. Douglas to John C. Breckinridge, September 14,1854, Breckinridge Papers, Library of Congress.

20. Franklin Pierce to Stephen A. Douglas, September 25, 1854, Pierce Papers, Bowdoin College Library.

21. Ibid.

22. Holt, *Rise and Fall of the American Whig Party*, 880–84; Gienapp, *The Origins of the Republican Party*, 139–45; Anbinder, *Nativism and Slavery*, 60–61.

23. William L. Marcy to Franklin Pierce, July 9, 1854, Marcy Papers, Library Congress (hereafter cited as Marcy Papers).

24. "Tammany Hall Resolution of July 11, 1854," copy in Marcy Papers.

25. William L. Marcy to Franklin Pierce, July 9, 1854, Marcy Papers.

26. William L. Marcy to Horatio Seymour, July 12, 1854, Marcy Papers.

27. Ibid.

28. Horatio Seymour to William L. Marcy, September 9, 1854, Marcy Papers.

29. Horatio Seymour to Marcy, September 18, 1854, Marcy Papers.

30. Holt, *The Rise and Fall of the American Whig Party*, 899.

31. Daniel Dickinson to Edmund Burke, March 25, 1854, Burke Papers, Library of Congress.

32. *New Hampshire State Capital Reporter and Old Guard,* September 29, 1854.

33. Strong, *Diary of George Templeton Strong,* 2: 183.

34. Holt, *The American Whig Party,* 893–907; Gienapp, *The Origins of the Republican Party,* 148–158.

35. Horatio Seymour to William L. Marcy, February 28, 1855, Marcy Papers.

36. Holt, *The Rise and Fall of the American Whig Party,* 906.

37. Ibid., 886.

38. Gienapp, *The Origins of the Republican Party,* 134–37; Billington, *The Protestant Crusade,* 388.

39. Gienapp, *The Origins of the Republican Party,* 161.

40. *New Hampshire State Capital Reporter and Old Guard,* October 13, November 3, 1854.

41. Howell Cobb to James Buchanan, December 5, 1854, in Ulrich B. Phillips, ed., "The Correspondence of Robert Toombs, Alexander H. Stephens, and Howell Cobb," *Annual Report of the American Historical Association* 2 (1911): 348–49.

42. "Second Annual Message," December 4, 1854, in James A. Richardson, ed., *A Compilation of the Messages and Papers of the Presidents,* (Washington, D.C.: Government Printing Office, 1897), 5: 273, 275–77, 280–84.

43. Ibid., 284–85.

44. Ibid., 285–86.

45. Ibid., 286–87.

46. Ibid.

47. "Report of the Secretary of War," and "Report of the Secretary of the Navy," *Congressional Globe,* 33rd Congress, 2nd session, appendix, 13–19, 19–24.

48. Richardson, *A Compilation of the Messages,* 5: 292–93.

49. "To the Senate and House of Representatives," December 30, 1854 in Richardson, *A Compilation of the Messages,* 5: 257–71.

50. "Report of the Secretary of the Treasury," *Congressional Globe,* 33rd Congress, 2nd session, appendix, 6–10; *Senate Executive Documents,* 33rd Congress, 2nd session, August 29, 1854, vol. 2, 399–404 (hereafter cited as "Report of the Secretary of the Treasury"); *Senate Executive Documents,* 33rd Congress, 2nd session, appendix, 2, November 27, 1854, vol. 2, 256.

51. "Report of the Secretary of the Treasury," appendix, 8, 10.

52. "Report of the Secretary of the Interior," *Congressional Globe,* 33rd Congress, 2nd session, appendix, 11.

53. "Report of the Postmaster General," *Congressional Globe,* 33rd Congress, 2nd session, appendix 26–27.

54. Benjamin Brown French, *Witness to the Young Republic: A Yankee's Journal, 1828–1870,* ed. Donald B. Cole and John J. McDonough (Hanover, N.H.: University Press of New England, 1989), 255.

55. Virginia Clopton-Clay, *A Belle of the Fifties: Memoirs of Mrs. Clay of Alabama* (New York: Doubleday, Page, 1905), 27.

56. Abigail Means to Mrs. Mary Aiken, December 26, 1854, Pierce-Aiken Papers, Library of Congress (hereafter cited as Pierce-Aiken Papers).

57. French, *Witness to the Young Repubic*, 255.

58. Abigail Means to Mrs. Mary Aiken, December 26, 1854, Pierce-Aiken Papers.

59. M. Kimball to his father, January 8, 1855, Pierce Papers, New Hampshire Historical Society, Concord.

60. Ibid.

61. Jane Pierce to Mrs. Swan, January, 1855, Pierce Papers, Bowdoin College Library.

62. Samuel Eliot Morison, *"Old Bruin": Commodore Matthew Calbraith Perry* (Boston: Little, Brown, 1967), 412–24; Arthur C. Walworth, *Black Ships off Japan: The Story of Commodore Perry's Expedition* (Hamden, Conn.: Archon Books, 1966), 230–32.

63. French, *Witness to the Young Republic*, 253–54; a list of the gifts sent by Japan to the United States is published in Walworth, *Black Ships off Japan*, appendix L, 263–65.

64. Varina Davis, *Jefferson Davis*, 1: 541–44.

65. Franklin Pierce, personal checks written on the Riggs Bank of Washington, D.C., 1854–1855, in Pierce Papers, New Hampshire Historical Society, Concord.

66. Anne Atherton to Franklin Pierce, February 20, 1855, Pierce Papers, New Hampshire Historical Society, Concord.

67. City of Boston, *Marriages Registered in the City of Boston, 1867*, lists Flora Atherton born in Washington, D.C., age eighteen, father Charles G., mother Eliza, marrying Arthur F. Lincoln from Maine, on March 25, 1867. Records provided by Barry A. Billings of Nashua, New Hampshire, a direct descendant of Flora Atherton.

68. Anne Atherton to Franklin Pierce, February 19, 1855, Pierce Papers, New Hampshire Historical Society, Concord.

69. Cooper, *Jefferson Davis, American*, 251.

70. *Congressional Globe*, 33rd Congress, 2nd session, 714–15.

71. Ibid., 708.

72. Leonard D. White, *The Jacksonians: A Study in Administrative History, 1829–1861* (New York: MacMillan, 1954), 239–240; *Senate Executive Documents* 2, 34th Congress, 1st session, vol. 2, Part III, 10–13, 30–44.

73. White, *The Jacksonians*, 239.

74. Alfred T. Mahan, *From Sail to Steam: Recollections of Naval Life* (New York: Harper and Brothers, 1907), 23.

75. *Congressional Globe*, 33rd Congress, 2nd session, 105–14, 908.

76. White, *The Jacksonians*, 160.

77. Ibid., 157–61; Mark W. Summers, *The Plundering Generation: Corruption and the Crisis of the Union, 1849–1861* (New York: Oxford University Press, 1987), 161–62.

78. *Congressional Globe*, 33rd Congress, 2nd session, 246–47, 656, 916, 919.

79. Robert G. Scott, Consul at Rio de Janeiro, to William L. Marcy, April 18, 1855; D.A. Ogden, Consul at Honolulu, to William L. Marcy, April 20, 1855; John Y. Mason

to William L. Marcy, May 16, 1855; John L. O'Sullivan to Marcy, July 28, 1855; all in Marcy Papers.

80. William L. Marcy to John Y. Mason, June 3, 1855, Marcy Papers.

81. Nathaniel Hawthorne to Franklin Pierce, June 7, 1855, National Archives.

82. Caleb Cushing to William L. Marcy, "Ambassadors and Other Public Ministers of the United States," May 25, 1855, in C. C. Andrews, ed., *Official Opinions of the Attorneys General of the United States: Advising the Presidents and Heads of Departments in Relation to Their Official Duties* (Washington, D.C.: Robert Farnham, 1856), 7: 186–229.

83. Caleb Cushing to William L. Marcy, "Appointment of Consuls," June 1855, in Andrews, *Official Opinions*, 242–77.

84. Nathaniel Hawthorne to Franklin Pierce, June 7, 1855, National Archives.

85. Ibid.

86. *Congressional Globe,* 33rd Congress, 2nd session, 69, 94, 147–48.

87. Ibid., 191–92, 229, 294, 308.

88. Ibid., 212.

89. Caleb Cushing to Sen. Stephen Adams, "A Bill for the further Regulation of the Executive Department," January 1855, in Letters Sent by the Attorney General, RG60, T969, Roll 1, National Archives (hereafter cited as Letters Sent by the Attorney General).

90. *Ring v. Maxwell*, 58 U.S. 147 (1854), *U.S. Supreme Court Cases and Opinions,* vol. 58, http://supreme.justia.com/us/58/147/case.html; Caleb Cushing to James Guthrie, December 14, 1854, in Letters Sent by the Attorney General.

91. *Congressional Globe,* 33rd Congress, 2nd session, 583, 588, 796; "Veto Messages," February 17, 1855, in Richardson, *A Compilation of the Messages*, 5: 310, 322.

92. *Congressional Globe,* 33rd Congress, 2nd session, 816.

93. Henry Cohen, *Business and Politics in America from the Age of Jackson to the Civil War: The Career Biography of W. W. Corcoran* (Westport, Conn.: Greenwood Publishing, 1971), 110–12.

94. *Congressional Globe,* 33rd Congress, 2nd session, 797, 920; "Veto Messages," March 3, 1855, in Richardson, *A Compilation of the Messages*, 5: 322–29.

95. *Congressional Globe,* 33rd Congress, 2nd session, 1156–57.

96. Benjamin B. French to Henry F. French, March 25, 1855, French Papers, New Hampshire Historical Society, Concord (hereafter cited as French Papers).

97. *Congressional Globe,* 33rd Congress, 2nd session, 692.

98. William L. Marcy to John Van Buren, March 25, 1855; and A. O. P. Nicholson, *Washington Union*, to Marcy, March 23, 1855; both in Marcy Papers.

99. B. B. French to H. F. French, March 25, 1855, French Papers.

100. William L. Marcy to Horatio Perry, May 26, 1855; William L. Marcy to Horatio Perry, June 1855; William L. Marcy to Augustus C. Dodge, July 16, 1855; Horatio Perry to Marcy "and the press," July 12, 1855; Horatio Perry to William L. Marcy, August 21, 1855; all in Marcy Papers; Amos A. Ettinger, *The Mission to Spain of Pierre Soulé, 1853–1855: A Study in the Cuban Diplomacy of the United States* (New Haven, Conn.: Yale University Press, 1932), 467–71; *New York Herald*, May 23, 1855.

101. William L. Marcy to Augustus C. Dodge, July 16, 1855, Marcy Papers; William C. Davis, *Breckinridge: Statesman, Soldier, Symbol* (Baton Rouge: Louisiana State University Press, 1974), 126–28.

102. *New York Herald,* July 2, 1855; Pierre Soulé to James Buchanan, June 26, 1855, Buchanan Papers, Historical Society of Pennsylvania, Philadelphia.

103. *Congressional Globe,* 33rd Congress, 2nd session, 217.

104. William H. Goetzmann, *Army Exploration in the American West,1803–1863* (New Haven, Conn.: Yale University Press, 1959), 312, 336.

105. Franklin Pierce to John H. George, January 22, 1855, Pierce Papers, New Hampshire Historical Society, Concord.

106. Franklin Pierce to William L. Marcy, February, 1855, Marcy Papers.

107. William L. Marcy to Horatio Seymour, February 25, 1855, Marcy Papers.

108. Lex Renda, *Running on the Record: Civil War-Era Politics in New Hampshire* (Charlottesville, Va.: University Press of Virginia, 1997), 51; Thomas R. Bright, "The Anti-Nebraska Coalition and the Emergence of the Republican Party in New Hampshire, 1853–1857," *Historical New Hampshire* 27, no. 2 (Summer 1972): 75.

109. Renda, *Running on the Record,* 54; John H. George to Albert R. Hatch, March 8, 1855, Hatch Papers, New Hampshire Historical Society, Concord; Richard H. Sewell, *John P. Hale and the Politics of Abolition* (Cambridge,Mass.: Harvard University Press, 1965), 158.

110. Sidney Webster to John H. George, March 8, 1855, George Papers, New Hampshire Historical Society, Concord.

111. Ibid.

112. Franklin Pierce to John H. George, March 7, 1855, Pierce Papers, New Hampshire Historical Society, Concord.

113. Renda, *Running on the Record,* 54; Bright, "The Anti-Nebraska Coalition" 76.

114. Charles W. March to Caleb Cushing, March 18, 1855, Cushing Papers, Library of Congress.

115. Letter in Pierce's handwriting, James Campbell to Arthur S. Nevitt, New Orleans postmaster, March 1, 1856, Pierce Papers, New Hampshire Historical Society, Concord.

116. French recounted the story of his Know-Nothing connection and his resignation from office in great detail in his journal, French, *Witness to the Young Republic,* 254–65. The conversation with Pierce is on pages 258–259.

117. French, *Witness to the Young Republic,* 265.

Chapter 8: *Trouble in the Territories*

1. William L. Marcy to James Buchanan, May 28, 1855 in James Buchanan,, *The Works of James Buchanan,* ed. John Bassett Moore (Philadelphia: J. B. Lippincott, 1909), 9: 354–55.

2. James Buchanan to William L. Marcy, June 8, 1855, William L. Marcy Papers, Library of Congress (hereafter cited as Marcy Papers).

3. Michael F. Holt, *The Rise and Fall of the American Whig Party* (New York: Oxford University Press, 1999); 940–41.

4. Robert Kent Fielding, *The Unsolicited Chronicler: An Account of the Gunnison Massacre: Its Causes and Consequences* (Brookline, Mass.: Paradigm Publications, 1993), 4.

5. "Proclamation by the Governor, May 21, 1853," State Department, Territorial Papers of Utah, RG59, M12, Roll 1, National Archives.

6. Captain J. W. Gunnison to George W. Manypenny, May 21, 1853, Letters Received by the Office of Indian Affairs, RG75, M234, Roll 897, National Archives.

7. Fielding, *The Unsolicited Chronicler,* 121, 150–52, 157–59.

8. Jefferson Davis to Brigham Young, June 28, 1853, in Jefferson Davis, *Jefferson Davis Constitutionalist: His Letters, Papers, and Speeches,* ed. Dunbar Rowland (New York: J. J. Little and Ives, 1923), 2: 365–66.

9. Brigham Young, "An Account of the Massacre of Captain J. W. Gunnison and Some of His Party, . . ." November 30, 1853, Letters Received by the Office of Indian Affairs, RG75, M234, Roll 897, National Archives.

10. Fielding, *The Unsolicited Chronicler*, 210.

11. Ibid., 217–18; Gen. Samuel Cooper to Col. E. J. Steptoe, May 10, 1854, Letters Sent by the Office of the Adjutant General, RG94, M565, National Archives.

12. John F. Kinney to Franklin Pierce, October 1, 1854, in Fielding, *The Unsolicited Chronicler*, 242; Hubert Howe Bancroft, *History of Utah* (San Francisco: History Company Publishers, 1891), 492–93.

13. John F. Kinney to Franklin Pierce, October 1, 1854 in Fielding, *The Unsolicited Chronicler*, 242.

14. *Journal of the Executive Proceedings of the Senate*, 33rd Congress, 2nd session, vol. 9: 393.

15. *New York Herald*, January 31, 1855.

16. Fielding, *The Unsolicited Chronicler*, 240, 243.

17. Roy Nichols, *Franklin Pierce: Young Hickory of the Granite Hills*, rev. ed. (Philadelphia: University of Pennsylvania Press, revised 1969), 403.

18. Col. E. J. Steptoe to George W. Manypenny, April 5, 15, 1855, Letters Sent to the Office of Indian Affairs, RG75, M234, Roll 897, National Archives (hereafter cited as Letters Sent to the Office of Indian Affairs); Fielding, *The Unsolicited Chronicler*, 255–73; Bancroft, *History of Utah*, 493–94; *New York Herald*, May 18, 1855.

19. Col. E. J. Steptoe to George W. Manypenny, April 5, 15, 1855, Letters Received by the Office of Indian Affairs; *New York Herald*, May 18, 23,1855.

20. Col. E. J. Steptoe to Gen. Samuel Cooper, April 25, 1855, Letters Sent to the Adjutant General, RG94, M565, National Archives.

21. *New York Herald*, September 8, 1855.

22. *New York Herald*, September 8, 1855; Bancroft, *History of Utah*, 494.

23. Henry Cohen, *Business and Politics in America from the Age of Jackson to the Civil War: The Career Biography of W. W. Corcoran* (Westport, Conn.: Greenwood Publishing Company, 1971), 159–63; Robert W. Johannsen, *Stephen A. Douglas* (New

York: Oxford University Press, 1973), 435–36; William C. Davis, *Breckinridge: Statesman, Soldier, Symbol* (Baton Rouge: Louisiana State University Press, 1974), 97–98.

24. Return I. Holcombe, *Minnesota in Three Centuries,* vol. 2, *Minnesota as a Territory* (n. p. Publishing Society of Minnesota, 1908), 477; William Watts Folwell, *A History of Minnesota,* (Saint Paul: Minnesota Historical Society, 1921), 1: 329–330.

25. Davis, *Breckinridge,* 121.

26. "Alterations of the Text of House Bill no. 342," *U.S. House Reports,* 33rd Congress, 1st session, serial set 744, vol. 3, #352, 1–55; Cohen, *Business and Politics in America,* 182–86; Holcombe, *Minnesota in Three Centuries,* vol. 4, *Minnesota as a State* (n. p. Publishing Society of Minnesota, 1908), 340–41; Theodore C. Blegen, *Minnesota: A History of the State* (Minneapolis: University of Minnesota Press, 1963), 194–95; Samuel Trask Dana, John H. Allison, and Russell N. Cunningham, *Minnesota Lands: Ownership, Use and Management of Forest and Related Lands* (Washington, D.C.: American Forestry Association, 1960), 95–96.

27. Cohen, *Business and Politics* in America, 183–84; Holcombe, *Minnesota in Three Centuries, Minnesota as a State,* 340–41.

28. "Alterations of the Text of House Bill no. 342," 1–4, 18–20; Davis, *Breckinridge,* 122–23; *Congressional Globe,* 33rd Congress, 1st session, 2090; Cohen, *Business and Politics in America,* 187.

29. Cohen, *Business and Politics in* America, 187–89; Caleb Cushing to John E. Warren, December 30, 1854; Caleb Cushing to Franklin Pierce, January 1, 1855; both in Letters Sent by the Attorney General, RG60, T969, Roll 1, National Archives (hereafter cited as Letters Sent by the Attorney General); Holcombe, *Minnesota in Three Centuries, Minnesota as a State,* 341–42; Dana and others, *Minnesota Lands,* 95–96.

30. Cohen, *Business and Politics in America,* 190–91; Davis, *Breckinridge,* 130–31; Henry M. Rice to John C. Breckinridge, March 18, 20, 24, 26, 28; April 1, 12, 15, May 6, 1855; all in John C. Breckinridge Papers, Library of Congress (hereafter cited as Breckinridge Papers).

31. Cohen, *Business and Politics in America,* 190; James Guthrie to John C. Breckinridge, March 30–31, 1855, Breckinridge Papers, LC; George W. Manypenny to Willis Gorman, April 25, 1854, Letters Sent by the Office of Indian Affairs, RG75, M21, Roll 49, National Archives.

32. Henry M. Rice to John C. Breckinridge, April 12, 15 and May 6, 1855, Breckinridge Papers; Roy Nichols, *Franklin Pierce,* 406; Davis, *Breckinridge,* 130–31; Sidney Webster to John H. George, May 28, 1855, John H. George Papers, New Hampshire Historical Society, Concord. Webster's itinerary included Saint Louis, Chicago, Lakes Michigan and Superior, Saint Paul, Rock Island, and Detroit.

33. Holcombe, *Minnesota in Three Centuries, Minnesota as a Territory,* 472; Lester B. Shippee, "Willis A. Gorman," *Dictionary of American Biography,* (New York: Charles Scribner's Sons, 1931), 7: 435–36.

34. Henry M. Rice to John C. Breckinridge, May 6, 1855, Breckinridge Papers.

35. John W. Forney to John C. Breckinridge, April 17, 1855, Breckinridge Papers.

36. James A. Richardson, ed., *A Compilation of the Messages and Papers of the Presidents,* (Washington, D.C.: Government Printing Office, 1897), 5: 291.

37. "Treaty with the Oto and Missouri," March 15, 1854; "Treaty with Omaha," March 16, 1854; "Treaty with Delaware," May 6, 1854; "Treaty with the Shawnee," May 10, 1854; "Treaty with the Kickapoo," May 18, 1854; all in Charles J. Kappler, ed., *Indian Treaties, 1778–1883* (New York: Interland Publishing, 1972), 608–36.

38. Paul Wallace Gates, *Fifty Million Acres: Conflicts over Kansas Land Policy, 1854–1890* (Ithaca, N.Y.: Cornell University Press, 1954), 15–16.

39. Ibid., 16.

40. Ibid., 18–19.

41. Ibid., 39–40.

42. Ibid., 19.

43. Jefferson Davis to Rep. Zedekiah Kidwell, March 20, 1854 in Davis, *Jefferson Davis, Constitutionalist*, 2: 346–47.

44. W. Broadus Thompson to Caleb Cushing, January 11, 1855, Cushing Papers, Library of Congress (hereafter cited as Cushing Papers).

45. Ibid., Cushing added his answer as a note dated March 28, 1855, to the original January 11 letter.

46. Samuel D. Lecompte to Caleb Cushing, October 27, 1854, Cushing Papers.

47. *Congressional Globe*, 33rd Congress, 2nd session, appendix, 769; also quoted in Nicole Etcheson, *Bleeding Kansas: Contested Liberty in the Civil War Era* (Lawrence: University Press of Kansas, 2004), 27.

48. Samuel A. Johnson, *The Battle Cry of Freedom: The New England Emigrant Aid Company in the Kansas Crusade* (Lawrence: University of Kansas Press, 1954), 7–26.

49. David R. Atchison, quoted in James A. Rawley, *Race and Politics: "Bleeding Kansas" and the Coming of the Civil War* (Philadelphia: J. B. Lippincott, 1969), 81.

50. David R. Atchison to Jefferson Davis, September 24, 1854, in Jefferson Davis, *The Papers of Jefferson Davis*, ed. Lynda Lasswell Crist, (Baton Rouge: Louisiana State University Press, 1985), 5: 83–84.

51. Etcheson, *Bleeding Kansas*, 53; Allan Nevins, *Ordeal of the Union*, vol. 2, *A House Dividing, 1852–1857* (New York: Charles Scribner's Sons, 1947), 312–13; Rawley, *Race and Politics*, 86–87; "Speech at Vicksburg," June 6, 1855, in Davis, *The Papers of Jeffeson Davis*, 5: 110 note 7. Crist notes, "Reeder was a 'confidential friend' of Davis' niece's husband Richard Brodhead. Also, while visiting Easton in 1850 Varina Davis had been entertained by Reeder's wife."

52. Nevins, *Ordeal of the Union*: *A House Dividing*, 312.

53. Etcheson, *Bleeding Kansas*, 53.

54. Ibid

55. Ibid.; Mark W. Summers, *The Plundering Generation: Corruption and the Crisis of the Union, 1849–1861* (New York: Oxford University Press, 1987), 233–34; John Sherman, *Recollections of Forty Years in the House, Senate and Cabinet* (Chicago: The Werner Company, 1895), 1: 118; "Howard Report," House, *Executive Documents*, 34th Congress, 1st session, report 200, serial 869 (hereafter cited as "Howard Report"). The congressional investigating committee found 1,700 illegal voters in this election.

56. George Manypenny to Andrew H. Reeder, April 27, 1855, Letters Sent by the Office of Indian Affairs, RG75, M21, Roll 51, National Archives; Etcheson, *Bleeding Kansas*, 55; Gates, *Fifty Million Acres*, 39–40. Gates commented on Reeder's "fraudulently purchased" "half-breed" tracts in Paul Wallace Gates, "A Fragment of Kansas Land History: The Disposal of the Christian Indian Tract," *Kansas Historical Quarterly* 6, no. 3 (August 1937): 231, 233.

57. Samuel D. Lecompte to Caleb Cushing, January 13, 1855, Cushing Papers.

58. Gates, *Fifty Million Acres*, 58–59.

59. *Atchison Squatter Sovereign*, Gates, *Fifty Million Acres*, 60.

60. Samuel D. Lecompte to Caleb Cushing, January 13, 1855, Cushing Papers.

61. J. B. Chapman to George W. Manypenny, March 29, 1855, Letters Received by the Office of Indian Affairs, RG75, M234, Roll 364, National Archives.

62. Ibid.

63. *Atchison Squatter Sovereign*, March 20, 1855, copy in State Department, Territorial Papers of Kansas, RG59, M218, Roll 1, National Archives (hereafter cited as Territorial Papers of Kansas); "Memorial from the Legislature of Kansas to the President of the United States," July 26, 1855, State Department, Territorial Papers of Kansas.

64. *Atchison Squatter Sovereign* in Etcheson, *Bleeding Kansas*, 57.

65. Ibid., 56.

66. Ibid., 56–60; Alice Nichols, *Bleeding Kansas* (New York: Oxford University Press, 1954), 28; Nevins, *Ordeal of the* Union, A House Dividing, 2: 385–86; David R. Atchison to R. M. T. Hunter, quoted in Johannsen, *Stephen A. Douglas*, 474.

67. Etcheson, *Bleeding Kansas*, 59; S. C. Pomeroy to Amos A. Lawrence, April 6, 1855, Amos A. Lawrence Papers, Massachusetts Historical Society, Boston (hereafter cited as Lawrence Papers).

68. Charles Robinson to Amos A. Lawrence, April 4, 1855, Lawrence Papers.

69. Alice Nichols, *Bleeding Kansas*, 28; Etcheson, *Bleeding Kansas*, 58–61. Estimates were that even after the census four of five legal voters in the territory were proslavery. See Don W. Wilson, *Governor Charles Robinson of Kansas* (Lawrence: University of Kansas Press, 1975), 19.

70. "Howard Report," 637–47.

71. Roy Nichols, *Franklin Pierce*, 410–11.

72. George W. Manypenny to Andrew H. Reeder, April 27, 1855, Letters Sent by the Office of Indian Affairs, RG75, M21, Roll 51, National Archives.

73. Amos A. Lawrence to Franklin Pierce, April 11, 1855, Lawrence Papers.

74. Diary of Amos A. Lawrence, May 1, 1855, Amos A. Lawrence Diaries, Massachusetts Historical Society, Boston (hereafter cited as Lawrence Diaries).

75. Amos A. Lawrence to George T. Richards, June 11, 1855, Lawrence Papers.

76. "Howard Report," 936–46.

77. Franklin Pierce, "This outline to be filled out and signed by Governor Reeder," draft of a letter, May, 1855, Pierce Papers, New Hampshire Historical Society, Concord.

78. William L. Marcy to James Buchanan, May 28, 1855, in Buchanan, *The Works of James Buchanan*, 9: 354–55.

79. George W. Clarke to Alfred Cumming, May 8, 1855, Letters Received by the Office of Indian Affairs, RG75, M234, Roll 364, National Archives.

80. Caleb Cushing to Samuel W. Johnston, June 14, 1855, Letters Sent by the Attorney General.

81. Etcheson, *Bleeding Kansas,* 67; "Memorial from the Legislature of Kansas to the President of the United States," July 26, 1855, State Department, Territorial Papers of Kansas; Wilson, *Governor Charles Robinson*, 23.

82. "Veto of Gov. Reeder," July 6, 1855, State Department, Territorial Papers of Kansas.

83. Etcheson, *Bleeding Kansas,* 63–64; Wilson, *Governor Charles Robinson*, 26.

84. Etcheson, *Bleeding Kansas*, 67.

85. G. W. Brown to Amos A. Lawrence, April 30, 1855, Lawrence Papers; Wilson, *Governor Charles Robinson*, 21.

86. Charles Robinson to Amos A. Lawrence, July 20, 1855, Lawrence Papers.

87. Amos A. Lawrence to Prof. Packard, July 14, 1855, Lawrence Papers.

88. Amos A. Lawrence to Pierce, July 15, 1855, Lawrence Papers.

89. Ibid.

90. W. Hunter, Acting Secretary of State, to Andrew H. Reeder, July 28, 1855, Marcy Papers; Gates, "A Fragment of Kansas Land History," 231–33.

91. Ibid.

92. Caleb Cushing to Associate Justice Rush Elmore, August 6, 1855, Letters Sent by the Attorney General.

93. "Memorial from the Legislature of Kansas to the President of the United States," July 26, 1855, State Department, Territorial Papers of Kansas.

94. Jefferson Davis to D. B. Clayton, August 3, 1855, in Davis, *Jefferson Davis, Constitutionalist*, 2: 487–88.

95. Etcheson, *Bleeding Kansas,* 71; Wilson, *Governor Charles Robinson*, 29–30.

96. Etcheson, *Bleeding Kansas,* 74; Wilson, *Governor Charles Robinson*, 31.

97. Johannsen, *Stephen A. Douglas,* 480; Wendell H. Stephenson, "Wilson Shannon," *Dictionary of American Biography* (New York: Charles Scribner's Sons, 1935), 17: 20–21.

98. Amos A. Lawrence to Charles Robinson, August 16, 1855, Lawrence Papers.

99. Etcheson, *Bleeding Kansas,* 74–75; Wilson, *Governor Charles Robinson,* 31–32.

100. Diary of Amos A. Lawrence, May 26, 1856, Lawrence Diaries.

101. Johannsen, *Stephen A. Douglas,* 475.

Chapter 9: *Filibusters, Recruitment*

1. Ivor Debenham Spencer, *The Victor and the Spoils: A Life of William L. Marcy* (Providence, R.I.: Brown University Press, 1959), 352–53; Robert E. May, *Manifest Destiny's Underworld: Filibustering in Antebellum America* (Chapel Hill, N.C.:

University of North Carolina Press, 2002), 138–39; William O. Scroggs, *Filibuster and Financiers: The Story of William Walker and His Associates* (New York: MacMillan, 1916; reprinted by Russell and Russell, 1969), 100–101; *Washington Union*, January 9, 1855.

2. Spencer, *The Victor and the Spoils*, 354; *Washington Union*, February 7, 1855.

3. *Washington Union*, February 7, 1855.

4. Ibid.

5. Scroggs, *Filibusters and Financiers*, 102; May, *Manifest Destiny's Underworld*, 138–39; Caleb Cushing to John McKeon, Senate, *Executive Documents*, 34th Congress, 1st session, vol. 68: 9.

6. *New York Herald*, May 16, 1855; Scroggs, *Filibusters and Financiers*, 102–103.

7. Caleb Cushing to John McKeon, May 25, 1855, Letters Sent by the Attorney General, M12, T969, Roll 1, National Archives (hereafter cited as Letters Sent by the Attorney General).

8. *New York Herald*, June 6, 1855; Scroggs, *Filibusters and Financiers*, 104–105; John McKeon to Caleb Cushing, June 5, 6, 8, 11, 17, 1855, in Caleb Cushing Papers, Library of Congress (hereafter cited as Cushing Papers); Joseph Fabens to Henry L. Kinney, July 3, 1855, "copy sent by Cushing to McKeon to help in prosecution of Kinney," in Letters Sent by the Attorney General.

9. Joseph Fabens to Henry L. Kinney, July 3, 1855, Letters Sent by the Attorney General.

10. Scroggs, *Filibusters and Financiers*, 106–107; Caleb Cushing to John McKeon, July 12, 1855, Letters Sent by the Attorney General.

11. Joseph Fabens to Henry L. Kinney, July 3, 1855, Letters Sent by the Attorney General.

12. William L. Marcy to Franklin Pierce, May 11, 1855, Marcy Papers, Library of Congress (hereafter cited as Marcy Papers).

13. May, *Manifest Destiny's Underworld*, 218–19.

14. Spencer, *The Victor and the Spoils*, 358; Scroggs, *Filibusters and Financiers*, 108–9; Edward S. Wallace, *Destiny and Glory* (New York: Coward and McCann, 1957), 163–73.

15. Robert E. May, *John A. Quitman: Old South Crusader* (Baton Rouge: Louisiana State University Press, 1985), 294.

16. May, *Manifest Destiny's Underworld*, 231–32; James Dobbin to Charles S. McAuley, April 10, May 31, 1855, in K. Jack Bauer, ed., *The New American State Papers, Naval Affairs*, 1789–1860 (Wilmington, Del.: Scholarly Resources, 1981), 2: 123, 237–39.

17. May, *John A. Quitman*, 294–95.

18. William J. Cooper Jr., *Jefferson Davis: American* (New York: Alfred A. Knopf, 2000), 252; Allan Peskin, *Winfield Scott and the Profession of Arms* (Kent, Ohio: Kent State University Press, 2003), 219–20.

19. Peskin, *Winfield Scott*, 118.

20. Ibid., 220.

21. Ibid.; "Pay and Emoluments of Lt. Gen. Scott," Senate, *Executive Documents,* 34th Congress, 3rd session, Document 34, 14 (hereafter cited as "Pay and Emoluments of Lt. Gen. Scott"), 19–53.

22. Peskin, *Winfield Scott,* 220; "Pay and Emoluments of Lt. Gen. Scott," 19–53.

23. "Pay and Emoluments of Lt. Gen. Scott," 19–53.

24. *Journal of the Executive Proceedings of the Senate,* 34th Congress, 2nd session, vol. 9, 420.

25. George Templeton Strong, *The Diary of George Templeton Strong,* vol. 2, *The Turbulent Fifties,* ed. by Allan Nevins and Milton Halsey Thomas (New York: MacMillan, 1952), 212.

26. Jefferson Davis to Caleb Cushing, April 26, 1855, and Jefferson Davis to Winfield Scott, April 26, 1855, in Jefferson Davis, *Jefferson Davis, Constitutionalist: His Letters, Papers, and Speeches,* ed. Dunbar Rowland (New York: J. J. Little and Ives, 1923), 2: 457–59.

27. Winfield Scott to Caleb Cushing, June 22, 1855; and Caleb Cushing to Winfield Scott, June 23, 1855; both in Cushing Papers; "Pay and Emoluments of Lt. Gen. Scott," 71–131.

28. Jefferson Davis to Major R. Delafield, Major A. Mordecai, and Capt. George B. McClellan, April 2, 1855 in Davis, *Jefferson Davis Constitutionalist,* 2: 446–48.

29. Cooper, *Jefferson Davis,* 255–56; John F. Prout, Col./U.S.A. (Ret), e-mail message to author, February 13, 2003.

30. John F. Prout e-mail message to author; Colonel Richard Delafield, *Report on the Art of War in Europe in 1854, 1855, and 1856* (Washington, D.C.: George W. Bowman, 1861).

31. Major H. C. Wayne to Jefferson Davis, November 21, 1853, Davis, *Jefferson Davis, Constitutionalist,* 2: 288–91.

32. Jefferson Davis to Henry C. Wayne, May 10, 1855; Jefferson Davis to David Dixon Porter, May, 1855; both in Davis, *Jefferson Davis, Constitutionalist,* 2: 461–62, 464–66; Edward S. Wallace, *The Great Reconnaissance: Soldiers, Artists, and Scientists on the Frontier, 1848–1861* (Boston: Little, Brown, 1955), 243–44.

33. Jefferson Davis to Winfield Scott, July 12, 1855, in Davis, *Jefferson Davis, Constitutionalist,* 2: 472–73. In fact, the seventy-six-year-old Hitchcock had no intention of serving on the frontier and hoped to avoid his assignment entirely by receiving a lengthy leave of absence. When the leave was denied by Davis, Hitchcock resigned his commission in October 1855. See Ethan Allen Hitchcock, *Fifty Years in Camp and Field: Diary of Major-General Ethan Allen Hitchcock, U.S.A.,* W. A. Croffut (New York: G. P. Putnam's Sons, 1909), 414–18.

34. Winfield Scott to Jefferson Davis, July 17, 1855, in Davis, *Jefferson Davis, Constitutionalist,* 2: 472–73.

35. Jefferson Davis to Winfield Scott, July 25, 1855, in "Pay and Emoluments of Lt. Gen. Scott," 181–82.

36. Winfield Scott to Jefferson Davis, July 30, 1855, in "Pay and Emoluments of Lt. Gen. Scott," 159–63.

37. Jefferson Davis to Winfield Scott, September 7, 1855, in *Jefferson Davis, Constitutionalist,* 2: 491–508.

38. Winfield Scott to Jefferson Davis, September 29, 1855, in *Jefferson Davis, Constitutionalist,* 2: 511–24.

39. Caleb Cushing to Jefferson Davis, "Lieutenant General Scott's Case," August 24, 1855 in C. C. Andrews, ed., *Official Opinions of the Attorneys General of the United States: Advising the Presidents and Heads of Departments in Relation to Their Official Duties,* (Washington, D.C.: Robert Farnham, 1856), 7: 399–439.

40. Jefferson Davis to Franklin Pierce, October 12, 1855, in Davis, *Jefferson Davis, Constitutionalist,* 2: 527–41.

41. Franklin Pierce to Jefferson Davis, October 29, 1855, in Davis, *Jefferson Davis, Constitutionalist,* 2: 541–44.

42. Peskin, *Winfield Scott,* 221; "Pay and Emoluments of Lt. Gen. Scott," 131–43, 144.

43. Franklin Pierce to Jefferson Davis, n.d., Letters Sent to the President by the Secretary of War, M127, National Archives.

44. Caleb Cushing to Franklin Pierce, "Relation of the President to the Executive Departments," August 31, 1855, in Andrews, *Official Opinions of the Attorneys General,* 7: 453–82.

45. Varina Davis, *Jefferson Davis, Ex-President of the Confederate States of America: A Memoir by His Wife* (New York: Belford Company Publishers, 1890), 1: 569; Peskin, *Winfield Scott,* 224; E. D. Keyes, *Fifty Years' Observation of Men and Events: Civil and Military* (New York: Charles Scribner's Sons, 1885), 11.

46. Jefferson Davis to Winfield Scott, February 29, 1856; Winfield Scott to Jefferson Davis, May 21, 1856; both in Davis, *Jefferson Davis, Constitutionalist,* 3: 10, 36.

47. "Pay and Emoluments of Lt. Gen. Scott."

48. H. Barrett Learned, "William Learned Marcy," *The American Secretaries of State and Their Diplomacy,* ed. Samuel Flagg Bemis, (New York: Pageant Book Company, 1958), 6: 239; Spencer, *The Victor and The Spoils,* 345; Richard W. Van Alstyne, "John F. Crampton, Conspirator or Dupe?" *American Historical Review* 41 (April 1936): 492–93.

49. John F. Crampton to Lord Clarendon, February 8, 1855, in Van Alstyne, "John Crampton, Conspirator or Dupe?" 494–95.

50. Ibid., 496–97; J. W. Longley, *Joseph Howe,* The Makers of Canada Series (Toronto: Morang, 1904), 150–54. Howe claimed to have recruited nine hundred men for the British army and was paid £2000 by the British government.

51. John F. Crampton to Lord Clarendon, March 12, 1855, in Van Alstyne, "John F. Crampton, Conspirator or Dupe?" 495–96.

52. Spencer, *The Victor and the Spoils,* 346; "British Recruitment," *Senate Executive Documents 35,* 34th Congress, 1st session, 80–81.

53. Caleb Cushing to John McKeon, March 23, 1855, Letters Sent by the Attorney General.

54. Caleb Cushing to James C. Van Dyke, March 26, 1855, Letters Sent by the Attorney General.

55. Spencer, *The Victor and the Spoils*, 346.

56. John F. Crampton to Lord Clarendon, March 12, 1855, in Van Alstyne, "John F. Crampton, Conspirator or Dupe?" 496.

57. Spencer, *The Victor and the Spoils*, 347; Learned, "William Learned Marcy," 6: 249–53.

58. William L. Marcy to James Buchanan, May 28, 1855, in James Buchanan, *The Works of James Buchanan*, ed. John Bassett Moore, (Philadelphia: J. B. Lippincott, 1909), 9: 354–355.

59. Spencer, *The Victor and the Spoils*, 347.

60. Lord Clarendon to John F. Crampton, May 30, 1856, in Van Alstyne, "John F. Crampton, Conspirator or Dupe?" 496.

61. William L. Marcy to James Buchanan, June 9, 1855, "British Recruitment"; Learned, "William Learned Marcy," 6: 243; Spencer, *The Victor and the Spoils*, 348.

62. James Buchanan to William L. Marcy, June 29, 1855, Buchanan, *The Works of James Buchanan*, 9: 362–64.

63. Van Alstyne, "John F. Crampton, Conspirator or Dupe?" 500–1.

64. John F. Crampton to Lord Clarendon, July 16, 1855, "John F. Crampton, Conspirator or Dupe?" 501.

65. William L. Marcy to James Buchanan, July 15, 1855, "British Recruitment," 13–15; Spencer, *The Victor and the Spoils*, 348.

66. John F. Crampton to Lord Clarendon, August 7, 1855, in Van Alstyne, "John F. Crampton, Conspirator or Dupe?" 501–2.

67. Learned, "William Learned Marcy," 6: 249.

68. Franklin Pierce to William L. Marcy, August 4, 1855, Marcy Papers; Diary of William L. Marcy, July 22, 1853, Marcy Papers; Spencer, *The Victor and the Spoils*, 348.

69. Caleb Cushing to William L. Marcy, "Including affidavit of Max F. O. Strobel & documents," August 10, 1855, Letters Sent by the Attorney General.

70. Franklin Pierce to William L. Marcy, August 6, 1855, Marcy Papers.

71. Franklin Pierce to William L. Marcy, August 7, 1855; 2:00 p.m. August 7, 1855; both in Marcy Papers.

72. Caleb Cushing to Franklin Pierce, August, 9, 1855, "Foreign Enlistments in the United States," in Andrews, *Official Opinions of the Attorneys General*, 7: 367–90; also in "British Recruitment," 35, 74.

73. "British Recruitment," 68–80.

74. William L. Marcy to John F. Crampton, August 27, 1855, Marcy Papers. See also, William L. Marcy to John F. Crampton, September 5, 1855, "British Recruitment," 18–21.

75. Roy Franklin Nichols, *Franklin Pierce: Young Hickory of the Granite Hills*, rev. ed. (Philadelphia: University of Pennsylvania Press, 1931; revised 1969), 421; Sidney Webster to William L. Marcy, August 18, 1855; Franklin Pierce to William L. Marcy, August 25, 1855, Marcy Papers.

76. Sara A. R. (Mrs. Roger A.) Pryor, *Reminiscences of Peace and War* (New York: MacMillan, 1904), 27–28.

77. Franklin Pierce to James Buchanan, September 10, 1855, in Buchanan *The Works of James Buchanan,* 9: 403; William L. Marcy to James Buchanan, June 18, 1855, Marcy Papers.

78. John F. Crampton to William L. Marcy, September 7, 1855, "British Recruitment," 21–22; Spencer, *The Victor and the Spoils,* 350; Learned, "William Learned Marcy," 6: 245.

79. Caleb Cushing to James C. Van Dyke, September 17, 1855, Letters Sent by the Attorney General.

80. Claude M. Fuess, *The Life of Caleb Cushing* (New York: Harcourt Brace, 1923), 2: 171; John M. Belohlavek, *Broken Glass: Caleb Cushing and the Shattering of the Union* (Kent, Ohio: Kent State University Press, 2005), 268.

81. James Buchanan to William L. Marcy, November 9, 1855, in Buchanan, *The Works of James Buchanan,* 9: 449–57; Belohlavek, *Broken Glass,* 268–69.

82. Caleb Cushing to John McKeon, October 27, 1855, Letters Sent by the Attorney General.

83. Ibid. Belohlavek, *Broken Glass,* 269.

84. Caleb Cushing to John McKeon and James C. Van Dyke, December 12, 1855, in *Broken Glass,* 269.

85. James Buchanan to William L. Marcy, November 7, 1855, in Buchanan, *The Works of James Buchanan,* 9: 447–48.

86. William L. Marcy to James Buchanan, November 12, 1855, Marcy Papers.

87. Lord Clarendon to John F. Crampton, November 16, 1855, "British Recruitment," 38–43.

88. William L. Marcy to James Buchanan, October 13, 1855, "British Recruitment," 29–35.

89. Learned, "William Learned Marcy," 6: 257.

90. James Buchanan to William L. Marcy, November 16, 1855, in Buchanan, *The Works of James Buchanan,* 9: 463–64.

91. Michael F. Holt, *The Rise and Fall of the American Whig Party* (New York: Oxford University Press, 1999), 929–31; Tyler Anbinder, *Nativism and Slavery: The Northern Know Nothings and the Politics of the 1850s* (New York: Oxford University Press, 1992), 165–74.

92. Benjamin Brown French, *Witness to the Young Republic: A Yankee's Journal, 1828–1870,* ed. Donald B. Cole and John J. McDonough (Hanover, N.H.: University Press of New England, 1989), 266–67.

93. Holt, *The Rise and Fall of the American Whig Party,* 970.

94. John W. Forney to John C. Breckinridge, August 8, 1855, Breckinridge Papers, Library of Congress (hereafter cited as Breckinridge Papers).

95. Sidney Webster to John H. George, November 3, 1855, George Papers, New Hampshire Historical Society, Concord (hereafter cited as George Papers).

96. *New Hampshire Patriot,* November 21, 1855.

97. John W. Forney to John C. Breckinridge, November 15, 1855, Breckinridge Papers.

98. Sidney Webster to John H. George, November 7, November 20, 1855, George Papers.

99. John W. Forney to James Buchanan, November 25, 1855, Buchanan Papers, Historical Society of Pennsylvania, Philadelphia.

100. Sidney Webster to John H. George, November 23, 1855, George Papers.

Chapter 10: *Congress and Kansas in Chaos*

1. Thomas B. Alexander, *Sectional Stress and Party Strength: A Study of Roll-Call Voting Patterns in the U.S. House of Representatives, 1836–1860* (Nashville, Tenn.: Vanderbilt University Press, 1967), 90, 94.

2. Ibid., 91; *Congressional Globe,* 34th Congress, 1st session, 3–17, 20–21, 24–27, 29, 33, 37, 39, 42–44, 51, 54, 55, 58, 62, 67, 77, 79.

3. Franklin Pierce to H. D. Pierce, December 4, 1855, Pierce Papers, New Hampshire Historical Society, Concord.

4. Elizabeth McNeil's death and a sketch of her life were reported in the *New Hampshire Patriot,* May 2, 1855. Though she was living in Concord at the time of her death, the funeral took place in Washington, D.C. at the home of her son-in-law, Captain Benham of the U.S. Army, and she was buried next to her husband, General John McNeil, at the "Congressional burying ground." The press reports do not mention whether President Pierce attended the funeral or burial. *Washington Union,* April 29, 1855.

5. *Congressional Globe,* 34th Congress, 1st session, 5–6.

6. Ibid., 8.

7. Nichole Etcheson, *Bleeding Kansas: Contested Liberty in the Civil War Era* (Lawrence: University Press of Kansas, 2004), 69; Wilson Shannon to Col. Samuel Medary, September 26, 1855, in *New Hampshire Patriot,* October 17, 1855.

8. *New York Times,* September 13, 14, 1855.

9. Etcheson, *Bleeding Kansas,* 74–78.

10. Etcheson, *Bleeding Kansas,* 78; Don W. Wilson, *Governor Charles Robinson of Kansas* (Lawrence: University Press of Kansas, 1975), 33.

11. Etcheson, *Bleeding Kansas,* 79–81; Wilson, *Governor Charles Robinson,* 33; "Kansas Affairs," also known as the "Howard Report," *House Executive Documents,* 34th Congress, 1st session, Report 200, serial 869, 59–63, 96–99 (hereafter cited as "Howard Report"). According to historian Dale E. Watts, prior to January 1856, there had been only four deaths related to the political conflict in Kansas. Watts believes the Dow murder was entirely a land claim issue that only later became a political matter. Dale E. Watts, "How Bloody Was Bleeding Kansas? Political Killings in Kansas Territory, 1854–1861," *Kansas History* 18, no. 2 (Summer 1995): 119–20, 126.

12. Wilson Shannon to Franklin Pierce, telegram, December 1, 1855, in *New Hampshire Patriot,* December 12, 1855.

13. Franklin Pierce to Wilson Shannon, telegram, December 3, 1855, in *New Hampshire Patriot,* December 12, 1855.

14. Wilson Shannon to Franklin Pierce, December 11, 1855, "Howard Report," 99–101; *New Hampshire Patriot,* December 12, 1855; Wilson, *Governor Charles Robinson,* 34–35.

15. Etcheson, *Bleeding Kansas,* 85–88.

16. Wilson Shannon to Franklin Pierce, December 11, 1855, "Howard Report," 99–101.

17. Ivor Debenham Spencer, *The Victor and the Spoils: A Life of William L. Marcy* (Providence, R.I.: Brown University Press, 1959), 359–60; William O. Scroggs, *Filibusters and Financiers: The Story of William Walker and His Associates* (New York: MacMillan, 1916; reprinted by Russell & Russell, 1969), 113–26.

18. William L. Marcy to John H. Wheeler, November 8, 1855, William L. Marcy Papers, Library of Congress (hereafter cited as Marcy Papers).

19. Spencer, *The Victor and the Spoils,* 360.

20. James A. Richardson, ed., *A Compilation of the Messages and Papers of the Presidents,* (Washington, D.C,: Government Printing Office, 1897), 5: 388–89.

21. Spencer, *The Victor and the Spoils,* 360; Scroggs, *Filibusters and Financiers,* 137; Caleb Cushing to John McKeon, December 24, 1855, Letters Sent by the Attorney General, M12, T969, Roll 1, National Archives (hereafter cited as Letters Sent by the Attorney General); Albert Z. Carr, *The World and William Walker* (Westport, Conn.: Greenwood Press, 1963; reprinted 1975), 153–63.

22. Caleb Cushing to District Attorneys of the United States, December, 1855, Letters Sent by the Attorney General.

23. Scroggs, *Filibusters and Financiers,* 140–41; Robert E. May, *Manifest Destiny's Underworld: Filibustering in Antebellum America* (Chapel Hill: University of North Carolina, 2002), 140–41.

24. Caleb Cushing to John McKeon, December 24, 1855, Letters Sent by the Attorney General.

25. *New York Herald,* December 25, 26, 1855; Scroggs, *Filibusters and Financiers,* 141–42.

26. *New York Herald,* December 25, 26, 1855.

27. Ibid.; Scroggs, *Filibusters and Financiers,* 142–43.

28. *New York Herald,* December 25, 26, 1855.

29. John McKeon to Caleb Cushing, December 25, 1855, Caleb Cushing Papers, Library of Congress (hereafter cited as Cushing Papers).

30. May, *Manifest Destiny's Underworld,* 140; Scroggs, *Filibusters and Financiers,* 142–143; John McKeon to Caleb Cushing, January 22, 1855, Cushing Papers.

31. Scroggs, *Filibusters and Financiers,* 143. Cushing supplied the press with the facts that French had been guilty of forgery and embezzlement, and that during the gold rush "he had defrauded thousands of emigrants en route to California by wagon train." A Senate report had been made, attesting to his "misdeeds" in 1851. See Carr, *The World and William Walker,* 162.

32. Caleb Cushing to John McKeon, telegram, January 9, 1856, Letters Sent by the Attorney General; *New York Herald,* January 10, 1856.

33. *New York Herald*, January 10, 1856; Scroggs, *Filibusters and Financiers*, 144–45; Caleb Cushing to P. J. Joachimsson, Acting U.S. Attorney, New York, January 14, 1856, Letters Sent by the Attorney General.

34. James Buchanan to William L. Marcy, December 18, 1855, in James Buchanan, *The Works of James Buchanan*, ed. John Bassett Moore (Philadelphia: J. B. Lippincott, 1909), 9: 479–480.

35. William L. Marcy to James Buchanan, December 23, 1855, Marcy Papers.

36. James Buchanan to William L. Marcy, December 28, 1855, Marcy Papers.

37. Franklin Pierce, "Third Annual Message," Richardson, *A Compilation of the Messages*, 5: 328–29.

38. Ibid., 330–31.

39. Ibid., 333.

40. Ibid.

41. Ibid., 338–39.

42. Ibid., 340.

43. Ibid.

44. Ibid., 343–34.

45. Ibid., 349–50.

46. Ibid., 350.

47. James Buchanan to William L. Marcy, January 18, 1856, Buchanan, *The Works of James Buchanan*, 10: 9–11.

48. James Buchanan to William L. Marcy, January 25, 1856, Buchanan, *The Works of James Buchanan*, 10: 12–15.

49. Diary of Amos A. Lawrence, January 2, 1856, Amos A. Lawrence Diaries, Massachusetts Historical Society, Boston.

50. Benjamin Brown French, *Witness to the Young Republic: A Yankee's Journal, 1828–1870*, ed. by Donald B. Cole and John J. McDonough (Hanover, N.H.: University Press of New England, 1989), 267.

51. Richard H. Sewell, *John P. Hale and the Politics of Abolition* (Cambridge, Mass.: Harvard University Press, 1965), 165–66.

52. *Congressional Globe*, 34th Congress, 1st session, 133.

53. Ibid.

54. Ibid., 134.

55. Ibid., 135.

56. *Washington Union*, January 5, 1856; Sewell, *John P. Hale*, 166; *New York Herald*, January 23, 1856.

57. James A. Rawley, *Race and Politics: "Bleeding Kansas" and the Coming of the Civil War* (Philadelphia: J. B. Lippincott, 1969), 116–18.

58. Wilson Shannon to George W. Clark, January 4, 1856, copy in Marcy Papers; Watts, "How Bloody Was Bleeding Kansas?" 116–29.

59. Robert W. Johannsen, *Stephen A. Douglas* (New York: Oxford University Press, 1973), 488, 491.

60. William L. Marcy to James Buchanan, January 3, 1856, Marcy Papers.

61. William L. Marcy to James Buchanan, December 28, 1855, "British Recruitment," *Senate Executive Documents,* 34th Congress, 1st session, Document 35, 43–65 (hereafter cited as "British Recruitment"); Spencer, *The Victor and the Spoils,* 363–64.

62. William L. Marcy to James Buchanan, December 28, 1855, "British Recruitment," 43; James Buchanan to William L. Marcy, January 18, 1856, in Buchanan, *The Works of James Buchanan,* 10: 9–11; Spencer, *The Victor and the Spoils,* 363–64.

63. James Buchanan to William L. Marcy, February 1, 1856, in Buchanan, *The Works of James Buchanan,* 10: 23–26.

64. Ibid., and James Buchanan to William L. Marcy, February 8, 1856, in Buchanan, *The Works of James Buchanan,* 10: 35–40; John M. Belohlavek, *Broken Glass: Caleb Cushing and the Shattering of the Union* (Kent, Ohio: Kent State University Press, 2005), 269–70.

65. James Buchanan to William L. Marcy, February 8, 1856, in Buchanan, *The Works of James Buchanan,* 10: 35–40.

66. Ibid.

67. James Buchanan to William L. Marcy, February 5, 1856, in Buchanan, *The Works of James Buchanan,* 10: 30–34.

68. William L. Marcy to James Buchanan, January 27, 1856, Marcy Papers.

69. Etcheson, *Bleeding Kansas,* 91; Wilson, *Governor Charles Robinson,* 35.

70. J. H. Lane and C. Robinson to Pierce, January 21, 23, 1856, in *New Hampshire Patriot,* February 27, 1856.

71. Richardson, Franklin Pierce, "To the Senate and House of Representatives," *A Compilation of the Messages,* 5: 352–60.

72. Ibid., 354–55.

73. Ibid., 355.

74. Ibid., 356–58.

75. Ibid., 359.

76. Ibid., 360.

77. *New Hampshire Patriot,* February 6, 1856; *Congressional Globe,* 34th Congress, 1st session, 294–96; *New York Herald,* January 25, 1856. "At this time there was great commotion and excitement in the Hall, a large number of members addressing the Clerk, amid cries of 'Order! Order!.'"—*Congressional Globe,* 294.

78. *Journal of the House of Representatives,* 34th Congress, 1st session, 444. Banks received 103 votes to 100 for the Democrat William Aiken of South Carolina. The members then passed a resolution thanking Clerk John C. Forney for the impartial manner in which he presided over the House during the past two months; then they dismissed Forney and replaced him with a Republican clerk. See *Journal of the House of Representatives,* 34th Congress, 1st session, 452.

79. Draft of proclamation in Cushing's handwriting, Pierce Papers, Library of Congress; Franklin Pierce, "Proclamation," in Richardson, *A Compilation of the Messages,* 5:, 390–91; Belohlavek, *Broken Glass,* 278.

80. William L. Marcy to Wilson Shannon, February 15, 1856, *New Hampshire Patriot,* February 27, 1856; Samuel A. Johnson, *The Battle Cry of Freedom: The New*

England Emigrant Aid Company and the Kansas Crusade (Lawrence: University of Kansas Press, 1954), 148.

81. Jefferson Davis to Cols. Sumner and Cooke, February 15, 1856, in Jefferson Davis, *Jefferson Davis, Constitutionalist: His Letters, Papers, and Speeches*, ed. Dunbar Rowland (New York: J. J. Little and Ives, 1923), 2: 603–4.

82. Jefferson Davis to Franklin Pierce, February 25, 1856, "Letters Sent to the President by the Secretary of War," RG 107, M127, National Archives.

83. Horatio Seymour to William L. Marcy, February 28, 1856, Marcy Papers.

84. Etcheson, *Bleeding Kansas*, 93; Wilson, *Governor Charles Robinson*, 38.

85. February 25, 1856, *Congressional Globe*, 34th Congress, 1st session, 495–97.

86. Ibid. Hale made another lengthy speech about Kansas on February 28, 1856; see *Congressional Globe*, 34th Congress, 1st session, appendix 103–9.

87. Johannsen, *Stephen A. Douglas*, 491–93; Douglas's report is in *Senate Reports*, 34th Congress, 1st session, Report 34, 1–41.

88. Johannsen, *Stephen A. Douglas*, 493; Collamer's minority report is in *Senate Reports*, 34th Congress, 1st session, Report 34, 42–61.

89. *Congressional Globe*, 34th Congress, 1st session, 663; appendix 280–89.

90. *Congressional Globe*, 34th Congress, 1st session, 693.

91. Ibid, 286; appendix, 403; Etcheson, *Bleeding Kansas*, 97–98.

92. Etcheson, *Bleeding Kansas*, 97; *Congressional Globe*, 34th Congress, 1st session, 636, 675, 690–92, 710, 728.

93. J. W. Whitfield to G. W. Clark, March 1, 1856, letter forwarded to Marcy by Governor Wilson Shannon, Marcy Papers; Wilson, *Governor Charles Robinson*, 39.

94. John Slidell to James Buchanan, January 30, 1856, in Buchanan, *The Works of James Buchanan*, 10: 23.

95. William P. Gienapp, *The Origins of the Republican Party, 1852–1856* (New York: Oxford University Press, 1987), 306.

96. Robert Toombs to Thomas W. Thomas, February 9, 1856, in Ulrich B. Philips, "The Correspondence of Robert Toombs, Alexander H. Stephens, and Howell Cobb," *Annual Report of the American Historical Association* 2 (1911): 361.

97. Daniel Dickinson to Edmund Burke, March 20, 1856, Edmund Burke Papers, Library of Congress.

98. Sidney Webster to John H. George, March 23, 1856, George Papers, New Hampshire Historical Society, Concord. Democratic gubernatorial candidate John S. Wells lost to the incumbent Ralph Metcalf by little more than one hundred votes: 31,937 to 32,050. See *New Hampshire Patriot*, March 17, 1856.

99. Franklin Pierce to H. D. Pierce, March 17, 1856, Pierce Papers, New Hampshire Historical Society, Concord.

100. Mary E. Aiken to Mary Aiken, April 7, 1856, Pierce-Aiken Papers, Library of Congress; see also Norman Boas, ed., *Jane M. Pierce: The Pierce-Aiken Papers, Supplement* (Mystic, Conn.: Norman Boas, 1989), 47–48.

101. Eve Anderson, ed., *A Breach of Privilege: Cilley Family Letters, 1820–1867* (Rockland, Maine: Seven Coin Press, 2002), 381–89.

102. Ibid., 387–88.

103. Wilson Shannon to William L. Marcy, April 11, 1856, "Howard Report," 66–67.

Chapter 11: *More Crises and a Convention*

1. Alfred T. Mahan, *From Sail to Steam: Recollections of Naval Life* (New York: Harper and Brothers, 1907), 30–32.

2. *New Hampshire Patriot*, April 30, 1856. The *Merrimac* had a brief but important career. After serving as the flagship of the U.S. Pacific squadron, the frigate was undergoing repairs at the Norfolk navy yard when the Civil War broke out. Rather than allow the powerful ship to be taken by the enemy, the Navy burned and sank the hull in the harbor. The Confederates refloated the damaged ship, refitted it with iron plates, and rechristened it the *CSS Virginia*. The *Virginia* patrolled the water route to Richmond sinking several federal ships, before it was crippled in the famous battle with the Union ironclad, the *Monitor*.

3. "Thompson Case," Senate, *Executive Documents*, 34th Congress, 1st session, serial 822, vol. 13, 10, 58, 99–103, Document 72 (hereafter cited as "Thompson Case").

4. Ibid., 87.

5. Ibid., 84.

6. Henry Cohen, *Business and Politics in America from the Age of Jackson to the Civil War: The Career Biography of W. W. Corcoran* (Westport, Conn.: Greenwood Publishing, 1971), 205.

7. "Thompson Case," 103.

8. Ibid., 103, 105–7, 116–19.

9. Ibid., 155–57.

10. *Congressional Globe*, 34th Congress, 1st session, 1252, 1333–34.

11. William O. Scroggs, *Filibusters and Financiers: The Story of William Walker and His Associates* (New York: MacMillan, 1916; reprinted by Russell and Russell, 1969), 170; Albert Z. Carr, *The World and William Walker* (Westport, Conn.: Greenwood Press, 1963; reprinted 1975, 160.

12. Scroggs, *Filibusters and Financiers*, 149.

13. Franklin Pierce, "To Senate and House of Representatives," May 15, 1856, in James A. Richardson, ed., *A Compilation of the Messages and Papers of the Presidents* (Washington, D.C.: Government Printing Office, 1897), 5: 373–74; *New Hampshire Patriot*, May 7, 1856; Ivor Debenham Spencer, *The Victor and the Spoils: A Life of William L. Marcy* (Providence, R.I.: Brown University Press, 1959), 370–71; Carr, *The World and William Walker*, 160–62.

14. William L. Marcy to George M. Dallas, April 25, 1856, Marcy Papers, Library of Congress (hereafter cited as Marcy Papers).

15. Scroggs, *Filibusters and Financiers*, 172–73; William L. Marcy to George M. Dallas, May 12, 1856, Marcy Papers.

16. William L. Marcy to George M. Dallas, May 12, 1856, Marcy Papers.

17. William L. Marcy to George M. Dallas, June 16, 1856, Marcy Papers.

18. Franklin Pierce, "To the Senate and House of Representatives, 372.

19. Ibid., 374.

20. Franklin Pierce to William L. Marcy, May 12, 1856, Marcy Papers.

21. *Washington Union,* April 25, 1856; *New Hampshire Patriot,* April 30, 1856; Philip Shriver Klein, *President James Buchanan: A Biography* (University Park: Pennsylvania State University Press, 1962), 251–52.

22. William L. Marcy to George M. Dallas, May 12, 1856, Marcy Papers; Spencer, *The Victor and the Spoils,* 371.

23. *New Hampshire Patriot,* May 28, 1856; *New York Times,* May 24, 1856; *New York Herald,* May 24, 1856; Scroggs, *Filibuster and Financiers,* 173–74.

24. Alice Nichols, *Bleeding Kansas* (New York: Oxford University Press, 1954), 99–100; Nichole Etcheson, *Bleeding Kansas: Contested Liberty in the Civil War Era* (Lawrence: University Press of Kansas, 2004), 100–101; *New Hampshire Patriot,* May 7, 1856; Don W. Wilson, *Governor Charles Robinson of Kansas* (Lawrence: University Press of Kansas Press, 1975), 40.

25. Nichols, *Bleeding Kansas,* 102–3; Etcheson, *Bleeding Kansas,* 102–4; Wilson, *Governor Charles Robinson,* 41.

26. Etcheson, *Bleeding Kansas,* 104, 115.

27. Alice Nichols, *Bleeding Kansas,* 105–6; Etcheson, *Bleeding Kansas,* 104–5; Wilson, *Governor Charles Robinson,* 42–43; Samuel A. Johnson, *The Battle Cry of Freedom: The New England Emigrant Aid Company in the Kansas Crusade* (Lawrence: University of Kansas Press, 1954), 169–70, 181; *New York Herald,* May 26, 1856.

28. Franklin Pierce to William Shannon, May 23, 1856, in Charles Robinson, *The Kansas Conflict* (New York: Harper and Brothers, Franklin Square, 1892), 259.

29. Ibid., 259–60.

30. Etcheson, *Bleeding Kansas,* 109–11; Alice Nichols, *Bleeding Kansas,* 116; Wilson, *Governor Charles Robinson,* 43–44.

31. Alice Nichols, *Bleeding Kansas,* 118.

32. *Congressional Globe,* 34th Congress, 1st session, 543–544; *Washington Union,* May 20, 1856.

33. *Congressional Globe,* 34th Congress, 1st session, 544–547; Robert W. Johannsen, *Stephen A. Douglas* (New York: Oxford University Press, 1973), 502–4; *New Hampshire Patriot,* May 28, 1856; David M. Potter, *The Impending Crisis, 1848–1861* (New York: Harper and Row, 1976), 209–11.

34. *Congressional Globe,* 34th Congress, 1st session, 664–66, 1105–06.

35. Franklin Pierce, "Veto Messages," May 19, 22, 1856, Richardson, *A Compilation of the Messages,* 5: 386–87.

36. Roy Nichols, *Franklin Pierce: Young Hickory of the Granite Hills,* rev. ed. (Philadelphia: University of Pennsylvania Press 1931; revised 1969), 465.

37. Spencer, *The Victor and the Spoils,* 372; H. Barrett Learned, "William Learned Marcy," in *The American Secretaries of State and Their Diplomacy,* ed. Samuel Flagg Bemis (New York: Pageant Book Company, 1958), 6: 258.

38. William L. Marcy to George M. Dallas, May 19, 1856, Marcy Papers.

39. Caleb Cushing to Franklin Pierce, May 21, 1856, Letters Sent by the Attorney General, RG60, T969, Roll 1, National Archives.

40. Learned, "William Learned Marcy," 6: 259; Spencer, *The Victor and the Spoils*, 373; *Washington Union*, May 29, 30, 1856; *New York Herald*, May 27, 1856.

41. "To All Whom It May Concern," May 28, 1856, in Richardson, *A Compilation of the Messages*, 5: 391–93; *New York Herald*, May 28, 1856.

42. William L. Marcy to George M. Dallas, May 27, 1856, Marcy Papers.

43. Spencer, *The Victor and the Spoils*, 373–74; *New Hampshire Patriot*, June 4, 1856.

44. Varina Davis, *Jefferson Davis, Ex-President of the Confederate States of America: A Memoir by His Wife* (New York: Belford Company Publishers, 1890), 1: 569.

45. Charles H. Peaslee to John H. George, May 15, 1856; Sidney Webster to John H. George, May 1, 1856; both in John H. George Papers, New Hampshire Historical Society, Concord.

46. Johannsen, *Stephen A. Douglas*, 514; H. M. Rice to John C. Breckinridge, May 1, 1856, John C. Breckinridge Papers, Library of Congress (hereafter cited as Breckinridge Papers); Roy F. Nichols, *The Disruption of American Democracy* (New York: MacMillan, 1948), 12–14.

47. Roy F. Nichols, *The Disruption of American Democracy*, 12; Philip Auchampaugh, "The Story of New York Factions and the Buchanan Managers at Cincinnati, 1856," *New York State Historical Association* 24 (1926): 304–16.

48. Franklin Pierce to Mary Aiken, May, 1856, Pierce-Aiken Papers, Library of Congress.

49. Roy F. Nichols, *The Disruption of American Democracy*, 4.

50. Ibid., 4; Cohen, *Business and Politics in America from the Age of Jackson*, 203–4; Auchampaugh, "The Story of New York Factions, " 305–6, 313; Klein, *President James Buchanan*, 255.

51. Klein, *President James Buchanan*, 255; National Democratic Convention, *Official Proceedings of the Convention Held in Cincinnati, June 2–6, 1856* (Cincinnati: Enquirer Company, 1856), 10, 13.

52. John E. Ward to Howell Cobb, June 3, 1856, in Ulrich B. Phillips, ed., "The Correspondence of Robert Toombs, Alexander H. Stephens, and Howell Cobb," *Annual Report of the American Historical Association* 2 (1911): 367.

53. Klein, *President James Buchanan*, 255; Roy F. Nichols, *The Disruption of American Democracy*, 16; Stephen A. Douglas to William A. Richardson, June 3, 1856, *Letters, Stephen A. Douglas*, ed. Robert W. Johannsen (Urbana: University of Illinois Press, 1961), 361.

54. Roy F. Nichols, *The Disruption of American Democracy*, 15, 17; Auchampaugh, "The Story of New York Factions," 307; National Democratic Convention, *Official Proceedings*, 34–36. The vote to seat the Softs and the Hards on an equal basis was 137 to 123, reflecting almost precisely the relative delegate strength of Buchanan and Pierce.

55. *New Hampshire Patriot,* June 11, 1856; National Democratic Convention, *Official Proceedings,* 39–43.

56. *New Hampshire Patriot,* June 11, 1856; Roy F. Nichols, *The Disruption of American Democracy,* 17; Johannsen, *Stephen A. Douglas,* 518–19; National Democratic Convention, *Official Proceedings,* 44.

57. William C. Davis, *Breckinridge: Statesman, Soldier, Symbol* (Baton Rouge: Louisiana State University Press, 1974), 143–46; John Slidell to Breckinridge, June 17, 1856, Breckinridge Papers; National Democratic Convention, *Official Proceedings,* 66–67. Filibuster advocate and former Mexican War general John A. Quitman led the balloting for vice president on the first ballot. Pierce's Secretary of the Navy, James C. Dobbin, also received some votes.

58. *New Hampshire Patriot,* June 18, 1856; National Democratic Convention, *Official Proceedings,* 60.

59. *Washington Union,* June 7, 1856; *New Hampshire Patriot,* June 18, 1856.

60. William L. Marcy to George M. Dallas, June 10, 1856, Marcy Papers.

61. Allan Nevins, *Ordeal of the Union,* vol. 2, *A House Dividing, 1852–1857* (New York: Charles Scribner's Sons, 1947), 512.

62. Alexander H. Stephens to Thomas W. Thomas, June 16, 1856, in Phillips, "The Correspondence of Robert Toombs," 367–68.

63. Edmund Burke to James Buchanan, June 9, 1856, Edmund Burke Papers, Library of Congress.

64. George Templeton Strong, *The Diary of George Templeton Strong,* ed. Allan Nevins and Milton Halsey Thomas (New York: MacMillan, 1952), 2: 277.

65. John P. Hale to Lucy Hale, July 3, 1856, John P. Hale Papers, New Hampshire Historical Society, Concord.

66. Benjamin Brown French, *Witness to the Young Republic: A Yankee's Journal, 1828–1870,* ed. by Donald B. Cole and John J. McDonough (Hanover, N.H.: University Press of New England, 1989), 270.

67. George M. Dallas to William L. Marcy, June 13, 1856, Marcy Papers; Spencer, *The Victor and the Spoils,* 376–77.

68. Spencer, *The Victor and the Spoils,* 376; Learned, "William Learned Marcy," 6: 260.

69. Spencer, *The Victor and the Spoils,* 377.

70. George M. Dallas to William L. Marcy, June 20, July 8, 1856, Marcy Papers.

71. Learned, "William Learned Marcy," 6: 262.

72. Nathaniel Hawthorne to Horatio Bridge, June 20, 1856, in Horatio Bridge, *Personal Recollections of Nathaniel Hawthorne* (New York: Harper and Brothers, 1893), 151.

73. *Congressional Globe,* 34th Congress, 1st session, 1544, 1550, 1574.

74. Cohen, *Business and Politics in America from the Age of Jackson,* 205.

75. *Congressional Globe,* 34th Congress, 1st session, 1846, 1883–84, 1901.

76. *Congressional Globe,* 34th Congress, 1st session, 1980–84.

77. Etcheson, *Bleeding Kansas*, 113–115; Alice Nichols, *Bleeding Kansas*, 123; Johnson, *The Battle Cry of Freedom*, 181; Wilson, *Governor Charles Robinson*, 44–45.

78. Edward E. Hale to Caleb Cushing, June, 1856, Cushing Papers, Library of Congress; Nichols, *Bleeding Kansas*, 125; Johnson, *The Battle Cry of Freedom*, 190; Charles A. Jellison, *Fessenden of Maine: Civil War Senator* (Syracuse: Syracuse University Press, 1962), 92.

79. Etcheson, *Bleeding Kansas*, 115, 128; Alice Nichols, *Bleeding Kansas*, 127.

80. Jefferson Davis to Franklin Pierce, June 19, 1856, Letters Sent to the President by the Secretary of War, RG 107, M127, National Archives (hereafter cited as Letters Sent to the President by the Secretary of War).

81. *Congressional Globe*, 34th Congress, 1st session, 1381–82.

82. *Congressional Globe*, 34th Congress, 1st session, 1467, 1475; Johannsen, *Stephen A. Douglas*, 527; Etcheson, *Bleeding Kansas*, 126; James A. Rawley, *Race and Politics: "Bleeding Kansas" and the Coming of the Civil War* (Philadelphia: J. B. Lippincott, 1969), 153–55.

83. *Congressional Globe*, 34th Congress, 1st session, 1506, 1519–20.

84. *Congressional Globe*, 34th Congress, 1st session, 1572–74; Johannsen, *Stephen A. Douglas*, 527; Rawley, *Race and Politics*, 153–55.

85. Johannsen, *Stephen A. Douglas*, 527.

86. *Congressional Globe*, 34th Congress, 1st session, 1525; "Howard Report," *Executive Documents*, 34th Congress, 1st session, report 200, serial 869, 1–1188.

87. Johnson, *The Battle Cry of Freedom*, 189; Etcheson, *Bleeding Kansas*, 117–118.

88. Etcheson, *Bleeding Kansas*, 115.

89. Ibid., 116–17.

90. Robinson, *The Kansas Conflict*, 334, 337; Etcheson, *Bleeding Kansas*, 133.

91. Jefferson Davis to Franklin Pierce, May 21, 1856, Letters Sent to the President by the Secretary of War.

92. Robinson, *The Kansas Conflict*, 337.

93. *Congressional Globe*, 34th Congress, 1st session, 2091–93; Etcheson, *Bleeding Kansas*, 118.

94. *Congressional Globe*, 34th Congress, 1st session, 2091–93, 2095, 2230; Johannsen, *Stephen A. Douglas*, 527–28; Persifor F. Smith to Col. Samuel Cooper, August 6, 11, 1856, Letters Received by the Office of Adjutant General, RG 94, M567, National Archives.

95. *Congressional Globe*, 34th Congress, 1st session, 1913, 2095.

96. Etcheson, *Bleeding Kansas*, 125; Alice Nichols, *Bleeding Kansas*, 122; Wilson, *Governor Charles Robinson*, 43.

97. Amos A. Lawrence to S. C. Pomeroy, July 12, 1856, Amos A. Lawrence Papers, Massachusetts Historical Society, Boston (hereafter cited as Lawrence Papers).

98. Pomeroy to Lawrence, July 24, 1856, Lawrence Papers.

99. Ibid.

100. Johannsen, *Stephen A. Douglas*, 527; Amos A. Lawrence to Solomon Haven, July 28, 1856, Lawrence Papers.

101. Roy F. Nichols, "John White Geary," *Dictionary of American Biography* (New York: Charles Scribner's Sons, 1932), 7: 203–4.

102. Johannsen, *Stephen A. Douglas*, 527.

103. *Congressional Globe,* 34th Congress, 1st session, 2091–93, 2095.

104. "Special Session Message," August 21, 1856, in Richardson, *A Compilation of the Messages*, 5: 394–96.

105. Ibid., 395.

106. *Congressional Globe,* 34th Congress, 2nd session, 83.

Chapter 12: *Closing the Book on the Pierce Administration*

1. Franklin Pierce to John C. Breckinridge, July 22, 1856, John C. Breckinridge Papers, Library of Congress (hereafter cited as Breckinridge Papers).

2. Howell Cobb to James Buchanan, July 14, 1856, Ulrich B. Phillips, ed., "The Correspondence of Robert Toombs, Alexander H. Stephens, and Howell Cobb," *Annual Report of the American Historical Association* 2 (1911): 324–25.

3. Ibid.

4. James Buchanan to Howell Cobb, July 22, 1856, in Phillips, "Correspondence of Robert Toombs," 376–77; Philip Shriver Klein, *President James Buchanan: A Biography* (University Park: Pennsylvania State University Press, 1962), 259.

5. James Buchanan to Howell Cobb, July 22, 1856, in Phillips, "Correspondence of Robert Toombs," 376–77.

6. Howell Cobb to James Buchanan, August 3, 1856, in Phillips, "Correspondence of Robert Toombs," 378–79; James Buchanan to J. C. Dobbin, August 20, 1856, in George Ticknor Curtis, *Life of James Buchanan* I (New York: Harper and Brothers, 1883), 2: 179–80; Michael F. Holt, *The Rise and Fall of the American Whig Party* (New York: Oxford University Press, 1999), 969.

7. James Buchanan to J. C. Dobbin, August 20, 1856, in Curtis, *Life of James Buchanan*, 2: 179–80.

8. William L. Marcy to James Buchanan, August 21, 1856, and James Buchanan to William L. Marcy, August 27, 1856, William L. Marcy Papers, Library of Congress (hereafter cited as Marcy Papers).

9. Klein, *President James Buchanan*, 259; Robert W. Johannsen, *Stephen A. Douglas* (New York: Oxford University Press, 1973), 537.

10. Nichole Etcheson, *Bleeding Kansas: Contested Liberty in the Civil War Era* (Lawrence: University Press of Kansas, 2004), 121–22; Alice Nichols, *Bleeding Kansas* (New York: Oxford University Press, 1954), 140; Samuel A. Johnson, *The Battle Cry of Freedom: The New England Emigrant Aid Company in the Kansas Conflict* (Lawrence: University of Kansas Press, 1954), 198–201; Don W. Wilson, *Governor Charles Robinson of Kansas* (Lawrence: University Press of Kansas, 1975), 46.

11. Johnson, *The Battle Cry of Freedom*, 206; Telegram, F. A. Abbot to Franklin Pierce, August 22, 1856 (3:40 p.m.), State Department, Territorial Papers of Kansas, RG59, M218, Roll 1, National Archives (hereafter cited as Territorial Papers of

Kansas); a copy of the telegram is also found in Franklin Pierce Papers, Library of Congress.

12. Johnson, *The Battle Cry of Freedom*, 201–2.

13. Wilson Shannon to Acting Governor Daniel Woodson, August 25, 1856, accompanied by nineteen affidavits, in State Department, Territorial Papers of Kansas; Etcheson, *Bleeding Kansas*, 122–23.

14. Daniel Woodson, Acting Governor of Kansas Territory to Col. P. St. George Cooke, Commander U.S. Dragoons, September 1, 1856, State Department, Territorial Papers of Kansas.

15. Col. P. S. George Cooke to Acting Governor Daniel Woodson, Headquarters Camp Near Lecompton, September 2, 1856, State Department, Territorial Papers of Kansas.

16. Ibid.

17. Ibid.

18. Jefferson Davis to Gen. Persifor F. Smith, September 3, 1856, in Jefferson Davis, *Jefferson Davis, Constitutionalist: His Letters, Papers, and Speeches*, ed. Dunbar Rowland (New York: J. Little and Ives, 1923), 3: 48–49.

19. John H. Gihon, Secretary to Governor John W. Geary, in John H. Gihon, *Gihon's History of Kansas* (n.p.: Cone Publishers, 1856), 125; Etcheson, *Bleeding Kansas*, 131; Johnson, *The Battle Cry of Freedom*, 230–31; Alice Nichols, *Bleeding Kansas*, 145.

20. Gihon, *Gihon's History of Kansas*, 126–27; Alice Nichols, *Bleeding Kansas*, 153; Wilson, *Governor Charles Robinson*, 47.

21. Alice Nichols, *Bleeding Kansas*, 158; Johnson, *The Battle Cry of Freedom*, 232–33; Etcheson, *Bleeding Kansas*, 131–34; Wilson, *Governor Charles Robinson*, 47–48.

22. Alice Nichols, *Bleeding Kansas*, 166; Caleb Cushing to Andrew J. Isaacs, District Attorney of Kansas Territory, September 7, 1856; Andrew J. Isaacs to Caleb Cushing, October 22, 1856; both in Caleb Cushing Papers, Library of Congress (hereafter cited as Cushing Papers).

23. Amos A. Lawrence to Mrs. (Sara) Robinson, October 3, 1856, Amos A. Lawrence Papers, Massachusetts Historical Society, Boston.

24. Ibid.

25. Sidney Webster to John H. George, August 21, 1856, John H. George Papers, New Hampshire Historical Society, Concord (hereafter cited as George Papers).

26. *New Hampshire Patriot*, September 24, 1856; *New Hampshire State Capital Reporter*, September 26, 1856; *New Hampshire Independent Democrat*, September 25, 1856.

27. *New Hampshire Patriot*, September 24, 1856; *New Hampshire State Reporter*, September 26, 1856; *New Hampshire Independent Democrat*, September 25, 1856. New Hampshire Historical Society, Concord.

28. Franklin Pierce to William Butterfield, September 24, 1856, Pierce Papers, New Hampshire Historical Society, Concord.

29. "List of names of people who contributed to defray expenses of Pierce recep-

tion in Concord," September 25, 1856, Pierce Papers, New Hampshire Historical Society, Concord.

30. *New Hampshire Patriot,* October 8, 1856.

31. Ibid.

32. *New Hampshire Patriot,* October 8, 1856; *New Hampshire Independent Democrat,* October 9, 1856; *New Hampshire State Capital Reporter,* October 3, 1856.

33. William L. Marcy to George M. Dallas, October 6, 1856, Marcy Papers.

34. *New Hampshire Patriot,* October 8, 1856; Franklin Pierce to Fanny McNeil, October 5, 1856, Pierce Papers, New Hampshire Historical Society, Concord; Abigail A. Means to Mary Aiken, October 11, 1856, Pierce-Aiken Papers, Library of Congress (hereafter cited as Pierce-Aiken Papers).

35. Albert R. Hatch to John H. George, September 27, 1856, George Papers.

36. Robert McClelland to Senator Charles E. Stuart, October 20, 1856, McClelland Letterpress Book, Library of Congress (hereafter cited as McClelland Letterpress Book).

37. James C. Dobbin to Caleb Cushing, October 9, 1856, Cushing Papers.

38. Robert McClelland to John W. Forney, October 20, 1856, McClelland Letterpress Book.

39. Lex Renda, *Running on the Record: Civil War-Era Politics in New Hampshire* (Charlottesville: University Press of Virginia, 1997), 68–69.

40. Franklin Pierce to James Buchanan, November 20, 1856, Buchanan Papers, Historical Society of Pennsylvania, Philadelphia.

41. Isaac O. Barnes to John H. George, November 6, 1856, George Papers.

42. William L. Marcy to George M. Dallas, May 24, 1856, in William R. Manning, ed., *Diplomatic Correspondence of the United States, Inter-American Affairs, 1837–1860,* vol. 7, *Great Britain* (Washington, D.C.: Carnegie Foundation for International Peace, 1936), 128–36; William L. Marcy to George M. Dallas, July 26, 1856, Marcy Papers.

43. George M. Dallas to William L. Marcy, August 22, 1856, William L. Marcy to George M. Dallas, September 22, 1856, both in Marcy Papers; Ivor Debenham Spencer, *The Victor and the Spoils: A Life of William L. Marcy* (Providence, R.I.: Brown University Press, 1959), 378–79.

44. Spencer, *The Victor and the Spoils,* 380–81; William O. Scroggs, *Filibusters and Financiers: The Story of William Walker and His Associates* (New York: MacMillan, 1916; reprinted by Russell and Russell, 1969), 215–17; Albert Z. Carr, *The World and William Walker* (Westport: Conn.: Greenwood Press, 1963; reprinted 1975), 185–98; J. Preston Moore, "Pierre Soulé: Southern Expansionist and Promoter," *Journal of Southern History* 21, no. 2 (May 1955): 212–13.

45. Scroggs, *Filibusters and Financiers,* 216; Spencer, *The Victor and the Spoils,* 381; Carr, *The World and William Walker,* 199–200; Moore, "Pierre Soulé: Southern Expansionist and Promoter," 212–15.

46. William L. Marcy to George M. Dallas, January 20, 1857, Marcy Papers.

47. Scroggs, *Filibusters and Financiers,* 238–39; *New York Times,* December 19, 1856.

48. Scroggs, *Filibusters and Financiers,* 239; *New York Herald,* December 25, 1856.

49. *Congressional Globe,* 34th Congress, 3rd session, 10, 18; Franklin Pierce, "Fourth Annual Message," James A. Richardson, ed., *A Compilation of the the messages and Papers of the Presidents,* (Washington, D.C.: Government Printing Office, 1897), 5: 397–99.

50. Pierce, "Fourth Annual Message," 5: 399.

51. Ibid., 400–3.

52. Ibid., 405–6.

53. Ibid., 406–7.

54. Ibid., 407–8.

55. Ibid., 408–9.

56. Ibid., 411–12; William L. Marcy to Henry Bedinger, U.S. Consul at Copenhagen, November 5, 1855, and May 5, 1856, Marcy Papers; H. Barrett Learned, "William Learned Marcy," *The American Secretaries of State and Their Diplomacy,* ed. Samuel Flagg Bemis (New York: Pageant Book Company, 1958), 285–87; Charles E. Hill, *The Danish Sound Dues and the Command of the Baltic* (Durham, N.C.: Duke University Press, 1926), 278–85; Spencer, *The Victor and the Spoils,* 398–407.

57. Hill, *The Danish Sound Dues,* 285.

58. Pierce, "Fourth Annual Messages5: 412–14; Learned, "William Learned Marcy," 6: 283–85; Alan Dowty, *The Limits of American Isolation: The United States and the Crimean War* (New York: New York University Press, 1971), 60–62, 237; William L. Marcy to Count de Sartiges, French Minister to the United States, July 28, 1856, Marcy Papers.

59. Pierce, "Fourth Annual Message," 5: 417.

60. *Congressional Globe,* 34th Congress, 3rd session, 10.

61. Ibid., 26.

62. Ibid., 30.

63. Ibid., 11–14, 27–30.

64. *New York Evening Post* and *New York Times* quoted in *New Hampshire Independent Democrat,* December 11, 1856.

65. *Boston Post* and *National Intelligencer* quoted in *New Hampshire Patriot,* December 10, 1856.

66. James A. Rawley, *Race and Politics: "Bleeding Kansas" and the Coming of the Civil War* (Philadelphia: J. B. Lippincott, 1969), 175. According to Rawley, "Pierce's denigration of a major political party in a state message was deplorable. His reading of the election returns was sophistical, his insensitivity of anti-slavery sentiment was cold-hearted." But Pierce had said nothing new. For example, in his debate with Hale in June 1845, Pierce stated, "Point out to us, if you can, some feasible, practicable plan for emancipation, one which as things are will not prove ruinous both to the master and the slave. . . . *New Hampshire Patriot,* June 12, 1845. In a speech supporting the Compromise of 1850 given in Manchester, New Hampshire, in November 1850, Pierce said, "If we are precipitated into a war by fanaticism, we cannot conquer.

Both sections of the country may be immolated. Neither could come out of the contest short of ruin." *New Hampshire Patriot,* November 28, 1850.

67. Gen. Persifor F. Smith to Col. Samuel Cooper, Adjutant General, November 11, 1856, Letters Received by the Office of Adjutant General, RG94, M567, National Archives.

68. Ibid.

69. Etcheson, *Bleeding Kansas,* 137; Alice Nichols, *Bleeding Kansas,* 163; John W. Geary to Franklin Pierce, December 22, 1856, Pierce Papers, Library of Congress.

70. John W. Geary to Franklin Pierce, December 22, 1856, Pierce Papers, Library of Congress; James Guthrie to John C. Breckinridge, December 4, 1856, Breckinridge Papers; William C. Davis, *Breckinridge: Statesman, Soldier, Symbol* (Baton Rouge: Louisiana State University Press, 1974), 165.

71. John W. Geary to Franklin Pierce, December 22, 1856, Pierce Papers.

72. Ibid.

73. Ibid.

74. John W. Geary to Franklin Pierce, January 12, 1856, Pierce Papers.

75. Ibid.; John W. Geary to William L. Marcy, January 19, February 2, 1857, State Department, "Territorial Papers of Kansas"; Etcheson, *Bleeding Kansas,* 140–41; Alice Nichols, *Bleeding Kansas,* 176–81; Rawley, *Race and Politics,* 178; Wilson, *Governor Charles Robinson,* 50.

76. Etcheson, *Bleeding Kansas,* 140; Alice Nichols, *Bleeding Kansas,* 182–83; Gihon, *Gihon's History of Kansas,* 227–44; John W. Geary to Gen. Persifor F. Smith, February 9, 1857, in Gihon, *Gihon's History of Kansas,* 280.

77. Etcheson, *Bleeding Kansas,* 140; Alice Nichols, *Bleeding Kansas,* 182–83; Gihon, *Gihon's History of Kansas,* 227–44; *New York Herald,* February 27, 1855.

78. Gen. Persifor F. Smith to John W. Geary, February 11, 1857 in Gihon, *Gihon's History of Kansas,* 281.

79. William L. Marcy to John W. Geary, February 4, 1857, Marcy Papers; John W. Geary to William L. Marcy, February 20, 1857, State Department, Territorial Papers of Kansas.

80. John W. Geary to James Buchanan, February 20, 1857, State Department, Territorial Papers of Kansas.

81. Etcheson, *Bleeding Kansas,* 142–43; Alice Nichols, *Bleeding Kansas,* 185.

82. Diary of Amos A. Lawrence, January 6, 1857, Massachusetts Historical Society, Boston (hereafter cited as Lawrence Diaries).

83. Thomas W. Thomas to Alexander H. Stephens, January 12, 1857, in Phillips, "The Correspondence of Robert Toombs," 392.

84. Robert Toombs to Thomas W. Thomas, February 5, 1857, in Phillips, "The Correspondence of Robert Toombs," 394.

85. Dale E. Watts, "How Bloody Was Bleeding Kansas? Political Killings in Kansas Territory, 1854–1861," *Kansas History* 18, no. 2 (Summer 1995), 123.

86. Hudson Strode, *Jefferson Davis: American Patriot, 1808–1861* (New York: Harcourt Brace, 1955), 1: 293.

87. Varina Davis, *Jefferson Davis, Ex-president of the Confederate States of America, A Memoir by His Wife*, I (New York: Belford Company, Publishers, 1890), 1: 523.

88. William L. Marcy to George M. Dallas, February 6, and 9, 1857, Marcy Papers.

89. William L. Marcy to George M. Dallas, February 16, 1857, Marcy Papers.

90. Spencer, *The Victor and the Spoils*, 380.

91. Caleb Cushing to Franklin Pierce, December 24, 1856, in "Morton's Anaesthetic Patent," C. C. Andrews, ed., *Official Opinions of the Attorneys General of the United States: Advising the President and Heads of Departments in Relation to Their Official Duties* (Washington, D.C.: Robert Farnham, 1857), 269–79.

92. Ibid.; Claude M. Fuess, *The Life of Caleb Cushing* (New York: Harcourt Brace, 1923), 2: 183–84.

93. Telegram, John McKeon to Caleb Cushing, February 4, 1857, Cushing Papers.

94. Note in Pierce's handwriting, Caleb Cushing to John McKeon, February 5, 1857, Letters Sent by the Attorneys General, RG60, T969, Roll 1, National Archives (hereafter cited as Letters Sent by the Attorneys General).

95. Caleb Cushing to John McKeon, February 7, 1857, Letters Sent by the Attorneys General.

96. *New York Herald*, February 28, 1857; Telegram, John McKeon to Caleb Cushing, February 4, 1857, Cushing Papers. Webster's letter, written on April 24, 1855, read, "My Dear Fabens—I have received the document and with my associate here am grateful to you and your partner, and entirely satisfied. The Judge [A.O.P. Nicholson] is here and will be for a week within which time we hope to see you at Willard's. Don't try to figure in the newspapers." Fabens testified that Pierce was "interested with Sidney Webster" in Kinney's enterprise but presented no evidence to prove his accusation. See *New York Herald*, February 28, 1855.

97. Caleb Cushing to James Campbell, March 2, 1857, in "Yazoo City Post Office Case," Andrews, *Official Opinions*, 7: 489–502; Fuess, *The Life of Caleb Cushing*, 2: 185.

98. *Congressional Globe*, 34rd Congress, 3rd session, 721, 802.

99. *Congressional Globe*, 34rd Congress, 3rd session, 989, 990, 997.

100. Afred T. Mahan, *From Sail to Steam: Recollections of Naval Life* (New York: Harper and Brothers, 1907), 30–32.

101. Chester G. Hearn, *Circuits in the Sea: The Men, the Ships, and the Atlantic Cable* (Westport, Conn.: Praeger, 2004), 36–39, 52–53.

102. *Congressional Globe*, 34rd Congress, 3rd session, 258, 395, 397, 421, 870, 880.

103. Hearn, *Circuits in the Sea*, 54.

104. *Congressional Globe*, 34rd Congress, 3rd session, 425, 741, 908, 914, 1086; Hearn, *Circuits in the Sea*, 54, 61.

105. *Congressional Globe*, 34rd Congress, 3rd session, 315–16, 1096.

106. Charles March to Albert R. Hatch, January, 1857, and February 1, 1857, Albert R. Hatch Papers, New Hampshire Historical Society. March wrote from Washington, "I had a long conversation with the President yesterday. . . . The President seems more disposed to make our part of the State [Portsmouth] his future residence and

his presence would add in little to our social advantage, we must try to look up a place for him. He says, he would want a farm of some 200 acres." A few days later March wrote, "Gen. Pierce says that his wife would not like the long steps to the Williams house—and he tells me confidentially that she prefers a house in town. Frank says he wants a farm and must have it. The deal gains a pleasant companion in the General, as well as political ally."

107. Abigail A. Means to Mary Aiken, March 2, 1857, Pierce-Aiken Papers.

108. William L. Marcy, et. al., to Franklin Pierce, March 3, 1857, Pierce Papers, Library of Congress.

109. Ibid.

110. Ibid.

111. Franklin Pierce to William L. Marcy, and others, March 4, 1857, Pierce Papers, Library of Congress.

112. Varina Davis, *Jefferson Davis,* 1: 529.

113. Diary of William L. Marcy, March 3, 1857, Marcy Papers; Klein, *President James Buchanan,* 271–72; Davis, *Breckinridge,* 166–67; Roy F. Nichols, *The Disruption of American Democracy* (New York: MacMillan, 1948), 71.

114. Diary of Amos A. Lawrence, March 4, 1857, Lawrence Diaries.

115. Larry Gara, *The Presidency of Franklin Pierce* (Lawrence: University Press of Kansas, 1991), 183–84; Allan Nevins, *Ordeal of the Union,* vol. 2, *A House Dividing, 1852–1857* (New York: Charles Scribner's Sons, 1947), 42; John M. Belohlavek, *Broken Glass: Caleb Cushing and the Shattering of the Union* (Kent, Ohio: Kent State University Press, 2005), 282.

116. Belohlavek, *Broken Glass,* 282.

Chapter 13: *Travel and Travails of an Ex-President*

1. Mary M. Aiken to John Aiken, March, 1857, Pierce-Aiken Papers, Library of Congress (hereafter cited as Piere-Aiken Papers).

2. Diary of William L. Marcy, March 19, 1857, William L. Marcy Papers, Library of Congress (hereafter cited as Marcy Papers); see also, Thomas Maitland Marshall, ed., "Diary and Memoranda of William L. Marcy, 1857," *American Historical Review* 24, no. 4 (July 1919): 645.

3. Nathan Clifford to Edmund Burke, April 29, 1857, Edmund Burke Papers, Library of Congress. Buchanan later nominated Clifford to the U.S. Supreme Court, where he served until his death in 1881. Pierce declared the appointment, "a disgrace." See Pierce to Caleb Cushing, February 2, 1858, Caleb Cushing Papers, Library of Congress (hereafter cited as Cushing Papers).

4. Diary of William L. Marcy, March 17, 1857, William L. Marcy Papers; see also Marshall, "Diary and Memoranda of William L. Marcy," 642. A year later Buchanan "emphatically disclaimed" to Jefferson Davis that his purpose was "to discriminate against those who were especially your [Pierce's] friends." Jefferson Davis to Franklin Pierce, April 4, 1858, Pierce Papers, Library of Congress. For a thorough

analysis of the political motives behind Buchanan's patronage policy, see David Meerse, "Buchanan's Patronage Policy: An Attempt to Achieve Political Strength," *Pennsylvania History* 40, no. 1, (1973): 37–57.

5. *New York Herald,* March 23, 1857; Marshall, "Diary and Memoranda of William L. Marcy," 642; Leonard D. White, *The Jacksonians: A Study in Administrative History, 1829–1861* (New York: MacMillan, 1954), 313–14; Dorothy G. Fowler, *The Cabinet Politician: The Postmasters General, 1829–1909* (New York: Columbia University Press, 1943), 90.

6. William C. Davis, *Breckinridge: Statesman, Soldier, Symbol* (Baton Rouge: Louisiana State University Press, 1974), 171.

7. Ibid., 171–72.

8. Buchanan had appointed seven Hards to office in New York, the quality of these appointments often described as "wretched." See Meerse, "Buchanan's Patronage Policy," 38, 52–54; Diary of William L. Marcy, March 25, 1857, Marcy Papers; see also Marshall, "Diary and Memoranda of William L. Marcy," 646. The new collector was Augustus Schell. Buchanan's biographer describes Schell as not "very bright" and lacking in "leadership." The appointment of Rynders as marshal did signal a change in policy toward filibusters. In December 1857, after U.S. Navy ships under Commodore Paulding intercepted Walker's ship in Nicaraguan waters as Walker was about to disembark for another attempt to take over the Central American nation, the Buchanan administration freed him and disciplined Paulding for exceeding his authority by entering foreign waters to detain Walker. The Buchanan administration did not charge Walker with violating U.S. neutrality laws, and Walker later claimed that Buchanan himself had encouraged his expedition, only to back away from this promise. See Philip S. Klein, *President James Buchanan: A Biography* (University Park: Pennsylvania State University Press, 1962), 280–81, 319–20; Robert W. Johannsen, *Stephen A. Douglas* (New York: Oxford University Press, 1973), 616.

9. Diary of William L. Marcy, March 27, 1857, Marcy Papers; see also Marshall, "Diary and Memoranda of William L. Marcy," 647.

10. Roger B. Taney to Franklin Pierce, August 29, 1857, Pierce Papers, Library of Congress.

11. *New Hampshire Patriot,* April 1, 1857.

12. Diary of William L. Marcy, March 24, 1857, Marcy Papers; see also Marshall, "Diary and Memoranda of William L. Marcy," 645; *New Hampshire Patriot,* April 1, 1857.

13. Diary of William L. Marcy, March 27, 1857, Marcy Papers; see also Marshall, "Diary and Memoranda of William L. Marcy," 647.

14. Franklin Pierce to Henry D. Pierce, March 21, 1857; Franklin Pierce to John H. George, April 1, 1857; both in Pierce Papers, Library of Congress.

15. Franklin Pierce to William L. Marcy, April 5, 1857, Marcy Papers.

16. Diary of William L. Marcy, April 4, 1857, Marcy Papers; see also Marshall, "Diary and Memoranda of William L. Marcy," 648.

17. *New York Herald,* April 13, 18, 1857; Diary of William L. Marcy, April 18, 1857,

Marcy Papers; see also Marshall, "Diary and Memoranda of William L. Marcy," 651; *New York Herald*, April 13, 18, 1857.

18. *New York Herald*, April 18, 1857; Diary of William L. Marcy, April 18, 1857, Marcy Papers; see also Marshall, "Diary and Memoranda of William L. Marcy," 651; Henry Cohen, *Business and Politics in America from the Age of Jackson to the Civil War: The Career Biography of W. W. Corcoran* (Westport, Conn.: Greenwood Publishing Corp, 1971), 205.

19. Franklin Pierce to George W. Manypenny, July 17, 1857, George W. Manypenny Papers, Library of Congress. Thompson had a long and controversial public career. He joined the Republican Party during the Civil War and was appointed secretary of the navy under Hayes. While holding this office, Thompson accepted the chairmanship of the American Committee of the Panama Canal Company at a salary of $25,000. Hayes fired Thompson for this flagrant conflict of interest. In later years, Thompson served as a lobbyist for railroads and wrote several books attacking the Catholic Church, claiming the pope was attempting to influence American politics. William A. Shea concludes, "Few of his contemporaries . . . were so frequently attacked on ethical grounds." See William A. Shea, "Thompson, Richard Wigginton," *Dictionary of American Biography*, ed. Dumas Malone (New York: Charles Scribner's Sons, 1936), 28: 468–69; Mark E. Neely Jr., "Richard W. Thompson: The Persistent Know Nothing," *Indiana Magazine of History* 72, no. 2 (June 1976): 95–122.

20. Franklin Pierce to William L. Marcy, May 13, 1857, Marcy Papers; James Campbell to Franklin Pierce, June 23, 1857; both in Pierce Papers, Library of Congress.

21. *New York Daily Times*, May 20, 21, June 1, 1857.

22. *New Hampshire Patriot*, June 3, 1857.

23. Jefferson Davis to Franklin Pierce, July 23, 1857, Pierce Papers, Library of Congress.

24. Diary of William L. Marcy, June 6, 10, 11, 20, 27, 1857, Marcy Papers; Franklin Pierce to William L. Marcy, May 13, 1857, Marcy Papers. See also the account of Marcy's death written by Edward Chase in Marcy Papers.

25. Caleb Cushing to Franklin Pierce, July 9, 1857; James Guthrie to Franklin Pierce, August 17, 1857; both in Pierce Papers, Library of Congress.

26. B. B. French to Franklin Pierce, July 12, 1857, Pierce Papers, Library of Congress.

27. Franklin Pierce to William Aiken, July 15, 1857, Pierce Papers, Library of Congress.

28. James Campbell to Franklin Pierce, August 12, 1857, Pierce Papers, Library of Congress.

29. Franklin and Jane Pierce to Mary Aiken, August 5, 1857, Pierce-Aiken Papers.

30. Franklin Pierce to James Shields, July 25, 1857; James Shields to Franklin Pierce, August 8,1857; Benjamin Grover to Franklin Pierce, August 9, 1857; all in Pierce Papers, Library of Congress.

31. Pierce to ——, September 9, 1857, Pierce Papers, New Hampshire Historical Society, Concord.

32. Diary of Clement March, October 2, 8, 1857, Clement March Diaries, microfilm, Center for Southwest Research, University of New Mexico, Albuquerque (hereafter cited as Clement March Diaries).

33. Ibid.

34. Diary of Clement March, October 16, 19, 26, 1857, Clement March Diaries.

35. Diary of Clement March, October 23, 24, 1857, Clement March Diaries.

36. For a description of crime and vice in the notorious Hill district neighborhood of the West End see Barbara Meil Hobson, *Uneasy Virtue: The Politics of Prostitution and the American Reform Tradition* (New York: Basic Books, 1987), 11–45; Roger Lane, *Policing the City: Boston, 1822–1885* (Cambridge, Mass.: Harvard University Press, 1967), 23–24, 27, 29, 94, 174–75. To locate Fruit Street within this West End neighborhood see *The Boston City Directory, July 1, 1859* (Boston: Adams, Sampson, 1859), 11.

37. Diary of Clement March, October 17, November 10, 1857, Clement March Diaries; Franklin Pierce to Samuel S. Cox, September 14, 1857; Franklin Pierce to Henry D. Pierce, November 9, 1857; both in Pierce Papers, New Hampshire Historical Society, Concord.

38. Diary of Clement March, November 20, 21, 22, 1857, Clement March Diaries; Isaac Toucey to Franklin Pierce, October 21, 1857; M. B. Brady to Franklin Pierce, November 6, 1857; both in Pierce Papers, Library of Congress.

39. *New Hampshire Patriot*, November 4, 1857; Claude M. Fuess, *The Life of Caleb Cushing*, vol. I (New York: Harcourt, Brace, 1923), 2: 198–207.

40. Franklin Pierce to Caleb Cushing, November 4, 1857, Caleb Cushing Papers; Fuess, *The Life of Caleb Cushing*, 2: 204.

41. A. C. Dodge to Franklin Pierce, February 18, 1858, Pierce Papers, Library of Congress.

42. *New Hampshire Patriot*, December 9, 1857; Jane Pierce to Mary Aiken, "On Board the Steamer Powhatan off Norfolk," December, 1857; Jane Pierce to Mary Aiken, December 29, 1857; both in Pierce-Aiken Papers.

43. Jane Pierce to Mary Aiken, January 9, 1858; Franklin Pierce to John Aiken, March 10, 1858; both in Pierce-Aiken Papers.

44. Mary F. Ripley to Mary Aiken, February 15, 1858, Pierce-Aiken Papers.

45. Jane Pierce to Mary Aiken, February 23, 1858, Pierce-Aiken Papers.

46. Jane Pierce to Mary Aiken, January 9, August 9, 1858; Franklin Pierce to John Aiken, March 10, 1858; both in Pierce-Aiken Papers.

47. Franklin Pierce to John and Mary Aiken, November 6, 1858, Pierce Papers, New Hampshire Historical Society, Concord.

48. Johannsen, *Stephen A. Douglas*, 581–94; Klein, *President James Buchanan*, 296–312.

49. John W. Forney to Henry A. Wise, May 26, 1857, John W. Forney Papers, Library of Congress. Forney's bitter split with Buchanan was due more to Forney's failure to receive a suitable office in the new administration than to Buchanan's Kansas policy. See Klein, *President James Buchanan*, 264–68, 281–82.

50. Robert McClelland to Franklin Pierce, September 3, 1858, Pierce Papers, Library of Congress.

51. Franklin Pierce to John H. George, July 6, 1858, Pierce Papers, New Hampshire Historical Society, Concord.

52. Caleb Cushing to Franklin Pierce, April 9, 1858, Pierce Papers, New Hampshire Historical Society, Concord.

53. Pierce to Henry D. Pierce, January 13, 1859; Franklin Pierce to John H. George, July 6, 1858; both in Pierce Papers, New Hampshire Historical Society, Concord.

54. Franklin Pierce to John H. George, July 6, 1858, Pierce Papers, New Hampshire Historical Society, Concord.

55. Ibid.

56. Jane Pierce to Mary Aiken, September 24, 1858, Pierce-Aiken Papers.

57. Jane Pierce to Mary Aiken, August 13, October 9, 1858, Pierce-Aiken Papers.

58. Jane Pierce to Mary Aiken, September 24, 1858, Pierce-Aiken Papers.

59. Franklin Pierce to Henry D. Pierce, January 13, 1859; Franklin Pierce to John H. George, December 30, 1858; both in Pierce Papers, New Hampshire Historical Society, Concord.; Jane Pierce to Mary Aiken, October 9, 1858, Pierce-Aiken Papers.

60. James R. Mellow, *Nathaniel Hawthorne in His Times* (Baltimore: Johns Hopkins University Press, 1980), 473–77, 531; Nathaniel Hawthorne to Franklin Pierce, October 27, 1858, Pierce Papers, Library of Congress.

61. Julian Hawthorne, *Nathaniel Hawthorne and His Wife* (Boston: James R. Osgood, 1885), 2: 210.

62. Edwin Haviland Miller, *Salem Is My Dwelling Place: A Life of Nathaniel Hawthorne* (Iowa City: University of Iowa Press, 1991), 440.

63. Ibid., 441.

64. Ibid.

65. Franklin Pierce to Horatio Bridge, September 11, 1859, Pierce Papers, New Hampshire Historical Society, Concord.

66. Ibid.

67. Jane Pierce to Mary Aiken, April 25–May 6, and May, 1859, Pierce-Aiken Papers.

68. Jane Pierce to Mary Aiken, June 12, 1859, Pierce-Aiken Papers. Thomas H. Seymour reminisced about spending time with the Pierces in Brussels, Paris, and Brighton, England, in a letter written in 1863. Thomas H. Seymour to Franklin Pierce, July 8, 1863, Pierce Papers, Library of Congress.

69. [John Carlton?] to Franklin Pierce, House of Commons, July 17, 1859, Pierce Papers New Hampshire Historical Society, Concord.

70. Sidney Webster, *Franklin Pierce and His Administration* (New York: D. Appleton, 1892), 29–30; James Buchanan to Franklin Pierce, September 7, 1859, Pierce Papers, New Hampshire Historical Society, Concord.

71. James D. B. DeBow to Robert McClelland, July 8, 1859, Robert McClelland Papers, Library of Congress.

72. Jefferson Davis to Franklin Pierce, September 2, 1859, Pierce Papers, Library

of Congress; William J. Cooper, Jr., *Jefferson Davis, American* (New York: Alfred A. Knopf, 2000), 310.

73. Franklin Pierce to Eli S. Shorter, September 22, 1859, Pierce Papers, Library of Congress.

74. Diary of Clement March, September 12, 1859, Clement March Diaries.

75. Diary of Clement March, September 12, 14, October 11, 1859, Clement March Diaries.

76. Diary of Clement March, October 12, 13, 1859, Clement March Diaries.

77. Draft of letter, Franklin Pierce to William Appleton, and others, December, 1859, Pierce Papers, Library of Congress.

78. Franklin Pierce to Henry D. Pierce, December 21, 1859, Pierce Papers, Library of Congress.

79. Franklin Pierce to Jefferson Davis, January 6,1860, Pierce Papers, New Hampshire Historical Society, Concord.

80. Franklin Pierce to John H. George, January 7, 1860, Pierce Papers, New Hampshire Historical Society, Concord.

81. John H. George to Franklin Pierce, January 30, 1860, Pierce Papers, Library of Congress.

82. Franklin Pierce to John H. George, February 17, 1860, Pierce Papers, New Hampshire Historical Society, Concord.

83. Ibid.

84. Jefferson Davis to Franklin Pierce, June 13, 1860, Pierce Papers, Library of Congress.

85. Roy F. Nichols, *The Disruption of American Democracy* (New York: The MacMillan Company, 1948), 288–309; Johannsen, *Stephen A. Douglas*, 749–60; David M. Potter, *The Impending Crisis, 1848–1861* (New York: Harper and Row, 1976), 403, 409; Fuess, *The Life of Caleb Cushing*, 2: 253.

86. Jane Pierce to Mary Aiken, March 18, 1860, and n.d. 1860, Pierce-Aiken Papers; Franklin Pierce to John H. George, June 12, 1860, Pierce Papers, New Hampshire Historical Society, Concord.

87. Franklin Pierce to John H. George, June 8, 1860, Pierce Papers, New Hampshire Historical Society, Concord.

88. Thomas H. Seymour to Franklin Pierce, May 19–20, 1860, Pierce Papers, New Hampshire Historical Society, Concord.

89. J. W. Forney to Franklin Pierce, May 20, 1860, Pierce Papers, New Hampshire Historical Society, Concord.

90. Jefferson Davis to Franklin Pierce, June 13, 1860, Pierce Papers, Library of Congress; Caleb Cushing to Franklin Pierce, June 7, 1860, Pierce Papers, New Hampshire Historical Society, Concord.

91. Thomas H. Seymour to Franklin Pierce, June 18, 1860, Pierce Papers, New Hampshire Historical Society, Concord; Jefferson Davis to Franklin Pierce, June 13, 1860, Pierce Papers, Library of Congress.

92. Nichols, *The Disruption of American Democracy*, 314–21; Johannsen, *Stephen*

A. Douglas, 767–73; Fuess, *The Life of Caleb Cushing*, 2: 255–60; B. F. Hallett to Franklin Pierce, June 21, 1860, Pierce Papers, Library of Congress; Hans L. Trefousse, *Ben Butler: The South Called Him Beast* (New York: Twayne Publishers, 1957), 56.

93. Franklin Pierce to B. F. Hallett, June 29, 1860, Pierce Papers, Library of Congress.

94. Franklin Pierce to Albert R. Hatch, July 18, 1860, Pierce Papers, New Hampshire Historical Society, Concord.

95. Albert R. Hatch to Franklin Pierce, July 21, 1860, Pierce Papers, New Hampshire Historical Society, Concord.

96. Isaac I. Stevens, National Democratic Executive Committee, to Franklin Pierce, July 26, 1860, Pierce Papers, Library of Congress; Nichols, *The Disruption of American Democracy*, 339; Potter, *The Impending Crisis*, 395.

97. Franklin Pierce to Isaac I. Stevens, July 30, 1860, Pierce Papers, Library of Congress.

98. Lex Renda, *Running on the Record: Civil War Era Politics in New Hampshire* (Charlottesville: University Press of Virginia, 1997), 90; Franklin Pierce to Albert R. Hatch, October 13, 1860, Pierce Papers, New Hampshire Historical Society, Concord.

99. Nichols, *Disruption of American Democracy*, 346–50; Franklin Pierce to James Campbell, October 17, 1860, Pierce Papers, Library of Congress.

100. James Campbell to Franklin Pierce, October 20, 1860, Pierce Papers, Library of Congress.

101. Renda, *Running on the Record*, 91–92; Potter, *The Impending Crisis*, 432; Franklin Pierce to John H. George, November 10, 1860, Pierce Papers, New Hampshire Historical Society, Concord.

Chapter 14: *The Civil War Years*

1. Draft of a letter, Franklin Pierce to unknown recipient, November 24, 1860, Pierce Papers, Library of Congress.

2. Richard Carwardine, *Lincoln: A Life of Purpose and Power* (New York: Alfred A. Knopf, 2006), 140.

3. Franklin Pierce to John H. George, December 31, 1860, Pierce Papers, New Hampshire Historical Society, Concord.

4. Franklin Pierce to Jacob Thompson, November 26, 1860, Pierce Papers, Library of Congress.

5. Horatio King to Franklin Pierce, December 8, 1860, Pierce Papers, Library of Congress.

6. J. Archibald Campbell to Pierce, December 19, 1860, Pierce Papers, Library of Congress.

7. Franklin Pierce to Campbell, December 24, 1860, Pierce Papers, Library of Congress.

8. Ibid.

9. J. Archibald Campbell to Franklin Pierce, December 29, 1860, Pierce Papers, Library of Congress.

10. Caleb Cushing to Franklin Pierce, January 1, 1860 [1861; the letter is incorrectly dated], Pierce Papers, Library of Congress.

11. Philip S. Klein, *President James Buchanan: A Biography* (University Park: Pennsylvania State University Press, 1962), 388–90; David M. Potter, *The Impending Crisis: 1848–1861* (New York: Harper and Row, 1976), 542–43.

12. Franklin Pierce to Jane Pierce, January 10, 1861, Pierce Papers, New Hampshire Historical Society, Concord.

13. Jefferson Davis to Franklin Pierce, January 21, 1861, Pierce Papers, New Hampshire Historical Society, Concord.

14. Franklin Pierce to Rev. Henry E. Parker, January 23, 1861, in "The Letters of Henry Elijah Parker," courtesy of Lawrence Brown of Albany, Georgia,available online at http://freepages.genealogy.rootsweb.com/~henryeparker.

15. Potter, *The Impending Crisis*, 530–32, 545–47, 549–51; Carwardine, *Lincoln*, 139.

16. Amos A. Lawrence to Franklin Pierce, January 27, 1861, Pierce Papers, Library of Congress.

17. Franklin Pierce to Lawrence, February 4, 1861, Pierce Papers, Library of Congress.

18. *New Hampshire Patriot*, April 17, 1861.

19. *New Hampshire Patriot*, April 24, 1861.

20. Ibid.

21. Franklin Pierce to Thomas H. Seymour, June 22, 1861, Pierce Papers, Library of Congress; Franklin Pierce to Martin Van Buren, April 16, 1861; Martin Van Buren to Franklin Pierce, April 20, 1862, both in Martin Van Buren Papers, Library of Congress.

22. Robert W. Johannsen, *Stephen A. Douglas* (New York: Oxford University Press, 1973), 840–873; Carwardine, *Lincoln*, 166–67; Jeffrey Manber and Neil Dahlstrom, *Lincoln's Wrath: Fierce Mobs, Brilliant Scoundrels and a President's Mission to Destroy the Press* (Naperville, Ill.: Sourcebooks, 2005), 98–101, 243–46.

23. Diary of Clement March, April 28, 1861, Clement March Diaries, Center for Southwest Research, University of New Mexico, Albuquerque (hereafter cited as Clement March Diaries).

24. *New Hampshire Patriot*, May 1, 1861; William Marvel, "Answering Lincoln's Call: The First New Hampshire Volunteers," *Historical New Hampshire* 39, no. 3 (1984): 139–51; Thomas J. O'Neill to Franklin Pierce, October 16, 1861, Pierce Papers, New Hampshire Historical Society, Concord.

25. Franklin Pierce to Jane Pierce, n.d. [April or May 1861?], Pierce Papers, Library of Congress.

26. Diary of Clement March, July 7, 1861, Clement March Diaries.

27. Mark E. Neely Jr., *The Fate of Liberty: Abraham Lincoln and Civil Liberties* (New York: Oxford University Press, 1991), 4–9; Geoffrey R. Stone, *Perilous Times:*

Free Speech in Wartime (New York: W. W. Norton, 2004), 85–87; Roger B. Taney to Franklin Pierce, June 12, 1861, Pierce Papers, Library of Congress.

28. Pierce's constitutional interpretation was endorsed by the Supreme Court after the war when the Republican-dominated court ruled in *Ex parte Milligan* (1866) that military courts could not try civilians in areas where civil courts were open and functioning. The ruling applied only to military courts, did not address wartime restrictions on habeas corpus or martial law, and has had little impact, as presidents continued, in all succeeding wars, to claim broad emergency powers. Neely, *The Fate of Liberty*, 175–84; Stone, *Perilous Times*, 126.

29. *New Hampshire Patriot*, June 12, and May 1, 1861.

30. *New Hampshire Statesman*, June 1, 15, 1861; Kenneth Starr, "Press Opposition to Lincoln in New Hampshire," *New England Quarterly* 31 (March-December 1948): 327–41.

31. *New Hampshire Patriot*, July 3, 1861; *New Hampshire Statesman*, July 6, 1861; Henry F. French to Benjamin B. French, July 4, 1861, French Papers, New Hampshire Historical Society, Concord.

32. *New Hampshire Democratic Standard*, August 3, 1861; Lex Renda, *Running on the Record: Civil War-Era Politics in New Hampshire* (Charlottesville: University Press of Virginia, 1997), 102; Everett S. Stackpole, *History of New Hampshire* (New York: American Historical Society, 1916), 4: 17.

33. *New Hampshire Statesman*, June 1, 1861; *New Hampshire Patriot*, August 14, 1861; *New Hampshire Statesman*, August 17, 1861.

34. Manber and Dahlstrom, *Lincoln's Wrath*, 118–41; Neely, *The Fate of Liberty*, 186–88.

35. *New Hampshire Statesman*, May 25, 1861; "Treason in New Hampshire," June 22, 1861; August 17, 31, 1861; *New Hampshire Patriot*, September 11, 1861.

36. *New Hampshire Patriot*, September 4, 11, 1861; *New Hampshire Statesman*, September 14, 1861; Franklin Pierce to John H. George, August 19, 20, 1861; Franklin Pierce to niece (Fanny Potter), October 19, 1861; both in Pierce Papers, New Hampshire Historical Society, Concord. The Pierce family's investment in Michigan land was considerable. In August 1860, 640 acres of "McNeil Lands" were offered for sale in East Saginaw; some of the land was along Pierce Street. The land had been in the Pierce family since Gen. John McNeil had purchased it while in the army in Michigan following the War of 1812. McNeil's daughter, Fanny, was Pierce's niece; she and her husband, Charles Potter, lived in Saginaw. Pierce's nephew, John McNeil, lived in Hillsborough. See "Subdivision of 'McNeil Lands,'" broadsides (ca. 1860–61), in the collection of the New Hampshire Historical Society, Concord.

37. Henry McFarland to M. B. Goodwin, September 2, 1861, in Abraham Lincoln, *The Collected Works of Abraham Lincoln*, ed. Roy Basler, (New Brunswick, N.J.: Rutgers University Press, 1953), 4: 505.

38. Franklin Pierce to William H. Seward, December 24, 1861, Pierce Papers, Library of Congress; "Case of Messrs. Hopkins, Butler, Wattles," 1257–58. Ibid. Lincoln's comments were written on the letter of McFarland that was passed on to Lincoln by Cameron.

39. "Case of Messrs. Hopkins, Butler, Wattles and ex-President Pierce," *The War of the Rebellion: A Compilation of the Official Records of the Union and Confederate Armies*, 2nd series (Washington, D.C.: Government Printing Office, 1897), 2: 1246.

40. James Guthrie to Franklin Pierce, September 14, 1861, Pierce Papers, Library of Congress; "Case of Messrs. Hopkins, Butler, Wattles," 1255–56. The "Case of Berret" is in the same volume, page 596.

41. Quotes from the *Detroit Tribune* and *Detroit Free Press*, in "Case of Messrs. Hopkins, Butler, Wattles," 1256. See also Frank L. Klement, "Franklin Pierce and the Treason Charges of 1861–1862," *Historian* 23, no. 4 (1961): 436–48; Frank L. Klement, "The Hopkins Hoax and the Golden Circle Rumor in Michigan, 1861–1862," *Michigan History* 47, no. 1 (1963): 1–14.

42. Guy S. Hopkins to William H. Seward, Fort Lafayette, November 29, 1861, in "Conspiracy against the Government," *Senate Executive Documents*, 37th Congress, 2nd session, vol. 38, 5–6; "Case of Messrs. Hopkins, Butler, Wattles," 1250–51.

43. Ibid.

44. William H. Seward to Franklin Pierce, December 20, 1861, Pierce Papers, Library of Congress; "Case of Messrs. Hopkins, Butler, Wattles," 1257.

45. Franklin Pierce to Wiliam H. Seward, December 24, 1861, Pierce Papers, Library of Congress; "Case of Messrs. Hopkins, Butler, Wattles," 1257–58

46. Franklin Pierce to William H. Seward, December 24, 1861, Pierce Papers, Library of Congress; "Case of of Messrs. Hopkins, Butler, Wattles," 1257–58.

47. William H. Seward to Franklin Pierce, December 30, 1861, Pierce Papers, Library of Congress; "Case of . . . Messrs. Hopkins, Butler, Wattles," 1260–61.

48. Franklin Pierce to William H. Seward, January 7, 1862, Pierce Papers, New Hampshire Historical Society, Concord; "Case of Messrs. Hopkins, Butler, Wattles," 1261.

49. Franklin Pierce to Sen. James Pearce, January 15, 17, 1862, Pierce Papers; Franklin Pierce to Robert McClelland, January 4, 1862; both in Pierce Papers, Library of Congress.

50. Robert McClelland to Franklin Pierce, January 15, 1862, Pierce Papers, Library of Congress.

51. Nathaniel Hawthorne to Horatio Bridge, February 13, 1862, in Nathaniel Hawthorne, *Selected Letters of Nathaniel Hawthorne*, ed. Joel Myerson (Columbus: Ohio State University Press, 2002), 241–42.

52. Franklin Pierce to Abraham Lincoln, March 4, 1862, Pierce Papers, Library of Congress; Elwin L. Page, "Franklin Pierce and Abraham Lincoln—Parallels and Contrasts," *Abraham Lincoln Quarterly* 5, no. 8 (December 1949): 468–69.

53. *Congressional Globe*, 37th Congress, 2nd session, 1370–71. See also Klement, "Franklin Pierce and the Treason Charges of 1861–1862," 436–48; Klement, "The Hopkins Hoax and the Golden Circle Rumor in Michigan," 1–14. Guy Hopkins, author of the hoax letter, had already been released from prison by the time the letter appeared in the newspapers. See "The Case of Messrs. Hopkins, Butler, Wattles," 1263.

54. Sidney Webster to Franklin Pierce, March 22, 1862, Pierce Papers, Library of Congress.

55. Franklin Pierce to Sen. Milton Latham, March 24, 25, 1862, Pierce Papers, Library of Congress; *Congressional Globe*, 37th Congress, 2nd session, 1370–71.

56. "Conspiracy Against the Government," *Senate Executive Documents*, 37th Congress, 2nd session, 38; *Congressional Globe*, 37th Congress, 2nd session, 1489–90.

57. Frederic Bancroft, *The Life of William H. Seward*, II (New York: Harper and Brothers, 1900), 271–76; Neely, *The Fate of Liberty*, 191. Seward's most recent biographers call the charges against Pierce an "embarrassment" and claim that "Seward had fallen for" the hoax letter. See Glyndon Van Deusen, *William Henry Seward* (New York: Oxford University Press, 1967), 290, and John M. Taylor, *William Henry Seward: Lincoln's Right Hand* (New York: HarperCollins, 1991), 171.

58. Clement L. Vallandigham to Franklin Pierce, April 11, 1862, Pierce Papers, Library of Congress.

59. *New York Times* and *Philadelphia Press*, quoted in *New Hampshire Patriot*, April 2, 1862; Cornelia (Mrs. Charles) O'Conor to Franklin Pierce, May 3, 1862, Pierce Papers, Library of Congress; *New York Herald*, April 5, 1862.

60. Fitz-John Porter to Franklin Pierce, February 10, 1863, Pierce Papers, Library of Congress.

61. Sidney Webster to Franklin Pierce, July 10, 1863, January 20, 1864, Pierce Papers, Library of Congress.

62. Edward E. Cross to Franklin Pierce, February 19, April 14, 1863, Pierce Papers, Library of Congress.

63. "Paul R. George," in C. C. Lord, *Life and Times in Hopkinton, New Hampshire* (Concord, N.H.: Republican Press Associates, 1890), 382–83.

64. *New Hampshire Patriot*, July 8, 1863. The Edgerly case happened following the state election of March 1863. Edgerly voted on March 8 and was discharged, without explanation, on March 10. On hearing of it, Governor Horatio Seymour of New York wrote to Pierce, "Is it true that one of the officers of a New Hampshire Regt. was dismissed for voting a Democratic ticket? It is positively asserted but I cannot credit the statement. It is important to me that I should know what the truth is." See Horatio Seymour to Franklin Pierce, April 8, 1863, Pierce Papers, New Hampshire Historical Society, Concord; *Revised Register of the Soldiers and Sailors of New Hampshire in the War of the Rebellion, 1861–1866* (Concord, N.H.: Ira C. Evans, 1895), 169.

65. Capt. A. W. Bartlett, *History of the Twelfth Regiment New Hampshire Volunteers in the War of the Rebellion* (Concord, N.H.: Ira C. Evans, 1897), 9; Asa Bartlett, "History of the 12th Regiment of New Hampshire Volunteers," in *Revised Register of the Soldiers and Sailors of New Hampshire in the War of the Rebellion*, 1861–6 (Concord, N.H.: Ira C. Evans, 1895), 603; Charles E. Potter, *The Military History of the State of New Hampshire, 1623–1861* (Baltimore: Genealogical Publishing, 1869; reprinted 1972), note, 339–40.

66. Samuel S. Cox to Franklin Pierce, February 24, April 5, 1862, March 17, 1864, Pierce Papers, Library of Congress.

67. Franklin Pierce to John H. George, August 11, 1862, Pierce Papers, Library of Congress; Neely, *The Fate of Liberty*, 53, 62. Stanton's proclamation had implications

in New Hampshire with the arrest of Nathaniel Batchelder, a longtime Democrat, for disloyalty in making provocative antiwar speeches. There is no record of Pierce reacting specifically to Batchelder's case, though John H. George spoke out in Batchelder's defense. Neely, *The Fate of Liberty*, 56; Renda, *Running on the Record*, 112.

68. Erastus B. Bigelow to Franklin Pierce, August 30, September 17, October 4, 13, 22, November 7, 1860; all in Pierce Papers, Library of Congress.

69. Irving Bell, *Persistent Patriot: The New Hampshire Life and Letters of Franklin Pierce* (Concord, N.H.: New Hampshire Political Library, 2005), 59–64; J. D. Hoover to Franklin Pierce, January 5, 1863; January 1, 1864; February 10, 1864; all in Pierce Papers, Library of Congress; Diary of Clement March, July 9, 1863, Clement March Diaries.

70. Franklin Pierce to Joseph Dixon and Co., May 24, 1862; Franklin Pierce to Joseph Dixon, February 23, 27, 1865; Joseph Dixon to Franklin Pierce, March 3, 1865; all in Pierce Papers, Library of Congress.; Bell, *Persistent Patriot*, 64.

71. Franklin Pierce to F. N. Blood, January, 1861, Pierce Papers, New Hampshire State Historical Society, Concord. An example of Pierce's condescending attitude regarding his brother's finances is found in a letter to Henry of May 8, 1863: "I write to remind you that your sixty day note will become due the 15th inst. you must on no account sacrifice your own pride and sense of honor or my convenience on this account. The 15th will be Monday one week from today, and I shall call at the Mechanic's Bank, where you will find the notes, on Tuesday. Let me repeat on no account and on no pretense, let me call in vain." Franklin Pierce to Henry D. Pierce, May 8, 1863, Pierce Papers, New Hampshire Historical Society, Concord.

72. Franklin Pierce to John H. George, January 2, 1863; Franklin Pierce to Milton Latham, January 1, 1863; both in Pierce Papers, Library of Congress. Pierce also wrote an editorial condemning the Emancipation Proclamation; it appeared in the *New Hampshire Patriot*, January 7, 1863. It is almost verbatim from his letter to George of January 2.

73. Carwardine, *Lincoln*, 79–80, 215.

74. Loyal Publication Society, "The Venom and the Antidote," *Loyal Publication Society*, no. 9 (1864); Leon Burr Richardson, *William E. Chandler, Republican* (New York: Dodd, Mead, 1940), 18.

75. Renda, *Running on the Record*, 112–17.

76. See Renda, *Running on the Record*, 111–32, for a full account of the Democratic Party's racist appeals in New Hampshire.

77. Stone, *Perilous Times*, 101–13; Neely, *The Fate of Liberty*, 67–68; Frank L. Klement, *The Limits of Dissent: Clement L. Vallandigham and the Civil War* (Lexington: University Press of Kentucky, 1970), 148–84. Neely, who made the most exhaustive study of civilian arrests during the war, asserts that the total number of arrests will never be known as the records were inconsistently kept in each location under military rule. Estimates are between thirteen thousand and thirty-eight thousand, and Neely implies that the higher number is closer to the truth, but he also states that most of those arrested were in the border states and were deserters, draft

dodgers, fraudulent contractors, and blockade runners. Nevertheless, many arrests were made in the North of newspaper editors, politicians, and local characters, for speaking out or writing provocatively against the policies of the Lincoln administration. See, Neely, *The Fate of Liberty,* 232–35.

78. E. E. Cross to Franklin Pierce, February 19, 1863, Pierce Papers, Library of Congress.

79. Cross to Franklin Pierce, April 14, 1863, Pierce Papers, Library of Congress.

80. *New Hampshire Patriot,* June 24, July 1, 1863; Diary of Clement, June 30, 1863, Clement March Diaries.

81. *New Hampshire Patriot,* July 8, 1863.

82. Ibid.

83. Ibid.

84. Ibid.

85. Ibid.; Mrs. M. S. Perley to Franklin Pierce, October 16, 1862; July 14, 1863; both in Pierce Papers, Library of Congress. For Cross's military career, see Mike Pride and Mark Travis, *My Brave Boys: To War with Colonel Cross and the Fighting Fifth* (Hanover, N.H.: University Press of New England, 2001).

86. *New Hampshire Independent Democrat,* July 9, 1863.

87. *Proceeding of the Trustees of Dartmouth College, July 24, 1863* (Concord, N.H.: McFarlane and Jones, 1863); Leon Burr Richardson, *History of Dartmouth College* (Hanover, N.H.: Dartmouth College Publications, 1932), 2: 429–514; William Henry Duncan, *Memorial to Rev. Nathan Lord* (1871), New Hampshire Historical Society, Concord.

88. Franklin Pierce to Albert R. Hatch, November 14, 1863, Pierce Papers, New Hampshire Historical Society, Concord. Pierce had probably known Rev. Lord since the 1820s, when he served as minister in Amherst, New Hampshire, at the same time that Pierce's father was sheriff of the county, and young Pierce was studying law in the town.

89. Richardson, *History of Dartmouth College* 2: 513–14; two unsigned letters, Nathan Lord Papers, New Hampshire Historical Society, Concord; Nathan Lord to Franklin Pierce, January 14, 1864; William H. Lord to Franklin Pierce, February 11, 1864; both in Pierce Papers, Library of Congress.

90. Nathaniel Hawthorne, *Our Old Home: A Series of English Sketches* (Boston: Ticknor and Fields, 1863).

91. Nathaniel Hawthorne to James T. Fields, July 18, 1863, in Hawthorne, *Selected Letters,* 255–56.

92. Nathaniel Hawthorne to Elizabeth Palmer Peabody, July 20, 1863, in Hawthorne, *Selected Letters,* 252–55.

93. Anne Fields, *Authors and Friends* (Boston: Houghton Mifflin, 1897), 184.

94. James R. Mellow, *Nathaniel Hawthorne in His Times* (Baltimore: Johns Hopkins University Press, 1980), 570.

95. James T. Fields, *Biographical Notes and Personal Sketches,* ed. Anne Fields (Boston: Houghton, Mifflin, 1881), 85–86.

96. M. A. DeWolfe Howe, *Memories of a Hostess: A Chronicle of Eminent Friendships Drawn Chiefly from the Diaries of Mrs. James T. Fields* (Boston: Atlantic Monthly Press, 1922), 13.

97. Jane Pierce to Nathaniel Hawthorne, September 30, 1863, Pierce Papers, Library of Congress.

98. Harriet A. Lord to Mary Aiken, December, 1863, Pierce-Aiken Papers, Library of Congress; *New Hampshire Patriot,* December 9, 1863.

99. James T. Fields, *Hawthorne* (Boston: James R. Osgood, 1876), 112; Howe, *Memories of a Hostess,* 57.

100. Laura Holloway, *The Ladies of the White House, or, In the Homes of the Presidents* (Philadelphia: Bradley, 1882), 494.

101. Clement March, quoted from the unpublished memoirs of Sarah Parker Goodwin, in Margaret Whyte Kelly, *Sarah—Her Story: The Life Story of Sarah Parker Rice Goodwin, Wife of Ichabod Goodwin, New Hampshire's Civil War Governor* (Portsmouth, N.H.: Back Channel Press, 2006), 172.

102. William H. Gibbs to Editors *Democrat,* Natches, Mississippi, August 29, 1863, *New Hampshire Independent Democrat,* September 7, 1863.

103. Ibid.

104. *New Hampshire Independent Democrat,* December 31, 1863, January 7, 1864.

105. *New Hampshire Independent Democrat,* January 14, 1864.

106. "New Hampshire Peace Democracy, Vallandigham and Frank Pierce, Their True Relation and Objects," broadside [February 1864?]; "Copperheads in Council! Declarations of the Leaders!" broadside [1864]; both in New Hampshire Historical Society, Concord.

107. "The Record of a Month" (n.p.: 1864).

108. Horatio Seymour to Franklin Pierce, February 24, 1864; Robert McClelland to Franklin Pierce, April 13, 1864; Daniel Voorhees to Franklin Pierce, April 18, 1864, Pierce Papers, Library of Congress.

109. Lex Renda, *Running on the Record,* 119–123; *New Hampshire Patriot,* March 9, 1864.

110. Jessie Benton Frémont, *Souvenirs of My Time* (Boston: D. Lothrop, 1887), 106.

111. Sophia Hawthorne to Franklin Pierce, May 6, 1864, Pierce Papers, New Hampshire Historical Society, Concord.

112. Sidney Webster, *Franklin Pierce and His Administration* (New York: Appleton, 1892), 36–38. A nearly identical description of Hawthorne's death is found in a letter, Franklin Pierce to Mary Aiken, May 19, 1864, in private hands; it recently sold at auction for $25,000.

113. Franklin Pierce to Horatio Bridge, May, 1864, in Horatio Bridge, *Personal Recollections of Nathaniel Hawthorne* (New York: Harper and Brothers, 1893), 179.

114. Franklin Pierce to Horatio Bridge, November 27, 1865, copy in Horatio Bridge File, Bowdoin College Library (herafter cited as Bridge File).

115. Julian Hawthorne, *Memoirs of Julian Hawthorne,* ed. Edith Garrigues Hawthorne (New York, MacMillan, 1938), 190; Franklin Pierce to Horatio Bridge,

November 27, 1864, copy in Bridge File; Franklin Pierce to Hugh Anderson, August 14, 1864, Pierce Papers, Library of Congress.

116. Julien Hawthorne, *Memoirs*, 190–91; James Parton to Gen. Benjamin F. Butler, August 19, 1864, in Benjamin F. Butler, *The Private and Official Correspondence of Gen. Benjamin F. Butler During the Period of the Civil War* (privately printed, 1917), 5: 79–80; John W. Headley, *Confederate Operations in Canada and New York* (New York: Neale Publishing, 1906), 219–22; David Herbert Donald, *Lincoln* (New York: Simon and Schuster, 1995), 521–23.

117. Headley, *Confederate Operations in Canada and New York*, 219; Donald, *Lincoln*, 522.

118. Franklin Pierce to John J. Taylor, June 14, 1864, Pierce Papers, Library of Congress.

119. John M. Belohlavek, *Broken Glass: Caleb Cushing and the Shattering of the Union* (Kent, Ohio: Kent State University Press, 2005), 329.

120. Franklin Pierce to Richard Spofford, August 17, 1864, in *New Hampshire Patriot*, September 7, 1864; Headley, *Confederate Operations in Canada and New York*, 226.

121. Diary of Clement March, August 17, 1864, Clement March Diaries.

122. National Democratic Convention, *Official Proceedings of the Democratic National Convention held in 1864 in Chicago* (Chicago: Democratic National Convention, 1864), 29–30, 35, on microfilm at Dimond Library, University of New Hampshire, Durham.

123. Franklin Pierce to Richard Spofford, August 17, 1864, in *New Hampshire Patriot*, September 7, 1864; *New York Tribune*, September 9, 1864.

124. Franklin Pierce to General Robert Patterson, February 16, 1865, Pierce Papers, Library of Congress.

125. *New Hampshire Patriot*, April 19, 1865.

126. Ibid.

127. Ibid. Pierce's family expressed concern for his safety. A nephew, W. A. Aiken, wrote from Dartmouth College on April 18, "We had heard rumours of riotous proceedings at Concord on Saturday & were fearful that some fanatics or company of fanatics might have molested you. We were very glad to be relieved by yesterday's paper, & to see that you spoke so nobly & truly, so like yourself." W. A. Aiken to Franklin Pierce, April 18, 1865, New Hampshire Historical Society, Concord.

Chapter 15: *Final Years*

1. Diary of Nathan K. Abbott, May 10, 1865, Nathan K. Abbott Diaries, vol. 8, 17, copy in Pierce Papers, New Hampshire Historical Society, Concord.

2. J. D. Hoover to Howell Cobb, August 31, 1865, in Ulrich B. Phillips, ed., "The Correspondence of Robert Toombs, Alexander H. Stephens, and Howell Cobb," *Annual Report of the American Historical Society* 2: (1911): 666–67.

3. J. D. Hoover to Franklin Pierce, January 1, February 16, March 10, 1864, Pierce Papers, Library of Congress.

4. John J. Craven, M.D., *Prison Life of Jefferson Davis* (New York: G. W. Dillingham, 1905), 148.

5. Charles O'Conor to Franklin Pierce, July 5, 15, 18, December 9, 1865, Pierce Papers, Library of Congress; William J. Cooper Jr., *Jefferson Davis, American* (New York: Alfred A. Knopf, 2000), 534–50.

6. George Wm. Brown to Pierce, July 14, 1866, Pierce Papers, Library of Congress; Cooper, *Jefferson Davis*, 540–50.

7. Julian Hawthorne to Franklin Pierce, April 26, 1865; Franklin Pierce to nephew (Kirk), July 25, 1863, and December 21, 1864; Franklin Pierce to nephew (Frank), April 24, 1867; all in Pierce Papers, New Hampshire Historical Society, Concord.

8. Julian Hawthorne to Franklin Pierce, September 30, 1865; Sophia Hawthorne to Franklin Pierce, October 15, 1865; both in Pierce Papers, New Hampshire Historical Society, Concord.

9. Julian Hawthorne, *Hawthorne and His Circle* (New York: Harper and Brothers, 1903), 359.

10. Sophia Hawthorne to Horatio Bridge, November 25, 1865, in Horatio Bridge, *Personal Recollections of Nathaniel Hawthorne* (New York: Harper and Brothers, 1893), 195; Sophia Hawthorne to Franklin Pierce, December 14, 1865, Pierce Papers, New Hampshire Historical Society, Concord.

11. Franklin Pierce to Horatio Bridge, November 27, 1865, Pierce Papers, New Hampshire Historical Society, Concord.

12. Franklin Pierce to John Aiken, December 1, 1865, Pierce Papers, Library of Congress; "Baptisms," *Records of St. Paul's Church* [Concord, N.H.], 19 (hereafter cited as *Records of St. Paul's Church*).

13. "Pews owned, 1867," *Records of St. Paul's Church*, 91.

14. *New Hampshire Patriot*, June 5, 12, 19, 1861; *New Hampshire Independent Democrat*, June 6, 13, 1861.

15. *Records of St. Paul's Church*, 78–79, 86–88, 91. At a corporation meeting on April 29, 1867, Pierce moved to increase Dr. Eames's salary to $1,500, which was unanimously approved. At that same meeting Pierce was nominated for a minor church office, junior warden, and received seven of sixteen votes on the first ballot. His name does not appear on the second ballot, in which nineteen voted. It is likely that he arrived late to the meeting and withdrew his name from consideration. Later in the same meeting Pierce was elected a delegate to the annual diocesan convention. He also served in this capacity in 1866. See *Records of St. Paul's Church*, 86–88.

16. Diary of Clement March, January 13, 14, 1866, Clement March Diaries, Center for Southwest Research, University of New Mexico, Albuquerque.

17. William Plumer Fowler, "Looking Back at Little Boar's Head," *Shoreliner Magazine*, August, 1950, Tuck Library, New Hampshire Historical Society, Concord; William P. Fowler to Charlotte D. Conover, Librarian, New Hampshire Historical Society, June 18, 1954, New Hampshire Historical Society, Concord; Franklin Pierce to nephew (Frank), May 28, 1868, Pierce Papers, New Hampshire Historical Society, Concord; Franklin Pierce to Mary Aiken, April 30, 1868, Pierce-Aiken Papers, Library of Congress (hereafter cited as Pierce-Aiken Papers).

18. Eric Foner, *Reconstruction: America's Unfinished Revolution, 1863–1877* (New York: Harper and Row, 1988), 180–84.

19. Franklin Pierce to Andrew Johnson, April 13, 1866, Andrew Johnson Papers, Library of Congress.

20. Thomas Hendricks to Franklin Pierce, January 27, 1866, Pierce Papers, Library of Congress; *Congressional Globe*, 39th Congress, 1st session, 315–21.

21. Robert McClelland to Franklin Pierce, January 5, 1866; James Guthrie to Pierce, February 4, 1866; James Dixon to Franklin Pierce, May 1, 1866, Pierce Papers, Library of Congress; Eric Foner, *Reconstruction*, 216–27.

22. Franklin Pierce to Edmund Burke, June 15, 1866, Edmund Burke Papers, Library of Congress; Edmund Burke to Franklin Pierce, July 5, 1866, Pierce Papers, Library of Congress.

23. Lex Renda, *Running on the Record: Civil War Era Politics in New Hampshire* (Charlottesville: University Press of Virginia, 1997), 142–43; Foner, *Reconstruction*, 262–64.

24. *Richmond Whig* quoted in *New Hampshire Independent Democrat*, May 16, 1867; Jefferson Davis to Franklin Pierce, May 8, 1867, Pierce Papers, Library of Congress.

25. *New Hampshire Patriot*, May 15, 1867; *New Hampshire Statesman*, May 17, 1867.

26. Franklin Pierce to Varina Davis, May 14, 1867, in Jefferson Davis, *Private Letters, 1823–1889*, ed. Hudson Strode (New York: Harcourt, Brace and World, 1966), 271–72.

27. Ibid.

28. Anne Fields, ed., *James T. Fields: Biographical Notes and Personal Sketches* (Boston: Houghton and Mifflin, 1881), 143.

29. Diary of Clement March, August 14, 16, 1867, Clement March Diaries.

30. Franklin Pierce to Mary Aiken, April 30, 1868, Pierce-Aiken Papers; Franklin Pierce to nephew (Frank), May 15, 1868, Pierce Papers, New Hampshire Historical Society, Concord.

31. Franklin Pierce to J. D. Hoover, April 22, 1868, Pierce Papers, Library of Congress.

32. Elizabeth Grimes to Franklin Pierce, March 11, 1869, Pierce Papers, Library of Congress.

33. Franklin Pierce to J. D. Hoover, April 22, 1868, Pierce Papers, Library of Congress L.C.

34. Journal of Benjamin Brown French, August 26, 1868, Benjamin Brown French, *Witness to the Young Republic: A Yankee's Journal, 1828–1870*, ed. Donald B. Cole and John J. McDonough (Hanover, N.H.: University Press of New England, 1989), 580.

35. Franklin Pierce to Horatio Bridge, October 11, 1868, copy in Bridge File, Bowdoin College; Bridge, *Personal Recollections*, 180.

36. Franklin Pierce to Horatio Bridge, February 16, 1869, copy in Bridge File.

37. Franklin Pierce, "Speech to Cincinnati Convention," Baltimore, May 1869, Pierce Papers, Library of Congress.

38. Franklin Pierce to nephew (Frank), May 25, 1869, Pierce Papers, New Hampshire Historical Society, Concord.

39. Diary of Clement March, July 30, August 13, 18, 1869, Clement March Diaries.

40. Bridge, *Personal Recollections*, 181.

41. Todd W. Van Beck, "The Death and Funeral of Franklin Pierce," typed manuscript, 1990, 2, New Hampshire Historical Society, Concord; *New Hampshire Daily Monitor*, October 9, 1869.

42. Todd W. Van Beck, "Funerals of the Famous: Franklin Pierce," *The American Cemetery*, November, 1991, 26; *New Hampshire Daily Patriot*, October 8, 1869.

43. Van Beck, "Funerals of the Famous: Franklin Pierce," 32.

44. *New Hampshire Daily Patriot*, October 11, 1869; Van Beck, "Funerals of the Famous: Franklin Pierce," *The American Cemetery*, 35.

45. *New Hampshire Daily Patriot*, October 11, 1869; Van Beck, "Funerals of the Famous: Franklin Pierce," 36.

46. *New Hampshire Daily Patriot*, October 11, 1869; Diary of Clement March, October 11, 1869, Clement March Diaries.

47. Diary of Clement March, October 9, 1869, Clement March Diaries.

48. French, *Witness to the Young Republic*, 604.

49. Daniel Voorhees to John H. George, February 20, 1870, John H. George Papers, New Hampshire Historical Society. Richard Spofford a friend of Pierce's from Massachusetts wrote a poem which appeared in the local newspapers.

> Him no more shall malice wrong,
> Hate nor envy's shafts come nigh him,
> Sorrow, that he bore so long,
> Nevermore its pangs shall try him.

Epilogue

1. "Inventory of the Pierce Estate," Judge of Probate for the County of Merrimack, January, 1870, Pierce Papers, New Hampshire Historical Society, Concord; *New Hampshire Patriot*, October 27, 1869.

2. Edwin Haviland Miller, *Salem Is My Dwelling Place: A Life of Nathaniel Hawthorne* (Iowa City: University of Iowa Press, 1991), 440; Nathaniel Hawthorne to Elizabeth Palmer Peabody, July 20, 1863, in Nathaniel Hawthorne, *Selected Letters of Nathaniel Hawthorne*, ed. Joel Myerson (Columbus: Ohio State University Press, 2002), 252–55.

3. Nathaniel Hawthorne, "Fragments from the Journal of a Solitary Man," *Tales and Sketches* (New York: Literary Classics of the United States, Viking Press, 1982), 499.

BIBLIOGRAPHY

I. Manuscripts

Atherton, Charles G., Papers. New Hampshire Historical Society, Concord.

Bancroft, George, Papers. Massachusetts Historical Society, Boston.

Black, Jeremiah, Papers. Library of Congress.

Breckinridge, John C. Family Papers. Library of Congress.

Buchanan, James, Papers. Historical Society of Pennsylvania, Philadelphia.

Buchanan, James, Papers. Library of Congress.

Burke, Edmund, Papers. Library of Congress.

Burke, Edmund, Papers. New Hampshire Historical Society, Concord.

Chandler, William P., Papers. New Hampshire Historical Society, Concord.

Cushing, Caleb, Papers. Library of Congress.

Everett, Edward, Papers. Massachusetts Historical Society, Boston.

Forney, John W., Papers. Library of Congress.

French, Benjamin Brown, Family Papers. New Hampshire Historical Society, Concord.

George, John Hatch, Papers. New Hampshire Historical Society, Concord.

Guthrie, James, Papers. Library of Congress.

Hale, John Parker, Papers. New Hampshire Historical Society, Concord.

Hale-Chandler Papers. Dartmouth College.

Hatch, Albert R., Papers. New Hampshire Historical Society, Concord.

Hibbard, Harry, Papers. New Hampshire Historical Society, Concord.

Johnson, Andrew, Papers. Library of Congress.

Lawrence, Amos, Papers. Massachusetts Historical Society, Boston.

Lawrence, Amos A., Papers. Massachusetts Historical Society, Boston.

Lawrence, Amos A., Diaries, Massachusetts Historical Society, Boston.

Lord, Nathan, Papers. New Hampshire Historical Society, Concord.

McClelland, Robert, Papers. Library of Congress.

McKeon, John, Papers. Library of Congress.

Manypenny, George W., Papers. Library of Congress.

March, Clement, Diary, Center for Southwest Research, University of New Mexico, Albuquerque.

Marcy, William L., Papers. Library of Congress.

Means, Abigail Kent, Papers. Library of Congress.

O'Sullivan, John L., Papers. Massachusetts Historical Society, Boston.

Parker, Henry Elijah, Letters. http://www.freepages.genealogy.rootsweb.com/~henryeparker.

Peaslee, Charles H., Papers. New Hampshire Historical Society, Concord.

Phillips, Philip, Papers. Library of Congress.

Pierce-Aiken Papers. Library of Congress.

Pierce, Franklin, Letters. Hillsborough [N.H.] Historical Society, Franklin Pierce Homestead.

Pierce, Franklin, Papers. Library of Congress.

Pierce, Franklin, Papers. New Hampshire Historical Society, Concord.

Sanders, George N., Papers. Library of Congress.

Smith, Francis Ormand Jonathan, Papers. Maine Historical Society, Portland.

Stevenson, Andrew and John W., Papers. Library of Congress.

Tuck, Amos, Papers. New Hampshire Historical Society, Concord.

Van Buren, Martin, Papers. Library of Congress.

Webster, Daniel, Papers. New Hampshire Historical Society, Concord.

Welles, Gideon, Papers. Library of Congress.

II. Published Writings and Memoirs

Anderson, Eve. ed. *A Breach of Privilege: Cilley Family Letters, 1820–1867*. Rockland, Maine: Seven Coin Press, 2002.

Austin, James C. *Fields of the Atlantic Monthly: Letters to an Editor, 1861–1870*. San Marino, Calif.: The Huntington Library, 1953.

Bartlett, Samuel Colcord. *An Address on the Life and Character of the Late Henry Elijah Parker, D. D.* Cambridge, Mass.: John Wilson and Son, University Press, 1897.

Basler, Roy P., and others, eds. *The Collected Works of Abraham Lincoln.* 9 vols. New Brunswick, N.J.: Rutgers University Press, 1953–55.

Benton, Thomas Hart. *Thirty Years' View.* New York: D. Appleton, 1856.

Boas, Norman F. *Jane M. Pierce (1806–1863): The Pierce-Aiken Papers.* Stonington, Conn.: Seaport Autographs, 1983.

———. *Jane M. Pierce (1806–1863): The Pierce-Aiken Papers,* Supplement. Stonington, Conn.: Seaport Autographs, 1989.

Buchanan, James. *The Works of James Buchanan.* Edited by John Bassett Moore. 12 vols. Philadelphia: J. B. Lippincott Company, 1909.

Butler, Benjamin F. *Private and Official Correspondence of Gen. Benjamin F. Butler During the Period of the Civil War.* 5 vols. Privately printed, 1917.

Clay-Clopton, Virginia. *A Belle of the Fifties: Memoirs of Mrs. Clay of Alabama.* New York: Doubleday, Page, 1905.

Craven, John J. *Prison Life of Jefferson Davis.* New York: Carleton, 1866. Reprinted by G. W. Dillingham, 1905

Crist, Lynda Lasswell, ed. *The Papers of Jefferson Davis.* 11 vols. Baton Rouge: Louisiana State University Press, 1985, 1989.

Curtis, George Ticknor. *Life of James Buchanan.* 2 vols. New York: Harper and Brothers, 1883.

Davis, Jefferson. *Jefferson Davis Constitutionalist, His Letters, Papers, and Speeches.* Edited by Dunbar Rowland. 10 vols. New York: J. J. Little and Ives, 1923.

Jefferson, Davis. *Private Letters, 1823–1889.* Edited by Hudson Strode. New York: Harcourt, Brace and World, 1966.

Davis, Varina. *Jefferson Davis, Ex-President of the Confederate States of America; A Memoir by His Wife.* vol. 1. New York: Belford Company, 1890.

Dix, Morgan. *Memoirs of John A. Dix.* 2 vols. New York: Harper and Brothers, 1883.

Douglas, Stephen A. *Letters.* Edited by Robert W. Johannsen. Urbana: University of Illinois Press, 1961.

Fields, Annie, ed. *James T. Fields; Biographical Notes and Personal Sketches.* Boston: Houghton, Mifflin, 1881.

Forney, John W. *Anecdotes of Public Men.* 2 vols. New York: Harper and Brothers, 1889.

Frémont, Jessie Benton. *Souvenirs of My Time.* Boston: D. Lothrop, 1887.

French, Amos Tuck, ed. *Exeter and Harvard Eighty Years Ago: Journals and Letters of F. O. French, '57.* Chester, N.H.: Privately printed, 1932.

French, Benjamin Brown. *Witness to the Young Republic, A Yankee's Journal, 1828–1870.* Edited by Donald B. and John J. McDonough. Hanover, N.H.: University Press of New England, 1989.

Gihon, John H. *Gihon's History of Kansas.* N. P. Cone Publishers, 1857.

Hamilton, James A. *Reminiscences of James A. Hamilton.* New York: Charles Scribner, 1869.

Hawthorne, Julian. *The Memoirs of Julian Hawthorne.* Edited by his Wife, Edith Garrigues Hawthorne. New York: MacMillan, 1938.

Hawthorne, Nathaniel. *Selected Letters of Nathaniel Hawthorne.* Edited by Joel Myerson. Columbus: Ohio State University Press, 2002.

Hitchcock, Ethan Allen. *Fifty Years in Camp and Field: Diary of Major-General Ethan Allen Hitchcock, U.S.A.* Edited by W. A. Croffut. New York: G. P. Putnam's Sons, 1909.

Holden, Walter, William E. Ross, and Elizabeth Slomba. *Stand Firm and Fire Low: The Civil War Writings of Colonel Edward A. Cross.* Hanover, N.H.: University Press of New England, 2003.

Howe, M. A. DeWolfe. *Memoirs of a Hostess: A Chronicle of Eminent Friendships Drawn Chiefly from the Diaries of Mrs. James T. Fields.* Boston: Atlantic Monthly Press, 1922.

Howe, M. A. DeWolfe. *The Life and Letters of George Bancroft.* 2 vols. New York: Charles Scribner's Sons, 1908.

Kelly, Margaret Whyte. *Sarah—Her Story: The Life Story of Sarah Rice Goodwin, Wife of Ichabod Goodwin, New Hampshire's Civil War Governor.* Portsmouth, N.H.: Back Channel Press, 2006.

Keyes, E. D. *Fifty Years' Observations of Men and Events: Civil and Military.* New York: Charles Scribner's Sons, 1885.

Lathrop, Rose Hawthorne. *Memories of Hawthorne.* Boston: Houghton, Mifflin, 1897.

Lawrence, Amos. *Extracts from the Diary and Correspondence of the Late Amos Lawrence.* Edited by William R. Amos. Boston: Gould and Lincoln, 1855.

Lowell, James Russell. *The Letters of James Russell Lowell.* Edited by Charles Eliot Norton. 2 vols. New York: Harper and Brothers, 1894.

Mahan, Alfred Thayer. *From Sail to Steam: Recollections of Naval Life.* New York: Harper and Brothers, 1907.

Means, Anne M. *Amherst and Our Family Tree.* Boston: Privately printed, 1921.

Oliphant, Laurence. *Episodes in a Life of Adventure.* London: William Blackwood and Sons, 1887.

Perley Poore, Ben. *Perley's Reminiscences of Sixty Years in the National Metropolis.* 2 vols. Philadelphia: Hubbard Brothers, 1886.

Perry, Matthew Calbraith. *The Japan Expedition, 1852–1854: The Personal Journal of Commodore Matthew C. Perry.* Edited by Roger Pineau. Washington D.C.: Smithsonian Institution Press, 1968.

Pierce, Edward L., ed. *Memoir and Letters of Charles Sumner.* 4 vols. Boston: Roberts Brothers, 1893.

Pryor, Mrs. Roger A. (Sara A. R.). *Reminiscences of Peace and War.* New York: MacMillan, 1904.

Rolfe, Colonel Abial. *Reminiscences of Concord, or Personal Recollections of Seventy Years.* Concord, N.H.: Rumford Press, 1901.

Scott, Winfield. *Memoirs of Lieut.-General Winfield Scott, LL.D.* 2 vols. New York: Sheldon and Company Publishers, 1864.

Sherman, John. *Recollections of Forty Years in the House, Senate, and Cabinet.* 2 vols. Chicago: Warner Company, 1895.

Strong, George Templeton. *The Diary of George Templeton Strong.* Edited by Allan Nevins and Milton Halsey Thomas. 4 vols. New York: MacMillan, 1952.

Thompson, Richard W. *Recollections of Sixteen Presidents.* 2 vols. Indianapolis: Bowen-Merrill, 1894.

Tuck, Amos. *Memoir of Amos Tuck.* Exeter, N.H., 1875.

Tyler, Samuel. *Memoir of Roger Brooke Taney.* Baltimore: John Murphy, 1872.

Van Buren, Martin. "The Autobiography of Martin Van Buren," in *Annual Report of the American Historical Review for the Year 1918.* Edited by John C. Fitzpatrick. Washington, D.C.: Government Printing Office, 1920.

Walker, William. *The War in Nicaragua*. Mobile, Ala.: S. H. Goetzelt, 1860.

Watterson, Henry. *"Marse Henry": An Autobiography.* 2 vols. New York: George H. Daron, 1919.

Welles, Gideon. *Diary of Gideon Welles, Secretary of the Navy under Lincoln and Johnson.* 3 vols. Boston: Houghton Mifflin, 1911.

Wise, John S. *Recollections of Thirteen Presidents.* New York: Doubleday, 1906.

III. Contemporary Newspapers and Periodicals

Albany [N.Y.] *Argus*
Amherst [N.H.] *The Farmers' Cabinet*
Baltimore Sun
Boston Post
Charleston [S.C.] *Courier*
Concord [N.H.] *Herald of Freedom*
Concord [N. H.] *Hill's Patriot*
Manchester and Concord [N.H.] *Independent Democrat*
Daily Wisconsin
Concord [N.H.] *Democratic Standard*
Concord [N.H.] *New Hampshire Patriot*
Concord [N.H.] *New Hampshire State Capital Reporter*
Concord [N.H.] *New Hampshire Statesman*
Detroit Free Press
Detroit Tribune
Hillsborough [N.H.] *Messenger*
Lewiston [Maine] *Journal*
Manchester [N.H.] *American*
Manchester [N.H.] *Democrat*
New Orleans Courier
Newport [N.H.] *Argus & Spectator*
New York Commercial Advertiser
New York Evening Post
New York Herald
New York Times
New York Tribune
Philadelphia Public Ledger
Richmond Enquirer
Washington [D.C.] *National Intelligencer*
Washington [D.C.] *Sentinel*
Washington [D.C.] *Union*

IV. Other Primary Sources and Government Documents

Andrews, C. C., ed. *Official Opinions of the Attorneys General of the United States: Advising the Presidents and Heads of Departments in Relation to Their Official Duties.* 12 vols. Washington, D.C.: Robert Farnham, 1856–7.

Bauer, K. Jack, ed. *The New American State Papers. Naval Affairs.* 10 vols. Wilmington, Del.: Scholarly Resources, 1981.

The Boston City Directory. July 1, 1859. Boston: Adams, Sampson, 1859. *Student Profiles. Class of 1824; Class of 1825.* Bowdoin College Library.

Delafield, Richard. *Report on the Art of War in Europe, 1854, 1855, and 1856.* Washington, D.C.: George W. Brown, 1861.

Holzer, Hans, ed. *The Lincoln-Douglas Debates: The First, Complete Unexpurgated Text.* New York: HarperCollins, 1993.

Kappler, Charles J., ed. *Indian Treaties, 1778–1883.* New York: Interland Publishing, 1972.

Manning, William R., ed. *Diplomatic Correspondence of the United States, Inter-American Affairs, 1831–1860.* 12 vols. Washington, D.C.: Carnegie Foundation for International Peace, 1936–1939.

National Archives: Microfilm Records:

Despatches from Special Agents of the Department of State. 1794–1906. Microfilm, RG 59, M37. National Archives.

Diplomatic Instructions of the Department of State, 1801–1906. Microfilm, RG 59, M77. National Archives.

U. S. Interior Department. Territorial Papers of Utah, 1850–1902. Microfilm, RG 48, M428. National Archives.

Letters of Application and Recommendation During the Administrations of Franklin Pierce and James Buchanan, 1853–1861. Microfilm, RG 59, M967. National Archives.

Letters Received by the Office of Adjutant General, 1822–1860. Microfilm, RG 94, M567. National Archives.

Letters Received by the Office of Indian Affairs, 1824–1881. Microfilm, RG 75, M234. National Archives.

Letters Received by the Secretary of the Navy From the President and Executive Agencies, 1837–1886. Microfilm, RG 45, M517. National Archives.

Letters Received by the Secretary of War, Registered Series, 1801–1870. Microfilm, RG 107, M221. National Archives.

Letters Sent by the Office of Adjutant General, 1800–1890. Microfilm, RG 94, M565. National Archives.

Letters Sent by the Office of Indian Affairs, 1824–1881. Microfilm, RG 75, M21. National Archives.

Letters Sent by the Secretary of War Relating to Military Affairs, 1800–1869. Microfilm, RG 107, M6. National Archives.

Letters Sent to the President by the Secretary of War, 1800–1863. Microfilm, RG 107, M127. National Archives.

Letters Sent to the President by the Secretary of the Treasury ("A" Series), 1833–1878. Microfilm, RG56, M415. National Archives.

Letters Sent by the Attorney General. Microfilm, RG 60, T969, M12. National Archives.

Letters Sent by the Indian Division of the Office of the Secretary of the Interior, Microfilm, RG 48, M606. National Archives.

U. S. State Department. Territorial Papers of Kansas. Microfilm, RG 59, M218. National Archives.

U. S. State Department. Territorial Papers of Utah. Microfilm, RG 59, M12. National Archives.

New Hampshire Peace Democracy. *Vallandigham and Franklin Pierce. Their True Relation and Objects.* N.d.

Official Proceedings of the National Democratic Convention Held in Cincinnati, June 2–6, 1856. Cincinnati: Enquirer Company, 1856.

Official Proceedings of the Democratic National Convention Held in 1864 in Chicago. Chicago: Democratic National Convention, 1864. Microfilm. Dimond Library, University of New Hampshire, Durham.

Proceedings of the Trustees of Dartmouth College, July 24, 1863. Concord, N.H.: McFarlane and Jenks, 1863.

Records of St. Paul's Church [Concord, N.H.].

Revised Register of the Soldiers and Sailors of New Hampshire in the War of the Rebellion, 1861–1865. Concord: Ira C. Evans, 1895.

Richardson, James D., ed. *A Compilation of the Messages and Papers of the Presidents, 1897–1897.* 10 vols. Washington, D.C.: Government Printing Office, 1897.

U.S. Bureau of the Census. *Historical Statistics of the United States: Colonial Times to 1970.* Washington, D.C.: Government Printing Office, 1975.

U.S. Congress. *Congressional Globe.* 32nd–37th Congresses. The entire *Congressional Globe* is available online; see www.locc.gov: click on Law Library of Congress, and then click on "A Century of Lawmaking for a New Nation." 1897–1898.

———. *House Reports.* 33rd–35th Congresses. See notes for specific reports used.

———. *Journal of the Executive Proceedings of the Senate*, vol. 9. 33rd Congress, special session.

———. *Senate Executive Documents.* 33rd, 35th Congresses. See notes for specific reports used.

———. *Senate Reports.* 34th Congress.

U.S. Supreme Court Center. *U.S. Supreme Court Cases and Opinions.* http://supreme.justia.com/us.

The War of the Rebellion: A Compilation of the Official Records of the Union and Confederate Armies. 128 vols. Washington, D.C.: Government Printing Office, 1880–1901.

V. Biographies

Adams, Henry. *The Life of Albert Gallatin.* Philadelphia: J. B. Lippincott, 1880.

Bancroft, Frederic. *The Life of William H. Seward.* 2 vols. New York: Harper and Brothers, 1900.

Bartlett, D. W. *The Life of General Franklin Pierce of New Hampshire.* Auburn [no state]: Derby and Miller, 1852.

Bell, Irving. *Persistent Patriot: The New Hampshire Life and Letters of Franklin Pierce: The Pre-presidential Years.* Concord, N.H.: New Hampshire Political Library, 2005.

Belohlavek, John M. *Broken Glass: Caleb Cushing and the Shattering of the Union.* Kent, Ohio: Kent State University Press, 2005.

Blue, Frederick J. *Salmon P. Chase: A Life in Politics.* Kent, Ohio: Kent State University Press, 1987.

Bohner, Charles H. *John Pendleton Kennedy: Gentleman from Baltimore.* Baltimore: Johns Hopkins Press, 1961.

Boulard, Garry. *The Expatriation of Franklin Pierce: The Story of a President and the Civil War.* New York: iUniverse, 2006.

Bridge, Horatio. *Personal Recollections of Nathaniel Hawthorne.* New York: Harper and Brothers, 1893.

Brown, Thomas J. *Dorothea Dix: New England Reformer.* Cambridge, Mass.: Harvard University Press, 1998.

Capers, Gerald M. *Stephen A. Douglas: Defender of the Union.* Boston: Little, Brown, 1959.

Carr, Albert Z. *The World and William Walker.* New York: Harper and Row. Reprinted by Greenwood Press, 1975.

Carwardine, Richard. *Lincoln: A Life of Purpose and Power.* New York: Alfred A. Knopf, 2006.

Cohen, Henry. *Business and Politics in America from the Age of Jackson to the Civil War: The Career Biography of W. W. Corcoran.* Westport, Conn.: Greenwood Publishing, 1971.

Cole, Donald B. *A Jackson Man: Amos Kendall and the Rise of American Democracy.* Baton Rouge: Louisiana State University Press, 2004.

———. *Martin Van Buren and the American Political System.* Princeton, N.J.: Princeton University Press, 1984.

Cooper, William J., Jr. *Jefferson Davis, American.* New York: Alfred A. Knopf, 2000.

Corning, Charles R. *Amos Tuck.* Exeter, N.H.: News-Letter Press, 1902.

Dalzell, Robert F., Jr. *Daniel Webster and the Trial of American Nationalism, 1843–1852.* Boston: Houghton Mifflin, 1973.

Davis, William C. *Breckinridge: Statesman, Soldier, Symbol.* Baton Rouge: Louisiana State University Press, 1974.

Donald, David Herbert. *Lincoln.* New York: Simon and Schuster, 1995.

Fields, James T. *Hawthorne.* Boston: James R. Osgood, 1876.

Fuess, Claude M. *The Life of Caleb Cushing.* 2 vols. New York: Harcourt, Brace, 1923.

Gara, Larry. *The Presidency of Franklin Pierce.* Lawrence: University Press of Kansas, 1991.

Gollaher, David. *Voice for the Mad: The Life of Dorothea Dix.* New York: Free Press, 1995.

Hawthorne, Julian. *Hawthorne and His Circle.* New York: Harper and Brothers, 1903.

———. *Nathaniel Hawthorne and His Wife.* 2 vols. Boston: James R. Osgood, 1885.

Hawthorne, Nathaniel. *The Life of Franklin Pierce.* Boston: Ticknor, Reed, and Fields, 1852. Reprinted by Peter E. Randall Publisher, 2000.

Hinman, Marjory B. *Daniel S. Dickinson: Defender of the Constitution.* Windsor, N.Y.: Privately published, 1987.

Hunt, H. Draper. *Hannibal Hamlin of Maine: Lincoln's First Vice President.* Syracuse, N.Y.: Syracuse University Press, 1969.

Ireland, John Robert. *History of the Life, Administration and Times of Franklin Pierce.* Vol. 14. *The Republic.* Chicago: Fairbanks and Palmer, 1888.

Jellison, Charles A. *Fessenden of Maine: Civil War Senator.* Syracuse, N.Y.: Syracuse University Press, 1962.

Johannsen, Robert W. *Stephen A. Douglas.* New York: Oxford University Press, 1973.

Katz, Irving. *August Belmont: A Political Biography.* New York: Columbia University Press, 1968.

Kenneally, Thomas. *American Scoundrel: The Life of the Notorious Civil War General Dan Sickles.* New York: Doubleday, 2002.

King, Dan. *The Life and Times of Thomas Wilson Dorr.* Boston: Privately printed, 1859.

Klein, Philip Shriver. *President James Buchanan, A Biography.* University Park: The Pennsylvania State University Press, 1962.

Klement, Frank L. *The Limits of Dissent: Clement L. Vallandigham and the Civil War.* Lexington: University Press of Kentucky, 1970.

Klunder, Willard Carl. *Lewis Cass and the Politics of Moderation.* Kent, Ohio: Kent State University Press, 1996.

Lewis, Walker. *Without Fear or Favor: A Biography of Chief Justice Roger B. Taney.* Boston: Houghton, Mifflin, 1965.

Longley, J. W. *Joseph Howe.* The Makers of Canada Series. Toronto: Morang, 1904.

Lynch, Denis Tilden. *An Epoch and A Man: Martin Van Buren and His Times.* New York: Horace Liveright, 1929.

Mann, Mary. *Life of Horace Mann.* Boston: Walker, Fuller, 1865.

Mann, Robert E. *John A. Quitman: Old South Crusader.* Baton Rouge: Louisiana State University Press, 1985.

Mellow, James R. *Nathaniel Hawthorne in His Times.* Baltimore: Johns Hopkins University Press, 1980.

Metcalf, Henry Harrison, ed. *Dedication of a Statue of General Franklin Pierce, Fourteenth President of the United States.* Concord: State of New Hampshire, 1914.

Metcalf, Henry H. *Franklin Pierce and Edmund Burke: A President and A President Maker.* Concord, N.H.: Ranney Printing, 1930.

Miller, Edwin Haviland. *Salem Is My Dwelling Place: A Life of Nathaniel Hawthorne.* Iowa City, Iowa: University of Iowa Press, 1991.

Mitchell, Stewart. *Horatio Seymour of New York.* Cambridge, Mass.: Harvard University Press, 1938.

Morison, Samuel Eliot. *"Old Bruin": Commodore Matthew Calbraith Perry.* Boston: Little, Brown, 1967.

Nathans, Sydney. *Daniel Webster and Jacksonian Democracy.* Baltimore: Johns Hopkins University Press, 1973.

Nevins, Allan. *Hamilton Fish: The Inner History of the Grant Administration.* New York: Dodd, Mead, 1937.

Nichols, Roy Franklin. *Franklin Pierce: Young Hickory of the Granite Hills.* Philadelphia: University of Pennsylvania Press, 1931 and 1958.

Parrish, William E. *David Rice Atchison of Missouri: Border Politician.* Columbia: University of Missouri Press, 1961.

Peskin, Allan. *Winfield Scott and the Profession of Arms.* Kent, Ohio: Kent State University Press, 2003.

Rayback, Robert J. *Millard Fillmore: Biography of a President.* Buffalo, N.Y.: Henry Stewart, 1959.

Richardson, Leon Burr. *William E. Chandler, Republican.* New York: Dodd, Mead, 1940.

Sears, Louis Martin. *John Slidell.* Durham, N.C.: Duke University Press, 1925.

Sears, Stephen W. *George B. McClellan: The Young Napoleon.* New York: Ticknor and Fields, 1988.

Sewell, Richard H. *John P. Hale and the Politics of Abolition.* Cambridge, Mass.: Harvard University Press, 1965.

Simpson, Craig M. *A Good Southerner: The Life of Henry A. Wise of Virginia.* Chapel Hill: University of North Carolina Press, 1985.

Spencer, Ivor Debenham. *The Victor and the Spoils: A Life of William L. Marcy.* Providence, R.I.: Brown University Press, 1959.

Stevens, Hazard. *The Life of Isaac Ingalls Stevens.* 2 vols. New York: Houghton, Mifflin, 1900.

Strode, Hudson. *Jefferson Davis: American Patriot, 1808–1861.* 3 vols. New York: Harcourt, Brace, 1955.

Swisher, Carl Brent. *Roger B. Taney.* New York: MacMillan, 1936.

Taylor, John M. *William Henry Seward: Lincoln's Right Hand.* New York: HarperCollins, 1991.

Tiffany, Francis. *Life of Dorothea Lynde Dix.* Boston: Houghton, Mifflin, 1891.

Trefousse, Hans L. *Ben Butler: The South Called Him Beast.* New York: Twayne Publishers, 1957.

Tuckerman, Henry T. *The Life of John Pendleton Kennedy.* New York: G. P. Putnam and Sons, 1871.

Van Deusen, Glyndon G. *Horace Greeley: Nineteenth Century Crusader.* Philadelphia: University of Pennsylvania Press, 1953.

———. *William Henry Seward.* New York: Oxford University Press, 1967.

Von Abele, Rudolph. *Alexander H. Stephens.* New York: Alfred A. Knopf, 1946.

Webster, Sidney. *Franklin Pierce and His Administration.* New York: D. Appleton, 1892.

Weisberg, Barbara. *Talking to the Dead: Kate and Maggie Fox and the Rise of Spiritualism.* New York: Harper San Francisco, 2004.

Wilson, Don W. *Governor Charles Robinson of Kansas.* Lawrence: University Press of Kansas, 1975.

Wilson, Dorothy Clarke. *Stranger and Traveler: The Story of Dorothea Dix.* Boston: Little, Brown, 1975.

Wineapple, Brenda. *Hawthorne: A Life.* New York: Alfred A. Knopf, 2003.

Wise, Barton H. *The Life of Henry A. Wise of Virginia, 1806–1876.* New York: MacMillan, 1899.

Woodford, Frank B. *Lewis Cass: the Last Jeffersonian.* New Brunswick, N.J.: Rutgers University Press, 1950.

VI. Secondary Sources

Alexander, Thomas B. *Sectional Stress and Party Strength: A Study of Roll-Call Voting Patterns in the United States House of Representatives, 1836–1860.* Nashville, Tenn.: Vanderbilt University Press, 1967.

Allen, H. C. *Great Britain and the United States: A History of Anglo-American Relations, 1783–1952.* New York: St. Martin's Press, 1955.

Anbinder, Tyler. *Nativism and Slavery: The Northern Know Nothings and the Politics of the 1850's.* New York: Oxford University Press, 1992.

Bailey, Thomas A. *A Diplomatic History of the American People.* New York: F. S. Crofts, 1940.

Baker, Jean H. *Affairs of Party: The Political Culture of Northern Democrats in the Mid- Nineteenth Century.* Ithaca, N.Y.: Cornell University Press, 1983.

Baker, Nancy V. *Conflicting Loyalties: Law and Politics in the Attorney General's Office, 1789–1990.* Lawrence: University Press of Kansas, 1992.

Bancroft, Hubert House. *History of Utah, 1540–1887.* San Francisco: History Company, 1891.

Bartlett, A. W. *History of the Twelfth Regiment New Hampshire Volunteers in the War of the Rebellion.* Concord, N.H.: Ira C. Evans, 1897.

Bell, Carl Irving. *They Knew Pierce (And Others Thought They Did).* Springfield, Vt.: April Hill Publishers, 1980.

Bemis, Samuel Flagg. *A Diplomatic History of the United States.* New York: Holt, Rinehart and Winston, 1955.

Bemis, Samuel Flagg, ed. *The American Secretaries of State and Their Diplomacy.* New York: Pageant Book, 1968.

Berger, Mark L. *The Revolution in the New York Party Systems, 1840–1860.* Port Washington, N.Y.: Kennikat Press, 1973.

Billington, Ray Allen. *The Protestant Crusade, 1800–1860.* Chicago: Quadrangle Books, 1964.

Blegen, Theodore C. *Minnesota: A History of the State.* Minneapolis: University of Minnesota Press, 1963.

Blue, Frederick J. *The Free Soilers: Third Party Politics, 1848–1854.* Chicago: University of Illinois Press, 1973.

Bouton, Nathaniel. *The History of Concord.* Concord, N.H.: Benning W. Sanford, 1856.

Browne, George Waldo. *The History of Hillsborough, New Hampshire, 1735–1921.* 2 vol. Manchester, N.H.: John B. Clarke, 1921.

Bryan, Wihelmus Bogart. *A History of the National Capital.* 2 vols. New York: MacMillan, 1916.

Bullit, Susan Dixon (Mrs. Archibald Dixon). *The True History of the Missouri Compromise and Its Repeal.* Cincinnati: Robert Blake, 1899.

Burnham, Walter Dean. *Presidential Ballots, 1836–1892.* Baltimore: Johns Hopkins Press, 1955.

Campbell, Stanley W. *The Slave Catchers: The Enforcement of the Fugitive Slave Law, 1850–1860.* Chapel Hill, N.C.: University of North Carolina Press, 1968.

Caroli, Betty Boyd. *Inside the White House.* New York: Canopy Press, 1992.

Carstensen, Vernon, ed. *The Public Lands: Studies in the History of the Public Domain.* Madison: University of Wisconsin Press, 1963.

Carwardine, Richard J. *Evangelicals and Politics in Antebellum America.* New Haven, Conn.: Yale University Press, 1993.

Connolly, Michael J. *Capitalism, Politics, and Railroads in Jacksonian New England.* Columbia: University of Missouri Press, 2003.

Cooper, William J. Jr. *The South and the Politics of Slavery, 1828–1856.* Baton Rouge: Louisiana State University Press, 1978.

Dana, Samuel Trask, John H. Allison, and Russell N. Cunningham. *Minnesota Lands: Ownership, Use, and Management of Forest and Related Lands.* Washington: D.C.: American Forestry Association, 1960.

Desmond, Humphrey J. *The Know-Nothing Party.* Washington, D.C.: The New Century Press, 1904.

Dowty, Alan. *The Limits of American Isolation: The United States and the Crimean War.* New York: New York University Press, 1971.

Ellis, Edward S. *The Indian Wars of the United States.* New York: Cassell Publishing, 1893.

Etcheson, Nicole. *Bleeding Kansas: Contested Liberty in the Civil War Era.* Lawrence: University Press of Kansas, 2004.

Ettinger, Amos A. *The Mission to Spain of Pierre Soulé, 1853–1855: A Study in the Cuban Diplomacy of the United States.* New Haven, Conn.: Yale University Press, 1932.

Fielding, Robert Kent. *The Unsolicited Chronicler: An Account of the Gunnison Massacre, Its Causes and Consequences, Utah Territory, 1847–1859.* Brookline, Mass.: Paradigm Publications, 1993.

Filler, Louis. *The Crusade Against Slavery, 1830–1860.* New York: Harper and Row, 1960.

Fergurson, Ernest B. *Freedom Rising: Washington in the Civil War.* New York: Alfred A. Knopf, 2004.

Folwell, William Watts. *A History of Minnesota.* 4 vols. Saint Paul: Minnesota Historical Society, 1921.

Foner, Eric. *Reconstruction: America's Unfinished Revolution, 1863–1877.* New York: Harper and Row, 1988.

Fowler, Dorothy G. *The Cabinet Politician: The Postmasters General, 1829–1909.* New York: Columbia University Press, 1943.

Garber, Paul Neff. *The Gadsden Treaty.* Philadelphia: Press of the University of Pennsylvania. Reprinted by Peter Smith, 1959.

Gates, Paul Wallace. *Fifty Million Acres: Conflicts over Kansas Land Policy, 1854-1890.* Ithaca, N.Y.: Cornell University Press, 1954.

Gienapp, William E. *The Origins of the Republican Party, 1852–1856.* New York: Oxford University Press, 1987.

Goetzmann, William H. *Army Exploration in the American West, 1803–1863.* New Haven, Conn.: Yale University Press, 1959.

———. *When the Eagle Screamed: The Romantic Horizon in American Diplomacy, 1800–1860.* New York: John Wiley and Sons, 1966.

Hamilton, Holman. *Prologue to Conflict: The Crisis and Compromise of 1850.* Lexington: University of Kentucky Press, 1964.

Hawthorne, Nathaniel. *Our Old Home: A Series of English Sketches.* Boston: Ticknor and Fields, 1863.

———. *Tales and Sketches.* New York: Literary Classics of the United States, Viking Press, 1982.

Headley, John W. *Confederate Operations in Canada and New York.* New York: Neale Publishing, 1906.

Hearn, Chester G. *Circuits In The Sea: The Men, The Ships, and the Atlantic Cable.* Westport, Conn.: Praeger, 2004.

Heffernan, Nancy Caffey and Ann Page Stecker. *New Hampshire: Crosscurrents in Its Development.* Rev. Ed. Hanover, N.H.: University Press of New England, 1996.

Hill, Charles E. *The Danish Sound Dues and the Command of the Baltic.* Durham, N.C.: Duke University Press, 1926.

Hinsdale, Mary L. *A History of the President's Cabinet.* Ann Arbor, Mich.: George Wahr, 1911.

Hobson, Barbara Meil. *Uneasy Virtue: The Politics of Prostitution and the American Reform Tradition.* New York: Basic Books, 1987.

Holcombe, Return I. *Minnesota in Three Centuries.* 4 vols. Saint Paul: Publishing Society of Minnesota, 1908.

Holloway, Laura. *The Ladies of the White House, or, In the Homes of the Presidents.* Philadelphia: Bradley, 1882.

Holt, Michael F. *The Political Crisis of the 1850's.* New York: John Wiley and Sons, 1978.

Holt, Michael F. *The Rise and Fall of the American Whig Party.* New York: Oxford University Press, 1999.

Huebner, Timothy S. *The Taney Court: Justices, Rulings, and Legacy.* Santa Barbara, Calif.: ABC-CLIO, 2003.

Hyman, Harold M. and William M. Wiecek. *Equal Justice under Law: Constitutional Developments, 1835–1875.* New York: Harper and Row, 1982.

Jensen, Amy LaFollette. *The White House and Its Thirty-three Families.* New York: McGraw-Hill, 1958.

Johnson, Samuel A. *The Battle Cry of Freedom: The New England Emigrant Aid Company in the Kansas Crusade.* Lawrence: University of Kansas Press, 1954.

Klapthorn, Margaret Brown. *The First Ladies.* Washington, D.C.: White House Historical Association, 1975.

Klement, Frank L. *Dark Lanterns: Secret Political Societies, Conspiracies, and Treason Trials in the Civil War.* Baton Rouge: Louisiana State University Press, 1984.

Lane, Roger. *Policing the City: Boston, 1822–1885.* Cambridge, Mass.: Harvard University Press, 1967.

Learned, H. Barrett. "William Learned Marcy." In *The American Secretaries of State and Their Diplomacy,* edited by Samuel Flagg Bemis, vol. 6. New York: Pageant Book Company, 1958.

———. *The President's Cabinet.* New Haven, Conn.: Yale University Press, 1912.

Lyford, James O. *History of Concord, New Hampshire.* 2 vols. Concord, N.H.: Rumford Press, 1903.

Manber, Jeffrey and Neil Dahlstrom. *Lincoln's Wrath: Fierce Mobs, Brilliant Scoundrels and A President's Mission to Destroy the Press.* Naperville, Ill.: Sourcebooks, 2005.

May, Robert E. *Manifest Destiny's Underworld: Filibustering in Antebellum America.* Chapel Hill: University of North Carolina Press, 2002.

McCormick, Richard P. *The Second American Party System: Party Formation in the Jacksonian Era.* Chapel Hill: University of North Carolina Press, 1966.

Meyers, Marvin. *The Jacksonian Persuasion, Politics and Belief.* Stanford, Calif.: Stanford University Press, 1960.

Miller, William Lee. *Arguing About Slavery.* New York: Alfred A. Knopf, 1996.

Morrison, Michael A. *Slavery and the American West: The Eclipse of Manifest Destiny and the Coming of the Civil War.* Chapel Hill: University of North Carolina Press, 1997.

The Nebraska Question, Comprising Speeches in the United States Senate Together With the History of the Missouri Compromise. New York: Redfield, 1854.

Neely, Mark E., Jr. *The Fate of Liberty: Abraham Lincoln and Civil Liberties.* New York: Oxford University Press, 1991.

Nevins, Allan. *Ordeal of the Union: Fruits of Manifest Destiny, 1847–1852.* New York: Charles Scribner's Sons, 1947.

———. *Ordeal of the Union.* Vol. 2, *House Dividing, 1852–1857.* New York:Charles Scribner's Sons, 1947.

Nichols, Alice. *Bleeding Kansas.* New York: Oxford University Press, 1954.

Nichols, Roy Franklin. *The Democratic Machine, 1850–1854.* New York: Columbia University, 1923.

———. *The Disruption of American Democracy.* New York: MacMillan, 1948.

O'Connor, Thomas H. *Lords of the Loom: The Cotton Whigs and the Coming of the Civil War.* New York: Charles Scribner's Sons, 1968.

Parents Magazine. *The First Ladies Cookbook: Favorite Recipes of All the Presidents of the United States.* Parents Magazine Press, 1965.

Perret, Geoffrey. *Lincoln's War.* New York: Random House, 2004.

Potter, Charles E. *The Military History of the State of New Hampshire, 1623–1861.* Concord, N.H.: McFarland and Jenks, 1869. Reprinted by Genealogical Publishing, 1972.

Potter, David A. *The Impending Crisis, 1848–1861.* New York: Harper and Row, 1976.

Pride, Mike and Mark Travis. *My Brave Boys: To War with Colonel Cross & the Fighting Fifth.* Hanover, N.H.: University Press of New England, 2001.

Rauch, Basil. *American Interest in Cuba, 1848–1855.* New York: Columbia University Press, 1948.

Rawley, James A. *Race and Politics: "Bleeding Kansas" and the Coming of the Civil War.* Philadelphia: J. B. Lippincott, 1969.

Ray, P. Orman. *The Repeal of the Missouri Compromise: Its Origin and Authorship.* Cleveland, Ohio: Arthur H. Clark, 1909.

Remini, Robert V. *The Revolutionary Age of Andrew Jackson.* New York: Avon Books, 1976.

Renda, Lex. *Running on the Record: Civil War-Era Politics in New Hampshire.* Charlottesville: University Press of Virginia, 1997.

Richards, Leonard L. *The Slave Power: The Free North and Southern Domination, 1780–1860.* Baton Rouge: Louisiana State University Press, 2000.

Richardson, Leon Burr. *History of Dartmouth College.* 2 vols. Hanover, N.H.: Dartmouth College Publications, 1932.

Robinson, Charles. *The Kansas Conflict.* New York: Harper and Brothers, 1892.

Ryan, William and Desmond Guinness, *The White House: An Architectural History.* New York: McGraw-Hill, 1980.

Scroggs, William O. *Filibusters and Financiers: The Story of William Walker and His Associates.* New York: MacMillan, 1916. Reprinted by Russell and Russell, 1916.

Seale, William. *The President's House: A History.* 2 vols. Washington, D.C.: White House Historical Association and the National Geographic Society, 1986.

Sewell, Richard H. *Ballots for Freedom: Antislavery Politics in the United States, 1837- 1860.* New York: Oxford University Press, 1976.

Siegel, Martin. *The Supreme Court in American Life*. Vol. 3, *The Taney Court, 1836–1864*. New York: Associated Faculty Press, 1987.

Silbey, Joel H. *A Respectable Minority: The Democratic Party in the Civil War, 1860–1868.* New York: Norton, 1977.

———. *The Shrine of Party: Congressional Voting Behavior, 1841–1852*. Pittsburgh: University of Pittsburgh, 1967.

Sprout, Harold and Margaret. *The Rise of American Naval Power, 1776–1918.* Princeton, N.J.: Princeton University Press, 1939.

Stackpole, Everett S. *History of New Hampshire.* 4 vols. New York: American Historical Society, 1916.

Stampp, Kenneth M. *America in 1857.* New York: Oxford University Press, 1990.

Stone, Geoffrey R. *Perilous Times: Free Speech in Wartime.* New York: W. W. Norton, 2004.

Summers, Mark W. *The Plundering Generation: Corruption and the Crisis of the Union, 1849–1861.* New York: Oxford University Press, 1987.

Tansill, Charles C. *The Canadian Reciprocity Treaty of 1854*. Baltimore: Johns Hopkins University Press, 1922.

Von Frank, Albert. *The Trials of Anthony Burns: Freedom and Slavery in Emerson's Boston.* Cambridge, Mass.: Harvard University Press, 1998.

Wallace, Edward S. *Destiny and Glory.* New York: Coward-McCann, 1957.

———. *The Great Reconnaissance, Soldiers, Artists, and Scientists on the Frontier, 1848–1861.* Boston: Little, Brown, 1955.

Walworth, Arthur C. *Black Ships off Japan: The Story of Commodore Perry's Expedition.* Hamden, CT: Archon Books, 1966.

White, Leonard D. *The Jacksonians: A Study in Administrative History, 1829–1861.* New York: MacMillan, 1954.

Widmer, Edward L. *Young America: The Floundering of Democracy in New York City.* New York: Oxford University Press, 1999.

Willets, Gilson. *Inside History of the White House.* New York: Christian Herald, 1908.

Witcover, Jules. *Party of the People: A History of the Democrats.* New York: Random House, 2003.

VII. Articles

Ambler, Charles Henry. "Correspondence of Robert M. T. Hunter, 1826–1876." *Annual Report of the American Historical Association,* 2 (1916): II, 1–383.

Auchampaugh, Philip. "The Story of New York Factions and the Buchanan Managers at Cincinnati, 1856." *New York State Historical Association* 24 (1926), 304–16.

Balla, Wesley G. "Inheriting the Revolution: Benjamin Pierce's World, Ideals, and Legacy." *Historical New Hampshire* 59, no. 1, (Spring 2005): 7–22.

Bell, Irving. "One Hundred Years Ago in New Hampshire." *Historical New Hampshire* 1 (September 1946): 16–24.

Bourne, Edward G. And others, editors. "Diary and Correspondence of Salmon P. Chase." *Annual Report of the American Historical Association* 2 (1902): Washington, D.C.: Government Printing Office, 1903.

Bright, Thomas R. "The Anti-Nebraska Coalition and the Emergence of the Republican Party in New Hampshire, 1853–1857." *Historical New Hampshire* 27, no. 2 (Summer 1972): 57–88.

Cross, David. "Franklin Pierce, the Lawyer." *Proceeding of the Bar Association of New Hampshire* 1 (1900–1903).

Curti, Merle. "Young America." *American Historical Review* 32 (October 1926): 34–54.

Davis, Granville D. "Douglas and the Chicago Mob." *American Historical Review* 54 (April 1949), 533–36.

Dunning, Mike. "Manifest Destiny and the Trans-Mississippi South: Natural Laws and the Extension of Slavery into Mexico." *Journal of Popular Culture* 35, no. 2 (Fall 2001), 111–27.

Fowler, William Plumer. "Looking Back at Little Boar's Head." Reprinted from *Shoreliner Magazine,* August 1950. Tuck Library, New Hampshire Historical Society, Concord.

Gates, Paul Wallace. "A Fragment of Kansas Land History: The Disposal of the Christian Indian Tract." *Kansas Historical Quarterly* 6, no. 3 (August 1937), 227–40.

George, John H. "Paul R. George." *Life and Times in Hopkinton, New Hampshire,* 382–83. Concord, N.H.: Republican Press Associates, 1890.

Haebler, Peter. "Nativism, Liquor, and Riots: Manchester Politics, 1858–1859." *Historical New Hampshire* 46, no. 2 (Summer 1991): 67–91.

———. "Nativist Riots in Manchester: An Episode of Know-Nothingism in New Hampshire." *Historical New Hampshire* 39, no. 3 and 4 (Fall/Winter 1984), 122–38.

Hale, George S. "Harry Hibbard, A Memoir." *The Grafton and Coos Bar Association* 3 (1895–1896): 103–07.

Howe, George F. "The Clayton-Bulwer Treaty." *American Historical Review* 42, no. 3 (April 1937): 484–90.

Hunt, Elmer Munson. "Remarks Relating to the Hundredth Anniversary of the Inauguration of President Franklin Pierce." *Historical New Hampshire* 9 (August 1953): 23–48.

Johnson, Christopher M. "Franklin Pierce, Trial Lawyer." *Advocate, A Magazine for Alumni and Friends of the Franklin Pierce Law Center* 7, no. 2 (Summer 2003): 5–9.

Jones, Henry Lorenzo. "The Black Warrior Affair." *American Historical Review* 12 (January 1907): 280–98.

Klement, Frank L. "Franklin Pierce and the Treason Charges of 1861–1862." *Historian* 23, no. 4 (1961): 436–48.

———. "The Hopkins Hoax and the Golden Circle Rumor in Michigan, 1861–1862." *Michigan History* 47, no. 1 (1963): 1–14.

Langsdorf, Edgar. "S. C. Pomeroy and the New England Emigrant Aid Company, 1854–1858." *Kansas Historical Quarterly* 7, no. 3 (August 1938): 227–45, and no. 4 (November 1938): 379–98.

Learned, Henry Barrett. "Cabinet Meetings under President Polk." *Annual Report of the American Historical Association* 1 (1914): 229–42.

———. "The Relation of Philip Phillips to the Repeal of the Missouri Compromise." *Mississippi Valley Historical Review* 8, no. 4 (March 1922), 303–17.

Lowden, Lucy. "The Granite State for Lincoln." *Historical New Hampshire* 25, no. 1 (Spring 1970): 3–26.

———. "New Hampshire at Chicago—1860." *Historical New Hampshire* 29, no. 1 (1974): 20–41.

Marshall, Thomas Maitland. "Diary and Memoranda of William L. Marcy, 1857." *American Historical Review* 24, no. 4 (July 1919): 641–53.

Marvel, William. "Answering Lincoln's Call: The First New Hampshire Volunteers." *Historical New Hampshire* 39, no. 3 (1984): 139–51.

———. "New Hampshire and the Draft, 1863." *Historical New Hampshire* 36, no. 1 (Spring 1981): 58–72.

Meerse, David. "Buchanan's Patronage Policy: An Attempt to Achieve Political Strength." *Pennsylvania History* 40, no. 1 (1973): 37–57.

Miley, Cora. "Franklin Pierce, the Most Charming Personality of All the Presidents." *Americana*, 29 (April 1935): 156–80.

Moore, J. Preston. "Pierre Soulé: Southern Expansionist and Promoter." *Journal of Southern History* 21, no. 2 (May 1955): 203–23.

Morison, Elting E. "In Praise of Pierce." *American Heritage* 36 (August/September 1985): 46–48.

Neely, Mark E., Jr. "Richard W. Thompson: The Persistent Know Nothing." *Indiana Magazine of History* 72, no. 2 (June 1976): 95–122.

Page, Elwin L. "Franklin Pierce and Abraham Lincoln—Parallels and Contrasts." *Abraham Lincoln Quarterly* 5 (December 1949): 455–72.

Phillips, Ulrich B. "The Correspondence of Robert Toombs, Alexander H. Stephens, and Howell Cobb." *Annual Report of the American Historical Association* 2 (1911).

Ray, P. O. "Some Papers of Franklin Pierce." *American Historical Review* 10 (October 1904): 110–27; (January 1905): 350–70.

Renda, Lex. "Credit and Culpability: New Hampshire State Politics During the Civil War." *Historical New Hampshire* 48, no. 1 (Spring 1993): 3–84.

Suarez, Ana R. "The Precious, the Priceless Right of Way across the Isthmus of Tehuantepec." *Journal of Popular Culture* 35, no. 2 (Fall 2001): 153–60.

Scott, Kenneth. "Press Opposition to Lincoln in New Hampshire." *New England Quarterly* 21 (March–December 1948): 327–41.

Terrazas, Marcela. "The Regional Conflict, the Contractors, and the Construction Projects of a Road to the Pacific at the End of the War between Mexico and the United States." *Journal of Popular Culture* 35, no. 2 (Fall 2001): 161–69.

Van Alstyne, Richard W. "Anglo-American Relations, 1853–1857." *American Historical Review* 42, no. 3 (1937): 491–500.

———. "John F. Crampton, Conspirator or Dupe?" *American Historical Review* 41 (April 1936): 492–502.

Van Beck, Todd W. "Funerals of the Famous: Franklin Pierce." *American Cemetery*, November 1991, 24–40.

"The Venom and the Antidote." *Loyal Publication Society*, no. 9 (1864).

Venzke, Jane Walter and Craig Paul Venzke. "The President's Wife, Jane Means Appleton Pierce: A Woman of Her Time." *Historical New Hampshire* 49, no. 1 (Spring 2005): 45–63.

Wallner, Peter A. "Franklin Pierce and Bowdoin College Associates Hawthorne and Hale." *Historical New Hampshire* 49, no. 1 (Spring 2005): 23–43.

Warner, Lee H. "Nathaniel Hawthorne and the Making of the President, 1852." *Historical New Hampshire* 28 (Spring 1973): 21–36.

Watts, Dale E. "How Bloody Was Bleeding Kansas? Political Killings in Kansas Territory, 1854–1861." *Kansas History* 18, no. 2 (Summer 1995): 116–29.

Webster, Sidney. "Mr. Marcy, the Cuban Question and the Ostend Manifesto." *Political Science Quarterly* 8, no. 1 (March 1893): 1–32.

VIII. Unpublished Works

Amsden, Grace P. "A Capital for New Hampshire." 3 vols. New Hampshire Historical Society, Concord, 1950.

Cox, Stephen Lawrence. "Power, Oppression, and Liberation: New Hampshire Abolitionism and the Radical Critique of Slavery, 1825–1850." Ph.D. dis., University of New Hampshire, 1980.

Duncan, William Henry. "Memorial of Rev. Nathan Lord." 1870. New Hampshire Historical Society, Concord.

Gaffney, Thomas L. "Maine's Mr. Smith: A Study of the Career of Frances O. J. Smith, Politician and Entrepreneur." Ph.D. dis., University of Maine, 1979.

Lacy, Harriet S., Frank S. Mevers, Katherine Morrill, and Ruth L. Page. "Governors of New Hampshire: Biographical Sketches." New Hampshire Historical Society, Concord, 1977.

Mauck, Jeffrey Gordon. "The Gadsden Treaty: The Diplomacy of Transcontinental Transportation." Ph.D. dis., University of Indiana, 1991.

Martin, John Milton. "William Rufus King: Southern Moderate." Ph.D. dis., University of North Carolina, 1955.

McGiffen, Steven Paul. "Prelude to Republicanism: Issues of the Realignment of Political Parties in New Hampshire, 1835–1847." Ph.D. dis., The University of New Hampshire, 1984.

"The Record of a Month." N.p., 1864

Van Beck, Todd W. "The Death and Funeral of Franklin Pierce." Typed manuscript, 1990. Copy at Tuck Library, New Hampshire Historical Society, Concord.

PHOTO CREDITS

Page numbers refer to photosection pages.

Page i. White House, ca. 1846 (Library of Congress); Franklin Pierce, Jane Pierce, and Abigail Kent Means (New Hampshire Historical Society)

Page ii. Pierce Cabinet, engraving by S. Pierson (courtesy of Craig Schermer)

Page iii. Pierre Soulé, August Belmont, John Y. Mason, Daniel Sickles (Library of Congress)

Page iv. Horatio Seymour, reproduced from Alexander J. Wall, *A Sketch of the Life of Horatio Seymour* (New York, 1929), Page 22. John A. Dix, Daniel Dickinson, Francis B. Cutting (Library of Congress)

Page v. David Rice Atchison, John C. Breckinridge, R.M.T. Hunter, James M. Mason (Library of Congress)

Page vi. Stephen A. Douglas, Archibald Dixon, Philip Phillips (Library of Congress); Alexander H. Stephens, reproduced from Henry Cleveland, *Alexander H Stephens in Public and Private* (Philadelphia: National Publishing Company, 1866), frontispiece.

Page vii. Edmund Burke, John Hale (New Hampshire Historical Society); Richard W. Thompson, reproduced from Richard W. Thompson, *Recollections of Sixteen Presidents from Washington to Lincoln* (Indianapolis, 1894), II, frontispiece.

Page viii. Alfred O. Page Nicholson, John W. Forney (Library of Congress)

Page ix. Varina Davis, reproduced from Varina Davis, *Jefferson Davis: A Memoir by His Wife* (New York: Belford Company Publishers, 1890), II, frontispiece; Sara Agnes Rice (Mrs. Roger Pryor), (Library of Congress); Jessie Benton Frémont, reproduced from Alan Nevins, *Frémont: The West's Great Adventurer* (1928), II, Page 144. Dorothea Dix, reproduced from Francis Tiffany, *Life of Dorothea Dix* (Boston: Houghton, Muffin, 1891), frontispiece.

Page x. Andrew H. Reeder (The Kansas State Historical Society), John W. Geary (Library of Congress)

Page xi. John Slidell, Jesse David Bright (Library of Congress)

Page xii. "1856 Campaign" broadside (New Hampshire Historical Society)

Page xiii. Hoax Letter (Pierce Papers, New Hampshire Historical Society); William H. Seward reproduced from Frederic Bancroft, *The Life of William H. Seward* (New York: Harper & Brothers, 1900), II, frontispiece.

Page xiv. Col. Edward E. Cross, Col. Thomas J. Whipple (New Hampshire Historical Society); Clement L. Vallandigham, Samuel S. Cox (Library of Congress)

Page xv. 52 South Main Street, Concord (New Hampshire Historical Society); Little Boar's Head, 2 views reproduced from *Shoreliner Magazine*, August, 1950 (New Hampshire Historical Society)

Page xvi. Franklin Pierce (New Hampshire Historical Society)

INDEX

A

B

C

E

F

I

J

K

L

M

N

O

P

Q

R

S

T